PART II   Managing the Union

The Institutions of **the European Union**

THE NEW EUROPEAN UNION SERIES

Series Editors: **John Peterson and Helen Wallace**

The European Union is both the most successful experiment in modern international cooperation and one of its most controversial. What is clear is that it is a daunting analytical challenge to students of politics, economics, history, law, and the social sciences.

The European Union of the twenty-first century continues to respond to multiple crises such as the United Kingdom's intention to withdraw following its 2016 referendum and new policy challenges—particularly in transnational arenas such as climate change, migration, and management of the euro—as well as political and institutional controversies. The result is a truly new European Union that requires continuous reassessment.

THE NEW EUROPEAN UNION SERIES brings together the expertise of leading scholars writing on major aspects of EU politics for an international readership.

The series offers lively, accessible, reader-friendly, research-based textbooks on:

POLICY-MAKING IN THE EUROPEAN UNION

INTERNATIONAL RELATIONS AND THE EUROPEAN UNION

THE MEMBER STATES OF THE EUROPEAN UNION

THE ORIGINS AND EVOLUTION OF THE EUROPEAN UNION

*THE INSTITUTIONS OF THE EUROPEAN UNION

THE EUROPEAN UNION: HOW DOES IT WORK?

The Institutions of the European Union

FOURTH EDITION

Edited by

Dermot Hodson

John Peterson

OXFORD
UNIVERSITY PRESS

OXFORD
UNIVERSITY PRESS

Great Clarendon Street, Oxford, OX2 6DP,
United Kingdom

Oxford University Press is a department of the University of Oxford.
It furthers the University's objective of excellence in research, scholarship,
and education by publishing worldwide. Oxford is a registered trade mark of
Oxford University Press in the UK and in certain other countries

First edition published 2002
Second edition published 2006
Third edition published 2012

Impression: 2

Published in the United States of America by Oxford University Press
198 Madison Avenue, New York, NY 10016, United States of America

British Library Cataloguing in Publication Data
Data available

Library of Congress Control Number: 2016960623

ISBN 978–0–19–873741–4

Printed in Great Britain by
Bell & Bain Ltd., Glasgow

▍OUTLINE CONTENTS

▮ DETAILED CONTENTS

PART I Providing Direction

PART III   **Integrating Interests**

∎ PREFACE

The first edition of this book was only the second to appear in the Oxford University Press 'New European Union' series, after Helen and William Wallace's milestone in the EU literature, *Policy-Making in the European Union*. The shelf on which these two books once sat alone now groans under the weight of no fewer than five other volumes, including a seventh version of *Policy-Making* (2015). Whereas we once faced 'only' the (already daunting) task of living up to the high standards set by Wallace and Wallace (recently joined by Mark A. Pollack and Alasdair R. Young), we now find ourselves having to be good enough to avoid letting down a stable of other authors and editors who, together, have made the New European Union series an essential set of works for any student of European integration. Quite a lot of the blame for putting us under so much pressure lies with Professor Helen Wallace, the series co-editor, whose energy, enthusiasm, razor-sharp mind, and all-around good citizenship never cease to amaze us.

We owe a large debt to our colleagues at Oxford University Press for helping to keep the project on track. Francesca Mitchell has been an absolute joy with whom to work. She has worked hard to ensure that this book, along with others in the series, finds the audience that it deserves. And the past efforts of Francesca's predecessors—Ruth Anderson, Sue Dempsey, Angela Griffin, Sarah Iles, and Catherine Page—have not been forgotten.

Our authors have invariably worked to a high standard, while patiently coping with our active editorship and constant urgings to respect the next deadline. We have learned much from them and are enormously grateful to each for the part that they have played in making this project a success. Some of the work of some contributors to past editions—Andrew Byrne, Brian Crowe, Hussein Kassim, George Karakatsanis, Kathleen McNamara, Neill Nugent, and Michael E. Smith—may live on in this edition, so we must thank them for their past efforts.

This edition also sees Dermot Hodson take over from Michael Shackleton as co-editor. Words cannot do justice to Mike's contribution to the first three editions of this volume. We are delighted that he has stayed on for this edition to write the chapter on the European Parliament, an institution that he understands better than anyone.

Our final expression of thanks is to our families: Elizabeth, Miles, and Calum; and Emma, William, and Hugh. Their love and support is what matters most and we dedicate this final product to them.

Dermot Hodson and John Peterson
London and Edinburgh

New to this edition

- The book, in its fourth edition, has been fully updated to cover the institutional changes prompted by the eurozone and migration crises, and many other challenges facing the European Union (EU).

- A new introductory chapter explores broad trends in the EU's institutional development and theoretical perspectives thereof.

- This edition's increased focus on institutional theory is picked up on in all chapters, including in a substantially revised concluding chapter.

- Several chapters explore the multiple crises facing the EU, including the euro crisis, Europe's migration crisis, conflict in Syria and Ukraine, and the United Kingdom's referendum vote to leave the EU.

- A number of new contributors have been added to ensure that the book continues to bring together the foremost scholars in the field.

■ LIST OF BOXES

▮ LIST OF FIGURES

▌ LIST OF TABLES

■ LIST OF ABBREVIATIONS

ACER	Agency for the Cooperation of Energy Regulators
ACP	African, Caribbean, and Pacific countries
ADDE	Alliance for Direct Democracy in Europe
AECR	Alliance of European Conservatives and Reformists
AFSJ	area of freedom, security, and justice
ALDE	Alliance of Liberals and Democrats for Europe
ARLEM	Euro–Mediterranean Assembly of Local and Regional Authorities
Art./Arts	Article/Articles
BBC	British Broadcasting Corporation
BBI	Bio-based Industries Joint Undertaking
BCC	British Chamber of Commerce
Benelux	Belgium, the Netherlands, and Luxembourg
BEREC	Body of European Regulators for Electronic Communications
BIS	Bank for International Settlements
Brexit	UK (British) exit from the Union
BRIC	Brazil, Russia, India, and China
BSE	bovine spongiform encephalopathy
BVerfGE	German Federal Constitutional Court (*Bundesverfassungsgericht*)
CAP	common agricultural policy
CATS	Article 36 Committee (*Comité article trente-six*)
CCMI	Consultative Commission on Industrial Change
CCP	common commercial policy
CDU/CSU	German Christian Democratic Union/Christian Social Union
CEAD	coordination, evaluation, assurance, and development
Cedefop	European Centre for the Development of Vocational Training
CEECs	Central and Eastern European countries
CEPOL	European Police College
CEPS	Centre for European Policy Studies
CESR	Committee of European Securities Regulators
CFCA	Community Fisheries Control Agency
CFI	Court of First Instance
CFP	common fisheries policy

CFSP	common foreign and security policy
CHAFEA	Consumers, Health, and Food Executive Agency
CHMP	Committee for Medicinal Products for Human Use
CIVEX	Commission for Citizenship, Governance, Institutional and External Affairs (of the Committee of the Regions)
CJEU	Court of Justice of the European Union
Clean Sky2	Clean Sky 2 Joint Undertaking
COA	Court of Auditors
Cocor	Coordinating Commission of the Council of Ministers (*Commission de coordination du conseil des ministres*)
COMP	Committee for Orphan Medicinal Products
CONT	Committee on Budgetary Control (of the European Parliament)
CoR	Committee of the Regions
Coreper	Committee of Permanent Representatives
COSI	Standing Committee on Internal Security
COTER	Commission for Territorial Cohesion Policy and EU Budget
CPMP	Committee for Proprietary Medicinal Products
CPVO	Community Plant Variety Office
CSCE	Conference for Security and Cooperation in Europe
CSDP	common security and defence policy
CSO	civil society organization
CSP	Confederation of Socialist Parties of the European Community
CVMP	Committee for Veterinary Medicines
DAS	statement of assurance (also known as SOA)
DG ENV	Directorate-General for the Environment
DG	Directorate-General
EA	European Alliance
EACEA	Education, Audiovisual, and Culture Executive Agency
EASA	European Aviation Safety Agency
EASME	Executive Agency for Small and Medium-sized Enterprises
EASO	European Asylum Support Office
EAW	European arrest warrant
EBA	European Banking Authority
EBRD	European Bank for Reconstruction and Development
EC	European Community
ECA	European Court of Auditors
ECB	European Central Bank

ECDC	European Centre for Disease Prevention and Control
ECHA	European Chemicals Agency
ECHO	European Community Humanitarian Office
ECHR	European Convention on Human Rights
ECJ	European Court of Justice
Ecofin	Council of Economic and Finance Ministers
ECON	Commission for Economic Policy (of the Committee of the Regions); Economic and Monetary Affairs Committee (of the European Parliament)
ECOWAS	Economic Community of West African States
ECSC	European Coal and Steel Community
ECSEL	Electronic Components and Systems for European Leadership Joint Undertaking
ECtHR	European Court of Human Rights
EDA	European Defence Agency
EDC	European Defence Community
EEA	European Environment Agency
EEAS	European External Action Service
EEC	European Economic Community
EESC	European Economic and Social Committee
EFA	European Free Alliance
EFC	Economic and Financial Committee
EFCA	Community Fisheries Control Agency
EFDD	Europe of Freedom and Direct Democracy
EFGP	European Federation of Green Parties
EFSA	European Food Safety Authority
EGP	European Green Party
EGWG	Eurogroup working group
EHCA	European Chemicals Agency
EIB	European Investment Bank
EIGE	European Institute for Gender Equality
EIOPA	European Insurance and Occupational Pensions Authority
EIT	European Institute of Innovation and Technology
ELDR	European Liberal, Democrat, and Reform Party
EMA	European Medicines Agency
EMCDDA	European Monitoring Centre for Drugs and Drug Addiction
EMI	European Monetary Institute
EMS	European monetary system
EMSA	European Maritime Safety Agency

EMU	economic and monetary union
ENF	Europe of Nations and Freedom
ENISA	European Network and Information Security Agency
ENP	European Neighbourhood Policy
ENVE	Commission for Environment, Climate Change, and Energy (of the Committee of the Regions)
EP	European Parliament
EPA	Environmental Protection Agency (US)
EPC	European political community; European political cooperation
EPP	European People's Party; European public prosecutor
ERA	European Railway Agency
ERC	European Research Council
ERCEA	European Research Council Executive Agency
ESC	*See* EESC
ESCB	European System of Central Banks
ESDP	European security and defence policy
ESM	European Stability Mechanism
ESMA	European Securities and Markets Authority
ESS	European Security Strategy
ETA	*Euskadi ta Askatasuna*
ETF	European Training Foundation
EU	European Union
EU3	France, Germany, and the UK
EUISS	European Union Institute for Security Studies
eu-LISA	European Agency for the operational management of large-scale IT systems in the area of freedom, security, and justice
EUL–NGL	Confederal Group of the European United Left/Nordic Green Left
EU-OSHA	European Agency for Safety and Health at Work
Euratom	European Atomic Energy Community
Eurofound	European Foundation for the Improvement of Living and Working Conditions
Eurojust	EU Judicial Cooperation Unit
Europol	European Police Office
Eurostat	European Statistical Office
F4E	Fusion for Energy
FAC	Foreign Affairs Council
FCH 2	Fuel Cells and Hydrogen 2 Joint Undertaking
FRA	European Union Agency for Fundament Rights

Frontex	European Agency for the Management of Operational Cooperation at the External Borders
G/EFA	Greens/European Free Alliance
G20	Group of Twenty
G7	Group of Seven
GAC	General Affairs Council
GDP	gross domestic product
GNP	gross national product
GSA	European GNSS Agency
GSA	European GNSS Supervisory Authority
HMPC	Committee on Herbal Medicinal Products
IAS	Internal Audit Service
IGC	intergovernmental conference
IIA	inter-institutional agreement
IMF	International Monetary Fund
IMI2	Innovative Medicines Initiative 2 Joint Undertaking
INEA	Innovation and Networks Executive Agency
IR	international relations
IRA	Irish Republican Army
ISIS	Islamic State of Iraq and Syria
JHA	justice and home affairs
JPC	judicial and police cooperation
KPI	key performance indicators
LSE	London School of Economics and Political Science
MENA	Middle East and North Africa
MEP	member of the European Parliament
MFA	European Minister for Foreign Affairs
MFF	multiannual financial framework
MLG	multilevel governance
NAT	Commission for Natural Resources (of the Committee of the Regions)
NATO	North Atlantic Treaty Organization
NCVO	National Council for Voluntary Organizations (UK)
NGO	non-governmental organization
NPM	new public management
NRA	national regulatory authority
OHIM	Office for Harmonization in the Internal Market (Trade Marks and Designs)
OLAF	European Anti-Fraud Office (*Office de la lutte anti-fraude*)

OLP	ordinary legislative procedure
OMC	open method of coordination
OMT	outright monetary transactions
OSCE	Organization for Security and Cooperation in Europe
PACE	Parliamentary Assembly of the Council of Europe
PCA	partnership and cooperation agreements
PES	Party of European Socialists
PNR	passenger name record
PoCo	Political Committee
PSC	Political and Security Committee (also known as COPS)
QMV	qualified majority voting
REA	Research Executive Agency
RegLeg	Conference of Presidents of Regions with Legislative Power
RRF	rapid reaction force
S&D	Progressive Alliance of Socialists and Democrats
SAI	supreme audit institution
SAGE	Secrétariat général des affaires européennes
Satcen	European Union Satellite Centre
SCA	Special Committee on Agriculture
SCIFA	Standing Committee on Immigration, Frontiers, and Asylum
SEA	Single European Act
SEDEC	Commission for Social Policy, Education, Employment, Research and Culture (SEDEC) (of the Committee of the Regions)
SESAR2	Single European Sky Air Traffic Management Research 2
SG	Secretariat-General
SIS	Schengen information system
SJ	Legal Service
SMP	Securities Markets Programme
SOA	*See* DAS
SRB	Single Resolution Board
SSM	Single Supervisory Mechanism
SWIFT	Society for Worldwide Interbank Financial Communication
Syriza	Greek Coalition of the Radical Left
TCN	third-country national
TEC	Treaty Establishing the European Community
TEU	Treaty on European Union (Maastricht Treaty)
TFEU	Treaty on the Functioning of the European Union

TSCG	Treaty on Stability, Coordination, and Governance in the Economic and Monetary Union ('Fiscal Compact')
UCLAF	Anti-Fraud Unit (*Unité de coordination de la lutte anti-fraude*)
UK	United Kingdom
UKIP	United Kingdom Independence Party
UN	United Nations
US	United States
WEU	Western European Union
WTO	World Trade Organization

▮ LIST OF CONTRIBUTORS

Philippe de Schoutheete	University of Louvain
Renaud Dehousse	European University Institute
Andrew Geddes	University of Sheffield
Fiona Hayes-Renshaw	College of Europe (Bruges)
Niklas Helwig	Johns Hopkins University
Dermot Hodson	Birkbeck College (University of London)
Liesbet Hooghe	University of North Carolina (Chapel Hill)
Charlie Jeffery	University of Edinburgh
R. Daniel Kelemen	Rutgers University
Brigid Laffan	European University Institute
Jeffrey Lewis	Cleveland State University
Paul Magnette	Minister-President of Wallonia, Belgium
Giandomenico Majone	European University Institute
Niamh Nic Shuibhne	University of Edinburgh
John Peterson	University of Edinburgh
Christian Rauh	WZB Berlin Social Science Center
Tapio Raunio	University of Tampere
Carolyn Rowe	Aston University
Michael Shackleton	Maastricht University

CHAPTER 1

Theorizing EU institutions: Why they matter for politics and international relations

Dermot Hodson and John Peterson

▌ Summary

The European Union (EU) is an extraordinary—and extraordinarily controversial—case of cooperation between sovereign states that no student of politics and international relations (IR) can overlook. As with most international organizations, the EU is built on intergovernmental institutions tightly controlled by national governments. But its member states have also given supranational and transnational institutions, which often operate with considerable autonomy, significant powers over the past sixty years. EU institutions are involved in almost all policy decisions taken by member states, but

Cont. ➤

Cont.

they are neither well understood nor trusted by many Europeans. This chapter first shows how the EU's traditional Community institutions emerged, before it examines the proliferation of new bodies created by EU member states since the 1990s. It introduces the crises confronting EU institutions, including the referendum vote in the United Kingdom (UK) in 2016 to leave the Union. Three competing theoretical approaches to this field of study—integration theory, the new institutionalism, and the separation of powers tradition—are presented and interrogated, and debates about the accountability of EU institutions are reviewed.

Introduction

The EU is the most historically ambitious attempt at peacetime cooperation between liberal democracies. Neither a state nor a conventional intergovernmental organization, the EU is the case of a conventional cooperation closest to the ideal of 'global government' (Koenig-Archibugi 2002). EU member states have made Treaty commitments to a range of policy objectives that are as wide as those of most governments. The EU's institutions are the means through which its members seek to achieve their policy commitments and, in so doing, realize the Union's lofty aims of promoting peace, shared values, and the well-being of more than 500 million Europeans.[1]

In the 1950s, the decision of six founding member states of (what was then) the European Economic Community (EEC) to create the European Commission, Court of Justice, Council of Ministers, and what became the European Parliament (EP)—defined Europe's bold new political experiment. All live on in the EU. Today, newer, more specialist institutions, such as the European Central Bank (ECB), the European External Action Service (EEAS), and the European border agency Frontex share a pivotal role in the provision of collective goods for a membership that reached twenty-eight countries prior to the UK's vote in 2016 to leave.

At the time of writing, EU institutions are shaping European responses to a range of challenges, including Brexit (that is, British exit from the EU), the euro crisis, a migration crisis, and conflict in Syria and Ukraine. Whether the EU should wield such power is a matter of fierce dispute. EU institutions thus matter in debates about who governs Europe and how Europe shapes the world (Scharpf 1999; Avant *et al.* 2010; Jørgensen and Laatikainen 2013; Jones 2014). More generally, EU institutions are crucial for students and practitioners of international politics seeking to understand whether attempts by states to share power and sovereignty can endure at a time of great uncertainty for the international system (Hoffmann *et al.* 1990).

The study of EU institutions can be infuriating. Too often, scholars devote their efforts to describing EU institutions in detail at the expense of investigating the causes and consequences of creating such bodies. This shortcoming cannot be justified by appeals to complexity. EU institutions are not uniquely complex, as anyone who has tried to understand the UK's parliamentary procedures or the inner workings of the United Nations (UN) can attest (Weiss 2007; Norton 2013). Scholarship on EU institutions can also be defensive. Too often, those researching the EU shield 'their' institutions—or the Union as a whole—from accusations of inefficiency, illegitimacy, or, worst of all, irrelevancy.

Fortunately, a host of theories have emerged to help us to understand why and how EU institutions matter. This book provides a comprehensive introduction to this fascinating and controversial field of study. The present chapter sets the scene for what follows by introducing five foundational questions.

- What are EU institutions?
- How have different types of institution evolved?
- What are EU institutions for?
- What do they do?
- How should EU institutions be held to account?

Each question is explored in turn before offering a plan of the book.

Defining EU institutions

A classic definition of political institutions comes from Douglass North (1991: 97), who defines them as 'humanly devised constraints that structure political, economic and social interaction'. North's work encouraged political scientists to think again about the importance of institutions. A strength of this 'new institutionalism' is that it looks beyond bricks-and-mortar institutions at the rules that shape political choices and outcomes; a weakness is that it counts almost any routinized interaction as an institution. We steer a middle course in this book by defining EU institutions as formal and informal political bodies that govern EU policy-making.

Having defined EU institutions, can we offer a definitive list? The Treaties are the obvious place to start. The Treaty on European Union (TEU) identifies seven EU institutions: the EP, the European Council, the Council of Ministers, the European Commission, the Court of Justice of the EU, the European Court of Auditors, and the ECB.[2] These institutions are arguably the most important for understanding the EU. But this list certainly is not exhaustive. Several other political bodies are named in the Treaties—the Economic and Social Committee, the Committee of the Regions (CoR), and the European Investment Bank are cases in point—but many are not.

Member states' hesitancy about naming EU institutions in the Treaties is one reason to tread carefully. Another is that the Treaties have changed over time. The European Council, for instance, was set up on the basis of an informal agreement in

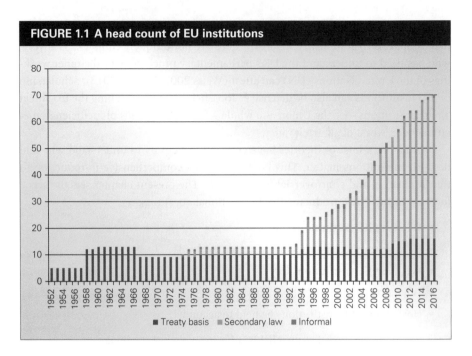

FIGURE 1.1 A head count of EU institutions

1974, but was not named as an EU institution until the Lisbon Treaty (2007). Another reason for caution is that many EU institutions, bodies, offices, and agencies derive their legal status not from the Treaties, but from secondary law or legislation. Frontex is one of many EU agencies that fit this bill. Other institutions have a murky status, as in the case of the European Stability Mechanism, a €500 billion fund created in response to the euro crisis underpinned by an intergovernmental treaty signed by some, but not all, EU member states.

A simple head count of EU institutions over time reveals some striking trends (see Figure 1.1). First, the number of institutions has grown significantly. At its launch in 1952, the European Coal and Steel Community (ECSC), a forerunner to the EU, had five institutions; by 2016, the EU had seventy.

Second, most EU institutions created since the 1990s derive their legal status from secondary law.[3] This trend is driven, in part, by an exponential increase in the number of EU agencies over the last two decades.

Third, the creation of informal bodies is rare and they are typically subsumed into the Treaties after their creation. Consider, for example, the Eurogroup, an informal body of finance ministers from EU states in the eurozone created in 1999 and later recognized in the Lisbon Treaty (2007).

EU institution-building might appear, on this basis, to be out of control. But it is modest compared to international trends. The head count of international organizations increased—by some measures—from fewer than ten in 1870 to tens of thousands in the 2010s (Union of International Organizations 2015: 2–15). The total number of staff working for EU institutions is, by our reckoning, around 54,000.

BOX 1.1	Perceptions of the EU institutions

Each man begins the world afresh. Only institutions grow wiser. They store up collective experience . . . From this experience and wisdom, men subject to the same laws will gradually find . . . not that their natures change . . . but that their behaviour does.

(Jean Monnet 1950, quoted in Duchêne 1994: 401)

What a model our institutions, which allow every country irrespective of its size to have its say and make a contribution, offer the nations of Eastern Europe.

(Jacques Delors 1989, quoted in Nelsen and Stubb 1994: 60–1)

Supranational institutions—above all, the European Commission, the European Court, and the European Parliament—have independent influence in policy-making that cannot be derived from their role as agents of state executives.

(Marks *et al.* 1996: 346)

All along [the] road, the European institutions—the Council, the European Parliament, the Commission, and the Court of Justice—have provided sterling service, to which we must pay tribute. At the same time . . . the process of European union is showing signs of flagging.

(Giscard d'Estaing 2002: 5)

From my own experience, the EU's institutions are far more autonomous than institutionalist theory (much of it focused on the American institutions) would lead one to believe. Much, much more.

(José Manuel Barroso 2007, quoted in Peterson 2008: 69)

The EU should be concentrated on adapting to globalization and global competitiveness, not building more powerful centralised institutions in Brussels.

(William Hague 2009, quoted in Winnett 2009)

Although this total is large by the standards of international organizations—the UN's Secretariat-General employs around 40,000 staff—it is minuscule compared to the estimated 14 million public employees in EU member states (Ministry of the President 2010: 7–8). Yet, although the EU employs only a modest share of all public servants in Europe, EU governments have been highly ambitious in delegating tasks, power, and autonomy to the Union's institutions (see Box 1.1).

EU institutions: A brief history and a taxonomy

Over four decades ago, Joseph Nye and Robert Keohane (1971) developed a theory of world politics focused on both state and non-state actors. At the time, developing a theory of IR that assumed non-state actors mattered was ground-breaking. The EU occupies an important, if neglected, place in this still vibrant research agenda because it is the site of a struggle between three ideal types of international institution. The first is *intergovernmental* institutions, which are directly accountable to national governments. The second type is *supranational* institutions, the leadership of which is appointed by—but thereafter independent from—national governments. The third is *transnational* institutions, which are accountable to societal actors, such as voters and pressure groups, rather than national governments. These societal actors influence intergovernmental and supranational institutions indirectly through domestic political channels such as elections and lobbying. But they exercise direct control of transnational institutions. In the terminology used by Keohane and Nye (1971), intergovernmental and supranational institutions are the products of inter-state politics between national governments. Transnational institutions, on the other hand, stem from transnational interactions between societal actors from different member states (see Figure 1.2).

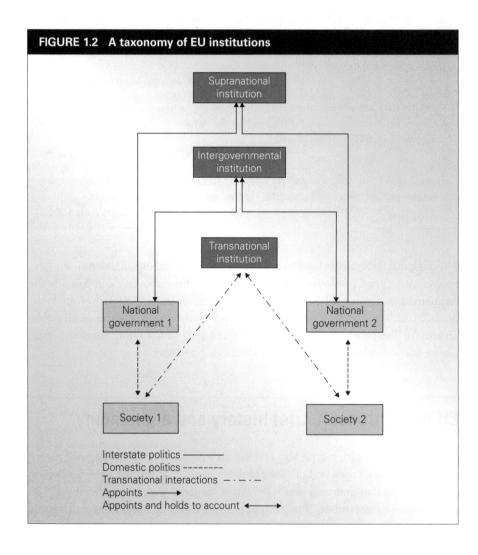

FIGURE 1.2   A taxonomy of EU institutions

The traditional Community institutions

The ECSC, created by the Treaty of Paris (1951), broke from previous attempts at international cooperation and set the mould for EU institutions that exist today in important respects (see Box 1.2). A key innovation was the High Authority. This institution was empowered to adopt decisions to create a common market for coal and steel. The High Authority was influenced—and initially led by—Jean Monnet, one of the true founding fathers of the EU (Duchêne 1994). The ECSC also had a supranational Court of Justice with the power to enforce European law and a Special Council of Ministers, an intergovernmental institution composed of national ministers of the member states.

BOX 1.2   The Council of Europe

The Council of Europe is commonly confused with the EU, but the two are distinct organizations. The Council of Europe was established in 1949 by the six original members of what became the EU (although not West Germany) plus Denmark, Ireland, Norway, Sweden, and the UK. Its central purpose was to encourage cooperation in 'economic, social, cultural, scientific, legal and administrative matters'.[4] The Council was equipped with a small secretariat and a large parliamentary assembly, but key decisions remained the reserve of a committee of (national) ministers. In this sense, the Council of Europe is a clear example of intergovernmental cooperation.

The Council of Europe is sometimes dismissed as a mere precursor to the EU—but this characterization is misleading (Urwin 1994: 38). For one thing, Council of Europe members agreed in 1959 to establish a European Court of Human Rights (ECtHR), a supranational judicial body that has become an important guarantor of rights in Europe. Although ECtHR rulings do not override national law, member states of the Council of Europe are expected to enforce them. Council members have signed up to the European Convention for Human Rights (1950), a treaty inspired by, and designed to reinforce, the UN Declaration on Human Rights (1948). The Council of Europe has played an important role in promoting democracy and the rule of law, especially after the end of the Cold War. Testament to that role is that the Council of Europe's membership now includes forty-eight member states, including Russia.

The ECtHR should not be mistaken for the Court of Justice of the EU, even though it frequently is. The same goes for the Council of Europe and the European Council, the EU institution that brings together the heads of state or government of the twenty-eight member states. One reason for such confusion, perhaps, is that all EU member states are members of the Council of Europe. The EU and Council of Europe also share the same flag (twelve yellow stars on a blue field) and the same anthem (Beethoven's *Ode to Joy*). Early meetings of the EP were even held in the Council of Europe's headquarters in Strasbourg. Thus it is little wonder that the institutions of the Council of Europe and EU are often confused one with the other. They are, however, two very separate international organizations.

The Treaty of Paris reflected a tentative belief in transnational institutions. Whereas intergovernmental and supranational institutions are accountable to national governments—directly (the former) or indirectly (the latter)—transnational institutions derive their authority from other actors. The Common Assembly (which became the EP in 1962) represented 'the peoples of the member states of the Community' rather than the national governments.[5] These representatives were seconded national parliamentarians at first, but the Treaty opened the door to direct elections. The Treaty also incorporated pressure groups through the creation of a Consultative Committee, an advisory body made up of representatives of coal and steel producers, workers, consumers, and dealers.

The ECSC served as an institutional blueprint for two other international organizations created under the Treaties of Rome (1957). The first was the EEC, which established a single market and common policies in areas such as agriculture, trade, and economic policy. The second was the European Atomic Energy Community (Euratom), which sought to develop Europe's nuclear industry. The EEC and Euratom came under the jurisdiction of the ECSC's Court of Justice and Common Assembly. Crucially, however, the roles of the High Authority and the Special Council of Ministers were not extended to the EEC (Euratom never amounted to much); instead, the Treaty of Rome created a new EEC Commission and an EEC-dedicated Council of Ministers.

The Commission was similar to, but less powerful than, the High Authority. While the High Authority could take decisions without the approval of the Special Council of Ministers in many areas, the Commission typically proposed decisions that could be taken only by the Council. In this sense, the EEC gave greater weight to intergovernmental institutions than the ECSC. The EEC's European Economic and Social Committee, meanwhile, had a similar institutional design to the ECSC's Consultative Committee.

A Merger Treaty (1965) created a single Commission and Council for all three Communities, thus forming a set of *traditional Community institutions* that remain vital to the EU. There have been only a few additions to the list since the early 1950s (see Table 1.1). One was the creation in 1958 of the Committee of the Permanent Representatives (Coreper), which brings together national EU ambassadors and officials based permanently in Brussels to prepare Council meetings. An awkward case for EU scholars, Coreper is seen as an intergovernmental counterweight to the Commission by some and a complicated mix of intergovernmental and supranational policy styles by others (Weiler 1981; Lewis 2005).

More important still was the creation in 1974 of the European Council, a regular summit of the heads of state or government of the member states. The European Council has emerged over the last four decades as the most powerful of the traditional Community institutions. When the EU faces a crisis, which it regularly does, all eyes look to the European Council as a site of intergovernmental bargaining and deliberation (Puetter 2014).

TABLE 1.1 The traditional Community institutions

Start of activities	Title of institution	Location
1952	Special Council of Ministers	Luxembourg
	ECSC High Authority	Luxembourg
	Court of Justice of the ECSC	Luxembourg
	ECSC Common Assembly	Luxembourg
	ECSC Consultative Committee*	Luxembourg
1958	European Commission	Brussels/Luxembourg
	ECSC Common Assembly becomes European Parliamentary Assembly	Strasbourg/Luxembourg
	Court of Justice of the ECSC becomes Court of Justice of the European Communities	Luxembourg
	Economic and Social Committee	Brussels
	Committee of Permanent Representatives (Coreper)	Brussels/Luxembourg
1962	European Parliamentary Assembly changes its name to European Parliament	Strasbourg/Luxembourg
1967	Merger Treaty (1965) creates a single Commission and Council of Ministers	Brussels/Luxembourg
1974	European Council	
1994	Committee of Regions	Brussels
1998	Eurogroup	Brussels
2009	Court of Justice of the European Communities changes name to Court of Justice of the EU	
	European Council becomes an EU institution with a permanent president	Brussels

* The ECSC Consultative Committee was incorporated into the Economic and Social Committee after the Treaty of Paris expired in 2002.

The Maastricht Treaty significantly increased the scope of EU decision-making. But it did so, by and large, without empowering the Commission or the Court of Justice (Bickerton *et al.* 2015a). Economic and Monetary Union (EMU) illustrates the point: it saw the ECB—a *de novo* body—assume responsibility for a new single currency, the euro, and monetary policy while member states retained control over their own economic policies. The common foreign and security policy (CFSP) and justice and home affairs (JHA) were created as 'intergovernmental pillars' in which national governments took decisions with little or no involvement from supranational institutions. Treaties agreed at Amsterdam (1997), Nice (2001), and Lisbon (2007) carried on in the same vein. A key exception was JHA (or internal security) policy: as of 2014, the Commission could propose legislation on immigration, asylum, and judicial cooperation, although member states retained agenda-setting powers in some sensitive areas.

At Amsterdam, EU member states agreed to appoint a High Representative for the CFSP—within the Council's own administration—to chair meetings of foreign ministers in the Council. But the Lisbon Treaty combined this post with that of the Commissioner for External Relations. Although this change puts the Commission at the heart of EU foreign and security policy cooperation, the High Representative is subject to more intergovernmental checks and balances than other Commissioners. Specifically, the European Council can dismiss the High Representative with the agreement of the Commission President.

In 1979, the EP became the world's first—and, to date, only—directly elected transnational parliament. A major role in Community decision-making came later. Under the Treaty of Rome (1957), the Parliament was given the right to censure— that is, dismiss—the college of Commissioners, and in the Budgetary Treaties (1970, 1975) it was given a role in the authorization of the Community budget. A significant change for the EP came in the Maastricht Treaty, which transformed the EP from a consultative body to a politically and legally equal co-legislator with the Council in specific policy areas. The new procedure—colloquially known as 'co-decision'—was gradually extended in subsequent Treaties to the point at which the EP and the Council play an equal role in almost all areas in which the EU legislates. Eventually, codecision was, revealingly, renamed the 'ordinary' legislative procedure (OLP).

The Maastricht Treaty also allowed the EP to veto the appointment of the college of Commissioners as a whole and the right to be consulted on the European Council's choice of Commission President. The Amsterdam Treaty turned this power of consultation into one of veto and the Lisbon Treaty (2007) required the EP to take account of the most recent EP elections when appointing a Commission President. Controversially, the European political parties used this provision to put forward nominees for Commission President before the EP elections in May 2014 rather than wait for the European Council to choose a nominee. This so-called *Spitzenkandidaten* process pushes the Commission in a more transnational direction and sits uneasily with its origins as a supranational institution.[6]

The EP's emergence as a powerful transnational institution contrasts with the status of the Economic and Social Committee (created to represent civil society interests, such as industry and labour), which plays much the same consultative role today as envisaged by the drafters of the Treaty of Rome. Other efforts to involve transnational actors in EU policy-making also have been made, including the creation by the Maastricht Treaty of the CoR. A consultative body, the CoR's members are chosen by member states from representatives—typically elected—to regional and local bodies. In sum, amongst the traditional Community institutions we find a mélange of bodies that are supranational, intergovernmental, and transnational.

De novo bodies

Traditional Community institutions are the cornerstone of cooperation between EU member states. But their evolution captures only part of the EU's institutional history. Another side of the story is the remarkable rise since the 1990s of, what Bickerton *et al.* (2015a) call *de novo*[7] bodies (see Table 1.2). Whereas the traditional Community institutions have acquired responsibility for a range of policies, *de novo* bodies are specifically created to carry out a much narrower range of tasks. The first such institution was the European Investment Bank, established under the Treaty of Rome to support investment projects for 'the balanced and steady development of the common market in the interest of the Community'.[8] The EIB was, and still is, a decidedly intergovernmental institution. Since the early 1990s, another forty-plus *de novo* bodies have been established. The institutional structure of these institutions is not identical, but most are essentially intergovernmental.

De novo bodies vary in size and the scope of their activities. But, taken as a whole, the number of staff working in these bodies has increased significantly. The combined staff of *de novo* bodies numbered 15,000 in 2013, which was greater than the combined staff of the EP, Court of Justice, and the Council (see Figure 1.3).

Another characteristic of *de novo* bodies is their geographic dispersion. At the time of writing, all EU member states, except Croatia (the EU's newest member state), were home to at least one agency. A recent evaluation of EU agencies concluded that the remote location of many of these bodies was a source of significant inefficiency. A case in point is the European Food Safety Authority, which reportedly spends €1 million per year on airport transfers for visitors and staff to its headquarters in Parma, an Italian city with a rich culinary history, but no international airport (European Commission 2009: 61). It is tempting to conclude that EU agencies have been headquartered on an intergovernmental 'share the spoils' (of jobs) basis.

European agencies are not the only form of *de novo* body. A case in point is the European Court of Auditors, which was established in 1977 to examine the accounts of all revenue and expenditure of the EU. Once appointed, the members of the Court of Auditors are independent and cannot be removed from office by the national governments. The European Court of Auditors is a *supranational* institution, albeit one that lacks powers of enforcement. The ECB is a more powerful institution,

TABLE 1.2 *De novo* bodies

Start of activities	Title of institution	Location
1958	European Investment Bank	Luxembourg
1960	European Supply Agency	Luxembourg
1975	European Centre for the Development of Vocational Training (Cedefop)	Thessaloniki (previously Berlin)
	European Foundation for the Improvement of Living and Working Conditions (Eurofound)	Dublin
1977	European Court of Auditors	Luxembourg
1993	European Environment Agency (EEA)	Copenhagen
1994	Translation Centre for the Bodies of the European Union	Luxembourg
	European Training Foundation (ETF)	Turin
	European Union Intellectual Property Office	Alicante
	European Monetary Institute*	Frankfurt
1995	European Ombudsman	Strasbourg
	European Agency for Safety and Health at Work (EU-OSHA)	Bilbao
	European Medicines Agency (EMA)	London***
	European Monitoring Centre for Drugs and Drug Addiction (EMCDDA)	Lisbon
1995	Community Plant Variety Office	Angers
1998	European Union Agency for Fundamental Rights (FRA)	Vienna
	European Central Bank	Frankfurt
1999	European Policy Office (Europol)	The Hague
2000	European Police College (Cepol)	Budapest (previously Bramshill)
	European Agency for Reconstruction**	Thessaloniki

2002	European Union's Judicial Cooperation Unit (Eurojust)	The Hague
	European Maritime Safety Agency (EMSA)	Lisbon
	European Food Safety Authority (EFSA)	Parma
	European Institute for Security Studies (EUISS)	Paris
	European Union Satellite Centre (Satcen)	Torrejón de Ardoz
2003	European Aviation Safety Agency (EASA)	Cologne
2004	European Data Protection Supervisor	Brussels
	European Network and Information Security Agency (ENISA)	Athens
	European Defence Agency (EDA)	Brussels
	Executive Agency for Small and Medium-sized Enterprises (EASME)	Brussels
2005	European Agency for the Management of Operational Cooperation at the External Borders (Frontex)	Warsaw
	European Centre for Disease Prevention and Control (ECDC)	Stockholm
	Consumers, Health and Food Executive Agency (CHAFEA)	Luxembourg
2006	Community Fisheries Control Agency (EFCA)	Vigo
	European Railway Agency (ERA)	Valenciennes/Lille
	Innovation and Networks Executive Agency (INEA)	Brussels
	Education, Audiovisual and Culture Executive Agency (EACEA)	Brussels
2007	European Chemicals Agency (ECHA)	Helsinki
	European Institute for Gender Equality (EIGI)	Vilnius
	European GNSS Supervisory Authority (GSA)	Prague

Cont. ➤

Cont.

	European Joint Undertaking for ITER—Fusion for Energy (F4E)	Barcelona
	Single European Sky Air Traffic Management Research 2 Joint Undertaking (SESAR2)	Brussels
2008	European Institute of Innovation and Technology (EIT)	Budapest
	Innovative Medicines Initiative 2 Joint Undertaking (IMI2)	Brussels
	Clean Sky 2 Joint Undertaking (Clean Sky2)	Brussels
2009	Research Executive Agency (REA)	Brussels
	European Research Council Executive Agency (ERC Executive Agency)	Brussels
2010	Body of European Regulators for Electronic Communications (BEREC)	Riga
	European External Action Service	Brussels
	European Financial Stability Facility	Luxembourg
2011	European Banking Authority (EBA)	London***
	European Securities and Markets Authority (ESMA)	Paris
	European Insurance and Occupational Pensions Authority (EIOPA)	Frankfurt
	European Asylum Support Office (EASO)	Valetta
	Agency for the Cooperation of Energy Regulators (ACER)	Ljubljana
2012	European Agency for the Operational Management of Large-scale IT Systems in the Area of Freedom, Security and Justice (EU-LISA)	Tallinn
	European Stability Mechanism	Luxembourg
2014	Electronic Components and Systems for European Leadership Joint Undertaking (ECSEL)	Brussels
	Fuel Cells and Hydrogen 2 Joint Undertaking (FCH 2)	Brussels

	Bio-based Industries Joint Undertaking (BBI)	Brussels
	Shift2Rail	Brussels
2015	Single Resolution Board (SRB)	Brussels
2016	Authority for European political parties and European political foundations	To be decided

* European Monetary Institute replaced by European Central Bank in 1998.

** European Agency for Reconstruction closed in 2008 after its mandate expired.

*** Prior to UK withdrawal from the EU.

responsible for the formulation and implementation of eurozone monetary policy, but it has closer ties to the national level. Specifically, the ECB's most important decision-making body, the Governing Council, includes national central bank governors who are independent from, but appointed by, national governments.

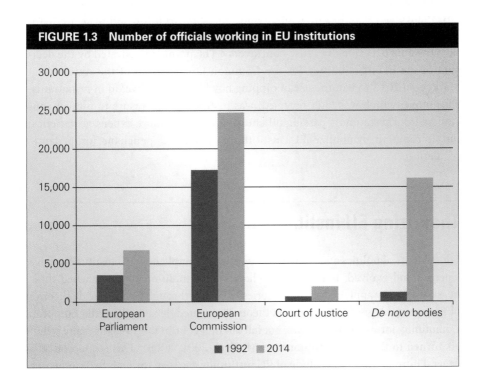

FIGURE 1.3   Number of officials working in EU institutions

The EU's implementation committees

Much of the detail of EU legislation is decided within committees, which work within a subterranean world of its institutional system. Simply put, *comitology* refers to a collection of specialist committees that watch over the implementation of EU law. Member states are responsible, in most cases, for ensuring that commitments agreed are reflected in national law. In some cases, EU policy-makers allow the Commission to determine the minimum requirements that member states must meet. Comitology committees, chaired by the Commission and chiefly comprising national officials, provide technical guidance on policy implementation that is non-binding in some cases and binding in others (Nugent and Rhinard 2015: 322–6).

Scholars are divided as to whether comitology serves as an intergovernmental brake on the Commission's supranational powers or a deliberative engine that can produce a convergence of views between national and EU officials (Blom-Hansen and Brandsma 2009). Either way, comitology committees are an increasingly important piece of the EU's institutional jigsaw. Between 2000 and 2014, the number of active comitology committees increased from 244 to 287.[9] In 2014, these committees met nearly 800 times and adopted some 3,600 opinions and implementing acts or measures (European Commission 2015b: 6–7).

Put simply, comitology points towards how technical and specialized much EU governance is, as well as how much takes place far from the political spotlight. Most decisions taken by comitology committees go unnoticed by the general public, but some occasionally cause controversy. The point is illustrated by the decision of the EU's Committee for the Common Organization of the Agricultural Markets in 2012 to ban the use of dipping bowls to serve olive oil in restaurants. This move, which was later reversed, was justified as a measure to protect consumers from restaurants passing off cheap olive oil for more expensive varieties, but it came to symbolize EU institutions' perceived penchant for pedantic regulation.

Theorizing EU institutions

For students of politics and IR, what matters is not simply how EU institutions have emerged and evolved, but why. EU scholars have traditionally approached these questions not by applying general theories of IR, but through custom-made theories of European integration. Integration theory dominated debates about the European Community for nearly forty years, but fell out of favour in the 1990s as many scholars turned to the new institutionalism (Pollack 2001, 2008). This section offers a general introduction to the study of EU institutions as seen through two competing lenses: integration theory and the new institutionalism.

Integration theory

Ernst Haas—a pioneer of neo-functionalism—was not the first to see why institutional cooperation between European states mattered for the study of IR. He was, however, the pioneer of theory-building in light of the European experience. Institutions and integration were inseparable for Haas (1958: 16), who defined political integration as 'the process whereby political actors in several distinct national settings are persuaded to shift their loyalties, expectations and political activities towards a new centre, whose institutions possess or demand jurisdiction over the pre-existing national states'. Unwieldy as this definition now appears, it focused the study of European integration on how and why states created new European institutions.

Neo-functionalism is often equated with Haas's concept of spillover, the process whereby integration in one policy domain gives rise to functional pressures for integration in another, for example creating a single market creates functional pressures for a single currency. But supranational institutions also played an important entrepreneurial role for Haas by brokering compromises between states in ways that furthered integration. He also hypothesized that transnational actors, such as political parties, businesses, or trade unions, would look to supranational institutions to serve and defend their interests. In the process, they would create demand for deeper integration.

Neo-functionalism fell into disfavour as the pace of European integration slowed in the 1960s and 1970s. Stanley Hoffmann's trenchant critique of neo-functionalism gave rise to his intergovernmental theory of European integration. Whereas neo-functionalism looked to non-state actors and supranational institutions to drive European integration, intergovernmentalism reasserted the importance of national governments. Insightful as Hoffmann's analysis was, it was built on a confusing conception of institutions, as evidenced by his claim that the Council was weak because the member states were strong and in his later suggestion that the European Council had 'decapitated' the Council (Hoffmann 1966; Hoffman 1995: 220).

The relaunch of European integration in the 1980s encouraged a second wave of theory-building based on a subtler and more sophisticated understanding of institutions. A high-water mark was Andrew Moravcsik's (1991, 1998) liberal intergovernmentalism. Simply put, liberal intergovernmentalism sees the delegation of policy-making powers to supranational institutions as a choice by member states to lock in the benefits of cooperation. Supranational institutions have little room to sway such institutional choices, with member states driven instead mainly by national (especially economic) interests.

European integration's revival encouraged scholars to revisit some of the central tenets of neo-functionalism. An important contribution was by Anne-Marie Burley (later Slaughter) and Walter Mattli (1993: 43), who offered a political theory of legal integration that 'correspond[ed] remarkably closely to the original neo-functionalist model developed by Ernst Haas in the late 1950s'. They emphasized not only the

Court of Justice's creation of a new legal order, but also the emergence of a transnational community of judges and lawyers with a shared understanding of, and commitment to, legal integration. Garrett (1995) led the intergovernmental backlash against this argument, suggesting that the Court took a stand only when large member states were unlikely to resist, thus ensuring that legal integration never strayed too far from national interests.

Another attempt to rework neo-functionalism was the so-called supranationalist school (Stone Sweet and Sandholtz 1998; Stone Sweet et al. 2001; Sandholtz and Stone Sweet 2012). Supranationalists argued that intergovernmental bargaining should be seen in a broader institutional context. European integration can produce a movement from intergovernmental to supranational decision-making, but only if supranational institutions, cross-border transactions, and institutionalization are sufficiently strong. Cross-border transactions occur when non-governmental actors, especially multinational firms, operate across European borders and demand closer cooperation between member states to facilitate their cross-border activities. Institutionalization refers to the tendency of EU institutions to spur institutional change as the potential and pitfalls of earlier institutional arrangements become apparent.

Classic integration theories offered more or less rationalist conceptions of IR in which individuals—and the institutions they populated—were driven by material self-interest. Constructivism, which emerged as a vibrant research agenda, challenged such simplistic assumptions (Ruggie 1982; Wendt 1992; Risse 2009). Jeffery Checkel (2005: 804) urged that greater attention be paid to the socialization effects of EU institutions, which he defined as 'the process of inducting actors into the norms and rules of a given community'. Curiously, work in this field suggests that socialization can be stronger in intergovernmental institutions, such as the Council (Beyers 2005) and Coreper (Lewis 2005) than in the Commission (Kassim et al. 2013).

Debates between intergovernmentalists, supranationalists, and constructivists boiled over in the 1990s and 2000s (Moravcsik 1999; Stone Sweet et al. 2001, Tsebelis and Garrett 2001). But general interest in integration theory cooled. Although important works of integration theory have emerged over the last two decades, the dominant paradigms remained largely unchanged (Mattli 1999; Niemann 2006). This continuity reflects the resilience of these theories, but also a lack of interest in the changing character of EU institutions during this period. At the time of writing, there are signs of a return to integration theory, as scholars seek to make sense of European Banking Union and other reforms enacted in response to the euro crisis (see Ioannou et al. 2015) and the changing institutional dynamics of European integration more generally (Bickerton et al. 2015a). Recurring risks that Greece and others might exit the eurozone has also encouraged scholars to theorize about disintegration (Vollaard 2014; Webber 2014), a literature that is likely to develop further in response to the UK's 2016 referendum vote to leave the EU.

The new institutionalism

Peter Hall and Rosemary Taylor (1996) famously identified three schools of new institutionalism, but, as Guy B. Peters (2011) shows, there are now at least five:

- normative institutionalism;
- rational choice institutionalism;
- historical institutionalism;
- sociological institutionalism; and
- discursive institutionalism.

They differ in several respects, but are united by an interest in institutions not only as conduits for politics, but also as catalysts and constraints. In this sense, the new institutionalism moves beyond integration theory's preoccupation with the question of why EU institutions are created to consider the wider importance of such political bodies in EU policy-making.

The oldest variant, normative institutionalism, was developed by James March and Johan Olsen (2004). Challenging the rational choice turn in political science, they argued that individuals are motivated not only by self-interest, but also by a logic of appropriateness, based on 'obligations encapsulated in a role, an identity, a membership in a political community or group, and the ethos, practices and expectations of its institutions' (March and Olsen 2004: 3). Normative institutionalism treats the Union's political bodies less as the product of political interests than as fora in which new conceptions of the national and European interest are forged. Bart Kerremans (1996: 231) sees the Council as shaping member states' preferences through routinized interaction between national officials and the depoliticization of decision-making. What seems appropriate within institutions may not seem so to the outside world, of course. This point relates to perennial worries that national officials 'go native' in Brussels and become socialized to find compromises rather than to defend the interests of their member state. Equally, concerns arise about the gendering of 'ethos, practices and expectations' within EU bodies that have traditionally been dominated by men (Chappell 2006).

Rational choice institutionalism sees EU institutions as created via calculated decisions taken by self-interested political actors. Member states choose to cooperate when it is in their interests and design institutions where they help to reduce the transaction costs—such as monitoring and compliance with agreed rules—associated with such cooperation. Rational choice institutionalism influenced Moravcsik's liberal Intergovernmentalism, but found wider application in Mark Pollack's (2003) principal–agent approach. Pollack (2003) asked not only why member state principals delegate to supranational agents, but also how the former can monitor and control the latter. The attraction of the principal–agent approach is that it can be applied to a range of institutional choices (Billiet *et al.* 2009). Tallberg (2003), for example, thinks of the Commission and Court of Justice not as agents, but as delegated monitors designed to ensure that member states meet their obligations under EU law. Hodson (2015a) goes further by conceptualizing the International Monetary Fund (IMF) as a *de facto* institution of the EU because of the important roles entrusted by the latter to the former in response to the euro crisis.

Historical institutionalism is interested in how EU institutions constrain political actors in ways that do not always serve their rational self-interest. It highlights emergent institutional norms, such as the Council's consensual working methods (Golub 1999; Hayes-Renshaw and Wallace 2006). Such norms can constrain political decision-making and produce 'path dependence', or an aversion to change existing practice because of the high costs of agreement in the first place (Armstrong and Bulmer 1998: 55). Pierson (1996) cites the Treaty of Rome's provision on gender pay equality, which was initially seen as symbolic by member states, but was eventually used by EU institutions to promote significant changes to national social policies.

Sociological institutionalism seeks to understand how 'culturally specific practices' become embedded in EU institutions (Hall and Taylor 1996: 946). A close cousin of constructivism, sociological institutionalism puts norms, conventions, and ideas at the centre of its analysis. For example, Neil Fligstein and Iona Mara-Drita's (1996) analysis of the single market stressed the Commission's success in putting forward the '1992 project' as a 'cultural frame' that broke the deadlock between member states in this policy domain. Ian Manners (2002) emphasized the EU's ability to project its norms on the international stage, as illustrated by the EU's collective campaign against the death penalty in the Council of Europe and the UN.

Discursive institutionalism, the newest of the new institutionalisms, views EU institutions through the lens of ideas and discourse. For Vivien Schmidt (2008), discursive institutionalism is about the meaning of ideas and ability of political actors to communicate them to one another and the wider public. This approach takes a dynamic view of institutions in which ideas and discourse serve as catalysts for change rather than a means of reinforcing the status quo. To illustrate, Schmidt's work with Amandine Crespy (2014: 1087) on the euro crisis contrasts German Chancellor Angela Merkel's public insistence that financial support for Greece be linked to greater EU oversight of national economic policies with French President Nicolas Sarkozy's appeals to European solidarity. This account departs from the logic of appropriateness in that actors are drawn towards ideas not necessarily because of their plausibility, but because they play well with domestic audiences.

The separation of powers tradition

Understanding how and why EU institutions have evolved are key questions in the study of European integration; fundamental, too, is the question of what EU institutions do. Faced with this puzzle, many scholars have turned to the separation of powers tradition by classifying EU bodies into executive, legislative, or judicial bodies.[10] This tradition was pioneered by Enlightenment philosopher Baron de Montesquieu (2011, first published 1748), who argued that giving responsibility for enacting law (legislative power), enforcing law (executive power), and interpreting law (judicial power) to a single institution brought a risk of tyranny. Montesquieu's arguments inspired the framers of the United States' (US) Constitution, who separated the powers of their new government in response to a perceived abuse of authority by the British monarch. But how has this political tradition inspired the design of EU institutions?

Executive pluralism

Under the US Constitution, the president's executive powers include command of the armed forces, the authority to make treaties, responsibility for appointing officers of the US, including Supreme Court Justices, and the right to recommend matters for consideration to Congress. Seen in these terms, few executive powers have been entrusted to the institutions of the EU and fewer still to the European Commission. And yet the Commission has long been referred to as an 'executive' body. Early work in the separation of powers tradition applied the concept of executive power in a rather inconsistent way, with Lindberg (1963) unclear as to whether executive power had been conferred to the Commission specifically or to the Community more generally. Pollack (2003) brought conceptual order by distinguishing between the Commission's legislative function—its right of initiative—and its executive functions—the power to monitor and enforce member states' commitments to EU law. However, neither instance of executive power is straightforward. The Commission's role in monitoring and enforcement is shared with the Court of Justice, while member states typically retain control over implementing EU policy 'on the ground' (Pollack 2003: 87).

The Commission enjoys sweeping executive powers in only a few cases. One is competition policy, where the Commission has authority on a par with that exercised by the US Department of Justice's Antitrust Division (Hawk and Laudati 1996). Elsewhere, the Commission's executive powers are limited. Under the Treaty of Rome, the Commission was given a prominent role in policy implementation, but, as Ludlow (1991: 105) notes, the reality of policy-making 'caution[s] against the slick identification of the Commission as the executive branch'.

For Hix and Høyland (2011), the Commission and the Council are two halves of a dual executive. Executive duality has arguably given way, however, to a system of executive pluralism. One reason for this shift is that the Council and European Council have emerged as distinctive bodies. The heads of state or government have assumed a more hands on role in EU policy-making. Between 1975 and 1995, the European Council met three times per year; since then, they have met much more frequently and as many as eleven times per year (Puetter 2015). Summits to deal with crises facing EU member states, from civil war in Libya to the euro crisis, are now commonplace. But the European Council is more than just a crisis manager; heads of state or government often find themselves involved in detailed policy-making in economic governance, JHA, and foreign and security policy (Puetter 2014).

The move towards executive pluralism can also be seen in the proliferation of bodies that exercise executive functions. The question of whether institutions other than the Commission can be so empowered is a sensitive one that has provoked a series of legal challenges since the 1950s. Recent rulings by the Court to try to clarify the place of agencies in the EU's institutional structure still leave the matter 'on shaky legal ground' (Chamon 2011: 1075).

A multicameral legislature

Students of EU institutions were initially reluctant to see the EP as a legislature even after the move to direct elections in 1979 (Palmer 1977; Herman and Lodge 1978). This reticence evaporated as the EP acquired more influence in EU policy-making. The Parliament is now commonly seen as exercising significant legislative powers (Maurer 2003). Still, there has been comparatively little reflection in the EU literature about what other legislative bodies do and whether the EP undertakes similar roles.[11] Part of the problem, perhaps, is that the roles played by legislatures vary from one political system to another (Blondel 1970; Norton 1990).

Nevertheless, it is clear that the EP is involved in many of the roles played by modern legislatures. First, the EP constrains the executive power (of the Commission and Council) through its ability to veto legislation that falls under the EU's 'ordinary' legislative procedure. Second, the EP plays a key role in the appointment and dismissal of the executive branch, albeit in relation to the Commission rather than the Council or European Council. Third, the EP provides parliamentary oversight through the work of its specialist committees. Finally, the EP is involved in the ratification of international agreements and treaties to which the EU is a signatory.

In other respects, the EP lacks powers typically associated with legislatures. Members of the EP have no war powers of the kind exercised by the US Congress. Legislatures play an important constitutional role in many cases. But the EP has limited powers here too. Congress can initiate and approve changes to the US Constitution before sending such amendments for ratification to the American states; in the EU, it ultimately falls to member states to agree all Treaty changes by unanimity and to ratify them in accordance with their constitutional tradition.[12]

The EP also is not the EU's only legislative body. A number of scholars see the Parliament and Council as two chambers in a bicameral legislative system (Hosli 1995; Crombez et al. 2000). In principle, the two chambers have an equal say under the OLP, but not always in practice (Hagemann and Høyland 2010). The Council can also legislate in some cases without the backing of the EP under the Treaty's so-called special legislative procedure, which covers sensitive policy areas such as the EU's common external tariff.

The right to initiate legislation is a key source of legislative power that both the EP and the Council lack. In the US, only members of the House of Representatives and Senate can formally introduce their own bills (even if many are written within the executive branch); in the EU, this role falls almost exclusively to the Commission. This monopoly on the right of initiative gives the Commission significant agenda-setting powers, although such powers are not exercised in a political vacuum. The European Council frequently 'invites' the Commission to come forward with legislative proposals, and the Council and Parliament are entitled to do likewise. Under the Lisbon Treaty, a new citizens' initiative means that members of the public—if they can put together a petition with a million signatures—can invite the Commission to put forward specific legislative proposals.

Traditionally seen as struggling to influence EU institutions, national parliaments have assumed a more prominent role on the European stage in recent decades. The Lisbon Treaty introduced a new 'yellow' card system to allow national parliaments to force the Commission to consider concerns over subsidiarity, or the idea that action should be taken at the most efficient level of government, but as close to the citizens as possible (Piris 2010: 128–9). Some commentators see sufficient potential to talk of 'emerging tricameralism' involving national parliaments alongside the EP and Council (Cooper 2013).

Judicial federalism

Viewing the EU through a separation of powers lens means looking hard to separate the executive and legislature trees from the institutional forest. This task is not as onerous when it comes to the judicial branch, but neither is it as obvious as it looks. Political scientists typically treat judicial review—the authority to decide whether a given law is consistent with a body of higher law—as the most important power exercised by the judiciary (Lijphart 2012). The Court of Justice of the EU has emerged as a more powerful judiciary than its architects arguably intended. Although the founding treaties gave the Court powers of judicial review, this provision was primarily concerned with keeping the High Authority and Commission in check. It was only over time, as Karen Alter (1998: 24) argues, that the Court assumed the right to subject national laws to judicial review.

While the Court of Justice is a powerful judicial institution, there are other boughs on the EU's judicial branch. National courts continue to play a major role in determining whether EU policy-making fits with national constitutional traditions. Germany's Federal Constitutional Court has emerged as a key player because of a series of challenges by German citizens against EU treaties and policies. A case in point is the 2009 Lisbon judgment in which the Federal Constitutional Court rejected a legal challenge to the ratification of the Lisbon Treaty, but nonetheless identified certain 'core state functions', including a monopoly over the use of force or issues related to taxation, of which EU institutions should steer clear (Steinbach 2010).

Meanwhile, national courts in the EU play a prominent role in the interpretation of Union law. Another feature of judicial federalism is that lower courts stake an independent claim to the protection of fundamental rights. The Court of Justice is generally deferential to national constitutional traditions in such matters. One reason is that EU judges have sought to enforce fundamental rights only insofar as they relate to acts of the EU rather than its member states (Weiler 1986).

In summary, the separation of powers tradition has pros and cons in guiding the study of EU institutions. The principal advantage is that it points towards a rich body of literature on executive, legislative, and judicial politics; the principal drawback is that EU institutions do not fit neatly into Montesquieu's triptych. Moreover, Montesquieu was, above all, interested in the normative question of how the separation of powers could ensure that no one institution would exercise undue influence. There is no such separation in the EU—in which powers are shared more than separated—and attempts by the Court of Justice to develop a doctrine of 'institutional balance' have clouded, rather than clarified, matters (Conway 2011).

Holding EU institutions to account

The last two decades have witnessed a debate over the perceived democratic deficit of EU institutions. This debate is a response to what Pollack (2008: 13) calls the EU's 'long constitutional crisis'. This crisis has been reflected in a string of 'no' votes in EU-related referenda since 1992, falling turnout in EP elections, and rising distrust in EU institutions (see Figure 1.4). This loss of trust has been exacerbated by the euro crisis, which saw EU institutions assume a new and controversial role in economic policy. The most serious step to date in the EU's constitutional crisis was the UK's referendum vote in 2016 to leave the EU, triggering concerns that other member states might follow suit.

A democratic deficit in the EU is inevitable, argues Robert Dahl (1999). Democracy, for Dahl (1999: 20), means:

... rule by the people, or rather the *demos*,[13] with a government of the state that is responsive and accountable to the *demos*, a sovereign authority that decides important political matters either directly in popular assemblies or indirectly through its representatives, chosen ... by means of elections.

For Dahl (1999: 30), Europe is simply too big and diverse for EU institutions to govern democratically, for example citizens question whether 'they exercise as much influence in the European Parliament as they do in their own'.

Governments frequently delegate powers to non-majoritarian institutions, a fact that Dahl (1999) seems to overlook. Such institutions operate at arm's length from politicians, as in the case of the US Federal Reserve System, which governs monetary policy. Drawing on this experience, Giandomenico Majone (1998) argues that the

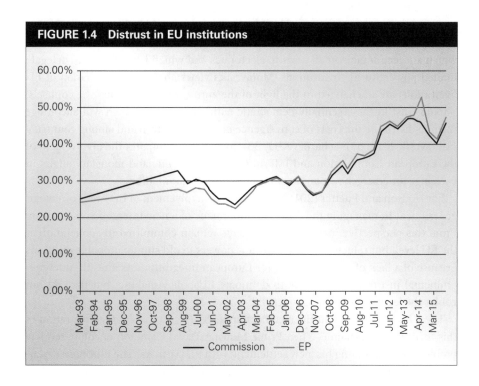

FIGURE 1.4   Distrust in EU institutions

—— Commission   —— EP

EU's democratic deficit is 'democratically justified' provided that the Union performs policy roles that are appropriate for non-majoritarian institutions.

Follesdal and Hix (2006) see EU regulation as creating winners and losers, and so question Majone's (1998) logic of delegation. The Commission, they argue, should divest itself of its regulatory functions and instead become a genuine political executive committed to 'initiating social, economic and environmental laws' (Follesdal and Hix 2006: 554). These policy choices should not be determined by the Commission in isolation, they argue, but by contestation between the Council and EP over who should lead the Commission and what his or her policy agenda should be. The *Spitzenkandidaten* process provides a powerful test of such claims and the EP's ability to bridge the EU's democratic deficit.

The long-standing idea of 'the European Parliament as a guarantor of democracy in the European system' (Dooge 1985: 38) is by no means endorsed by all. Hix and Bartolini (2006) warn that the EP is more likely to split along pro–anti EU lines rather than the left–right axis traditionally associated with national parliaments. The result, they suggest, would be contestation over the question of what powers EU institutions should have rather than how this power should be exercised. The results of the 2014 EP elections spoke to this point, with about a third of MEPs elected on a Eurosceptic ticket.

Amid clamour to reform EU institutions, some voices defend the institutional status quo. Moravcsik (2002) suggests that the Union's institutional crisis is premised, in part, on a misunderstanding of how its institutions should be legitimated. The EU derives a large measure of its legitimacy, he argues, from national governments, which are accountable in all cases to electorates and which have chosen to delegate limited powers to EU institutions. Moravcsik's views about the legitimation of EU institutions are unchanged in the light of the euro crisis. 'Europeans', he counsels, 'should trust in the essentially democratic nature of the EU, which will encourage them to distribute the costs of convergence more fairly within and among countries' (Moravcsik 2012: 55). Scharpf (2011: 35), in contrast, compares the involvement of the European Commission and IMF in Greece's economic and monetary affairs in exchange for emergency loans as a form of 'external domination'.

For Hodson and Puetter (2016), the intensive involvement of EU heads of state or government in managing the crisis is symptomatic of a new intergovernmentalism. From this perspective, national governments remain committed to cooperation at the EU level, but reluctant to delegate new powers to old supranational institutions because of a lack of public support for European integration. As a result, intergovernmental institutions continue to dominate EU policy-making, but they do not confer the legitimacy that they once did.

The UK's referendum on EU membership in 2016 is, arguably, one illustration of this institutional dynamic. Then Prime Minister David Cameron encountered few problems in negotiating his 'new settlement' with EU partners. The European Council did what it typically does during crises and hammered out a deal that satisfied most member states. The real challenge was selling this deal—or any deal—to a British electorate that was deeply distrustful not only of EU institutions, but also national ones. After a tumultuous referendum campaign, British voters opted by a narrow margin to leave the EU. The result was little short of catastrophic for Europe: the Union had never before lost a member state, even though the Treaty provides for such a possibility.[14] And yet, within days of the vote, even British politicians who led the campaign to leave the EU were looking towards new forms of institutionalized cooperation between the UK and EU (Johnson 2016). The precise terms and timing of Brexit—the UK's formal exit from the EU—were yet to be decided at the time of writing. But these matters would, once again, be worked out in intergovernmental institutions by the heads of state or government.

Conclusion and plan of the book

This chapter has explored five fundamental questions.

- What are EU institutions?
- Where did they come from?
- What are EU institutions for?
- What do they do?
- How should EU institutions be held to account?

The key message of this chapter and volume are that the answers to the questions can be found by resorting to a variety of theoretical perspectives, even though different theories often provide different answers. Nevertheless, EU institutions matter not only for those who seek to understand the EU, but also for those interested in politics and IR more generally. Although the EU remains institutionally slight by the standards of a state, it has arguably become the most powerful international organization in the world (Josselin and Wallace 2001; Cowles 2003).

As with earlier efforts at institutionalized cooperation in Europe, the EU is built on intergovernmental institutions. But its member states broke from the past by giving supranational and transnational institutions significant policy-making powers. The EU's two traditional supranational institutions, the Commission and Court of Justice, remain strong after sixty years. The more dramatic story set out in this chapter, however, concerns the rise of new intergovernmental institutions, including the European Council and many *de novo* bodies, such as EU agencies, as well as the empowerment of the EP, the EU's directly elected transnational institution. More dramatic still are the chronic crises of effectiveness and legitimacy facing these institutions, the latest—but likely not the last—phase of which saw the UK vote to leave the EU.

Most texts on the EU's institutions offer a straight review of what the Treaty designates as institutions, with one chapter each on the Council, Commission, EP, and so on. Less weighty institutions, such as the Court of Auditors and CoR, are covered in a composite, 'lest we forget', chapter. This book does not present a simple, standard, one-institution-per-chapter dash across the EU's institutional landscape; instead, after further historical discussion (Chapter 2), we offer three guided tours of how different institutions provide political direction (Part I), manage the Union (Part II), and integrate interests (Part III).

Each of the chapters begins with an analysis of the origins and development of the institution specified, followed by an overview of its structure and functions. Each author then reflects on the institution's powers, before considering how it fits into the EU's long wider institutional system. Each considers which theories help us best to understand the institution. None ignores the crucial questions of how the institution is likely to be changed by the EU's long constitutional crisis and continued turmoil over the euro. A final chapter draws the various strands of this discussion together to reflect on how EU institutions and the study thereof have evolved over the last sixty years, and where they might be headed in a new and uncertain phase for the Union.

Some EU institutions—particularly the Commission, Council, and EP—perform more than one function, hence analysis of them is spread across more than one chapter. The reader who wants to understand the institutions 'one by one' (or the teacher who wants to teach them that way) should not hesitate to read, say, Chapter 5 on the college of Commissioners together with Chapter 8 on the Commission's services. But we encourage reading chapters together in the sections into which they are grouped. The effect is to encourage a coming to grips with the intensity of both inter-institutional cooperation *and* competition in the performance of the Union's policy functions. Above all, we seek not simply to give readers 'the facts' about EU institutions, but rather to invite more rigorous reflections on why EU institutions matter.

ENDNOTES

1. Art. 3 TEU.
2. Art. 13 TEU.
3. Primary law flows from the Treaty. Sources of secondary law include regulations proposed by the Commission and adopted by the Council and EP.
4. Art. 1 of the Treaty of London.
5. Art. 20 of the Treaty Establishing the European Coal and Steel Community.
6. *Spitzenkandidaten* is a German term that, in this context, means top, or preferred, candidate for Commission President.
7. *De novo* is a Latin term that translates (loosely) to 'afresh, anew, again, from the beginning' in English. See http://translation.babylon.com/english/de%20novo/
8. Art. 130 of the Treaty Establishing the European Economic Community.
9. See European Commission (2001a: 8); European Commission (2015b: 4).
10. The separation of powers tradition is sometimes referred to in the original Latin as the *trias politica* tradition. For applications to the EU, see Sandalow and Stein (1982); Pinder (1992); Lenaerts (1991); Hix and Høyland (2011).
11. For exceptions, see Voermans (2010); Conway (2011).
12. Under the Lisbon Treaty, the EP can also propose changes to the Treaties, but it falls to the European Council to decide on whether to take such changes forward (Art. 48 TFEU).
13. Joseph Weiler (1999: 337) uses the term 'demos' to describe the citizens that make up a democracy. Nicolaïdis (2013: 351) views the EU as a 'demoicracy', i.e. 'a Union of peoples . . . who govern together but not as one'.
14. See Art. 50 TEU.

FURTHER READING

For alternative perspectives on the EU's institutions, see Hix and Høyland (2011), Doutriaux and Lequesne (2013, in French), and Wallace and Reh (2015). The best and most comprehensive coverage of the institutions given in any basic EU text is Nugent (2010). Peters (2011) provides an excellent overview of institutionalist theory. Rosamond (2000) and Wiener and Diez (2009) are essential reading on integration theories. Bickerton *et al.* (2015a) explore the rise of *de novo* bodies and the changing character of EU institutions more generally since the Maastricht Treaty.

Bickerton, C.J., Hodson, D., and Puetter, U. (eds) (2015a) *The New Intergovernmentalism: States and Supranational Actors in the Post-Maastricht Era* (Oxford and New York: Oxford University Press).

Doutriaux, Y., and Lequesne, C. (2013) *Les institutions de l'Union européenne après la crise de l'euro* (9th edn, Paris: La Documentation Française).

Hix, S., and Høyland, B. (2011) *The Political System of the European Union* (3rd edn, Basingstoke: Palgrave).

Nugent, N. (2010) *The Government and Politics of the European Union* (7th edn, Basingstoke: Palgrave Macmillan).

Peters, B.G. (2011) *Institutional Theory in Political Science* (3rd edn, New York: Continuum).

Rosamond, B. (2000) *Theories of European Integration* (Basingstoke: Palgrave Macmillan).

Wallace, H., and Reh, C. (2015) 'An institutional anatomy and five policy modes', in H. Wallace, M.A. Pollack, and A.R. Young (eds) *Policy-Making in the European Union* (7th edn, Oxford and New York: Oxford University Press): 72–112.

Wiener, A., and Diez, T. (2009) *European Integration Theory* (2nd edn, Oxford and New York: Oxford University Press).

WEB LINKS

http://europa.eu/

Europa, the official website of the EU, is the best place to begin any search for basic information on the EU's institutions. It has links to the websites of all EU institutions, a newsroom containing all EU press releases and statements, and databases and access to the Treaties and official documentation.

http://www.ft.com/world/europe/brussels

Among English language newspapers, the *Financial Times* offers the best news coverage of EU affairs. It is *the* journal of record for those working in EU institutions.

http://www.politico.eu

Politico's European edition offers in-depth, high-octane news coverage of EU affairs. Its journalists have a reputation for securing scoops from EU policy-makers and @POLITICOEurope is well worth following on Twitter.

CHAPTER 2

The history of EU institutions: Six decades of institutional change

Renaud Dehousse and Paul Magnette

▌ Summary

Its institutions have frequently been reformed since the origins of what is now the European Union (EU)—and particularly so in the last twenty years. This chapter explains why and how this quasi-constant change has taken place. It begins by identifying five phases in this history: the founding, consolidation, adaptation, and reform of the institutional system, and the brief 'constitutional' moment at the turn of the century. Following a discussion of the euro crisis and Brexit, it then assesses the

Cont. ➤

> **Cont.**
>
> respective weight of state interests, ideas, and institutions in the evolution of EU institutions. In retrospect, institutional change in the EU appears to have followed a functionalist logic, leading to complex compromises that, in turn, prompt regular calls for 'simplification' and democratization.

Introduction

It is widely recognized that the dynamics of European integration owe much to the originality of its institutional structure, in which the delegation of powers to supranational institutions has been more intensive than in 'classical' international organizations (see Chapter 1). However, European institutions themselves have changed significantly since the creation of the European Coal and Steel Community (ECSC) by six countries in 1951. The EU of today, which reached twenty-eight member states before the United Kingdom (UK) voted to leave, has a population of roughly 500 million people. Several Treaty changes have taken place since the 1990s and new institutions have been created. The EU deals with a much wider range of issues than its forerunners did some fifty years ago. New problems—such as the need to democratize the European political system—have emerged.

The aim of this chapter is to understand how the institutional setting has evolved. To this end, we will begin by reviewing the main changes that have taken place, covering not only the grand 'constitutional moments'—that is, the intergovernmental conferences (IGCs) that have marked the history of European integration—but also the changes that have taken place in the meantime. We will then briefly review the economic and financial crises that have shaken the EU in recent years, to assess the impact they may have on the structure of the Union. Finally, we will discuss the main factors that have affected the dynamics of institutional change.

The five phases of institutional development

The institutional system of the EU has been in constant evolution since its creation in the 1950s. The IGCs that were concluded by the signing of the Treaties of Paris (1951) and Rome (1957) were merely the first of a long series of inter-state negotiations. Indeed, institutional change can be seen as a quasi-permanent feature of the integration process, with many institutional adaptations taking place without Treaty reform in the periods between IGCs. The EU's institutional history can be divided into five phases. These 'stages' are not precisely delimited, but each does have its own peculiarities and consequently its own dynamics of change.

The foundations

Contrary to many other polities, the EU's institutional system was not brought about by a dramatic revolution inspired by a clear doctrine. The long decade between the end of the Second World War and the signature of the Treaty of Rome in 1957 was, in hindsight, a period of trial and error, which gave rise to an unprecedented system via the accumulation of partial compromises. Contrary to what the official historiography would lead us to believe, what is now called the 'Community method' (Dehousse 2011) was not born overnight; there was no sudden conversion of European elites to Jean Monnet's plans. Between 1948 and 1957, European leaders were actually torn between competing visions of Europe's future, each reflecting a particular institutional model.

For example, the 'constitutional approach' was a widely shared objective in the founding years. At the Congress of Europe held in The Hague in May 1948 (a private initiative gathering dozens of European movements that had mushroomed in the two preceding years), many voices supported the idea that a European constitutional assembly should be convened to define the basic rules governing relations among European countries. The institutional conceptions of these federalist movements were largely inspired by the American model; the idea that Europe should have its own 'Philadelphia'[1] was their leitmotif. In the following months, however, a clear opposition emerged between governments supporting a federal vision and those conceiving Europe's future in more classical intergovernmental terms. This divide, which echoed the debates of the interwar period, showed that Europe was not ready to adopt anything like the United States' (US) Constitution (1787). Ultimately, in May 1949, ten European governments managed to sign the Treaty establishing the Council of Europe (see Chapter 1). Even before it was signed, however, it was clear for most of its members that the consensus on which it was based was so narrow that it would end in deadlock.

The Schuman Declaration of May 1950, which launched the idea of a more modest European Coal and Steel Community (ECSC), signalled a change of strategy; the states most interested in deeper European cooperation shifted to an apparently more modest functional approach, confining cooperation to a limited field. Although very classical in some respects, this approach was founded on an original institutional blueprint. The cornerstone of ECSC institutional architecture was the delegation of powers to an international High Authority, the independence of which was guaranteed, and to a court with much wider powers than other international jurisdictions. In addition, the governments gathered in the Council of Ministers could renounce the classic international practice of unanimity in favour of qualified majority voting (QMV). By virtue of these 'supranational' elements (a word used in the ECSC Treaty), the 'Community model' entailed greater transfers of powers than other international organizations. It nevertheless fell short of a federal model, given, among other things, the absence of a direct link to the people (although there was a provision in the Treaty for member states to create such a link—see Chapter 6).

A hybrid institutional system always gives rise to competing interpretations and the Community model was no exception. Many supporters of the functionalist approach hoped that integration would be a dynamic process—that cooperation would extend to other fields as a result of issue linkages and spillover effects, so that, ultimately, the functionalist approach could lead to the adoption of a real constitution. In the months following the signing of the Paris Treaty, the dynamics of European integration did, in fact, seem to accelerate. In an international context marked by the intensification of the Cold War, the six member states of the ECSC ('the Six') agreed to try to extend their cooperation to the military field and negotiated a new Treaty establishing a European Defence Community (EDC). In the framework of these negotiations, the governments of the Six also agreed to set up a constitutional assembly (prudently called an 'ad hoc assembly') to define a broader institutional framework inspired by federal principles, referred to as the European Political Community (EPC). In March 1953, the assembly chaired by Paul-Henri Spaak adopted a draft constitution inspired by federalist principles (Griffiths 2000). However, this constitutional phase was short-lived. Only a year later, the French National Assembly rejected the EDC Treaty following a heated public campaign and the EPC sank with it. The 'relaunch' of European integration at the Messina Conference and the subsequent creation of the European Economic Community (EEC) in March 1957 were, in part, a functionalist reaction to this failure.

The negotiations that gave rise to the Treaties of Paris and Rome were but the first in a long series of diplomatic bargains between the member states. They took the classic form of IGCs, rather than constitutional assemblies. Formally, the governments never departed from the canons of international practice. The outcome, arrived at through discrete and complex negotiations, was not a constitution, but a treaty agreed upon by 'the High contracting parties'. As such, it could enter into force only after being ratified by all member states. In these conferences, in which each country was represented by a delegation of government officials, mixing diplomats and experts drawn from economic ministries, everything had to be decided by consensus. National experts gathered in working groups to examine the details of the arrangements, while the heads of delegation—usually senior diplomats—met regularly to assess the progress of the negotiations and settle the most sensitive issues in close consultation with foreign ministers. In addition, the heads of state and governments met bilaterally or multilaterally to provide the political impetus and address the most contentious issues. Mindful of the political crisis generated by the ratification of the EDC Treaty, the national delegations worked in closer contact with national parliamentarians, party leaders, and interest groups during the Brussels IGC of 1956–57. But the conference nevertheless remained classically intergovernmental. Its deliberations took place behind closed doors and were almost entirely invisible to ordinary citizens, while the Community institutions merely acted as outside advisers.

In retrospect, this founding decade seems characterized by a constant oscillation between a 'constitutional way' and a functionalist approach. In the end, the repeated failures of the former consolidated the latter (Magnette 2005a). The governments of the member states accepted some limitations on their sovereignty in order to improve the efficiency of their cooperation. But governments nevertheless retained control of the process of institutional change.

The consolidation of the Community model

The first decade after the foundation was a period of sharp differences among the Six, which paradoxically strengthened the European Community (EC)'s institutional system. Several governments still hoped to expand the scope of their cooperation and to strengthen the Community institutions, whereas France, under President Charles de Gaulle, was fundamentally concerned with preventing encroachments on its sovereignty. In these circumstances, the Community model was subjected to both centripetal and centrifugal forces.

In the early 1960s, two well-known episodes of the European saga—the rejection of the Fouchet Plans and the 'empty chair' crisis—showed that any attempt to alter the balance between intergovernmentalism and supranationalism in the Community model would be opposed by at least one member state. In 1961–62, de Gaulle thought that he could reassert French hegemony by creating a political community based on pure intergovernmental cooperation. The Fouchet Plans, named after de Gaulle's special envoy to European capitals, contemplated both the extension of the scope of European cooperation to military issues and the creation of an administrative secretariat, which was largely seen as a potential rival for the supranational European Commission. These plans were thwarted, however, by the opposition of the Benelux countries (Belgium, the Netherlands, and Luxembourg). Although they had initially feared the supranational High Authority, which they saw as a Trojan horse of French influence, the three small states now realized that a strictly intergovernmental Community would weaken them. In the absence of a supranational agenda-setter and independent monitoring of Treaty implementation, it would be harder to resist French dominance.

Advocates of supranationalism were no more successful. In 1964, the ambitious Commission President Walter Hallstein sought to strengthen the Commission and the European assembly's powers, believing that he could force France to accept more supranationalism in exchange for a consolidation of the common agricultural policy (CAP). But Hallstein had underestimated de Gaulle's capacity for resistance. France deserted Council meetings for six months, before imposing on its partners the so-called Luxembourg compromise, a declaration (released only in the form of a press release) that stated that any member state could block any proposal that threatened its 'vital' national interest. The agreement made the use of QMV practically impossible, thereby significantly reducing the Commission's room for manoeuvre (see Chapter 5).

Similarly, the European Court's foundational case law, which gave the Community legal order a quasi-constitutional authority, was paralleled by the reinforcement of intergovernmental influence over decision-making. In a series of landmark cases, and in spite of opposition from several governments, the Court ruled that European law could be invoked directly by private plaintiffs (*direct effect*) even where this was not explicitly contemplated by the Treaties, and that it should enjoy *supremacy* in case of conflict with national law (see Chapter 7). This jurisprudence enhanced the pressure on national governments, which now realized that decisions taken in common could limit their freedom of action. In this new legal context, the Commission's prerogatives took on a new dimension; its powers to set the agenda upstream and to monitor the implementation of EU decisions by the national administrations downstream seemed less innocuous (Stein 1981). Moreover, during the same period, a number of Court of Justice rulings enabled integration to proceed irrespective of deadlocks in the Council (Dehousse 1998). However, these developments in the legal sphere were compensated for by the evolution of policy-making structures. The creation of the Committee of Permanent Representatives (Coreper) and the gradual extension of its tasks enabled governments to control the Commission's power of initiative (see Chapter 14). Their influence in the executive phase was made possible by another ad hoc development, the establishment of an ever-denser network of committees composed of national civil servants to 'assist' the Commission—a phenomenon known in Eurospeak as 'comitology' (Pedler and Schaefer 1996; Joerges and Vos 1998). Like the Luxembourg compromise, these developments confirmed the Community's partly intergovernmental character, in the face of an ever-stronger legal supranationalism (Weiler 1981).

The 1960s was thus a paradoxical period in terms of institutional development. Divergences between member states prevented any major amendment of the Treaty, except for the 1965 decision to merge the institutions of the three European communities—the ECSC, the EEC, and the European Atomic Energy Community (Euratom)—without altering their powers. Nonetheless, crucial developments did take place during this same period; the 'constitutionalization' of the Community legal order compensated for the member governments' stronger grip over the policy process. Ultimately, these tensions ended up strengthening the original matrix; the Community model demonstrated its stability by resisting any attempt to strengthen either intergovernmentalism or supranationalism.

The 'relaunch': Institutional change through task extension

The two decades that followed saw considerable expansion of the European Community. Three consecutive enlargements doubled the number of member states, rendering decision-making more difficult. At the same time, they also created demands for new policies, which ended up pushing in favour of substantial changes.

The 1970s were perceived as a period of relative stagnation resulting from a severe economic crisis and the institutional strains created by the first enlargement. However, the resignation of Charles de Gaulle created a political climate more favourable to change. The Treaty revision agreed in Luxembourg in 1970 endowed the EC with its own financial resources, thereby ensuring the financing of the CAP. It also saw an increase—the first in a long series—in the powers of the European Parliament (EP), which was given a significant role in the adoption of the EC budget. At the Paris Summit of 1972, heads of state and government decided to 'relaunch' the integration process by developing policies more in tune with citizens' expectations, such as environmental and consumer protection, and regional development. This decision served to justify the development of a series of policies that went beyond economic integration.

While reflections on the institutional development of the Community were not entirely absent, they failed to trigger any real momentum. At Monnet's instigation, the meetings of heads of state and government were institutionalized with the creation—amid some controversy—of the European Council (Wessels 2016). A 1976 decision made the direct election of members of the European Parliament (MEPs) possible, realizing an idea first mooted three decades earlier at the Hague Congress. The first directly elected Parliament rapidly pressed for bolder reforms. In 1984, it presented a 'Draft Treaty on European Union' that was clearly inspired by federalist ideas. While several of the ideas contained in that project were picked up in ensuing reforms, it was not even discussed by most of the national parliaments to which it had been sent for consideration.

The Parliament's pressure in favour of institutional reform was, however, exploited by another actor. As soon as Jacques Delors was nominated President of the Commission in 1985, he began searching for a new strategic concept capable of imparting a fresh dynamic to the integration process. Many of the options contemplated at the time—monetary union, joint defence, or institutional reforms—seemed out of reach, because each faced opposition in some national capitals. Delors and his aides therefore settled for a seemingly more modest plan: the completion of the internal market by the end of 1992 (Delors 2004). As much of the preparatory work had already been done by the previous Commission, a road map detailing a long series of directives aiming to remove obstacles to free movement was presented to the European Council within a few months. The strength of this approach was that it did not appear to require any major transfer of legal competence or budgetary resources to the European level. Moreover, the emphasis placed on the concept of mutual recognition of national standards, developed by the Court of Justice of the EU in its famous 1979 *Cassis de Dijon* ruling,[2] gave the programme a deregulatory flavour. This idea appealed to the UK's Conservative government, headed by Margaret Thatcher, which strongly opposed further transfers of power to the Community (Dehousse 1988).

Having secured the member states' support for its 1992 programme, the Commission was then in a good position to obtain the Treaty changes that were needed to facilitate its implementation. A large majority of governments supported the Commission's agenda in a vote (the first ever) during the 1985 Milan European Council, where it was decided to convene an IGC. Despite the initial furore among those countries that opposed such a move (the UK, Denmark, and Greece), fears were soon allayed by the pragmatic nature of the proposals tabled by the Commission, which for the most part focused on making it possible to implement the 1992 programme (De Ruyt 1987). The 1985 IGC was both short and largely structured by the Commission's proposals—two features that were absent from the IGCs that were to follow (Moravcsik 1998). The 1986 Single European Act (SEA), which it elaborated, contained mostly incremental changes: new tasks for the Community (environmental, research, and regional development policies); a closer association of the EP with law-making through the establishment of the so-called cooperation procedure (see Chapter 6); and, above all, the shift to QMV for much of the 1992 legislation. The harvest seemed meagre to the pro-integration camp (Pescatore 1987), but it was sufficient to inject the EC with a new dynamic. Thanks in part to the open texture of several new legal bases, a number of new policy areas were able to develop, which themselves conveyed to European people the feeling that the Community could influence their daily lives.

This episode suggests that when the Commission, acting as a 'policy entrepreneur', is able to 'soften up' the relevant policy community by getting it used to new ideas, it may then make the most of opportunities to push forward its preferred reform proposals (Kingdon and Thurber 1984). This dynamic was confirmed in the lead-up to economic and monetary union (EMU). When it appeared that the single market was making substantial progress, the Commission began to argue that it needed to be supplemented by greater coordination of macroeconomic policies; otherwise, the liberalization of capital movements would lead to major disruption (Padoa-Schioppa *et al.* 1987). Because monetary union had little chance of materializing without the support of central bankers, Delors convinced the European Council to create a working party, made up of the governors of the central banks, to discuss the establishment of EMU. This committee, chaired by Delors himself, proposed a gradual move towards a single currency (Committee for the Study of Economic and Monetary Union 1989), endorsed by the European Council in June 1989, despite British reservations (compare Box 3.7 in Chapter 3).

While there is a scholarly debate as to who shaped the Committee's conclusions,[3] it is fair to say that the IGC that led to the Maastricht Treaty (1991) largely followed the Committee's blueprint on EMU, emphasizing the establishment of a European Central Bank (ECB), the autonomy of which was protected by the Treaty, and a process of economic policy convergence that was regarded as indispensable prior to the creation of a single currency. But it did not stop there. In the meantime, the collapse of communism in Eastern Europe and the rapid move towards German unification completely modified the context in which the integration process was taking place. Eager to anchor Germany firmly in Europe, French President Mitterrand and German Chancellor Kohl suggested convening a second IGC to deal with the creation of a 'political union' (that is, a pact on non-economic policies and institutional questions), but achievements in this framework were less spectacular. Incremental changes were made to the Community's institutional structure: more majority voting, the opening of new areas to Community intervention, and the advancement of the legislative prerogatives of the EP, notably through the creation of a codecision procedure (see Chapter 6). In addition, the EP was granted the right to approve the appointment of the Commission, a power that went largely unnoticed at the time, but subsequently proved to be of great importance. In contrast, the member states did not consent to any delegation of power in relation to issues of 'high politics', such as foreign policy or immigration policy. The newly created EU was therefore given a complex structure, the EC being supplemented by two intergovernmental 'pillars' in which the role of supranational institutions was strictly limited. In the view of the masters of the Treaty, 'political decisions' were therefore to remain primarily in the hands of national governments.

This mixed result confirmed the experience of the previous decades: transfers of sovereignty are more readily accepted when they are approached in a functional manner, the emphasis being on substantive issues. When institutional issues are handled separately, however, negotiations are likely to end up with a lowest-common-denominator result, as subsequent IGCs were to confirm.

Adjusting the institutional system

After the monumental changes decided in Maastricht and the intense debates that followed, a period of relative institutional stability might have been expected. In fact, the opposite happened; two IGCs took place in the second half of the 1990s, leading to the Treaties of Amsterdam (1997) and Nice (2000). Even before the latter was ratified, pressure for further reforms led to the convening of a European Convention, which drafted a 'Treaty establishing a Constitution for Europe', signed in Rome in October 2004. How can one account for this acceleration in the pace of change?

Contrary to the previous phase, this period was not characterized by major new projects. The difficult ratification of the Maastricht Treaty had revealed widespread dissatisfaction within the European public and generated a 'spirit of subsidiarity', with many European leaders arguing that the EU should resist the temptation to regulate all matters from Brussels and leave more discretion to national authorities. Instead, institutional change was motivated by two concerns: a desire to respond to criticism of the EU's 'democratic deficit' by bringing the EU institutional architecture closer to European democratic standards; and the need to prepare for the enlargement to Central and Eastern European countries (CEECs).

Meeting these two challenges proved tricky, given the considerable heterogeneity of member states' preferences. The divergences between these preferences largely explain the sustained pace of Treaty changes (Moravcsik and Nicolaïdis 1999). The Maastricht Treaty had, in fact, foreseen the 1996 IGC. Forced to accept the 'pillar' structure by a minority of their peers, several pro-integration governments obtained the guarantee that the institutional setting would be revisited four years later. This scenario was repeated in Amsterdam in 1997 and in Nice in 2000. Unable to reach a comprehensive agreement, but unwilling to abandon their claims, a group of governments ensured that the process of institutional revision continued.

Democratic concerns were not the main difficulty. As will be seen, European governments tend to share a vision of democracy in which the parliamentary element plays a key role, which makes compromises easier. Indeed, from the SEA to the Lisbon Treaty, the most stable trend in institutional change has been the increase in the powers of the EP.

The reforms aiming to help the EU to adjust to its new membership have proved much more controversial. This problem was unprecedented: whereas earlier enlargements had meant incorporating a maximum of three countries at a time without altering the initial balance between large and small states, the 2004 enlargement involved ten countries, of which nine were small states. Mechanical adjustments were therefore not sufficient; they would have led to an excessive increase in size of both Commission and the EP, and given too much influence to the small states in the Council. Since unanimity was required for Treaty changes, the pro-integration camp, which found support in the Commission and the Parliament, argued that consolidating the institutional structure was a necessary precondition of enlargement. In contrast, the CEECs, having recently recovered their sovereignty, were anxious not to have it diluted in the EU. Other countries, such as the UK, Denmark, and Sweden, hoped that enlargement would counterbalance the integrationist drift of the previous decade.

The problem was addressed unsuccessfully during the Amsterdam and Nice negotiations. The large countries tried to reassert their influence to avoid being constrained by coalitions of smaller states, while the latter resisted attempts to reduce their weight in the EU institutions. The classic federal dilemma between equality of states and equality of population became tenser than ever. Because the EU regime is based on a complex balance of state representation in the three poles of the institutional triangle, changes made at the level of one institution rendered adaptations indispensable in the others, as well as in the balance of power among the institutions. The large states were willing to abandon their right to appoint a second Commissioner (see Chapter 5), but only to the extent that this loss was compensated by having their positions strengthened in the two other institutions. This crucial issue could not be solved in Nice. After protracted bickering, a complex compromise was reached, including a redistribution of seats in the EP, the eventual downsizing of the Commission, and a re-weighting of votes in the Council. This agreement was the focus of intense criticism, however, so that these issues re-emerged as one of the central contentions of the Treaty reform negotiated in the years that followed.

The 'constitutional' moment

On 9 May 2000, Joschka Fischer, then German Minister for Foreign Affairs, made a speech in Berlin, calling for the adoption of a European constitution—and thereby sparking intense debate on the institutional future of the EU. In the ensuing months, the leaders of most member states made their own views public.

Those who advocated transforming the procedure of Treaty change made a two-fold argument: in terms of substance, the EU's institutional system had to undergo thorough reform before the next enlargement (Dehaene *et al.* 1999); in terms of process, the Nice Summit had demonstrated the limits of the IGC process—hence more inclusive and more transparent methods were required. The precedent of the first Convention—set up in 1999 to draft a Charter of Fundamental Rights—offered an alternative model consistent with a 'constitutional' perspective on the issues at stake, given that it comprised European and national parliamentarians, and operated in public. The assumption underlying this argument was that a new process would produce a new outcome. One year after the bitter compromise reached in Nice, the governments of the member states seemed to subscribe to this idea when, at the Laeken European Council (2001), they agreed to create a new body to prepare a blueprint for the next IGC and to reflect, among other things, on the constitution-alization of the EU. The European Convention comprised a broader range of actors, a number of whom were independent from national governments (the two Commis-sioners, most of the MEPs, and MPs drawn from the domestic opposition, making up about a third of the members). Half a century after its foundation, the EU ap-peared ready to resume the constitutional work abandoned after the abortive at-tempts of the 1950s.

Of course, supporters of the convention model had a vested interest in this pro-cess. The EP and the Commission which, until then, were deprived of a formal role in Treaty reforms, expected their representatives to be associated as full and equal partners with governments. Likewise, the representatives of the smaller member states had discovered in previous IGCs that their ability to shape the final outcome of the negotiations was limited (Moravcsik and Nicolaïdis 1999): while possible in theory, a veto was extremely costly. They hoped that the framework of the Conven-tion (in which government representatives would have to negotiate with other ac-tors) would offer broader opportunities to forge alternative coalitions. Obviously, expectations of this kind were strongest among those governments who wanted to go beyond the status quo—namely, the Benelux countries, Finland, Greece, and Portugal. On the other side of the fence, governments from bigger member states (with the exception of Germany) were less inclined to change the rules of the game.

The setting up of the Convention was therefore accompanied by safeguards ena-bling governments, acting collectively and individually, to remain in control of fu-ture developments. The Convention was a preparatory body only insofar as all decisions remained with the IGC and national representatives made up three-quar-ters of the membership. Finally, the Convention's President was appointed by, and reported to, the European Council. However, it was free to organize its own work and it had to deliberate in public—a factor that, according to students of constitution-making, renders the crude expression of naked interests more difficult (Elster 1998). The Convention was thus a middle ground between the intergovernmental tradition and the constitutional approach that had been supported by the federalist move-ments since the 1950s.

From his inaugural speech on, former French President Valéry Giscard d'Estaing dwelled on the originality of this experience and tried to convey what he called a more genuinely deliberative 'Convention spirit' (Giscard d'Estaing 2002: 14). To some extent, this strategy was successful, at least in the first part of the Convention's work. The 'conventioneers' took the time to deliberate on each and every issue in plenary sessions, and to examine the most technical issues in more detail within smaller working groups. The flexibility of this organization, the absence of obvious pressures from governments, and the collective willingness of most members to reach an ambitious outcome, as well as the 'constitutional ethos' surrounding their work, all combined to make compromises possible on several issues that former IGCs had been unable to settle. These included the abolition of the pillars, the consolidation of the Treaties, the EU's legal personality, the simplification of decision-making procedures, and the incorporation of the Charter on Fundamental Rights into the draft Constitution (Magnette 2005b). True, none of these elements was totally new and original, and the legal clarity of the text was often disputable (Jacqué 2004), but the Convention nevertheless succeeded where the three previous IGCs had failed.

By the autumn of 2002, however, when discussions on institutional issues were initiated, the pendulum had moved back to traditional forms of diplomatic bargaining. Most government representatives started openly to defend their briefs, to build coalitions among themselves, and to use thinly veiled threats of vetoing in the ensuing IGC. Neither political parties nor institutional representatives were able to develop coherent positions, except in a few specific instances. Instead, two classic cleavages dominated the debate (Magnette and Nicolaïdis 2004): the traditional opposition between 'federalist' and 'intergovernmentalist', and that between large and small countries. With the exception of Germany, large countries sought to strengthen the role of the European Council, and thereby the role of governments in the decision-making process, while most small states defended supranational institutions and the rotating presidency of the Council. The final compromise, reached through typical intergovernmental negotiation (with MEPs kept on the sidelines), largely reflected a Franco–German proposal tabled in January 2003. When a change was supported by a very large majority, a government that was isolated on points that could not easily be presented as non-negotiable 'red lines' (as was the UK on the incorporation of the Charter of Fundamental Rights) was generally forced to make unilateral concessions.

The Presidium played an important role in shaping the final outcome; being a collective organ rather than a single presiding member state, it could present its viewpoints as 'the best possible compromise'. Potential vetoes were forestalled and actual ones ignored—such as the Spanish and Polish opposition to the idea of a double majority (50 per cent of states; 60 per cent of population) that would replace the system of weighted votes agreed on in Nice. These tactics succeeded in bringing about a 'consensus' that might have eluded a traditional IGC. But they also left a decidedly bitter taste for many delegates. Unsurprisingly, the governments of Poland

and Spain, the objections of which had been ignored, fought back. The ensuing IGC rejected some of the Convention's innovations and added new ones.

As regards substance too, continuity was the main theme of the eventual compromise, even though the reference to a Constitution suggested a radical break with the past. Not only did the 'Constitutional Treaty' require ratification by all member countries before it could come into force, but also intergovernmental negotiations and unanimous ratification were deemed necessary for future modifications. Many of the innovations contained in the text had actually been discussed in previous IGCs and the elements that consolidated the supranational institutions (more QMV and more codecision) were similar to those of earlier inter-state bargains. Above all, several of the changes introduced, from the full-time President of the European Council to the status of the 'double-hatted' Foreign Minister (at the same time a member of the Commission and accountable to the European Council) showed a clear reluctance to allow the development of a strong executive at the European level.

Despite (or perhaps because of) its fundamental ambiguity, the Constitutional Treaty became a source of concern in some circles, particularly among those who felt left behind by an integration process that did not seem to respond to their day-to-day problems. These feelings of alienation appear to have played a major role in the rejection of the Treaty in France and the Netherlands, where referenda were organized (Dehousse 2005; Sauger *et al.* 2007). This was not the first time that a proposed reform had been rejected in a referendum: the Danes, at the time of the Maastricht Treaty, and the Irish, on the occasion of the Nice Treaty, had done so in the past. Yet the shock was particularly brutal in this case. Not only did the failure of the draft Constitutional Treaty leave the Union with the institutions carved in Nice, which many argued could not work efficiently, but also the campaign had brought to the fore a deep mistrust vis-à-vis European institutions that appeared too remote to be controlled. To make things worse, given the intensity of the debate in countries in which referenda were held, it could hardly be argued that the negative outcome was to be attributed to a lack of interest. At the same time, no threat of exclusion was deemed to be possible against France or the Netherlands, as founding members of the EU. These elements are recalled here for they largely conditioned the way out of the crisis. On the one hand, the Commission reverted to a functionalist rhetoric, advocating an emphasis on a 'Europe of results' (Barroso 2007); on the other, in his successful bid for the French presidency, Nicolas Sarkozy announced that he would, if elected, seek his partners' support for a 'modifying treaty' that, while abandoning the state-like symbolism of the Constitutional Treaty, would preserve most of its substance. Having rallied a large majority of voters, he could legitimately claim to have been given a mandate to implement this solution, which the other member states were broadly happy to accept.

The Lisbon Treaty therefore appeared as a return to the logic of incremental change that had dominated the history of European integration and marked the end of the short-lived 'constitutional moment'. Technically, it consisted of amendments to its forerunners. In substance, it extended earlier reforms: more majority voting in the Council, more powers to the EP, and the completion of the transfer of justice and home affairs (JHA) to the 'first pillar', as well as an attempt to improve synergy between the 'Community method' and the policy regime applied to foreign policy. All are certainly important reforms, but none appeared to have been designed to achieve a major transformation of the EU policy system. While typical features of the Community method were extended, the newly created President of the European Council was seen as a potentially powerful rival of the Commission. Once more, ambiguity appeared to be one of the essential attributes of compromise.

The uncertain legacy of the euro crisis and Brexit

It is sometimes said that European integration has made big leaps forward on the occasion of crises, be they economic or political. What, then, will be the legacy of the momentous turmoil that started with the bankruptcy of US bank Lehman Brothers in September 2008? The protracted recession that it triggered, with its adverse social consequences, severely undermined support for European institutions in most member states. Equally importantly, the crisis exposed major structural flaws in the design of EMU, which threatened the viability of the jewel in the crown of the European project—that is, the common currency. On the one hand, the eurozone was deprived of any solidarity mechanism that could be used in the event that one of its members ran into serious difficulty; on the other, the absence of a real macroeconomic coordination beyond the purely fiscal parameters foreseen by the Maastricht Treaty and the weakness of enforcement mechanisms acted as a strong disincentive to establish such assistance mechanisms. Northern European countries were reluctant to accept financial transfers in what appeared to be a bottomless pit. At the same time, however, interdependence among eurozone countries (not least in the banking sector) was such that financial markets feared a total collapse of EMU should a country abandon the euro (a possibility that Greece seriously considered).

This context largely explains the changes that took place in the wake of the crisis. The countries in trouble, which were mostly from the periphery, benefited from various financial assistance packages, and a large backstop scheme—the European Stability Mechanism (ESM)—was established in 2012. In exchange, however, the 'creditor countries', led by Germany, demanded a significant tightening of macroeconomic policy, which took the form of two legislative packages (the 'Six Pack' and the 'Two Pack', in Eurospeak) and of a new treaty, the 'Fiscal Compact', all adopted in 2011–12. Likewise, in the field of banking regulation—of crucial importance for the European economy, which, unlike the US, is largely financed by banks—the creditor countries insisted that the supervision of banks be removed from the hands of national authorities and entrusted to a strong European regulator—in this case, an entirely new branch of the ECB, separated from the monetary branch (Epstein and Rhodes 2014).

The institutional implications of the reforms are, once again, striking in terms of their ambiguity. As far as process is concerned, the key deals made during the period were decided in numerous meetings of the European Council (which convened eleven times in 2011). Intergovernmental agreements concluded outside the framework of the EU Treaties were often preferred over standard Treaty reforms, be it to neutralize the opposition of some governments (in the case of the 'Fiscal Compact'), or because of disputes over their status under EU law (in the case of the Single Resolution Mechanism). In addition, the Commission often appeared to be sidelined, with the European Council President playing a crucial agenda-setting role; hence the idea of a shift to further intergovernmentalism, advanced by some authors (Fabbrini 2013; Bickerton *et al.* 2015a). At the same time, however, the powers of supranational institutions have been greatly enhanced. The ECB has been very entrepreneurial, expanding its range of instruments at its disposal and acquiring *de facto* the role of lender of last resort, which everyone thought it had been denied by the Maastricht Treaty (Buiter and Rahbari 2011), as well as a primary role in European macroeconomic policy. The 'hardening' of economic policy coordination was essentially achieved by strengthening the Commission's surveillance and enforcement powers. Were it not for the British Prime Minister's refusal to endorse any modification of the EU Treaty, the German government and its allies would, in all likelihood, have secured an extension of the Court of Justice's oversight in the realm of economic policy.

Finally, taking advantage of the growing unpopularity of the EU, the EP succeeded in forcing heads of state and government to accept the indirect election of the Commission President with the so-called *Spitzenkandidaten* system (Garcìa and Priestley 2015). While the implications of this 'politicization' process on the interaction between the EU institutions remain to be seen, it appears to be in direct contrast with the other big changes of the past few years; the main reason underpinning the delegation of control powers to supranational bodies was their independence. If the Commission were electorally accountable, supporters of fiscal discipline would not have pleaded in favour of granting it stronger enforcement powers. While presenting a road map for reforms aiming at strengthening the eurozone, the 'Five Presidents' Report', adopted in 2015, carefully avoided such fundamental issues (Juncker *et al.* 2015). Time will tell which of these contradictory pulls will eventually prevail.

The prospect of deeper integration among eurozone member states was a pretext for—although probably not the principal reason underpinning—UK Prime Minister David Cameron's decision to hold a referendum in June 2016 on his country's continued membership of the EU. 'The European Union that emerges from the eurozone crisis is going to be a very different body', he had argued when he committed to this referendum three years earlier (Cameron 2013). In truth, Mr Cameron called this referendum under pressure from those within his own Conservative Party who had campaigned for an EU referendum since the 1990s and the in light of the rise of the UK Independence Party (UKIP), which, by 2014, had become the largest British party in the European Parliament.

Mr Cameron's pledge helped him to secure a second term as prime minister and, campaigning for a 'Remain' vote, he probably expected to win the EU referendum. Yet those in favour of continued UK membership had not counted on a pro-Brexit 'Leave' campaign led by senior members of the Conservative Cabinet that tapped into popular disenchantment with political elites and urged citizens to 'take back control' from EU institutions. In the end, 52 per cent voted to leave the EU, prompting Cameron to resign and setting Brexit in motion. The result came as a profound shock to the EU, which was confronted with the prospect of protracted negotiation over UK withdrawal from the Union and a risk of similar referenda in other member states. This new political reality began to impact upon EU institutions immediately, with British member of the European Commission Lord Hill resigning within hours of the referendum result being announced (see Chapter 5). But the process of extricating the UK from the EU's institutions and reconfiguring these bodies for an EU of twenty-seven is, at the time of writing, unfolding more slowly.

The dynamics of institutional change

The history of institutional change in the EU shows that its motivations and dynamics vary widely over time. It is nevertheless possible to identify three permanent factors of change and the conditions under which they may influence the negotiation. The classical trilogy of interests, institutions, and ideas (Hall 1997) serves as a helpful guide.

The weight of state interests

That institutional change has largely been shaped by state interests should not come as a surprise. After all, when the EU was created, it took the form of an inter-state agreement that, like most treaties, could be modified only with the assent of all parties. Economic interests played a key role in this process, because the states saw the construction of Europe as a means to reassert their influence in an increasingly interdependent world (Milward 1992). Domestic concerns clearly impinged upon governments' attitudes whenever reforms were contemplated. France's farming interests, Germany's industries, and the need to foster free trade for export-oriented Benelux countries featured prominently in the European agenda of their respective governments. The most important stages of the integration process have therefore been associated with the key interests of the member states. Institutional changes have generally responded to an instrumental logic rather than to some kind of grand design. Governments, having defined a series of objectives, bargained to reach 'substantive agreements concerning cooperation, and finally selected appropriate international institutions in which to embed them' (Moravcsik 1998: 5).

The contours of institutional evolution have also been shaped by states' desire to retain some control over the process. Intergovernmental bodies were thus given a central role: the position of the Council of Ministers in decision-making was consolidated by structures such as Coreper, the web of intergovernmental committees, and the European Council. More recent developments, such as the Maastricht pillar system or the creation of the High Representative for foreign policy, were clearly inspired by reluctance to relinquish power in sensitive areas. Representative concerns are apparent in the design of every European institution, including the supranational ones; nationals of all member countries sit in the Commission and on the Court's bench. Balance among states has certainly been a key point in most institutional negotiations and, from the outset, QMV within the Council of Ministers was based on a system of weighted votes balancing the equality of states and demographic size. The three biggest states made sure that they would need only one ally to block a decision, while preventing the three small ones from forming a blocking minority. Fifty years later, the same strategic concerns informed the lengthy pre-enlargement discussions; the debates on the composition of the Commission (should it include one national of each member state, or should it be reduced in size?), on the presidency of the Union (should the system of rotation among member states be maintained, or should it be replaced by a permanent chair?), and on the reform of QMV (should the system of weighted votes be maintained, or should it be replaced by a more proportional double majority?) were all clearly dominated by the governments' ambitions to maximize their (individual and collective) weight in the EU institutions.

While the emphasis on states' interests has occupied a central place in the analysis of European integration, it should not blind us to the importance of other factors. On several occasions, states have decided that their interests were better served by mechanisms that could facilitate their negotiations (the Commission's monopoly of initiative), reduce transaction costs (majority voting in the Council), or ensure that joint decisions would be implemented fairly by everyone (the enforcement powers of the Commission and the Court). Furthermore, supranational actors have often used their (formal or informal) powers to foster their own interests as institutions, as discussed next.

The role of institutions

Understood in their broadest sense as the rules that structure political relationships (Steinmo 2004), institutions have also considerably influenced the dynamics of change. This point is quite clear in the case of formal rules: the requirement of unanimity for any amendment to the Treaties means that governments must take the final crucial steps in the negotiations. They can also use the threat of non-ratification by their legislature to obtain concessions from their partners. Such constraints largely explain both the piecemeal character of the reform process and its deep ambiguity. Likewise, the change in the rules of the game reflected in the setting up of the

Convention allowed for the development of a new dynamic, which largely explains why the Convention could reach an agreement on issues where previous IGCs had failed. There are also informal rules affecting the way in which actors behave (see Chapter 14). Smaller countries know that the veto power they enjoy can be used only sparingly—and preferably not without allies when a major reform is at stake. This explains why Belgium in Nice, or even Poland at the 2004 IGC, ended up accepting agreements that they had forcefully opposed.[4]

While these principles are valid in many international regimes, the weight of institutions is of particular relevance at EU level, because of the political clout enjoyed by its supranational organs. They are endowed with a substantial degree of autonomy and thus are naturally inclined to promote interests of their own. As was seen earlier, in its rulings on direct effect and supremacy, the Court of Justice has conferred a federal structure on the European legal order. In so doing, however, it has considerably increased its own role in the integration process (Dehousse 1998). The Parliament's stubborn insistence on the need to address the 'democratic deficit' was, of course, underpinned by its eagerness to improve its own institutional position, and this helped it to secure important changes as regards the appointment of the Commission (not least with the invention of the *Spitzenkandidaten* system in 2014) or the codecision procedure.[5] Likewise, we have seen that even if it is deprived of any formal role in IGCs, the Commission can at times shape the contours of the final agreement by acting as a policy entrepreneur or as a mediator between national preferences. The SEA is the best illustration of this kind of dynamic. One year before the conclusion of that treaty, several governments had opposed any extension of majority voting in the so-called Dooge Committee. It was the Commission that developed the idea that enabled a breakthrough, and it did so by drawing inspiration from principles laid down in the ground-breaking 1979 *Cassis de Dijon* case. Thus even if one accepts the centrality of inter-state negotiations in the cumbersome process of institutional change, one must recognize that state preferences are not static and can be influenced by the action of supranational institutions (Dehousse and Majone 1994).

When do ideas matter?

In addition to state interests and institutional constraints, ideas can, at times, help to shape the EU's institutional system. All of the actors of the EU political system have their own views of what the system should look like. In some cases, those views derive from the actors' broader perceptions of the nature of the EU. Since its origins, two competing interpretations of the 'meaning' of European integration have proved very significant. The federalist doctrine 'is still required to account for the general institutional structure of the EC' and particularly 'its quasi-constitutional form' (Moravcsik 1998: 153). Whereas this perspective remains influential in some circles, particularly in the founding member states; others rather see the EU as a functional organization, designed to maximize states' economic interests in an increasingly interdependent economy—a view that is also widespread in Nordic and Central European countries. These two 'models' are, in key respects, the poles of the debate. They structure, positively or negatively, the ongoing discussion on the EU's *raison d'être*, very much like the 'federalist' and 'anti-federalist' doctrines that dominated constitutional debates in the US for decades. As such, they bear their own institutional patterns; governments may support an institutional reform that defies their own short-term interests—such as when the Benelux countries defended the extension of the EP's prerogatives, although they are less overrepresented in this institution than in the Council—because it is part of their broader vision of the EU.

States preferences will very often also reflect their own national political culture. When German leaders support the parliamentarization of the EU's regime, they tend, explicitly or not, to project the constitutional balance of the Federal Republic (Kohler-Koch 2000). French politicians, on the other hand, tend to perceive the European Council as a collective 'head of state' and to consider the Commission–European Council duopoly as a European equivalent of the Fifth Republic's dualist executive. The Nordic insistence on the transparency-enhancing mechanisms of the EU system (the Ombudsman, parliamentary scrutiny, and the publicity of the Council's deliberations) is another example of importing national traditions into the EU (Grønbech-Jensen 1998).

Although some of these ideas have found their way into the EU Treaties, they remain secondary factors of change. In most cases, the governments' positions depend on how they perceive their own interests. When the long-term implications of an institutional decision are unclear, however, ideas may be influential. This phenomenon may notably explain the gradual consolidation of the EP's powers—one of the most original aspects of the EU's institutional evolution, strengthened even though it may undermine the influence of member states. Some governments were prompted to support this consolidation by an ideological bias in favour of parliamentary democracy (Dehousse 1995); others made what they considered symbolic concessions with no foreseeable impact on their interests (Pollack 1997; Moravcsik 1998; Rittberger 2001). Needless to say, governments' expectations can, at times, prove misplaced. One of the 'minor' concessions made to parliamentary orthodoxy in the Maastricht Treaty—the conferral on the EP of the right to approve the appointment of the Commission—allowed the assembly to gain significant leverage over the European executive (Magnette 2001). In situations of crisis, notwithstanding their reservations, they may be constrained to adopt suggestions made by supranational actors; hence the 'hardening' of macroeconomic policy cooperation decided in 2011–12, for instance, essentially consisted of reforms suggested by the Commission in the previous decade and rediscovered by 'creditor' countries in search of better monitoring devices (Dehousse 2016). Similarly, the 'democratization' narrative promoted by the EP in its strenuous defence of the *Spitzenkandidaten* system proved to be hard to oppose (Garcia and Priestley 2015).

When they think of the EU's overall institutional order, governments tend to reason, like the lawyers of the EU institutions, in the conceptual terms with which they are familiar. This reasoning has facilitated agreement on reforms designed to 'simplify' the institutional and legal order of the EU by making it more compatible with classic constitutional canons. Like most other polities, the EU oscillates between institutional complexity prompted by pragmatic concerns to accommodate divergent interests and institutional rationalization driven by the leaders' will to clarify the rules of the game (Olsen 2002). This oscillation may help us to understand why, at the turn of the century, EU leaders collectively flirted with the 'constitutional' idea, only to abandon it as soon as it appeared that it met with sustained opposition in some countries. All in all, therefore, the 'ideational' stream can significantly shape the process of institutional change.

Conclusion

The institutional history of the EU can be read in several ways. On the one hand, the system has substantially evolved. Successive enlargements and expansion of the tasks delegated to the Union have created regular pressures for adaptation. On the other, it has demonstrated remarkable stability: the EU has not become a centralized superstate nor have member states done away with the atypical powers enjoyed by the European Commission (such as its right to initiate legislation). On several occasions, attempts to consolidate the powers of the supranational institutions have been balanced by governments' determination to see their role in the system preserved.

Institutional change has been mostly incremental. For all of the surrounding rhetoric, even the Constitutional Treaty signed in 2004 could not really be seen as marking a rupture in the history of European construction, given that it largely built on innovations introduced at earlier stages. IGCs have been the key moments in this evolution, but they cannot be understood independently from the rest of the process. Their successes have owed much to the institutional adjustments that have taken place between conferences (Héritier 2007). Their failures have paved the way for continuing tensions.

This gradualism is largely the result of a process in which governments retain the central role because they must agree to all formal changes. For the same reason, functionalism has been the main force in this evolution. Governments had to agree on joint objectives prior to any major transfer of powers to the European level. Agreed objectives, however, are but one part of the story. The complexity of the system has generated pressures for simplification and legitimation as part of a process in which ideational factors play an important role. The European Commission has, at times, succeeded in influencing the preferences and negotiation strategies of the member states. The coexistence of these contrasting forces largely accounts for the schizophrenic nature of an institutional evolution simultaneously characterized by a consolidation of intergovernmentalism and the conferral of ever-larger powers onto the EP. The rigidity of the 'constitutional charter' is another explanation for the fundamental ambiguity of most reforms; unanimity being required for any change, such reforms must appeal both to supranationalists and supporters of states' rights. In all likelihood, the same structural factors will impinge upon future changes and prevent a radical simplification of European institutional architecture as long as each member country retains a right of veto on proposed changes. Calls for more flexibility have been made, advocating, for example, more transparency in the Treaty revision process or stressing the need to do away with unanimity. To some extent, they have been heard, owing to the dramatic character of the recent financial crisis; unanimity was not required for the coming into force of the ESM Treaty or the 'Fiscal Compact'.

However, a decade of institutional discussions has made clear that there is no real consensus on what the ultimate organization of the Union should look like. Enlargement has made the Union more diverse and the many changes brought about by globalization appear to have created in public opinion a strong ambivalence vis-à-vis the integration process. In such conditions, the prospects for large-scale reform remain limited unless external factors decide otherwise once more. The UK's vote to leave the EU could provide such an exogenous shock, but it remains to be seen how Brexit will ultimately reshape the EU's institutional structures.

ENDNOTES

1. The US Constitution was drafted by delegates of the thirteen states gathered in Philadelphia in 1787.
2. Case 120/78 *Rewe-Zentral AG v Bundesmonopolverwaltung für Branntwein* ECLI:EU:C:1979:42.
3. See, e.g., Moravcsik (1998: 432–5) for a classical intergovernmental account.
4. In Nice, as part of the new Treaty, Belgium was asked to accept fewer votes under QMV than the Netherlands, with which it had always had numerical parity in the past (despite Belgium's population being only about two-thirds that of the Netherlands). Poland had to accept a new QMV system in the Constitutional Treaty that was far less favourable to it numerically than the system in the Treaty of Nice.
5. This, however, does not mean that the EP is systematically able to impose its views upon the governments. In many cases, claims supported by the majority in the EP (e.g. approval of appointments to the Court of Justice and consolidating budgetary power by giving the EP rights over revenue) were not followed up by governments (Costa 2001).

FURTHER READING

There is no systematic overview of institutional change in the EU available in the current literature. In-depth historical accounts can be found in Moravcsik (1998), which remains the classic presentation of the liberal intergovernmentalist interpretation. For more recent periods, see Moravcsik and Nicolaïdis (1999) and Magnette and Nicolaïdis (2004). Analyses of individual institutions can be found in Kassim *et al.* (2013) for the European Commission, Costa (2001, in French) and Corbett *et al.* (2016) for the EP, Hayes-Renshaw and Wallace (2006) for the Council, and Dehousse (1998) for the Court. Fabbrini (2015) offers a critical analysis of the changes brought about by the economic and financial crisis. On the role of ideas in the founding period, Parsons (2003) offers a stimulating view, as does Rittberger (2001), who offers an institutionalist reading.

Corbett, R., Jacobs, F., Neveille, D., and Shackleton, M. (2016) *The European Parliament* (9th edn, London: John Harper).

Costa, O. (2001) *Le parlement européen, assemblée délibérante* (Brussels: Editions de l'Université de Bruxelles).

Dehousse, R. (1998) *The European Court of Justice: The Politics of Judicial Integration* (Basingstoke and New York: Palgrave).

Fabbrini, S. (2015) *Which European Union? Europe after the Euro Crisis* (Cambridge: Cambridge University Press).

Hayes-Renshaw, F., and Wallace, H. (2006) *The Council of Ministers* (2nd edn, Basingstoke and New York: Palgrave).

Kassim, H., Peterson, J., Bauer, M., Dehousse, R., Hooghe, L., Connolly, S., and Thompson, A. (2013) *The European Commission of the 21st Century* (Oxford and New York: Oxford University Press).

Magnette, P., and Nicolaïdis, K. (2004) 'The European Convention: Bargaining under the shadow of rhetoric', West European Politics, 27/3: 381–404.

Moravcsik, A. (1998) *The Choice for Europe: Social Purpose and State Power from Messina to Maastricht* (Ithaca, NY: Cornell University Press).

Moravcsik, A., and Nicolaïdis, K. (1999) 'Explaining the Treaty of Amsterdam: Interests, influence, institutions', *Journal of Common Market Studies*, 37/1: 59–85.

Parsons, C. (2003) *A Certain Idea of Europe* (Ithaca, NY: Cornell University Press).

Rittberger, R. (2001) 'Which institutions for post-war Europe? Explaining the institutional design of Europe's first Community', *Journal of European Public Policy*, 8/5: 673–708.

 WEB LINKS

http://www.eui.eu/Research/HistoricalArchivesOfEU
The website of the Historical Archives of the European Union provides details about the official archives of the EU institutions, which are held by the European University Institute.

http://aei.pitt.edu/
Maintained by the University of Pittsburgh, the Archive of European Integration (AEI) makes available online a wide range of historical documentation on European integration.

http://onlinelibrary.wiley.com/journal/10.1111/(ISSN)1468-5965
Each year, the *Journal of Common Market Studies* publishes an Annual Review of the European Union, which includes an in-depth analysis of key developments across a range of EU institutions in the preceding year.

PART I

Providing Direction

CHAPTER 3

The European Council: A formidable locus of power

Philippe de Schoutheete

▌ Summary

Since its creation in 1974, the European Council has played a fundamental role in the development of European integration. It gives political guidance and impetus to the European Union (EU), takes the most important decisions, gives high visibility to external policy positions and declarations, and plays a major role in amending the Treaties. Its composition gives it an intergovernmental character, yet successive decisions at that level have increased the supranational character of the Union. The European Council has been, for more than thirty years, a formidable locus of power, and the Lisbon Treaty gave it the formal status of an institution of the Union under the leadership of a full-time President.

Introduction

With the entry into force of the Treaty of Lisbon (2007), the European Council became an institution of the EU. It brings together heads of state or government (a formula designed to cover the situation of chief executives who are also heads of state) together with its own President and the President of the Commission. The High Representative of the Union for Foreign Affairs and Security Policy is also present. Ministers or a member of the Commission or the president of the European Central Bank (ECB) can be invited to attend when the agenda so requires. Apart from a very small number of European civil servants, nobody else is allowed in the meeting. This is the essence of the European Council: a limited number of political figures, including the chief executives of all member states, meeting in a closed room with no assistants.

The Treaty specifies that the European Council 'shall provide the Union with the necessary impetus for its development and shall define the general political directions and priorities thereof'.[1] Over the years, it has been involved in detailed decision-making on a great number of issues. The Treaty and the Rules of Procedure indicate that the European Council shall meet at least four times a year. In practice, regular use of informal meetings and occasional meetings in the margins of summits with third countries lead to more frequent contacts, particularly in times of crisis. European Council meetings have traditionally been held in Brussels in the Justus Lipsius building, which also houses the Council. Since 2016 they have been held in the purpose-built Europa building next door. In exceptional circumstances, meetings may be organized outside Brussels.

Two points about the European Council should be kept in mind:

- As an institution of the Union, the European Council has, in some circumstances, the power and the obligation to adopt acts having legal effect, which was not the case before the Lisbon Treaty. The Court of Justice of the EU has the power to rule on the legality of such acts. The new legal situation led the European Council to adopt formal rules of procedure in December 2009 (see Box 3.2).

- When adopting Treaty changes, as in Maastricht, Amsterdam, Nice, and Lisbon, the participants meet not as a European Council, but as an intergovernmental conference (IGC) at the level of heads of state or government.[2] This legal distinction is not generally understood by the public and is frequently ignored even by participants.

Origins

Heads of state or government have always played an important role in the development of European integration. The legendary Belgian Foreign Minister Paul-Henri Spaak (1969: II.95) described a meeting in Paris in February 1957, on the eve of the signature of the Treaty of Rome, in which heads of state or government had to settle the last politically sensitive issues: 'It went on day and night. I had to run from one to the other, pleading, looking for compromises. Finally at dawn on 20 February a solution was found.' This sounds no different from some present-day meetings of the European Council. But regular meetings of what was to become the European Council were decided only at a summit in Paris in December 1974 (see Box 3.1) and the first such meeting was held in Dublin in March 1975.

At the time, two reasons were put forward as justifications for the decision. In the first instance, Community institutions were felt not to be working as well as they should, especially since the Luxembourg compromise of 1965 was in practice blocking majority voting (see Chapter 4). In the second, the first enlargement of the Community (the UK, Ireland, and Denmark) was likely to make decision-making more ponderous. The creation of a regular (as opposed to an occasional) source of strategic direction and political impulse made sense in this context.

Foreign ministers were finding it difficult to coordinate the activities of a growing number of Council formations. Moreover, the first efforts at foreign policy coordination, or European political cooperation (EPC), posed a problem. Some member states—France in particular—were insisting that Community institutions should have no authority whatsoever in this new activity. Clearly, some form of overall coordination would be needed if the 'European Union', as it was beginning to be called, were to develop in a coherent manner in various directions. Introducing the heads of state or

---

BOX 3.1	The origins of the European Council

Conclusions of the Paris Summit meeting, December 1974

[. . .]

2. Recognizing the need for an overall approach to the internal problems involved in achieving European unity and the external problems facing Europe, the Heads of Government consider it essential to ensure progress and overall consistency in the activities of the Communities and in the work on political co-operation.

3. The Heads of Government have therefore decided to meet, accompanied by the Ministers of Foreign Affairs, three times a year, whenever necessary, in the Council of the Communities and in the context of political co-operation.

The administrative secretariat will be provided for in an appropriate manner with due regard for existing practices and procedures.

In order to ensure consistency in Community activities and continuity of work, the Ministers of Foreign Affairs, meeting in the Council of the Community, will act as initiators and co-ordinators. They may hold political cooperation [sic] meetings at the same time.

[. . .]

Source: Bulletin of the European Communities, December 1974, No. 12

government as the ultimate source of authority, with, at the time, foreign ministers at their side, was felt to be a way in which to ensure coordination and consistency.

As is frequently the case for important decisions, personalities also played a role in the creation of the European Council. Newly elected French President Valéry Giscard d'Estaing (1988) wanted to continue playing a significant role in European affairs, as did the new West German Chancellor Helmut Schmidt. Jean Monnet, whose influence in all Community countries was considerable, came to the conclusion that regular meetings of heads of state or government were needed and his views were instrumental in securing the agreement of the smaller member states.

In any institutional framework, the regularity of meetings makes a fundamental difference. Before 1974, summit meetings were important occasions on which significant decisions were taken, but with little or no lasting impact on the working of Community institutions. Since then, and increasingly as time has gone by, European Council meetings have come to mark the rhythm of EU activities. The Council has played a leading role in the European integration process and crisis management. By the end of the twentieth century, it was being called the arbiter of systemic change, the principal agenda-setter, and the core of the EU's executive (Ludlow 1992), or the primary source of history-making decisions (Peterson and Bomberg 1999). At that time, however, the European Council was not an institution of the Union: it exercised great power without any legal Treaty basis for that power. That is a paradox to which the Lisbon Treaty put an end.

Composition

The Lisbon Treaty has significantly altered the composition of the European Council. Foreign ministers, who had been *de jure* participants in the European Council, lost that capacity. Now, they get a sort of proxy presence in the European Council through the presence of the High Representative, who is chair of the Foreign Affairs Council. Moreover, foreign ministers, as well as finance ministers, can be called to take part in the discussion of agenda points relevant to their competence. Practice allows a small amount of flexibility: in the absence of a head of state or government, a minister may take a seat. Over the years, a limited number of officials from the presidency, the Council Secretariat, or the Commission have gained a seat in the room or at the table (see Figure 3.1). Two delegates per delegation are issued red badges, which allow them to enter and submit a note or whisper a message, but they may not stay. Other members of national delegations, who should number no more than twenty, do not have access to the conference room; instead, they are confined to a 'blue' zone.

The debate in the European Council is relayed to the outside world by a system of note-takers, who are officials from the Council Secretariat sitting in the conference room. At regular intervals, they are replaced and then give an oral briefing to the Antici group (personal assistants of the permanent representatives), sitting in an adjacent room.[3] Each Antici then transmits his or her notes to his or her own delegation, in the 'blue' zone. This indirect dissemination of information guarantees that national delegations know something of the proceedings inside, but with considerable delay and in a way that makes direct attribution of specific words to any participant nearly impossible. Peter Ludlow (2000: 15) has compared the physical arrangements at a European Council 'to a vast temple in some oriental rite', in which high priests officiate in seclusion, while lesser participants remain in other parts of the building. Such an extraordinary system would not have survived if heads of state or government were not happy with the result—namely, that they operate at some distance, both in space and time, from the views and comments of their assistants.

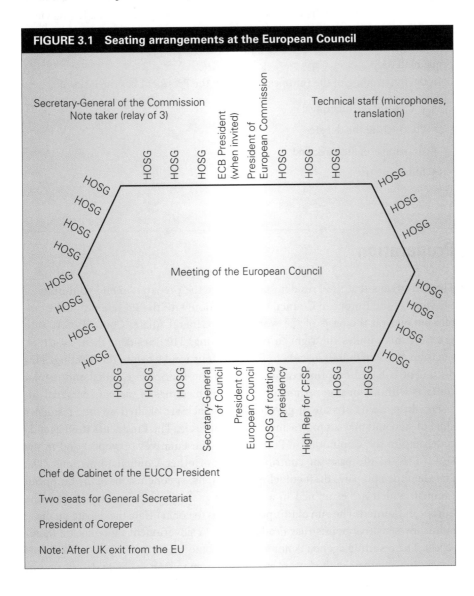

FIGURE 3.1   Seating arrangements at the European Council

The President

The European Council is chaired by a President elected for a two-and-a-half-year period, renewable once. Prior to the Lisbon Treaty, it had been chaired by the head of government of the country holding the rotating presidency. Combining the duties and responsibilities of a national head of government with the duties and responsibilities linked to the preparation and chairmanship of the European Council had always been somewhat problematic. The difficulty obviously increased with the enlargement of the Union. The main advantage of a 'dedicated' President is that he or she has more time to establish personal relationships and understand differing views and interests. Shortly after his appointment as the first full-time President of the European Council, Herman Van Rompuy (2010) noted that 'time is a politician's prime material'.

In the functioning of the European Council, the President has the tasks of:

- preparing the meetings;
- conducting the debates;
- drawing conclusions; and
- following up.

Preparation

The Treaty says that the President shall ensure the preparation and continuity of the work of the European Council in cooperation with the President of the Commission and on the basis of the work of the General Affairs Council (GAC). In practice, this implies the right to call a meeting. The President then, as a rule, sends an annotated draft agenda to the GAC four weeks before the meeting. This document is based on prior commitments of the European Council and regular contacts with national governments, including meetings of *sherpas* (personal advisers of the heads of state or government), which are chaired by the President's chief of staff and play an increasingly important role. The President's draft agenda is debated in the Committee of Permanent Representatives (Coreper) and in the GAC, also on the basis of contributions from other Council formations. The President then prepares draft guidelines, decisions, or conclusions of the European Council, which are examined in a last GAC meeting held five days before the European Council. The aim of this procedure is to concentrate the debate on those politically sensitive points that heads of state or government must decide themselves. The resulting agenda is not absolutely binding, because there is no way of preventing members of the European Council from raising a subject that they want to raise. In general terms, however, the authority of the President is respected.

Debates and decision-making

Proceedings of the European Council are now formalized by the Rules of Procedure adopted on 1 December 2009 (see Box 3.2). Most European Councils extend over a two-day period. They will usually begin in the afternoon, with an exchange of views with the President of the European Parliament (EP). A working session will frequently be held before dinner. At the dinner table, the heads of state or government can have a free-wheeling discussion on European affairs, recalling the fireside chats of the early European Councils, or have a preliminary exchange on politically sensitive issues. Typically, a second working session, regularly concentrating on the text of conclusions, will be held the next morning, ending with press conferences. At some point, a 'family' photograph will be taken. According to expediency, any number of variants of this usual framework can be, and have been, tried out.

It is up to the President to ensure the smooth conduct of meetings. If the discussion gets bogged down, the President may well interrupt the meeting and hold bilateral conversations (known as 'confessionals') with each delegation, or a group of delegates. The President can also encourage two or more delegations to get together to solve a specific problem. As a rule, decisions are taken in the European Council by consensus. Rules of procedure, however, are adopted by a simple majority, as is the decision to call an IGC. Major appointments, such as the President of the Commission or the High Representative, require a qualified majority. If absent, a member of the European Council can delegate his or her voting power to another member, but

---

BOX 3.2   Rules of procedure for voting

[. . .]

2. In those cases where, in accordance with the Treaties, the European Council adopts a decision and holds a vote, that vote shall take place on the initiative of its President.

The President shall, furthermore, be required to open a voting procedure on the initiative of a member of the European Council, provided that a majority of the members of the European Council so decides.

3. The presence of two thirds of the members of the European Council is required to enable the European Council to vote. When the vote is taken, the President shall check that there is a quorum. The President of the European Council and the President of the Commission shall not be included in the calculation of the quorum.

4. Where a vote is taken, any member of the European Council may also act on behalf of not more than one other member.

Where the European Council decides by vote, its President and the President of the Commission shall not take part in the vote.

[. . .]

Source: Art. 6 of the Rules of Procedure, adopted on 1 December 2009

none may exercise more than two votes. On urgent matters, and if all members agree, decisions may be taken by written procedure at the initiative of the President.

Consensus is obtained when a proposal is put on the table and no objection is formulated. Unanimity implies that a proposal be put to a vote and that no negative vote be registered. In theory, the difference therefore lies in the formality of the procedure; in practice, formal votes are extremely rare, so the difference is meaningless.

Treaty texts normally specify a procedure other than consensus when decisions by the European Council are to have legal effects (see Box 3.3).

BOX 3.3   European Council decisions that are not taken by consensus

- Art. 7(2) TEU: Persistent breach of Union values*
- Art. 14(2) TEU: Composition of the EP*
- Art. 15(5) TEU: Election and ending the term of office of the President of the European Council**
- Art. 17(5) TEU: Modifying the number of Commissioners*
- Art. 17(7) TEU: Proposal for President and appointment of the Commission**
- Art. 18(1) TEU: Appointment and ending the term of office of the High Representative**
- Art. 22(1) and (6) TEU: Identification of strategic interests, objectives, and general guidelines for CFSP*
- Art. 31(3) TEU: *Passerelle* clause for CFSP*
- Art. 42(2) TEU: Establishment of a common defence*
- Art. 48(3) TEU: Decision to examine amendments to the Treaty and decision not to convene a Convention***
- Art. 48(6) TEU: Simplified Treaty revision for internal EU competences (TFEU Pt III)*
- Art. 48(7) TEU: Simplified Treaty revision (general *passerelle* clause)*
- Art. 50(3) TEU: Withdrawal of a member state (extension of the period)*
- Art. 86(4) TFEU: Powers of the Public Prosecutor*
- Art. 236 TFEU: Configurations and presidency of the Council**
- Art. 244 TFEU: Rotation of Commissioners*
- Art. 253(3) TFEU: Rules of Procedure of the European Council***
- Art. 283(2) TFEU: Appointment of the board of the European Central Bank**
- Art. 312(2) TFEU: *Passerelle* clause for multiannual financial framework*
- Art. 355(6) TFEU: Amending the status of overseas territories*

* Unanimity; ** Qualified majority; *** Simple majority

TEU =Treaty on European Union; TFEU =Treaty on the Functioning of the European Union

Following up

Conclusions reached by the European Council are encapsulated in a final document. In one exceptional case (Athens in 1983), disagreement was such that no conclusions could be drafted. Time spent on drafting conclusions shows that everyone is aware of their importance for the daily working of the Union. In practice, if a conclusion of the European Council can convincingly be quoted in support of any argument, at any level of the Union, it is most likely to be decisive. The Rules of Procedure now imply that the drafting, and later approval, of minutes of each meeting contain references to the conclusions and the official text of statements and declarations.

The last, but certainly not least important, act of a European Council is to give press conferences. The President of the European Commission is the first to speak, but most heads of state or government and the President of the Commission give their own press conferences to journalists who commute from one delegation to another. By comparing notes, experienced hands will frequently get a clear picture of the actual debate. This practice led Roy Jenkins (1989: 75), President of the Commission from 1977 to 1981, to call European Councils 'a restricted meeting with full subsequent publicity'.

In the days following a European Council, the President, accompanied by the President of the Commission, reports to the EP on the meeting. Although this exercise tends to repeat information already available in the press, it has contributed to a better understanding between the institutions. Various voices in the EP have requested that the European Council not simply report, but also be accountable, to Parliament for the conclusions adopted. Such a procedure would, however, have no basis in the Treaty.

The Lisbon Treaty gives the President of the European Council a new and most important task: to see that European Council decisions and conclusions are effectively implemented. As a result, the President is now frequently entrusted with follow-up tasks that would probably, in previous years, have been given to the Commission. In 2010, the President chaired a task force on economic governance; in 2012, he chaired a group of 'Four Presidents' (of the European Council, Commission, ECB, and Eurogroup) on a 'genuine economic and monetary union'. The President is thus the major player in the follow-up of the European Council.

By the end of his five-year term of office (2010–14), Herman Van Rompuy had clarified the nature of the job. He had authority to call meetings, prepare the agenda, lead debates and negotiations in and around the meetings, draft conclusions, and, when necessary, implement them. Van Rompuy avoided institutional rivalries and, under his guidance, the European Council found its place within, and no longer outside, the framework of the Union. He made a point of establishing personal relationships with national leaders, irrespective of the size and weight of their countries, and of listening to them on European or national political problems. He also found some balance between his public visibility and the obvious desire of heads of state or governments to remain in the limelight. His largely consensual and discreet style won applause. The present incumbent Donald Tusk, former prime minister of Poland, with a different style and background, is exercising the function along basically the same lines.

Meetings

The European Council holds four scheduled meetings a year, in March, June, October, and December. Special meetings can be called at short notice, as was the case in September 2001 after the '9/11' terrorist attacks on the United States (US), in February 2003 at a crucial moment in the Iraq crisis, in September 2008 when war erupted in Georgia, and in March 2011 when war broke out in Libya. In 2015, a special meeting was called on 23 April on migratory pressures in the Mediterranean.

Heads of state and government also hold informal meetings, chaired by the President of the European Council. They are usually short one-day meetings. There are no formal conclusions, but declarations or presidency statements may be issued. Their initial purpose was to allow for a confidential exchange of views and brainstorming, but in practice they deal mostly with current affairs. The first informal meeting was called by the Spanish presidency at Formentor (Mallorca) in September 1995. In 2015, three informal meetings were held, dealing with subjects ranging from terrorism, migration, and EMU, to Ukraine, Turkey, and the UK referendum, confirming the importance of informal gatherings among EU heads of state or government.

Taking into account occasional meetings in the margin of the United Nations (UN) and other international gatherings, and (for members concerned) euro summits, it is reasonable to say that no other group of heads of state or government in the world meets as regularly and frequently as the members of the European Council.

In the course of accession negotiations, it has been customary to invite heads of state or government from candidate countries for lunch and/or a brief session on the second day of a summit. Special guests may be invited to a meeting in the margins of a European Council. In 2015, for example, Petro Poroschenko, prime minister of Ukraine, met the members of the European Council in Brussels in February 2015; Ahmet Davutoğlu, prime minister of Turkey, was their guest at the November summit. The practice is time-consuming and is practised only with the unanimous agreement of the members.

Legal nature and characteristics

For many years, the European Council met, and exercised significant power on European affairs, without any legal basis in the Treaties. Its status remained ambiguous until the Lisbon Treaty clarified the matter: the European Council is now an institution of the Union.

The European Council needs to be considered not only as an institution, in legal terms, however, but also as an essential locus of power. This explains some key characteristics such as its authority, informality, and flexibility, and the impact of seniority and of the size of member states.

- *Authority* The European Council brings together political personalities who, in their national capacity, are ultimate decision-takers. Collectively, they consider themselves, in the European context, as having a similar task. Essentially, they come together to take decisions and they expect these decisions to be respected. That is a fact that other players have to take into account.

- *Informality* The European Council has always attached importance to the informality of its meetings. It works on the basis of restricted sessions in which heads of state or government sit alone, face to face, frequently addressing each other by their first names. In the 1970s, West German Chancellor Willy Brandt wanted summit meetings to be like a fireside chat (*Kamingespräch*). Roy Jenkins (1989: 74) considered the European Council to be 'a surprisingly satisfactory body, mainly because it is intimate'. With time, and as a result of enlargement, meetings have tended to become more structured and more formal. Specific papers are, in practice, actively debated. But the principle of privacy and direct contact—quite frequently confrontational—remains.

- *Flexibility* In the past, European Councils did not have formal rules of procedure and did not hesitate to depart from those rules that they themselves had formulated. They now have formal rules of procedure (see Box 3.2), but flexibility remains. It has accommodated the gradual emergence of euro summits without excessive difficulty.

- *Seniority* Because participants are relatively few in number and personal relations are important, the balance of power in the European Council is influenced by seniority. Newcomers will not be able to pull their full weight at first meetings. Heads of state or government from smaller member states can expect to exert more influence after several years of being present, particularly after they have led a successful presidency.

- *Size* In the abstract, all heads of state or government are equal, just as their states have equal status in international law. But because the European

Council is a locus of power, the fact that some participants in fact have more power (because they lead a more powerful country) is immediately apparent and implicitly understood by all.

Functions

The Treaty says that the European Council 'shall provide the Union with the necessary impetus for its development and shall define the general political directions and priorities thereof. It shall exercise no legislative function.[4]' In foreign policy, it should 'identify the Union's strategic interest, determine the objectives of and define general guidelines'.[5] It should discuss the broad guidelines of the economic policies of the member states and the Union.[6] Other Articles specify competences for the European Council in Treaty revision, breaches of human rights, appointments, Council formations, and so on. These texts undoubtedly give a clearer view of its tasks than was the case in the Treaties pre-Lisbon. But it can be argued that they still do not adequately reflect its role of ultimate negotiator and, at times, detailed decision-maker. The fact is that functions of the European Council go well beyond the official texts. They can be described under the following headings.[7]

- Strategic guidelines
- Decision-making
- Economic governance
- Foreign policy
- Justice and home affairs (JHA)
- Amending the Treaties

Strategic guidelines

The most traditional function of the European Council is to provide political guidance and impetus across the whole spectrum of Union activities. Indeed, this was the main reason given for its creation. It is mentioned both by the Tindemans Report (1976)[8] and by the Stuttgart Declaration (1983). In the early texts, the accent was put on ensuring consistency between Community affairs and other forms of European activity. Before the Treaty of Maastricht introduced a 'pillar' structure to encompass activities of different natures, the European Council was indeed the only place where some form of consistency could be ensured.

This task implies the right to launch new fields of activities. In Rome, in December 1975, the European Council decided to initiate cooperation in the fight against terrorism and organized crime. In Hanover, in June 1988, it appointed a group to look into economic and monetary union (EMU). At Lisbon, in March 2000, it opened up a new field of action in social affairs and economic policy. Gradually, it has acquired a sort of monopoly in this respect: 'Nothing decisive can be proposed or undertaken without its authority' (Taulègne 1993: 481).

Basically, the European Council fixes the agenda of the EU and is the place where strategic orientations are given. This is true for all fields of activity. It is the European Council that approves common strategies in the framework of CFSP, as it has done vis-à-vis Russia and Ukraine. As far as the Community is concerned, orientations leading to the completion of the internal market and EMU were defined at that level. Political guidance in the enlargement process was given at Copenhagen in December 1993 on Central and Eastern European countries (CEECs), and in Brussels in December 2004 on Turkey. At the onset of the Greek sovereign debt crisis in February 2010, heads of state or government issued a statement that gave guidance to the Economic and Financial Affairs Council (Ecofin), the Commission, Greece, and other eurozone members. In December 2015, they addressed unprecedented migration flows, and gave guidelines to the Council and Commission (see Box 3.4).

Decision-making

It was certainly not the initial intention of the member states that the European Council should serve as ultimate decision-taker nor as a court of appeal for settling problems too complex or too politically sensitive to be resolved at the Council level. Quite the contrary: both the Tindemans Report (1976) on European Union and the Dooge Report (1985)[9] on institutional reform stated that this should *not* be the case.

BOX 3.4   Strategic guidelines on migration

Over the past months, the European Council has developed a strategy aimed at stemming the unprecedented migratory flows Europe is facing. However, implementation is insufficient and has to be speeded up . . .

2. The Council should continue work on the crisis relocation mechanism taking into account experience gained, and rapidly decide on its position on the list of safe countries of origin. The Council is invited to rapidly examine the situation concerning Afghanistan. The Council should rapidly examine the Commission proposals of 15 December on a 'European Border and Coast Guard', the Schengen Borders Code, 'voluntary humanitarian admission scheme', and travel documents for returns. The Council should adopt its position on the 'European Border and Coast Guard' under the Netherlands Presidency. The Commission will rapidly present the review of the Dublin system; in the meantime, existing rules must be implemented. It will also soon present a revised proposal on Smart Borders.

Source: European Council Conclusions, 18 December 2015

Official texts, such as the Stuttgart Declaration (1983), steer clear of giving the European Council a decision-making capacity. But, over the years, that is exactly what it has acquired and exercised—although it has, in recent years, avoided time-consuming discussion of long texts and detailed numbers.

Examples abound. The British budgetary problem found a detailed solution at the top level at Fontainebleau in 1984. Decisions concerning the seat of European institutions are decided at the same level: at Edinburgh in December 1992; at Brussels in October 1993 and December 2003. The 'packages' around the finances of the Union, which involve an element of distributive bargaining between member states, were settled at the top level. It was obvious, in 2016, that decisions relevant to Brexit could be taken only at that level.

In part, it has been the weakness of Community decision-making, and in particular the incapacity of the GAC (composed of foreign ministers) to coordinate the activities of other councils, which has transferred the role of ultimate decision-maker to the European Council. But it should be noted that heads of state or government, although accepting in principle that their role should be one of mere guidance, have in practice not refused to deal in substance with the growing number of problems arising on their agendas. After all, decision-making is a sign of power—and power is not something that successful politicians tend to eschew.

Economic governance

The European Council has always considered a range of socio-economic challenges. In 2000, the Lisbon process gave it a specific responsibility in coordinating different national experiences in economic reform, making use of benchmarks, periodic monitoring, and peer review. In an evaluation document in 2010, the Commission noted tactfully that 'ambitions endorsed at the highest political level have not always resulted in faster decision-making or in avoiding dilution'.[10]

Under the presidency of Herman Van Rompuy, after 2010, the European Council nonetheless emerged as the principal decision-maker in the management of the eurozone crisis, initiating and promoting a surprising variety of legal procedures and instruments. In December 2011, it chose the ordinary legislative method to establish a fiscal and macroeconomic surveillance system applicable to all member states (known as the 'Six Pack'). It used Article 136 TFEU in May 2013 to complete the budgetary surveillance cycle and economic governance of eurozone members (known as the 'Two Pack'). It used a special legislative procedure under Article 127(6) TFEU in October 2013 to establish a single supervisory system (SSM) led by the ECB. In September 2012 it used the simplified Treaty revision procedure to modify Article 136 TFEU, to create the European Stability Mechanism (ESM), an international organization based in Luxembourg providing, when necessary, financial assistance to eurozone member states. Following the threat of a British veto, in January 2013 it made use of an intergovernmental procedure whereby twenty-five member states adopted a Treaty on Stability, Coordination and Governance (known as the 'Fiscal Compact').

Underlining this 'multifaceted performance', Wolfgang Wessels (2016: 207–8) concludes that the European Council has arguably emerged as a kind of economic government. But it should be noted that these new instruments of economic governance have also considerably increased the implementation powers of the Commission.

Foreign policy

Formulation of foreign policy has always been one of the primary tasks of the European Council. Its very first meeting at Dublin in March 1975 approved a declaration on Cyprus and one on the Conference for Security and Cooperation in Europe (CSCE). Over the years, European Councils have approved a great number of statements on foreign policy, covering events in all parts of the world and developments in all fields of diplomacy. Many of these statements were made at a time of existing or impending crisis: in March 1999, on the eve of NATO air strikes in Yugoslavia; in September 2008, when armed conflict was breaking out in Georgia; in March 2011, just before intervention in Libya; or in June 2014, on Ukraine (see Box 3.5).

BOX 3.5   **Statement of the Heads of State or Government on Ukraine, Brussels, 6 March 2014**

We strongly condemn the unprovoked violation of Ukrainian sovereignty and territorial integrity by the Russian Federation and call on the Russian Federation to immediately withdraw its armed forces to the areas of their permanent stationing, in accordance with the relevant agreements. We call on the Russian Federation to enable immediate access for international monitors. The solution to the crisis in Ukraine must be based on the territorial integrity, sovereignty and independence of Ukraine, as well as the strict adherence to international standards. We consider that the decision by the Supreme Council of the Autonomous Republic of Crimea to hold a referendum on the future status of the territory is contrary to the Ukrainian Constitution and therefore illegal . . .

The solution to the crisis should be found through negotiations between the Governments of Ukraine and the Russian Federation, including through potential multilateral mechanisms. Such negotiations need to start within the next few days and produce results within a limited timeframe. In the absence of such results the EU will decide on additional measures, such as travel bans, asset freezes and the cancellation of the EU-Russia summit. The Commission and the EEAS will take forward preparatory work on these measures.

Source: Statement of the Heads of State or Government on Ukraine, Brussels, 6 March 2014, © European Union 2016

The present Treaty confirms the tradition by saying that the European Council should identify the Union's strategic interest in, determine the objectives of and define general guidelines for the CFSP, including for matters with defence implications. It adopts the necessary decisions by unanimity. The Treaty adds that, if international developments so require, 'the President of the European Council shall convene an extraordinary meeting of the European Council in order to define the strategic lines of the Union's policy in the face of such developments'.[11]

It can be argued that, in the past, European Council conclusions contained an excessive number of foreign policy declarations (between fifteen and twenty, in some cases) and that this proliferation diminished the impact of such statements. There is no doubt, however, that member states have, at times, used the European Council effectively as a means of forcefully expressing common positions on international affairs.

When acting in this external capacity, the European Council operates as a 'collective head of state'. This was used in the Convention as an argument in favour of a stable presidency for that body, to avoid the disadvantages of the six-month rotation. The Lisbon Treaty says that:

[T]he President of the European Council shall, at his level and in that capacity, ensure the external representation of the Union on issues concerning its common foreign and security policy, without prejudice to the powers of the High Representative of the Union for Foreign Affairs and Security Policy.[12]

This is not the clearest of Treaty texts nor the easiest to implement, as was shown when the UN General Assembly refused in September 2010 to give the floor to Herman Van Rompuy in a debate at head-of-government level. Areas of potential conflict clearly exist: with the High Representative, with the President of the Commission, and with the rotating presidency. But, in practice, frequent and regular contact, deliberate avoidance of institutional rivalry, and practical arrangements on external representation have prevented the emergence of conflicts.

Justice and home affairs (JHA)

The European Council occasionally dealt with matters in the field of JHA even before the Maastricht Treaty created a specific 'pillar' to deal with it. The Amsterdam Treaty established Community competence in these matters. But it was a special meeting of the European Council, held in 1999 at Tampere (Finland), which defined the goal of establishing an area of freedom, security, and justice, and approved policy orientations and priorities to that effect. They were reinforced by five-year programmes adopted in 2004 (Hague Programme), 2009 (Stockholm Programme), and again in 2014. In the twenty-first century, the rise of wide-scale international terrorism and, more recently, massive migration have concentrated the attention of heads of state or government on these issues. In practice, most recent meetings of the European Council had to deal with immigration and counter-terrorism.

The Lisbon Treaty, while extending qualified majority voting (QMV) and codecision to this area, introduced a specific institutional competence for the European Council (Piris 2010: 180–90). In a procedure known as the 'emergency brake', a member state that considers that a draft legislative act would affect fundamental aspects of its criminal justice system is allowed to suspend the procedure by transferring the matter to the European Council. In the event of disagreement in the European Council and if at least nine member states wish to establish an enhanced cooperation on that basis, they will be automatically allowed to do so (known as the 'accelerator mechanism'). Thereby the European Council is formally recognized, in this field, as an institution of political appeal.[13]

Amending the Treaties

Heads of state or government have always played some role in Treaty negotiations. This tradition began with the negotiation of the Treaty of Rome. But, over time, that role has become predominant: their meeting has become 'the key forum for determining treaty reforms' (Wallace and Wallace 2000: 20). The present Treaty text gives a central role in amending the Treaties to the European Council. It allows different procedures, but, in all cases, the trigger mechanism for a Treaty revision of any sort is a decision by the European Council.

In the *ordinary revision procedure*, the European Council decides by simple majority on a proposal by the Council, after consulting the EP and the Commission. If the decision is positive, the President of the European Council convenes a convention, unless the European Council decides to give a direct mandate to convene an IGC. If convened, the convention examines the proposals for amendments and transmits its decisions to the IGC. Heads of state or government are represented in the convention and present in the IGC, so that they are in control at each stage of this procedure.

A *simplified revision procedure* allows Treaty amendment by unanimous decision of the European Council, subject to ratification by member states, without going through the process of an IGC.[14] This procedure applies exclusively to internal policies and actions (that is, the third Part of the TFEU). As indicated above, that procedure was used in September 2012 to create the ESM, an important instrument of economic and financial governance.

The European Council, again, is allowed to change the decision-making procedure foreseen in Treaty Articles from unanimity to qualified majority, and from special to ordinary legislative procedure.[15] Similar clauses, known as *passerelle* clauses in EU jargon, exist for foreign and security policy and for the multiannual financial framework.[16] In all cases, they imply a unanimous decision of the European Council that therefore remains central to any form of Treaty modification.

Euro summits

The first meeting of heads of state or government of the eurozone was called on 12 October 2008 by President Nicolas Sarkozy, then chairing the European Council. The argument that he gave was that 'only heads of state and government have the necessary democratic legitimacy' to face the ongoing international monetary crisis (quoted in Duthel 2010: 28). Other governments, including Germany, were reluctant to establish a new forum and considered the meeting to be a unique event. However, since 2010 and under the pressure of the euro crisis, regular meetings have been held in that format. Such meetings are requested at least twice a year under the 'Fiscal Compact', signed by twenty-five member states in March 2012, to deal with the governance of the eurozone and give strategic orientations.

The press and public opinion frequently consider euro summits to be a special format of the European Council. In legal terms, however, they are not. They are obviously powerful and important gatherings, but they remain informal, as is confirmed by the 'Fiscal Compact'. Euro summits bring together the heads of state or government of the contracting parties whose currency is the euro. The President of the European Commission is a member. The President of the ECB is invited.

Much effort has been made to control and limit potential tensions between eurozone and non-eurozone member states. The presidency of both bodies is, and was, entrusted to the same person, Herman Van Rompuy, and later, Donald Tusk, irrespective of the fact that the latter comes from a non-eurozone member state. The President is specifically tasked with keeping non-eurozone member states closely informed of the preparation and outcome of euro summits. He or she also informs the EP. Meetings typically take place after European Council meetings and procedures are largely similar.

Other than differences in membership, there is some difference in preparation. It is the Eurogroup (not GAC) which prepares euro summit meetings, assisted by the Eurogroup Working Group (not Coreper, which is nonetheless kept informed). Notwithstanding initial reservations, euro summits have become a key element for crisis management in the eurozone, as demonstrated by the three meetings held in summer 2015 (see Box 3.7).

Theorizing the European Council: Intergovernmental or hybrid?

The traditional view is that the intergovernmental nature of the European Council is more marked than that of the sectoral councils (Hayes-Renshaw 1999: 25). It should be noted, however, that the President of the Commission, who is not an intergovernmental figure, is *de jure* an influential member of the European Council. Moreover, the full-time President of the European Council is not dependent on any specific government and it is debatable whether he or she should be considered as strictly intergovernmental. Everybody knows that highly important decisions favouring supranational integration, such as the creation of the euro, were taken at this level and could not have been taken at any other. There is therefore a good deal of ambivalence in the institutional nature of the European Council and, perhaps because of this ambivalence, theories of European integration have some difficulty in accommodating the role of the European Council.

Its composition and the power that it wields would seem, at first sight, to confirm liberal intergovernmentalist theory, best developed by Andrew Moravcsik, who sees European integration as a succession of bargains between the bigger member states, based on national interests and domestic politics. According to this view, 'the creation of the European Council was explicitly designed to narrow rather than to broaden the scope for autonomous action by supranational actors' (Moravcsik 1998: 488). One may indeed consider, as does Moravcsik, successive IGCs to be 'bargains' concluded by member states at the highest level. However, the fact is that the Union has obviously more supranational elements today than it did in 1974. If supranational actors 'have only a rare and secondary impact' on negotiations (Moravcsik 1998: 485), how is this transfer of power to be explained?

A somewhat similar interpretation is given by Uwe Puetter (2014) under the name of 'deliberative intergovernmentalism'. He explains the rise of power of the European Council as an answer to the paradox that member states are willing to expand and further develop the EU's policy agenda, but insist upon excluding the transfer of competences to supranational institutions. He underlines that the post-Maastricht EU focuses more on policy coordination than on the traditional community method of legislative decision-making (Puetter 2014: 56). It should be noted, however, that in the 1970s, well before the rise of the European Council, intergovernmentalism (that is, the EPC) was accepted as an alternative to the Community method in significant fields such as foreign policy and counter-terrorism.

Wolfgang Wessels (2016: 18) favours a 'fusion model', asserting that the European Council derives its power from the pivotal role that it plays simultaneously in the institutional architecture of the Union and in the relationship between the Union and member states. He underlines the fact that members of the European Council wear two hats: a national one and a European one. This point is also made by Luuk Van Middelaar (2013: 30), who speaks of 'dual capacity': 'Of all the bodies representing the circle of member states the European Council alone measures up to the jungle outside and has authority over the community world within.' It would seem that the European Council is powerful because it is a hybrid (see Box 3.6).

> **BOX 3.6**   **A hybrid political animal**
>
> At Milan, on 29 June 1985, Chair of the European Council Bettino Craxi, prime minister of Italy, called a vote on the convening of an IGC to modify the Treaty. Facing the outcry of some member states, Craxi referred to the Treaty Article indicating that, for procedural questions, the Council shall act by a majority of its members.[17] The implication was that the European Council was operating as the Council of Ministers. Scholars had previously noted that this possibility existed in the Treaty, but the observation remained a relatively irrelevant legal nicety until it was unexpectedly put into use. The vote was carried by seven votes to three.
>
> Luuk Van Middelaar (2013: 107) underlines the significance of that event: 'It is a magnificent moment of passage . . . Craxi exposed the dual capacity of the European heads of government and pulled those two capacities apart.' He also notes that the outvoted member states (the UK, Denmark, and Greece) did not later question the legitimacy of the vote: they attended the IGC when it convened.

Strengths and weaknesses

For over a quarter of a century, the European Council has been the guiding force of the European integration process. Time and time again, the most difficult problems have been debated, and solutions have been found, at that level. The EU would not be what it is today had heads of state or government not been systematically involved in major decisions.

But top-level decision-making has its limits and its dangers. Dangers relate to the irretrievable character of mistakes; limits include the nature and the quantity of decisions to be taken. Moreover, negotiation at the highest level is risky: miscalculations or tactical errors occur and cannot, in most cases, be corrected (see Box 3.7).[18]

The decision-making capacity of the European Council, is limited by the number of meetings and the search for consensus.

- *Meetings* In view of their other obligations, it will always be difficult for heads of state or government to meet regularly more than six or seven times a year, as they do at present.[19] It is far from clear that such a limited number of meetings, however intense, are sufficient to deal effectively with the governance of an increasingly complex multinational entity. European Councils are frequently short of time and dominated by unforeseen current events.

- *Consensus* As a general rule, decision-making in the European Council is based on consensus—that is, on a relatively inefficient procedure. European Councils frequently fail to reach decisions on time, and 'too little, too late' is a frequently heard criticism.

BOX 3.7	**Miscalculations and tactical errors**

Miscalculations or tactical errors come with a high cost, not least in credibility and good-will. Two examples illustrate this, at an interval of twenty-five years.

- *Rome European Council, 27–28 October 1990* The main point on the agenda was whether the future European currency should be a common currency (circulating in parallel with national currencies) or a single currency (taking the place of national currencies). The Italian presidency took the view that the British prime minister would in no circumstances accept conclusions based on a single currency and therefore initially proposed draft conclusions implying a *common* currency. On the second day, Mrs Thatcher declared unexpectedly that those conclusions were unacceptable and that she required a separate paragraph in which the British point of view would be described. Italian Prime Minister Giulio Andreotti, who was in the chair, then stated that, given that the UK would have a separate paragraph of its own, it could hardly expect to influence the formulation preferred by other member states. Redrafted conclusions thus read, 'The Community will have a single currency which will be an expression of its identity and unity'—precisely the statement that Britain had sought to avoid. Three days later, in the House of Commons, Deputy Prime Minister Geoffrey Howe implied in his resignation speech that the Prime Minister had given an 'impulsive answer'.[20]

- *Brussels Euro Summit, June–July 2015* On 26 June, Greek Prime Minister Alexis Tsipras abruptly left the euro summit, which was addressing the monetary crisis in his country, and flew to Athens. To other participants, the decision seemed impulsive and unprepared. Tsipras called, without prior notice, a referendum on the suggested bailout programme, scheduled for 5 July, and recommended that voters reject it. A majority of Greek voters followed that advice. The procedure created dismay and resentment in the Union. It fuelled market speculation on the insolvency of the banking system, and on Greece defaulting on public debt and exiting the eurozone. On 30 June, even before the referendum, the Greek government had to renew its request for assistance. The euro summit met again on 7 July, in a tense atmosphere, and asked for specific and detailed Greek proposals in a matter of days. A third meeting on 12 July sat in an all-night session and, at dawn on 13 July, agreed a bailout programme that was in several respects more stringent for Greece than that which had been so spectacularly rejected two weeks before.

It is interesting to note that, in both examples, observers used the word 'impulsive'.

The limits of the European Council are particularly apparent when it is amending the Treaties because its task as Treaty negotiator is different in nature from its other functions. When it gives political guidance or impetus, when it makes foreign policy statements, or when it debates economic governance or financial frameworks, decisions are political, not legal, in nature. When it acts as Treaty negotiator, however, the European Council is directly modifying the basic law of the Union. It is, in fact, legislating.

The structure and the *modus operandi* of the European Council are well adapted to collective bargaining, the crafting of compromises, the definition of general guidelines, and the drafting of political statements; they are less well adapted to a legislative function. Hectic night sessions with no assistants in the room, multilingual debate on texts that appear and disappear from the negotiating table without having been studied in depth, and across-the-board compromises on unrelated issues at the break of dawn cannot lead to clear legal texts. The complexity and confusion of the Treaties (with numerous protocols and declarations annexed to the final act of each IGC) must be partly attributed to the way in which they are negotiated. It regularly takes legal and linguistic experts, under the guidance of Coreper, several weeks to establish in legal terms what has been decided. The fact is that no civilized nation legislates in such an uncoordinated and risky way. Tony Blair famously remarked at the end of the Nice European Council, 'We cannot go on like this.'

In 2002, critical voices began to be heard in academic circles, in the institution itself, and in the Convention, which was then meeting. In March of that year, the Barcelona European Council heard strong words from the Secretary-General of the Council. Javier Solana considered that, for some years, the European Council had been side-tracked from its original purpose and had spent too much time on low-level drafting work, and that its meetings had been reduced to 'report-approval sessions or inappropriate exercises in self-congratulation' (Solana 2002: 2). This led to the Rules of Procedure adopted at Seville in June 2002. The very substantial modifications, proposed in the Constitutional Treaty and finally introduced by the Treaty of Lisbon, have been described in this chapter.

While the European Council has undoubtedly been strengthened by becoming a formal institution, with a reduced number of participants, a full-time President, and some clarification of its competences and decisions, some observers consider that it has been excessively strengthened to the detriment of the Commission and institutional balance. But those modifications tend to bring law in line with reality and to remedy perceived weaknesses in the previous construction.

Conclusion

In many ways, 'the whole European Union system revolves round the European Council' (Ludlow 2000: 15). It is 'the only institution which has overall political leadership on all EU affairs' (Piris 2010: 208). The dates of its meetings, announced well in advance, mark the rhythm of the Union's various activities. Foreign governments, the press, and business organizations study conclusions to gauge the health, the dynamics, future orientations, and potential actions of the Union. When that rhythm is interrupted, such as in the aftermath of the UK's 2016 referendum decision to leave the EU, it is the European Council that meets to take decisions at the highest political level in Europe about what happens next.

In successive meetings over the years, it has largely fashioned the Union as we know it today. The fact is that even if the European Council is basically intergovernmental in nature, the system of the establishment to which it has so largely contributed is not mainly intergovernmental. Forty years later, the Union is much larger, much more integrated, and more supranational than it was in the 1970s. With hindsight, therefore, it is clear that Monnet was justified in advocating its creation. What are the underlying reasons that have led to this result? For most of the time since 1974, France and Germany have been governed by leaders strongly committed to mutual cooperation and to furthering European integration. They found enough support, at their level, among other leaders to push the Union forward, even if some members preferred to opt out. The Maastricht Treaty, with monetary union, is an example; the 'Fiscal Compact' is another. The role of the President of the Commission has been crucial in some circumstances. For example, Jacques Delors developed a real talent for harnessing the power of the European Council to further the dynamics of integration. In the absence of any of these conditions, the results would have been very different.

There is no doubt that, over the years, the growing number of member states has weighed on the working of the European Council, as it does on other institutions of the Union. The informality, direct contact, and personal trust that characterized early meetings are difficult to maintain in a larger body. Unofficial preparatory caucuses or other forms of *directoire* become more tempting and cause dismay. The Lisbon Treaty sought to adapt the European Council to new challenges in an enlarged Union. The institutional innovations were immediately tested by the critical environment in which they were born. The first European Council chaired by Herman Van Rompuy had to deal with the crisis in Greece. His last meeting, five years later, had the same point on its agenda. He notes that, when entering uncharted territory and new rules need to be established, the European Council is well placed to fulfil that role.

Major decisions on EMU and an impressive array of new legal instruments were approved in that period. They originated in, or were promoted by, the European Council. There was also adopted a significant institutional innovation: euro summits. Timing and effectiveness is always debatable, but the fact is that, contrary to the expectations of many, the eurozone did not break down. A major upheaval for the whole Union was avoided. Where else could those decisions have been taken?

 ENDNOTES

1. Art. 15 TEU.
2. See Arts 15 and 48(4) TEU.
3. This group, which plays an important role in the coordination of Coreper II activities, is named after Massimo Antici, an Italian diplomat who was its first chairman in 1975.

4. Art. 15(1) TEU.

5. Art. 26 TEU.

6. Art. 121(2) TFEU.

7. These distinctions are somewhat arbitrary and they frequently tend to overlap. Some authors identify no fewer than nine different functions (Bulmer and Wessels 1987: 76–80); elsewhere, they are counted as three (Dinan 2000: 190), six (Nugent 1999: 201), or even twelve (Werts 1992: 120–2). In all instances, the ground covered is basically the same.

8. Leo Tindemans was prime minister of Belgium in December 1974 when he was asked by the Paris Summit to draft a report on European Union, which he presented in early 1976.

9. James Dooge, a former Irish foreign minister, was asked by the Fontainebleau European Council in June 1984 to chair a group to draft a report on institutional reform. The report, presented in 1985, prepared the negotiation of the SEA.

10. COMM SEC(2010) 114 final.

11. Art. 15(3) TEU.

12. Art. 15(6) TEU.

13. Arts 82(3), 83(3), and 86(1) TFEU. A similar brake applying to eurozone decisions was part of a new settlement requested by David Cameron in view of the then-impending UK referendum, adopted by the European Council on 18 February 2016.

14. Art. 48(6) TEU.

15. Art. 48(7) TEU.

16. Art. 31(3) TEU and Art. 312(2) TFEU (respectively).

17. Art. 31(5) TEU.

18. Information on the European Council in Rome is provided by interviews conducted in 1997 by the British Broadcasting Corporation (BBC) for the preparation of a documentary on monetary union called *The Money Makers*.

19. In 2014, there were four scheduled: three extraordinary and one informal meetings of the European Council. In 2015, there were four scheduled meetings: one special and three informal.

20. A full text of Howe's speech is available online at http://www.britpolitics.co.uk/speeches-sir-geoffrey-howe-resignation

 FURTHER READING

Wessels (2016) is a recent and in-depth analysis of the history and performance of the institution, its impact on decision-making in the Union, and its activities in different fields. Puetter (2014) considers both the European Council and Council of Ministers together to be the centre of a post-Maastricht institutional dynamic that he describes in detail and calls the 'new intergovernmentalism'. Van Middelaar (2013) makes a very thoughtful contribution to the debate on European institutions, underlining the distinction between three spheres: European sovereign states (the outer sphere); treaty-based institutions (the inner sphere); and member states operating in the Union (the intermediate sphere). A lively historical description of key meetings of the European Council is given in a collective work drafted by former high-level Council officials in de Boissieu *et al.* (2015), while Van Rompuy (2014) is the contribution of a major actor.

de Boissieu, P., Cloos, J., Skytte Christoffersen, P., van Middelaar, L., Keller-Noëllet, J., Milton, G., Roger, C., Blanchet, T., Galloway, D., and Gillissen, A. (2015) *National Leaders and the Making of Europe: Key Episodes in the Life of the European Council* (London: John Harper).

Puetter, U. (2014) *The European Council and the Council: New Intergovernmentalism and Institutional Change* (Oxford: Oxford University Press).

Van Middelaar, L. (2013) *The Passage to Europe: How a Continent Became a Union* (New Haven, CT: Yale University Press).

Van Rompuy, H. (2014) *Europe in the Storm: Promise and Prejudice* (Leuven: Davidsfonds).

Wessels, W. (2016) *The European Council* (Basingstoke: Palgrave Macmillan).

WEB LINKS

http://www.consilium.europa.eu

The Council website gives detailed information on the European Council and its activities, including press releases, basic documents, and presidency conclusions since 1993. The home page of the President includes major speeches and a number of videos.

https://councillibrary.wordpress.com/bibliographies/

The website of the central library of the Council hosts an exhaustive bibliography on the European Council in a great variety of languages.

CHAPTER 4

The Council of Ministers: Conflict, consensus, and continuity

Fiona Hayes-Renshaw

▌ Summary

As one of the original traditional Community institutions, the Council of Ministers has always occupied a central position among the European institutions and in European policy-making. It is involved in all areas of European Union (EU) activity, usually by legislating in tandem with the European Parliament (EP), but also by coordinating the member states' policies in particular fields. The Council meets in ten different configurations that bring together ministerial representatives from each of the member states,

Cont. ➤

Cont.

who articulate, defend, and aggregate the interests of the EU's member governments. The decisions they take are prepared by national officials in numerous meetings at various levels, the most important being that of the Committee of the Permanent Representatives (Coreper), the subject of Chapter 14. The Lisbon Treaty (2007) institutionalized a tri-presidency system designed to ensure continuity and consistency in the Council's work. A new 'double majority' voting system has also been introduced for legislative decision-making within the Council, but most decisions continue to be taken by consensus.

Introduction

Visitors to the reception area of the Council's official seat in Brussels in the second half of 2015 were met with a moveable display of twenty-eight deckchairs in the colours of the flags of each of the member states. This rather incongruous installation—the brainchild of then Council presidency Luxembourg—was designed and arranged to promote the idea of sitting together in a sociable and friendly way, and presumably by extension to serve as a basic metaphor for Council deliberations. The reality of the meetings of national governmental representatives that take place on a daily basis in the Council's Justus Lipsius building is understandably rather different, given the various national interests that have to be taken into account when agreeing a common Council position. However, the inherent conflict that characterizes the Council and its working methods coexists with a degree of consensual behaviour that might surprise outside observers.

Nationality is, obviously, important in the Council of Ministers. Each delegate is identified by the member state they represent, and this determines where they sit at the negotiating table and when they undertake the six-month presidency of the Council. National interests determine the positions they adopt in the Council, national administrative systems affect how these positions are reached, and the size of their national population affects the weight attached to the votes they cast. Once these interests have been articulated in the Council and votes have been cast, however, national positions are subsumed into a so-called Council position, which is then defended against that (or those) of the EP. Consequently, participants in Council meetings frequently act and interact in ways that owe more to supranationalism than to intergovernmentalism.

This chapter examines the inhabitants of, and working visitors to, the Council's headquarters in Brussels. First, the present-day Council is traced back to its origins in the 1951 Treaty of Paris. Second, the structure of the institution is explored to identify those individuals who, together, constitute its horizontal and hierarchical layers. Because this volume contains separate chapters on the European Council (see Chapter 3) and Coreper (see Chapter 14), this chapter will concentrate on the remaining layers of the Council hierarchy: the ministerial Council; the preparatory bodies (the working parties and senior committees other than Coreper); the Council presidency; and the Council Secretariat. Third, this chapter describes the formal and informal powers of the Council and its members, the ways in which its work is coordinated, and the means available to its members to exert influence and affect its output. The often-vexed question of the Council's accountability is also addressed. The Council's relationships with the European Council, the Parliament, and the Commission are subsequently examined, while the final part of the chapter analyses the Council's role in the context of the EU as a whole, and describes some of the theoretical approaches advanced to describe and explain the Council.

The origins of the Council

The Council of the European Union can trace its origins back directly to the Special Council provided for in the 1951 Treaty of Paris, which established the European Coal and Steel Community (ECSC). The creation of a body representing the governments of the member states was a direct and rather obvious attempt to temper the powers of the ECSC's innovative supranational High Authority, the forerunner of the present-day European Commission. When the founding Treaties of the European Economic Community (EEC) and the European Atomic Energy Community (Euratom) were negotiated and adopted six years later, a slightly altered version of the ECSC's institutional blueprint was agreed. The two new Communities were granted their own Council and Commission, while sharing the ECSC's already established Assembly and Court.

   Despite the shared name, the powers of the old and new Councils could not have been more different. The ECSC's Special Council was required merely to exchange information with and consult the High Authority; in contrast, Article 145 of the 1957 Treaty of Rome provided that the Council should 'ensure coordination of the general economic policies of the member states and have power to take decisions'. This enhanced role, similar to that still exercised by the Council today, derived from the increased assertiveness of member governments vis-à-vis the more supranational elements of the new European Communities. In 1967, in a move to coordinate the activities and institutions of the three Communities, the so-called Merger of the Executives resulted in the creation of a single Council (and a single Commission) for all three European Communities. The Council of the European Communities subsequently and formally became the Council of the European Union with the entry into force of the Maastricht Treaty in November 1993, but continues to be referred to informally as 'the Council', or 'the Council of Ministers'.

Over the decades, the Council's membership has increased almost fivefold from six to twenty-eight (to be twenty-seven post-Brexit) and, as a result, its areas of responsibility have expanded dramatically. Simultaneously, it has had to adapt to the additional budgetary and legislative powers acquired over time by the EP, with which it must now work closely. In response, the Council has adapted its structure and working methods on a number of occasions, documenting the changes in successive Treaties and in revisions to its internal rules of procedure.

The Council hierarchy

Until 2009, it was possible to represent the Council hierarchy as a layered triangle, with the European Council at the top, followed by the ministerial councils, then by Coreper and several other senior preparatory bodies, and, at the base, a large number of working parties. Each of these levels was headed by the rotating Council presidency and the whole structure was underpinned by a General Secretariat. The 2007 Lisbon Treaty established the European Council as a separate institution with its own full-time President (see Chapter 3) and created a cross-institutional High Representative, who now chairs the Foreign Affairs Council. As will become clear, both the European Council and the High Representative continue to be connected via political and administrative ties to the remaining layers of the Council hierarchy.

The ministerial Council

Although we speak of 'the' Council of Ministers, in practice it now meets in ten different configurations, each dealing with one or more policy areas. There is no formal hierarchy between the different configurations, although the General Affairs Council (GAC) has a special coordinating role, and the Economic and Financial Affairs and Foreign Affairs Councils (Ecofin and FAC, respectively) are viewed as the most senior formations because of their membership and the frequency of their meetings (see Box 4.1). Each Council is composed of the relevant and responsible governmental representative(s)—ministers or state secretaries—from each member state and (with the exception of the FAC) is chaired by a representative of the member state currently holding the rotating Council presidency (see 'The presidency'). The Commission is represented by one or more Commissioners, and the meetings are also attended by officials from the member states, the Commission services, and the Council Secretariat.

The Council is a busy body. It meets formally between seventy and eighty times a year, normally at the Council's headquarters in Brussels. During the months of April, June, and October, the Council's meetings are held in Luxembourg—the enduring and inefficient result of a 1965 political agreement on the seat of the institutions. Should the need arise for certain Councils to convene at short notice in response to unexpected events, extraordinary Council meetings may be inserted into the already busy

BOX 4.1	Council configurations and frequency of meetings, 2010 and 2015

The Council meets in ten different configurations (see Table 4.1), some of which are responsible for a number of related policy areas. In such cases, the agendas are divided up according to policy area to enable ministers with distinct portfolios to attend separate parts of the session. Different aspects of some policy areas are dealt with in more than one configuration. Some configurations meet almost monthly, while others may be convened only once or twice during a presidency.

TABLE 4.1   Council configurations and number of formal meetings, 2010 and 2015

		Number of formal meetings	
Configurations		**2010**	**2015**
AGRIFISH	**Agriculture and fisheries**	11	10
COMPET	**Competitiveness** Single market International trade and customs Enterprise and industry Research and technological development	6	5
ECOFIN	**Economic and financial affairs** Economy and finance Euro area Budget Single market Enlargement	11	10
EYCS	**Education, youth, culture and sport**	3	2
EPSCO	**Employment, social policy, health and consumer affairs**	4	4
ENV	**Environment**	4	5
FAC	**Foreign affairs** Foreign affairs and international relations Security and defence International trade and customs Enlargement	14	13
GAC	**General affairs** Institutional affairs Regional affairs Enlargement Budget	11	9
JHA	**Justice and home affairs**	6	10
TTE	**Transport, telecommunications and energy**	4	7
Total		74	75

Source: Information obtained from http://www.consilium.europa.eu/en/council-eu/configurations/

timetable drawn up by each presidency in advance of its term in office. This was the case for the Justice and Home Affairs Council, which met more often than usual in 2015 in response to the migration crisis in Europe. Each presidency also schedules a number of informal ministerial meetings, normally in its member state, where participants have the opportunity to exchange views on issues of importance to their particular Council configuration. A total of twenty-six such meetings were held in 2015.

Special mention should be made of the Eurogroup, a rather different 'informal' and now rather powerful ministerial gathering, which was created by means of a European Council decision in 1997 (see Puetter 2006) and officially recognized in the Lisbon Treaty. It brings together the finance ministers of the eurozone member states, along with the Vice-President of the Commission with responsibility for the euro and the President of the European Central Bank (ECB), to discuss matters arising from the members' shared responsibilities related to the euro. They normally meet on a monthly basis, the day or evening before the full Ecofin Council, and additional meetings take place when necessary. They met twenty-two times in 2015. The group is presided over by one of its members who is appointed for a period of two-and-a-half years, although the idea of creating a full-time post of Eurogroup president has been mooted.

The preparatory bodies

Council meetings are prepared by more than 150 specialized committees and working parties, composed of officials from each of the member states and a representative of the Commission. Coreper, the most senior of these committees, is formally responsible for preparing the work of the entire Council and fulfils an important horizontal coordination function (see Chapter 14). Other senior bodies coordinate work in particular policy areas, such as the Economic and Financial Committee (EFC), the Political and Security Committee (PSC), and the Special Committee on Agriculture (SCA).

Officials from the national ministries represent their governments in the many working parties that constitute the base of the Council hierarchy. Some of these officials are based in Brussels in their national permanent representations (see Chapter 14), while others travel to the Belgian capital from their member states for meetings. All are experts in their policy fields, operating on the basis of instructions from their home ministries. The Commission is represented by officials from the relevant Directorate-General (DG) in the 3,400 or so Council working party meetings that take place every year.

While the chairmanship of most of the preparatory bodies changes every six months in accordance with the rotating Council presidency (see next section), some have a more permanent leadership arrangement. A small number have a fixed (elected or appointed) chair, while others are presided over by a member of the High Representative's staff or are headed by an official from the Council Secretariat.

The presidency

The presidency of the Council rotates every six months among the member states according to a pre-established order (see Box 4.2), which also determines the place their representatives occupy at the table in meetings throughout the Council hierarchy (see Figure 4.1). The current order of rotation, which was drawn up to coincide with the accession of Bulgaria and Romania, came into effect on 1 January 2007 and covers the period to the end of June 2020. A decision determining the order of rotation from the second half of 2020 onwards will be taken by July 2017.

Taking on the Council presidency is an onerous task for national officials. Both a chair and a national spokesperson must be provided for virtually every meeting at each level of the Council hierarchy over the six-month period—a particular challenge for smaller member states with limited personnel. While the Council Secretariat provides valuable administrative support and expertise both before and during

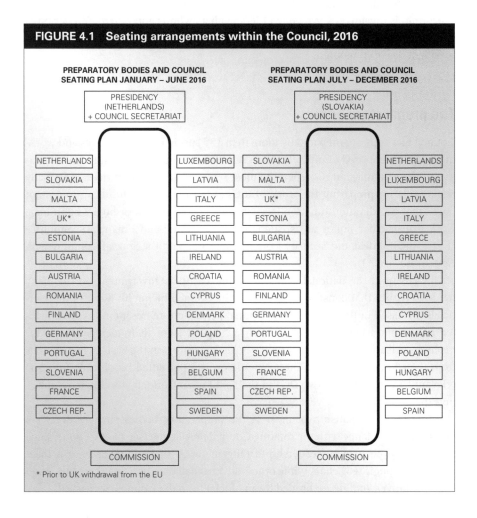

FIGURE 4.1   Seating arrangements within the Council, 2016

BOX 4.2	Order of presidency rotation, 2007–20

The Lisbon Treaty institutionalized what had already existed in embryonic form in the years preceding its entry into force—that is, a system of team presidencies, whereby groups of three member states are responsible for exercising the Council presidency over a period of eighteen months. The teams are intended to reflect a general balance of geographical situation, economic weight, and 'old' and 'new' member states. Each team presidency agrees a common work programme spanning the entire eighteen-month period and each of the members of the trio is responsible for the details of the work programme during its particular term in office. Each member state takes its turn in the chair for a period of six months and is expected to provide material support to its team colleagues during their time in office (see Table 4.2).

TABLE 4.2 Council presidency rotation, 2016–20

Trio period	Member states	Presidency dates
1 January 2016–30 June 2017	Netherlands	1 January–30 June 2016
	Slovakia	1 July–31 December 2016
	Malta	1 January–30 June 2017
1 July 2017–31 December 2018	UK*	1 July–31 December 2017
	Estonia	1 January–30 June 2018
	Bulgaria	1 July–31 December 2018
1 January 2019–30 June 2020	Austria	1 January–30 June 2019
	Romania	1 July–31 December 2019
	Finland	1 January–30 June 2020

*Scheduled prior to 2016 UK referendum

the presidency in order to ensure coherence and consistency across the entire range of issues being discussed in the Council hierarchy, additional national personnel are also required on the ground to deal with the sheer volume of work associated with leadership of virtually all areas of Council activity during the term in office.

The Council Secretariat

The General Secretariat of the Council (to give it its official title) is a relatively small and ostensibly politically neutral body that is also responsible for assisting the European Council. It employs some 3,000 staff, most of whom are permanent officials recruited by open competition from among the nationals of the member states. A small number of national officials and experts are seconded to the Secretariat from the member states. The Secretariat has increased in size over the years as a direct result of successive enlargements and has undergone reorganization in response to changes in the scope of the Council's activities.

The Council Secretariat is headed by a Secretary-General, the incumbent at the time of writing being Jeppe Tranholm-Mikkelsen, a former Danish permanent representative, who has been appointed to serve for the period from July 2015 until the end of June 2020. The main body of the Secretariat is divided into seven DGs, the largest of which is that responsible for Administration (DG A). Five DGs are organized on a functional basis, according to the Councils they serve, and the seventh is responsible for communication and document management. A horizontal legal service serves all levels of the Council hierarchy and a number of specialized units are directly answerable to the Secretary-General.

What does the Council do?

The Council has five main functions, as follows.

- *It negotiates and adopts EU laws* (legislative acts), mostly legislating jointly with the EP under the ordinary legislative procedure (OLP), also known as 'codecision'.
- *It coordinates member states' policies* in particular fields (economic and fiscal policy; education, culture, youth, and sport; employment policy), usually taking decisions by unanimity.
- *It develops the EU's common foreign and security policy (CFSP)*, working closely with the European Council and the High Representative.
- *It concludes international agreements* negotiated by the Commission with non-EU countries and international organizations, and with the consent of the EP and the member states.
- It *adopts the EU budget* together with the EP.

Formal and informal powers

The Council fulfils its functions mainly by reference to formal rules laid down in the Treaties and in its own internal rules of procedure. These formal rules have been supplemented over the years by informal conventions and rules that govern the work of all levels of the Council, and its relations with the Commission, the EP, and the European Council.

The ministers and preparatory bodies

The Council is the EU's principal legislative and policy-making institution, being formally charged with decision-making across virtually all areas of Union activity. Specific decision-making procedures and voting rules apply to the different areas of Council activity, entailing a greater or lesser role for the EP and, in most cases, some form of majority voting in the Council itself.

In fulfilling its legislative decision-making functions, the Council as a body represents and attempts to aggregate the interests of all of the member governments in order to arrive at a common 'Council position', which it then defends vis-à-vis the other EU institutions, in particular its co-legislator, the EP. The reconciliation of conflicting interests within the Council is achieved through a continuous process of negotiation. Throughout this process, the Commission proposal on the table is discussed in detail, national positions are articulated and defended, coalitions are formed, and compromises are advanced until agreement is reached. In addition and parallel to these internal deliberations, the Council must also negotiate with the other institutions involved in the legislative process—in particular, the EP (see 'The Council and Parliament'; see also Chapter 6).

In the Council hierarchy, most of the detailed negotiation and much of the actual agreement tends to occur at various levels below that of the ministerial Council itself. Every dossier undergoes a first detailed examination at a series of meetings at working-party level. National officials work through the Commission's proposal, article by article, until such time as no further agreement can be reached at that level. This may mean that consensus has been achieved on the entire document, or that certain parts of the document have proved too contentious to agree at that level and need the input of more senior officials, or even the ministers themselves. In any event, the dossier passes through Coreper (with or without further discussion, depending on how much agreement has been reached at working-party level) on its way to the agenda of the relevant Council, which is divided into two distinct parts.

At their meetings, the ministers adopt without discussion those items listed in the first part of the agenda that have been the object of agreement at Coreper or working-party level (the so-called A points), and engage in detailed discussions on those still requiring deliberation and agreement (the so-called B points). About a third of all Council agenda items fall into the latter category. Any issues that find their way to the Council table for ministerial discussion are accompanied by an indication of the main opposing positions that have emerged during the preparatory discussions, along with recommendations from Coreper for possible compromise solutions. Following discussion in the Council, an agenda item may either be the subject of agreement or else referred back down to a senior committee or a working party for further discussion, before reappearing on the Council's agenda for final adoption.

Insiders have estimated that, in some Council configurations, the ministers actively discuss only between 10 and 15 per cent of all of the items on their agendas, with the rest being discussed by Coreper and the working groups. Häge (2007, 2008) has produced figures to show that the decision-making input of ministers may in fact be much higher than this, particularly in some configurations, but acknowledges the inherent difficulty in identifying the level within the Council hierarchy at which agreement is actually reached.

There is no controversy, however, about who legally takes the final decision. The calculation of possible positive and negative votes occurs throughout the Council hierarchy, and there may even be implicit indicative voting in the more senior preparatory bodies, but it is the ministers themselves who take—and they alone who are legally authorized to take—the final decision in the name of the Council. Ministers vote in the Council on the basis of simple majority, qualified majority, or unanimity, depending on the Treaty rules governing the issue in question. Under simple majority voting, which is normally used for procedural issues, each member state has a single vote and fifteen votes in favour are required to adopt a measure in the EU of twenty-eight. In the small number of policy areas in which unanimity is now required (such as indirect taxation, foreign policy, citizenship, and social security), an unhappy member state can either exercise a veto by voting against, or can choose to abstain from voting without preventing agreement by the others (under unanimity rules, an abstention, in effect, counts as a 'yes').

Qualified majority voting (QMV) is now the standard voting rule in the Council, accounting for some 90 per cent of all legislative acts adopted annually in recent years. Figure 4.2, which depicts Council votes taken on legislative acts in the period 1999–2015, indicates the cyclical nature of the EU's decision-making process, which is driven by the electoral cycle of the EP and the related terms of successive Commissions. A peak in legislative output is evident in the years of and immediately preceding EP elections (1999, 2004, 2009, and 2014 in Figure 4.2), which act as an incentive to complete many of the legislative procedures in the pipeline. This is normally followed by a fall in output as a new Commission gets into its stride, inserting new proposals into the system. The marked drop in overall legislative output in recent years is the direct result of a commitment on the part of the Commission to 'do less and do it better', which has entailed fewer new proposals being tabled and some existing ones being withdrawn or

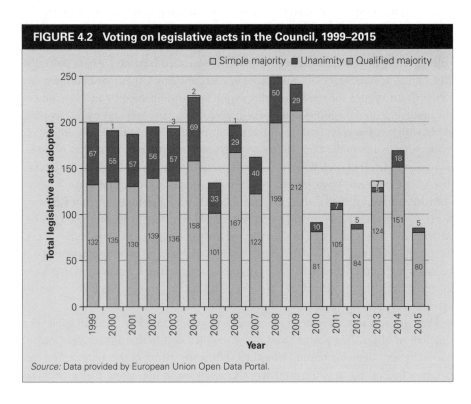

FIGURE 4.2 Voting on legislative acts in the Council, 1999–2015

Source: Data provided by European Union Open Data Portal.

replaced. About 90 per cent of all Commission draft legislative acts are adopted by the Council and EP, with the other 10 per cent being withdrawn or replaced because of a lack of agreement between the Council, EP, and Commission (Häge 2011).

Until November 2014, the Council's QMV system was based on weighted votes, according to which each member state was allocated a set number of votes in approximate relation to its size and specific thresholds had to be attained in order to adopt or block a measure.[1] The threshold for the achievement of a qualified majority was always set at about 70 per cent of the total number of votes, implicitly also requiring a majority of the member states. With every enlargement of the EU, a number of votes had to be attributed to each acceding state and agreement had to be reached on the level of votes required to achieve a qualified majority or blocking minority. These often-protracted discussions gave rise to some of the bitterest bargaining ever witnessed among the member states.

Concerns about the lack of proportionality inherent in the system resulted in a population requirement being introduced by the Nice Treaty in 2001, although it could be deployed only if specifically requested by one or more member states when a vote was being taken. The 2007 Lisbon Treaty sought to further simplify the process by attributing a single vote to each member state and stipulating fixed percentages for a new 'double majority' QMV system, based on the number of member states and the overall size of the EU's population. This obviated the need for protracted discussions in the event of future enlargements, but, as a compromise, it was agreed that the Nice Treaty rules could be applied on a case-by-case basis for a short transitional period (see Box 4.3). Official (Eurostat) population figures for each member

---

BOX 4.3   **Qualified majority voting (QMV) in the Council**

The 2001 Treaty of Nice laid down the following three conditions for the achievement of a qualified majority in the Council (amended, in view of Croatian accession, to provide for twenty-eight member states):

- a minimum of 260 of the 352 votes are cast in favour by
- a majority of the member states (15 out of 28)
- (if requested) representing at least 62 per cent of the total EU population.

It follows that ninety-three votes would constitute a blocking minority, thereby preventing the adoption of a measure. The 2007 Lisbon Treaty introduced a double-majority system, in which a qualified majority is attained if a vote in favour is registered by:

- 55 per cent of the member states (16 out of 28)
- representing 65 per cent of the total EU population.

Importantly, a blocking minority (representing more than 35 per cent of the total EU population) must be composed of at least four member states—a stipulation designed to ensure that the three largest member states alone cannot determine outcomes.

Cont. ➤

Cont.

The Lisbon Treaty voting rules entered into force on 1 November 2014, but member states were permitted to request the use of the Nice Treaty voting rules on a case-by-case basis until 1 April 2017 (see Table 4.3). A year after the entry into force of the Lisbon Treaty, no recourse had been made to the Nice Treaty rules.

TABLE 4.3 Qualified majority voting in the Council

Member state	Percentage of EU population (2016)	Weighted votes (Nice Treaty rules)
Germany	15.93	29
France	13.04	29
UK*	12.73	29
Italy	12.07	29
Spain	9.12	27
Poland	7.47	27
Romania	3.90	14
Netherlands	3.37	13
Belgium	2.21	12
Greece	2.13	12
Czech Republic	2.05	12
Portugal	2.04	12
Hungary	1.94	12
Sweden	1.92	10
Austria	1.69	10
Bulgaria	1.42	10
Denmark	1.11	7
Finland	1.08	7
Slovakia	1.06	7
Ireland	0.91	7
Croatia	0.83	7
Lithuania	0.57	7
Slovenia	0.41	4
Latvia	0.39	4
Estonia	0.26	4
Cyprus	0.17	4
Luxembourg	0.11	4
Malta	0.08	3
Total	**100.00**	**352**

*Prior to 2016 UK referendum

state are now published in a Council decision in December every year and used for the calculation of the population criterion for the following twelve months. The current figures are available on the Council's website as part of its ingenious voting calculator.

Much time and effort has been expended over the years by national officials and academics alike on the details of the Council's voting rules, the implications for the relative voting strength of individual member states, and the identification of possible winning coalitions. In the run-up to, and aftermath of, the 2016 UK referendum on membership of the EU, these rules were once again in the spotlight as speculation inevitably arose about whether the Union would feature fewer winning coalitions that were (say) pro-market, deregulatory, or US-friendly post-Brexit. Yet a perusal of the systematic voting records produced by the Council since 1999 (see 'Ensuring accountability in the Council') indicates that most decisions subject to QMV are actually taken by consensus (uncontested) and only a small number of abstentions or negative votes are logged annually in contested votes (see Figure 4.3). Although still low, the number of such instances has increased slightly in recent years, as has the practice of member states including formal statements in the minutes or providing explanations of their decision to vote in favour, abstain, or vote against a particular measure (Hagemann 2008; VoteWatch Europe 2012). The actual levels of disagreement within the Council are therefore certainly higher than the raw voting

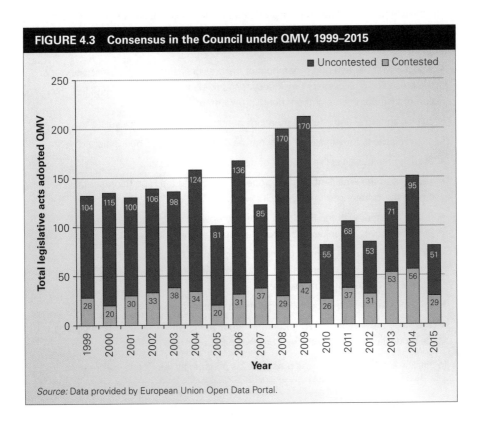

FIGURE 4.3   Consensus in the Council under QMV, 1999–2015

■ Uncontested   □ Contested

Source: Data provided by European Union Open Data Portal.

statistics would suggest, but the basic consensual attitude that underlies Council decision-making ensures that any deep-seated dissatisfaction is normally dealt with before the final decision is taken. Council members sometimes use consensus rather than formal voting as a strategy of blame avoidance (Novak 2013) and unanimous agreement continues to be the general trend under QMV.

The presidency

Exercising the rotating presidency of the Council has always been an important task, but the list of its overall duties has expanded over time, in line with the Council's extended scope of activities, and is now rather extensive (see Box 4.4). Successive enlargements have also increased the number of member states, meaning that negotiations have become more time-consuming and, at times, more conflictual. Exercising the presidency today can therefore be a rather daunting prospect, not only for small or new member states, but also for those faced with other pressing national or non-EU concerns or commitments during their presidency term.

BOX 4.4   Duties of the Council presidency

The main formal task of the Council presidency is the management of the Council's business during its six-month period in office. This involves a number of different duties, including:

- working with the two other members of the presidency trio (and, where necessary, the preceding or successor presidency team) to elaborate, and then carry out, its part of their common eighteen-month programme;
- convening formal and informal meetings at ministerial and official levels;
- providing chairs for virtually all meetings held throughout the Council hierarchy;
- ensuring the business-like conduct of discussions at meetings;
- liaising with the President of the European Council and the High Representative to ensure the coherence of the Council's work;
- acting, together with the President of the European Council and the High Representative, as spokesperson for the Council within and outside the Union;
- constituting the main point of Council contact for the Commission, EP, and other bodies involved in decision-making, including speaking on behalf of the Council in trilogues and conciliation meetings;
- ensuring that all of the Council's legislative and other obligations are met; and
- facilitating the reaching of agreement in negotiations within the Council, including the production of 'compromises from the chair'.

In fulfilling all of these tasks, the presidency is assisted by the Council Secretariat.

Arguably, the main task of the rotating presidency is to be—or at least to be seen to be—neutral. Specifically, this is achieved by the presidency member state fielding two delegates for each meeting it chairs: one to chair and manage the meeting; the other to articulate and defend the national position. The introduction of 'compromises from the chair' (often with substantive input from the Council Secretariat) when negotiations get bogged down is further evidence of the neutrality of the presidency, as is the fact that the President does not vote.

The presidency can and does play a critical role in shaping the Council's agenda (Tallberg 2010; Warntjen 2008), but its ability to impose its own interests on the rest of the EU is limited by the fact that Council activities are now programmed on a multi-annual basis, requiring close cooperation within and between presidency trios. A presidency member state needs to tread carefully in attempting to highlight certain issues, since its colleagues will not look kindly on a presidency that appears to use (or abuse) the office too flagrantly for its own ends.

It has become a point of pride for outgoing office-holders to be viewed by their colleagues as having conducted a 'good' presidency. Such judgements are obviously subjective, but a number of objective criteria can be employed as measuring devices. For example, it is possible to gauge whether Council business was dealt with efficiently and impartially, whether the main objectives outlined in the presidency programme were achieved, and whether unpredictable events were dealt with calmly, efficiently, and effectively. All presidencies produce a 'scoreboard' at the end of their period in office, seeking to show that they have indeed fulfilled these criteria in carrying through EU business.

The Council Secretariat

The changing role of the Council Secretariat is evident in the description of its basic formal functions contained in both the earliest and the most recent versions of the Council's internal rules of procedure. Originally charged with 'assisting' the Council, it is now required to be 'closely and continually involved in organising, coordinating and ensuring the coherence of the Council's work and implementation of its 18-month programme. Under the responsibility and guidance of the Presidency, it shall assist the latter in seeking solutions.'[2] Indeed the very permanence of the Council Secretariat has facilitated its emergence as the 'institutional memory' of the Council, making it an invaluable resource for all Council members, but particularly for the rotating presidency.

Some 85 per cent of the Secretariat's staff is engaged in the technical and logistical organization of the Council's work. This task involves convening meetings, preparing meeting rooms, and producing and distributing documents (including their translation, photocopying, archiving, and, in recent years, release to the public—see 'Ensuring accountability in the Council'). The remainder of the Secretariat's staff is engaged in the substantive preparation of the Council's work: drawing up agendas; preparing briefing notes for the presidency; advising the presidency on questions of substance, procedure, and legality; helping to draft amendments; and producing reports, minutes, and press releases on meetings held within the Council hierarchy. In fulfilling all of these functions, the Secretariat is at the service of the presidency, but is independent of both it and the member governments, its main master being the Council as a whole. In the 1990s and early 2000s, the Council Secretariat also acquired a number of executive and leadership functions in the intergovernmental areas of justice and home affairs (JHA) and the CFSP (Beach 2008; Dijkstra 2010), but these were transferred elsewhere with the coming into force of the Lisbon Treaty.

Coordinating the Council's work

The division of the Council into distinct configurations has facilitated specialization, but given rise to problems of coordination, both vertical and horizontal. The need for coordinating bodies to ensure coherence and consistency in the Council's work was recognized from the beginning, and was rapidly addressed at official level with the creation of Coreper, which subsequently carved out, and continues to occupy, a central position in the Council hierarchy (see Chapter 14). For their part, the rotating presidency and the permanent Council Secretariat have also shouldered some of the responsibility for horizontal and vertical coordination as a result of the overview of all Council areas that they enjoy owing to their respective positions and roles in the Council hierarchy.

Overall responsibility for coordinating the work of the Council at ministerial level has historically been the preserve of the GAC, which for many years was also responsible for the foreign affairs portfolio and comprised the foreign ministers of the member states. Unsurprisingly, the foreign ministers proved more interested in the growing number of foreign policy issues on the GAC's agenda, while some specialist Councils (most notably Ecofin) and the nascent European Council began to play an increasingly lead role in important policy discussions. The inevitable result was the gradual undermining of the GAC's central coordinating role, which was addressed by both the Seville reforms of 2002 and the Lisbon Treaty.

The result is a General Affairs Council that is now functionally distinct from the Foreign Affairs Council. It is tasked with ensuring consistency in the work of all Council formations, is responsible for a number of cross-cutting policy areas, such as enlargement and cohesion policy, and is involved in the preparation and follow-up of European Council meetings. It comprises a mixture of national ministers for Europe (in those member states in which the position exists), foreign ministers, junior ministers, and state secretaries—a fact that raises questions about its profile and its ability to exercise authority over other formations. It is chaired by the rotating Council presidency, which constitutes a useful link to the other Council formations, with the important exception of the FAC, which is now chaired by the High Representative. On paper at least, the new GAC would appear to be central to the work of the Council, in effect acting as the political equivalent of Coreper vis-à-vis the European Council. However, its potential political role is open to challenge by the powerful members of the FAC and Ecofin, while the existence of a full-time President of the European Council with his or her own staff ensures that it is neither the only nor the most influential body engaged in preparing what have now become much more frequent European summits (see Chapter 3).

Exerting influence in the Council

The Council's central position in the EU's decision-making process endows upon it a significant degree of influence over other institutions and authorities. But the Council is not a monolithic body: it is composed of the representatives of very different governments, whose member states differ in size, economic weight, length of EU membership, administrative culture, negotiating style, and attitude to European integration. Despite these differences, they continue to reach agreement on an impressive number of legislative and non-legislative measures every year. So who wields influence within the Council and what form does this influence take?

In the small number of areas in which unanimity is now the rule, influence is shared equally among the Council members. Since any national representative can unilaterally block agreement by voting 'no', the interests of all have to be taken into account if a measure is to be adopted. Under QMV, numbers matter, and those member governments with the largest number of votes or biggest populations are clearly at an advantage, since their support can be vital for the adoption or rejection of a draft piece of legislation. The formation of coalitions within the Council is an intrinsic part of the decision-making process under QMV, in which qualified majorities and blocking minorities matter, if only for the purposes of calculating which member states need to be won over in order to achieve a consensus. Nonetheless, individual member states, even the largest ones, can find themselves an outvoted minority, as Council voting records demonstrate—a point that pro-Brexit campaigners made frequently in the run-up to the 2016 UK referendum on membership of the EU, claiming that 'Brussels' often imposed legislation on the UK against its will (and vote). But raw voting figures need to be treated with caution, since they are not an accurate reflection of an individual member state's overall amount of influence in EU-level decision-making; rather, they constitute a type of snapshot as regards the position adopted at the end of a process, revealing nothing about the reasons that underlie it nor the other ways in which that member state may have had an influence over the final shape of the agreement.

Influence can also be exerted by large and small member states alike in more informal and less easily quantifiable ways. Representatives of member governments can contribute to compromise proposals acceptable to a majority of the member governments, they can form coalitions with like-minded states, or they can make their government's point of view known to the Commission, the presidency, or the Council Secretariat in an effort to influence the outcome of the decision-making process.

Safeguards have historically been built into the Council's decision-making system to encourage the formation of broad coalitions and to try to avoid the total domination of the process by the interests of the larger member states. For example, under the old weighted voting system, a qualified majority had to consist of around 70 per cent of the total number of votes, while the Lisbon Treaty stipulates that a blocking minority must be composed of at least four member states. The Lisbon Treaty also explicitly allows a group of member states to demand that negotiations continue on issues in regard to which they feel their concerns have not been sufficiently addressed—in effect, delaying a vote. This mechanism draws on previous agreements reached in 1994 (the Ioannina compromise) and 1966 (the Luxembourg compromise), aimed at assuaging concerns about the consequences of moving to a more widespread use of QMV, under which member states could be outvoted.[3]

For many years, it was customary to claim (based on anecdotal evidence) that coalitions in the Council were constantly shifting and tended to be issue-driven rather than power-driven. The publication of systematic records of Council voting, however, has enabled some emerging patterns of coalition formation to be identified (Naurin and Lindahl 2008). Again, such findings need to be approached with caution: while roll-call votes represent a precise public choice on the part of national representatives in the Council, they constitute only one aspect of a member state's preferences and bargaining behaviour at EU level.

The continuous process of discussion and negotiation at all levels that has epitomized the work of the Council for more than six decades now has resulted in a generally cooperative approach to the resolution of common problems. This is not to say that real and serious conflicts do not arise within the Council, or that individual member states are not frequently unhappy about the outcomes of specific decisions; rather, the emphasis is on using informal contacts to understand national positions and to engage in behind-the-scenes bargaining to gain support for a collective approach. This ingrained and now routine intergovernmental cooperation has transformed the Council into a body that is frequently more than the sum of its constituent national parts.

Ensuring accountability in the Council

Accountability in the Council can be addressed by asking two different, but related, questions.

1. To whom is the Council answerable?
2. How easy is it to find out what goes on inside the Council?

These questions relate, respectively, to its democratic legitimacy and the transparency of its procedures.

At first sight, the Council does not fare particularly well in terms of democratic legitimacy in comparison to the other EU core institutions. While the members of the European Parliament (MEPs) can rightfully claim to be directly elected by, and answerable to, a constituency of national voters (although turnout rates in European elections are often dismally low) and the members of the Commission hold office only with the explicit approval of the EP, the members of the Council take their seats *ex officio* in their capacity as national ministers and the Council as a body has permanent tenure. Therefore the Council, as a whole, cannot be dismissed, and its individual members are democratically accountable only to their respective citizens and national parliaments. The EP's lack of direct control over the Council has been a source of some frustration over the years for MEPs, who have instead sought to increase their public contacts with Council representatives. As a result, the rotating Council presidency is now the EP's main interlocutor at EP plenary sessions and EP committee meetings, both of which are open to the public.

The Council's record as regards transparency is also subject to some qualification. Its historic and much-criticized habit of conducting its business behind closed doors was long justified by the avowed need for privacy while compromises resulting in perceived gains and losses for different actors were being negotiated. While admissible at one level, this argument could not long withstand a protracted campaign to shed light on the decision-making processes of all the EU's institutions. Transparency provisions first introduced in the 1990s, subsequently strengthened and then enshrined in the Council's rules of procedure and the Lisbon Treaty, have increasingly required the Council to open up its internal processes to public scrutiny.

The Council is now obliged to deliberate and vote in public on draft legislative acts and to maintain a public online document register; it fulfils both of these obligations via its website, which has been updated and much improved in recent years. Thanks to live streaming, interested members of the public can now watch ministers deliberating and voting on draft legislative acts in so-called open sessions of the Council, and can gain access, also via the Council's website, to a wide range of Council documents, including draft agendas, minutes, and voting records. Depending on their nature, most Council documents are now made available directly to the public, either wholly or partially, online or by request, shortly after they are circulated within the Council or else after the final adoption of the legislative act under discussion, while special rules apply for sensitive documents (Curtin 2014; Galloway 2014; Council of the European Union 2015).

However, the existence of both pro- and anti-transparency factions in the Council means that it has proved somewhat resistant to opening up its proceedings beyond what it views as being strictly necessary to comply with the current transparency rules. Indeed, a recent report for Transparency International identified a 'culture of reluctance to interpret transparency regulations in a more liberal light' (Hancisse *et al.* 2014: 72). The EU's transparency rules make it theoretically possible to hold national decision-makers to account by monitoring how ministerial representatives defend their positions and exercise their votes in the Council. However, there is as yet no public access, even via live streaming, to meetings below ministerial level and no public record of the discussions in working party or trilogue meetings (see 'The

Council and Parliament') on draft legislative acts, despite the fact that most of the pre-agreement discussion and negotiation, and indeed a good deal of the actual decision-making, continues to take place in these forums. In addition, the Council has resisted pressure from the Commission and the EP to participate in the common Transparency Register that they administer to track lobbying activity vis-à-vis the EU's institutions. The system—currently voluntary, but expected to become mandatory—therefore does not apply to the Council Secretariat or the permanent representations. The nagging feeling persists that the transparency provisions, far from shining a spotlight on decision-making in the Council, have instead had the effect of moving the real negotiations out of the range of the cameras and the microphones, or indeed of making negotiations even more complicated by encouraging 'grandstanding', whereby ministers take more extreme positions when they know they are being observed by outside parties (Cross 2013).

Dealing with the other institutions

The notion of an inherent institutional balance within the EU is a popular one, particularly when new powers are at stake, or when treaties or inter-institutional agreements are being negotiated or implemented. At such times, the members and supporters of individual EU bodies watch even more carefully than usual in order to gauge the effect the new arrangements will have on 'their' institution. When assessing inter-institutional relations in the EU, however, it is important to distinguish between outward protestations or manifestations of discord, and a close and cooperative working relationship that has developed over the years between the various institutions, particularly since the introduction of the codecision procedure.

The Council and European Council

The Lisbon Treaty's institutionalization of the European Council and its full-time President has had the effect of finally and formally setting the European Council apart from the Council of Ministers (see Chapter 3). Now recognized as a legally separate entity and no longer merely the notional tip of the Council hierarchy, the European Council nevertheless remains closely linked to the Council, both administratively and physically. The two bodies are served by the same General Secretariat and shared the Council's headquarters in Brussels until the European Council's own dedicated building was completed next door in 2016.

As the main agenda-setter in the EU, the European Council provides the political impetus for driving the Union forwards, defining its priorities and initiating or endorsing its main policy initiatives. It therefore feeds into the internal processes of the Council, the Commission, and the EP. Of these three institutions, its links to the

Council are perhaps the strongest, since it also operates as the forum for the resolution of disputes that have proved irreconcilable at the level of the ministers. The European Council's work continues to be prepared by the GAC and Coreper, supported by the Council Secretariat, and (a point driven home repeatedly in the European Council's internal rules of procedure) in cooperation with the rotating presidency of the Council of Ministers. The draft conclusions of each European Council meeting are discussed in advance in a restricted session of Coreper, which is attended by one or more officials from the European Council President's private office. By means of these conclusions, the European Council frequently 'tasks' the Council with specific obligations by a certain date, and it falls to the GAC and Coreper to ensure that these obligations are duly fulfilled. A good deal of Council–European Council cooperation is therefore inherent to, and already written into, the relationship. It helps too that the members of the European Council—the heads of state or government of each of the member states—are also the political masters of the members of the Council in their domestic settings.

The altered dynamics between the Council and the newly institutionalized European Council are still in the process of being defined and refined.[4] Much depends on the personality and approach of the serving President of the European Council, which to a large extent informs the way in which the two institutions interact. One potential friction point is the relationship between the latter and the head of state or government in the member state holding the rotating Council presidency, whose formerly rather public international role is now substantially reduced by the existence of the President of the European Council. Both presidents to date have appeared to be sensitive to this issue and have endeavoured to establish a close working relationship with the senior political figures in successive Council presidencies, recognizing their importance as the vital link between the Council and the European Council, which continues to be interdependent.

The Council and Parliament

The Council–Parliament relationship is based on the natural rivalry that exists between all executives and legislatures, even though neither institution closely resembles national models of such bodies. Such inherent rivalry is exacerbated in the EU setting by the EP's historically unremitting and largely successful campaign to wrest increasing amounts of legislative and budgetary power from the reluctant grasp of the Council (see Chapter 6).

Successive inter-institutional agreements (IIAs) on budgetary discipline and the introduction of multi-annual financial frameworks (MFFs) have done much to reduce the number and ferocity of the disputes between the two arms of the budgetary authority in recent years. Budgetary rows still flare up from time to time, but the hostilities have tended to be muted by agreed rules of engagement and intense inter-institutional negotiations. It remains to be seen whether a prolonged period of economic hardship will result in a resumption of hostilities and what effect this will have on Council–Parliament relations overall.

In contrast, the EP has had to fight harder and longer for its legislative powers, which it has won in increments via court cases, IIAs, and Treaty reform. The Council–Parliament relationship in the legislative arena has evolved from a state of permanent confrontation to one of both formal and informal cooperation, in which the EP is now a real co-legislative authority with the Council. Tensions persist between them, however, and sometimes flare up into battles over their respective powers—such as in the EP's 2010 refusal to grant its consent to the Society for Worldwide Interbank Financial Telecommunication (SWIFT) agreement that the Council wished to conclude with the United States (US)—or, less frequently, outright failures in decision-making—such as in the case of their non-agreement in 2011 on amendment of the Novel Foods Regulation.[5] The EP's habit of attempting to extract the maximum amount of influence from newly acquired formal powers was in evidence in the years immediately following the entry into force of the Lisbon Treaty, causing blockage for a time on certain dossiers under negotiation with the Council.

The bedrock of the Council–Parliament relationship is the now well-established OLP, which requires intense and sustained cooperation between all levels of both institutions in order to reach agreement on the wide range of legislative proposals put forward annually by the Commission (Hayes-Renshaw 2015). In most cases, agreement is now reached at an early stage in the process: 85 per cent at first reading and a further 8 per cent at early second reading during the legislative period 2009–14 (European Parliament 2014b). These early agreements are driven by the practice of convening informal tripartite meetings between small numbers of representatives of the Council, the EP, and the Commission to discuss the elements of a compromise agreement before the EP has completed its first reading. These so-called trilogues have become the arena for a form of secluded decision-making that has facilitated early agreements, but at the price of transparency and accountability (Roederer-Rynning and Greenwood 2015). A number of factors have been identified to try to explain this 'puzzling trend',[6] which is a source of much concern to those who advocate a more open and inclusive decision-making process. Indeed, the EU Ombudsman opened an own-initiative inquiry into the transparency of the trilogue system in May 2015 and launched a public consultation on the matter in December of that year.

Whatever the underlying reasons for the marked increase in early agreements between the Council and the EP, they constitute real evidence of growing levels of cooperation and mutual trust between the two institutions, at least in those areas in which codecision is well established. The experience of codecision has led the Council to view the EP as a mature and responsible co-legislator in areas subject to the OLP, although some tensions persist in other areas in which cooperation is less well established. Another wrinkle in the relationship is the EP's claim of a persistent imbalance between them as regards access to one another's meetings and internal documents, which, in its view, gives the Council an unfair advantage in the decision-making process.

The Council and Commission

Council–Commission relations have always been typified by a complex mixture of cooperation and competition. Public skirmishes between the Council and Commission have frequently been presented as battles for dominance between a more supranationalist and a more intergovernmentalist concept of the integration process. Yet this political rhetoric coexists with very real cooperation, the result of a long and close working relationship across all areas of EU activity.

The implementation of the provisions of the Lisbon Treaty from 2009 onwards have required new forms of Council–Commission cooperation, the long-term effects of which as yet remain to be discerned. The remodelled post of High Representative for Foreign Affairs and Security Policy, originally located firmly within the Council, now straddles both institutions, the incumbent being both a member (indeed, Vice-President) of the Commission and the President of the FAC. As such, he or she constitutes the formal institutional link between the Council and the Commission where European foreign policy is concerned. The High Representative oversees the European External Action Service (EEAS), composed of permanent officials drawn from both the Commission services and the Council Secretariat, as well as seconded officials from the national foreign ministries. The creation of this new position and innovative body gave rise to long and complex negotiations between the two institutions about administrative issues that might appear trivial (even petty) to outsiders, but which had very real resonance for serving officials (Smith 2013). Relations between the High Representative and the EEAS, on the one hand, and the Council (specifically the rotating presidency and the Council Secretariat), on the other, got off to a probably predictably rocky start, but a suitable *modus vivendi* is gradually emerging between these bodies as the relationship settles down and acquires its own distinctive rhythm (Juncos and Pomorska 2013; Vanhoonacker and Pomorska 2013).

The day-to-day reality of Council–Commission relations at the level of officials is much more mundane and reassuring, bearing in mind that the relationship differs between policy arenas. As regards issues subject to the so-called Community method, the two institutions are required to cooperate because they are so clearly interdependent (see Chapter 17). Thanks to its right of initiative, the Commission is responsible for producing the proposals on which most Council debates are based, but it is reliant on the Council (increasingly in tandem with the EP) to adopt the measures it has proposed. Accordingly, it attends meetings at all levels of the Council hierarchy, acting both as protagonist and mediator in an attempt to have its proposals adopted. As one of the potential architects of compromise between conflicting positions in the Council, the Commission delegation can be regarded by beleaguered member governments in the Council as their greatest ally on particular issues under discussion. Indeed, the support of the Commission can be helpful for both the Parliament and the Council in their dealings with one another, and the Commission is well placed to play a brokerage role between them. One increasingly common forum in which it exercises this role is that of the trilogues, which have become an established feature of the legislative process and the locus for detailed inter-institutional negotiations that generally give rise to early agreements.

In some cases, however, and despite its best efforts, agreement on a legislative proposal put forward by the Commission proves elusive and the draft legislative act has to be withdrawn. This could be because of deep-seated divisions within or between the Council and the EP, the convergence of their positions in a direction that is fundamentally unacceptable to the Commission, or simply a realization that the proposal is no longer fit for purpose, for whatever reason. This exercise of weeding out weak or conflict-ridden proposals that stand little chance of adoption is undertaken in consultation with the Council and the EP when a new Commission takes up office and draws up its work programme for the next five years. It is one of the public acknowledgements of the fact that sustained levels of cooperation and coordination are required if all three institutions are to fulfil their respective and interdependent functions in the overall EU system.

Theorizing the Council

In this chapter, the Council has been presented both as a club of member governments and as the locus of persistent competition among them for influence. The Council is regarded as the central body by those who stress the importance of national interest as the factor explaining outcomes in the EU. Indeed, the Council as it exists and operates today may be viewed as one of the living symbols of the continuing power of the member states in the EU and of the desire of the national governments to remain at the centre of the process of European integration. Since it also represents the member governments who constitute the intergovernmental conferences (IGCs) that initiate constitutional reform in the EU, we can expect the Council to endure and to continue to play a central role in any future enlarged EU.

Despite being the EU's longest-serving intergovernmental institution, however, this chapter has also attempted to show that, in reality, the Council is a unique blend of the intergovernmental and the supranational. It represents member state interests that are aggregated under conditions frequently owing more to supranationalism than to intergovernmentalism and it is not necessarily the interests of the larger member states that determine the final outcomes. In addition, the Council as an institution works closely with the Commission and the EP, the views of both of which inform its work and impinge in important ways on its output.

Spanning as it does the supranational and intergovernmental camps, the Council embodies the enduring tension between the two approaches as explanatory tools for understanding the construction of the EU. Realist and liberal intergovernmentalist observers can find plenty of instances in which 'state interests' inform negotiating preferences (Høyland and Hansen 2014), while constructivists and rational choice scholars argue that the predominant modes of decision-making are based on deliberation and bargaining (Warntjen 2010). The behaviour of the ministerial and official representatives who comprise the Council may be better explained by sociology and anthropology than by regional integration or negotiation theories, but the outcome of their conduct continues to be a testimony to 'collective purpose, collective commitment and collective ideas' (Hayes-Renshaw and Wallace 1997: 2).

Throughout the Council hierarchy, the reconciliation of conflicting national interests is pursued by means of a continual process of negotiation. The norm-rich, collective decision-making environment attributed to Coreper by Lewis in Chapter 14 is also evident to different extents in the Council's working parties and ministerial gatherings—particularly those that meet most regularly or, in the case of the working parties, those whose members are based in Brussels. However, the consensual reflex in the Council is tempered by the fact that the ministers are more high-profile actors than either the permanent representatives or the officials in the working parties. As domestically elected representatives, the ministers are required to justify their actions to their national constituents and, given the transparency rules that now govern their formal meetings, they can be directly monitored to ensure that they are indeed 'defending the national interest'. Thus while consensus is the most usual mode of ministerial agreement whatever the formal rule, abstentions, 'no' votes, and statements in the Council minutes are all utilized to signal national dissatisfaction with the legislative act being adopted when earlier negotiation has not succeeded in having the national viewpoint taken into account, for whatever reason.

Two opposing suggestions for the Council linger in the debate over EU institutional reform: one advocates that it should become an explicitly representative and legislative, rather than an executive, institution; the other asserts that the Council should be made even more explicitly dominant, as the core of executive power within the EU. The Lisbon Treaty has neither resolved this argument nor clarified the situation. It is likely that the Council will have to continue to serve both camps, with all of the constitutional and operational ambiguities that this implies.

Conclusion

The Council has always occupied a central position in the institutional structure of the EU, both because of its composition and because of the functions attributed to it. Successive Treaty changes have altered some aspects of its role and relationships with the other institutions, while repeated enlargements of the EU have compelled the Council to assess the way in which it transacts its business and to introduce reforms to its operating procedures. The implementation of the Lisbon Treaty is but the latest stage in this ongoing process of adaptation.

The Lisbon-inspired changes to the Council's internal presidency arrangements require sustained coordination between the various bodies in order to ensure a coherent and consistent approach in decision-making. The double-majority system of voting which came into effect in November 2014 has not changed the fact that (apparent) consensus continues to be the most usual means of reaching agreement on legislative acts in the Council, as can be verified from the voting figures now routinely produced by the Council Secretariat.

The institutionalization of the European Council, the addition of the role of Vice-President of the Commission to that of the High Representative, and the extension of the EP's legislative powers under the Lisbon Treaty have all had, and will continue to have, implications for the Council's relationship with each of these institutions. A state of flux in the so-called institutional balance is to be expected until such time as a mutually acceptable *modus operandi* is agreed, whether formally or informally. In the meantime, outward protestations or manifestations of inter-institutional discord are likely to coexist with the close and cooperative working relationship that has developed behind the scenes between the EU's core institutions over the years, particularly since the introduction of codecision.

ENDNOTES

1. For a historical overview, see Hayes-Renshaw and Wallace (2006: 264–5).
2. Art. 23(3) of the Rules of Procedure of the Council, OJ L 325/36, 11 December 2009.
3. See Hayes-Renshaw and Wallace (2006: ch. 10).
4. See Puetter (2014), particularly as regards policy coordination.
5. Regulation (EC) No. 258/97 of the European Parliament and Council of 27 January 1997 concerning novel foods and novel food ingredients, OJ L 43/1.
6. See, e.g., Reh *et al.* (2013); European Parliament (2014b).

FURTHER READING

The two most comprehensive books on the Council—Hayes-Renshaw and Wallace (2006) and Westlake and Galloway (2005)—are now somewhat dated, but still contain much useful and detailed material. The excellent edited volume by Naurin and Wallace (2008) focuses on conflict dimensions, modes of interaction, and power and leadership in the Council, while Puetter (2014) analyses the role of both the Council and the European Council in the coordination of the EU's newest and more intergovernmental areas of non-legislative decision-making. Novak (2013) provides a fascinating account of how decisions are actually taken 'by consensus' within the Council, while Roederer-Rynning and Greenwood (2015) illuminate the shadowy world of the inter-institutional trilogue.

Hayes-Renshaw, F., and Wallace, H. (2006) *The Council of Ministers* (2nd edn, London: Palgrave Macmillan).

Naurin, D., and Wallace, H. (eds) (2008) *Unveiling the Council of the European Union: Games Governments Play in Brussels* (London: Macmillan).

Novak, S. (2013) 'The silence of ministers: Consensus and blame avoidance in the Council of the European Union', *Journal of Common Market Studies*, 51/6: 1091–1107.

Puetter, U. (2014) *The European Council and the Council: New Intergovernmentalism and Institutional Change* (Oxford: Oxford University Press).

Roederer-Rynning, C., and Greenwood, J. (2015) 'The culture of trilogues', *Journal of European Public Policy*, 22/8: 1148–65.

Westlake, M., and Galloway, D. (eds) (2005) *The Council of the European Union* (3rd edn, London: John Harper).

WEB LINKS

http://www.consilium.europa.eu

The comprehensive and much-improved Council website contains a wealth of information on the Council's structure, working methods, and output, including voting records and direct access to many of its legislative documents. It also contains a link to the website of the current Council presidency.

CHAPTER 5

The College of Commissioners: Supranational leadership and presidential politics

John Peterson

▌ Summary

No other institution—national or international—closely resembles the European Commission. It is a distinct hybrid: the largest administration and main policy manager within the European Union (EU), but also a source of political and policy direction. This chapter focuses on the college of Commissioners—the Commission's most political level. Yet these Commissioners—who form a 'college'—are unelected, independent (in theory) of member governments, and often portrayed as unaccountable technocrats. The Commission seemed to be in a permanent state of decline after 1999, after being headed by presidents who were perceived as weak, ineffective, or both. The appointment of Jean-Claude Juncker as President in 2014—according to an unprecedented and highly contested process—produced fresh debates about what it

Cont. ➤

> **Cont.**
> might mean for the EU to have (in Juncker's words) a 'political Commission'. Whatever comes of the idea, the fact that the EU faced multiple and vexed political crises during Juncker's early years in office revealed the ways in which the Commission's fate is largely determined by factors over which it has little or no control.

Introduction

The European Commission may be the strangest administration ever created. Despite brave attempts to compare it to other bureaucracies (Page 1997), the Commission is in many respects a *sui generis* institution. Legally, the Commission is a single entity. In practice, it is a unique hybrid. It is given direction by a political arm—or college—of Commissioners. But the college is unelected, which (for example) made the Commission an object of ire for the 'Leave' camp during the 2016 referendum campaign in the United Kingdom (UK). Commissioners act independently of the states that appoint them (at least in theory) and even swear an oath of independence. The college exists alongside a permanent, apolitical administration—what are known as the Commission's services, or Directorates-General (DGs). This book squarely confronts the Commission's duality by focusing here on the college and devoting a separate chapter to the services (see Chapter 8).

Even if they are unelected, Commissioners 'are appointed via a highly politicised process . . . are almost invariably national politicians of senior status, and are expected to provide the Commission's political direction' (Nugent and Rhinard 2015: 2–3). At times, the college—the President, Commissioners, and their advisers—has provided political direction to European integration, particularly during the earliest days of the European Economic Community (EEC) and again in the 1980s. More recently, it has become almost accepted wisdom that 'the decline of the Commission . . . has continued . . . and there seems little possibility that the situation will be reversed' (Kassim and Menon 2004: 102).[1] The Commission has always been powerful as a designer and manager of EU policy. But its role has never been uncontested (Spence and Edwards 2006; Kassim *et al.* 2013). The central theme of this chapter is that the Commission and most of what it does have always been highly politicized despite its ambitions to be an honest broker between national interests and an independent guardian of the EU's Treaties.

The origins and history of the college

The forerunner of today's European Commission was the High Authority of the European Coal and Steel Community (ECSC). Its first President was the legendary Jean Monnet (1978).[2] Provisions in the 1951 Treaty of Paris that gave the High

Authority significant independent powers to regulate markets for coal and steel bore Monnet's own fingerprints. The ECSC thus established that common European policies would be managed, and European integration given political impulse, by a non-partisan central authority.

The High Authority's own college was larger than Monnet wanted it to be: nine members—two from France and West Germany, and one from all other member states (plus a co-opted ninth member). Thus a precedent was set for national representation in what was meant to be a supranational administration. Over time, the High Authority became much less nimble and more bureaucratic than Monnet wanted it to be (Nugent and Rhinard 2015: 24–5). Partly in protest, Monnet resigned before the end of his term.

The design of common institutions for the new EEC was one of the most difficult issues in negotiations on the Treaty of Rome. A Dutch proposal sought a supranational EEC administration that would be even more independent of member governments than the ECSC's High Authority. However, it ran into opposition, particularly from France, and ended up being 'almost the reverse of what was finally decided' (Milward 1992: 217–18). Compared to the High Authority, the new European Commission (the label 'High Authority' was discarded as too grandiose) was balanced by a more powerful intergovernmental institution in the form of a Council of (national) Ministers.

The Treaty assigned three basic functions to the Commission:

- overseeing the implementation of policies;
- representing Europe in external trade negotiations; and
- most importantly, proposing new policies.

The Commission's monopoly on the right of legislative initiative, along with its prerogative to formulate recommendations and deliver opinions, gave it licence to act as a sort of engine of integration, or a source of ideas on new directions that the Community might take. Alongside the Court of Justice, the Commission was also designated guardian of the Treaty, and tasked with ensuring that its rules and injunctions were respected.

The early Commissions were small (nine members) and united by a 'dominating sense of team spirit' (Narjes 1998: 114).[3] Between 1958 and 1967, only fourteen different men[4] served as Commissioners, supported by two cabinet advisers (with four advising the President). Walter Hallstein, foreign policy adviser to the first West German Chancellor, Konrad Adenauer, became the Commission's first President. Hallstein was both a political heavyweight and a forceful leader, repeatedly referring to himself as the equivalent of a 'European prime minister'. The Commission achieved considerable policy success during this period, laying the foundations for the common agricultural policy (CAP), mere agreement on which was considered a success, representing the Community in the successful Kennedy Round of world trade talks, and convincing member government to accelerate the timetable for establishing the EEC's customs union.

A watershed in the history of the Commission was reached in 1965. A year from a scheduled extension of qualified majority voting (QMV) as a decision rule in the Council, the Hallstein Commission proposed a new system of financing the CAP through 'own resources', or revenue directly channelled to the Community rather than cobbled together from national contributions. The plan proposed to give new budgetary powers to both the Commission and the European Parliament (EP). It became a pretext on which French President Charles de Gaulle would pull France out of nearly all EEC negotiations for more than six months. De Gaulle's hostility to Hallstein's federalist rhetoric and actions, which included receiving foreign ambassadors to the EEC with a red carpet, was highly personal, but also reflected deep French anxieties about a resurgent Germany (de Gaulle 1970: 195–6).

The so-called empty chair crisis ended and France returned to EEC negotiations after the Luxembourg compromise was agreed in 1966 (with Luxembourg holding the Council presidency). The agreement, made public only in the form of a press release, stated that 'where very important interests are at stake the discussion must be continued until unanimous agreement is reached' (Council of Ministers 1966). Any member government could invoke the compromise in any negotiation if it felt its 'very important interests' were at risk. The upshot was to give political blessing to unanimous decision-making in the Council and generally to hobble the Commission.[5]

De Gaulle insisted that Hallstein be replaced as President of the Commission, which itself became a single integrated administration for all three previously distinct 'Communities'—the EEC, ECSC, and the European Atomic Energy Community (Euratom)—in 1967. Headed by the low-key Belgian Jean Rey, the new Commission initially contained fourteen members (reduced to nine in 1970). The next decade was a lean time for the Commission, because of both weak presidential leadership (Nugent and Rhinard 2015: 37–8; see also Table 5.1) and the EEC's more general lack of dynamism. In retrospect, the Community may have actually achieved more in the 1970s than it appeared at the time. Still, Western Europe suffered through a series of economic crises and the Community itself was widely seen as dilapidated.

By the late 1970s, a critical mass of member governments was persuaded that the Commission should be led by a political figure who was a potential prime minister in his or her own country. Thus Roy Jenkins, a senior figure in the UK's then-governing Labour Party, was appointed as President in 1977. Jenkins was the first President to be nominated in advance of the college as a whole, thus giving him scope to influence the composition of his team.

Jenkins' record was ambiguous (Ludlow 2016). On the one hand, member governments frequently disregarded his advice. There is little dispute that he 'was not a great success at running or reforming the Brussels machine' (Campbell 1983: 195). On the other, Jenkins raised the external profile of the Commission by insisting (against French resistance) that the Commission President should attend Group of Seven (G7) economic summits. Jenkins also worked tirelessly with German Chancellor Helmut Schmidt and French President Valéry Giscard-d'Estaing to

TABLE 5.1 The presidents of the Commission	
Presidents (nationality*)	**Period of tenure**
Walter Hallstein (German)	1958–67
Jean Rey (Belgian)	1967–70
Franco Maria Malfatti (Italian)	1970–72
Sicco Mansholt (Dutch)	1972–73
François Xavier-Ortoli (French)	1973–77
Roy Jenkins (British)	1977–81
Gaston Thorn (Luxembourger)	1981–85
Jacques Delors (French)	1985–95
Jacques Santer (Luxembourger)	1995–99
Romano Prodi (Italian)	1999–2004
José Manuel Barroso (Portuguese)	2004–14
Jean-Claude Juncker (Luxembourger)	2014–present

*Note that the presidency has been held by a non-national of one of the original EEC-6 only twice.

build support for the European Monetary System (EMS). The EMS helped to keep European currency values stable in the 1980s after enormous exchange rate turbulence in the 1970s. It was an important forerunner to both the freeing of the Community's internal market and, later, monetary union.

Before the 1979 election of Margaret Thatcher as UK prime minister, Jenkins seemed a candidate to be the first Commission President since Hallstein to be reappointed to a second four-year term.[6] However, reappointing Jenkins became politically untenable when Thatcher doggedly pursued the so-called British budgetary question (arising from the size of its net EU budgetary contribution), which preoccupied the Community for no fewer than five years. It cast a dark cloud over the Commission presidency of former Luxembourg Prime Minister Gaston Thorn, whose tenure marked a retreat in the direction of the lacklustre post-Hallstein Commissions.

Thorn was replaced in 1985 by former French Finance Minister Jacques Delors. Thatcher accepted the nomination of Delors, a French Socialist, on the strength of his role in France's economic policy U-turn of the early 1980s, when it abandoned protectionism and increased public expenditure in favour of market liberalism. Delors carefully reflected on how the Community could be relaunched via a headline-grabbing political project. Working closely with Lord (Arthur) Cockfield (1994), former British trade minister and Commissioner for the internal market, Delors opted for an integrated programme to dismantle most barriers to internal EU trade by the end of 1992. Seizing on converging preferences amongst the EU's largest member states for economic liberalization (Moravcsik 1991), as well as the strong support of the European business community, the 1992 project gave European integration renewed momentum. A substantive overhaul of the Community's founding Treaties was agreed in the 1986 Single European Act (SEA), which empowered the Commission, notably by extending the use of QMV in the Council.

Delors then convinced European leaders, despite the scepticism of many, to allow him to chair a high-level committee of (mostly) central bankers and to relaunch long-dormant plans for economic and monetary union (EMU). Progress towards EMU was uninterrupted—and probably accelerated—by the geopolitical earthquakes that shook the European continent in late 1989. German unification was handled with skill and speed by the Delors Commission (Spence 1991; Ross 1995), which also stepped forward to coordinate Western economic aid to the former Warsaw Pact states. By spring 1990, with a round of Treaty revisions to create EMU on course, French President François Mitterrand and German Chancellor Helmut Kohl threw their combined political weight behind the idea of a separate, parallel set of negotiations to create a political union. By this point, Delors was accepted by Kohl, Mitterrand, and even Thatcher as a political equal in the European Council.

The second half of Delors' ten-year reign was a far less happy time for the Commission. Member governments agreed mostly intergovernmental mechanisms for making new internal security and foreign policies via the (Maastricht) Treaty on European Union (TEU), denying the Commission its traditional prerogatives in these areas. Delors also shouldered some of the blame for the 1992 Danish rejection of the new Treaty, after suggesting that the power of small states would inevitably be weaker in a future EU (Nugent and Rhinard 2015: 46–7). By the time Delors left Brussels in 1995, most EU member governments wanted a less visionary successor.

After a tortured selection process,[7] Jacques Santer, prime minister of Luxembourg, was chosen to replace Delors. Santer promised that his Commission would 'do less but do it better'. Yet it inherited a full agenda, including the launch of the euro, eastern enlargement, another round of Treaty reforms, and negotiations on the Union's multi-annual budget and structural funds for regional development. The Santer Commission generally handled these issues well. Its stewardship of the launch of EMU in particular seemed 'enough to earn any Commission President a proud legacy' (Peterson 1999: 61).

In fact, Santer's legacy was hardly a proud one. For all of the dynamism of the Delors era, the Commission had become far more focused on policy initiation than on effective management. Santer presided over an administration that had become inefficient and sometimes chaotic; the Santer era culminated in the dramatic mass resignation of the college in March 1999 after the publication of a report of a Committee of Independent Experts (1999a), convened by the EP, on charges of fraud, mismanagement, and nepotism (see Box 5.1).

BOX 5.1	The fall of the Santer Commission

Jacques Santer's troubles began in earnest in late 1998 after the publication of a damning Court of Auditors' report, which suggested that large amounts of EU funding had gone missing. Around the same time, press reports appeared alleging that Research Commissioner (and former French Prime Minister) Edith Cresson had given plum advisers' jobs in the services to unqualified personal cronies (including her dentist). Characteristically, Cresson dismissed them as part of an Anglo-German 'conspiracy'. A motion of censure tabled under the EP's Treaty powers to sack the entire Commission was defeated (by 293 votes to 232) after Santer accepted that a Committee of Independent Experts would investigate charges of fraud and mismanagement within the Commission. At this point, according to Leon Brittan (2000: 10), a veteran of the Delors and Santer Commissions, the Commission began 'to sleepwalk towards its own destruction'. Santer told the EP that the college would implement the recommendations of the Experts' report, regardless of what they were, in a sign of the Commission's political weakness.

The Experts had only five weeks in which to investigate the Commission, yet produced a report that was painstaking in detail. Its most serious charges—leaving aside those against Cresson—concerned improprieties that had occurred during the Delors years. Bitter animosity between Delors and the Experts' chair, former head of the Court of Auditors André Middlehoek, was palpable in the report, which drew conclusions that seemed to go well beyond its evidence. It built to a crescendo with the devastating charge that it was 'becoming difficult to find anyone who has even the slightest sense of responsibility' for the work of the Commission (Committee of Independent Experts 1999a: 144). The EP's largest political group at the time, the Socialists, announced that it would vote to sack all twenty Commissioners, thus making the outcome of any vote all but inevitable.

A series of efforts were mounted by individual Commissioners to isolate Cresson, including a bid by Santer to convince French President Jacques Chirac and Prime Minister Lionel Jospin to ask her to step down. None succeeded. Thus Santer insisted that the entire Commission, as a collegial body, had to resign. The President was defiant in a subsequent press conference, claiming that the Experts' report was 'wholly unjustified in tone'.[8] Whether or not Santer's combativeness was ill-judged, his fate was sealed by bad luck: an English interpreter mistakenly communicated Santer's claim (in French) that he was *blanchi*, or exonerated, from personal charges against him to the non-French press as a claim that he was 'whiter than white'. It became seen as a political necessity that Santer had to go, and quickly.

Ironically, the Commission under Santer had undertaken reforms that made it—on balance—better-managed than it had been under Delors (Peterson 1999; Metcalfe 2000; Nugent and Rhinard 2015: 48–9). But the efforts were far from enough to cure the Commission of pathologies that had festered under Delors. The Experts' report exposed the Commission as everyone's favourite scapegoat in Brussels. More generally, the fall of the Santer Commission showed, in the words of one of its members, that 'in economic and monetary terms Europe is a giant in the world. But politically we are very young.'[9]

Santer's resignation in spring 1999 came at a particularly difficult moment. The Berlin summit, at which a series of major decisions needed to be made on the EU's seven-year budget, structural funds, and agricultural reform, was about a week away. A political crisis over Kosovo was deepening. The German Council presidency thus undertook a whirlwind tour of national EU capitals to seek a swift decision on replacing Santer. In Berlin, after ten minutes of discussion, the European Council agreed that the new Commission President should be former Italian Prime Minister Romano Prodi.

Prodi was by no means free to choose his own college. Nevertheless, armed with new powers granted to the Commission President by the Treaty (see 'The structure of the college'), Prodi had more influence over its composition than had most of his predecessors. He ended up with a less charismatic college than Santer's, but one in which expertise was matched to portfolio to an extent unseen in the Commission's history.

One EU ambassador spoke for many in Brussels in claiming that Prodi's economic team was 'collectively the best the Commission has ever had'.[10] One of two Vice-Presidents, Neil Kinnock, was charged with implementing an ambitious series of internal reforms of the Commission (Schön-Quinvalin 2011). Prodi himself helped to shift the debate on eastern enlargement to the point at which EU governments—at the 1999 Helsinki summit—decided to open accession talks with twelve applicant states on a more or less equal basis.

Yet Prodi's weakness as a political communicator was probably his Commission's most glaring liability (Peterson 2004). Kinnock's administrative reform programme encountered resistance in the services, where morale seemed to sink ever lower. The Commission was marginalized in the negotiations that yielded the Treaty of Nice. It appeared chaotic in the 2002–03 Convention on the Future of Europe that drafted a new Constitutional Treaty, with Prodi unable to contain divisions in the College about what the Commission's strategy should be and doing little or nothing to ensure that Commission staff working on the Constitutional Treaty—numbering more than the Convention's own secretariat—worked together (Norman 2003: 267). The most charitable comments that could be made about Prodi himself were that he mostly avoided interference in the work of a highly competent college.

The leading candidate to replace Prodi in 2004, Belgium's Prime Minister Guy Verhofstadt, received powerful Franco–German backing, but was opposed by the UK, thus reawakening divisions over the previous year's invasion of Iraq. Eventually, Portuguese Prime Minister José Manuel Barroso emerged as a consensus candidate to lead a new, expanded college, with each of (now) twenty-five member states appointing one member. Barroso's allocation of powerful economic portfolios to economic liberals and previous support for the Iraq War were both controversial. Barroso found himself on the sharp end of muscle-flexing by the EP, which threatened to reject his Commission after the initial Italian nominee, Rocco Buttiglione, outraged MEPs by airing his conservative views on women and gay men (see Box 5.2). By most accounts, Barroso handled the affair badly, before finally securing the EP's approval of a redesigned college. Hopes that Barroso could restore the Commission's position sank—and fell yet further when French and Dutch voters rejected the Constitutional Treaty in May 2005 referenda.

Barroso's first term in office focused on the Commission's buoyant policy agenda, but launched no new major initiative besides deciding to recommend Bulgaria and Romania as the EU's newest member states (they joined in 2007). Barroso himself dominated the College as perhaps no other President previously had, transforming the Commission's Secretariat-General—its service responsible for management of the Commission—into almost an extension of his private office. A survey of Commission officials in 2008 found widespread agreement that the 'Sec-Gen', as it is known in Commission parlance, had become both more 'political and influential' in the life of the Commission (see Figure 5.1). Despite resentment of his personal dominance of the Commission and allegations that he lacked ambition (Hodson 2013a), Barroso worked to ensure the ratification of the Lisbon Treaty, showing considerably better political communication skills than had Prodi. Barroso was renominated for a second term by member states in 2010, thus becoming the first Commission President since Delors to serve two terms.

Inevitably, Barroso's second term was consumed by the fallout from the worst global recession since the 1930s, with multiple (southern) EU member states requiring large rescue packages policed in part by the Commission. Under Barroso, the Commission acquired new powers to scrutinize national draft budgets and supervise EU banks. Ultimately, however, the Barroso decade saw the Commission occupy a considerably more modest role than it had under Delors, the only other President in EU history to serve as long.

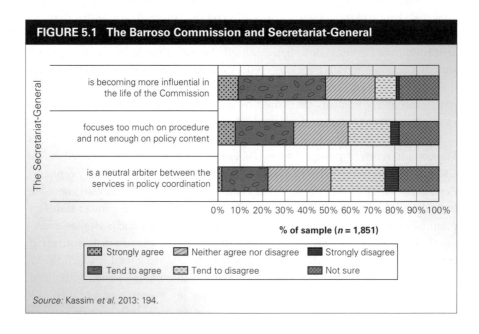

FIGURE 5.1   The Barroso Commission and Secretariat-General

Source: Kassim *et al.* 2013: 194.

The choice about Barroso's successor became highly politicized. It became caught up with both the UK's renegotiation of the terms of its membership (and subsequent referendum) and new provisions in the Lisbon Treaty that EP party groups interpreted (controversially) as giving them the right to nominate *Spitzenkandidaten*, or nominees to head the Commission that led their 2014 EP election campaigns, with the Commission presidency then awarded to the leader of the group that had won the most seats. When the centre right European People's Party (see Chapter 15) emerged as largest party group, its *Spitzenkandidat*—Jean-Claude Juncker, former Luxembourg prime minister—was presented by the EP as the logical choice for Commission President. The UK's Prime Minister David Cameron was infuriated and accused the EP of a 'backdoor power grab' for foisting Juncker on the European Council in a form of 'stitch up'.[11] Yet Angela Merkel returned from a Brussels summit at which she appeared to back Cameron to a pro-Juncker firestorm in Germany (Peterson 2016). Subsequently, the European Council approved Juncker with its first-ever formal vote to choose the Commission President. Only Hungary's Victor Oban joined Cameron in voting 'no', before the EP predictably confirmed Juncker.

The structure of the college

The Spitzenkadidaten controversy—and Juncker's subsequent structuring of what he called a 'political Commission' (see Box 5.3)—marked rare departures from basic norms established over fifty years to govern appointments to the college and the relationship between its three basic elements: the President, the college itself, and Commissioners' *cabinets*.

The President

A biographer of Roy Jenkins starkly concluded that:

The Presidency of the ... Commission is an impossible job. Indeed it can hardly be called a job at all—the President has a number of conflicting responsibilities, but no power. By no stretch of the imagination does it resemble the Prime Ministership of Europe.

(Campbell 1983: 181)

The claim initially seemed to be challenged by the appointment of Prodi, the first former prime minister of a large member state. Yet, less than a year after his appointment, Prodi was denying rumours that he was considering leaving the Commission to fight a forthcoming Italian domestic election. The only other Italian to have been Commission President, the barely remembered Franco Maria Malfatti, had done precisely that and left Brussels early in the 1970s. Had the Commission gone back to the future?

In a sense, the legacy of Delors continued to haunt Brussels at the turn of the millennium, both in terms of the aversion of many member governments to a powerful Commission *and* the reality of a Commission that was irreversibly powerful. The internal market was, if by no means complete, a political fact. The Commission was responsible for policing it, suggesting steps towards its full realization, and representing the EU in international trade diplomacy. The enormously powerful market forces unleashed by open commerce in the world's largest single capitalist market were often able to overwhelm public power unless it was wielded collectively, with the Commission usually in the lead (Pollack 1997; Peterson and Bomberg 1999: 67). The freeing of the internal market truly transformed the Commission's institutional position.

Moreover, the EU was increasingly powerful as a player in international politics (Hill and Smith 2011). Over time, the Council Secretariat became a formidable institutional rival and clear superior to the Commission on most questions of foreign policy. Yet the Commission still packed a punch as purveyor of the EU's programmes for development aid and humanitarian assistance, and particularly through its lead role in international economic diplomacy. After the post-2004 enlargements, the Commissioner for External Trade could plausibly be considered more powerful than perhaps twenty or so prime ministers of the EU's smaller states. The Commission also remained an honest broker between diverse and competing interests in a system that relied fundamentally on consensus. Arguably, the Commission was empowered in an expanded EU of twenty-eight member states, around three-quarters of which were small states (with about 17 million or fewer citizens), since the Commission had always been the traditional defender of the 'smalls'.

The days when the President's job could 'hardly be called a job at all' may be gone, but no Commission President ever makes his or her own luck; how much any President can accomplish is determined by a variety of factors over which he or she has little or no control. Even Delors was successful only because of three propitious contextual variables: a (brief) receptivity to European solutions; international changes (especially German unification); and a favourable business cycle from 1985 to 1990 (Ross 1995: 234–7). These factors helped Delors to exert 'pull' within the European Council, within which the Commission President is the only member who does not head a state or government. At the time of writing, whether Juncker matched Delors' influence at the EU's top table was unclear. But the confluence of multiple crises over the UK's exit, Greece, and the threat of another refugee crisis, combined with Juncker's unmatched wealth of experience in the European Council, enhanced his position (see Box 5.3).

In any case, the Commission has become more *presidential* over time. Successive Treaty revisions gave the Commission President—only 'first amongst equals' during Delors' time—a progressively stronger grip over the college. Prodi tried to focus on broad political themes, giving himself no specific policy portfolio, while also seeking to expand his own influence by inserting many of his 'own people' into key positions of authority within the Commission's services. The collective identity of the college seemed a secondary consideration, with Prodi declaring, 'I want each Commissioner to be a star, a big star, in his or her own policy area'.[12]

Yet few argued that it was also more effective or cohesive. Prodi's political misjudgements were frequent and his communication skills poor. His inability to form coalitions with (especially large-state) European leaders led to charges that he had failed to reverse 'the weakness of a Commission that ha[d] not fully recovered from the trauma of the Santer resignation' (de Schoutheete and Wallace 2002: 17).

Promising that his college would be more policy-focused with a strong presidential lead, Barroso argued that any effort to restore the position of the Commission had to respect the premise that 'the basic legitimacy of our union is the member states'.[13] Yet even after recovering from the Buttiglione affair (see Box 5.2), Barroso's defence of small and new EU states provoked French President Jacques Chirac to respond to rising Euroscepticism in France (in advance of the failed 2005 referendum on the Constitutional Treaty) by attacking the Commission. Nonetheless, Barroso's reappointment to a second term was testimony to his skills as a consensus-builder and political communicator. He also ranked well above his predecessors—although (predictably) behind Delors—when Commission officials were asked to rate his performance in an extensive survey of officials (see Figure 5.2).

The college

The appointment of the college is often a fraught politicized exercise. The compositions of the Jenkins and Prodi Commissions were shaped in important ways by the nominees for President himself. Still, provisions in the Amsterdam Treaty that formally lent weight to Prodi's own preferences in 1999 did not mean that several of his 'specific requests [for nominees] fell on deaf ears', even after he toured EU capitals to meet national leaders to try to influence the composition of his College (Nugent and Rhinard 2015: 101).

Barroso did not appear to influence many choices about who was nominated to his first Commission (or his second) until he was forced to ask for fresh nominees following the Buttiglione affair (see Box 5.2). After the EP's *Spitzencandidaten* power grab in 2014, most member states made their own decisions about whom to nominate with little input from Juncker, besides a few influenced by his pleas for political or gender balance. The College that emerged contained a large crop of former prime or foreign ministers, but also others with little high-level political experience (see Table 5.2).

The institutional design of the EU gives rise to collective, inter-institutional responsibility for what the Union does. Over time, that has extended to a strengthening of the EP's right to vet the choice of member governments' nominees to the college. The Santer, Prodi, and Barroso I and II Commissions all were ultimately confirmed by large margins (of around 300 votes), with the large influx of Eurosceptic MEPs in 2014 reducing Juncker's margin to 172. Yet the controversy surrounding Juncker's

---

BOX 5.2   The Rocco Buttiglione affair

Views on José Manuel Barroso's prospects fluctuated wildly in the first days after his nomination as Commission President. Barroso was hardly anyone's first choice for the Commission presidency. Immediately after he was chosen, he was lobbied by France and Germany to designate their nominees as 'super-Commissioners', provoking fears of another weak Commission President.

Barroso's surprise early announcement of the distribution of jobs in his college and his wry comment that he needed *everyone* in his college to be a 'super-Commissioner' temporarily silenced his critics. After offering the powerful justice and home affairs (JHA) portfolio to French nominee Jacques Barrot (who was firm in wanting an economic job), Barroso designated Italian nominee Rocco Buttiglione as JHA Commissioner. An arch-Catholic and close confidant of the Pope, Buttiglione aired ultra-conservative views on homosexuality (calling it a 'sin') and women (who 'belonged in the home') at his EP confirmation hearing, leading the Parliament's civil liberties committee to vote to recommend his rejection. Barroso tried to appease MEPs by delegating Buttiglione's responsibilities for civil liberties to a committee of other Commissioners. Yet opinion within the EP did not shift. Barroso then made things worse, stating that he was 'absolutely convinced' that his Commission would be approved since only 'extremist' MEPs could possibly vote against it.[14] Ultimately, he had no choice but to withdraw his team from consideration by the EP in order to avoid a humiliating rejection.

Barroso's political instincts seemed to return in subsequent weeks. He was helped by Buttiglione's decision to stand down, as well as Latvia's withdrawal of its original nominee, Ingrida Udre, who was dogged by allegations of corruption. Fresh nominations by both states—particularly Italy's choice of its foreign minister, Franco Frantini, to replace Buttiglione—allowed Barroso to propose a new-look College, which was overwhelmingly approved by the EP. Afterwards, Barroso could claim that 'we have come out of this experience with strengthened institutions',[15] including a stronger Commission and, of course, an emboldened EP.

For their part, religious organizations were outraged, with one insisting that the affair showed 'how little trust there is at the heart of the EU'.[16] Supporters of the Parliament accused Barroso of going too far to try to appease European leaders, particularly Italy's Prime Minister Silvio Berlusconi. A more mundane conclusion was that as long as each state in an EU of twenty-eight or more nominates one Commissioner, any nominee for President will find himself or herself trying to build a team from a large group that includes many (in Barroso's case, a majority) whom they have never met. In Barroso's words, 'it is like a blind date'.[17]

---

nomination reflected how the Lisbon Treaty reinforced the formal powers of the EP: it now officially elects the presidential nominee and member states are legally obliged to take account of the results of the most recent EP election in choosing a nominee. Even these changes, however, pose no threat to the basic principle that 'each national government is free to select a national Commissioner' (Devuyst 2005: 53).

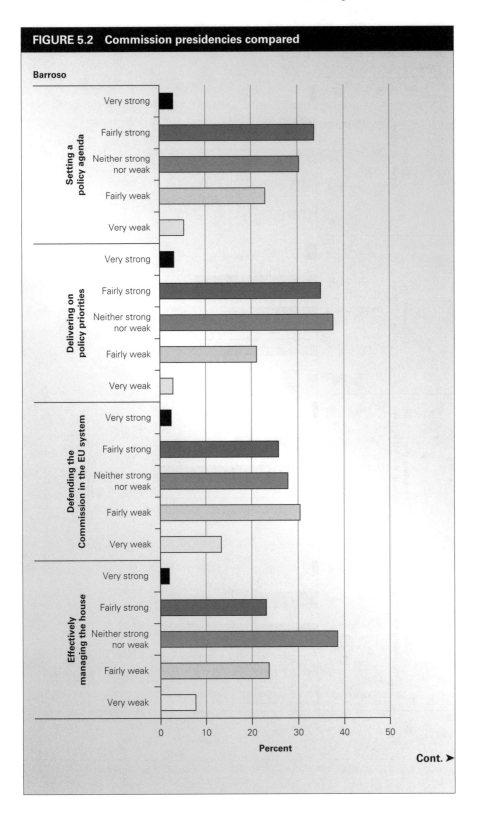

FIGURE 5.2   Commission presidencies compared

Cont. ➤

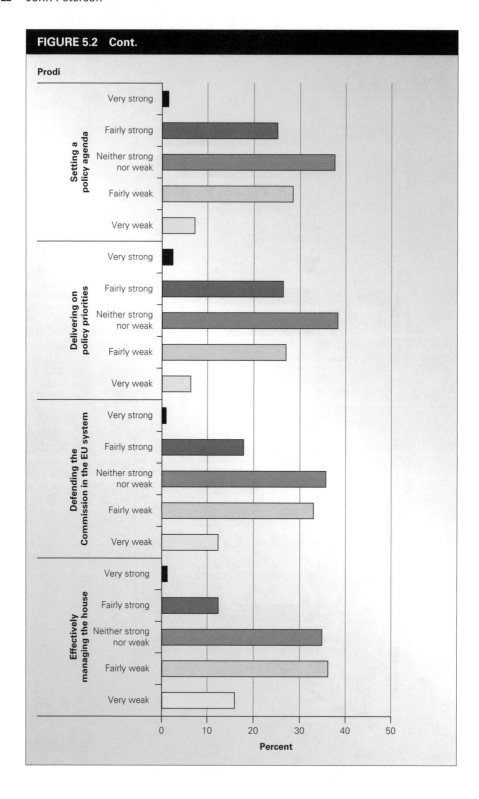

FIGURE 5.2 Cont.

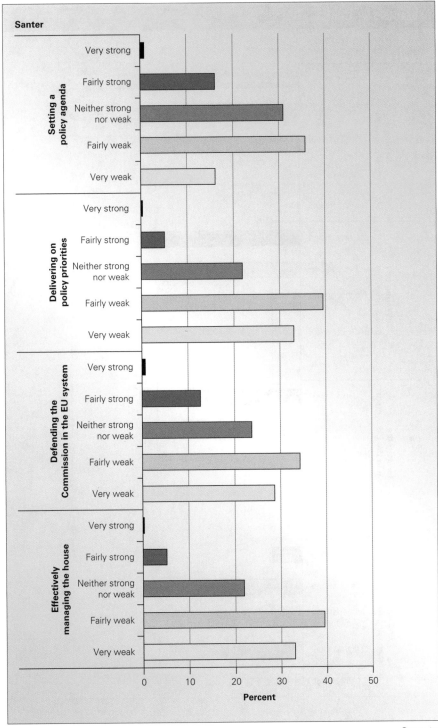

Cont. ➤

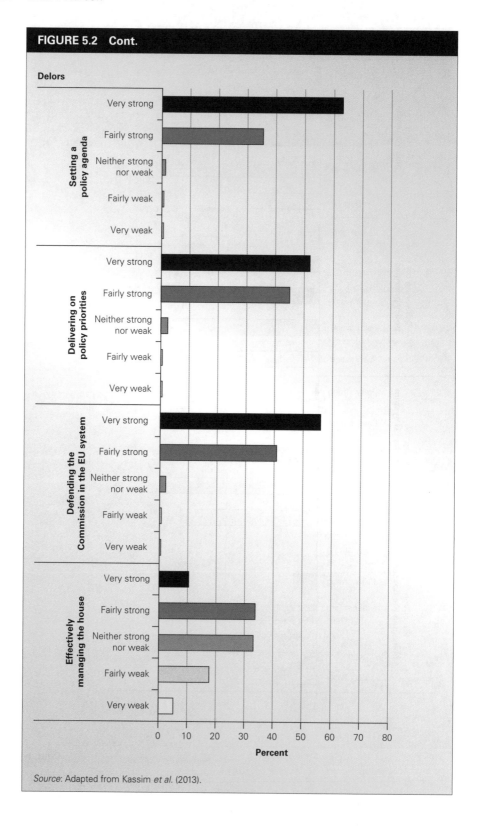

FIGURE 5.2 Cont.

Source: Adapted from Kassim et al. (2013).

Collective responsibility is not only built into the EU's institutional system generally, but also a cardinal principle *within* the college. All members must publicly support all decisions and actions of the Commission. The principle is often difficult to uphold. In contrast to cabinet governments, the college is never united by shared party political, national, or ideological affinities. In fact, no one has ever really explained what is meant to hold it together besides a commitment to Europe (Coombes 1970).

Formally, the college decides by simple majority votes. In a College of twenty-eight (or twenty-seven, post-Brexit), as many as thirteen Commissioners could vote against a motion, but then have to support it publically. Our knowledge about how often the college votes is primitive[18] and frequent voting cannot necessarily be equated with more division in the college. However, when the college votes, it is usually an admission that the majority view must be forced on at least a few Commissioners. By most accounts, voting was more frequent in the Santer Commission than in Delors', perhaps because the latter was more clearly dominated by its President. In the Prodi Commission, insiders noted 'a culture of avoiding votes' in a college whose members were 'very focused on their own responsibilities and relatively unconcerned with some larger "big vision" ' (Peterson 2008: 69). Barroso took pride in noting that his first college never resorted to a single vote and that there were 'probably five votes' in his second (Peterson 2016).

Barroso's colleges reflected a new political reality in an enlarged EU—that is, that even if all Commissioners are formally equal, the idea that no Commissioner is more powerful than another is now a fiction. If Commissioners from large member states tend to be more successful or powerful, it may be less because of blatant political activism by their national capitals than because they operate in wider networks of contacts (Joana and Smith 2002). Commissioners from small states can 'punch above the weight' of their home country if their performance earns them the respect of their peers and EU member governments. Still, no one pretends that Commissioners from, say, Germany and Malta start out as equals.

To their credit, member governments of the 2004–13 accession states mostly appointed top members of their political classes to the college. Of the first thirteen appointed by new EU states, six were former prime, foreign, or finance ministers, and several others had been European affairs ministers or national ambassadors to the EU. Four of seven of Juncker's Vice-Presidents hailed from post-2004 accession states (see Table 5.2).

The institutional effects of the twenty-first-century enlargements on the Commission, as well as the rest of the EU, are still bedding down. Yet there were reasons to think that enlargement had been digested more easily by the Commission than other EU institutions, whose numbers were swelled by a relatively larger influx of new and inexperienced members (Best *et al.* 2008). Enlargement made the Commission a younger, more female, and more economically liberal institution (Kassim *et al.* 2013: 260–4), with the latter point extending to Commissioners whose states had undergone radical, often painful, reforms to enter the EU. At the level of the college, and even more so within the services, enlargement held out the prospect of revitalizing and renewing the Commission with a new breed of reform-minded Europeans.

TABLE 5.2   The Juncker Commission

Commissioner (Nationality)	Position/portfolio	Relevant previous post(s)	Party group (EP*)
Jean-Claude Juncker (Luxembourg)	President	Prime Minister, Luxembourg	European People's Party (EPP)
Frederica Mogherini (Italy)	Vice-President and High Representative for CFSP	Foreign Minister, Italy	Party of European Socialists (PSE)
Frans Timmermans (Netherlands)	First Vice-President for Better Regulation, Inter-institutional Affairs, the Rule of Law and Charter of Fundamental Rights	Foreign Minister, Netherlands	Party of European Socialists (PSE)
Kristalina Georgieva (Bulgaria)	Vice-President for Budget and Human Resources	EU Commissioner, World Bank	European People's Party (EPP)
Andrus Ansip (Estonia)	Vice-President for Digital Single Market	Prime Minister, Estonia; MEP	Alliance of Liberals and Democrats for Europe (ALDE)
Maroš Šefčovič (Slovakia)	Vice-President for Energy Union	EU Commissioner, Ambassador to the EU	Party of European Socialists (PES)
Valdis Dombrovskis (Latvia)	Vice-President for Euro and Social Dialogue	Prime Minister, Latvia; MEP	European People's Party (EPP)
Jyrki Katainen (Finland)	Vice-President for Jobs, Growth, Investment and Competitiveness	Prime Minister, Finland	European People's Party (EPP)
Günther Oettinger (Germany)	Digital Economy and Jobs	EU Commissioner	European People's Party (EPP)
Johannes Hahn (Austria)	European Neighbourhood Policy and Enlargement Negotiations	EU Commissioner	European People's Party (EPP)
Cecilia Malmström (Sweden)	Trade	EU Commissioner; MEP, Minister for Europe (Sweden)	Alliance of Liberals and Democrats for Europe (ALDE)
Neven Mimica (Croatia)	International Cooperation and Development	EU Commissioner	Party of European Socialists (PES)

Miguel Arias Cañete (Spain)	Climate Action and Energy	Minister for Agriculture, Food & Environment, Spain; MEP	European People's Party (EPP)
Karmenu Vella (Malta)	Environment, Maritime Affairs and Fisheries	Minister for Tourism and Aviation, Malta	Party of European Socialists (PES)
Vytenis Andriukaitis (Lithuania)	Health and Food Safety	Minister for Health, Lithuania	Party of European Socialists (PES)
Dimitris Avramopoulos (Greece)	Migration, Home Affairs and Citizenship	Foreign Minister, Greece	European People's Party (EPP)
Marianne Thyssen (Belgium)	Employment, Social Affairs, Skills and Labour Mobility	MEP; leader of Flemish Christian-Democratic Party	European People's Party (EPP)
Pierre Moscovici (France)	Economic and Financial Affairs, Taxation and Customs	Minister for Economy and Finance, France	Party of European Socialists (PES)
Christos Stylianides (Cyprus)	Humanitarian Aid and Crisis Management	MEP	European People's Party (EPP)
Phil Hogan (Ireland)	Agriculture and Rural Development	Minister for Environment, Ireland	European People's Party (EPP)
Jonathan Hill (UK)**	Financial Stability, Financial Markets and Capital Markets Union	Leader, House of Lords, UK	European Conservatives and Reformists
Violeta Bulc (Slovenia)	Transport	Deputy Prime Minister, Slovenia	Alliance of Liberals and Democrats for Europe (ALDE)
Elżbieta Bieńkowska (Poland)	Internal Market, Industry, Entrepreneurship and SMEs	Deputy Prime Minister, Poland	European People's Party (EPP)
Věra Jourová (Czech Republic)	Justice, Consumers and Gender Equality	Regional Development Minister, Czech Republic	Alliance of Liberals and Democrats for Europe (ALDE)
Tibor Navracsics (Hungary)	Education, Youth, Culture and Sport	Foreign Minister, Hungary	European People's Party (EPP)

Cont. ➤

Cont.			
Corina Crețu (Romania)	Regional Policy	MEP; Vice-President, EP	Party of European Socialists (PES)
Margrethe Vestager (Denmark)	Competition	Economic Affairs Minister, Deputy Prime Minister, Denmark	Alliance of Liberals and Democrats for Europe (ALDE)
Carlos Moedas (Portugal)	Research, Science and Innovation	Secretary of State to Prime Minister, Portugal	European People's Party (EPP)

*All twenty-eight Commissioners are members of national political parties that are represented in EP party groups.

**Resigned on 15 July 2016 following the UK referendum vote to leave the EU.

The single most important factor in determining the cohesiveness of the college—regardless of its size—remains the strength of presidential leadership. The Prodi Commission was the first in which, according to the Amsterdam Treaty, the college worked 'under the political direction of the President'. Nevertheless, one of its members denied ever having a single substantive discussion with Prodi on any issue related to his own (economic) portfolio, adding 'Prodi got out of the way, but we needed a sort of control tower. We only avoided a lot of plane crashes at the last minute, and some we did not avoid.'[19]

Barroso appeared to think that his college needed more of a collective identity and more teamwork on actual policy. Yet he very much dominated his college, even though clashes between Commissioners sometimes erupted. There was little evidence that the five 'clusters' of Commissioners he created in key areas—the Lisbon agenda, external relations, communications, equal opportunities, and competitiveness—made much difference.

For his part, Juncker imposed a radical restructuring of the College, which was split between Vice-Presidents with broad policy remits (see Table 5.2) and 'portfolio Commissioners' who reported directly to a Vice-President. Former Dutch Foreign Minister Frans Timmermans was made the first-ever 'First VP' and given prerogative to veto any Commission proposal. In mission letters that Juncker wrote to all members of his new college, he made clear that Timmermans' approval was needed for any initiative to have 'political ownership' by the Commission.

Collective responsibility has become more difficult to enforce as the college has become, over time, a more politically weighty group of individuals. The Santer Commission reinforced the trend towards 'increasing politicisation of the college' (MacMullen 2000: 41), with its inclusion of six former prime ministers, foreign ministers, or finance ministers. Prodi's college contained more policy specialists, with a majority coming to the Commission after being national ministers for agriculture, finance, European affairs, and so on. The Barroso I Commission pushed back in the direction of high-powered generalists, with three former prime ministers, five former foreign ministers, and three former finance ministers, although nearly all who had held such high-level posts hailed from small states. Barroso's second college was more populated by low-key technocrats and thus even easier to dominate by the President himself. Juncker's team counted four former prime ministers (including himself), a wealth (five) of former foreign or deputy prime ministers, and—perhaps crucially—no fewer than six repeat Commissioners. All seven Vice-Presidents had such high-level pedigree. While the College remained governed by the principle of 'one Commissioner, one vote' (when and if the College did vote), the new division between Vice-Presidents and portfolio Commissioners made it clear that some were now even more equal than others.

The *cabinets*

One of the Commission's most vexed problems in the past has been the role of *cabinets*. In principle, *cabinets* are meant to act as a bridge between the college and the services, and thus between the political and technical. Most national civil services contain some analogue in the form of party-political, temporary appointees to civil services. Yet members of *cabinets* in the Commission have tended to be vilified as agents of their member state, as opposed to the Commission as an institution. In the past, *cabinets* were usually (not always) packed with officials—often quite young— who shared their Commissioner's nationality, leaving aside a few non-nationals. Many were hand-picked by governments in national capitals. Tensions between the *cabinets* and services were rife, especially during the Delors years. One abiding complaint was that *cabinets* intervened aggressively in personnel decisions, acting as lobbyists for national capitals.

Prodi himself was accused of violating the spirit of his own new meritocratic rules on appointments by placing hand-picked operatives in powerful posts. Still, Prodi instituted major changes at the level of *cabinets*, which were reduced to six officials from as many as nine previously (Prodi's own *cabinet* numbered nine). Each Commissioner was required to appoint a head (*chef*) or deputy head (*adjoint*) who hailed from a member state other than his or her own. Leading by example, Prodi chose as his own *chef* an Irishman, David O'Sullivan (later to become Commission Secretary-General).

Under Prodi, a significant number of new faces appeared in the *cabinets*, with only about a third having previous *cabinet* experience.[20] The Commission trumpeted the fact that all *cabinets* had officials of at least three different nationalities and that almost 40 per cent were women (a big increase on past totals). *Cabinets*, along with their Commissioners, were moved out of a central office in Brussels by Prodi and into the same buildings as the services for which their Commissioner was responsible, thus making Commissioners more like national ministers.

Barroso brought Commissioners and *cabinets* back together when the Commission's Berlaymont headquarters were reopened (after being refurbished) in 2004.

The move was widely expected after complaints that separating Commissioners' offices made it harder for them to strike deals and build coalitions. However, Barroso stuck with Prodi's rules on *cabinet* appointments and the influx of (thirteen) Commissioners from post-accession states made for an unusually large influx of fresh faces at this level. Juncker's decision to have the Commission's Secretariat-General 'service' his college's Vice-Presidents, who (unlike portfolio Commissioners) oversaw no Commission services themselves, led to questions about whether Vice-Presidential *cabinets*—with no service with whom to liaise—might become more like the national agents of old. Yet survey data presented in Kassim *et al.* (2013: 197–205) suggested that, at least under Barroso, there existed far less animosity between the *cabinets* and services than had once been the case.

The Commission's powers

The main source of the Commission's power has always been its monopoly right to propose legislation. The Commission also has significant independent powers within the CAP, and on external trade and (especially) competition policy. In the latter case, the college often acts as judge and prosecuting attorney—and sometimes jury—on cases of state aid to industry, mergers, and anti-competitive practices by firms. The Commission has considerable powers to set the agenda for policies that flank the internal market, such as cohesion or research policies.

Two important sources of Commission influence—as opposed to power—are its prerogative to deliver opinions on any EU matter and its obligation to publish an annual report on the activities of the EU. Both give the Commission scope to influence policy debates or to steer the EU in specified directions. Generally, however, the Commission must earn its respect by the quality of its analysis, and particularly its judgement of what will play in national capitals and with relevant policy stakeholders (including industry and non-governmental lobbies). To illustrate, the Juncker Commission was criticized heavily by (especially) eastern EU member states for forcing a vote by QMV on the sharing out of migrants during the refugee crisis of 2015 (see Box 5.3).

Over time, the Commission has become increasingly accountable to the EP. Besides its powers to confirm the college (and its President) and to sack the Commission (but only as a whole), the EP retains the informal right to scrutinize the activities of the Commission, with individual Commissioners expected to appear regularly before its policy-specialized committees. The emergence of the codecision procedure (see Chapter 6) as the 'ordinary' legislative procedure (OLP) post-Lisbon has had the effect of upgrading the institutional position of the EP at the expense of the Commission. When the EP and Council cannot agree, the Commission risks being marginalized unless it is sensitive to the positions of both of the other institutions and acknowledges their dominance of the procedure. More generally, the Parliament has

BOX 5.3	Juncker's crises

Almost immediately after the (contested) selection of Jean-Claude Juncker as Commission President, the EU was plunged into crises on a dizzying array of different fronts, to the extent that its very durability became subject to question. As head of a 'political' Commission, Juncker—and his powerful *chef*, Martin Selmayr—were in the thick of nearly all of them. A prime example was the Commission's politically noxious proposal in September 2015 to share out an estimated 120,000 migrants arriving in Greece, Italy, and Hungary. Despite bitter exchanges between member states, the proposal was approved (although soon overtaken by events). Juncker's forcing of a vote on quotas, as well as his personal investment in the Greek crisis, led one senior Commission official to contend, 'this Commission takes political risks in a way Barroso never did . . . Juncker is far more ambitious. Barroso never would've proposed quotas.'[21]

Juncker pushed hard to expand the Commission's powers to supervise the euro and European banks, while also (perhaps cleverly) telling the EP that its oversight was crucial: '[T]hese are all political decisions that require a political Commission that accounts for its actions before this Parliament.'[22] The report of the 2015 'Five Presidents'—of the Commission, European Central Bank (ECB), Eurogroup, EP, and European Council—on completing EMU was written mostly within Juncker's private office, with one *cabinet* official insisting: 'Martin [Selmayr] wrote it himself. Dombrovskis [Vice-President for the euro—see Table 5.2], the poor guy, had to present it to the media even though he had nothing to do with it.'

Chairing the European Council, Donald Tusk mostly brokered the settlement of the UK's demands for 'renegotiation' ahead of its 2016 referendum on EU membership. But—again—Selmayr was widely expected to take a leading (if backroom) role in negotiating the terms of the UK's exit from the EU. Only on Ukraine did Juncker (and Selmayr) step back to let Mogherini take the lead in brokering tough EU sanctions on Russia after its 2014 annexation of Crimea. Her successful chairing of talks on Iran's nuclear programme was widely viewed as revealing her basic competence to be EU High Representative and a Commission Vice-President, while doing nothing to dispel the impression that Juncker's Commission was truly a 'political' one.

Juncker also was unafraid to link the various crises into a single, existential one for the EU, arguing that failure to solve the migrant crisis would have dismal consequences: 'Schengen is one of the biggest achievements of the European integration process . . . whoever kills Schengen carries the internal market to its grave . . . the euro [will] make no sense.'[23] Commission insiders admired Juncker's inclination to 'work the phones' and speak directly to EU leaders, implicitly reminding them of his vast experience at the highest political levels as prime minister of Luxembourg for eighteen years and chair of the Eurogroup for eight. One of his top advisers summarized his leadership style thus: '[H]e will sometimes lead on process like a Prime Minister. He won't wait for consensus but will push for it, doing things as a [head of] government does.'

No system of government is very good at solving multiple crises at the same time, let alone one as convoluted as that of the EU. Juncker appeared determined to assert the Commission's role in finding solutions, even if it risked deep fissures between EU governments. However much capacity the Union had to escape its period of crisis, Juncker was clearly determined that his Commission had to be part of the solutions.

'gained a greater ability not only to hold the Commission more accountable, but also to get the Commission to do things it would not otherwise do' (Stacey 2003: 951).

Historically, the Court of Justice of the EU has usually ruled in the Commission's favour when it has been asked to settle competence disputes. Several underpinnings of the 1992 project became doctrine as the result of individual Court decisions, which the Commission then used in the design of new policies (Armstrong and Bulmer 1998). However, a landmark case in early 1994 saw the Court rule against the Commission in a dispute with the Council over competence on new external trade issues such as services and intellectual property (Peterson and Bomberg 1999: 100). The Commission also suffered a series of painful Court defeats on its competition policy judgements under Prodi, leading to a sweeping overhaul of the EU's regime for state aid to industry under Barroso.

The Commission's most important power may be its right of initiative, but increasingly the Commission's most important role is that of a *manager* of policies set by other institutions. The twenty-first century has found the Commission sharing responsibility for more EU policies, often acting as a broker and facilitator within organizational networks linking the member states and other EU institutions. To illustrate, the launch of the Lisbon agenda of economic reform in 2000 granted few significant new competences to the Commission. However, it allowed just enough room for the Commission to catalyse new initiatives to convince Barroso (five years later) that a revamped Lisbon strategy focused on jobs and growth—which lived on in the Europe 2020 strategy—should be his Commission's top priority. More than ever, the Commission's work was concerned with advocacy and persuasion within horizontal policy networks, rather than hierarchical compulsion or coercion.

Theorizing the college

The mass resignation of the Santer Commission was clearly a defining event in the life of the institution. Six years later, Trade Commissioner Peter Mandelson claimed that the Barroso college still found its position eroded by a 'pincer movement': a loss of leadership to the Council and loss of the internal Commission agenda to the services, which had become more autonomous in the void created by the demise of the Santer Commission.[24] If the Commission was really so weak, intergovernmental accounts of EU politics—which tend to make three arguments about the Commission— could be marshalled to explain why. First, it makes little difference who is Commission President. Second, the Commission is powerful only when and where national preferences converge. Third, the Commission is empowered only to the extent that member governments want to ensure the 'credibility of their commitments' to each other (Moravcsik 1998: 492).[25] There is little dispute—amongst scholars, as well as practitioners—that the Commission has traditionally had little influence over most 'history-making' decisions about the broad sweep of European integration.

In contrast, institutionalist theory—arguably 'the leading theoretical approach in EU studies' (Cowles and Curtis 2004: 305)—paints a portrait of a Commission that is often powerful in day-to-day policy debates (Pierson 1996). According to this view, policy decisions in complex systems such as the EU are difficult to reverse, and policy often becomes locked into existing paths and is 'path-dependent'. Thus even as the Stability and Growth Pact, the economic rulebook governing EMU, was rewritten in 2005 amidst frustration over the Commission's reprimands of governments running profligate budget deficits, the Commission lost none of its existing mandate or authority over EMU (Heipertz and Verdun 2010).

Some variants of institutionalism combine insights from rational choice and principal–agent theories (Pollack 2003, 2008). They hold that the principal authorities in EU politics—the member governments themselves—make rational choices to delegate tasks to the EU's institutions, which then become their agents in specific policy areas. This body of theory sheds light on the tendency of the EU to make policy by means other than the traditional Community method of legislating (Devuyst 1999), according to which only the Commission can propose. One of the least flattering features of the Prodi Commission was its frequent insistence that the Community method was the only legitimate path to making EU policy, even in areas such as common foreign and security policy (CFSP), where its use was politically unthinkable. There was little dispute that some policy modes—particularly the so-called open method of coordination (OMC), relying on benchmarking, league tabling, and designating the Commission as a scrutinizer of national policies rather than a proposer of EU policies—produced few tangible results (Borràs and Jacobsson 2004; Dehousse 2004). Yet EU principals (national governments) were clearly moving towards new kinds of delegation such as voluntary codes and other 'soft' forms of regulation, particularly in line with the Europe 2020 strategy, with the Commission cast as a different kind of agent.

Increased affinity for new policy modes is also reflected in the creation of a variety of new regulatory agencies, some of which have assumed some of the traditional roles of the Commission (see Chapter 10). EU governments increasingly seem to want *de novo* institutions—not only the Commission—to whom they can delegate cooperative policy tasks. Usually, however, the Commission 'has had little reason to protest delegation to European agencies . . . because most operate in areas where the Commission's powers are weak and most offer resources the Commission both needs and lacks' (Peterson 2015: 202). In many cases, the Commission still identifies and seeks to solve coordination problems within policy networks of (among others) private actors, consumer and environmental groups, and national and European agencies.

Advocates of multilevel governance have long contended that the Commission enjoys a privileged place at the 'hub of numerous highly specialized policy networks of technical experts', even retaining 'virtually a free hand in creating new networks' (Marks *et al.* 1996: 355, 359), especially ones that bring together national regulatory officials. At the beginning of the twenty-first century, Metcalfe (2000: 838) argued that 'the Commission will have to be reinvented as a network organization adept at designing the frameworks of governance and developing the management capacities needed to make them work effectively'. There is little doubt that, insofar as the Commission provides direction to the EU of the future, it will largely do so as a coordinator of networks that seek to make national policies converge (Kohler-Koch and Eising 1999; Peterson 2009)—as has taken place, say, in competition policy (Maher 2007)—as opposed to replacing them with EU policies.

Conclusion

Any analysis of the Commission must consider the normative question of what kind of organization the college should be: a policy entrepreneur; an honest broker; a manager of decisions taken by others; or an engine of integration?

Increasingly, the Commission has outgrown the last of these roles. It might be argued that there is no other institution that has the independence to identify the new directions that European integration needs to take. Juncker's designation of his as a political Commission might be viewed as a sign of more boldness than under Barroso at a time when Europe clearly needed radical rethinking. Moreover, there is historical evidence suggesting that the Commission's declining fortunes can be reversed: after all, it appeared entirely moribund after Hallstein and before Delors.

The Commission spent much of the Prodi era focused on its own institutional position. With its basic role preserved, it can be argued that the Commission now needs to focus on policy, as opposed to grand designs. Yet it has become increasingly difficult, especially in an EU of twenty-eight (or twenty-seven, post-Brexit), to design single policy solutions in Brussels. In this context, the EU's added value may now be mostly as a laboratory for policy learning and transfer. Logically, the new EU will have to adopt new policy modes and particularly more, and more intensive, exchange and cooperation within networks of national, or even subnational, agencies (Wallace and Reh 2015). The Union's institutions—including the Commission—will need to embrace more collective types of leadership and advocacy of new policy ideas. Article 9 of the Lisbon Treaty gives a clear political signal that the EU's institutions must 'practise full mutual cooperation' if the Union is to thrive.

In an enlarged EU, the Commission may be even better placed than it was in the past to act as a truly honest broker. It may rarely exercise control over new networks or reclaim its old function as an engine of integration, but it will logically remain at the centre of many EU policy networks. In any event, it will often find itself in a unique position to steer debates in ways that serve collective European interests, as difficult as they may be to identify clearly in the new EU.

ENDNOTES

1. See also Dinan (2011: 117–18); Nugent and Rhinard (2015: 382–91).

2. See also Duchêne (1994).

3. See also Dumoulin (2007).

4. The college remained a men-only club for a shockingly long time. The first women Commissioners were Christiane Scrivener (France) and Vasso Papandreou (Greece), who were appointed to the Delors Commission in 1989. By 2014, Juncker's college consisted of nine women and nineteen men.

5. The Luxembourg compromise was accompanied by a range of new restrictions on the Commission, including a bar on making proposals public before the Council could consider them and the requirement that the Commission could receive the credentials of non-EEC ambassadors to the Community only alongside the Council.

6. It is not clear that Jenkins wished to serve another term. His 1979 Dimbleby lecture (halfway through his term as Commission President) foreshadowed his ambition to form a new British political grouping—eventually, the Social Democratic Party (SDP)—of which he became co-leader three years later. By 1980, even Belgium—which originally favoured his reappointment—decided that the 'gap between [Thatcherite] Britain and the rest of the Community was so great that the time had not arrived when any Englishman could be President of the Commission indefinitely' (Jenkins 1989: 601). The Commission's term in office was later extended to five years by the Maastricht Treaty so as to align its tenure with that of the EP.

7. Santer was literally no one's first choice, but was chosen after the nominations of Ruud Lubbers (Prime Minister of the Netherlands), Leon Brittan (Commissioner under Delors), and Jean-Luc Dehaene (Prime Minister of Belgium) were all rejected, with the UK under John Major prominently vetoing Dehaene.

8. Santer was not alone in making this claim. Respected Belgian Commissioner for Competition Policy Karel van Miert attacked the Experts' report as 'unjust and incorrect' (Santer and van Miert, both quoted in *Financial Times*, 17 March 1999). For his part, Brittan (2000: 11) insisted that the Experts had added 'unnecessary and crude journalistic icing . . . to what was a perfectly well-baked and freestanding cake'.

9. Unattributed quote in *Financial Times*, 17 March 1999.

10. This quote (and all others not referenced as otherwise in this chapter) is taken from interviews conducted as part of the research for this chapter between November/December 2000 and October 2015.

11. Quoted in *Daily Telegraph*, 10 June 2014.

12. Quoted in *Financial Times*, 19 July 1999, p. 9.

13. Quoted (respectively) in *Financial Times*, 2 March 2005, p. 6, and 7 February 2005, p. 17.

14. Quoted in *Financial Times*, 22 October 2004, p. 1.

15. Quoted in BBC News (2004).

16. See Catholic Educator's Resource Centre, 'The New Europe: Catholics no longer need apply', available online at http://www.catholiceducation.org/en/controversy/persecution/the-new-europe-no-catholics-need-apply.html. See also National Secular Society, 'Christian onslaught on EU Parliament continues', available online at http://www.secularism.org.uk/christianonslaughtoneuparliament.html

17. Quoted in *Financial Times*, 19 December 2004, p. 8.

18. To illustrate the point, one former Commissioner interviewed for this chapter insisted that there were 'far more votes under Delors and tight votes'; another indicated that 'voting wasn't very frequent' in the Delors Commission. Previous interviewees with experience of successive Commissions estimated that there were more votes taken under Santer than Delors (see Peterson 1999: 62).

19. Quoted in Peterson (2006: 505).

20. As is generally the case in the Commission, personnel records on *cabinet* members are incomplete, making precise comparisons impossible. However, using data presented in Hill & Knowlton (2000) on the Prodi college, a total of thirty-four (out of all 123 *cabinet* officials) had previous experience working in *cabinets*, or 28 per cent of the total, compared to seventy-four with no previous *cabinet* experience, or 60 per cent of the total.

21. This official and others in this box quoted in Peterson (2016).

22. Quoted in Livingstone (2015).

23. Quoted in *Irish Times*, 16 January 2016.

24. See Mandelson (2005).

25. See also Bickerton *et al.* (2015a).

 FURTHER READING

The most comprehensive works on the Commission are Kassim *et al.* (2013), based on a large dataset on the attitudes of Commission officials, and Nugent and Rhinard (2015). Spence and Edwards (2006) is also useful. Good on the history of the Commission is Dumoulin (2007), while Delors (2004) offers an insider's view. Coombes (1970) and Ross (1995) are classics that are worth revisiting. A typically downbeat assessment of the declining position of the Commission is Tsakatika (2005), while Peterson (2015, 2016) offers a view of the position of the Commission within the 'new intergovernmentalism' and what a 'political Commission' might look like under Juncker, respectively.

Coombes, D. (1970) *Power and Bureaucracy in the European Community* (London: Croon Helm).

Delors, J. (2004) *Mémoires* (Paris: Plon).

Dumoulin, M. (ed.) (2007) *The European Commission, 1958–72: History and Memories* (Brussels: European Commission).

Kassim, H., Peterson, J., Bauer, M., Dehousse, R., Hooghe, L., Connolly, S., and Thompson, A. (2013) *The European Commission of the 21st Century* (Oxford and New York: Oxford University Press).

Nugent, N., and Rhinard, M. (2015) *The European Commission* (2nd edn, Basingstoke and New York: Palgrave).

Peterson, J. (2015) 'The Commission and the New Intergovernmentalism: Calm within the Storm?', in C. Bickerton, D. Hodson, and U. Puetter (eds) *The New Intergovernmentalism: States and Supranational Actors in the Post-Maastricht Era* (Oxford and New York: Oxford University Press), 185–207

Peterson, J. (2016) 'Juncker's political commission and an EU in crisis', *Journal of Common Market Studies*, at http://onlinelibrary.wiley.com.ezproxy.is.ed.ac.uk/doi/10.1111/jcms.12435/full

Ross, G. (1995) *Jacques Delors and European Integration* (New York and London: Polity Press).

Spence, D., and Edwards, G. (eds) (2006) *The European Commission* (London: John Harper).

Tsakatika, M. (2005) 'The European Commission between continuity and change', *Journal of Common Market Studies*, 43/1: 193–220.

WEB LINKS

http://ec.europa.eu/index_en.htm

The Commission's own website is a treasure trove that handles millions of 'hits' per month.

http://www.politico.eu/
http://www.epc.eu/

The sites of *Politico* (the European, not the American version; formerly *European Voice*) and the European Policy Centre offer insiders' insights from Brussels.

http://ec.europa.eu/unitedkingdom/
http://www.euintheus.org/

It is often useful to see how the Commission's delegations in EU member states (such as the UK) and non-EU member states (such as the United States) present the Commission's line in capitals beyond Brussels.

CHAPTER 6

The European Parliament: The power of democratic ideas

Michael Shackleton

▌ Summary

The European Parliament (EP) is the only directly elected institution of the European Union (EU). It derives its authority from national electorates rather than national governments and is therefore a transnational institution in the terms of this book. For much of its history, it was relatively weak; since the first direct elections in 1979, its powers and status have grown with remarkable speed, culminating in the changes agreed under the 2007 Lisbon Treaty. It is now arguably one of the most powerful parliaments in the world, enjoying a relationship of equals with governments in the Council, as well as the ability to exercise significant control over the Commission. And yet many argue that, despite the changed status of its one directly elected body, the EU still suffers from a 'democratic deficit' (Dahl 1999; Hix and Bartolini 2006; Moravcsik 2012). This chapter examines these issues, looking at how the EP has evolved, how it aggregates interests, what influence it exercises, and what kind of body it is becoming.

Introduction

The election of Jean-Claude Juncker as President of the European Commission (see Box 6.1) represented a dramatic use of the provisions of the Lisbon Treaty by the EP. It showed how the Parliament could act to shape the institutional structure of the EU, even when confronted by the heads of state or government in the European Council. It was an outcome that should not be seen as simply the product of a single Treaty; rather, it was the result of developments stretching back over the whole history of the EP, which differentiate it from all of the other institutions discussed in this book. The Parliament is the only one of the EU bodies created in the 1950s whose role has been radically revised over the last half-century, with tasks and responsibilities that very few imagined likely before the 1990s.

BOX 6.1   **The election of Jean-Claude Juncker as Commission President**

On 15 July 2014, Jean-Claude Juncker was elected President of the European Commission with 422 votes in favour, 250 against, forty-seven abstentions, and ten spoiled ballot papers. The result was not dissimilar to those that had seen José Manuel Barroso elected President in 2004 and 2009, but the process was completely different. Juncker did not emerge as the result of a bargain between the heads of state or government in the European Council, but was already known as a candidate for the job in advance of the 2014 EP elections. Five European political parties proposed the person (in the case of the Greens, two people) whom they considered should be Commission President if their party were to gain the most votes in the elections. Their argument, supported by a majority in the Parliament, was that only in this way could the European Council propose a candidate 'taking account of the European elections', as laid down in the Lisbon Treaty.[1] Such an interpretation was resisted inside the European Council and considered by some to be a crude power grab by the Parliament. However, the main groups in the Parliament made it plain, after it became clear that the European People's Party (EPP) had emerged as the largest party in the elections, that the EPP candidate, Juncker, should have the first opportunity to obtain majority support. Indeed, they went further, stating that no candidate who had not been known before the elections would be able to obtain such a majority. It proved extremely difficult for the heads of state or government to resist this line of argument—particularly those in the EPP. Their parties had been involved in the selection of Juncker as the candidate at a party congress in Dublin back in March 2014. Juncker himself spoke on the phone to Angela Merkel, telling her that, unless she supported him, he would resign and explain publicly why (Garcia and Priestley 2015: 162). In the event, the European Council voted by twenty-six to two (the British and Hungarian prime ministers, Cameron and Orban, voting against) to propose Juncker to the Parliament. It was agreed in the European Council that the system should be looked at again in 2019, but there is a strong likelihood that the precedent set in 2014 will be repeated before and after the next elections (Garcia and Priestley 2015: 184).

The chapter addresses the following three main issues:

- how and why the Parliament has been able to acquire such a range of additional powers;
- what difference the inclusion of a directly elected institution has made to the evolution of the EU; and
- whether the evolving EP can close the so-called democratic deficit by improving the accountability of EU decisions.

The election of Jean-Claude Juncker is relevant to all three of the questions to be discussed in this chapter. First, it reinforces the claim that the growth in influence of the EP can be explained by the fact that it has consistently proved easier to agree an extension of the institution's role than to say no to the claims of a representative institution with democratic credentials based on direct elections. Such a claim constitutes a challenge to those who argue that the EU is becoming more intergovernmental in character (Bickerton et al. 2015a). Second, it underlines that the Parliament can make a difference to the direction of the EU, thus inviting us to consider the conditions under which it can have influence. Third, it raises the issue of whether the EU will seem more legitimate in the eyes of its citizens if the election of the Commission President is made dependent on the outcome of European elections. Can what is often called the 'democratic deficit' in the EU be resolved by modifying the process by which its decision-makers are chosen? Will a more politicized EU be one that is seen as more democratic, more accountable to its citizens?

Historical evolution

The story of the Parliament has been told as a transition from 'fig-leaf to co-legislature' (Corbett et al. 2016: 1). The change is reflected symbolically in the Parliament's physical surroundings: it has moved from renting premises in Strasbourg that it shared with the Parliamentary Assembly of the Council of Europe (PACE), to become the effective owner of two substantial building complexes in Brussels and Strasbourg, each with parliamentary chambers, or 'hemicycles', equipped to seat 751 members. At the same time, as Table 6.1 indicates, the formal powers of the EP developed dramatically between 1951, when 'the Six' (Belgium, France, Italy, Luxembourg, the Netherlands, and West Germany) signed the European Coal and Steel Community (ECSC) Treaty, and 2009, when the Lisbon Treaty, signed by twenty-seven states, came into force.

When the ECSC was established, a parliamentary body was not at the centre of the discussions (Smith 1999: 27–44). The crucial institution was the High Authority, which was given supranational powers in the management of coal and steel. The issue of how best to hold this new body to account was much discussed in the Treaty

TABLE 6.1	Main Treaty changes affecting the European Parliament		
	Election of MEPs	**Legislative and budgetary role**	**Appointment and scrutiny of executive**
ECSC Treaty (1950)	Choice between direct elections or national parliaments to select members		Right to dismiss High Authority
Rome Treaty (1957)	Specific provision for direct elections (implemented in 1979)	Right to be consulted and to give its opinion to the Council	
Budgetary Treaties (1970 and 1975)		Right to reject budget, modify level of expenditure, and approve/disapprove accounts ('discharge')	
Single European Act (1986)		'Cooperation procedure' providing right to a second reading of legislation; 'assent procedure' to approve enlargement and some international agreements	
Maastricht Treaty (1992)		'Codecision procedure' with conciliation to apply to 15 legal bases; right to invite Commission to present a legislative proposal	Right to approve Commission as a whole; Committees of inquiry; appointment of Ombudsman; ECB President to report to EP Committee
Amsterdam Treaty (1997)		Simplification and extension of codecision to 32 legal bases	Right to approve Commission President
Nice Treaty (2000)		Extension of codecision to 37 legal bases	
Lisbon Treaty (2007)		Extension of codecision to 90 legal bases and now called 'ordinary legislative procedure'; budget procedure amended to give joint control with Council over whole budget; consent procedure (formerly 'assent') for international trade agreements; joint control with Council over delegated legislation	Commission President elected by EP on basis of proposal of European Council that 'takes into account the elections to the European Parliament'

negotiations, with many feeling that it was national ministers who should play the central role. However, there was eventually agreement to create a parliamentary institution, called the Common Assembly, but with powers limited to the exercise of supervisory control via a censure motion. It was not expected to play a significant role in the new institutional structure (Rittberger 2003: 213).

The potential for the Assembly to evolve was, however, reflected in the provisions governing its election. Member states could choose whether to have direct elections to the Assembly or to allow their national parliaments to select members.[2] The possibility of a direct link to the electorate distinguished the institution from the outset from other international parliamentary bodies, such as PACE, established three years earlier in 1949. The absence of any supranational element in the structure of the Council of Europe eliminated any possible move away from having an Assembly made up of national parliamentarians.

The Treaty of Rome brought significant change. Specific provision was made under Article 138(3) for the Assembly to draw up a proposal for elections by direct universal suffrage, which the Council was called to act upon. No timetable was laid down, but the commitment to abolish the system of nominated members was awarded Treaty status. The Assembly was also given advisory, as well as supervisory, powers and thus was given its first glimpse of legislative power. These two changes did not have an immediate effect. It took more than twenty years for direct elections to be organized and the Parliament's formal legislative powers were not altered for nearly thirty years. Nevertheless, a trajectory for further development in the Parliament's powers was laid down, creating a form of 'path dependency' (see Chapter 1).

Subsequent changes in the Parliament's role were closely linked with other modifications to the EU's structure. Treaty revisions introduced in 1970 and 1975 gave the EP budgetary powers, including the right to reject the budget (a right it exercised in 1979 and 1984), to amend it within certain fixed limits, and to approve (or not) the annual accounts. The essential source of these changes was the decision to alter the basis for financing the European Community. It was agreed that the EU would move away from a system of national contributions linked to each country's gross national product (GNP) to a system of 'own resources', whereby the revenue available for financing European policies legally belonged to the Community. Under these circumstances, there was a strong body of opinion amongst the governments of the Six—notably the Dutch—that national parliaments could no longer exercise effective control over Community finance and the task should be passed onto the EP. Already in the 1960s, the idea of the EP enjoying the kind of rights at EU level traditionally exercised at national level by parliamentarians was proving difficult to resist, with sceptics faced with the task of suggesting a convincing alternative.

The argument about an increase in the powers of the Parliament was inextricably linked with the issue of how its members should be elected. As the Vedel Report noted:

[I]f one cannot imagine a Parliament with real powers which does not draw its mandate from direct universal suffrage, it is even more difficult to imagine the election through direct universal suffrage of a Parliament without extended powers. In this way, two equally desirable objectives are making each other's implementation impossible.

(Vedel 1972: 59)

The dilemma persisted until the elections of French President Valéry Giscard d'Estaing and West German Chancellor Helmut Schmidt within five days of each other in May 1974. The subsequent Paris Summit agreed to hold direct European elections after 1978, which in turn paved the way for an extension of the Parliament's legislative powers. A critical moment was the 1980 *Isoglucose* judgment of the Court of Justice.[3] The judgment annulled a piece of Community legislation adopted by Council on the grounds that the EP had not yet given its opinion. The Court made it clear that Council could not adopt Community legislation before receiving Parliament's opinion. Moreover, the Court made a link between the democratic character of the Community and the Parliament's right to be consulted, which the Court described as:

... the means which allows the Parliament to play an actual part in the legislative process of the Community. Such a power represents an essential factor in the institutional balance intended by the Treaty. Although limited, it reflects at Community level *the fundamental democratic principle* that the peoples should take part in the exercise of power through the intermediary of a representative assembly.[4]

The right to be more than simply consulted came in 1986 with the Single European Act (SEA), which provided the Treaty base for the establishment of a single European market by 1992. To accelerate the process, member states created a new 'cooperation' procedure, with more majority voting, under which Parliament was entitled to two readings of proposed legislation, rather than one. Moreover, provided that the Commission was persuaded to back Parliament's amendments, the Council could overrule the EP only by unanimity.

The precise form of Parliament's involvement in the legislative procedure was not preordained. The Vedel Report had argued against the idea that the Parliament should be given the right to amend legislation and instead suggested giving it the right to say 'yes' or 'no' to legislation presented to it by the Council. In fact, such a power of 'assent' was granted to the Parliament under the SEA for non-legislative issues. Although restricted to the accession of new member states and the conclusion of a limited number of agreements with non-EU countries, the Parliament was called to give its assent to international agreements thirty times within the first two years of the SEA being ratified. It was subsequently asked to vote on all ensuing new accessions.

The Maastricht Treaty ushered in a new and transformational procedure that made the EP and Council legal equals in the legislative process. The procedure provided for joint decision-taking and direct negotiations between Parliament and Council, as well as the possibility that the EP might reject draft legislation if such negotiations were to fail. Supporters of stronger EP powers argued, successfully, that more majority voting in Council weakened the position of national parliaments. A greater role for the EP would improve the democratic legitimacy of EU legislation by ensuring that it had the support of European citizens and not only their governments.

Maastricht also gave the EP a number of additional rights, including to:

- approve (or not) the Commission before it took office;
- establish committees of inquiry to consider issues of maladministration;
- appoint a European Ombudsman every five years; and
- invite the Commission to present a legislative proposal.

Member states thereby proved receptive to the argument that the broader agenda set for the EU at Maastricht should be matched by a reinforced role for the Parliament. Not all governments were enthusiastic—the United Kingdom (UK), for example, insisted that the word 'codecision' should not appear in the Treaty (Corbett 1993: 58)—but the new role was accepted as part of the deal on the overall shape of the Treaty.

The process of parliamentarization was still only partial, but the ongoing process of Treaty revision provided the EP with the opportunity to continue pressing for an expansion of its role—and it did so with considerable success. Under the Amsterdam Treaty, codecision was extended from fifteen to thirty-two Treaty legal bases and simplified to make it possible to reach agreements more quickly. The development can be partly explained by the Parliament proving more 'responsible' than some in EU national capitals had imagined or predicted it would be, readily accepting the obligations imposed by the Treaty. At the same time, the direct negotiations provided for under codecision proved remarkably successful in facilitating agreement. As a result, more reticent member states, such as the UK and Denmark, became less nervous about extending the Parliament's prerogatives and accepting the arguments of those such as Germany that its powers needed to be expanded to increase the democratic legitimacy of the Union.

The Amsterdam Treaty also legitimized existing practice by giving the EP the formal right to approve the European Council's nominee as Commission President. Thus, by 1999, the Parliament possessed a set of rights to influence the nomination of the Commission. These rights complemented the power of dismissal that originated in the ECSC Treaty, nearly fifty years earlier.

Negotiations over the Nice Treaty were dominated by the dispute over the relative weight of member states in the Council and Commission in an enlarged Union, with a related, but less central, argument about the number of seats that each member state should have in the Parliament. However, agreement emerged to extend codecision, if only marginally, to thirty-seven Treaty legal bases, with the possibility of limited further extension thereafter by unanimous Council decision.

The position of the Parliament was subject to major debate and revision in the course of the European Convention and in the 2004 Constitutional Treaty. Although the Treaty was rejected, following negative votes in referenda in France and the Netherlands in 2005, the process that led four years later to the Lisbon Treaty saw no one seriously contest the changes proposed for the EP. The most significant of these was the acceptance of the link between qualified majority voting (QMV) in the Council and the application of codecision. The procedure was extended to ninety legal bases, including the common agricultural and fisheries policies (CAP and CFP, respectively), the common commercial policy (CCP), and justice and home affairs (JHA). The centrality of codecision as a way of making EU laws was recognized by renaming it the 'ordinary legislative procedure' (OLP).

The Treaty gave the Parliament two other important powers: the right to share power with the Council over all EU spending in the annual budget negotiations; and the right to approve virtually all international agreements, including all trade agreements. In addition, the Lisbon Treaty laid down that the Commission President should be elected by the Parliament on the basis of a European Council proposal, '[t]aking into account the elections to the European Parliament and after having held the appropriate consultations'.[5] The EP was not given the right to elect the Commission President on its own, but the suitability of a candidate would henceforth be judged in the light of the political composition of the Parliament after direct elections. Such a link had effectively already been established in 2004 when the largest group in the Parliament (the EPP) insisted that the new President come from their ranks, thereby establishing a precedent that was repeated in 2009, when Barroso was reappointed. However, the new phrase took on a quite different significance in 2014, as noted in Box 6.1, with competing candidates being put forward by several European political parties in advance of the European elections.

How can we explain this constant accretion of powers to the Parliament? It can be suggested that it occurred by a process of spillover from one area to another, generating a momentum that no government was willing or able to stop, in a manner similar to the way in which neo-functionalists explain the extension of EU competences. It has been described as a 'habitual response' on the part of the member states (Goetze and Rittberger 2010). Others have argued that parliamentarization now constitutes a core value in the constitutionalization of the EU. Those opposed to the reinforcement of the powers of the Parliament have proved unable to develop an effective counter-narrative (Rittberger and Schimmelfennig 2006). In any case, the increase in powers presents an 'integration paradox' to those who argue in favour of an intergovernmental approach whereby important decisions are reserved for representatives of national governments (Pollak and Slominski 2015).

However, it would be a mistake to assume that the increase in formal powers has resulted automatically in an increase in the influence that the Parliament can exercise. The Lisbon Treaty can be seen as the pinnacle of success for the institution in achieving its goals, in particular, to become a co-legislator with the Council. Yet it can also be portrayed as underlining the limits of what the Parliament can influence and the kind of compromises it has to make to have an impact. The Treaty is not a charter to parliamentarize the EU nor to make the EP the EU's legislature, in the terms of a separation of powers as discussed in Chapter 1; rather, it sets the ground rules for Parliament's work for the medium term—rules that have been sorely tested in the context of the financial crisis that hit the EU in 2008 and which has continued to cast a shadow over the eurozone in particular ever since. This crisis, along with the ongoing conflicts in Ukraine and in the Middle East, the latter provoking mass migration into the EU, have underlined what the EP cannot do as much as what it can do. The EP will also play a key role in Brexit, following the result of the UK's 2016 referendum on EU membership. Under the Treaty, the EP's consent is required for any agreement concerning the withdrawal of a member state from the Union.

Decision-making in the European Parliament

One central problem for the Parliament in using the powers that it has effectively and exercising influence is that of aggregating interests. The Parliament is more diverse and more heterogeneous than any other EU institution. Before the first direct EP elections, there were 198 members from nine states; by 2014, the number of members had more than tripled to 751 from twenty-eight states, coming from more than 200 national parties. No elected parliamentary chamber in Europe had as many members, with such major differences in the number of citizens that each member is expected to represent (see Table 6.2).

How can such a large, heterogeneous institution take effective decisions? The EP does not contain a government and cannot rely on those parliamentarians who belong to the party, or parties, of a government to ensure that a particular political programme is enacted. Instead, it has constructed a complex structure whereby the bulk of its activity is driven by the interrelationship between political groups and parliamentary committees, with a leadership that seeks to manage that relationship without being able to influence it significantly.

At the apex at the Parliament sits the President, who is elected every two-and-a half years. She or he has the task of chairing the plenary (with the help of fourteen Vice-Presidents), representing the institution vis-à-vis other institutions and the outside world, and overseeing the Parliament's internal functioning. She or he also chairs two leadership bodies: the Conference of Presidents and the Bureau. The Conference, composed of the chairs of all of the political groups, amongst other things, agrees the draft agenda of plenary sessions, settles conflicts of competence between committees, and determines whether or not to send delegations outside the EU. The Bureau, composed of the Parliament's fourteen Vice-Presidents, deals with internal financial, organizational, and administrative matters.

The role of the President has witnessed some significant development in recent times. The present incumbent, Martin Schulz, is the first President since direct elections to have been re-elected a second time. He was able to benefit from his position

TABLE 6.2 Number of MEPs per member state and ratio to population

Country	Population (in millions)	Seats in 2014 elections	Inhabitants per MEP (2014)
Germany	81.0	96	844,000
France	66.1	74	894,000
UK*	64.5	73	884,000
Italy	60.7	73	832,000
Spain	46.4	54	859,000
Poland	38.4	51	754,000
Romania	19.9	32	623,000
Netherlands	16.9	26	650,000
Belgium	11.2	21	535,000
Greece	10.8	21	515,000
Czech Republic	10.5	21	501,000
Portugal	10.3	21	494,000
Hungary	9.8	21	469,000
Sweden	9.7	20	489,000
Austria	8.6	18	477,000
Bulgaria	7.2	17	423,000
Denmark	5.6	13	436,000
Finland	5.4	13	421,000
Slovakia	5.4	13	416,000
Ireland	4.6	11	419,000
Croatia	4.2	11	388,000
Lithuania	2.9	11	263,000
Slovenia	2.0	8	257,000
Latvia	1.9	8	247,000
Estonia	1.3	6	218,000
Cyprus	0.8	6	143,000
Luxembourg	0.5	6	93,000
Malta	0.4	6	69,000
TOTAL EU 28	**507**	**751**	**675,100**

*As of 2014 EP election and prior to 2016 referendum and Brexit

Source: Adapted from Corbett (2016)

as a candidate for Commission President before the 2014 elections and from the post of Parliament President becoming part of the overall bargain between the main European political families over the distribution of important jobs. As a result, he has had the advantage of enjoying extended tenure and has used it to adopt a more prominent position in European policy discussions. He was, for example, the first European leader to visit Alexis Tsipras, leader of Syriza, after he was elected Greek prime minister in January 2015 and among the first to respond to the UK's 2016 referendum vote to leave the EU.

However, the key agents in the aggregation of interests are the EP's political groups (see also Chapter 15). Since 1952, members have sat not in national groups, but in groups created to reflect shared political affiliation. The structure serves to counteract the logic of the Council within which national interests dominate. It is also a structure that has proved remarkably stable, with members of the European Parliament (MEPs) from new member states normally being assimilated into existing groups rather than forming completely new ones. In 2015, there were eight political groups—only two more than in 1979 before direct elections.

Within the group structure, there is a mixture of competition and cooperation. On the one hand, there is evidence of high levels of group cohesion, with members eager to find agreement with their colleagues in the same group. Hix *et al.* (2007) have drawn attention to a substantial increase in Left–Right competition in the EP. They have shown that party allegiance is much more important than nationality in determining how members vote and that members vote the party line more often than do, for example, legislators in the United States (US). Contrary to the expectations of many, the addition of members from thirteen new member states has not served to undermine significantly the coherence of the groups. In practice, being a member of a group encourages all to follow the group line in most circumstances.[6]

The obligations imposed by the Treaties also create strong incentives for groups to find agreement across party lines. Consider the measures that require an absolute majority of MEPs (half of all members plus one) to vote in favour:

- to reject or adopt amendments to the Council's draft budget or to its position at second reading under the OLP (codecision);
- to give consent to international agreements;
- to approve the accession of new member states; and
- to adopt a motion of censure on the Commission.

No group has anything approaching such a majority: the largest group, the EPP, would be 150 votes short even if all of its members were to be present and were to vote in the same way.

However, it is a system that came under strain in the 2014 European elections. These elections witnessed the arrival of a large number of Eurosceptic members who did not share the views of the main political groups about the desirability of closer integration. Of the eight groups in the Parliament, two were strongly Eurosceptic: the Europe of

Freedom and Direct Democracy, with forty-five MEPs, the largest component of which was the UK Independence Party (UKIP); and the Europe of Nations and Freedom, with thirty-nine members, the strongest element of which was the French *Front national*. In addition, there were two less strongly Eurosceptic groups, the European United Left (known as the GUE), with fifty-two members, and the European Conservatives and Reformists, with seventy-four members, including the British Conservative Party, making it the third largest group in the Parliament. The response of the other four groups, the EPP, the Socialists and Democrats (S&D), the Liberals (ALDE), and the Greens, was to make a distinction between the first and second category of Eurosceptic groups, blocking positions of influence for the two most Eurosceptic groups. As a result, it has proved possible to maintain a structure that enables the Parliament to obtain majorities and to retain an effective voice with regard to other institutions.

Most of the detailed work of the EP is conducted not inside the groups, but rather within twenty policy-specialized committees, the political composition of which closely reflects that of Parliament as a whole. These committees enjoy a high level of autonomy under the Parliament's rules. All legislative proposals are referred directly, without debate, from the plenary to one of the committees, which then organizes the examination of a proposal before it returns to the plenary for a vote. Only one committee can normally be responsible for a proposal (a procedure for associating other committees can be applied in special cases) and only its amendments can be considered in plenary. Other committees can table amendments in the responsible committee, but do not get a second chance in plenary. The responsible committee appoints a *rapporteur* who follows a legislative proposal from its inception to the conclusion of the procedure. On the basis of a report prepared by the *rapporteur*, the committee comes to adopt a position that will normally prevail in the plenary, unless the vote in committee is close. In February 2016, for example, the plenary narrowly rejected a proposal by the Environment Committee to veto a plan to temporarily raise the nitrogen oxides emissions limits from diesel cars.

The committees provide an effective mechanism for finding agreement across political groups. But they also embody two other important features that differentiate the Parliament from the Council. First, all committee meetings are—and, since 1999, must be—held in public. The Parliament has traditionally offered a contrast between its own way of operating and the often-less-transparent mechanisms of the Council. The result can be very full meeting rooms, with all those who wish to influence the shape of proposals—lobbyists, national governments, or officials from the Council Secretariat—free to observe the evolution of debate. Second, the detailed work in the committees provides an opportunity for those interests that fail to win the argument in the Council or the Commission to have a second chance. The fact that the Parliament does not necessarily mirror the majorities in the Council, with opposition parties often making up the largest number of MEPs from a member state, means that such efforts to influence policy can sometimes succeed. In both respects, the Parliament offers a distinctive model for reaching political agreement at the EU level.

The European Parliament's role

As a result of the Lisbon Treaty, the Parliament now codecides virtually all normal EU laws, covering ninety Treaty Articles, with the exception of those relating to taxation and the revenue of the EU, for both of which decisions in the Council have to be taken by unanimity. Between 2009 and 2014, codecision constituted 89 per cent of all legislation (European Parliament 2014b). The outline of the legislative process in Figure 6.1 reveals the implications of the procedure for the Parliament.

First, the figure shows that neither Parliament nor Council can be overruled by the other—that is, that there is a significant level of parity between the two institutions. Unless both agree on the outcome of negotiations, there can be no agreement. In practice, there have been very few such cases: in total, since codecision was established in 1993, there have been more than 1,500 laws adopted, but in fewer than ten cases have negotiations failed to lead to an agreement. Both sides have adapted to working with the other to find the way to an accord, which they are then obliged to act together to defend should it be challenged in the Court of Justice, as in the example shortly to be discussed in Box 6.2.

Second, it underlines that agreement can be reached at different moments in the procedure, after one, two, or three readings, the last following a formal conciliation procedure between the two sides. Over time, there has been a relentless move towards reaching agreements earlier in the procedure, without having to go to conciliation. In the five years between 2009 and 2014, those procedures that went to three readings comprised only 2 per cent, whereas those concluded at first reading comprised 85 per cent (European Parliament 2014b). The comparative figures for the period 1999–2004 were 22 per cent and 29 per cent, respectively. In the process, it has proved possible to reduce the length of time that each procedure takes to a total of nineteen months. As we shall see, these changes have raised questions about the procedure's transparency.

Third, the figure shows that different majorities and different time limits apply at different stages of the procedure. Parliament amendments at first reading can be adopted by simple majority, whereas amendments at second reading require an absolute majority of members, which, in a Parliament of 751, totals 376. It is a relatively high hurdle, forcing negotiation between political groups, and establishes a threshold that enables EP negotiators in a conciliation to argue that they speak on behalf of a majority of the institution. However, it has also encouraged the move to first readings, at which stage it is easier to get the plenary to support a position that has been negotiated with the Council despite significant opposition in the Parliament. First-reading agreements are also encouraged by the fact that there are no time limits, so negotiations are not under the same pressure as applies once second reading starts.

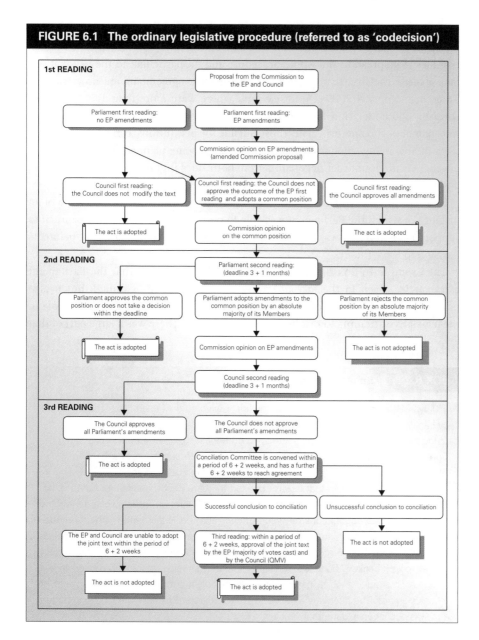

FIGURE 6.1   The ordinary legislative procedure (referred to as 'codecision')

1st READING

Proposal from the Commission to the EP and Council

Parliament first reading: no EP amendments

Parliament first reading: EP amendments

Commission opinion on EP amendments (amended Commission proposal)

Council first reading: the Council does not modify the text

Council first reading: the Council does not approve the outcome of the EP first reading and adopts a common position

Council first reading: the Council approves all amendments

The act is adopted

Commission opinion on the common position

The act is adopted

2nd READING

Parliament second reading: (deadline 3 + 1 months)

Parliament approves the common position or does not take a decision within the deadline

Parliament adopts amendments to the common position by an absolute majority of its Members

Parliament rejects the common position by an absolute majority of its Members

The act is adopted

Commission opinion on EP amendments

The act is not adopted

Council second reading (deadline 3 + 1 months)

3rd READING

The Council approves all Parliament's amendments

The Council does not approve all Parliament's amendments

The act is adopted

Conciliation Committee is convened within a period of 6 + 2 weeks, and has a further 6 + 2 weeks to reach agreement

Successful conclusion to conciliation

Unsuccessful conclusion to conciliation

The EP and Council are unable to adopt the joint text within the period of 6 + 2 weeks

Third reading: within a period of 6 + 2 weeks, approval of the joint text by the EP (majority of votes cast) and by the Council (QMV)

The act is not adopted

The act is not adopted

The act is adopted

Finally, it is worth pointing out that the figure does not mention anywhere (nor does the Treaty) perhaps the most significant institution in the legislative procedure—namely, the trilogues. These provide the most important mechanism through which the Council and Parliament talk to each other and reach negotiated agreements. In the 1990s, conciliations were already starting to be prepared by small groups of negotiators from the Council—in particular, the country holding the presidency—and Parliament, both being assisted by the Commission. The innovation has now spread to the whole procedure and, in particular, to the negotiations that precede the first reading at which point most agreements are now reached. Thus, in the period 2009–14, for example, there were more than 1,500 trilogues covering 350 codecision files. Again, it is a development that raises questions of transparency—no one, especially those outside the institutions, can adequately keep track of how many trilogues are in progress or are being planned at any one time— but there is no doubt that negotiators from both sides find them a very convenient, if not essential, means for reaching agreement.

How has the procedure worked in practice? Box 6.2 provides an example of an instance in which the Parliament was able to persuade a majority in the Council to support a position that was fiercely resisted by one member state, the UK, before its decision to leave the EU.

The example in Box 6.2 illustrates the kind of influence that the Parliament can exercise, even in the face of strong opposition in the Council, but it also points towards the limits of the procedure. First, despite the Parliament's role in the legislative attempts to resolve the financial crisis, there was a large part of that

---

BOX 6.2   Bankers' bonuses

In July 2011, as part of its response to the financial crisis and in particular the role played by banks, the Commission published a proposal for a directive designed to improve the prudential supervision of credit institutions. Both Parliament and Council considered the Commission proposal; in the former, the committee responsible, the Economic and Monetary Affairs Committee (ECON), adopted in May 2012 a draft report outlining its position and making plain that it was opposed to guaranteed bonuses for bankers, because these were not consistent with sound risk management. There followed a lengthy period of trilogue negotiations between Council and the Parliament, led by the Parliament's *rapporteur*, Austrian EPP MEP Othmar Karas. The negotiations were concluded in May 2013—twenty-two months after the proposal was presented—when the Council agreed to limit bankers' bonuses, stipulating that they should not normally exceed annual salaries and should reach twice the annual salary only if authorized by holders of half of a bank's shares. The deal was endorsed by the Parliament plenary the following month and was published in June that year.

The UK government, outvoted in the Council, decided to take the matter to the Court of Justice, arguing that the EU was overstepping its remit by legislating on bonuses. In November 2014, the Court rejected the British argument and George Osborne, then Chancellor, decided to withdraw the challenge. While the issue did not disappear, because banks were tempted to increase basic salaries as a way of circumventing the bonus cap, the European Parliament had nonetheless successfully pushed through a significant change in financial legislation that would have been very unlikely to have emerged had the Council alone decided.

crisis which was out of its reach. The European Semester, the Euro Plus pact, and the Treaty on Stability, Coordination and Governance in Economic and Monetary Union (EMU), including the 'Fiscal Compact', were all overarching issues on which the Parliament could and did express its opinion very vociferously, but on which decisions were in the hands of the European Council and, to a lesser degree, the European Commission. Such structural decisions were much more difficult for the Parliament to get a hold on, despite its increased legislative competences (Fasone 2012). They underline the fact that the Parliament is not faced by a single executive and is often confronted by decisions of the European Council over which it has little or no control.

Second, the trilogue format in the bonus case generated an outcome that found strong support in the institution. However, it is a format that has been the source of a considerable level of disquiet, in part because negotiations before first reading give considerable leeway to *rapporteurs* and those from other political groups negotiating with them, known as 'shadow *rapporteurs*'. Other MEPs have only limited opportunities to express their views or to seek changes before a first-reading vote. Hence there has been much debate as to whether the decisions taken in trilogues are representative of the Parliament as a whole and are therefore legitimate (Farrell and Héritier 2007; Rasmussen 2007; Rasmussen *et al.* 2013). The format is also disputed because it is difficult for outsiders to follow the discussions and influence them. A plenary debate creates more opportunities for those beyond the institutions to make their voices heard. If agreement with the Council has already been reached before the plenary discusses a proposal, there is little scope for external scrutiny. The rules of the Parliament have been modified to make it possible for the plenary to be invited to give a mandate for negotiations with the Council, but the mechanism has been used so far in only a relatively small number of cases.

Third, the opportunity to influence outcomes depends on the Commission presenting proposals for legislation. Following the 2014 elections, the Juncker Commission decided to reduce radically the number of proposals that it would present to the legislative authority, thereby responding to concerns about the extent of EU interference in domestic affairs. It decided in March 2015 to restrict itself to twenty-three new legislative proposals, in contrast with the 316 presented by President Barroso in 2009. Reluctantly, the Parliament acquiesced and thereby effectively limited its opportunity to exercise legislative influence. Previously, it had looked as though the Parliament's enhanced role had brought to an end the Commission's position as the privileged interlocutor of the Council and had undermined the right of the Commission to withdraw a proposal—but such a position of strength depends on there being proposals in the first place. Such proposals cannot come from the Parliament, despite the declared willingness of the Commission to take account of its legislative suggestions. For the moment at least, the ability of the Parliament to influence legislation will therefore be exercised over a smaller range of proposals.

Potential limitations on the Parliament's role have also become clear in other areas. In the case of the budget, the Lisbon Treaty gave the institution an equal say with the

Council over all expenditure (which it had not enjoyed before) and also introduced a conciliation procedure similar to that which applies in codecision. Several commentators have noted that, in practice, these provisions have made it harder for the Parliament to alter the draft budget presented by the Council (Benedetto 2013). Equally, the ability to share responsibility with the Council for the implementation of legislation has opened up a new struggle over whether secondary legislation should be carried by delegated or implementing acts. The choice makes a major difference: delegated acts, like the proposal to raise the emission limits referred to earlier, can be vetoed by the Parliament, but implementing acts escape parliamentary control. A 'victory' in a Treaty does not necessarily resolve an issue where institutions are competing for power and influence.

In contrast with the budget and legislative implementation, there was one area in which few anticipated that the Parliament would exercise influence after Lisbon. The Treaty gave the Parliament the power of consent—that is, the right to say 'yes' or 'no'—on virtually all international agreements between the EU and third countries. In February 2010, only three months after the Treaty came into force, the EP had already rejected the Society for Worldwide Interbank Financial Telecommunication (SWIFT) agreement between the US and the EU. The agreement was designed to give the US access to data about the international money transactions of EU citizens as part of its efforts to combat terrorism. A large majority in the Parliament (378 to 196) considered that the provisions of the agreement did not provide an adequate balance between security needs and civil liberties. In particular, members felt that the agreement was unfair in that it did not apply to US citizens, was not firmly restricted in time, and did not provide for the right of appeal against misuse of data.

A striking feature of the debate was the greater seriousness with which the US government appeared to treat the EP as compared with EU governments. Then US Secretary of State Hilary Clinton rang the President of the EP in advance of the vote to express her concerns and, some weeks after the vote, US Vice-President Joe Biden visited Europe and spoke to the full Parliament to allay its worries, and to prepare for the revision of the agreement. In July 2010, the Parliament gave its approval to a new version that provides for judicial redress, as well as for a limited period of data retention.

Theorizing the democratic deficit

For more than two decades, there has been an ongoing argument about the democratic credentials of the EU. The argument has become even more acute in recent years in the face of major crises that have served to undermine the level of support that the EU enjoys amongst European citizens in nearly all countries. This final section considers how far the Parliament, particularly in light of the changes in its powers discussed so far, can provide the link of accountability between citizens and the EU, and thereby strengthen the legitimacy of the whole institutional structure. It will outline four theoretical perspectives that offer us very different views of the future evolution of the Parliament.

The first and most radical perspective is often referred to as the 'no demos' thesis. It suggests that democracy is a chimera outside the national context because the peoples of Europe are not bound together in the same way as national communities—which form a *demos*, or common people or populace, and share common histories and cultures (Cederman 2001; Siedentop 2001). When it comes to big decisions such as whether to provide financial support to Greece or to admit more refugees from Syria, European citizens will always look to their national politicians and not to MEPs. If there is indeed no European demos, then there can be no democracy at the European level. The EP can be only an expensive irrelevance that cannot hope to reinforce accountability in the EU, however much its powers are increased.

Proponents of the 'no demos' thesis argue that there is no evidence of the loyalties of European citizens being transferred upwards from the national level. Thus the development of the powers of the Parliament has not been matched by an increase in participation in European elections. As Table 6.3 shows, the overall level of turnout has declined at every election since 1979 and fell again in 2014, if only by a small amount, to 42.6 per cent. The figures for individual countries vary considerably, but are consistently lower than turnouts at elections to national parliaments.

One response is to point out that EU citizens recognize that more is at stake in national elections, where governments are made and undone, and so are bound to show less interest in EP elections, which have a limited effect on the shape of the EU executive. Moreover, because the EU is not characterized by a classic separation of powers, with a recognizable and distinct executive and legislature, the difference in electoral behaviour is unlikely to change markedly. Equally, one can argue that the level of democracy in the EU is a matter of degree, with the Parliament offering a level of accountability that would be absent if it did not exist. However, the power of the 'no demos' thesis is reflected in the growing strength of populist movements in many EU countries that contest the value of the EU and its institutions, and which would seem to prefer a return to international cooperation limited to the non-binding variety of the kind found in the Council of Europe.

A second perspective suggests that accountability in the EU can be increased by a more developed level of politicization. The collective character of decisions in the EU makes it difficult for voters to identify whom to reward or punish for particular policy outcomes when they participate in European elections. Hence people will be more inclined to vote in European elections if and when they see that it can make a difference, and such a change requires the differences between parties at European level to be made clearer. Hix (2008) made this argument in advance of the 2009 European elections when he offered a scenario of political competition for the post of Commission President. It was a philosophy that guided the *Spitzenkandidaten* campaign in 2014—the first time that the electorate was given a chance to see different presidential candidates in advance of the EP elections. Here was an opportunity to introduce a more politicized, less consensual style into the appointment of the President of the European

TABLE 6.3   Turnout in European Parliament elections, 1979–2014

	1979	1981	1984	1987	1989	1994	1995	1996	1999	2004	2007	2009	2013	2014
EU	62.0	–	59.0	–	58.4	56.7	–	–	49.5	45.5	–	43.0		42.6
Belgium	91.4	–	90.7	–	90.7	90.7	–	–	91.0	90.8	–	90.4		89.6
Luxembourg	88.9	–	88.8	–	87.4	88.6	–	–	87.3	91.3	–	90.8		85.6
Malta	–	–	–	–	–	–	–	–	–	82.4	–	78.8		74.8
Greece	–	81.5	80.6	–	80.0	73.2	–	–	70.2	63.2	–	52.6		60.0
Italy	85.6	–	82.5	–	81.1	73.6	–	–	69.8	71.7	–	65.0		57.2
Denmark	47.8	–	52.4	–	46.2	52.9	–	–	50.5	47.9	–	59.5		56.3
Ireland	63.6	–	47.6	–	68.3	44.0	–	–	50.2	58.6	–	58.6		52.4
Sweden	–	–	–	–	–	–	41.6	–	38.8	37.8	–	45.5		51.1
Germany	65.7	–	56.8	–	62.3	60.0	–	–	45.2	43.0	–	43.3		48.1
Lithuania	–	–	–	–	–	–	–	–	–	48.4	–	21.0		47.3
Austria	–	–	–	–	–	–	–	67.7	49.4	42.4	–	46.0		45.4
Cyprus	–	–	–	–	–	–	–	–	–	72.5	–	59.4		44.0
Spain	–	–	–	68.5	54.7	59.1	–	–	63.0	45.1	–	44.9		43.8
France	60.7	–	56.7	–	48.8	52.7	–	–	46.8	42.8	–	40.6		42.4
Finland	–	–	–	–	–	–	–	57.6	30.1	39.4	–	38.6		39.1
Netherlands	58.1	–	51.0	–	47.5	35.7	–	–	30.0	39.3	–	36.7		37.3

Estonia	–	32.3	–	–	–	–	26.8	–	43.9	36.5
Bulgaria	–	–	–	–	–	–	–	29.2	39.0	35.8
UK	–	32.6	–	36.4	36.4	24.0	38.5	–	34.7	35.6
Portugal	–	–	72.4	51.1	35.5	39.9	38.6	–	36.8	33.7
Romania	–	–	–	–	–	–	–	29.5	27.7	32.4
Latvia	–	–	–	–	–	–	41.3	–	53.7	30.2
Hungary	–	–	–	–	–	–	38.5	–	36.3	29.0
Croatia	–	–	–	–	–	–	–	20.8		25.2
Slovenia	–	–	–	–	–	–	28.3	–	28.4	24.5
Poland	–	–	–	–	–	–	20.9	–	24.5	23.8
Czech Republic	–	–	–	–	–	–	28.3	–	28.2	18.2
Slovakia	–	–	–	–	–	–	17.0	–	19.6	13.0

Source: Adapted from Corbett (2016)

Commission whereby the winning party or parties would have a chance to get their electoral programme implemented in the same way as would happen at national level.

However, there are significant obstacles to such an approach. It requires that national parties give their full support to nominations for Commission President (in the UK, in 2014, none of the three main parties wanted to see 'their' candidate campaign in the country). All parties are likely to be reluctant fully to support nominations that weaken their own control of the electoral process. They are, for example, unlikely to devote financial resources to promote a candidate who is not of their nationality and whose manifesto they may not fully agree with. In addition, the Commission is not an executive in the same sense as a national government. As this volume makes plain, the EU is marked by executive pluralism, with the balance of power evolving in favour of the European Council. It remains outside the traditional mechanisms of parliamentary control and accountability, despite the regular appearances of its President in front of the Parliament. Hence, although the Parliament's success in obliging the European Council to propose Jean-Claude Juncker as President of the Commission may well have ensured that a similar procedure will be followed in 2019 and may generate more interest in the EP elections, it will not make the Parliament the overseer of the whole executive apparatus of the EU as national parliaments are in their own countries. Elections to the European Parliament can never provide the opportunity to 'throw the rascals out' in the same sense as national elections do. This point was not lost during the campaigns ahead of the UK's 2016 referendum on EU membership, in which the EP's claims to democratic legitimacy were insufficient to counter concerns that the EU was run by an 'unelected elite'. It is thus difficult to see how the EP can become more than part of the accountability structure of the EU.

A third perspective suggests that the partial hold of the EP on the executive necessarily means that national parliaments need to have their role reinforced (Auel 2007). It is a point of view widely shared at national level and was one of the least contested of the positions that the UK put forward in 2015–16 in its effort to renegotiate its terms of membership. Some have argued that a second parliamentary chamber, composed of national parliamentarians, should be established at European level. This was the position of Giscard d'Estaing during the Constitutional Convention between 2002 and 2003, but it did not win majority support. However, the Lisbon Treaty did reinforce the position of national parliaments and gave them, for the first time, a Treaty-based role in the legislative procedure. They are now explicitly invited to state whether a draft legislative act complies with the principle of subsidiarity, whereby action at European level should be restricted to areas in which an EU objective can be better achieved at the Union level. If sufficient parliamentary chambers consider the principle to be breached, then the EU institutions are obliged to confirm whether they think the proposal should go forward. So far, a majority of national parliaments objecting to an EU proposal in this way has been found on only two occasions, but some would like to go further and give national parliaments collectively the right of veto over legislation.

It is not clear that a veto for national parliaments of this kind will necessarily improve the accountability of the EU institutions. It gives the parliaments the possibility of substituting themselves for their national governments in the Council and thereby makes it still less clear who governs in the EU. It is also difficult to see how such a power can be reconciled with the existing power of the EP and the Council as the bicameral legislature of the EU. What would full-blooded 'tricameralism' look like? Could national parliaments act at any point in the procedure and would their power be limited to saying 'no'? Could they introduce amendments? The risk of creating a third layer in the legislative process is that it would be still harder to reach agreements and for those outcomes to be explained to national electorates. Nevertheless, there is no doubting the pressure to give national parliaments a wider role that would certainly weaken the position of the Parliament as the privileged interlocutor of the Council.

Finally, we might ask, from a wider international relations (IR) perspective, how far the EU has progressed in establishing a democratic system. The remarkable evolution of the EP is not matched within any other framework of international cooperation. By comparison, the role of PACE, for example, has hardly changed since its inception in the late 1940s. As Corbett (2012: 157) has commented, 'the EU is unique in how far it goes to try to apply democratic principles above the nation state'. It is a system that provides for very extensive involvement of parliamentary assemblies in the adoption of legislation, which assures a high level of parliamentary scrutiny of the action of the executive and which goes to considerable lengths to guarantee the rights of minorities. The democratic added value of the system derives from the high premium that it places on the search for compromise among competing interests, and the opportunities it offers to challenge decisions and procedures.

Two examples illustrate how the democratic development of the system extends beyond strengthening the EP. The Lisbon Treaty included provision for the 'European citizens' initiative', which now enables 1 million citizens from seven member states to participate directly in the development of EU policies, by calling on the Commission to make a legislative proposal. The first such initiative to gain the necessary number and range of signatures called for the right to water to be guaranteed to all citizens (European Commission 2016). Similarly, the European Ombudsman, elected every five years by the Parliament, provides a means to challenge the way in which the institutions are working. Emily O'Reilly, the present Ombudsman, for example, began an inquiry in May 2015 into the use of trilogues in codecision, a topic discussed earlier, with a view to promoting the transparency of the legislative process (European Ombudsman 2015).

At the same time, many outside the Parliament continue to see its evolution as an important part of improving the democratic credentials of the EU. The German and French finance ministers, for example, recognizing the risk of the eurozone not being subject to adequate democratic control, have argued for a eurozone Parliament, alongside or within the EP, underlining once again that member states find it easier to look for solutions to the 'democratic deficit' in further development of the existing parliamentary structures. Whatever its limitations, the Parliament remains, from this perspective, central to making the EU more democratic now, just as it has been for the last sixty years.

These four perspectives are in competition with each other both as sets of ideas and as the source of practical proposals for reform. It is the relative success of each that will determine the place of the Parliament inside the EU over the next decade.

Conclusion

This chapter has pointed towards four general insights into the workings of the Parliament. First, it has shown the power of the democratic idea as driving change in the Parliament's powers. Even those governments opposed to reinforcing the position of the Parliament have found it extremely difficult to resist, because they have not easily been able to formulate an alternative for addressing the 'democratic deficit'. The force of such ideas has to be integrated into any explanation of institutional change.

Second, we have seen that the shape of the EU's institutions is 'path-dependent', or heavily influenced by earlier decisions. Direct elections can be traced back to the provisions of the ECSC Treaty in the early 1950s. Similarly, the establishment of co-decision in the Maastricht Treaty established a trajectory for the Parliament effectively to become one branch of a bicameral legislature under Lisbon.

Third, the chapter has contested the notion that major decisions in the EU are taken exclusively by governments. The Parliament has been able to use its legislative powers to alter the shape of outcomes sought by the Council and has started to exercise influence over the choice of the Commission President, as well as the shape of the Commission. Such developments are difficult to reconcile with an intergovernmentalist perspective (Pollak and Slominski 2015: 261). At the same time, the framework of executive pluralism within which the Parliament operates does not suggest that the EU is evolving towards a classic separation of powers between an executive and a legislature.

Finally, we have stressed the importance of consensus mechanisms within the Parliament, as well as those that link it to the other institutions. The result is the spreading of responsibility to ensure that support for policy change is broad amongst a very diverse set of competing interests. Democracy in the EU seems unlikely to develop on the basis of the same kind of majoritarian processes as exist at national level.

 ENDNOTES

1. Art. 17.7 TEU.
2. Art. 21 of the ECSC Treaty.
3. Case 138/79 *SA Roquette Frères v Council of the European Communities* ECLI:EU:C:1980:249 (*Isoglucose*).

4. *Ibid.*, 3360, emphasis added.
5. Art. 7 TEU.
6. See also Ringe (2010).

FURTHER READING

There is a growing range of books and articles on the EP. Corbett *et al.* (2016) is the ninth edition of a book that provides a detailed account of the internal workings of the institution. Judge and Earnshaw (2008) place the role of the Parliament in a wider perspective, considering its formal and informal influence, as well as its effectiveness as a representative body. Rittberger (2005) offers an in-depth analysis of the reasons why governments have been willing to delegate powers to the institution. Ringe (2010) considers how policy choices are made inside the Parliament and why the political groups are able to overcome their internal heterogeneity. Rasmussen *et al.* (2013) provide a wide-ranging set of views of the impact of codecision twenty years after its introduction. Corbett (1998) offers a more historical account of how the institution consciously set out to develop its powers during the 1980s and 1990s—a view that can be compared with Vedel (1972), a report that looked forward to an unknown future for the institution.

Corbett, R. (1998) *The European Parliament's Role in Closer Integration* (Basingstoke: Palgrave).

Corbett, R., Jacobs, F., and Neville, D. (2016) *The European Parliament* (9th edn, London: John Harper).

European Commission (2016) 'European Citizens' Initiative, Official Register', available online at http://ec.europa.eu/citizens-initiative/public/basic-facts

European Ombudsman (2015) 'Ombudsman opens investigation to promote transparency of "trilogies" ', Press release no. 9/2015, 28 May.

Judge, D., and Earnshaw, D. (2008) *The European Parliament* (2nd edn, London: Palgrave Macmillan).

Rasmussen, A., Burns, C., and Reh, C. (2013) 'Twenty years of legislative codecision in the European Union', *Journal of European Public Policy*, 20/7: Special Issue.

Ringe, N. (2010) *Who Decides, and How? Preferences, Uncertainty, and Policy Choice in the European Parliament* (Oxford: Oxford University Press).

Rittberger, B. (2005) *Building Europe's Parliament: Democratic Representation beyond the Nation-State* (Oxford: Oxford University Press).

Vedel, G. (1972) 'Report of the Working Party Examining the Problem of the Enlargement of the Powers of the European Parliament', *Bulletin of the European Communities*, S4/72 (the 'Vedel Report').

WEB LINKS

http://www.europarl.europa.eu
The EP's website provides up-to-date material on the workings of the institution. It is divided into five sections, looking at the news from the Parliament, what the EP is and how

it is structured, who the MEPs are, what the EP produces (reports, amendments, minutes, records of debates, etc.), and an online video link to parliamentary debates.

http://www.europarltv.europa.eu

Since 2008, the Parliament has also run a web television channel that offers (in twenty-three languages, using subtitles) background interviews and analysis on what is happening in the Parliament, and enables the viewer to discover more about how the Parliament works. The channel is fully integrated into the Parliament's main website.

http://votewatch.eu

The Parliament website hosts access to Votewatch, a project run from the London School of Economics and Political Science (LSE) that provides a means of checking how MEPs have voted, as well as verifying how cohesive the groups have been on particular issues and over time.

CHAPTER 7

The Court of Justice: European integration and judicial institutions

Niamh Nic Shuibhne

▌ Summary

This chapter provides an overview of the structure and functions of the Court of Justice of the European Union (EU). It outlines how the Court is composed, 'who' the Court is, and how judges are appointed. It then focuses on what the Court does and how the Court functions in a practical sense. How is its workload organized? How long does it take before the Court issues a judgment? The chapter reflects changes brought about by successive EU enlargements and the Lisbon Treaty. The Court was not radically reformed by Lisbon; arguably, it is the sheer increase in its size as a result of EU enlargement that created the practical difficulties that the Court now faces. The wider political environment

Cont. ➤

Cont.

in which the Court operates is another important factor to consider. For example, the Court has been called upon to evaluate some of the regulatory steps taken to manage the ongoing euro crisis, and to consider the reach of EU citizenship and shared financial solidarity in the midst of increasingly divided opinion on the enduring worth of free movement rights. The chapter also offers some reflections on the nature and influence of the Court, and locates it within a wider institutional picture in terms of its relationship with the Strasbourg-based European Court of Human Rights (ECtHR).

Introduction

The Court of Justice of the European Union (CJEU) is the EU's judicial institution. Although confusingly depicted in the singular, the CJEU actually comprises two distinct courts: the Court of Justice and the General Court. Both courts have their institutional seat in Luxembourg, in a burgeoning complex of buildings. Because of the broad span of its work and also its particular connection with national courts through the preliminary rulings procedure, this chapter concentrates primarily on the Court of Justice. However, particular features of the functioning and tasks of the General Court will be addressed where relevant.

History and development

The Court of Justice—often still referred to as the 'European Court of Justice' (ECJ)—is the most well known of the EU courts and it is the EU's original judicial institution. It was established in 1952 to resolve disputes for the European Coal and Steel Community (ECSC). Its role was then consolidated and expanded with the adoption of the Treaty of Rome, when it became the sole judicial institution of the European Economic Community (EEC) too. Mainly because of long-held concerns about workload, a second court, the Court of First Instance (CFI), was established in 1989. The Lisbon Treaty renamed this second court the 'General Court'.

Through reforms implemented by the Nice Treaty, the European Community (EC) Treaty was amended in 2003 to provide also for the establishment of 'specialized courts'. The intention was to offer a structure for the creation of new courts that would focus only on certain types of case. On that basis, the Civil Service Tribunal was created in 2005. The purpose of this seven-judge court was to resolve employment disputes between the EU and the staff of its institutions, bodies, and agencies. However, both the cases and most personnel of the Tribunal were transferred to the General Court in September 2016.

Structure and functions

The composition of the Court

Both the Court of Justice and the General Court have always included one judge from each EU member state, but this principle has been articulated as an express requirement only since the Nice Treaty. However, the wording of the Treaty reflected a difference between the rule for the Court of Justice ('one judge from each Member State') and for the General Court ('*at least* one judge per Member State').[1] In 2015, the European Parliament (EP) and Council adopted significant reforms to double—through appointments to be made in three stages—the number of General Court judges by 1 September 2019.[2] At the completion of this reform process, it is intended that the General Court will consist of two judges from each member state.

Inspired by a similar feature of the judicial process in some of the member states and reflecting the French legal tradition in particular, the Court of Justice also has eleven Advocates General (AGs).[3] When a case that arrives before the Court is thought to raise an especially complex or new legal question, an AG is instructed to prepare an advisory opinion to assist the Court in reaching its decision. These opinions set out in detail both the factual background to the case and the possible legal options available to the Court. But the AG's views are not binding; the Court is always free to depart from either the reasoning used or the actual decision proposed—but, typically, it does not. However, while we often speak of the Court 'following' its AG, in fact, judgments rarely make express reference to opinions.

At present, six member states—France, Germany, Italy, Poland, Spain, and the United Kingdom (UK), until it formally exits the EU—have a permanent AG. The remaining five spaces rotate as non-renewable six-year positions across the other twenty-two member states. Notwithstanding the contrast with the Treaty-guaranteed equality of member state representation that is built into judicial appointments to the Court of Justice, the unevenness of the AG appointment process has never caused serious political discord. This situation may be contrasted with tensions evident in the procedure for appointments to the executive board of the European Central Bank (ECB), as discussed in Chapter 9.

The General Court does not have distinct AGs; rather, its rules of procedure provide that General Court judges can themselves perform this function. They do so on an ad hoc basis, whenever an advisory opinion is felt to be necessary.

Judicial appointments

At the time of writing, the Court of Justice is composed of twenty-three male and five female judges, with nine male and two female AGs. The age range of its members spans 39 to 78, and members' biographies reflect a diverse range of professional backgrounds in legal practice, public service, other (national and international) institutional roles, and academia.[4] The judges themselves elect a President of the Court of Justice and a President of the General Court, each for a renewable three-year term. Koen Lenaerts, Belgium's judge, was elected President of the Court of Justice in 2015; Marc Jaeger, Luxembourg judge at the General Court, first became its President in 2007 and was re-elected for a fourth term in 2016.

How are judges and AGs chosen and appointed? Most importantly of all, they are required by the Treaty to be 'persons whose independence is beyond doubt'.[5] Independence is an essential characteristic of the judicial function in general. In the EU context, each member state is represented by having 'its' judge at both the Court of Justice and General Court, but, critically, each judge must then be an independent member of the EU judiciary.

Judicial independence at the CJEU is enhanced by the fact that both courts operate as *collegiate* institutions. The publication of just one judgment in each case exemplifies this collective responsibility, by ensuring that the views or arguments put forward by any of the individual judges when the case was being discussed are never revealed. This feature is a point of contrast with most national judicial systems, in which dissenting opinions, directly attributed to the relevant individual judge, are often published alongside the majority judgment. Interestingly, dissenting opinions are also part of the system at the ECtHR.

Apart from the five rotational AG positions, all other judicial appointments are made for a period of six years and are renewable. Partial replacements of Court of Justice and General Court membership take place every three years. This practice is designed to ensure a degree of institutional continuity notwithstanding any new appointments.

According to the Treaty, all judges and AGs must be appointed 'by common accord of the Member States'.[6] Since Lisbon, however, a panel must first assess the suitability of proposed judicial candidates. The panel must consist of seven persons chosen from among former members of the Court of Justice and the General Court, members of national supreme courts, and lawyers of recognized competence, one of whom shall be proposed by the EP. This new step in the approval of judicial appointments fits with broader Lisbon ambitions of greater accountability, representation, and transparency.

Finally, there is a subtly nuanced difference in the Treaty-specified basis of qualification for judicial appointment to each court. The requirement of independence is common to all CJEU judicial appointments. To be eligible for appointment to the Court of Justice, candidates must 'possess the qualifications required for appointment to the *highest* judicial offices in their respective countries or be jurisconsults of recognised competence'.[7] This requirement would typically be understood to mean eligibility for supreme court positions. For the General Court, it is possession of 'the ability required for appointment to *high* judicial office'.[8] This sliding scale of required expertise reflects a sort of hierarchy. More specifically, it suggests that the Court of Justice sits at the institutional apex of the EU judicial architecture, with a line of authority then flowing downwards to the General Court. This notion of a functional hierarchy of courts fits with how we understand national legal systems too.

What the Court does

Lawyers talk about what courts can and cannot do in the language of 'jurisdiction'. A court's jurisdiction normally has two important meanings: substantive and procedural. First, *substantive jurisdiction* means the subject matter on which a court is permitted to hear disputes. The Court of Justice and General Court can hear cases on any aspect of EU law unless the EU Treaties expressly exclude something from their jurisdiction. One of the most basic rules here is that disputes must typically have a factor linking them to EU law, often as a result of the given situation having a cross-border dimension. In other words, the CJEU normally has no jurisdiction to hear disputes in which the facts are wholly internal to one member state. The Treaty provides for only very limited exceptions to this general rule, for example claims about gender discrimination in employment.

The Lisbon Treaty made some fundamental changes to substantive jurisdiction. These reforms were generally praised for their unification of the different parts of the EU's post-Maastricht structure (notably, through the merging of the EC and EU) and for managing the implications of this unification in policy terms. Under the former three-pillar EU structure, the jurisdiction of the Court of Justice and General Court was very limited with respect to police and judicial cooperation in criminal matters, and also disputes involving visas, asylum, and immigration. Since 2014, after a transitional period of five years, these limitations have largely dissolved and the Court has greater jurisdiction on legal questions that arise from action in these policy fields. This development is subject to an important exception, in that the Court cannot review:

... the validity or proportionality of operations carried out by the police or other law-enforcement services of a member state or the exercise of the responsibilities incumbent upon member states with regard to the maintenance of law and order and the safeguarding of internal security.[9]

This proviso recognizes a protected sphere of national security sovereignty for the member states.

Restrictions on jurisdiction also remain in place in relation to common foreign and security policy (CFSP). The default position here is that the Court does *not* have jurisdiction, but the Lisbon Treaty did introduce significant exceptions. The Court does have jurisdiction to monitor the delimitation of Union and member state competences in this field. Again, this provision fits with the broader Lisbon Treaty objective of setting out more clearly how the exercise of exclusive and shared competences should be worked out. The Court may also hear actions brought against Council decisions providing for restrictive measures against natural or legal persons in connection with, for example, combating terrorism. Overall, this enhanced role for the Court reflects its significant contribution towards ensuring both institutional and member state compliance with principles of constitutional importance, such as the boundaries of EU competence and the protection of fundamental rights.

Second, the jurisdiction of the CJEU has an important *procedural* meaning. The legal vocabulary for procedural jurisdiction speaks of 'forms of action' before the Court. This boils down to two critical questions: what types of legal action can each of the courts hear; and who can initiate them?

As a general rule, and addressing the second question first, the Court of Justice is typically the court to which only the EU institutions and the member states have access for *direct actions* (that is, legal actions actually initiated in the Court of Justice itself). By contrast, the General Court is the forum in which direct actions initiated by a natural (that is, human) person or legal person (that is, a company or an organization) are heard. Because of this, the substantive jurisdiction of the General Court mainly produces cases connected to commercial practice, such as competition proceedings or disputes concerning intellectual property rights. Both the complexity and volume of these cases contributed to the ongoing expansion of the General Court.

However, other disputes arrive in Luxembourg following their initiation elsewhere. The most important of these *indirect actions* before the Court of Justice is the preliminary rulings procedure (see 'The preliminary rulings procedure').

The Court of Justice also has jurisdiction to hear appeals (only on points of law, not fact) against judgments of the General Court. This *appellate jurisdiction* is a further marker of hierarchy within the CJEU.

Finally, the Court of Justice also has jurisdiction to hear a number of special procedures, such as disciplinary actions, for example dismissal of the European Ombudsman, or actions for damages against EU institutions.

To unpack the first question in more detail—*what* the forms of action are—the following sections first look at two direct actions (enforcement proceedings before the Court of Justice and actions for judicial review), then outline the key features of the preliminary rulings procedure—a vitally important indirect action.

Enforcement proceedings

Legal discourse on EU integration often centres on the idea and objective of *effectiveness*. In other words, if the EU were a purely political organization, without any input from law or any culture of legal obligation, could European integration have been achieved as effectively or intensively as it has been to date? Is it more effective to persuade member states to act in a certain way or to force them to do so? After all, it is a hallmark of modern Western democracies that their courts are obeyed (Weiler 1999).

In fact, enforcement proceedings (also known as 'infringement proceedings') combine both political persuasion and legal obligation.[10] The action is initiated against a member state when there is an alleged failure to fulfil binding obligations to which the state has committed under EU law. In theory, member states can launch proceedings against each other, but the Commission initiates almost all of these actions in practice (see Box 7.1).

BOX 7.1	**Enforcing state commitments**

The enforcement proceedings mechanism provides an interesting example of how the Commission and the Court work together and share responsibility for ensuring that the member states fulfil the obligations they assume under EU law. The political phase managed by the Commission is essential. Ultimately, however, the bite of law lies in wait.

The Commission can commence infringement proceedings against a member state either on its own initiative or in response to a complaint that it has received. Failure to fulfil an obligation can arise only where the relevant commitment is a legally binding one. The mechanism enables, and indeed encourages, the resolution of enforcement issues through channels of political negotiation between the Commission and the state involved. The judicial phase is, in other words, the stage of last resort. Moreover, even when disputes have not been resolved satisfactorily at the political stage, the Commission still retains discretion about whether to proceed to the Court of Justice or not. The political stage involves a series of letters and other communications (detailed in the Treaty) between the Commission and the relevant member state. Firm time limits within which a state must respond to the case set out against it by the Commission are also stipulated.

If the situation is not resolved to the satisfaction of the Commission after the necessary political steps have been exhausted, the Commission may then decide to go ahead and launch legal proceedings against the member state. If the Court of Justice finds against the member state, which it does in more than a hundred enforcement actions annually (typically, more than half of all such cases initiated), and if, even then, the state fails to remedy the breach of its EU obligations, the Commission can embark on a second round of enforcement proceedings, with the added step that the Court can then impose steep financial sanctions.

The Commission has published guidance on the calculation of these financial penalties, which can involve per diem penalty payments or lump sums. The Commission recommends the amount of financial sanction that it wishes to apply in each case, but the decision rests ultimately with the Court. However, the Court can vary, but not exceed, the amount proposed by the Commission. Moreover, if the infringement of EU law at issue involves a state's failure to notify the Commission that it has transposed an EU directive (which it is legally obliged to do), sanctions may be imposed at the end of 'round one'. Member states defaulting on their obligations under EU law are regularly presented with a 'bill' running into hundreds of millions of euro.[11]

Actions for judicial review

Direct actions for judicial review require the input of the Court in determining the legal propriety of binding EU acts (a regulation or directive, for example).[12] As noted, member states and the other EU institutions initiate their actions for judicial review before the Court of Justice. Actions brought by natural or legal persons must begin in the General Court.

The purpose of judicial review is to ensure that the EU legislative institutions comply with Treaty rules (on law-making procedures and voting requirements, for example) and with general principles of EU law (such as the requirements of proportionality and non-discrimination on the grounds of nationality) when carrying out their law-making activities—in legal vocabulary, to check that they have not acted *ultra vires* (that is, beyond the extent of their authority) in fulfilling their functions. The ultimate objective of the action is to have either the entire EU act or the offending part of that act annulled.

Four conditions must be met in order to bring a successful action for judicial review. First, the act in question must be a 'reviewable act'. The Court has interpreted this provision to mean that the act must be intended to produce legal effects. A directive or regulation will always fall into this category, but even a letter, for example, might be looked at by the Court and tested for any binding legal intention.

Second, anyone bringing an action for judicial review must have *locus standi* (that is, the legal standing to do so). Different actors have different levels or degrees of legal standing before—and therefore different levels of access to—the Court. Member states, the Council, the Commission, and the EP are *privileged applicants*—that is, they can challenge *any* legal act before the Court of Justice; importantly, they do not have to show that the act has any particular impact on them. The Court of Auditors, the ECB, and the Committee of the Regions (CoR) are *semi-privileged applicants*. This means that they can challenge acts only on the basis of protecting their prerogatives—that is, the act in question must have a potential impact on their own powers or functions.

The legal standing of natural and legal persons is the most difficult—and contentious—aspect of judicial review. No court is an absolutely open forum; all litigants have to establish their legal standing to bring an action for judicial review in national courts too. The critical question is whether the conditions for access to the courts, and thus access to justice, are properly balanced between the need to ensure an appropriate workload for courts (on the basis of the 'floodgates' argument—that is, that if courts were completely open, then they would be overwhelmed with mostly nonsensical claims), on the one hand, and appropriate respect for the fundamentally important right to effective judicial protection, on the other.

Natural or legal persons normally have standing to challenge acts that have been directly addressed to them (for a company, for example, a decision of the Commission imposing a fine on it for breach of EU competition rules). If natural or legal persons want to challenge acts of more general application (such as an EU regulation or directive), the odds are stacked against them. In such a scenario, the person in question must fulfil the criteria of 'direct and individual concern', which signify two distinct tests.

The test of *direct concern* demands a clear relationship of cause and effect between the act in question and its impact on the applicant, with no intervening discretion on the part of member states. A significant consequence of this test is that it rules out any individual challenges to EU directives through the direct action for judicial review, since directives must *always* be transposed into national law through the adoption of national (thus intervening) measures. EU regulations, on the other hand, are self-executing: as soon as the institutions adopt them, they have legal effect in the member states. This direct applicability suggests that individuals have standing to challenge their legality before the General Court. Normally, however, the second test—of *individual concern*—rules this out. The Court of Justice has determined that any applicant seeking to challenge an EU regulation will have to show himself, herself, or itself to be a member of a closed class—that is, a finite group of persons affected by the measure to which not even a future or hypothetical expansion of membership is possible.[13] Ironically, then, the greater the number of persons affected or *potentially* affected by an EU measure, the smaller the chance that any of them can actually challenge that act directly before the General Court.

There has been stringent criticism of this situation within the academic literature and also from some of the Court of Justice's own AGs.[14] Nevertheless, the Court has held fast to its narrow understanding of direct, and especially individual, concern. First, it has always stressed that the system of judicial remedies available under EU law must be looked at in the round. Thus, although individuals have more limited access to the Court of Justice through direct actions, the possibility of raising questions about the validity of EU law in national courts through the preliminary rulings procedure has always existed in parallel. But this solution is an imperfect one, since it demands that someone must get involved in a national dispute in the first place and must then persuade the national court about the possibility of illegality, so that the court will decide to refer the question to Luxembourg.

Second, the Court of Justice has pointed out repeatedly that the tests of direct and individual concern are both in the Treaty. In its view, if the member states wish to amend the Treaty so as to soften the rules on legal standing, it is entirely within their powers to do so. This claim is difficult to argue with and, in fact, the Treaty was finally altered to some extent at Lisbon to enable natural or legal persons to 'institute proceedings against . . . a regulatory act which is of direct concern to them and does not entail implementing measures'.[15] It was hoped that this change would cover EU regulations, thus going some way towards restoring the balance in favour of judicial protection and lending more credence to the Court's claim about the completeness of the EU forms of action when they are taken together as a comprehensive system of remedies. However, the Court has continued to take a strict stance to the scope of legal standing in its first interpretations of a 'regulatory act'.

The third of the four conditions for direct actions of judicial review is that the applicant must adhere to a strict time limit: the action must be initiated within two months (normally, of the publication of the measure or of its notification to the applicant).

The fourth and final condition is that there must be actual grounds for review. In other words, the applicant must have good arguments regarding the illegality of the act being challenged. This test might involve, for example, an argument that the institution in question did not have legal authority to adopt the act being challenged, or that the act is not compatible with the substantive provisions of the Treaty on which it has been based.[16]

Overall, if the challenge is well founded, the Court will declare that the act (or the relevant part of the act) is void. The action for judicial review thus represents the provision of legal checks on the exercise of political power. EU law sets down the substantive and procedural parameters within which the institutions can develop and implement their policy choices; the action for judicial review enables the Court to ensure that these parameters are respected.

The preliminary rulings procedure

Accounting for more than half of the Court's entire caseload,[17] its judgments under the preliminary rulings procedure have pronounced some of its most significant statements on the nature and purpose of EU law. The profoundly important principles of the primacy of EU law (meaning that, in the case of a conflict, EU law must prevail over national law) and of its direct effect (meaning that EU law can be invoked directly by litigants in national court proceedings) both emerged in cases decided under this form of indirect action.

The purpose underlying the preliminary rulings procedure is to ensure uniform application and interpretation of EU law by the national courts and tribunals in all of the EU member states.[18] The procedure establishes a vital line of communication between national judicial institutions and the Court of Justice that can be invoked in two instances:

- *interpretation* of the Treaties or of acts of the institutions, bodies, offices, or agencies of the Union; and
- assessment of the *validity* of those acts.

In the former scenario, a national court or tribunal is typically asking the Court of Justice for clarification on the meaning or scope of EU law to the extent that EU law is relevant to the dispute before it. In situations concerning validity, the national court is essentially raising the same questions as those considered under a direct action for annulment—but, crucially, without the same constraints regarding legal standing or time limits. For example, if the legality of an EU directive adopted thirty years ago is relevant to a case before a national court involving two private individuals, then that court can still send questions about the validity of the measure to Luxembourg today.

Whether the issue before the national court relates to interpretation or validity, that body formulates a question, or questions, for transmission to the Court of Justice. The Court publishes an online guide to help national courts in making their references. It will not answer questions in a limited range of circumstances: those in which there is no genuine dispute at national level (that is, a case contrived purely to ascertain the Court's interpretation of EU law); those in which the questions sent are too vague; or those in which the referring court has not supplied the Court with sufficient information.

The ruling given by the Court of Justice under this procedure is 'preliminary' in the sense that the practical application of the ruling—that is, the final resolution of the national dispute—rests with the referring national court. Indeed, proceedings before that body have to be suspended pending the Court of Justice's judgment. But that judgment *is* legally binding on the national court: the latter is the only court that can resolve the dispute, but it must apply the legal interpretation given by Luxembourg. The Court has also established that an interpretation of EU law given in the context of one particular preliminary ruling has binding legal effects throughout all member states in any future cases. The Court has thus constructed a system akin to precedent within EU case law.

The average duration of the Court of Justice phase, from receipt of question(s) to publication of judgment, is now approximately fifteen months. The reduction of delay in Court proceedings has emerged as a clear institutional priority for the CJEU, as evidenced by its annual reports. The Court of Justice's rules of procedure also make provision for both an accelerated preliminary rulings procedure and an urgent preliminary rulings procedure. The latter mechanism was first used in 2008. It has enabled the Court, where the requisite conditions for urgency are genuinely established (five times in 2015), to respond to questions from national courts in just over two months. These cases often involve questions about compliance with fundamental rights in situations of detention or the wrongful removal of children across borders in family disputes.

As for the interpretation of EU law, most national courts have discretion about whether or not to refer questions to the Court of Justice. National judges are obliged to trigger the preliminary rulings procedure only if they deem the input of the Court of Justice to be *necessary* to enable them to resolve the national dispute before them. They are perfectly entitled to interpret EU law themselves. For final courts of appeal, however, the referral of questions is mandatory, unless the correct application of EU law is so obvious as to leave no scope for reasonable doubt. This safeguard is in place to ensure that 'bad' interpretations of EU law do not get trapped in national law because of the mistaken interpretation offered by national supreme courts (which all other national courts would then be obliged to follow, except for a subsequent reference to Luxembourg). But national courts can never themselves declare EU acts to be invalid, and thus if any credible doubts about the validity of an EU legal measure are raised, the question must be referred to the Court of Justice.

In terms of uptake, the preliminary rulings procedure has been an astounding success. National courts and tribunals at all levels in all member states (some more than others, of course) continue to engage with the mechanism and the number of pending preliminary rulings remains consistently high. The access to the Court of Justice given to lower courts and tribunals within national judicial hierarchies has been a particularly significant feature of the procedure. This level of openness has gone some way towards the embedding of EU law in national legal structures and also, to some extent at least, in national legal culture. It has also seen the effective application of EU rights in lower-level cases involving individuals (through the access to Luxembourg afforded, for example, to employment and also immigration tribunals). The Court of Justice continues to build its substantive contribution to EU law primarily through its judgments in such cases.

How does the Court work?

Judicial chambers

Since the Court of Justice and General Court both have a minimum of twenty-eight judges, we can immediately dispel any image of 'the Court' in trying to understand the organization of its work in practical terms. Instead, both courts function mainly through a system of three-judge or five-judge *chambers*. A single judge can also hear cases under limited circumstances in the General Court.

The 'Grand Chamber' is the formation used when a member state or an institution that is a party to the proceedings so requests, or for more legally difficult or significant cases. It comprises fifteen judges. The method for deciding which judges sit for a given Grand Chamber case is detailed in the rules of procedure.[19] The 'Full Court' of twenty-eight judges still exists in theory (and must sit for certain hearings, such as in disciplinary hearings provided for by the Treaties), but it is very rarely assigned any cases in practice.

The organization of the Court of Justice and General Court into chambers is clearly essential in ensuring that their respective workloads can be managed both effectively and efficiently. In the majority of cases, three or five judges can resolve the dispute appropriately. The Court has also been under constant pressure to reduce the duration of its proceedings, especially in the preliminary rulings procedure, so that pending national disputes can be resumed and resolved more speedily, which should in turn encourage more national courts to engage with the process.

With so many chambers delivering so many judgments at any one time, however, and with few opportunities for all members of the Court of Justice or of the General Court to engage in meaningful collective debate or discussion sitting as the full Court, there is also a growing concern about the need to ensure consistency and coherence in judicial decision-making. The 2014 Annual Report of the Court of Justice (2015) showed that, in 2014, five-judge chambers resolved just over half of all cases (54.49 per cent) and chambers of three judges determined just over a third of cases. The Grand Chamber delivered only 8.56 per cent of the Court's judgments and the Full Court sat only once. As noted, the Court applies a system akin to precedent in effect, which means that it does refer to its own previous judgments to explain its reasoning. Its decisions should therefore 'add up' coherently overall. At the Court of Justice, the burden of piecing the developing case-law narratives together as systematically as possible falls increasingly on the shoulders of the AGs (see Box 7.2).

Judgments of the Court of Justice are sometimes criticized because of the absence of detailed reasoning. Especially when compared to the more discursive (and often

---

BOX 7.2   From case to judgment at the Court of Justice

Once a case is lodged, the preliminary documents (national court questions, for example) are translated into the EU's twenty-four official languages. This first step reflects the logistical complexities of applying EU case law uniformly in twenty-eight member states. Each case is assigned a 'language of the case' into which all case documents are translated. As a general rule, the applicant selects the language of the case, unless the defendant is a member state or a natural or legal person.

For preliminary rulings, the parties, as well as any of the member states or the institutions, have two months within which to submit written observations. Several submissions will be received in contentious cases. For direct actions, the application is served on the defendant, who has one month in which to lodge a defence. The applicant may then lodge a reply and the defendant, a rejoinder, both, again, within one month.

In all cases, a Judge-*Rapporteur* is appointed by the President. The Judge-*Rapporteur* prepares an initial report summarizing all aspects of the case. The parties are asked to state whether (and, if so, why) they wish an oral hearing to be held. The Court of Justice decides collectively to what type of chamber the case should be assigned and whether a hearing should be held. If an oral hearing is held, the parties present strictly time-limited arguments in public.

Some weeks later, the AG delivers his or her opinion in open court. But if it was considered that the case raised no new question of law, the Court will have proceeded to judgment without an opinion. Originally, an opinion was delivered in all cases before the Court; in 2014, approximately half of the cases in which a judgment was delivered were resolved without an opinion.

The judges deliberate on the basis of a draft judgment prepared by the Judge-*Rapporteur*. Judicial deliberations take place in private, however, in the Court's common working language (French). Decisions are taken by majority according to the voting mechanism outlined in the rules of procedure[20]—but no record of dissent is ever made public.

The judgments themselves are quite formulaic. They begin with an outline of national (where relevant) and EU law, which is followed by a summary of the dispute, the legal arguments, and any observations submitted, and then the findings of the Court—that is, its legal reasoning and the decision actually taken on the various questions of EU law raised. The legal kernel of the judgment is repeated briefly in bold at the end of the text.

Judgments are published on the Court's website on the day on which they are delivered, though not always in every official language on the day of delivery, reflecting the demands of the translation effort that underpins the work of the CJEU. The judgment in the language of the case has authoritative legal effect if there is any question about diverging meanings across different languages. Print copies of the *European Court Reports* (ECR) are no longer published; in 2014, the CJEU updated its case law citation system to reflect exclusively online publication.

much lengthier) AG opinions, they can appear 'clipped' in style. Neither does the Court make as much effort as it might to relate the case to relevant previous case law, so that the bigger jurisprudential picture is not always as clear as it could be. From a different perspective, however, when the application of a legal solution that works both for the specific case at issue and as a precedent across twenty-eight states, in mostly translated versions, is taken into account, then perhaps the simpler the text, the better. This point also demonstrates why it is essential to try to ensure a good balance of representation of the different legal systems and legal approaches of the member states in the composition of the chambers.

From the outside, we can only imagine what deliberations are actually like: polite and ordered exchanges of concise views, or passionate exchanges of detailed arguments? No doubt the walls of the Court have seen both, depending on the case at hand. Is the flow of judicial discussion inhibited by the need to use one common language, with which judicial competence and comfort levels must surely vary, at least initially? We will never really know. Judges pledge to preserve the independence of the Court through an oath of secrecy. Moreover, the force of this oath outlasts the tenure of their appointment.

Theorizing the Court

How can we assess the Court of Justice in institutional terms? Can the Court's contribution to European integration be quantified? How can we measure the influence of its case law? These questions are critical. However, they tend to be tackled by lawyers through very different theoretical and practical lenses from the integration criteria usually applied in political science.

As a starting point, lawyers tend to *assume* the relevance and value of both law and judicial institutions. In particular, law is conceptualized as having a neutral quality. It is a product of rational reasoning and it is thereby, ideally, insulated from political vagaries. This neutrality is seen then to confer a considerable perception of authority on legal decisions that, in turn, feeds into a neutral perception of courts in institutional terms. But it is not that simple and there are a series of interrelated questions on which lawyers persistently disagree, reflecting discourse on court behaviour in general. Is the Court of Justice an activist court or not? (Should *any* court be an activist court or not?) Does the Court of Justice evaluate the law or does it also make law? (*Should* courts make law?) And if courts do make law, is this function an expression of, or rather an undue trampling on, legitimate political functions? Here, we are mainly in the territory of well-developed—although sharply contested—debates about the balance between legislative and judicial functions, and the respective roles of elected and unelected officials.[21] In particular, in a polity besieged by charges of a democratic deficit, unelected Court of Justice judges annulling legislative decisions of, collectively, the Commission, Council, and EP can be all the more difficult to swallow.

There is an added edge to discourse on the Court of Justice, however, as we try to decipher whether it has its own integrationist agenda. Even if that could be shown to be true—and both the size and structure of the EU Court, which means that multiple chambers produce judgments largely in parallel rather than collectively, as well as its deliberative, collegiate system of decision-making, arguably suggest otherwise—the question arises as to whether the progression of such an agenda is acceptable, or even possible, in the interests of institutional legitimacy and overall institutional balance.

At a very basic level, Article 19(1) TEU establishes the core function of the Court of Justice: 'It shall ensure that in the interpretation and application of the Treaties the law is observed.' This deceptively clear sentence has generated controversies of its own: notably, what is 'the law'? The Court has always applied an expansive interpretation of 'the law' to include more amorphous legal sources (such as the historically unwritten 'general principles of EU law'—which provided the basis for developing EU standards of fundamental rights protection in the case law, for example, long before the drafting of the Charter of Fundamental Rights). It is also an empirical fact that many of the Court's judgments have resulted in the outcome that best fits with a preference for deeper levels of European integration. It is also true, however, that those decisions have often required very sparse or ambiguous Treaty provisions to be 'interpreted'. Moreover, in both the classic foundational decisions that established core legal principles (notably, primacy and direct effect) and more recent judgments that have determined the fate of significant political questions—especially the opinion of the Court that stalled EU accession to the European Convention on Human Rights and Fundamental Freedoms (ECHR), discussed further shortly (see 'The Court of Justice and the European Court of Human Rights')—what remains constant is the Court's articulation and affirmation not of some overtly political conception of European integration, but rather of the autonomy and distinctiveness of the EU's *legal order*, a key feature of which is, according to the Court, protection of the rights of individuals.

It would be astonishing if the judges and AGs at the CJEU were not aware of broader political issues and considerations underpinning the cases before them. We can be sure that they are. Important judgments—for example on the compatibility with the EU Treaties of measures taken by eurozone member states to establish the European Stability Mechanism (ESM)[22]—continue to demonstrate the fine line between law and politics that the Court often treads. But it does not automatically follow that the Court somehow abuses its position within the overall EU institutional balance. It should be remembered, too, that the Court is *required* to answer all disputes and questions brought before it. It does not have the luxury of declining to resolve a dispute on the grounds that the questions the case might raise are just too difficult or too politically sensitive.

Additionally, it may also be recalled that member state courts and tribunals are the institutions raising most of these questions in the first place. Over the years, courts and tribunals at the lower levels of the national judicial ladder, in particular, have engaged very healthily with the preliminary rulings procedure. But the measure of success indicated here is somewhat superficial, reflecting simply the volume of questions sent. It would entail empirical research on a massive scale (both geographically and linguistically) to discover what happens when the judgments from Luxembourg are then applied back in the referring court forum—in other words, how 'obedient' national courts are. The Commission instigated enforcement proceedings against one member state (Italy) for persistent failures on the part of its national courts to engage with EU law; it is more difficult to get an accurate, as well as widespread, sense of how well (or otherwise) EU law is applied across the legal orders of the twenty-eight states. Moreover, such an assessment would also have to consider cases in which national courts determine that a reference to the Court of Justice is not 'necessary' at all and instead interpret (or dismiss) the relevant EU legal issue by themselves.

The reception of EU case law within national constitutional courts or other courts at the apex of national judicial hierarchies, such as the *Bundesverfassungsgericht* (BVerfG), or Federal Constitutional Court, in Germany, is a more documented phenomenon. Lower courts are, in general, used to being lower: they can resolve the legal dispute before them, but they are still links in an appellate court chain. The highest courts within national systems have more to lose within the supranational EU legal order. They give up their more typical role of having the final say on legal questions, especially on questions closely connected to national constitutional principles.

Taking the primacy of EU law as an example, the Court of Justice attributes this principle to the supranational nature of the EU bargain itself, made voluntarily by the member states through their ratification of the Treaties. But by placing the tenets of EU law at the apex of this multilevel system, the Court also created the situation in which it has exclusive authority to determine the outcome of any cases of conflict between EU law and national law. It is critical to remember, however, that the resulting 'new legal order' is the Court's own description of things.[23] National constitutional courts tend to take a different stance. They *allow* rather than subjugate themselves to primacy, permitting the operation of primacy in practice more to accommodate the (reversible) tolerant will of their national parliaments. This point is extremely clear in the *Solange* doctrine of the BVerfG in particular,[24] a position that has been altered subtly over the years, but which nonetheless continues to inform how that Court characterizes its relationship with the Court of Justice. This perspective was articulated once again in the BVerfG's 2009 decision on ratification of the Lisbon Treaty,[25] which reaffirmed the sovereignty of the member states by referencing the temporary transfer of limited sovereignty to the EU so that agreed political objectives can be achieved through the actions of the Union's institutions, where appropriate. The BVerfG acknowledged the purpose of primacy in securing the effectiveness of progress towards realizing those objectives. But it located these decisions at the level of the states themselves—not the EU in general, and not the Court of Justice more specifically.

However, in 2014, the BVerfG referred questions to the Court of Justice under the preliminary rulings procedure for the very first time—a development that demonstrates its commitment to the cooperation that ultimately underpins its relationship with the Court in Luxembourg.[26] The danger is that cooperation works only while it works. The shadow of national court revolt continues, however faintly, to shade the Court of Justice's perception of the primacy of EU law specifically, and its monopoly on the 'final say' on questions of EU law more generally.

The Court of Justice and the European Court of Human Rights

The ECtHR, based in Strasbourg, was established in 1959 to adjudicate on both state and individual applications concerning alleged violations of the ECHR. The ECHR is the flagship instrument of the Council of Europe—an organization distinct from, although often unfortunately confused with, the Council of the European Union. The Strasbourg and Luxembourg courts have also been frequently mixed up.

The ECHR binds all twenty-eight of the EU member states, but it also applies to the additional nineteen states that are members of the Council of Europe. The connection between the two legal spaces could become even more complex in the future, because the Lisbon Treaty compelled the EU to seek formal accession to the ECHR. Completion of that process would, for the first time, introduce a layer of external judicial supervision over the work of the Court of Justice. However, a 2014 opinion of that Court erected fundamental legal barriers to political progress by rejecting the proposed accession agreement, largely on the premise of the autonomy of EU law.[27]

It is sometimes suggested that the Court of Justice invented the idea of fundamental rights as general principles of EU law as a compromise to respond to challenges from national constitutional courts in the 1970s. At that time, it was trying to bed down the nascent principle of EU law's primacy over national rules, including national constitutional protection of rights. Whatever the motivation(s), however, this profoundly important judicial work led ultimately to the drafting and adoption of the EU Charter of Fundamental Rights, which acquired the same legal standing as the EU Treaties through Lisbon.

Importantly, the Court of Justice had drawn from the ECHR, and the jurisprudence of the ECtHR interpreting the Convention, as sources of inspiration for its separate system of EU fundamental rights protection. It thus recognized the authoritativeness and expertise of the Strasbourg Court, while ensuring that it could nonetheless develop its own distinct case law. This approach also threads through the Charter, which makes it clear that the standards of protection as set by the ECHR and Strasbourg Court are the threshold below which EU law cannot go, while emphasizing that EU protection can, however, go further. But we saw that the Lisbon Treaty also requires the EU to accede to the ECHR, raising fascinating questions about the next phase of the relationship between the two courts.

In reality, there are not many examples of Court of Justice case law that depart from ECtHR jurisprudence. This process of mutual judicial engagement works both ways: although not, of course, as a legally binding source, the ECtHR actually referred to the Union's Charter of Fundamental Rights before the Court of Justice did so itself, and it has continued to cite examples from the Charter when it wishes to show how understandings of fundamental rights have evolved since the ECHR was drafted in the 1950s.

However, in another line of case law, the ECtHR demonstrated that it is also prepared indirectly to review EU measures for compatibility with ECHR standards of fundamental rights protection. This technique is designed to ensure that the member states—that is, Council of Europe members acting 'behind' the EU measure—have not unduly relinquished their responsibilities under the ECHR when crafting EU obligations. But that is not the same as a more direct supervisory role. And it is not the same as having one definitive institutional voice on standards of fundamental rights protection in the EU legal space.

How will the Court of Justice cope with the changes that EU accession to the ECHR would inevitably bring? Meanwhile, has lasting damage been done to relations between the Court of Justice and the ECtHR because of the Court's placing of priority on the autonomy of EU law? On these questions and noting the increasingly apparent divisions among the member states on the political priorities of the EU more generally, it will certainly be interesting to watch this next chapter in the story of the Court of Justice unfold, which may include observing its responses to legal instruction and not only charting its profile as the legal instructor.

Conclusion

The contribution of the Court of Justice's case law to the furtherance of EU integration may well be controversial, but, at least at the level of fact, it is probably uncontested. Through the development of the primacy and direct effect of EU law in particular, the Court copper-fastened the idea that EU law was going to be *effective* law. The Court has consistently emphasized the seriousness of the commitments entered into by the member states of their own volition. It has striven also to ensure the uniform application of EU law across all of the member states insofar as is practically possible. The Court has rationalized this objective on the basis of the promises committed to in the Treaties and especially for the eradication of any differential treatment that stems from nationality discrimination. In doing so, however, it has inevitably established, consciously or otherwise, its own critical role in fulfilling these functions.

The Court of Justice is, in practical terms, very different from its ancestor 1952 institution. For starters, it is now a considerably enlarged institution comprising two constituent courts of multiple chambers, which must balance the application of effective and efficient working methods against fundamental requirements such as coherence of the case law. It is not yet apparent that the enlarged Court has really grappled with these challenges in a systematic way. The scale of the challenges facing the soon-to-be radically expanded General Court will be all the more difficult to manage.

Finally, it is worth remarking that few lawyers have engaged seriously with theories of European integration or governance in their analyses of the Court of Justice. Equally, few political scientists have engaged seriously with the Court's own extensive outputs (that is, its judgments) in shaping their perspectives of the Court as an institution. Notable exceptions are included in the guide to further reading at the end of this chapter. But there remains much scope for meaningful and rich interdisciplinary research on all of these questions.

ENDNOTES

1. See European Commission, 'Summary of the treaty *[sic]* of Nice', available online at http://europa.eu/rapid/press-release_MEMO-03-23_en.htm, emphasis added.

2. Regulation (EU, Euratom) 2015/2422 of the European Parliament and of the Council of 16 December 2015 amending Protocol No. 3 on the Statute of the Court of Justice of the European Union, [2015] OJ L 341/14. In the preamble to the Regulation, it is explained that these reforms were adopted '[a]s a consequence of the progressive expansion of its jurisdiction since its creation' on the basis that 'the number of cases before the General Court is now constantly increasing'.

3. Following Declaration No. 38 attached to the Lisbon Treaty, the number of Advocates General was increased from eight to nine on 1 July 2013, and to eleven on 1 October 2015. Declaration No. 38 also provided that Poland has become the sixth member state to have a permanent Advocate General at the Court of Justice.

4. The biographies of all members of the Court of Justice can be found online at http://curia.europa.eu/jcms/jcms/Jo2_7026/; for the General Court, see http://curia.europa.eu/jcms/jcms/Jo2_7035/

5. Art. 253 TFEU.

6. *Ibid.*

7. *Ibid.*, emphasis added. There is no official definition of the term 'jurisconsult', but it is normally considered simply to mean someone who has legal expertise. This might refer to a practising lawyer, for example, or to a legal academic.

8. Art. 254 TFEU, emphasis added.

9. Art. 276 TFEU.

10. The details of this procedure are set out in Art. 258 TFEU.

11. The action is detailed in Art. 263 TFEU.

12. The Commission provides an overview of the outcomes of infringement proceedings in its Annual Report on Monitoring the Application of Union Law; for 2014 statistics, see COM(2015) 329 final, pp. 15–17. At p. 14, it is noted that '[w]hile in 2014 the number of open infringement cases increased slightly, overall the figure has fallen since 2010'.

13. The Court expressed this principle as follows in its classic decision in Case 25/62 *Plaumann v Commission* ECLI:EU:C:1963:17:

   . . . if that decision affects them by reason of certain attributes which are peculiar to them or by reason of circumstances in which they are differentiated from all other persons and by virtue of these factors distinguishes them individually just as in the case of the person addressed.

14. For a classic account of the problems caused by the Court's stance, see the Opinion of AG Jacobs in Case C-50/00 P *Unión de Pequeños Agricultores* ECLI:EU:C:2002:197. Reflecting on these issues following the Lisbon Treaty, see the Opinion of AG Kokott in Case C-583/11 P *Inuit Tapiriit Kanatami and others v Parliament and Council* ECLI:EU:C:2013:21.

15. Art. 263(4) TFEU.

16. A famous example of a legislative act being annulled occurred in the *Tobacco Advertising Case* (Case C-376/98 *Germany v Parliament and Council* ECLI:EU:C:2000: 544), in which the Court found that a directive prohibiting several forms of tobacco advertising, including advertising methods confined to one member state, such as cinema adverts, exceeded the competence to harmonize internal market standards provided for in the Treaty. In 2014, the Court annulled an EU directive on data retention on the basis of the legislation's non-compliance with the EU Charter of Fundamental Rights (Case C-293/12 *Digital Rights Ireland* ECLI:EU:C:2014:238).

17. In 2014, there were 428 references for a preliminary ruling, of a total of 622 new cases (Court of Justice of the European Union 2015).

18. The procedure is outlined in Art. 267 TFEU.

19. The Rules of Procedure for the Court of Justice are available online at http://curia.europa.eu/jcms/upload/docs/application/pdf/2012-10/rp_en.pdf

20. In the original EEC of six member states, there were seven Court of Justice judges for precisely this reason.

21. For further discussion of these themes and related debates, see Adams *et al.* (2013) and Weiler (1999).

22. Case C-370/12 *Thomas Pringle v Government of Ireland* ECLI:EU:C:2012:756.

23. This depiction comes from the landmark decisions in Case 26/62 *Van Gend en Loos v Nederlandse Administratie der Belastingen* ECLI:EU:C:1963:1 and Case 6/64 *Costa v ENEL* ECLI:EU:C:1964:66.

24. In a series of cases, the BVerfG suggested that it would not review EU law for compatibility with the German Constitution 'so long as' threshold levels of protection of fundamental rights and other basic constitutional principles were embedded in EU law and the EU institutional structure: see Order of 29 May 1974 (*Solange I*) 37 BVerfGE 271; Order of 22 October 1986 (*Solange II*) 73 BVerfGE 339; Order of 12 October 1993 (*Maastricht*) 89 BVerfGE 155.

25. Judgment of 30 June 2009, 2 BvE 2/08, 2 BvE 5/08, 2 BvR 1010/08, 2 BvR 1022/08, 2 BvR 1259/08, 2 BvR 182/09; available in English online at https://www.bundesverfassungsgericht.de/SharedDocs/Entscheidungen/EN/2009/06/es20090630_2bve000208en.html

26. Case C-62/14 *Gauweiler and others* ECLI:EU:C:2015:400; the questions referred concerned the governance of the eurozone crisis and, in particular, powers conferred on the ECB and the European System of Central Banks.

27. *Opinion 2/13 pursuant to Article 218(11) TFEU* ECLI:EU:C:2014:2454.

 FURTHER READING

Craig and de Búrca (2015) is one of the most comprehensive texts on EU law. There are specific chapters on the Court of Justice and also on, for example, the primacy of EU law. For classic accounts of, and debate on, the role of the Court from the perspective of political science, compare Burley and Mattli (1993) with Garrett *et al.* (1998); see also Alter (2001) for a political science perspective on the evolution of primacy. The Maduro and Azoulai (2010) edited collection first selects cases that are considered to be 'classics' within the Court of Justice's output, then offers parallel comments on each from a range of different perspectives (present and former members of the Court, for example, but also academics who are not specialists in EU law). Weiler (1999) has written extensively on the Court's relationship with the broader development and integration of the Union. Burrows and Greaves (2007) is one of the few in-depth studies of the role of the Advocates General. Looking outwards from Luxembourg, Lock (2015) locates the Court of Justice within a wider global context. Finally, the contributions in Adams *et al.* (2013) provide comprehensive and critical analyses of the case law and functioning of the Court from the perspective of the institution's past and continuing legitimacy, progressing classic debates about the existence, degree, or propriety of the Court's judicial activism considerably further forward.

Adams, M., de Waele, H., and Meeusen, J. (2013) *Judging Europe's Judges: The Legitimacy of the Case Law of the European Court of Justice* (Oxford: Hart).

Alter, K.J. (2001) *Establishing the Supremacy of European Law* (Oxford and New York: Oxford University Press).

Burley, A.-M., and Mattli, W. (1993) 'Europe before the Court: A political theory of legal integration', *International Organization*, 47/1: 41–76.

Burrows, N., and Greaves, R. (2007) *The Advocate General and EC Law* (Oxford: Oxford University Press).

Craig, P., and de Búrca, G. (2015) *EU Law: Text, Cases and Material* (6th edn, Oxford: Oxford University Press).

Garrett, G., Kelemen, R.D., and Schulz, H. (1998) 'The European Court of Justice, national governments, and legal integration in the European Union', *International Organization*, 51/1: 149–76.

Maduro, M., and Azoulai, L. (eds) (2010) *The Past and Future of EU Law* (Oxford: Hart).

Lock, T. (2015) *The European Court of Justice and International Courts* (Oxford: Oxford University Press).

Weiler, J.H.H. (1999) *The Constitution of Europe* (Cambridge: Cambridge University Press).

 WEB LINKS

http://curia.europa.eu/

The Court's website provides access to all cases brought before the Court of Justice since 1953 and the General Court since 1989. The annual reports of the Court of Justice are also available on this website. It is a hugely valuable source of statistics, and also institutional commentary, on both the functioning and case law of the three CJEU courts. The annual reports detail the types of case that have arrived before the Court, how long it takes to get to judgment, which countries have enforcement proceedings pending against them, and so on. There are also valuable tables and charts covering statistical trends over the Court's history.

PART II

Managing the Union

CHAPTER 8

The Commission services: A powerful permanent bureaucracy

Liesbet Hooghe and Christian Rauh

▌ Summary

The European Commission has always been torn between its roles as an international secretariat and as an 'engine of integration'. Its expanding scope of activities, allegations of mismanagement, the challenge of eastern enlargement, and an increasingly attentive and sceptical public continuously compel the Commission services to rethink these roles. The institution has embarked on internal reforms that have moved it closer to a 'normal bureaucracy', but the Commission services remain a bureaucracy with unique agenda-setting powers at the heart of the European Union (EU) polity. This

Cont. ➤

Cont.

chapter describes the functions and organization of the Commissions services and highlights what the officials themselves think about the challenges the institution faces. We conclude that while the Commission bureaucracy has become more circumspect of bold political initiatives, neither its capacity nor its will to play a strong policy role in Europe have been significantly weakened.

Introduction

Commentaries on the European Commission[1] tend to focus more on the college, the political arm of the Commission (see Chapter 5), than on the services, the Commission's permanent bureaucracy. This emphasis is not surprising: commentaries on national political systems also tend to pay more attention to political executives than to bureaucracies. But in the case of the Commission, it is unwise to focus overly on the college, for the Commission services are not a normal bureaucracy. They exercise a central role—sometimes in a leading and sometimes in a supporting capacity—in virtually everything the EU does. Few European initiatives are launched, few legislative proposals are made, and few decisions are taken without being extensively prepared, examined, and approved by the Commission services.

The Commission was originally designed by the founding fathers to be one of the 'engines' of European integration and it has often lived up to this role. But, over past decades, the context of European integration has changed. Three exogenous shocks—a sharp increase in tasks and managerial workload, the 2004 'Big Bang' enlargement, and a deepening politicization of European integration—have intensified the contradictions between Commission officials' administrative and political roles.

This chapter examines how the Commission services deal with these tensions. We outline the evolution of Europe's central bureaucracy, discuss its functions and internal procedures, highlight the major responses to a changing context, and finally scrutinize what the Commission officials themselves think about the roles of their institution. We conclude that while the Commission bureaucracy has become warier of bold political initiatives, neither its capacity nor its will to play a strong policy role in Europe have been significantly weakened.

Origins and evolution

The Commission services have their origins in the High Authority of the European Coal and Steel Community (ECSC). Jean Monnet, the High Authority's first President, wanted it to be small and informal. Shortly after becoming President, Monnet

(1978: 405) remarked to a fellow member of the High Authority: 'If one day there are more than two hundred of us, we shall have failed.'

Monnet's hopes were quickly dashed. Following its foundation in 1952, the High Authority rapidly acquired more staff, a more formal organization, and more bureaucratic procedures than Monnet had envisioned. When, in 1957–58, the Commissions of the European Economic Community (EEC) and the European Atomic Energy Community (Euratom) were established, their administrations were built on the High Authority model. With the mergers of the High Authority and the two Commissions in 1967, the single Commission that we know today came into existence. Over the intervening years, the Commission services have expanded their tasks as the EU has come to touch upon many aspects of European citizens' lives. Yet core features of the services have remained durable:

- The services have always emphasized their impartiality (that is, their neutrality in policy stances, save perhaps for a certain pro-integration bias) and independence (that is, autonomy from national interference). This neutrality has facilitated close working relationships with a host of governmental and non-governmental organizations (NGOs). More than any national or international administration, the work of the Commission is intimately interwoven with that of national, regional, and local administrations, and stakeholder groups.

- The administrative structure, organized around the Brussels equivalent of ministries, Directorates-General (DGs), has remained essentially unchanged, except that the number of policy DGs and services increased from fifteen in 1958 to forty-four in 2016.[2]

- The Commission has always been small in size compared to national administrations. The Commission rarely implements EU policies and does not undertake much routine administration, the two most common bureaucratic activities that require large numbers of civil servants. In 1959, there were just over 1,000 full-time staff in the EEC Commission for a population of 172 million; in 1970, there were close to 5,300 in the merged Commission; by 1990, the number had increased to 16,000 for 343 million; by mid-2015, there were 23,500 full-time officials for more than half a billion EU citizens in twenty-eight member states (twenty-seven, post-Brexit). In addition, the Commission employs annually some 7,600 temporary agents, contract agents, and seconded officials, as well as about 1,200 trainees (*stagiaires*).[3]

- Recruitment has been primarily meritocratic. Officials are recruited through competitive procedures, although this method has not always been applied strictly at the most senior levels. National governments have often insisted on a broadly proportional representation of their nationals in the top layers of the bureaucracy and some key posts, such as the Directors-General for development, or trade, were until recently reserved for particular nationalities (for years, the Director-General for Agriculture was always French). Commissioners, too, sometimes bend the rules of competitive recruitment to reward *cabinet* members with a permanent appointment.

- The services consistently have been involved in administrative, as well as political, activities—with the relative importance of the political being much greater than in national administrations. Preparing EU legislation, managing funds, conducting trade negotiations, or leading accession talks—tasks undertaken mainly by the services—often require policy choices with significant political ramifications. Monnet intended the Commission to set the agenda for Europe and the services have generally lived up to his expectations.

So what kind of bureaucracy does this make the Commission—or 'the House', in the language of Commission officials? The outlined core features can be traced to three diverse models of bureaucracy.

The Monnet model

Jean Monnet had a strong hand in shaping the early years of the Commission services. His vision was to recreate at European level a planning commission, based on the French *Commissariat du Plan* he had headed after the Second World War. The *Commissariat* was composed of a small high-level team of civil servants and experts outside the normal bureaucratic hierarchy, whose main job was to produce five-year national economic plans. In the same vein, Monnet wanted the High Authority to be made up of a small, organizationally flexible and adaptable, multinational nucleus of individuals. It was to be their role to develop ideas, and stimulate and persuade others, but to leave implementation to national administrations. Monnet did not want a permanent core of civil servants.

This Monnet spirit is still palpable. By and large, Commission officials focus on designing policies and rely on national or regional administrations to implement most EU legislation. The services (along with Commissioners and their *cabinets*) bring together an exceptionally diverse and multinational collection of people. And although officials have career tenure, the Commission is more inclined than national administrations to attract experts from outside, not least because its resources are so limited.

National bureaucratic models

Monnet was never able to mould the High Authority wholly according to his vision. From the start, the nature and range of its responsibilities and the watchful, sometimes suspicious, eye of member states meant that it came to have much in common with national bureaucracies—that is, from an early stage, the services were strongly shaped by Weberian principles and modes of operation. Hierarchy, formality, and impartiality became key organizational principles.

Particular national bureaucratic traditions have also fed into the shaping of the services. The strongest national signature remains French, which, while weaker now than in the early years of European integration, is still apparent in the Commission's organizational structure and terminology. For example, the terms for senior positions are borrowed from the French model: *directeur-général*; *directeur-général-adjoint*; *directeur*; *conseiller*; and *chef de cabinet*.

International organization models

The Commission also has features of an international bureaucracy. In important respects, the League of Nations and the United Nations (UN) secretariats were models for the High Authority. The influence of international organization bureaucratic models is evident in the special work conditions of Commission officials, such as their relatively high pay and special status in the host country. Generous terms of employment are designed to help officials to resist outside pressures. In return, Commission officials pledge neither to seek nor to receive instructions from their home state. Like international civil servants, Commission officials also benefit from tax privileges and limited immunity against prosecution, although some of these privileges have been curtailed by the most recent personnel reform.

These diversified legacies are evident in persistent conundrums that the Commission services face, including:

- how to wed meritocracy with national representation;
- how to guarantee officials' impartiality and independence, while recognizing their national and sectoral allegiances; and
- how to provide political leadership in the absence of electoral accountability.

The Commission has always been an amalgam of diverse traditions, but over time the resulting tensions have become more evident. As the EU's tasks have expanded, its membership has diversified. As its decisions have become politicized, the Commission has found it more difficult to reconcile its various roles. However, as we describe next, the threads of continuity appear as strong as those of change.

Powers, structure, and functioning

Administrative routines and political tasks are built into the Commission services' day-to-day work. The basic tasks of the European Commission are described in the 1992 Treaty on the European Union (TEU, or Maastricht Treaty), especially Article 17. The Treaty instructs the Commission to serve the European interest, provides the institution with an encompassing right to set and manage the European legislative agenda, and requires the Commission to be independent. More specifically, the Commission's powers and functions can be grouped under six headings—as:

- policy initiator;
- legislative facilitator;
- executor;
- legal guardian;
- mediator and broker; and
- external representative and negotiator.

These powers apply to both the college of Commissioners and the Commission services, which puts the latter in a position that is unparalleled among international and national bureaucracies. The ultimate political responsibility for Commission action lies with the college (see Chapter 5). However, in practice, the services have considerable leeway to act on behalf of the institution.

If political and administrative tasks could be disentangled clearly, the College would be responsible for politics and the services for administration. But there are a number of reasons why the role of the services is not easily separated from that of Commissioners and their *cabinets*. To begin with, the distinction between what is a 'political decision' and what is 'routine' or 'administration' is blurred. So, for example, deciding whether a new product is subject to an existing EU law on product standards may appear to be purely administrative—but the decision may be contested by important economic or social interests. Likewise, ensuring the smooth functioning of Europe's internal market by harmonizing national rules on, say, the regulation of consumer contracts is a technical task—but the particular choices the services make invariably affect the distribution of rights and resources across and within societies.

Second, Commissioners often rely heavily on the services for information and advice. Before a decision is finally tabled in the college, the services usually scrutinize it in a multilayered process that involves various departments and hierarchical units in the Commission (Hartlapp *et al.* 2013). Here, the services operate as the main repository of accumulated wisdom in the Commission. While Commissioners and *cabinets* come and go, the services hold the fort.

Third, Commission officials tend to be the hub of multilevel policy networks that connect EU institutions, national administrations, interest groups, and policy experts. They often create, run, and maintain these networks, and develop long-term relationships, while Commissioners and their *cabinets* typically drop by to defend a particular proposal and then disappear. Thus the services are positioned well to detect potential political ramifications, which provides them with a unique steering capacity (Beyers and Kerremans 2004; Suvarierol 2009; Metz 2015).

Finally, and arguably most importantly, Commissioners have to contend with a strong tradition of policy entrepreneurship among Commission officials, which has a legal basis in the Commission's monopoly on the right of initiative: no EU legislative decision may be adopted unless the Commission decides to propose it. Monnet's intent to create a team of creative thinkers echoes powerfully. This ethos is reinforced by internal career incentives: in contrast to the unglamorous work of administering existing programmes, designing European policy boosts personal satisfaction, status, and prestige, as well as chances of promotion.

In summary, Commissioners and their *cabinets* simply do not have the time, information, or political will to closely monitor their civil servants or control their actions. That is why the services have a notable influence on each function that the Commission performs in the political system of the EU.

Policy initiator

The single most important power of the Commission is its virtually exclusive Treaty right to draft legislative proposals. This prerogative guarantees a pole position in initiating and designing the content of European policy. The Commission maintains this position whether it deals with broadly based policy initiatives or proposals to develop or revise narrow 'technical' measures.

Clearly, many others actors besides the Commission may also attempt to initiate EU policy. The European Council and the Council of Ministers regularly request policy papers from the Commission. The European Parliament (EP) can prod the Commission to start initiatives. Member states table policy documents and proposals at Council meetings. Interest groups make policy submissions to relevant DGs. However, to be turned into a binding European rule, such proposals must be picked up and fleshed out by the services of the Commission. No other body can formally draft legislation or direct the Commission on how it should respond to emerging regulatory or legal demands.

Certainly, the Commission's monopoly of initiative has received a few dents over recent decades. Most importantly, the Commission does not initiate legislation in common foreign and security policy (CFSP) and in some areas of police cooperation. In most other fields, the Council and Parliament may request legislation, although the Commission has the power to refuse, and it has occasionally done so. Since the 2007 Lisbon Treaty, EU citizens have also been able to request the Commission to legislate in an area via a petition carrying 1 million signatures spanning at least seven member states. But even where other actors successfully push the Commission into drafting a proposal, they still have to rely on the Commission services to formulate the substantial legal rules (Hartlapp *et al.* 2014).

Legislative facilitator

The Commission also acts as a legislative facilitator. It is the only institution present throughout the whole legislative process—at meetings in the Council of Ministers, in the Parliament, and at inter-institutional meetings. This continuing presence, often personified by the same officials who have drafted a legislative proposal, adds to the services' knowledge not only of what the legislators in the Council and the EP ideally want, but also what they are prepared to accept.

The bulk of EU legislation now uses the ordinary legislative procedure (OLP)—formerly known as codecision. The Commission initiates a proposal and, after consultation with national parliaments and (where required by the Treaty) the Committee of the Regions (CoR) or the Economic and Social Committee (EESC), it engages in a layered negotiation game with the EP and the Council of Ministers that can stretch over three rounds. In the first and second readings, the Commission's legislative role is pivotal: it can withdraw its proposal, amend it, or raise the voting hurdle in the Council of Ministers by accepting amendments passed by the Parliament. Once the Council and the EP convene in a conciliation meeting, which is the third and final stage, the Commission loses the right to withdraw its proposal and it can no longer raise the bar to unanimity in the Council if it disagrees with the Parliament's amendments. At that point, it is charged with taking 'all the necessary initiatives with a view to reconciling the positions of the European Parliament and the Council'.[4] These are the legal rules, but their exercise in practice has been progressively eroded by the expansion and normalization of the OLP (Ponzano et al. 2012). Indeed, it has become increasingly difficult for the Commission to withdraw its proposal if not so requested by the Parliament or the Council. The last case in which the Commission withdrew a proposal for political reasons—that is, to prevent it from being altered against the Commission's wishes—dates back to 1994 (Ponzano et al. 2012: 39).

The bottom line, however, is pretty clear: with the exception of the few policy areas mentioned, every initiative begins with the Commission. No national bureaucracy and virtually no other international governmental organization has this kind of authority. Comparative examples that spring to mind are the Commission in the Economic Community of West African States (ECOWAS) and, within much narrower parameters, the Staff of the International Monetary Fund (IMF) (Hooghe et al. forthcoming).

Executor

In a few areas, the Commission implements policy directly. The most important of these is competition, in which it has to decide, for example, whether state aids and certain types of takeover or merger are permissible. In most policy areas, however, the Commission relies on national or regional governments, or external agencies, to do the work. Some 76 per cent of the EU budget is implemented by third parties.[5] Here, the Commission's role is largely limited to putting an implementation framework in place—that is, rules that tell national or regional governments or agencies how to implement EU legislation.

Such implementation frameworks—for example rules prescribing how to test technical product standards or how to set prices for agricultural products—must normally be channelled through a so-called comitology committee, of which there were 287 in 2014 (European Commission 2015b). The comitology network is densest in internal market and industry, environment, transport, justice, and consumer, as well as agricultural, policy. Here, member state representatives, scientific experts, and interest group representatives watch closely how the Commission monitors the implementation of EU policies by third parties. Comitology is the living embodiment of how different institutions and different levels of government have become intertwined. Unilateral action by one institution has become virtually impossible (Marks *et al.* 1996).

Legal guardian

The Commission—along with the Court of Justice of the EU—is also charged with ensuring that EU law is applied uniformly. The Commission is heavily dependent on 'whistle-blowing' to be made aware of possible breaches of EU law. Its limited resources mean that only a relatively small number of likely breaches can be pursued all the way to the Court; the usual approach is to resolve the matter informally. From time to time, however, the Commission organizes dawn raids on suspected firms, which (if found guilty) may end up paying hefty fines. The Commission may impose fines of up to 1 per cent of a company's total turnover for the preceding business year for failure to provide accurate information or refusal to submit to an inspection.

Since the 1992 Maastricht Treaty, the Commission has also been able to take member states to the Court. The first fine imposed on a member state was in July 2000, when the Court of Justice ordered the Greek government to pay €20,000 for each day of continued non-compliance with a 1992 Court judgment concerning the disposal of toxic and dangerous waste at a plant on the island of Crete.[6] This power has been invoked sparingly, but the threat of Court proceedings hangs as a shadow over the Commission's use of softer instruments to compel member states into compliance, such as shaming or withholding funds (Falkner 2016).

Mediator and broker

EU decision-making involves a multiplicity of actors eager to influence policy. Within this multilevel system, there is a strong need for mediation and brokerage, for which the Commission is particularly well placed. The Commission staff tends to have a good overall understanding of the positions of decision-making actors— knowledge that stems from its contacts across the EU and its extensive involvement in EU policy processes. It is also more likely to be perceived as impartial, compared, for example, to the Council presidency, parliamentary groups, or interest group representatives. In fact, Commission officials spend large amounts of their time organizing consultation procedures, building policy-related networks, and engaging in bilateral meetings with external interests to hammer out the politically most feasible path to European policy (Hartlapp *et al.* 2014).

External representative and negotiator

Finally, the Commission and its services negotiate trade matters on behalf of the EU. The institution also takes the lead during enlargement negotiations, and shares responsibilities with member states in foreign policy, development policy, and the external dimensions of such policies as transport, environment, and competition. Here, the Commission's influence depends on the character of the policy. The influence of the services is greatest in areas that:

- fall under what used to be called the 'first pillar' (of the EC)—notably, trade and the single market;
- have been subject to extensive transfer of competence, such as enlargement;
- do not normally raise too much political sensitivity, such as development;
- require impartial leadership, such as competition; and
- require technical expertise, such as agriculture or environment.

Structure of the Commission services

The Commission services are organized into DGs, and general and internal services. Directorates-General are normally concerned with specific policies, but their mandates vary in breadth and specificity. Some have a sectoral focus, such as Mobility and Transport (DG MOVE), Energy (DG ENER), or Agriculture and Rural Development (DG AGRI). Others have cross-cutting responsibilities, such as Internal Market, Industry, Entrepreneurship and SMEs (small and medium-sized firms) (DG GROW), or Employment, Social Affairs and Inclusion (DG EMPL). A range of services handles horizontal tasks, such as the Secretariat-General (SG), the Legal Service (SJ), and the Publications Office (OP), and others have specific duties, such as fighting fraud (the European Anti-Fraud Office, or OLAF) or compiling statistics (Eurostat).

The Commission's most senior official is the Secretary-General. There have been only six Secretaries-General in the history of the Commission at the time of writing: Émile Noël (1958–87, French); David Williamson (1987–97, British); Carlo Trojan (1997–2000, Dutch); David O'Sullivan (2000–05, Irish); Catherine Day (2005–15, Irish); and Alexander Italianer (2015–, Dutch). In principle, the Secretary-General is the captain on the ship. He or she and his or her services aim to ensure that all parts of the Commission coordinate activities, act in accordance with formal procedures, and liaise with other institutions. Under Émile Noël and, to a lesser extent, David Williamson, the Secretary-General was also a formidable policy-shaper. Several important new policy ideas—including cohesion policy, justice and home affairs (JHA) policy, asylum policy, and foreign policy—were nursed in the Secretariat-General. The two subsequent Secretary-Generals interpreted their role in more strictly managerial terms. Catherine Day steered between these poles and, perhaps more than her predecessors, understood her role to be the extended arm of the Commission President in the services (Kassim *et al.* 2013: 171, 282; Peterson 2015: 185–207).

Each individual DG or service is headed by a Director-General, who may be assisted by one or more deputies. Directors-General give instructions to directors, who head a directorate within DGs. Exact administrative setups on budgets, administrative costs, staff figures, or legislative output vary considerably. But an average-sized DG has between three and five directorates, each of which is composed of between three and seven units—the lowest organizational level in the Commission. A typical unit contains between twelve and fourteen officials, of whom, aside from its head of unit, between four and six work on policy development. These people are assisted by clerks, or secretarial or administrative officials, often supplemented by one or two contractual positions.

It is in this complex machinery of the Commission services that new ideas for policies emerge, are tested, negotiated, and scrutinized, and finally are pushed onto the broader agenda of European integration.

The Commission under pressure

In the first half of the twenty-first century, the role of the Commission services came under intense external pressure. This pressure was largely a consequence of three external shocks. The first was the expansion of Commission powers and responsibilities over consecutive Treaty reforms. For example, the number of provisions in which the Commission holds the sole right of legislative initiative rose from sixty-eight in the 1958 Rome Treaties to 172 in the 2009 Treaty of Lisbon (Biesenbender 2011). Deeper European integration has provided Commission officials with powerful political tools for shaping European societies, but the Commission has also been nudged to take on a more traditional administrative role. As the policy portfolio has widened and grown more complex, so has pressure grown to beef up coordination within the services and with outside stakeholders. As the EU budget has expanded, so have demands for managing these funds efficiently.

Parts of the Commission services were ill-prepared for this new reality, which became evident when alleged malpractice in the Commission services led to the resignation of the Santer Commission in March 1999. The immediate cause was the publication of a report by a Committee of Independent Experts (1999a), established by the European Parliament to investigate accusations of maladministration in the Commission (Hooghe 2002; see also Chapter 5). Media attention was mostly directed towards those parts of the Committee report that detailed favouritism by some Commissioners. But the message to the services was that there were serious problems of administrative performance in the organization (Committee of Independent Experts 1999b).

The second shock, enlargement to include the Central and Eastern Europe countries (CEECs), was a game changer. No institution was left unaffected, but the impact on the Commission has been particularly great. Political interests have diversified, resources have become scarcer, and implementation more haphazard. These changes have made it harder for the Commission to play its roles of initiator, mediator, and legal guardian. The Commission's internal organization has also been profoundly affected; for example it had to overhaul its own organization to make space for new nationals (Ban 2013). Such an exercise is never popular among existing staff because it diminishes promotion opportunities. In this case, it also led to considerable disillusionment among recruits from the new member states. Personnel reforms by the Commission that adversely affected both pay and promotion came into force on the same day as the accession of ten new members. The Commission has invested extensive personnel resources in the accession process and it will continue to do so for some time to come (Kassim *et al.* 2013).

Perhaps the most enduring challenge is the politicization of European integration (Hooghe and Marks 2009). 'Politicization' refers to the increasing contentiousness of decision-making in the EU. The early neo-functionalists, who invented the term, believed that politicization would lead to more regional integration; a federal polity, or something like it, would result. The process of legitimating the Maastricht Treaty proved this assumption to be wrong. It opened a complex elite bargain to public inspection, and precipitated referenda and a series of national debates that alerted the public to the fact that European integration was diluting national sovereignty. The rejection of the Maastricht Treaty in Denmark and its near-rejection in France (in 1992) revealed an elite–public gap, and sustained the populist notion that important EU decisions could no longer be legitimized by the executive and legislature operating in the normal way; rather, direct popular approval was required (Hooghe and Marks 2012). Given the deep societal challenges that the Union faces, for example with the euro crisis or the refugee crisis, a more attentive and sceptical public is likely to remain an important constraint on the European Commission (De Wilde and Zürn 2012; Rauh and Zürn 2014). Politicization may weaken the Commission's claim to be the primary agenda-setter for Europe. In a polity that struggles to be democratic, decisions by unelected Commission officials have questionable legitimacy. However, they also generate strong incentives for the Commission services to actively demonstrate their added value to the wider European public (Hartlapp *et al.* 2014: ch. 9; Rauh 2016).

The Commission has always struggled to reconcile its role as administrative manager with its political agenda-setting role. But politicization, enlargement, and task expansion have certainly made this more difficult. In response, the institution has embarked on comprehensive internal reform to strengthen both its managerial capacity and its responsiveness to stakeholders and European citizens. As we shall see, these efforts have not fundamentally altered the balance between administration and political agenda-setting. The Commission remains an institution with a pronounced hybrid personality.

Internal Commission reform

After the resignation of the Santer Commission and under the cloud of nepotism, fraud, and mismanagement in 1999, the incoming Prodi Commission made internal reform a top priority. The reform process, which was mainly driven by Commission Vice-President Neil Kinnock, kept the basic organizational structure of the Commission services, but sought to make them more professional, efficient, and focused by strengthening managerial systems and principles.[7]

Four elements of the reform speak directly to the services' hybrid role. First, the Commission's financial management and control were overhauled. Under the old system, policy-making took place in one part of the Commission and financial planning, in another. There was no incentive for policy initiators to incorporate value for money in their decisions. The reform created bridges between policy design and financial management by decentralizing financial responsibility to units, and even to individual officials, separating financial control and auditing, simplifying accounting, and reorganizing cooperation with national administrations, which are often the culprits when EU funds are mismanaged.

Second, senior recruitment was made more meritocratic. The new procedures made it more difficult for national governments to interfere with the hiring and firing of senior officials (Egeberg 2003). The reforms also mandated mobility through the services to discourage national governments or particular industrial interests from 'capturing' a service. Directors-General can no longer spend more than five years in the same post and management training is mandatory.

Meritocracy has always been strongly entrenched at the entry level. The reform tightened rules on temporary hires and reinforced the *concours*—a series of written and oral examinations—as the primary recruitment mechanism. Competition in the *concours* is intense and there are usually, for each vacancy, well over a hundred qualified candidates—that is, people with a good academic qualification and high proficiency in at least one language in addition to their mother tongue. Candidates who pass the *concours* are placed on a reserve list from which they may be cherry-picked by an interested DG. Nationality is, in principle, not a criterion, but overrepresented nationalities, such as Belgians and Italians, find it more difficult to jump from the reserve list to a permanent job.

Third, the reform streamlines rules on the 'externalization' of support tasks to non-core Commission services. Tasks may be externalized to EU agencies or national administrations, or outsourced to private parties. For each category, rules of engagement and oversight have been standardized and tightened. The basic idea is that external agents take on implementation so that the Commission can concentrate on making policy.

A final set of measures is aimed at making the Commission more 'service-oriented' and accountable to its principals—the EP, member states, interest groups, and also Europe's citizens. The Commission pays its invoices more quickly, has increased electronic access to documents, and has adopted guidelines for consultation with civil society.

The thrust of the reform reflects new public management (NPM) philosophy, which applies principles and practices from the private sector, such as competition, cost-effectiveness, outsourcing, and customer satisfaction, to public service (Hood 1991). At first blush, this emphasis appears to shift the Commission in the direction of the more service-oriented Anglo-Saxon bureaucracies and away from the more politically inspired Franco–German influences that have historically shaped its practices (Balint *et al.* 2008; Kassim *et al.* 2013: ch. 8). However, the new system is not at odds with policy activism and political entrepreneurship. To the extent that the services' energies are refocused on 'core functions such as policy conception, political initiation and enforcing Community law' and 'away from managing programmes and projects and directly controlling the latter' (European Commission 2000: 5), the services may end up doing *less* standard routine administration and *more* policy initiation—and that would be close to Monnet's heart.

Balancing diverging external and internal interests

As a result of task expansion, enlargement, and politicization, the services face an extraordinarily diverse set of internal and external interests, all of which try to influence the policies that the Commission feeds into the EU system. Coordinating, balancing, and communicating with internal and external stakeholders are key challenges for Europe's bureaucracy.

Greater diversity affects internal coordination within the Commission services. Officials do not think alike on how to conduct policy or what kind of policy should be proposed. Divisions may run along sectoral perspectives and constituencies, competence-seeking motives, and DG allegiances, or sometimes even ideology or nationality. For example, DG GROW thinks very differently about regulating gender equality from, say, DG EMPL. Societal contention sometimes tends to spill over into the Commission services. Finding a common policy position is not a trivial matter for the organization.

In practice, the services' day-to-day operation fluctuates between efficient problem-solving and bureaucratic politics. Efficiency necessitates a fair balancing of contending interests, but bureaucratic politics, whereby coordination is approached much more strategically among the Commission services, can get in the way (Hartlapp *et al.* 2013). Undoubtedly, policy initiation within the Commission is highly formalized. Typically, drafting starts in a single DG—the lead department or *chef de file*—whereby a unit gathers relevant facts, communicates with external stakeholders, and sets an initial legal position. At this stage, which often stretches out over months or years, the lead DG may or may not decide to include other services. In a second, formal, coordination stage—the inter-service consultation—the lead DG is required to collect opinions on the initial draft from all 'concerned' DGs. There is some leeway on who to invite, but it must include the SG, the Legal Service, and often also the DG for the Budget (DG BUDG). DGs need to respond within fifteen days with one of three opinions: a disapproving *avis négatif* (which happens very rarely); a direct *accord* (approval); or an agreement subject to certain amendments (the most frequent answer). Usually, bilateral talks follow, and if no agreement is reached, the lead DG can withdraw its proposal, draft a new text, or hand over the conflictual points to higher tiers of coordination—that is, directors, the *cabinets*, or ultimately the Commissioners. But even this densely formalized process opens up multiple opportunities for the lower echelons of the Commission services—and in particular the lead DG—to set the basic political parameters of a Commission initiative.

The managerial reforms brought greater predictability to this coordination process. First, the Commission is required to develop a multi-annual policy programme, which makes it easier to see which DGs work on which issues at any given point in time and thus which ones should be included in a coordination exercise. Second, the lead DG is now required to involve other services in its impact assessments, which scrutinize the likely effects of its proposed policy across various dimensions. Impact assessments tend typically to draw in DGs EMPL and GROW. Third, the reforms have considerably strengthened the coordinative capacity of the SG. Besides being a key actor in setting up the multi-annual policy programmes, the SG beefed up the so-called upstream coordination by setting up central posts for coordination—sectorally responsible SG officials who monitor the activities of DGs with overlapping policy mandates. These rules enable the SG to acts as legislative gatekeeper. Yet research into a broad array of policies indicates that, under these new rules, the services still rarely achieve a representative balance of the diverse policy perspectives that persist inside in the Commission (Hartlapp *et al.* 2014).

Greater diversity of interests and perspectives also affects coordination of external stakeholder interests. The Commission services are the target of varying lobbying interests who attempt to influence drafting officials through bilateral contacts, working groups and expert committees, broad-scale stakeholder meetings, public consultations, or public relations (PR) campaigns. With their scarce resources, the services depend heavily on the policy-related information that these interests convey.

In this context, politicization of European integration poses particular challenges. A more attentive and often sceptical public necessitates that the Commission acts more carefully with regard to the immediate distributional consequences and the public reception of its procedures and policies. Making the Commission more accountable and responsive to public interests was arguably one of the key motivations for the *Spitzenkandidaten* process (see Chapter 5). But political sensitivity has also grown among the lower echelons of the Commission services. Policy officials who work on issues that have traditionally been considered purely technical—for example contract rules, product standards, or food safety—have become aware that their regulatory choices may have political implications (Rauh 2016). They rebalance their stakeholder contacts, monitor public opinion and media debates, engage in long-term PR activities to prepare their initiatives, and even revise extant European law in response. This behaviour sometimes clashes with an administrative approach that gives precedence to managing the European market rather than attuning it to changing political demands. However, since the politicization of European integration is likely to stay, the Commission services will need to walk the fine line between political agenda-setting and efficient administration for years to come.

What do Commission officials think about their institution's role?

The Treaty creates clear expectations for the officials working in the Commission services. It prescribes that they must put the Union's interest first, set the agenda for the EU, and promote the Union's interest independently from national pressures. The Commission's autonomy, its all-European focus, and its exclusive power of initiative were central to Monnet's conception of the Commission as the engine of European integration. Already in the early 1960s, Émile Noël, the Commission's first Secretary-General, had institutionalized them in Commission staff rules, which state that:

[A]n official shall carry out his duties and conduct himself *solely with the interests of the Communities* in mind; he shall neither seek nor take instructions from any government, authority, organization or person outside his institution. . . . *He shall carry out the duties assigned to him objectively, impartially and in keeping with his duty of loyalty to the Communities.*

(Commission Staff Regulations 2005, Art. 11, emphasis added)

Several observers anticipated that increased managerial challenges streaming from task expansion, enlargement, and politicization would cool the political agenda-setting ambitions of Commission officials. Administrative reform in particular, which was designed to buttress the Commission's managerial capacity, was seen to reinforce this trend. In other words, the expectation is that the Commission's bureaucracy would become more like a normal civil service executing orders given elsewhere. In fact, the 2000 White Paper on Reforming the Commission (2000: 7) still emphasized that:

[T]he original and essential source of the success of European integration is that the EU's executive body, the Commission, is supranational and independent from national, sectoral or other influences. This is at the heart of its ability to advance the interests of the European Union.

So to what extent do Commission officials still subscribe to Monnet's core philosophy sixty years after the Commission's inception? Have administrative reform and politicization dampened officials' ambition in acting as European agenda-setters? And have officials from the new member states adopted the traditional norms?

We bring to bear evidence from four surveys of Commission officials in 1996, 2002, 2008, and 2014. The first two surveys were conducted among the senior ranks of the Commission bureaucracy: Director-Generals, Deputy Director-Generals, directors, and principal advisers (Hooghe 2002, 2005). The 2008 and 2014 surveys polled a representative sample of the Commission bureaucracy (Hooghe 2012; Kassim *et al.* 2013).[8]

Agenda-setting, nationality, and EU governance

We first need to be clear about what we mean by 'Monnet's ideas'. One understanding emphasizes features of the Commission's immediate environment:

1. that the Commission has the sole power of initiative;
2. that it should develop new policies rather than administer existing ones; and
3. that its composition should be meritocratic rather than reflect the EU's multiple nationalities.

A broader conception also considers the role of the European Commission in the future EU institutional architecture:

4. that the Commission is not simply subservient to the member states as central players of the EU; and
5. that it should become Europe's government in an ever closer Union.

The four surveys provide a glimpse of how Commission officials' beliefs on these Monnet norms have evolved against the backdrop of profound change in EU politics. The first survey, conducted in 1996, took place before the eastern enlargement, before monetary union and the expansion into non-economic policy areas, and at a time that European integration was only minimally politicized. The last two surveys of 2008 and 2014 were conducted in the full glare of a politicized, expanded, and more supranational EU. How, if at all, did these changes affect Commission officials' beliefs in Monnet norms?

The short answer is: 'Not much.' Figure 8.1 reports support among senior officials for these five norms over nearly two decades. Each bar indicates the percentage of senior officials who agree or agree strongly with a norm.

The most robust estimates are the figures that express average support for the five norms—the four bars at the bottom of the figure. Average support increased—but statistically not significantly—from 59 per cent in 1996 to 68 per cent in 2014. Support for Monnet norms *in the aggregate* barely budged, which is remarkable given the dramatic changes in the Commission services' political environment.

Let us now take a closer look norm by norm. There is consistent and overwhelming support for a characteristic that distinguishes the Commission from other bureaucracies: its monopoly of legislative initiative. Between 62 and 84 per cent supported the principle. When asked for justification, most Commission officials explained the need for strong Commission agenda-setting power in pragmatic terms. They argued that Commission leadership tends to produce better results than

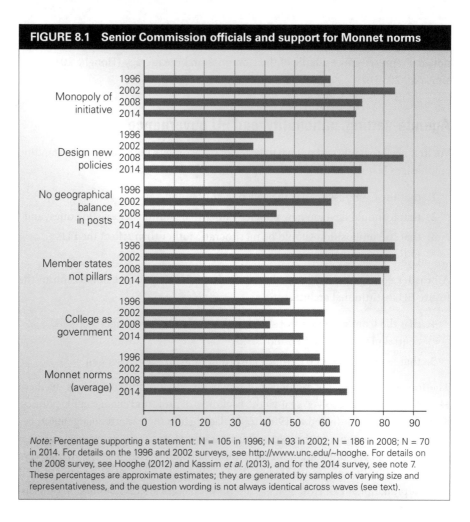

FIGURE 8.1   Senior Commission officials and support for Monnet norms

Note: Percentage supporting a statement: N = 105 in 1996; N = 93 in 2002; N = 186 in 2008; N = 70 in 2014. For details on the 1996 and 2002 surveys, see http://www.unc.edu/~hooghe. For details on the 2008 survey, see Hooghe (2012) and Kassim *et al.* (2013), and for the 2014 survey, see note 7. These percentages are approximate estimates; they are generated by samples of varying size and representativeness, and the question wording is not always identical across waves (see text).

member state guidance. During interviews, officials contrasted the relatively smooth handling of enlargement or climate change, in which the Commission has taken the lead, with well-documented examples of inefficient or botched member state guidance, such as the failure to manage the break-up of Yugoslavia, the aborted attempt to negotiate external trade in services, deadlocks in immigration and asylum policy (including, recently, the failure of Frontex to secure Europe's southern borders and safeguard Schengen), and, of course, the euro crisis. Many top officials essentially warned that enlargement and crisis will grind EU decision-making to a halt unless the Commission gains power and can preserve its right of initiative.

Next come two norms that go to the heart of the Commission's daily operation: the balance between designing new policies and management, and the role of nationality in personnel policy.

One major objective of the administrative reform programme was to focus attention on administrative management. This move ran counter to Monnet, who saw a contradiction between the need to provide political leadership and the duty to administer, and, when forced, relegated the Commission's administrative and managerial tasks to second place—a choice not always appreciated by his colleagues. By the mid-1990s, the Commission's senior officials were not so sure about the wisdom of Monnet's choice. The glorious years of Commission leadership under Jacques Delors (1985–95) left a sour aftertaste when, a few years later, accusations of mismanagement and nepotism were slung at the college and the Commission bureaucracy. Many senior officials had seen it coming and supported a correction (Hooghe 2002). As Figure 8.1 shows, in 1996—before the Santer crisis—a majority of senior Commission officials already wanted to make management and administration a priority. By 2002, at the cusp of the administrative reform, support for this view had grown, with only 37 per cent of officials agreeing with the statement that designing new policies should have priority over administering existing ones. But, by the end of 2008, after the administrative reform had been implemented, the overwhelming majority of senior officials (86 per cent) wanted the Commission to focus *more* on initiative again—and this trend continued into 2014. We may speculate that the administrative managerial pendulum had swung too far or that the challenges of enlargement, monetary union, and politicization had made the Commission leadership change its mind. Be that as it may, it is clear that the changing context has not corroded the officials' determination to act as an agenda-setter of European integration.

Monnet also emphasized the need for officials to be independent of national interests. The strongest tool for realizing this aspiration is a personnel policy that allocates posts on the basis of merit instead of nationality. Administrative reform has reinforced this shift by asserting that merit, not national quotas, should determine promotion and recruitment, especially at the highest ranks. In Figure 8.1, support among senior officials for this principle is considerable, but it softened from 75 per cent in 1996 to 62 per cent in 2002. In 2008, the support base had shrunk to a plurality of senior officials (44 per cent, with another 17 per cent neither agreeing nor disagreeing). Direct comparison is complicated because the question wording changed between 2002 and 2008. In 2008, the question was whether posts should be 'distributed according to geographical balance'; in 2002, it was whether posts should be 'distributed across nationalities proportionate to their respective populations'. So the sharp dip in support may be caused in part by a change in the question—but it is difficult to believe that this alone explains the sea change.

Interviews reveal that many top officials take a more nuanced view than either the Monnet idea or the administrative reform on nationality suggest. Officials resent *parachutage*—the practice of appointing individuals outside the normal recruitment procedures—but see merit in geographical balance. As late as the mid-1990s, 35–40 per cent of top positions were filled by outsiders parachuted in from national administrations, diplomatic services, or from Commissioners' *cabinets* into the Commission's top bureaucracy. These individuals bypassed competitive examinations and blocked career paths for officials who had worked their way up through the ranks.

Moreover, there were no guarantees that these parachuted officials had the necessary skills or that they would be independent from the national capital that landed them the job. One outcome of the 2002 personnel reform was the virtual elimination of *parachutage* and, on the rare occasions on which it is still used, it is subject to competitive examination. Because *parachutage* has thus become a thing of the past, the once-deep suspicion against national colonization has mellowed—which provides one plausible explanation for the dip in the 2008 attitudes on geographical balance.

Geographical variation among Commission officials, on the other hand, ensures a range of views in policy-making and may bestow greater legitimacy on EU policy. A policy blind to the realities of a diverse multilevel polity could do more harm than good. Senior officials' instincts about how to balance national sensitivities and impartiality have been honed by the hard school of the last decades. A Commission that speaks in foreign tongues is vulnerable to Eurosceptic rhetoric, while a Commission perceived to be the handmaiden of particular national interests loses credibility. That is one reason why officials make a sharp distinction between talking with compatriots and making policy for compatriots. While the former finds broad approval, the latter meets with widespread reticence. When asked in 2002, only 12 per cent believed that Commission autonomy would be better served if officials were to avoid contact with compatriots, while 80 per cent agreed that national policy dossiers are better *not* handled by officials of the same nationality.

In 2008, we asked a more probing question: whether it is problematic for Commission officials to manage dossiers of special interest to their own member states. We found that an absolute majority (53 per cent) finds it unproblematic. Allocating national dossiers to nationals remains contested, but sometimes it is wise to strike a balance between the ideal and the practical. As a top official observed, there are not many non-Estonian officials who speak Estonian and so, to the extent that good policy relies on local knowledge, one needs to use the human capital that one has. Moreover, one major outcome of the new personnel policy is that even when geographical balance influences hiring and promotion, it happens after candidates have gone through the fire of meritocratic examination.

The last two statements in Figure 8.1 gauge senior officials' attitudes on the constitutional future of Europe. The first statement—member states should be the central pillars of the EU—echoes de Gaulle's call for intergovernmentalism.[9] The second—the Commission's college should be government of Europe—taps Monnet's (or Hallstein's—see Chapter 5) notion of supranationalism. If Monnet's political ideas were to determine Commission views on Europe's architectural design, one would expect to see solid majorities opposing member states being central pillars and solid majorities supporting the idea of the Commission as 'government for Europe'. The expectation that member states should *not* run the EU is confirmed (from 65 per cent in 1996, to 84 per cent in 2002, 82 per cent in 2008, and 79 per cent in 2014), but support for the Commission as the embryonic European government is less widespread than expected (49, 60, 42, and 52 per cent, respectively). On basic issues of EU governance, senior Commission officials are distinctly divided.

A minority of Commission officials can be called supranationalist—that is, they agree that the college of Commissioners should be the government of Europe and disagree that member states should remain the central pillars. A smaller minority are intergovernmentalists who disagree with the former and agree with the latter positions. But many officials believe that *neither* the college of Commissioners *nor* the member states should be the kernel of European government, or they believe that *both* should lead Europe. This third group does not want to be lumped in with the other two. We call them 'institutional pragmatists' on account of the fact that they prefer to side-step institutional battles. They favour a multilevel polity in which the Commission and member state institutions are conceived as complementary: the Commission, on account of its monopoly of initiative; member states, on account of their legitimacy to legislate and implement EU policy (Hooghe 2012). Table 8.1 shows how each of these visions has found a constituency among senior Commission officials since the mid-1990s. Plurality, not polarity, continues to describe most aptly the political views of senior Commission officials.

It may come as a surprise that a majority of the Commission's bureaucratic leadership is, at best, lukewarm on a federal Europe with a government-like Commission. After all, liberal intergovernmentalists saw the Commission mainly as an agent of the member states (Moravcsik 1993), while neo-functionalists conceived it as biased to supranationalism (Pollack 1997). But the mixed picture that we find is consistent with a conceptualization of the EU polity as multilevel (Marks *et al.* 1996). The system of multilevel governance in which Commission officials operate primes them to develop views that internalize the Commission's interdependence with other actors and institutions.

Rank-and-file vs top, and East vs West

The 2008 and 2014 polls surveyed the whole Commission, and thus give us an opportunity to explore the breadth and depth of Monnet norms across the Commission services as a whole.

TABLE 8.1   Supranationalists, institutional pragmatists, and intergovernmentalists among senior Commission officials

	1996 (%)	2002 (%)	2008 (%)
Supranationalists	35.2	53.1	39.3
Institutional pragmatists	37.0	26.1	33.5
Intergovernmentalists	22.2	8.8	12.6

Note: n = 105 (1996), 93 (2002), 186 (2008); data not available for 2014

Source: Kassim *et al.* (2013)

Source: http://europa.eu/agencies/index_en.htm

Source: http://eca.europa.eu

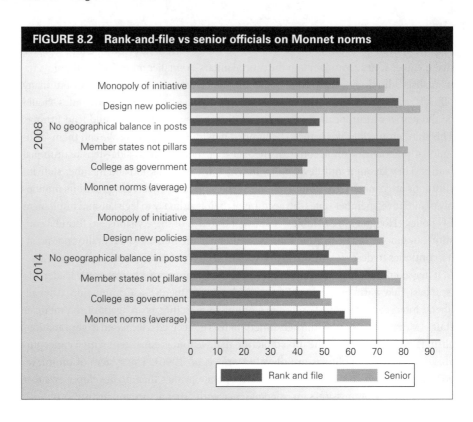

FIGURE 8.2   Rank-and-file vs senior officials on Monnet norms

Figure 8.2 compares rank-and-file with senior officials. In all but one instance, junior and middle management is less in favour of Monnet norms than senior officials. The greatest difference relates to the Commission's agenda-setting power, in which regard the rank-and-file seem much less insistent on maintaining the Commission's monopoly of initiative. The gap between top management and the rest of the Commission appears to have widened—from 5 per cent in 2008 to 10 per cent in 2014.

By mid-2015, 27 per cent of Commission policy-makers (AD grades) hailed from the thirteen newest member states. They appeared to think somewhat differently compared to officials from the EU15, but the gap seems to be narrowing (see Figure 8.3). In 2008, officials from the new member states were less supportive of Monnet norms in every instance—on average, nearly 10 per cent. By 2014, that overall difference had halved (see Figure 8.3).

There is only one exception: a deep and persistent gap on the desirability of geographical balancing in allocating Commission posts. Just 30 per cent of new member state recruits believe it to be a bad idea and nearly half (49 per cent) positively support the policy. Not so in the old member states: 55 per cent oppose geographical balancing and just 27 per cent support it. This finding appears to be a direct

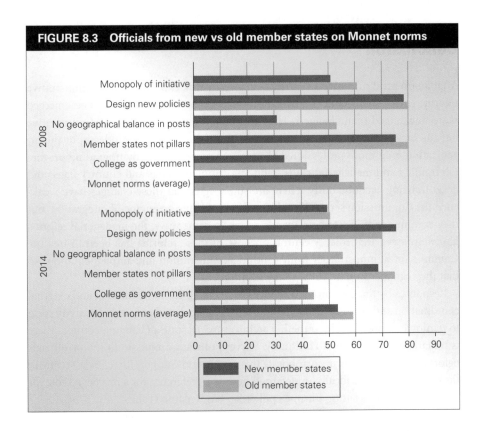

FIGURE 8.3   Officials from new vs old member states on Monnet norms

effect of the Commission's hiring policy since 2006 to meet target quotas for na-tionals of the new member states. The policy both diminished promotion opportu-nities for EU15 officials and generated uncertainty among recruits from the new member states, who often felt they had to prove themselves doubly to escape 'the logic of tokenism: the assumption by their colleagues that even those with excel-lent credentials [were] there only because of nationality' (Ban 2013: 199). As one newly minted director from a new member state recounted of his first staff meeting:

And then I had a meeting with my staff, and that was something like, I saw seven new faces, all people working here for years, very experienced, knowing the system and so on. And I am and I was comparatively younger than they are. So I had a feeling they are looking on me as something exotic, coming from the east, very young, without experi-ence. So, 'show what you know' – you know, this feeling, [of being] on the spot.

(Quoted in Ban 2013: 142)

Ten years after the Commission embarked on the largest personnel renewal since its inception, neither 'new' or 'old' officials have found an angle of repose.

Conclusion

After an eventful turn of the century—shaped by task expansion and administrative reform, enlargement, and politicization—the Commission services have emerged more unchanged than changed. They continue to be a hybrid of an administrative bureaucracy and a political agenda-setter. Internal reforms have indeed put the organization on a more professional footing, most particularly by upgrading on-the-job training and managerial skills, reducing national quotas and country flags, and decentralizing accountability. There are some signs that these changes have weakened the Commission services' traditional role of being an engine of integration, but they continue to be a strategic agenda-setter. In some ways, the managerial reforms have reinforced that role. A central purpose of these reforms has been to free the Commission administrators from routine administration and implementation, so that they can focus on drafting policy solutions.

Responses by the Commission services to demands for more internal and external coordination and changes in staff policy, work practices, and political sensitivity seem to reinforce its special role in the EU architecture. Despite a changing context, there is remarkable institutional continuity. Surveys of the Commission's senior officials before and after the reform corroborate this conclusion. Support for agenda-setting in the spirit of Monnet's ideal—understood here as a preference for a privileged role for the Commission in setting Europe's policies—has remained robust.

Does this trend suggest that more policy may flow from the services? The answer is 'not necessarily', because the changing context of European integration is likely to constrain the Commission's penchant for policy entrepreneurship. New internal procedures such as the Commission's annual policy strategy and management programme are designed to entrench this restraint, by compelling Commission officials to pursue initiatives within the guidelines set by the college and the Secretary-General. These measures may keep the Commission services' entrepreneurship within bounds. But perhaps of most consequence is that a political environment of resurgent nationalism and sceptical public debates is sending powerful signals to the Commission services to tread lightly.

ENDNOTES

1. http://ec.europa.eu/about/ds_en.htm
2. There are thirty-three Directorates-General, which are equivalent to departments or ministries at the national level, and eleven services, which usually perform a more specialized task and tend to have a more arms-length relationship with the core administration.
3. http://ec.europa.eu/civil_service/about/figures/index_en.htm
4. Art. 294(11) TEU.
5. http://ec.europa.eu/budget/library/biblio/publications/glance/budget_glance_en.pdf

6. Case C-45/91 *Commission v Hellenic Republic* ECLI:EU:C:1992:164.

7. For an overview, see Kassim (2004).

8. Data for 2008 collected as part of The European Commission in Question project, funded by the UK Economic and Social Research Council (Grant No. RES-062-23-1188) and conducted by the first author, along with Michael Bauer, Sara Connolly, Renaud Dehousse, Hussein Kassim, John Peterson, and Andrew Thompson. For further information, see online at http://www.uea.ac.uk/psi/research/EUCIQ or see Kassim *et al.* (2013). The data for 2014 were collected as part of the project, 'European Commission: Facing the Future', by a team of researchers led by Hussein Kassim and Sara Connolly, and including Michael W. Bauer, Renaud Dehousse, and Andrew Thompson. It is drawn from an online survey (*n* = 5,545), conducted between March and April 2014: see https://www.uea.ac.uk/political-social-international-studies/facing-thefuture. We are grateful to the principal investigators for sharing preliminary data for the purpose of this chapter.

9. The item reads as 'Member states—not the European Commission nor the European Parliament—should be the central players in the European Union'. Figure 8.1 reverses the direction of the wording to make it consistent with Monnet norms.

FURTHER READING

The academic literature on the Commission has grown considerably in recent years. The list of further reading provided here concentrates on sources that include extensive discussions and analyses of the services. The full findings from the 2008 survey of Commission officials is reported in Kassim *et al.* (2013).

Balint, T., Bauer, M., and Knill, C. (2008) 'Bureaucratic change in the European administrative space: The case of the European Commission', *West European Politics*, 31/4: 677–700.

Egeberg, M. (2003) 'Organising Institutional Autonomy in a Political Context: Enduring Tensions in the European Commission's Development', ARENA Centre for European Studies Working Paper No. 02/04.

Hartlapp, M., Metz, J., and Rauh, C. (2014) *Which Policy for Europe? Power and Conflict inside the European Commission* (Oxford and New York: Oxford University Press).

Hooghe, L. (2002) *The European Commission and the Integration of Europe: Images of Governance* (Cambridge: Cambridge University Press).

Hooghe, L. (2005) 'Many roads lead to international norms, but few via international socialization: A case study of the European Commission', *International Organization*, 59/4: 861–98.

Hooghe, L. (2012) 'Images of Europe: How Commission officials conceive their institution's role', *Journal of Common Market Studies*, 50/1: 87–111.

Kassim, H., Peterson, J., Bauer, M., Connolly, S., Dehousse, R., Hooghe, L., and Thompson, A. (2013) *The European Commission of the 21st Century* (Oxford and New York: Oxford University Press).

WEB LINKS

http://europa.eu/about-eu/institutions-bodies/european-commission/index_en.htm
The Commission's website.

http://ec.europa.eu/reform/index_en.htm

Provides access to European Commission (2004) *Reforming the Commission: Reform of Europe's Public Services.*

http://ec.europa.eu/civil_service/docs/toc100_en.pdf

Provides access to European Commission (2005) *Staff Regulations of Officials of the European Communities: Conditions of Employment of Other Servants of the European Communities.*

CHAPTER 9

The European Central Bank: New powers and new institutional theories

Dermot Hodson

▌ Summary

With the launch of the single currency in January 1999, the European Central Bank (ECB) assumed complete control over eurozone monetary policy. A powerful *de novo* body, the Bank boasts a higher degree of independence than either the European Commission or the Court of Justice and yet it assigns national central banks a key role in its decision-making structures. The euro crisis has been a major test for the ECB, which responded cautiously at first, before pursuing unconventional monetary policies, and taking on new and controversial roles in relation to crisis management and financial supervision. The ECB's transformation has encouraged a new wave of institutional theorizing about the Bank. It emphasizes, among other things, the importance of credible commitments, path-dependence, strategic discourse, and the changing politics of European integration.

Introduction

Few institutions of the European Union (EU) wield more power in their respective policy domains than the ECB, which opened the doors of its Frankfurt-based headquarters in May 1998.[1] Given responsibility for maintaining price stability and, without prejudice to this goal, supporting economic policy, the ECB assumed complete responsibility for monetary policy when the single currency was finally launched in January 1999.[2] The establishment of the ECB was provided for under the Maastricht Treaty (1992), but the Bank was not formally recognized as an institution of the EU until the Lisbon Treaty (2007). The euro's first decade thus bore witness to a lively debate over the ECB's exact status in EU law, with some scholars claiming that economic and monetary union (EMU) involved the creation of a new institutional order in its own right (Torrent 1999; Zilioli and Selmayr 2000). Even the ECB itself sought to establish a *sui generis* institutional status in its dealings with the Court of Justice (Goebel 2005) and the Convention on the Future of Europe (Hodson 2011).

The ECB's initial strategy of institutional isolationism can be viewed as an attempt by a *de novo* body (see Chapter 1) to test the scope and limits of its statutory independence. The Bank enjoys considerable autonomy under the Treaty, which prohibits monetary authorities from seeking or taking instructions from member states or from institutions, bodies, offices, or agencies of the EU.[3] The limits of ECB autonomy were soon discovered, however, with the Court of Justice ruling in 2004 that central bank independence 'does not have the consequence of placing the ECB beyond the reach of the rules of the Treaty'.[4] The ECB's new designation under the Lisbon Treaty implies, furthermore, that the Bank is bound to practise 'sincere mutual cooperation' with other EU institutions and to uphold the objectives, interests, and values of the people and member states of the Union.[5]

Economically, the first decade of the euro appeared to be a reasonably successfully one for the ECB, which gained a reputation as a credible central bank (Geraats 2008). The ECB's second decade has been a tumultuous one, with global financial turmoil in 2007–08 exposing severe fiscal problems in Greece and other eurozone members.[6] The ECB's initial response to the euro crisis was cautious, with its policy choices constrained by its unique institutional design (Cour-Thimann and Winkler 2012). However, the ECB was eventually drawn into unconventional monetary policies, including large-scale government bond purchases, and given important new roles in relation to crisis management and financial supervision. ECB President Mario Draghi's promise in July 2012 to do 'whatever it takes' to save the euro had a powerful palliative effect on the euro crisis, but it was never intended as a cure (Hodson 2013b). As such, the ECB remains on the front line of efforts to save the eurozone and, ultimately, its own powerful place in EU policy-making.

This chapter examines the ECB's emergence and evolution as an institution of the EU. It begins with an overview of the Bank's mandate, tasks, and key decision-making bodies, before examining how this institution has been tested—and transformed—by the euro crisis. Alternative theoretical perspectives on the ECB are explored, followed by a brief excursion into debates about the legitimation of eurozone monetary policy.

The ECB's mandate and tasks

Not to be confused with the 'other' European banks (see Box 9.1), the ECB is responsible for monetary policy in the eurozone. Monetary policy, conventionally, involves the setting of one or more official interest rates, which influence the cost of borrowing for individuals and firms, as well as the exchange rate, which in turn affects price

---

BOX 9.1	The 'other' European banks: The European Investment Bank and the European Bank for Reconstruction and Development

Established by the Treaty of Rome in 1958, the overarching objective of the European Investment Bank (EIB) is to 'contribute . . . to the balanced and steady development of the internal market in the interest of the Union'.[7] To this end, the Bank gives loans and guarantees for a wide range of projects, financed not through the EU budget, but by borrowing on financial markets.

The projects funded by the EIB vary according to the EU's shifting policy priorities. In July 2015, the EIB was given a central role in the European Commission's new European Fund for Strategic Investment. Under the 'Juncker Plan', as this fund was known, EU member states agreed to put up €16 billion in funding, which, combined with a €5 billion contribution from the EIB's funds, would be used to unlock at least €315 billion in public and private investment in smaller companies and infrastructure projects. It was too soon, at the time of writing, to say whether the Juncker Plan would meet its overarching objective of boosting growth and jobs, but the scheme was undoubtedly a boon for the EIB (Claeys 2015).

The EIB is, alongside the EU and some sixty-four countries, a shareholder in one of the 'other' European banks: the European Bank for Reconstruction and Development (EBRD). Founded in 1991, the EBRD was assigned a key role in promoting the transition from central planning to market economics in Central and Eastern Europe following the end of the Cold War. Today, the EBRD functions as a development bank for 'countries committed to and applying the principles of multiparty democracy, pluralism and market economics'.[8] The Bank's original mandate referred specifically to investments in Central and Eastern European countries (CEECs), but this remit was extended to the Southern and Eastern Mediterranean Region in 2011 as part of investment efforts in Egypt, Jordan, Morocco, and Tunisia following the Arab Spring (EBRD 2012: 14). In 2015, the EBRD announced a five-year investment programme in Greece—an unusual move designed to support Greek business (Williams 2015). Such support may be indicative, too, of more fundamental concerns that the euro crisis is fuelling a 'broader crisis of democracy' in which extremist groups are gaining ground on the traditional governing elite (Matthijs 2014: 106).

levels and, in the short-term, economic activity (Taylor 1995). Monetary policy is thus a powerful instrument of macroeconomic stabilization, particularly when it comes to controlling inflation, a term that describes sustained increases in prices.

The Treaty puts price stability above all other goals for the ECB, but it does not specify what is meant by 'price stability'. The ECB's own definition—a year-on-year increase in the harmonized index of consumer prices for the eurozone of below 2 per cent—has been criticized for lacking precision (Buiter 1999). A particular concern here is that the Bank will pay insufficient heed to deflation—that is, a sustained fall in the price level that can discourage consumption and investment, and add to the real burden of paying back debt (Arestis and Sawyer 2001). The Bank offered a partial concession on this point when it announced that it would pursue inflation rates 'below, but close to, 2 per cent over the medium term' (ECB 2003). But this statement offered guidance, rather than a formal revision to its definition of price stability.

The Treaty is even more opaque about how the ECB is supposed to support economic policy, stating only that such efforts should contribute to the objectives of the Union.[9] That the objectives in question include such lofty aims as peace, social justice, and human rights, as well as more grounded objectives such as balanced growth and full employment,[10] makes it virtually impossible to judge the ECB's compliance with its secondary objectives. For its critics, the ECB's mandate is biased towards the pursuit of low inflation at the expense of higher growth and employment (Randzio-Plath 2000), although the Bank's supporters insist that no such trade-off exists, in the long term at least (Issing 2008). One point is clearer: the Treaty's so-called no-bailout clause prevents the ECB from directly taking on the debts of member states or EU institutions.[11]

Compared with other central banks, the ECB is more independent, but less transparent, than most. As for its independence, the ECB's statutes are embedded in a hard-to-revise Treaty, as compared with the more malleable legislative acts underpinning the United States' (US) Federal Reserve, the Bank of Japan, and the Bank of England. That the ECB can choose its own definition of 'price stability' gives it an added layer of independence that monetary authorities such as the Bank of England lack, since the latter is assigned an inflation target by the Chancellor of the Exchequer (the British equivalent of a finance minister). As regards transparency, the ECB has a less clear-cut price stability definition than the Federal Reserve, Bank of Japan, and the Bank of England, all of which were targeting a rate of inflation of 2 per cent at the time of writing. The ECB's definition is vaguer, because it commits the eurozone monetary authority to deliver inflation of below 2 per cent.

The ECB's primary task is to define and implement eurozone monetary policy.[12] The ECB, furthermore, holds and manages the official foreign reserves of the member states, which includes the foreign currency and gold reserves of national central banks. The Bank also promotes the smooth operation of European payments and settlements systems, which (among other things) allow individuals to use debit and credit cards in different eurozone countries and to transfer money between eurozone accounts (Quaglia 2009).

The ECB is required under the Treaty to contribute to 'the smooth conduct of policies pursued by the competent authorities relating to the prudential supervision of credit institutions and the stability of the financial system'.[13] This cumbersome phrase gives the Bank a role in financial supervision, although it does not say exactly what this role should be. Having kept the ECB at arm's length in this area in the early years of EMU, EU leaders' initial response to the global financial crisis was to put the Bank in charge of a new European Systemic Risk Board (ESRB). This new body has a nebulous mandate and gives the ECB powers to issue non-binding warnings only in the event of risks to the financial system. When the euro crisis intensified (see 'The ECB and the euro crisis'), eurozone members eventually agreed to create a European banking union, a key element of which is the Single Supervisory Mechanism (SSM). Under the SSM, the ECB is responsible for the licensing and supervision of all financial institutions in the eurozone (see Box 9.2). When a bank is found to be

---

BOX 9.2   The Single Supervisory Mechanism

With the launch of the SSM in November 2014, the ECB assumed responsibility for 'contributing to the safety and soundness of credit institutions and the stability of the financial system within the EU and each Member State'.[14] This task means, in practice, that the ECB is now responsible for licensing financial institutions, enforcing prudential standards, and carrying out supervisory reviews in all eurozone members.[15] In other words, the SSM is now responsible for ensuring that Europe's banks behave prudently rather than taking the kinds of risks that contributed to the euro crisis.

Situated within the ECB's decision-making structures, the SSM nonetheless operates at one remove from the Bank's governing structures. The Supervisory Board is responsible for day-to-day tasks and for preparing decisions to be approved by the ECB Governing Council (see 'The decision-making bodies of the ECB'). The Supervisory Board's right of initiative here is powerful: the ECB Governing Council is able to object to, but not modify, the Board's draft decisions.

The SSM has direct responsibility for the supervision of the eurozone's 120 largest banking groups, the rest being supervised by national supervisory authorities under the gaze of the ECB. This division of labour ensures that national authorities continue to play a major role in relation to financial supervision. Another way in which the ECB's powers over the SSM are constrained concerns the conduct of supervisory missions. Day-to-day supervision is carried out by so-called joint supervisory teams, which include officials from both the SSM and national supervisors.

In its first full year of operation, the SSM held thirty-eight meetings and took around 1,500 decisions on various aspects of financial supervision. These included a stress test of the eurozone banks, as a consequence of which several financial institutions were required to raise additional capital so as to prevent against future financial crises. The SSM also announced an investigation into parts of the Italian banking system, amidst concerns over financial stability and management in this sector. This area of policy-making is a sensitive one, wherein money meets power, confirming just how radically the ECB's powers have been transformed in recent years.

failing—or being close to doing so—it falls to the Supervisory Board, another new institution, to take charge of this bank. In principle, this means that all eyes will look not only towards national governments, but also towards the EU, when eurozone banks run into difficulties. All of these changes add onerous and politically sensitive new responsibilities to the ECB's already encumbered shoulders. The fact that the Bank hired nearly 1,000 additional staff to run the SSM is a sign of how complex and challenging this new role is (ECB 2015: 38–9).

The task of conducting eurozone exchange-rate policy, finally, is shared by the ECB and the Economic and Financial Affairs Council of Ministers (Ecofin). The authority to enter the single currency into an exchange-rate regime with a third country—if, for example, it were decided to peg the euro against the dollar—lies with Ecofin, but this decision must be based on a recommendation from the ECB or the Commission.[16] Ecofin is also empowered to formulate general orientations on the exchange-rate policy of the eurozone in relation to third countries, although it falls to the ECB to carry out specific foreign-exchange operations.[17] In practice, Ecofin has been reluctant to issue formal recommendations on the exchange rate of the euro for fear that they might be seen as impinging on the independence of the ECB; instead, eurozone finance ministers have developed an informal approach based on the adoption of 'terms of reference' by eurozone finance ministers.

The decision-making bodies of the ECB

Responsibility for eurozone monetary policy formally lies with the Eurosystem, which includes the ECB and the national central banks of eurozone member states.[18] The Eurosystem, in turn, is a member of the European System of Central Banks (ESCB), which also consists of monetary authorities from member states that do not share the single currency. The ESCB is made up of three key decision-making bodies—the Executive Board; the Governing Council; and the General Council—the composition of all three confirming just how prominent national authorities remain within eurozone monetary policy (see Table 9.1).

The ECB Executive Board runs the Bank on a day-to-day basis. Among its most important tasks is the preparation of ECB Governing Council meetings, thus giving the Executive Board significant agenda-setting powers in relation to Eurosystem business. The Executive Board also plays a lead role in policy implementation, putting monetary policy decisions into practice through measures taken by Frankfurt in close cooperation with national central banks.

The six members of the ECB Executive Board are appointed for an eight-year, non-renewable term of office by the European Council. This decision is based on a qualified majority vote (QMV) on a recommendation from the Council of Ministers following consultation with the European Parliament (EP) and the ECB Governing

TABLE 9.1 Composition of key ECB decision-making bodies

General Council	Governing Council	Executive Board	SSM Board	Official/Institution Represented
x	x	x		ECB President
x	x	x		ECB Vice-President
			x	SSM Supervisory Board Chair
	x	x	x	ECB Executive Board Member / SSM Vice-Chair
	x	x		ECB Executive Board Member
	x	x		ECB Executive Board Member
	x	x		ECB Executive Board Member
			x	Four ECB representatives on the SSM Board
				National Central Banks of Eurozone Members
x	x		x	Oesterreichische Nationalbank (Austria) · National Bank of Belgium · Central Bank of Cyprus · Bank of Estonia
x	x		x	Bank of Finland · Banque de France (France) · Deutsche Bundesbank (Germany) · Bank of Greece
x	x		x	Central Bank of Ireland · Banca d'Italia (Italy) · Bank of Latvia · Bank of Lithuania
x	x		x	Banque Centrale du Luxembourg (Luxembourg) · Central Bank of Malta · De Nederlandsche Bank (Netherlands) · Banco de Portugal

Cont. ▶

Cont.

National Bank of Slovakia	x x	The Bank of Slovenia	Banco de España (Spain)	

National Central Banks of Other Member States

Bulgarian National Bank	x	Czech National Bank	Bank of Croatia	Danmarks Nationalbank (Denmark)
Magyar Nemzeti Bank (Hungary)	x	National Bank of Poland	National Bank of Romania	Sveriges Riksbank (Sweden)
Bank of England	x			

National Financial Supervisors of Eurozone Members (operating independently from national central banks)

Bundesanstalt für Finanzdienstleistungsaufsicht (Germany)	x	Finantsinspektsioon (Estonia)	Finanšu un kapitāla tirgus komisija (Latvia)	Commission de Surveillance du Secteur Financier (Luxembourg)
Malta Financial Services Authority	x	Finanzmarktaufsich (Austria)	Finanssivalvonta (Finland)	

Council.[19] The only formal criteria for selecting ECB Executive Board members is that they should be chosen from persons of recognized standing and professional experience in monetary or banking matters. In practice, appointments to the Executive Board have been subject to informal deals, especially between the eurozone's largest member states (see Box 9.3).

By far the most important Executive Board member is the ECB President, who is responsible for chairing meetings of the Governing Council and representing the ECB externally.[20] The ECB President's signature also adorns euro banknotes, making him or her the public face of the single currency. The first President of the ECB was Wim Duisenberg, former head of Dutch central bank *De Nederlandsche Bank*.

| BOX 9.3 | Appointments to the ECB Executive Board |

In May 1998, an eleventh-hour bilateral agreement between French President Jacques Chirac and German Chancellor Helmut Kohl in the margins of the European Council saw Germany's preferred candidate, Wim Duisenberg, become the first ECB President. Known as 'the longest lunch in EU history', this agreement saw Wim Duisenberg then step aside in the middle of his eight-year term, allowing France's nominee, Jean-Claude Trichet, to become ECB President in November 2003.

Subsequent appointments to the ECB Executive Board sought, not without controversy, to 'reserve' a seat for candidates from the four large member states, with Eugenio Domingo Solans (Spain), Tommaso Padoa-Schioppa (Italy), Otmar Issing, Jürgen Stark, and Jörg Asmussen (all from Germany) each replaced by a compatriot. The two remaining seats on the Executive Board have generally been rotated between candidates from smaller eurozone countries, although the decision in 2012 to replace a Spaniard, José Manuel González Paramo, with a Luxembourger, Yves Mersch, created a more equitable balance between officials from large and small member states. The vice-presidency of the ECB was initially held by a Frenchman, Christian Noyer, but this role has been occupied by a central banker from a smaller state since 2002.

To date, only three out of a total of nineteen Executive Board members have been women. To underline this imbalance, the EP voted against Yves Mersch in October 2012, there being no woman on the ECB Executive Board at this point. Although finance ministers appointed Mersch anyway—the EP having no formal say in such matters—the ECB Governing Council subsequently agreed to introduce gender targets for senior management appointments. The appointment of Danièle Nouy as chair of the SSM and Elke König as chair of the Supervisory Board suggest that attitudes may be changing, although it should be noted that the SSM regulation explicitly requires appointments to the Supervisory Board to respect the principles of gender balance, experience, and qualification.[21]

It was initially assumed that a German candidate would succeed Jean-Claude Trichet as ECB President in 2012, with Axel Weber considered the heir apparent until his unexpected resignation as president of the Bundesbank in April 2011. Germany proved unable or unwilling to field an alternative, leaving Mario Draghi to emerge as a compromise candidate. Draghi won the backing of EU finance ministers in 2011, paving the way for his investiture as the third President of the ECB in November 2011.

Duisenberg took office in 1998 and was succeeded in 2003 by Jean-Claude Trichet, former governor of *Banque de France*. Trichet served his full eight-year term before being succeeded in November 2011 by Mario Draghi, similarly, former president of *Banca d'Italia*.

The ECB's authority over the SSM is constrained by the presence of national authorities on the latter's Supervisory Board (see Box 9.2). The SSM chair is not an internal appointment; instead, it falls to the ECB Governing Council to propose a candidate on the basis of an open procedure, who is then approved by the EP and confirmed by the Council. The vice-chair of the Supervisory Board is chosen from the members of the ECB Executive Board, although he or she must be approved by the EP. The other members of the Supervisory Board include four representatives of the ECB and a representative from each national financial supervisor, which is the national central bank in some cases and a government agency in others. These arrangements sound complex, but their complexity has a simple explanation: member states were prepared to increase the ECB's powers over financial supervision in light of the euro crisis, but not to eliminate the role of national financial supervisors entirely.

The ECB Governing Council includes the six members of the ECB Executive Board and the national central bank governors of eurozone members. The Governing Council's most important function is to formulate the monetary policy of the eurozone. It also determines the ECB's role in international financial institutions, such as the International Monetary Fund (IMF), and fulfils its advisory function, which allows the ECB to submit opinions on EU and national legislation that may be relevant to its sphere of competence.

Originally, all members of the Governing Council retained the right to cast a single vote on monetary policy matters, with decisions approved, in most cases, by a simple majority. Under this arrangement, the ECB Executive Board saw its relative voting power diminish as the number of eurozone members (and, by implication, national central bank governors on the ECB Governing Council) increased from eleven in 1999 to nineteen in 2015. A new system, which came into effect in 2015, rotates votes between national central bank governors, the speed of rotation varying according to the relative size of a member state's economy and financial sector (Meade 2003). Rotating voting is not unusual among central banks—not all members of the US Federal Reserve Open Markets Committee have a vote all of the time—but this arrangement is unique among EU institutions.

The General Council of the ECB consists of the Bank's President and Vice President, and the national central bank governors of the twenty-eight EU member states (twenty-seven, post-Brexit). Initially designed as a transitional body, the General Council was given responsibility for certain practical aspects of the ECB's work, such as the collection of statistical information, until such time as all EU member states have adopted the single currency.[22] This seldom-seen body came to prominence during the 2008 global financial crisis by virtue of its advisory role in relation to financial supervision. It was on the basis of this role that EU finance ministers decided in 2009 that the President and vice-chairs of the ESRB should be chosen from the ECB General Council. This decision opened the door for the Governor of the Bank of England, a central bank from outside the eurozone, to serve as one of two vice-chairs of this new body.

Explaining the ECB's institutional design

Several variants of new institutionalism (see Chapter 1) can explain different aspects of the ECB's distinctive design. *Historical institutionalism*, with its belief that past institutional choices influence present policies, for example, can help us to understand the prominent role played by national central banks in the governance of the Eurosystem. *Rational choice institutionalism*, with its emphasis on intergovernmental bargaining and commitment devices, helps to explain the very high degree of independence granted to the ECB. Finally, *sociological institutionalism* offers important insights into the influence of economic ideas on the governance of the ECB.

If we apply historical institutionalism, the role of national central banks in EMU shows signs of path-dependence that can be traced back to the signature of the Treaty of Rome in 1957. No reference was made at the outset of the European Economic Community (EEC) to the goal of monetary union. But the Treaty's modest provisions on macroeconomic policy coordination did authorize the European Commission to promote collaboration between national central bankers on matters related to the balance of payments (Maes 2006). National central bankers were wary about the Commission encroaching on their turf and they moved quickly to initiate discussion on their own terms (Andrews 2003). The result was the creation of the Committee of Governors of the Central Banks of EEC member states in May 1964.

Few central banks were independent of national governments during this period—the Bundesbank was a notable exception—but these circumstances did not prevent the Committee of Governors from keeping its distance from Brussels. Significant in this respect was the decision of the Committee of Governors to meet in the margins of the Bank for International Settlements (BIS) in Basle, Switzerland, far from the gaze of EEC institutions. The Commission was given observer status on the Committee of Governors, but its official was excluded from discussions in Basle of highly sensitive policy matters (Andrews 2003).

In December 1969, EEC leaders finally agreed on the goal of EMU, inviting Luxembourg Prime Minister Pierre Werner to work out a detailed policy plan. Such was the influence of the Committee of Governors by this point that its chair, Hubert Ansiaux, was invited by Werner to produce an opinion on the technical aspects of preparations for monetary union. It was in the light of this opinion that the Werner Committee proposed, in effect, to upgrade the Committee of Governors to the status of an EEC institution with responsibility for the conduct of monetary policy in EMU.

The international economic turmoil that followed the first oil shock in October 1973 shelved the Werner Plan, but the Committee of Governors continued to wield significant influence in EEC macroeconomic policy. This influence was evident, for example, in the Committee's key role in the management of the European monetary system (EMS), a fixed exchange-rate regime launched by member states in March 1979. The relaunch of EMU at the Hanover European Council in June 1988 saw national central banks given a still more significant role, with the governors invited to draw up a blueprint for a single currency under the leadership of Commission President Jacques Delors.

The reluctance of national central banks to cede control over monetary policy was evident in the final report of the Delors Committee. It called for the creation of a European System of Central Banks that would include a central monetary authority and national central banks (Committee for the Study of Economic and Monetary Union 1989). EC leaders endorsed this vision of EMU, even inviting the Committee of Governors to draw up the statutes of the ESCB in the intergovernmental conference (IGC) on EMU launched in December 1990.

The Maastricht Treaty, signed in February 1992, codified a three-stage plan for EMU in which national central banks played a central role. Stage 1, which began in July 1990, saw the Committee of Governors given a more hands-on role in the coordination of monetary policies. Stage 2, which began in January 1994, saw the Committee of Governors integrated into the Council of the European Monetary Institute (EMI), which took charge of practical preparations for EMU. These preparations culminated in June 1998 with the launch of the ECB, which saw the Council of the EMI transformed into the ECB Governing Council. Stage 3 of EMU, which was launched in January 1999, saw the Governing Council take charge of eurozone monetary policy, thus giving national central bank governors a major say in EU macroeconomic policy a little over four decades after informal cooperation between these institutions was initiated.

Historical institutionalism can explain the involvement of national central banks in the decision-making structures of the Eurosystem. But it is arguably less clear about the reasons why EMU involved such a dramatic increase in central bank independence in the EU. Rational choice institutionalism fares better here, with Moravcsik (1998) pointing towards the importance of preference formation, intergovernmental bargaining, and institutional choice in the design of EMU's governance architecture.

Moravcsik's essential point about preference formation regarding EMU is that Germany had only a little to gain from a single currency, while France stood to gain a lot. In the case of the former, it seemed unlikely that EMU could outperform domestic macroeconomic policy. The Bundesbank, in particular, had a formidable track record at achieving price stability, even if some in the business community saw a single currency as a response to the progressive appreciation of the Deutschmark against some European currencies. In the case of the latter, the Banque de France was already shadowing the monetary policy of the Bundesbank as part of its efforts to keep inflation under control. EMU was therefore seen by political leaders and interest groups alike as a way in which to reassert a degree of shared sovereignty over French macroeconomic policies.

The intensity of France's preferences for EMU was such, Moravcsik (1998) contends, that its negotiators were willing to make significant concessions to Germany during intergovernmental bargaining over the Maastricht Treaty. A deal breaker in this regard was Germany's demand that EMU attach a very high degree of importance to the pursuit of price stability. This commitment was essential in allaying domestic concerns—especially in the upper echelons of the Bundesbank—that a single currency would be soft on inflation. To this end, it was agreed not only that the Maastricht Treaty would assign an unequivocal price-stability mandate to the ECB, but also that EU member states would be required to keep inflation under control and to meet convergence criteria before being admitted to the eurozone.

On the issue of institutional choice, Moravcsik (1998) rejects the argument, neofunctionalist in its reasoning, that the delegation of monetary policy to the ECB was a matter of necessity for the successful management of the single currency. He suggests, rather, that the framers of the Maastricht Treaty chose to delegate policy-making powers in this area to an independent institution, rather than a political forum such as Ecofin, because the former provided a more credible commitment to the anti-inflationary intergovernmental bargain on which EMU rests. The ECB, in other words, was given a high degree of autonomy over monetary policy because member states willed it so.

Scholars looking at these issues through the lens of sociological institutionalism challenge this line of reasoning. The economic case for an independent ECB, McNamara (2002) suggests, is a 'rational fiction' that is based on a narrow reading of the causes of inflation and the distributional consequences of interest-rate decisions. The emergence of independent central banks in the eurozone and elsewhere, she suggests, can be viewed as a symbol of economic credibility aimed at financial markets, as well as the product of an epistemic community with a shared understanding of monetary policy.

Verdun (1999) also sees an epistemic community at work in the design of the ECB's price stability mandate. The Delors Committee, she argues, consisted not only of policy-makers with an authoritative claim to knowledge about central banking issues, but also a shared set of causal beliefs about the importance of stable prices for sustainable economic growth. It was by virtue of these beliefs, Verdun argues, that the Delors Report insisted on the pursuit of price stability above all other goals as a *sine qua non* for EMU.

The ECB and the euro crisis

The global financial crisis was a major institutional test for the ECB. The euro crisis proved more testing still, because it continued to cast doubt on the future of the single currency and hence the Bank itself. The single currency's existential difficulties came to light in late 2009, when the newly elected Greek government revealed previous systematic and widespread misreporting of Greek debt and deficit data (Savage and Verdun 2016). A sharp upward revision of budget deficit and government debt figures in Greece triggered a sovereign debt crisis, as financial markets demanded higher and higher interest rates on Greek government debt to allay concerns that the country might default.

By late 2010, the euro crisis had engulfed Ireland, which found itself on the brink of sovereign default after the Irish government stepped in to support the country's banks following the bursting of its national housing bubble (Donovan and Murphy 2013). Portugal soon faced similar problems for different reasons, the global financial crisis having amplified pre-existing fiscal and political problems (Pereira and Wemans 2012). Serious fiscal problems emerged in 2012 in Cyprus, which was heavily exposed to Greece, as well as dependent on a precarious financial model reliant on foreign borrowers (Zenios 2013). But the bigger worry was that the sovereign debt crisis would spread to two large eurozone members, Spain and Italy. Spain suffered a similar fate to Ireland after its decade-long housing boom came to an end (Ortega and Peñalosa 2012). Although Italy's problems of low growth and high debt were long-standing, this fact did not prevent financial markets from reacting to them with a newfound sense of alarm in light of developments elsewhere in the eurozone (Pagoulatos and Quaglia 2013).

Sovereign debt crises happen in—and to—monetary unions and are invariably messy. Even in advanced economies, as Carmen Reinhart and Kenneth Rogoff (2013) note, such crises historically involve some combination of fiscal retrenchment (that is, tax increases and expenditure cuts), debt restructuring (such as an agreement with creditors to pay back only a percentage of what is owed), inflation (to reduce the real debt burden), and financial repression (including controls on capital movements or government borrowing from pension funds). In 2013, for example, the city of Detroit filed for bankruptcy to cancel more than a third of its US$18 billion municipal debt. Even after this move, Detroit faced swingeing expenditure cuts to get its borrowing under control, even as it received $300 million in federal aid in September 2013 (Davey and Walsh 2013).

The EU, in comparison, entered the euro crisis with limited instruments for crisis management. There is no bankruptcy code for eurozone members, which are also prohibited by the no-bailout clause from being liable for—or assuming–each other's debt.[23] The Treaty does provide 'mutual assistance' to member states facing (certain types of) economic crisis, but this provision applies only to EU member states that have not yet adopted the euro.[24] All of this raises the question of whether eurozone members that find themselves facing a sovereign debt crisis might not be better off exiting the euro and whether the eurozone could survive such an exit (Eichengreen 2010).

Faced with the global financial crisis, the ECB was quick to provide emergency loans to eurozone banks, but slow to cut interest rates and engage in large-scale bond purchases of the kind undertaken by the US Federal Reserve, Bank of Japan, and

Bank of England during the financial crisis. Tensions within the ECB's decision-making structures played a role here, with Bundesbank President Axel Weber and his successor Jens Weidmann both openly critical of unconventional monetary policies (Moschella and Lombardi 2015). As the euro crisis worsened, the ECB went against Bundesbank wishes. In 2010 came the Securities Markets Programme (SMP), under which the ECB committed to the limited purchase of government bonds, thus providing a valuable line of support to those member states facing rising costs of borrowing on government debt. The SMP was superseded in 2012 by the Outright Monetary Transactions (OMT), which gave effect to ECB President Mario Draghi's promise two months earlier 'to do whatever it takes' to preserve the euro (Hodson 2013b). Although the OMT had yet to be used at the time of writing, its potential for the unlimited purchase of government bonds for eurozone members facing fiscal crisis had a dramatic effect on market sentiment. By 2014, the euro crisis had de-escalated (but not disappeared). Still, annual increases in the consumer price index were close to zero. Fearing a prolonged period of deflation, the ECB finally embraced quantitative easing in early 2015 with its expanded asset purchase programme. Thus the ECB agreed to purchase up to €60 billion in public and private bonds per month, some seven years after the US Federal Reserve had embarked on a similar course of action (Dunne *et al.* 2015).

The euro crisis has pushed the ECB not only into unconventional monetary policies, but also into a wider and more controversial role in crisis prevention and management. The launch of the SSM gave the Bank important new powers in the area of crisis prevention (see Box 9.2). An early sign of the ECB's increased responsibilities for crisis management came from an informal summit of EU leaders in early 2010, which invited the Commission to monitor fiscal efforts in Greece 'in liaison with the ECB . . . and drawing on the expertise of the IMF' (EU Heads of State or Government 2010). As Greece's fiscal problems mounted, the 'Troika', as this highly unusual informal institutional arrangement came to be known, led negotiations with Greek authorities on a package of €110 billion loans from the EU and IMF, and took charge of monitoring the policy commitments attached to such support (Panagiotarea 2013). Greece received a second loan package from the EU and IMF in 2011, worth €109 billion, and shortly after reached a deal with its creditors to write off most of the Greek government debt held by private investors. These measures were significant, but they fell well short of restoring fiscal sustainability to an economy that contracted by more than a quarter between 2007 and 2014. Discredited, the mainstream parties lost power in a general election in January 2015 to a government led by Greece's Coalition of the Radical Left, Syriza. Having refused to deal with the Troika and after holding a referendum on the deal on offer for the disbursement of the final tranche of the second loan deal (which Greek voters rejected), there followed a long night of negotiation in the European Council in which Germany tabled plans for Greece to take a 'time out' from the eurozone in return for further debt structuring (Hodson 2016). A political deal was eventually reached to keep Greece in the eurozone, but at the expense of even more draconian reform commitments and the return of the Troika. It shortly afterwards reached agreement with Greek officials on a third round of loans, this time valued at €85 billion.

The Troika played a central, if not quite as dramatic, role in negotiating and overseeing loan deals from the EU and/or IMF for Ireland (2010), Portugal (2011), Spain (2012), and Cyprus (2013). Officials from the Commission, ECB, and IMF became familiar faces in the national media of these states through their regular meetings with government representatives. Familiar too were 'Troika Go Home' placards and graffiti from anti-austerity protestors (Kousis 2014). Such protestors made their presence felt at the inauguration of the ECB's new headquarters in 2015, which saw violent exchanges between members of the so-called Blockupy movement and Frankfurt riot police (Pianta and Gerbaudo 2015).

Theorizing the euro crisis

The ECB may be an idiosyncratic institution, but, as noted above, its institutional idiosyncrasies can be explored using many of the theories surveyed in this volume. These variants of institutional theory, and others, are relevant too for understanding the ECB's response to the euro crisis, as can be seen in a new wave of institutionalist scholarship on the Bank.

Historical institutionalism sees the euro crisis as a critical juncture, and policy responses to it as exemplary of path-dependence and institutional layering (Verdun 2015). Paradoxically, Yiangou *et al.* (2013) see path-dependence under EMU as a catalyst for change. The ECB's strict adherence to the no-bailout clause, they argue, pushed member states' hands into institutional reforms to address governance 'gaps' in the eurozone's institutional design. Peter Hall (2012: 190) offers a more conventional view of path-dependence in which the ECB's preoccupation with price stability discouraged large-scale bond purchases in the early stages of the euro crisis and so pushed eurozone members into protracted intergovernmental negotiations that further alarmed financial markets about the unsustainability of member states' public finances. In a similarly historical institutionalist vein, Braun (2015) sees the ECB as responding to—and ultimately benefiting from—the unintended consequences of EMU's lack of preparedness for a sovereign debt crisis. 'True, policy-makers did act as *bricoleurs* [handymen or women] who made use of the tools that were at hand,' he writes, 'yet as it turned out, during the emergency phase of the crisis the ECB was virtually the only tool at hand' (Braun 2015: 434).

From a rational choice institutionalist perspective, the ECB is viewed as a commitment device designed to lock in the benefits of price stability (Moravcsik 1998). A puzzle posed by the euro crisis is why Germany would jeopardize this commitment by giving the ECB new and more complex responsibilities that go beyond the pursuit of price stability. One explanation concerns the lack of ready-made alternatives; another points to the fact that the ECB's new powers are not as expansive as they might seem at first glance. The institutional design of the SSM significantly constrains the involvement of the ECB in financial supervision. This can be seen, for example, in the Supervisory Board's powerful right of initiative vis-à-vis the ECB Governing Council and in the continued involvement of national supervisors in the operation of the SSM (see Box 9.2). A key question from a rational choice institutionalist perspective is not only why the ECB was given new responsibilities by member states, but also why the Bank consented. For Héritier (2015), the ECB can be seen as an opportunistic agent that responded to an unexpected external shock (specifically, the euro crisis) by reinterpreting its mandate in ways that led to a covert deepening of integration. Henning (2015) sees the ECB as being involved in a strategic game with member states in which the Bank seeks to insulate itself from political interference.

Discursive institutionalism, the newest of the new institutionalisms, is readily applicable to a crisis in which words have been more plentiful than deeds (Crespy and Schmidt 2014; Karyotis and Gerodimos 2015). Schmidt (2014) sees the ECB as being by far the most important institution in the euro crisis because of its capacity for subtle communication with financial markets in contrast to what she sees as ill-judged interventions by national leaders. A key insight from discursive institutionalism is that policy-makers draw their ideas not from a particular paradigm, but from a complex collection of ideas that remain in flux, particularly during moments of crisis.

Given the scale and speed of reforms to EMU's institutional architecture in response to the euro crisis, it is not surprising to see scholars returning to integration theory. Niemann and Ioannou (2015) offer a neo-functionalist reading of the crisis that highlights the ECB's role in championing integrationist measures. The Bank, they suggest, was a vocal supporter of European Council President Herman Van Rompuy's plans for a 'genuine' EMU, as well as an early champion of European banking union (Niemann and Ioannou 2015: 211). For Schimmelfennig (2015a), who offers a liberal intergovernmentalist account of the euro crisis, reforms such as European banking union are an attempt to boost the credibility of supranational oversight in those areas in which decentralised forms of decision-making fell short. The ECB may have bought time for member states to make this choice, he contends, 'but it does not seem to have had a noteworthy agenda-setting role in institutional reform' (Schimmelfennig 2015a: 189). Traditional theories of integration treat supranational institutions as being hardwired for the pursuit of European integration—even if they disagree over their ability to realize this goal. But the new intergovernmentalism challenges this view (Bickerton *et al.* 2015a): the ECB was a consistent—if cautious—champion of a more centralized approach to financial supervision, but it was critical of many integrationist initiatives in response to the crisis, including plans for a financial transactions tax and Eurobonds.

Legitimating the ECB

Compared to other EU institutions, the ECB is subject to comparatively few checks and balances. While members of the European Commission and Court of Justice serve renewable terms of five and six years, respectively, members of the ECB Executive Board are appointed for eight years, after which they cannot be rehired. This rule gives the ECB an added layer of political protection, as does the fact that the EP is powerless to remove members of the Bank's Executive Board. Only the Court of Justice can call for the removal of Executive Board members who are guilty of serious misconduct or otherwise in breach of the requirements for the performance of their duties, and only then with the prior approval of the ECB Governing Council.[25]

The ECB's remarkable degree of statutory independence has understandably raised concerns about its legitimacy. For Verdun and Christiansen (2000), the problem is not so much that the ECB lacks democratic accountability, because this characterization is true to a greater or lesser extent of all independent central banks; rather, it is that the Bank lacks the societal embeddedness of other monetary authorities. In other words, the ECB is unable to look to the kinds of beliefs and values that allowed the Bundesbank, for example, to seek legitimacy by appealing to collective memories of hyperinflation and through the interaction of its conservative monetary policies with Germany's coordinated welfare state policies.

The failure of EMU's architects to embed the ECB in a 'wider European polity', Verdun and Christiansen (2000) warn, leaves the euro's legitimacy dangerously dependent on its perceived economic benefits and hence on short-term economic fluctuations. Subsequent empirical work chimes with this analysis, with Deroose *et al.* (2007) finding a correlation between popular support for the euro, on the one hand, and expectations about future economic developments, on the other. The perception that the euro cash changeover in 2002 caused prices to rise sharply, although not borne out by the economic data, also appears to have weighed heavily on support for the single currency in some countries.

For its part, the ECB has sought to enhance its legitimacy by reaching out to the EP. The Treaty envisages only a limited role for the EU legislature in the oversight of the Bank. For example, the ECB President is required to present an annual report on its activities to the EP and, along with other Executive Board members, to appear before competent committees if requested to do so.[26] But these provisions have not stopped the two sides from developing a close working relationship. An illustrative example is the monetary dialogue, which sees the ECB President appear before ECON at least four times per year to present the Bank's views on the economic situation.

Few commentators expected the monetary dialogue to amount to much, but it has proved to be a mutually beneficial forum. For the ECB, the monetary dialogue offers further evidence of the Bank's commitment to transparency and a public platform from which to expound on policy issues in a non-technical way. For the EP, the monetary dialogue offers a chance to (be seen to) hold the ECB to account, as well as a foothold in an area of EU policy-making in which the legislature has limited competence. Although it is difficult to measure the precise impact of the monetary dialogue, Amtenbrink and Van Duin (2009) argue that the EP has achieved a level of oversight for eurozone monetary policy beyond that envisaged in the Treaty, even if doubts remain about whether the ECB is being held sufficiently to account.

The surprising success of the monetary dialogue can be explained by a number of factors. First, the ECB President has demonstrated a commitment to this forum by presenting carefully prepared statements, and answering most questions in a full and frank way. Second, the Bank offered concessions to members of ECON (the main EP committee responsible), agreeing, in 2000, for example, to make public the macroeconomic forecasts prepared by ECB staff. In 2015, similarly, the ECB began to publish minutes of Governing Council meetings, a move for which the EP had long pushed. Third, ECON has upgraded its expertise on monetary policy by inviting high-profile economists to contribute to the preparation of the monetary dialogue. Fourth, the ECON Committee has itself operated in a highly transparent manner, publishing a transcript of the monetary dialogue, as well as the briefings of its outside experts, on its external website.

The ECB has been altogether more guarded in its dealings with other EU institutions. A case in point is the Bank's uneasy relationship with the Eurogroup, an informal meeting of eurozone finance ministers that meets in advance of Ecofin. A key rationale for the launch of the Eurogroup in 1997 was to facilitate a dialogue behind closed doors between eurozone finance ministers and the ECB President, with the Commissioner for Economic and Monetary Affairs also in attendance. Initially, such discussions were said to have been fairly one-sided, with the ECB President keen to lecture finance ministers on the importance of fiscal discipline, but finance ministers reluctant to criticize the ECB openly out of respect for its independence (Puetter 2006).

The appointment of then Luxembourg Prime Minister Jean-Claude Juncker as the first permanent President of the Eurogroup in early 2005—prior to which eurozone finance ministers had taken it in turns to chair—marked the beginning of a more combative approach to the ECB. Tensions came to a head before the end of the year when Juncker let it be known in public that eurozone finance ministers saw the ECB's anticipated increase in interest rates as 'not particularly necessary' (Atkins *et al.* 2005). Such comments did not deter the ECB from increasing interest rates in December 2005, but neither did they discourage Juncker from publicly seeking an enhanced dialogue on eurozone issues with the ECB President. This request received short shrift from ECB President Jean-Claude Trichet, who insisted that the proposed measures were incompatible with the independence of the Bank. Juncker's reincarnation as Commission President raises the possibility that this controversy could be rekindled. Noteworthy in this regard was Juncker's call in his Commission presidency 'mission statement' 'to re-balance the relationship between elected politicians and the European Central Bank in the daily management of the eurozone' (2014).

Juncker may be trying to settle old scores here. But the question of whether there are sufficient checks and balances on the ECB in view of the new roles acquired during the euro crisis is a legitimate one. The accountability of the Troika is a particular point of contention here. The Commission and ECB are accountable in their own ways to the EP (see Chapter 5, 6, and 8), but the IMF—even though it has, in some sense, become a *de facto* institution of the EU (Hodson 2015a)—is bound only by its own governance structures. There is, moreover, no mechanism for holding all three members of the Troika to collective account. The ECB has tended to keep its counsel on the Troika, but the Commission President has publicly called for the Troika to be replaced in due course with a 'democratically legitimate and more accountable structure, based around European institutions with enhanced parliamentary control both at European and at national level' (Juncker 2014). Germany has thus far insisted on the continued involvement of the Troika, but an open question is whether the IMF will remain a willing participant. Although the IMF has been empowered by the eurozone crisis, it has come at the cost of significant compromises over the conditions of EU–IMF support and increasingly vocal concerns that EU member states have a disproportionate say within the Fund's decision-making bodies.

The ECB's new role in financial supervision is quite different—although not unproblematic—from the point of view of accountability. Under the SSM regulation, the ECB is subject to much more stringent checks and balances on its supervisory activities than is the case for monetary policy. A key difference here is that the EP, as noted above, has power of approval over the appointment of the SSM chair and vice-chair. The ECB nonetheless brings a very high degree of independence to its role as financial supervisor by virtue of its autonomy under the Treaty. This arrangement is far from being the norm for financial supervisors worldwide, which routinely face political interference in decision-making (Quintyn *et al.* 2007). The question that arises is whether the ECB confers too much independence on the SSM for such a politicized area of policy-making or whether the ECB's independence might be at risk from the activities of the SSM.

Conclusion

Under the Lisbon Treaty, the ECB has finally been recognized as an EU institution—but it remains an unusual one. The autonomy afforded to the ECB in the pursuit of this goal also goes well beyond the independence enjoyed by the Commission and the Court of Justice, leading Pollack (2003: 392) to describe the Bank as 'without doubt the most spectacular example of delegation in the European Union since the EEC Treaty of 1957'. Like many *de novo* bodies (see Chapters 1 and 10), the ECB also has a decentralized governance structure, with national central bank governors outnumbering Executive Board members.

The ECB presided over a seemingly successful first decade for the single currency before being hit by the worst global financial crisis for nearly a century and a sovereign debt crisis that continues to cast doubt on the viability of EMU. The Bank's initial response to the euro crisis was characteristically cautious, but—as fiscal turmoil spread from one eurozone member to another—it eventually pursued a panoply of unconventional policy responses, including large-scale bond buying. The euro crisis also brought new and onerous roles for the ECB through its involvement in the Troika, which plays a lead role in the provision of financial support to eurozone members and its stewardship of the SSM.

The ECB faces few checks and balances compared to other EU institutions. And yet the ECB has gone further than the Treaty requires in developing a close working relationship with the EP. Whether the ECB–ECON monetary dialogue can be said to hold the ECB to account is a matter of debate, but it has proved to be a mutually beneficial exercise for both sides. The ECB's new role in relation to financial supervision has brought with it greater accountability; for example through the EP's role in appointing the SSM chair and vice-chair. Such accountability sits uneasily with the ECB's still-high degree of independence in relation to monetary policy and it remains to be seen how this role will fit with its potentially more politicized responsibilities as financial supervisor.

Although all EU institutions face an uncertain future, the fate of the ECB is particularly opaque. Further eurozone integration is a possibility, but eurozone disintegration cannot be discounted. Although an agreement was ultimately reached in 2015 on further financial support for Greece, the country came within hours of exiting the euro. Having done so once, it could do so again, and there is no guarantee that loans will continue to flow or that Greece will remain resigned to the exacting conditions attached to such funding. Greece's exit from the eurozone could lead to the dissolution of EMU as financial markets question the inviolability of other member states' commitment to the euro. The reintroduction of national currencies would see national central banks exit the Eurosystem, and hence end the ECB's role in monetary policy and, presumably, financial supervision. As such, the euro crisis is an existential one not only for the single currency, but also for the ECB, which may ultimately explain why this conservative institution accepted member states' calls to take on new and complex competences as the economic problems facing the eurozone became steadily more serious.

ENDNOTES

1. Thanks to John Peterson and Ivo Maes for helpful comments on an earlier draft of this chapter. The usual disclaimer applies.
2. Art. 127 TFEU.
3. Art. 130 TFEU.
4. Case C-11/00 *Commission of the European Communities v European Central Bank* ECLI:EU:C:2003:395, [126].
5. Art. 13 TEU.

6. The term 'eurozone' is widely used in the press, but 'euro area' is the preferred term in Brussels and appears in the Treaties.

7. Art. 309 TFEU.

8. Art. 1 of the Agreement establishing the European Bank for Reconstruction and Development.

9. Art. 105 TFEU.

10. Art. 3 TEU.

11. Art. 125 TFEU.

12. Art. 127 TFEU.

13. Art. 127 TFEU.

14. Art. 1 of Council Regulation (EU) No. 1024/2013 of 15 October 2013.

15. The SSM is, in principle, open to EU member states that have not adopted the euro, but none joined at the outset.

16. Art. 219 TFEU.

17. Arts 219 and 127 TFEU.

18. Art. 282 TFEU.

19. Art. 11, Protocol 4 TFEU.

20. Art. 11, Protocol 4 TFEU.

21. Art. 26 of Council Regulation (EU) No. 1024/2013 of 15 October 2013.

22. Art. 46, Protocol 4 TFEU.

23. Art. 125 TFEU.

24. Art. 143 TFEU.

25. Art. 11, Protocol 4 TFEU.

26. Art. 285 TFEU.

 FURTHER READING

See Hodson (2015b) for a short introduction to EMU and its relevance for debates about EU policy-making. For a detailed introduction to the economics of EMU, see De Grauwe (2016). Howarth and Quaglia (2016) examine the design of European Banking Union and Jones (2014) offers a series of short, lucid essays written at the height of the euro crisis. For a discussion of the euro crisis from competing theoretical perspectives, see Ioannou *et al.* (2015). Hodson (2011) includes a detailed discussion of the ECB's ambivalent relationship with the EU's institutional order. Dyson and Featherstone (1999), Moravcsik (1998), and McNamara (1998) offer alternative perspectives on the ECB's creation.

De Grauwe, P. (2016) *The Economics of Monetary Union* (11th edn, Oxford and New York: Oxford University Press).

Dyson, K., and Featherstone, K. (1999) *The Road to Maastricht: Negotiating Economic and Monetary Union* (Oxford and New York: Oxford University Press).

Hodson, D. (2011) *Governing the Euro Area in Good Times and Bad* (Oxford: Oxford University Press).

Hodson, D. (2015) 'Policy-making under economic and monetary union: Crisis, change and continuity', in H. Wallace, M. Pollack, and A. Young (eds) *Policy-making in the European Union* (7th edn, Oxford University Press): 166–95.

Howarth, D., and Quaglia, L. (2016) *The Political Economy of European Banking Union* (Oxford: Oxford University Press).

Ioannou, D., Leblond, P., and Niemann, A. (eds) (2014) 'European integration in times of crisis: Theoretical perspectives', *Journal of European Public Policy* 22/2: Special Issue.

Jones, E. (2014) *The Year the European Crisis Ended* (Basingstoke: Palgrave MacMillan).

McNamara, K. (1998) *The Currency of Ideas: Monetary Politics in Europe* (Ithaca, NY: Cornell University Press).

Moravcsik, A. (1998) *The Choice for Europe: Social Purpose and State Power from Messina to Maastricht* (Ithaca, NY: Cornell University Press).

 ## WEB LINKS

http://ec.europa.eu/dgs/economy_finance
http://www.ecb.eu
http://www.europarl.europa.eu/committees/en/econ/home.html
https://www.bankingsupervision.europa.eu

Key official websites include those of the European Commission's Directorate-General for Economic and Financial Affairs, the ECB itself, the SSM, and the EP's ECON Committee.

http://www.economist.com
http://www.ft.com

The *Financial Times* is *the* journal of record on EU economic and political affairs, with *The Economist* counting as another important publication.

CHAPTER 10

European agencies: Managing Europeanization

R. Daniel Kelemen and Giandomenico Majone

▮ Summary

Over the past three decades, the European Union (EU) has instituted more than forty agencies in a wide variety of policy areas, with headquarters spread out across the member states. EU agencies are now well established as an integral part of the EU's model of governance. This chapter analyses why EU agencies have been created and what impact they are having on European governance. EU leaders have delegated regulatory powers to agencies both in response to functional pressures and because of political motivations relating to inter-institutional politics in the EU. The chapter spotlights the development and operation of three particular European agencies: the European Environment Agency (EEA); the European Medicines Agency (EMA); and the European Food Safety Authority (EFSA).

Introduction

This chapter examines the rise of EU agencies. EU agencies—sometimes also la-belled 'authorities' or 'centres'—can be defined as 'EU level public authorities with a legal personality and a certain degree of organizational and financial autonomy that are created by acts of secondary legislation in order to perform clearly specified tasks' (Kelemen 2005: 175). Over the past three decades, the EU has established more than forty agencies in a wide variety of policy areas, with headquarters spread out across the member states. With the establishment of these agencies, along with the creation of other *de novo* bodies as described by Hodson and Peterson in Chapter 1, the EU has quietly managed to expand its regulatory capacity without directly increasing the size or capacity of the EU's primary executive organ—the European Commission. EU agencies are now well established as an integral part of the EU's model of govern-ance. This chapter analyses why they have been created and what impact they are having on European governance.

Development

The first EU agencies—the European Centre for the Development of Vocational Training (Cedefop) and the European Foundation for the Improvement of Living and Working Conditions (Eurofound)—were created in the 1970s, but these were operational, rather than regulatory, bodies. The 1990s produced a second wave of agencies, this time dealing with regulatory issues, including the European Environ-ment Agency (EEA) and the European Medicines Agency (EMA). A third wave of agency creation started at the beginning of the twenty-first century with the creation of the European Food Safety Authority (EFSA), the European Maritime Safety Agency (EMSA), the European Aviation Safety Agency (EASA), and the European Railway Agency (ERA). It has continued with the recent creation of EU authorities in the fields of securities, banking, and pension regulation. Most European regula-tory-type agencies of the second and third generation advise the Commission on the technical or scientific aspects of regulatory problems, but have not been given the formal authority to take final and binding regulatory decisions.

   In addition to the regulatory agencies on which we focus in this chapter, the EU has also established a handful of executive agencies that perform managerial tasks on behalf of the Commission, such as the Education, Audiovisual and Culture Executive Agency (EACEA), the European Research Council Executive Agency (ERC Executive Agency), and the Executive Agency for Small and Medium-sized Enterprises (EASME). It has also set up a number of agencies focusing on foreign and security policy, such as the European Union Institute for Security Studies (EUISS), the

European Defence Agency (EDA), and others focused on justice and policing, such as the EU Judicial Cooperation Unit (Eurojust), the European Asylum Support Office (EASO), and the European Agency for the Management of Operational Cooperation at the External Borders (Frontex). While this chapter focuses exclusively on EU agencies with some regulatory dimension (see Table 10.1), the creation of these regulatory agencies should be understood as part of a broader trend in the EU toward delegating authority to autonomous bodies outside the structure of the European Commission.

Why EU agencies? Theories of agency creation

When they agree to regulate a field at the EU level, EU law-makers in the Council of Ministers and European Parliament (EP) have a number of options in setting up bodies that can be tasked with making and implementing regulation (Coen and Thatcher 2008; Kelemen and Tarrant 2011). First, they can simply delegate to the European Commission, as member state governments did for most of the EU's history when they decided to delegate regulatory tasks to the EU level. Second, law-makers can delegate tasks to specially established networks of national regulatory authorities (NRAs), as did securities regulators when they delegated certain regulatory tasks to the Committee of European Securities Regulators (CESR) in 2001. Finally, they can delegate to EU agencies outside the structure of the European Commission, as in the case of the EEA, the EMA, or the more recently created ESMA. What, then, explains law-makers' design choices and the increasing popularity of EU agencies?

Delegation and policy credibility

First, compelling functional reasons exist for delegating regulatory powers to agencies—namely, to enhance the credibility of long-term policy commitments. *Political uncertainty* and *time inconsistency* are the main causes of the credibility problem. Political uncertainty is a direct consequence of the democratic process. One of the defining characteristics of democracy is that it is a form of government *pro tempore* (Linz 1998). The requirement of elections at regular intervals implies that the policies of the current majority can be subverted by a new majority with different, and perhaps opposing, interests; hence the uncertainty about future policies.

The other threat to policy credibility—time inconsistency—occurs when a government's optimal long-run policy differs from its preferred short-run policy, so that the government in the short run has an incentive to renege on its long-term commitments. In the absence of some binding commitment, the government will use its discretion to pursue what appears now to be a better policy. If the policy-makers have the possibility of revising the original policy to achieve such short-term gains, economic actors will recognize this incentive and change their behaviour accordingly.

TABLE 10.1 European regulatory agencies

Agency	Start of activities	Mission	Location	Official website
European Environment Agency (EEA)	1990	To collect and disseminate information on the state and trends of the environment at European level; to cooperate with relevant scientific bodies and international organizations	Copenhagen	http://www.eea.europa.eu/
Office for Harmonization in the Internal Market (Trade Marks and Designs) (OHIM)	1993	To contribute to harmonization in the domain of intellectual property and, in particular, the domain of trade marks	Alicante	http://oami.europa.eu/
European Medicines Agency (EMA)	1993	To protect and promote public and animal health through the evaluation and supervision of medical products for human and veterinary use	London*	http://www.ema.europa.eu/
Community Plant Variety Office (CPVO)	1994	To implement the regime of Community plant variety rights, a specific form of intellectual property rights relating to new plant varieties	Angers	http://www.cpvo.europa.eu/
European Agency for Safety and Health at Work (EU-OSHA)	1994	To provide the Community bodies, the member states, and stakeholders with all relevant technical, scientific, and economic information; to create a network linking national information networks, and to facilitate the provision of information in the field of health and safety at work	Bilbao	http://osha.europa.eu/
European Union Agency for Fundament Rights (FRA)	1997/2007	To provide EU and member state institutions with assistance and expertise on fundamental rights when implementing Community law, and to support them in formulating and taking measures	Vienna	http://fra.europa.eu/

Cont.

European Food Safety Authority (EFSA)	2002	To provide independent scientific advice on all matters with a direct or indirect impact on food safety; to carry out assessments of risks to the food chain; to give scientific advice on genetically modified (GM) non-food products and feed	Parma	http://www.efsa.europa.eu/
European Aviation Safety Agency (EASA)	2002	To assist the Community in establishing and maintaining a high level of civil aviation safety and environmental protection in Europe; to promote cost-efficiency in the regulatory and certification processes; to promote worldwide Community views regarding civil aviation safety standards	Cologne	http://easa.europa.eu/
European Maritime Safety Agency (EMSA)	2002	To provide technical and scientific advice to the Commission in the field of maritime safety and prevention of pollution by ships; to contribute to the process of evaluating the effectiveness of Community legislation	Lisbon	http://emsa.europa.eu/
European Network and Information Security Agency (ENISA)	2004	To assist the Community in ensuring particularly high levels of network and information security; to assist the Commission, the member states, and the business community in meeting the requirements of network and information security, including those of present and future Community legislation	Heraklion	http://www.enisa.europa.eu/
European Railway Agency (ERA)	2004	To provide the member states and the Commission with technical assistance in the fields of railway safety and interoperability, in particular by carrying out continuous monitoring of safety performance, and producing a public report every two years	Lille/Valenciennes	http://www.era.europa.eu/

European Centre for Disease Prevention and Control (ECDC)	2004	To work with national health protection bodies to strengthen and develop continent-wide disease surveillance and early warning systems; to develop authoritative scientific opinions on risks posed by new and emerging infectious diseases	Stockholm	**http://www.ecdc.europa.eu**
European GNSS Agency (GSA)	2004	To manage the public interests and to be the regulatory authority for the European GNSS (Global Navigation Satellite Systems) programmes	Brussels	**http://www.gsa.europa.eu/**
European Fisheries Control Agency (EFCA)	2004	To strengthen the uniformity and effectiveness of enforcement by pooling EU and national means of fisheries control, and monitoring resources and coordinating enforcement activities	Vigo	**http://cfca.europa.eu/**
European Institute for Gender Equality (EIGE)	2006	To support the work of EU institutions in promoting gender equality by collecting and analysing data, facilitating dialogue between stakeholders, and raising public awareness	Vilnius	**http://www.eige.europa.eu/**
European Chemicals Agency (ECHA)	2007	To coordinate registration, evaluation, authorization, and restriction processes under REACH; to ensure consistency in chemicals management across the EU; to provide technical and scientific advice and information on chemicals	Helsinki	**http://echa.europa.eu/**
European Securities and Markets Authority (ESMA)	2010	To safeguard the stability of the EU's financial system by ensuring the integrity, transparency, efficiency, and orderly functioning of securities markets, as well as enhancing investor protection	Paris	**http://www.esma.europa.eu/**

Cont. ▶

Cont.

European Banking Authority (EBA)	2010	To safeguard the stability of the financial system, the transparency of markets and financial products, and the protection of depositors and investors; to work with national regulators to prevent regulatory arbitrage, strengthen supervisory coordination, and promote supervisory convergence; to provide advice to the EU institutions on banking and financial regulation	London*	**http://www.eba.europa.eu/**
European Insurance and Occupational Pensions Authority (EIOPA)	2010	To support the stability of the financial system, and the transparency of markets and financial products, as well as the protection of insurance policyholders, pension scheme members, and beneficiaries	Frankfurt	**https://eiopa.europa.eu/**
Body of European Regulators for Electronic Communications (BEREC)	2010	To promote consistent implementation of EU regulations on electronic communications, based on best practices	Riga	**http://berec.europa.eu/**
Agency for the Cooperation of Energy Regulators (ACER)	2011	To provide advice to EU institutions on energy-related issues; to take binding individual decisions on terms and conditions for access, and operational security for cross-border infrastructure if the NRAs national authorities cannot agree	Ljubljana	**http://www.acer.europa.eu/**
Single Resolution Board (SRB)	2015	To ensure the orderly resolution of failing banks; to establish standard rules and procedures for resolution; to take decisions on resolution within the Banking Union	Brussels	**http://www.srb.europa.eu**

*Prior to UK withdrawal from the EU

Source: Official home page of the Agencies: http://europa.eu/agencies/index_en.htm © European Union, 1995-2016

One way of enhancing the credibility of long-term policy commitments is to delegate the implementation of those objectives to politically independent institutions. The delegation of regulatory powers to some agency distinct from the government itself can serve as a means whereby governments can commit themselves to regulatory strategies that would not be credible in the absence of such delegation (Gatsios and Seabright 1989). In the EU context, member states may agree that it is in their long-term interests to cooperate on harmonizing regulation in a particular area so as to integrate the market, but they will face short-term incentives to defect from their agreements. To make their policy commitments credible, member states may have an incentive to delegate to a politically independent, supranational regulatory authority. Indeed, in a general sense, this is the very *raison d'être* for the European Commission.

These considerations explain why there may be a functional need for independent regulatory bodies at the European level, but they do not by themselves explain the creation of EU agencies. They do not tell us how agencies will be structured, what powers will be delegated to them, or why new autonomous agencies—rather than the European Commission itself—will be tasked with regulation. While functional considerations play a key motivating role, the process of agency design is ultimately driven by political considerations. The design of EU agencies is the result of political compromises involving EU law-makers in the Council of Ministers, the EP, and the European Commission.

The politics of agency design

With the drive to complete the single market project by 1992, the EU's regulatory agenda expanded rapidly—increasing significantly the scale of regulatory functions (information-gathering, analysis, issuance of rules to implement directives, monitoring of enforcement, and so on) that needed to be performed (or at least coordinated) at the European level. These regulatory burdens might have been dealt with simply by expanding the European Commission—and as Hodson and Peterson point out in Chapter 1, the Commission has grown substantially over the past two decades. The Commission itself and its allies in the EP would likely have preferred to address the EU's need for added capacity by expanding the Commission even further, but there was widespread opposition among the member states to giving the European Commission control over the level of staff and resources that would have been necessary to that end. Quite simply, many governments did not want to see a large, powerful, and centralized EU bureaucracy in Brussels.

In this political context, Commission President Jacques Delors proposed what would become the first in a wave of new EU agencies: the EEA. For the Commission and EP, the idea of establishing autonomous European agencies was an attractive second-best means through which to expand the EU's regulatory capacity—given that expansion of the Commission itself was unacceptable to member governments. Delegating routine information-gathering and regulatory tasks to agencies was attractive to the Commission, because it allowed the Commission to focus its limited resources better on its core tasks, such as policy development and enforcement. Moreover, many of the responsibilities granted to EU agencies would not actually be taken away from the European Commission; instead, agencies would perform tasks that might otherwise have been performed by so-called comitology committees, which advised the Commission. Comitology committees were composed of technical experts who represented member state governments; they served not only to provide expert advice, but also to exert intergovernmental control over the Commission in its policy implementation activities. EU agencies would replicate many of the functions of comitology committees, but they would control far more resources, have additional powers, and operate in a more transparent manner. When they agreed to establish these new agencies, the member states insisted that they be subject to considerable intergovernmental oversight, through the creation of management boards that were to be dominated by appointees of member state governments. In other words, with the creation of EU agencies, the European Commission got the expansion of EU regulatory capacities that it wanted, while the member states maintained substantial intergovernmental control over these new entities.

Over the course of the past two decades, the politics of agency design have shifted as a result of the growing power of the EP. Along with the growth of its legislative power, the Parliament has strengthened its oversight of the Union's executive organs—including the EU agencies. The EP has scrutinized agency budgets, and has demanded that agencies follow formal and transparent regulatory procedures. In essence, the Parliament is acting to ensure that the European agencies will operate in a far more transparent manner than the obscure comitology committees that for so long operated in the shadows of EU governance.

Finally, in a broader sense, the rise of EU agencies has coincided with, and facilitated, a shift in the role of the European Commission. The Commission used to be viewed as the EU's independent, regulatory bureaucracy, but just as more and more routine regulatory tasks were being delegated to EU agencies, so too the Commission itself was experiencing a progressive politicization, which culminated in 2014 with the introduction of the so-called *Spitzenkandidat* ('lead candidate') process that explicitly linked the selection of the Commission President to the outcome of the European Parliament elections. As the Commission comes to depend on the political support of the EP, it begins to look less like a politically independent supranational regulatory bureaucracy and more like a nascent parliamentary government.

Legal obstacles to delegation

European agencies do not have the powers granted to American regulatory bodies and even lack the more limited competence enjoyed by the regulatory authorities of many member states. Thus, for instance, the regulation setting up the EEA did not include regulatory functions in the agency's mandate.[1] The task of the EEA is mainly to provide information that may be useful in framing and implementing environmental policy. Even those agencies with more substantial regulatory powers, such as the

EMA, the EASA, or the more recently established ESMA, do not, formally speaking, have discretionary decision-making powers. For example, the EMA does not take decisions concerning the safety and efficacy of new medicinal drugs, but submits opinions concerning the approval of such products to the European Commission, which takes the final legal decision.[2] Similarly, EFSA is allowed only to assess risk, not to manage it.[3] Only the Commission can make final determinations concerning the safety of the food that Europeans—and others who enjoy EU exports—eat.

Ostensibly, the primary reason why European agencies are not granted broader powers is that the Court of Justice has prohibited it. In a 1958 ruling,[4] the Court of Justice established the 'Meroni doctrine', holding that Community law prohibits the delegation of discretionary powers to bodies—including European agencies—that are not established in the EU Treaties. Thus member states can establish new bodies with discretionary powers—such as the European Central Bank (ECB) or Europol— in EU Treaties, but they cannot do so through normal secondary legislation. The European Commission (2001b: 23) has interpreted the doctrine as follows: 'Agencies cannot be granted decision-making power in areas in which they would have to ar- bitrate between conflicting public interests, exercise political discretion or carry out complex economic assignments.'

However, a 2014 Court of Justice ruling may mean that the legal landscape govern- ing the delegation of authority to agencies is changing.[5] The ruling concerned the EU's Short Selling Regulation,[6] which had granted ESMA the power to ban short sell- ing during market emergencies. The United Kingdom (UK)—before its 2016 referen- dum on EU membership—brought a legal action before the Court of Justice seeking to strike down this provision, claiming that it had delegated discretionary rule-mak- ing power to ESMA in violation of the Meroni doctrine. The Court of Justice rejected the UK's claims. Although the Court of Justice did not explicitly overrule Meroni, it offered a very expansive reinterpretation of how much decision-making authority could be granted to an EU agency without this constituting 'excessive' discretionary power. In other words, the Court of Justice's ruling seems to open up the way for the delegation of greater regulatory powers to EU agencies. Indeed, the impact of the Court of Justice's new, more expansive, reading of Meroni could be detected almost immediately in the context of negotiations over the establishment of a Single Resolu- tion Mechanism (SRM) for failed banks as part of European banking union. The Court of Justice decision came down just as member states were holding these nego- tiations and governments agreed to delegate to a new Single Resolution Board (SRB) far-ranging powers to wind down failed credit institutions—powers that would have been unthinkable under the Court's previous stricter reading of the Meroni doctrine.

But even if the legal obstacles to greater delegation of power to agencies have been reduced, political obstacles remain. Some of the political actors involved in the de- sign of European agencies prefer not to see them take on discretionary regulatory powers. While some member states would be happy to transfer more rule-making power from the Commission to agencies, the design of EU agencies and decisions over which powers they will exercise require the agreement of the Commission and

EP as well. The Commission, for its part, prefers to maintain ultimate decision-making authority; it is enthusiastic to see routine regulatory tasks delegated to EU agencies in large part because it knows (or in the past knew) that, under the *Meroni* doctrine, it retained the last word. A number of the EU agencies established in recent years—from EASA to the European Chemicals Agency (ECHA), to the SRB and ESMA—have been granted regulatory powers that would seem to push them into the realm of discretionary decision-making. With the relaxation of the *Meroni* doctrine, this trend is likely to continue. Indeed, in the context of Europe's recent refugee crisis, member states have already agreed to a far-reaching expansion of Frontex's operational capacity and duties, and the Commission is considering proposing a dramatic centralization of asylum policy in the hands of the EASO. Nevertheless, political opposition to granting EU agencies extensive regulatory powers will continue to act as a limit on their delegated authority.

The growing role of agencies

The EEA and the other agencies established in the mid-1990s were ad hoc experiments in institutional innovation. But, over the past decade, EU agencies have become an integral aspect of the EU's regulatory landscape. Today, proposals to expand EU regulation substantially are regularly accompanied by plans for the establishment of an EU agency, which may take on regulatory, informational, or executive tasks (Rittberger and Wonka 2010). As plans for new agencies proliferated, the Commission called for the establishment of a common framework on which to model them. The 2001 White Paper on European Governance (European Commission 2001b) contained a section on 'Better application of EU rules through regulatory agencies', and called for the establishment of a common framework for the creation, operation, and supervision of agencies. The following year, the Commission proposed such a framework for the agencies and, in 2005, a draft inter-institutional agreement on EU agencies was published. However, adoption of the agreement was blocked in the Council. In 2008, the Commission finally withdrew the stalled agreement and presented a new communication on European agencies that promised to relaunch the debate about their place in governance. Representatives of the Commission, EP, and Council subsequently met to discuss issues concerning the structure, supervision, and operations of the agencies—but they did not agree on a uniform framework for European agencies.

While the Council, Commission, and Parliament have been unable to agree on a standard template for agencies, they nonetheless have continued to create new ones. In recent years, agencies have been created in sectors such as energy—the European Agency for the Cooperation of Energy Regulators (ACER), financial market regulation (ESMA, the EBA, and the European Insurance and Occupational Pensions Authority, or EIOPA), and banking (the SRB), in which member states had long resisted the establishment of new agencies (see Table 10.1). In these fields, in which regulatory decisions entail substantial distributional consequences, member states had previously sought to rely on networks of NRAs to provide the necessary coordination without establishing EU bodies that might constrain national regulatory discretion. However, disastrous regulatory failures and a growing acceptance that the network model alone was inadequate led member states to agree to link these networks to powerful EU agencies (Kelemen and Tarrant 2011).

The politics of institutional choice: The birth of the European Environment Agency

In January 1989, Commission President Jacque Delors proposed the establishment of a European Environment Agency, to strengthen the Community's information-gathering, monitoring, and implementation capacity. Member states, European institutions, and environmentalist groups all voiced support for the proposal, but were deeply divided over specific structural choices—especially those concerning the regulatory powers and effective independence of the new agency. Many in the EP favoured a body with regulatory 'teeth'. In varying degrees, all member states opposed the idea that the agency could monitor the implementation of European environmental legislation by national regulators, preferring to restrict its task to the collection of environmental information and to networking with national, European, and international research institutions. The position of the Commission was ambivalent. On the one hand, officials in the Directorate-General for the Environment (DG ENV) were concerned about the criticism of industry and some member states that the Commission's environmental proposals were not grounded in 'good science'. They were even more concerned by the poor implementation of environmental directives. Hence the idea that the EEA could become a sort of inspectorate of national environmental inspectorates had a number of influential supporters within the Commission. On the other hand, this institution was reluctant to surrender regulatory powers to an agency operating at arm's length. In a 1989 proposal, the Commission outlined four functions for the new body:

- to coordinate the enactment of European Community (EC) and national environmental policies;
- to evaluate the results of environmental measures;
- to provide modelling and forecasting techniques; and
- to harmonize the processing of environmental data.

Because of the expected opposition by the member states, no inspection tasks were contemplated.

This proposal was quite distant from the EP's 'ideal point'. The fact that Beate Weber, *rapporteur* of the EP's Environmental Committee, travelled to Washington

DC to gain first-hand knowledge of the United States' (US) Environmental Protection Agency (EPA) suggests the model of regulatory agency that European parliamentarians had in mind. The EP Environmental Committee maintained that the EEA should be given power to police environmental abuses, to supervise national enforcement of EC environmental regulations, and to carry out environmental impact assessments (EIAs) on certain Community-funded projects. Also, the composition of the management board became a point of contention. According to the EP, environmental groups should be represented on the board, alongside representatives from the member states, the Commission, and the EP itself, and the board should be allowed to take decisions by majority vote.

Comparing the preferences of the main political actors—member states, Commission, EP—with the provisions of the regulation setting up the agency, we see that the member states clearly won the contest over the structure and powers of the agency. The decisive influence of the national governments is revealed by the composition of the management board, which was to be dominated by member state appointees. As mentioned, the main task assigned to the agency is to provide the EU and the member states with environmental information and, in particular, 'to provide the Commission with the information that it needs to be able to carry out successfully its tasks of identifying, preparing, and evaluating measures and legislation in the field of environment'.[7] The wording is sufficiently vague, however, to make it unclear whether the agency would be allowed to directly influence policy formulation, for example by evaluating alternative proposals for regulatory measures. Political compromise produced an institutional design characterized by uncertain competences, unresolved conflicts, and failure to deal with the serious implementation problems of EU environmental policy. The compromise over the creation of the EEA established a model that then provided a rough template for subsequent agency proposals. Each agency was created in distinctive political circumstances, and the details of the powers granted to agencies and the oversight structures put in place varied as a result. However, a number of key elements of the design of the EEA have been replicated in other agencies. For example, agency management boards have continued to be dominated by representatives of member state governments and the agencies have served as hubs of regulatory networks that include (rather than replace) NRAs.

From committees to agency: The development of the European Medicines Agency

Our next example provides valuable insights into how obscure comitology committees have been transformed into a structure in which they become the operational arm of European agencies and link with national authorities to form transnational regulatory networks. The first attempt by the EC to regulate the testing and marketing of pharmaceutical products was a directive introduced in 1965 with the dual objective of protecting human health and of eliminating obstacles to intra-Community trade. This directive established only the principle that no medical drug should be placed on the market without prior authorization, and defined the essential criteria of safety and efficacy for drug approval.

The second phase of regulatory developments began in 1975, with another directive setting up the 'multi-state drug application procedure' and establishing the Committee for Proprietary Medicinal Products (CPMP). This Committee composed of national experts has played, and continues to play, a key role in the EU's approach to the regulation of pharmaceuticals. Under the multi-state procedure, a firm that had received a marketing authorization from the regulatory agency of a member state could ask for the recognition of that approval by at least five other member states. The agencies of these countries had to approve or raise objections within 120 days. In the event of objections, the CPMP had to be notified and would express its non-binding opinion within sixty days. The procedure did not work well: the national agencies did not appear to be bound either by the decisions of other regulatory bodies or by the opinion of the CPMP. Subsequent simplifications failed to streamline the approval process, as national regulators continued to raise objections against each other almost routinely. Hence firms generally chose to continue to seek authorization from each national agency separately.

A different approval process was introduced in 1987 for biotechnology and other high-tech products. This new 'concertation procedure' required that the application for the authorization be filed both with the national authorities and with the CPMP. The country in which the authorization had been filed acted as *rapporteur*, but, unlike under the old multi-state procedure, no decision on the application was to be made by any member state before the CPMP had expressed its opinion. The final decision remained with the member states, however. The evaluation of the application, led by the *rapporteur* country, was carried out at the same time in all of the member states—hence the name 'concertation procedure'. The new process was an advance with respect to the old practice, but was nevertheless problematic for firms because, as with the previous procedure, there was a tendency for delays in the notification of decisions following the CPMP opinion. Waiting for all countries to notify their decisions following the Committee's opinion could result in serious delays in a firm's ability to start marketing a new drug.

In 1995, the problematic multi-state and concertation procedures were replaced by three new approaches and a new agency (see Box 10.1). The multi-state procedure was replaced by a decentralized procedure, which continues and reinforces the principle of mutual recognition introduced in 1975; the concertation procedure was replaced by the centralized procedure set out in the same regulation that also established the EMA (see Box 10.2).[8]

Under the centralized procedure, applications are made directly to the agency, leading to the granting of a European marketing authorization. Use of this procedure is compulsory for products derived from biotechnology and optional for other innovative medicinal products. The EMA is also called on to arbitrate disputes arising

> ### BOX 10.1 An overview of the European authorization system
>
> #### Human and animal health
>
> The European system for the authorization of medicines for human and veterinary use has been in place since 1995. It is designed to promote both public health and the free circulation of pharmaceuticals. Access to the European market is facilitated for new and better medicines—benefiting users and European pharmaceutical research.
>
> #### EMA: A network agency
>
> The European system is based on cooperation between the nationally competent authorities of the member states and the EMA. The EMA acts as the hub of the system, coordinating the scientific resources made available by member state national authorities, including a network of thousands of European experts.
>
> The EMA is designed to coordinate the scientific resources of the member states, acting as an interface between the national competent authorities rather than as a highly centralized organization.
>
> #### The European procedures
>
> The European system offers two routes for authorization of medical products, as follows.
>
> | **Centralized procedure** | **Decentralized procedure** |
> |---|---|
> | Applications are made directly to the EMA, leading to the granting of a European marketing authorization. Use of this procedure is compulsory for products derived from biotechnology. | Applicable to the majority of conventional medicinal products. Applications are made to the member states selected by the applicant and the procedure operates by mutual recognition of national marketing authorizations. Where mutual recognition is not possible, the EMA is called upon to arbitrate. |
>
> Opinions adopted by the EMA scientific committees in either the centralized procedure or following arbitrations lead to binding decisions adopted by the European Commission. Purely national authorizations remain available for medicinal products to be marketed in one member state.

under the decentralized (mutual recognition) procedure. Opinions adopted by the EMA in either the centralized procedure or following arbitration lead to binding decisions formally adopted by the Commission.

The technical work of the agency is carried out by the Committee for Medicinal Products for Human Use (CHMP, the successor of the old CPMP), by the Committee for Veterinary Medicines (CVMP), and by two smaller and newer bodies: the Committee for Orphan Medicinal Products (COMP), established in 2001 and charged with reviewing designation applications from persons or companies who intend to

> **BOX 10.2   The EMA mission statement**
>
> The mission of the European Medicines Agency (EMA) is to foster scientific excellence in the evaluation and supervision of medicines, for the benefit of public and animal health.
>
> Working with the member states and the European Commission as partners in a European medicines regulatory network, the [EMA]:
>
> - provides independent, science-based recommendations on the quality, safety and efficacy of medicines, and on more general issues relevant to public and animal health that involve medicines;
>
> - applies efficient and transparent evaluation procedures to help bring new medicines to the market by means of a single, EU-wide marketing authorisation granted by the European Commission;
>
> - implements measures for continuously supervising the quality, safety and efficacy of authorised medicines to ensure that their benefits outweigh their risks;
>
> - provides scientific advice and incentives to stimulate the development and improve the availability of innovative new medicines;
>
> - recommends safe limits for residues of veterinary medicines used in food-producing animals, for the establishment of maximum residue limits by the European Commission;
>
> - involves representatives of patients, healthcare professionals and other stakeholders in its work, to facilitate dialogue on issues of common interest;
>
> - publishes impartial and comprehensible information about medicines and their use;
>
> - develops best practice for medicines evaluation and supervision in Europe, and contributes alongside the member states and the European Commission to the harmonisation of regulatory standards at the international level.
>
> *Source:* European Medicines Agency, Annual Report 2015

develop medicines for rare diseases ('orphan drugs'); and the Committee on Herbal Medicinal Products (HMPC), established in 2004 to provide scientific opinions on traditional herbal medicines. A network of some 3,500 European experts underpins the scientific work of the EMA, and of its committees and working groups.

The CHMP (with similar rules applying to the CVMP) is composed of two members nominated by each member state for a three-year renewable term. These members, in fact, represent the NRAs. Although Commission representatives are entitled to attend the meetings of the Committee, the Commission is no longer represented, no doubt to emphasize the independence of the CHMP.

In keeping with the political compromise common to the establishment of all EU agencies, the new EMA was put under the control of a management board dominated by member state appointees. When the EMA was restructured in 2004, member states acquiesced to the Parliament's demand that EP and stakeholder representatives be added to the Agency's management board, although member state representatives still held a majority. The Council also agreed to the Parliament's demand that the nominee for the position of agency executive director appear before the Parliament prior to her or his formal approval by the Council.

In fact, the Committee has become more important, as well as more independent, since the establishment of the EMA. In the new situation, Committee members have greater incentives to establish the agency's, and their own, international reputation than to defend national positions. Using Alvin Gouldner's (1957: 58) terminology, we may say that the agency creates a favourable environment for the transformation of national regulators from 'locals' (that is, professionals who have primarily a national orientation) to 'cosmopolitans', who are likely to adopt an international reference-group orientation. It does so by providing a stable institutional focus at the European level, and a forum in which different risk philosophies are compared and mutually adjusted, and by establishing strong links to national and extra-European regulatory bodies. Overall, the EMA has been highly successful at least insofar as pharmaceutical manufacturers report satisfaction with the agency's centralized procedure and many companies seek centralized authorizations (Kelemen and Tarrant 2011). In spite of this success, the EMA will have to move from its home in London once the UK leaves the EU in light of its 2016 referendum vote on membership.

The pursuit of regulatory credibility: The European Food Safety Authority

The food sector is an area in which EC regulation dates back to the earliest days of the Community. Traditionally, policy on food safety was developed by the Commission, assisted by a large number of comitology and expert committees. Several regulatory failures—of which the bovine spongiform encephalopathy (BSE), or 'mad cow disease', epidemic attracted the greatest public attention—revealed the inadequacy of the traditional approach. The BSE outbreak exposed serious shortcomings in the overall coordination of European policies on agriculture, the internal market, and human health. In 1996, the EP set up a temporary committee of inquiry into BSE. The committee concluded that both the Council and the Commission had neglected their duties, and that the UK government had exerted pressures on the Commission's veterinary services in order to avoid Community inspections and to prevent the extent of the epidemic being made public. The Commission was criticized for having given priority to the management of the beef market rather than to the risks to human health posed by BSE and for having downplayed the problem despite concerns raised by a number of experts. The Committee of Inquiry also noted that there had been severe problems with the workings of the Commission's Scientific Advisory Committee.

BOX 10.3	The EFSA mission statement

The Authority shall provide scientific advice and scientific and technical support for the Community's legislation and policies in all fields which have a direct or indirect impact on food and feed safety. It shall provide independent information on all matters within these fields and communicate on risks.

The Authority shall contribute to a high level of protection of human life and health, and in this respect take account of animal health and welfare, plant health, and the environment, in the context of the operation of the internal market.

The Authority shall collect and analyse data to allow the characterization and monitoring of risks which have a direct or indirect impact on food and feed safety.

Source: Regulation (EC) No 178/2002 of 28 January 2002

Responding to these and other criticisms, in 1997 the Commission issued a Green Paper on the general principles of food law in the EU. It was followed in 2000 by a White Paper on food safety, proposing the creation of what became the EFSA in the context of a reform of the entire food safety system, 'from farm to table'. EFSA was to take on responsibilities relating to the risk assessment and risk communication parts of the regulatory system envisaged by the Commission. However, risk management, comprising legislation and control, was not to be transferred to the agency. EFSA was to be guided by the best science, independent of industrial and political interests, open to public scrutiny, scientifically authoritative, and closely linked to national scientific bodies. The reform proposals contained in the White Paper formed the basis of a regulation that laid down the general principles and requirements of food law, established EFSA, and sets out its mission (see Box 10.3).

The organizational design of EFSA is broadly similar to that of the EMA: a management board, an executive director, a scientific committee, and a number of scientific expert panels and their working groups. There are, however, some important differences that are best understood in light of the credibility crisis of EU food safety regulation in the aftermath of BSE and the rising power of the EP. The BSE crisis exposed the potential dangers of interference by national officials in objective risk assessments. Under pressure from the Parliament, the member states agreed to put EFSA under control of a management board that did not guarantee each member government a representative. The board comprises fourteen members appointed by the Council—in consultation with the Parliament, from a list drawn up by the Commission—plus an additional representative of the Commission. Four members must have a background in organizations representing consumer and other interests in the food chain, and no member is an official government representative. The principle of one representative per country has instead been retained in the composition of the advisory forum, which assists the executive director and advises on scientific matters, priorities, and work programmes.

The tension between the desire to enhance regulatory credibility by appealing to independent scientific expertise and the refusal to delegate regulatory powers to EFSA has been temporarily resolved by the doubtful expedient of an organizational separation of risk assessment (the function assigned to the authority) and risk management, which remains the responsibility of the Commission. However, the separation of risk assessment and risk management is problematic, because while the two functions are conceptually distinct—one dealing with scientific issues; the other, with economic, legal, and political issues—they are closely intertwined in practice. The setting of rational regulatory priorities, for example, entails economic, political, and scientific judgements that cannot be easily separated. Again, the determinations of the risk analysts can effectively pre-empt the decisions of the risk managers. Thus it is often impossible to determine with certainty whether a 'dose–response function'—measuring the probability of an organism's response to different levels of toxicity—follows a linear or a non-linear model, yet the scientists' choice of one or the other model is crucially important to the determination of an acceptable level of risk (Majone 2003). Because risk assessment and risk management are so difficult to separate in practice, the refusal to set up a regulatory agency fully responsible for food safety entails a serious accountability deficit without solving the credibility problem.

Independence and accountability

In any democracy, there is a tension between the desire for regulatory bodies to be simultaneously independent and accountable. As we saw at the beginning of this chapter, the desire for policy credibility provides an important functional motivation for agency independence. However, in a democratic polity, when regulatory powers are entrusted to a non-elected body, there is understandably a desire to balance this independence with a healthy dose of accountability. The basic problem is always how 'to control and validate the exercise of essentially legislative powers by administrative agencies that do not enjoy the formal legitimacy of one-person, one-vote election' (Stewart 1975: 1688). Law-makers can try to ensure some measure of accountability by giving the agency very specific instructions in the laws that they ask it to implement, putting in place a variety of oversight and judicial review mechanisms, and imposing rigid administrative procedures that force the agency to act in an open and transparent manner (McCubbins et al. 1987).

From the outset, EU agencies have been subject to a variety of control mechanisms designed to ensure that they cannot deviate too far from the will of their political masters. This oversight has long been evident in the composition of agency management boards, whereby member states ensured that their representatives could keep a watchful eye over agency operations. As the power of the EP has grown over the past two decades, it too has asserted itself as a political master of the EU agencies. This assertion has been evident both in the EP's scrutiny of agencies' budgets and in the Parliament's demands that the agencies adopt more formal, transparent, and judicially enforceable administrative procedures. The impact of these demands is evident in the regulations founding a number of the recently created EU agencies. For example, the EASA and the ECA, both of which have been given authority to make decisions concerning the safety of products, are required to follow detailed, transparent procedures, to give reasons for their decisions, and to provide applicants access to a board of appeal to contest decisions. Substantial accountability mechanisms have been put in place, and certainly the EU agencies operate in a far more transparent and accountable manner than the comitology committees that preceded them.

The network model

It is clearly impossible to transpose to the EU the American model of federal agencies operating independently from the regulatory authorities of the states. Regardless of what one thinks of the alleged legal obstacles to the adoption of such a model, it is certain that the member states would reject it. However, again and again, member states have proven themselves willing to construct systems in which the national regulators become components of EU-wide networks, coordinated by European agencies.

The model in which an EU agency serves as the coordinating hub of a network of NRAs should not be confused with a model of governance that relies exclusively on a network of NRAs in the absence of a European agency. Some scholars (Eberlein and Grande 2005) and many practitioners have argued that EU-wide networks of NRAs provide an effective alternative to establishing more formal, centralized EU agencies. In some sectors, such as energy and financial market regulation, many national governments long resisted calls for the establishment of EU agencies by insisting that networks of NRAs could achieve the needed cooperation and harmonization. However, the actual experience with such networks—in fields from pharmaceuticals, to telecoms, to energy, to financial market regulation—has been unimpressive. EU networks regularly fail to deliver regulatory harmonization because pursuit of national self-interests regularly trumps the impact of 'professionalization' and other normative pressures that network governance theorists claim should facilitate effective cooperation. Indeed, it is for this very reason that some of these loose, ineffectual networks were eventually subsumed into more centralized structures under the leadership of a European agency (as in the fields of medicines, energy, and financial services regulation).

The network model has been crucial to the proliferation of EU agencies. By relying on networks of NRAs, EU agencies render themselves less threatening to those who oppose centralization of power. Nevertheless, by creating and coordinating networks of NRAs, the EU agencies can encourage the spread of common regulatory norms and practices across the member states. Ultimately, the agencies manage to harness the capacities of existing NRAs to serve European ends.

Conclusions

As shown by most chapters in this volume, the rate of institutional innovation in the EU, after six decades of integration, is still remarkable. This is certainly true in the case of European regulatory agencies. The quantitative growth of EU agencies since the 1990s and, with it, expansion of the range of policy areas in which agencies play a role in governance is striking. More recently, we have also seen an increase in the substantive powers of at least some EU agencies, with doctrinal change at the Court of Justice opening the way for a greater delegation of regulatory powers to these agencies.

Inter-institutional politics continues to play a crucial role in the design of EU agencies. In most areas of regulation, design of new regulatory agencies today requires the agreement of the Council, the EP, and the Commission, each of which can simply refuse to propose reforms that would undermine its own authority. The precise terms of the compromise between these institutions varies in the case of each agency and they have failed thus far to agree on a standard template. Nevertheless, the basic outlines of a model of EU agencies has emerged and is now a vital feature of the Union's regulatory landscape. EU agencies rely heavily on NRAs, but the agencies provide central leadership and harness these authorities into pan-European networks. The two most dramatic crises faced by the EU in recent years—the euro crisis and the refugee crisis—have each revealed the need for greater centralization of regulatory authority in their respective fields, and these crises have prompted the establishment of new agencies (such as ESMA, the EBA, EIOPA, the SRB) or the dramatic scaling up of existing ones (Frontex and EASO). It seems highly likely that the number and authority of EU agencies will continue to grow in the decade to come.

ENDNOTES

1. Council Regulation 1210/90 of 7 May 1990 on the establishment of the European Environment Agency and the European Environment Information and Observation Network, OJ L 120/1.
2. Council Regulation 2309/93 of 22 July 1993 laying down Community procedures for the authorization and supervision of medicinal products for human and veterinary use and establishing a European Agency for the Evaluation of Medicinal Products, OJ L 214/1.
3. Regulation 178/2002 of the European Parliament and the Council of 28 January 2002 laying down the general principles and requirements of food law, establishing the European Food Safety Authority and laying down procedures in matters of food safety, OJ L 31/1.
4. Case 9/56 *Meroni v High Authority* ECLI:EU:C:1958:7.
5. Case 270/12 *United Kingdom v Parliament and Council* ECLI:EU:C:2014:18.

6. Regulation 236/2012 of 14 March 2012 on short selling and certain aspects of credit default swaps, OJ L 86/1.

7. Art. 2 of Regulation 1210/90.

8. See Regulation 2309/93.

FURTHER READING

Recent examples of the burgeoning literature on regulatory agencies in Europe are the volumes edited by Zwart and Verhey (2003) and Gerardin *et al.* (2005). Freedman (1978) considers only US institutions, but still provides the most extensive discussion of the legitimacy problems of regulatory agencies. Recent developments in risk regulation, with special emphasis on food safety, are discussed in Majone (2003). The Community method and its implications for institutional reform are analysed by Majone (2005). Shapiro (1997) and Kelemen (2002) provide early accounts of the politics of EU agency design. Kelemen and Tarrant (2011) and Rittberger and Wonka (2010) provide more recent analyses, while Groenleer (2009) provides a detailed book-length analysis of the development of EU agencies.

Freedman, O. (1978) *Crisis and Legitimacy* (Cambridge: Cambridge University Press).

Gerardin, D., Munoz, R., and Petit, N. (eds) (2005) *Regulation through Agencies: A New Paradigm of European Governance* (Cheltenham: Edward Elgar).

Groenleer, M. (2009) *The Autonomy of European Union Agencies: A Comparative Study of Institutional Development* (Delft: Eburon).

Kelemen, R.D. (2002) 'The politics of "Eurocratic" structure and the new European agencies', *West European Politics*, 25/4: 93–118.

Kelemen, R.D., and Tarrant, A. (2011) 'The political foundations of the Eurocracy', *West European Politics*, 34/5: 922–47.

Majone, G. (ed.) (2003) *Risk Regulation in the European Union: Between Enlargement and Internationalization* (Florence: European University Institute).

Majone, G. (2005) *Dilemmas of European Integration: The Ambiguities and Pitfalls of Integration by Stealth* (Oxford: Oxford University Press).

Rittberger, B., and Wonka, A. (2010) 'Credibility, complexity and uncertainty: Explaining the institutional independence of 29 EU agencies', *West European Politics*, 33/3: 730–52.

Shapiro, M. (1997) 'The problems of independent agencies in the US and the EU', *Journal of European Public Policy*, 4/2: 279–91.

Zwart, T., and Verhey, L. (eds) (2003) *Agencies in European and Comparative Law* (Antwerp: Intersentia).

WEB LINKS

http://europa.eu
http://europa.eu/agencies
The official EU website is the place to start any search for basic information on its institutions and bodies, and this page links directly to the various different European agencies. (See also Table 10.1 for more specific links.)

CHAPTER 11

The Court of Auditors and the European Anti-Fraud Office: The politics of financial accountability

Brigid Laffan

▌ Summary

This chapter analyses two of the organizational entities of the European Union (EU) designed to protect its financial interests: the European Court of Auditors (ECA), also known as the 'Court of Auditors', which was created in 1977 before becoming a full EU

Cont. ➤

Cont.

institution since the 1992 Treaty on European Union (TEU, or Maastricht Treaty); and the European Anti-Fraud Office (OLAF, from the French *Office européen de lutte antifraude*), which is a department (service) of the European Commission. These bodies are part of the scrutiny and accountability framework of the Union. The chapter examines their origins, how their internal structures have evolved, their powers, and their place in the institutional landscape of the Union. Their growing importance arises from the expansion of the EU budget, evidence of mismanagement and fraud against the financial resources of the Union, the emergence of an accountability culture in the EU, and enlargement. Notwithstanding institution-building and a tightening of the regulatory environment, there remains a lack of clarity in roles under shared management practices between the Commission and the member states—especially since the costs of controls principally burden the latter, while effective implementation of reforms is still in question. There is, of course, significant EU spending outside shared management in other parts of the world. Entering a new phase in its evolution as an institution, the Court of Auditors has begun a reform process designed to increase its visibility and presence in the Union's institutional landscape. This has been prompted by two international peer reviews, and a report and resolution from the European Parliament (EP) on the Court of Auditors.

Introduction

The focus in this chapter is on those EU bodies that were created to protect the interests of Europe's taxpayers in relation to the Union's public finances: the European Court of Auditors and the European Anti-Fraud Office.[1] The two bodies are very different. The Court of Auditors, established as one of the institutions of the EU under the Maastricht Treaty, is a public audit institution that, as the Union's external auditor, is charged with carrying out the audit of EU finances, while OLAF is not an EU institution; rather, it is a specialist body with a remit to combat fraud. The Court of Auditors, based in Luxembourg, is already almost forty years old, dating back to 1977. In contrast, OLAF is a much newer body, created only in 1999. The EP, exercising its role of fostering political accountability, played an important part in the establishment of both institutions.

   The question of how EU institutions should be held to account is an important one (see Chapter 1). All polities have institutions and mechanisms designed to ensure that organizations and individuals may be held to account: actors are obliged to explain and to justify their actions, answer questions, and face the consequences in the event of failure (Bovens 2007a: 445). Part of the accountability process is gathering evidence, evaluating action, and providing reports to parliamentary and other bodies that form part of a chain of accountability. The core tasks of the Court of Auditors are to investigate how EU monies are spent and to provide the Union's parliamentary arm with the raw material to further financial accountability. The Court of Auditors' stated strategic objective for the period 2013–17 is 'to maximise the value of the Court's contribution to EU public accountability' (European Court of Auditors 2014c: 44). Being part of the Union's system of public accountability is constitutive of the Court; OLAF is an investigative unit with a limited remit in relation to fraud and corruption. Its work clearly also falls within the remit of scrutiny and accountability.

In the mid-1970s, member states were persuaded that an independent audit body was warranted given the emergence of an EU budget with supranational characteristics. The creation of the Court represented polity-building at the EU level. The fight against fraud assumed greater salience as the size and reach of the EU budget expanded. Peterson (1997) highlights the challenge facing the EU that arises from the coexistence of pooled sovereignty and divided accountability. The two bodies are part of an important contribution to improving the accountability for EU spending, while taking account of pooled sovereignty.

Financial management—and, in fact, management more generally—tends to be marginalized in scholarly discussions of the EU (Bauer 2002). We should not forget, however, that it was a pronounced failure of management that led to the first resignation in the history of the Union of an entire college of Commissioners. The political crisis that culminated in March 1999 with the departure of the Santer Commission (see Chapter 5) had its origins in deep-rooted and perennial problems of financial management in the EU (MacMullen 1999; see also Chapter 5). Moreover, a continuing stream of sensational newspaper headlines highlighting the smuggling of animals, cigarettes, or liquor acted to undermine public confidence in the effectiveness of EU institutions and its policy regimes. Whistle-blowers working in European institutions have featured prominently in public disclosures about financial management in the Union. One of the most prominent of these, Marta Andreasen, who worked for some time as an accountant of the Commission, was subsequently elected in 2009 as a member of the European Parliament (MEP) and was a member of the Parliament's Committee on Budgetary Control (CONT) until 2014. Following the 1999 crisis, the next Commission under Romano Prodi was given a strong mandate by the European Council to make financial management more robust in the Commission. The Prodi Commission embarked on a series of structural and managerial reforms, known as the 'Kinnock reforms', because Vice-President Neil Kinnock was given the lead role in the Commission reform programme (see Chapter 8).

Effective management of the EU budget poses a considerable challenge to the EU and the member states. While overall responsibility for management rests at EU level (that is, with the Commission), over 80 per cent of expenditure management is shared with the member states. The budget amounted to some €141.2 billion in payment appropriations in 2015, with approximately 5 per cent spent on the administrative costs of running the institutions.[2] Management and control of the budget is therefore not only—or even primarily—a task for the EU's institutions, but it can occur only if member states have the capacity and willingness to protect the financial interests of the Union.

OLAF's annual reports highlight various cases of fraud and corruption, such as misuse of parliamentary expenses by an ex-MEP and fraudulent import activities (OLAF 2014: 15–19). OLAF also continues to have to assert its right to conduct investigations involving the EU institutions. In March 2011, following allegations that a number of MEPs had accepted money for amending legislation, OLAF attempted to launch an investigation. The EP questioned OLAF's legal right to investigate the MEPs, but appeared to back down when faced with a legal justification from OLAF. Subsequently, a new OLAF regulation was agreed that codified and strengthened OLAF's investigative powers and practices.[3]

Combating fraud, corruption, and waste—much of it transnational—is a formidable task. The Court of Auditors and OLAF operate in a challenging environment, given the complexity and reach of the EU budget. The future of OLAF has become bound up with discussion of the establishment of a European public prosecutor, an office designed also to protect the financial interests of the Union.

The origins of the institutions

Both the Court of Auditors and OLAF evolved from pre-existing bodies with responsibility for financial control and fighting fraud. The Court of Auditors replaced two audit bodies: the European Communities Audit Office and the Auditor of the European Coal and Steel Community (ECSC). OLAF evolved from the Commission's internal anti-fraud unit known as UCLAF (from the French *Unité de coordination pour la lutte anti-fraude*), established in 1988 by the Delors Commission. Both were created as a response to the perceived weakness of their precursors, as well as to broader changes in the EU as a whole.

The provision for a Court of Auditors in the 1975 Budget Treaty was directly related to the transition from national contributions to a system based on 'own resources'—that is, an independent revenue base. In addition, the granting of the power of the purse to the EP was seen to require a related shift in the locus of financial auditing. The political argument in favour of a Court of Auditors was made in 1973 by Heinrich Aigner, then president of the EP's Budgetary Committee, who argued that a more centralized EU budget necessitated an independent EU audit body. His case was reinforced by a series of well-publicized frauds against the EU budget, and the limited and patchy nature of the financial investigation undertaken by the Audit Board and the ECSC Auditor (Wallace 1980: 101–2; Strasser 1992). The establishment of OLAF in 1999 can be traced back to 1988 when the Delors Commission felt compelled to create UCLAF in response, notably, to repeated requests from the Parliament to the Commission to enhance its fight against fraud.

The decision to transform UCLAF into OLAF was taken as the relationship between the Commission and Parliament worsened on the whole question of the

Commission's management capacity. After the Santer Commission resigned in March 1999, the Prodi Commission immediately identified an European Anti-Fraud Office (which became OLAF) as a central plank in its response to the criticisms of the Commission's ability to combat fraud (Pujas 2003: 778–97). The Committee of Independent Experts (1999a: 143) had been critical of UCLAF, finding that 'its intervention sometimes slows the procedures down, without necessarily improving the end result'. This was followed by a 2005 special report of the Court of Auditors highlighting the potential for improved efficiency in the operations of UCLAF's successor body (OLAF).[4] In March 2011 and after OLAF had carried out approximately 4,500 investigations since its establishment, the Commission adopted a proposal to reform the organization with the aim of improving its efficiency, effectiveness, and accountability, while safeguarding its investigative independence. When it began, OLAF was focused on the Commission, but subsequently expanded its role to other EU institutions. This transition was not smooth with other institutions—notably, the European Central Bank (ECB), which was forced by the Court of Justice to open its doors to OLAF (Hodson 2011).

As the external auditor of the EU budget, the Court of Auditors audits the accounts of all revenue and expenditure of the Union, and all bodies, offices, or agencies set up by the Union. This function is typical of any external audit body, but what is atypical is the obligation conferred on the Court by the Treaties to provide assurance not only as to the reliability of the accounts, but also as to the legality and regularity of the underlying financial transactions. In doing the latter, the Court of Auditors conducts detailed on-the-spot checks in the places where expenditure has actually taken place. It is through this provision that many irregularities are revealed and reported in the Court of Auditors' annual reports. In the event that the Court happens to run across a fraudulent case through its examination of underlying transactions, it reports it to OLAF for assessment, investigation, and action (if OLAF decides that action is necessary having carried out a triage of incoming reports to see which should be followed up). OLAF's role is more functional, with the emphasis on protecting the financial interests of the Union via combating fraud, corruption, or any other illegal activity.

The structure of the institutions

The European Court of Auditors

The Court of Auditors consists of one member per member state, the members' cabinets (up to four staff per member, usually a head of private office, and an *attaché*, plus one/two assistants), and about 550 auditors, who form the operating core of the organization. There are five chambers: three are related to internal EU policies, one to external actions, and the other is a chamber that deals with horizontal issues such as

coordination and audit methodology and quality control. Although the precise arrangements were being re-considered as part of ongoing reforms at the time of writing,
the assignment of both members and staff resources to chambers with audit responsibilities is likely to remain the key plank of the division of audit work within the ECA.
The Council of Ministers appoints the members of the Court of Auditors to a six-year
renewable term after consultation with the EP. The members of the Court of Auditors
elect a President from amongst their number for a three-year renewable term.

The EP's CONT holds formal investiture proceedings on appointments to the
Court of Auditors, which have led, on two occasions, to a candidate being replaced.
In 1989, when the Parliament issued an opinion objecting to two nominees from a
total of six, one of the two member states concerned agreed to nominate another
candidate (Strasser 1992: 271). In 2004, the Cypriot government withdrew its candidate following a negative vote in Parliament. In 2013, despite a promise to withdraw
from consideration if rejected, Croatia's Neven Metes became the newest Court auditor in spite of a negative parliamentary vote, which underlines the consultative nature
of the role of the EP. In April 2016, the Council agreed to press ahead with the appointment of a nominee of the Polish government, despite a negative opinion of the
Parliament. At the same time, the appointment of a Maltese nominee did not proceed
after a similar negative opinion. Clearly, the investiture proceedings established a
right of parliamentary involvement, but not a veto, which was later followed in relation to the appointment of the Commission (see Chapters 5 and 6).

The members of the Court of Auditors must be from the national external audit
bodies or have 'special qualifications' for the office, which means that the Court of
Auditors consists mainly of a mixture of professional senior auditors, senior officials,
and former politicians.[5] The President of the Court of Auditors is essentially *primus
inter pares*: his or her authority rests on the fact that fellow members of the Court elect
him or her. The President oversees the operation of the Court of Auditors and is the
public face of the institution, presenting an annual report to the EP and to the Economic and Financial Affairs Council (Ecofin), and representing the Court vis-à-vis
national audit offices. The role of the President has been enhanced by the growing
importance of financial control in the Union. Since its inception, the Court of Auditors
has had ten Presidents (see Table 11.1). Vítor Manuel da Silva Caldeira of Portugal was
elected President in 2008, then re-elected in 2011 and again in 2014, making him the
longest-serving head of this institution. One of the most outspoken presidents was
André Middelhoek, who served until 1995. As a member of the Court of Auditors from
the outset, President Middelhoek was also determined to heighten the profile of the
Court and to give greater salience to the issue of financial management. Middelhoek
went on to play a major role in the 1999 Commission resignation crisis when he
chaired the Committee of Independent Experts in a particularly muscular fashion.

Regardless of the personality of its President, the Court of Auditors is a collegiate
body characterized by a vertical hierarchy between the auditing staff and the college of
members, and a horizontal division between the sectoral auditing areas. From the outset, the Court of Auditors had organizational autonomy, and was solely responsible for

TABLE 11.1 Presidents of the European Court of Auditors	
President (Country)	Period
Sir Norman Price (UK)	1977
Michael Murphy (Ireland)	1977–81
Pierre Lelong (France)	1981–84
Marcel Mart (Luxembourg)	1984–89
Aldo Angioi (Italy)	1990–92
Andre Middelhoek (Netherlands)	1993–95
Bernhard Friedmann (Germany)	1996–98
Jan O. Karlsson (Sweden)	1999–2001
Juan Manuel Fabra Vallés (Spain)	2002–05
Hubert Weber (Austria)	2005–08
Vítor Manuel da Silva Caldeira (Portugal)	2008–present

Source: European Court of Auditors, http://eca.europa.eu © European Union, 1995–2016

the organization of its work and rules of procedure. In June 2010, the Court of Auditors replaced the rules of procedure under which it had operated since December 2004. It is now organized into audit chambers to facilitate the more efficient adoption of certain categories of report and opinion (see Box 11.1).[6] The areas of responsibility of each chamber are decided by the Court of Auditors as a collegial body on a proposal of the President. Each chamber elects one of its members as dean, and can adopt reports and opinions, with the exception of annual reports on the general EU budget and the European development funds. The Court of Auditors retains the right to consider a document that has been adopted by a chamber, for a short period after adoption, after which it is deemed to be adopted on behalf of the Court of Auditors. Chambers have a preparatory responsibility for the adoption of documents—notably, the annual reports that are still adopted by the Court of Auditors as a collegial body. This new organizational structure gives the institution more flexibility, enabling it to address the problem of size, and has been designed to improve its efficiency in decision-making.

The size of the Court of Auditors has developed on the basis of one member per state, thus giving it an increasingly top-heavy structure over time. The size of the institution grew from nine to twenty-eight as the number of member states expanded—and before implementation of the negative outcome of the 2016 referendum on EU membership in the United Kingdom (UK), known as 'Brexit'. The Treaty of Nice made explicit provision for 'one national from each Member State'.[7] Following successive enlargements, the Court of Auditors gained thirteen additional members and their supporting cabinets. Given the disparate backgrounds and management challenges of auditing of the members of the Court of Auditors, ensuring that the college works

BOX 11.1	Distribution of responsibilities in the Court of Auditors, April 2016

Presidency: Supervision of the performance of the Court of Auditors' work; relations with the institutions of the European Union; relations with the supreme audit institutions (SAIs) and international audit organizations; legal matters; internal audit

The President is not a member of a Chamber. Twenty six members are assigned to Chambers.

Chamber I: Preservation and management of natural resources (six members)

Chamber II: Structural policies, transport, and energy (six members)

Chamber III: External actions (five members)

Chamber IV: Revenue, research and internal policies, and institutions, and bodies of the European Union (six members)

CEAD Chamber: Coordination, evaluation, assurance, and development (CEAD) (three members)

Secretariat-General: Human resources, finance and support, information technology, and translation

Source: http://eca.europa.eu

effectively and to the highest professional standards required in an auditing institution is a genuine challenge.

OLAF

OLAF's structure grew out of UCLAF, the office that it replaced in 1999. The key difference between UCLAF and OLAF is that the latter was given a special independent status in the regulations that led to its establishment. It remains, however, a part of the Commission under the responsibility of the Commissioner in charge of the budget. Its independence is clear in its investigative powers and OLAF's Director-General (the Italian Giovanni Kessler, at the time of writing) is independently responsible for its investigations. The Director-General is appointed by the Commission for a five-year period, renewable once following a favourable opinion from the supervisory committee of OLAF, the Council, and the EP. He or she may neither seek nor take instructions from any government or EU institution, including the Commission, and may uphold its prerogatives before the Court of Justice of the EU (see Chapter 7). The management of the Office is under the guidance of a supervisory committee of five persons who have no links to EU institutions and are specialists in its area of work. After its creation, OLAF underwent a process of rapid expansion and had a staff of 500 by 2010.

The relationship between the Commission and OLAF is ambiguous. On the one hand, OLAF has independent powers of investigation; on the other, it works closely with the Commission concerning its responsibility for advising on anti-fraud measures. Yet, in the conduct of its work, it has to investigate Commission officials on occasion. This hybrid nature of OLAF was raised as a serious issue in a report by the UK's House of Lords (2004). It pointed to the absence of an independent investigating body in the EU and the continued contestation around the idea of a European public prosecutor.

Powers of the institutions

The European Court of Auditors

Notwithstanding its title, the Court of Auditors does not perform judicial functions; rather, it is an auditing body that relies on the credibility of its methods and findings, and by providing other accountability arenas, particularly the EP, with the analysis that enables it to perform its role in financial and budgetary accountability. The Court of Auditors performs its audits within an inter-institutional framework laid down mainly by the 2012 Treaty on the Functioning of the European Union (TFEU) and a financial regulation.[8] Article 287(2) TFEU states that the 'Court of Auditors shall examine whether all revenue has been received and all expenditure incurred in a lawful and regular manner and whether the financial management has been sound'. In addition, under Article 287, the Court of Auditors may submit observations particularly in the form of special reports on specific questions that provide the legal basis for its special reports. Its task is a vast one given that the EU's financial instruments are deployed in the member states and in third countries throughout the world. The Commission estimates that, in any one budgetary year, it engages in 400,000 individual budgetary transactions (Laffan 1997).

The Court of Auditors has developed a number of non-Treaty-based practices. The President of the Court may issue what is known as a 'President's letter' to a concerned institution to raise important issues arising from an audit, but which are not considered significant enough to be published as a special report. These letters, at times, provide chilling accounts of the challenges of financial management in the EU and reveal the politicized nature of the Commission when faced with high-level national intervention.

Output of the Court

The Court of Auditors is a prolific producer of reports (see Table 11.2). From 2011–2015, it published 147 special studies and reports and eight annual reports. The Court of Auditors' work programme and auditing cycle enters the policy process in the form of the Court's annual report, published in the autumn of each

TABLE 11.2 Reports of the European Court of Auditors, 1977–2015					
Years	**1977–86**	**1987–96**	**1997–2004**	**2005–10**	**2011–2015**
Annual reports	10	10	8	6	8*
Special reports and studies	47	55	112	71	147
Landscape reviews	0	0	0	0	2
Total	**57**	**65**	**120**	**77**	**157**

*European Development Fund is reported separately as another annual report; in addition, the Court produces reports each year on each of the agencies and joint undertakings of the EU

Source: European Court of Auditors, http://eca.europa.eu © European Union, 1995–2016

year for the preceding year and mainly comprising the statement of assurance, which has been drafted since 1994, specific annual reports on particular EU bodies, myriad special reports on policy programmes or financial processes, and opinions when requested by the Council or observations on the initiative of the Court.

The Court of Auditors' annual report is a large document running to some 240 pages each year. It includes detailed observations on different spending programmes, and the replies of the Commission and other EU institutions to its observations. The length of the report and the level of detail that it contains has been a deterrent to all but the most eager followers of EU finances. An attempt was made to produce shorter and sharper annual reports towards the end of the 1990s, and to focus more on special reports dealing with the results of audits on specific sectors, such as agriculture and natural resources, or specific aspects of financial control, such as financial regulations. A report on the Court of Auditors by the UK's House of Lords (2001) found Special Reports to be of more value than the Annual Report, although variations in the quality of the former were noted.

Since 2005, there has been a concerted attempt to add clarity and consistency among chapters to facilitate ease of reading, and the annual report is now supplemented by a concise introduction as a summary of the detailed report. There has also been a recent tendency to include in the annual report issues affecting sound financial management and not only those revolving around the traditional financial audit work. In 2014, the Court of Auditors produced two 'landscape reviews', a new kind of publication with the objective of considering big issues and bringing together the lessons that should be drawn from the accumulated work of the Court of Auditors. One of the two reviews was entitled *Gaps, Overlaps and Challenges: A Landscape Review of EU Accountability and Public Audit Arrangements* (European Court of Auditors 2014a). This publication was an effort by the Court of Auditors to raise its profile and to contribute to wider deliberations on accountability in the Union. Another feature of the work of the Court of Auditors is its growing emphasis not only on the big spending programmes, but also on the new financial instruments that have evolved in response to the euro crisis. The Court of Auditors' 2015 work programme sets out the intention to analyse how crisis interventions worked, notably in relation to: the implementation of balance of payments and the European Financial Stabilization Mechanism (EFSM); the implementation of the excessive deficit procedure; intervention in the Greek financial crisis; the reform of European Securities and Markets Authority (ESMA); and the ECB's Single Supervisory Mechanism (SSM) (European Court of Auditors 2015: 7).

From the outset, there has been considerable consistency in the findings of the Court of Auditors. In 1981, its benchmark study of the financial systems of the European Communities (European Court of Auditors 1981) reported key findings including the effects of limited staff resources devoted to financial management, delays in the clearance of accounts, difficulty defining the task of the Commission's financial controller, and financial accounts that were hardly intelligible to users. These criticisms have been repeated regularly in the annual report, the special reports, and, since 1994, in the statement of assurance.

However, progress has been made. In 2010, the Court of Auditors published an opinion that stated:

In recent years, the Court has reported improvements in the internal control at the Commission and an overall reduction in the level of irregular payments. However, the Court continues to report a high level of irregular payments in substantial areas of the budget and scope for improving important aspects of diverse EU expenditure programmes and schemes.
(European Court of Auditors 2010: 2)

The second 2014 landscape review of the Court focused on the risks to the financial management of the EU budget (European Court of Auditors 2014a). The focus of the review in addition to legality, regularity, and reliability of expenditures and accounts was on sound financial management and what added value comes from the EU budget. This focus underlines the growing political and popular demand that the EU and its institutions justify what they are doing (see Box 11.2).

In 2008 and 2012, the Court of Auditors engaged in two international peer review exercises that had an important impact on its internal functioning and external positioning. The 2008 review was followed by a period during which the Court of Auditors developed key performance indicators (KPIs) to assist it in assessing its own work. The KPIs were reviewed and adopted for the period 2013–17. The 2008 review also made strong recommendations concerning the need for the Court of Auditors to develop a stronger communications strategy. This request led to a new communications strategy, and to the appointment of an official in charge of relations with the EP and the Council, located in the unit for communication and institutional relations under a new head appointed in 2014.

The 2012 peer review focused on the follow-up to the 2008 recommendations and an assessment of the Court of Auditors' performance auditing practices. The review made a number of recommendations on strengthening performance auditing, better

BOX 11.2	Statements of assurance

Since the coming into force of the 1992 Maastricht Treaty, the Court of Auditors has been required to include a statement of assurance in its annual report. The statement has two elements:

- an audit of the reliability of the accounts; and
- an audit of the legality and reliability of the underlying transactions.

Much has been made in the EP, national parliaments, and the media of the failure of the Court of Auditors to give positive assurances of the Union's accounts for many years. Headlines such as 'European Union STILL wasting billions every year as auditors refuse to sign off accounts for 18th year in a row' (Chorley 2012) reflect the manner in which Eurosceptic media use the Court of Auditors' annual reports to highlight problems in the management of EU funding.

There has been a tendency in the press and among some parliamentarians to conflate the Court of Auditors' identification of problems of financial management with fraud and corruption. In fact, there has been significant improvement in the management of EU funds, which is captured in the Court of Auditors' statements of assurance since 2008. The 2013 annual report launched in November 2014 represented the seventh consecutive year during which the Court of Auditors found the accounts to be reliable. Concerning legality and regularity, the Court found that the revenue side of the budget was free from material error, as were commitments. Payments remain the key problem area in which the Court of Auditors continues to find material levels of error, particularly in relation to agriculture and natural resources, with a level of error of between 2 per cent and 5 per cent, and cohesion policy, with error levels of over 5 per cent. The continuing evidence of errors in these two big spending areas underlines the continuing challenges facing EU financial management, notwithstanding improvements. The complexity of the spending programmes, decentralized management systems, and myriad rules make improvements in EU financial management a work in progress.

programming, shortening auditing duration, and improved relations with the Court of Auditors' stakeholders (European Court of Auditors 2014c). There is a pronounced focus on the Court of Auditors' relations with other institutions in the EU system and the length of time it takes to produce a report based on the audit. For example, the EP expects that it should take an average of thirteen months to the point of adoption of a special report. The growing emphasis on speed is intended to enable the EP to follow up on findings quickly.

The Court's institutional position

In analysing the Court of Auditors' position in the Union's institutional landscape, it is important to distinguish between its relationship with its auditees, on the one hand, and its place in the Union's system of financial control, on the other. Inevitably, tensions exist between the Court of Auditors as an audit institution and the other EU institutions that are subject to its audits. Although the work of the Court of Auditors covers all EU institutions and bodies, it does so to varying extents. Both the European Investment Bank (EIB) and the ECB are only partially audited by the Court. Partial coverage also extends to the SSM, while other financial instruments created in response to the euro crisis—notably the European Financial Stability Facility (EFSF) and the EFSM—are outside the scope of the Treaty structure and thus not audited by the Court of Auditors. It is only when the EU budget and financial resources are deployed that the Court of Auditors has a right to audit. The most critical relationship for the Court is the one with the Commission as the institution that is responsible for EU expenditure (even if it directly manages only a small part of it). The relationship with the Commission was very difficult for many years as the young Court of Auditors strove to find its niche in the Union's institutional landscape. One of the first controversial issues with the Commission related to a 'right of reply' to the Court of Auditors' observations. In the early years, the Commission never fully reconciled itself to the role of the Court in 'value for money' auditing and clearly felt that the Court was straying from its audit function into policy or political judgements. Gradually, however, in the 1980s, the two institutions developed a working relationship as the latter came to accept that the audit body was a permanent feature of the Union—a relationship that has continued to the present, albeit with the expected tensions between auditor and auditee.

Relations with the Commission deteriorated again during Jacques Delors' term as President of the Commission. During the negotiations of the Delors II budgetary package (covering 1993–99), the Commission was furious at a report from the Court of Auditors to the Council on management problems in the structural funds. Delors complained that the report made it more difficult for him to get the member states to agree to a larger budget. The Santer Commission made improving relations with the Court of Auditors one of its main objectives, Santer himself having had considerable contact with the Court of Auditors during his time as prime minister of Luxembourg. It is paradoxical, then, that the Court of Auditors contributed to the resignation of the entire Santer Commission in March 1999 when the 1996 discharge procedure became embroiled in a wider debate on management problems in the Commission.

The Court of Auditors is not the only cog in the wheel of financial management in the Union; such management is also the responsibility of the internal auditors in all of the EU institutions, the authorizing officers in each Commission Directorate-General (DG), OLAF, the national authorities that manage EU finances, and the national audit offices. Within the Commission, until recently, there was both a Commission Internal Audit Service (IAS) and internal auditors at the DG level; the latter were subsumed into the IAS in 2014. Given the extent and range of the Union's budgetary activities, the Court of Auditors cooperates with the national audit offices, taking account of the independence of each body. Audits in the member states are carried out in liaison with the national audit authorities, all of which have appointed a liaison official with the Court of Auditors. In the period since the ratification of the

Maastricht Treaty in 1993, the Court of Auditors has devoted considerable energy to improving its links to the national audit offices, especially given the latter's staffing resources and responsibility for national financial interests. But a key factor has been a provision introduced by the 2007 Lisbon Treaty stating that:

In the Member states the audit shall be carried out in liaison with national audit bodies or, if these do not have the necessary powers, with the competent national departments. The Court of Auditors and the national audit bodies of the Member states shall cooperate in a spirit of trust while maintaining their independence.[9]

In practice, a significant part of this cooperation happens within the annual contact committee meetings between the Court of Auditors and the national audit bodies, which can be traced to a provision of a declaration in the Treaty of Nice.

The Court of Auditors' formal relations with the Council and the EP take place within the so-called discharge procedure. Under this procedure, the EP has the power to grant or postpone approval for the Commission's implementation of the annual budget. The Council also offers a recommendation, but the Parliament takes this decision alone. The Commission is legally bound to take the EP's discharge resolutions into account. The procedure is based on the analysis by CONT of the Court of Auditors' annual report, its statement of assurance, and any special reports published during the budgetary year in question. The EP drafts a discharge report largely based on the work of the Court of Auditors and hearings of Commissioners. Because of the discharge procedure, contact is continuous between the Court of Auditors and CONT. The Parliament refused to grant a discharge in 1984 with respect to the 1982 budget and has delayed the discharge on a number of occasions since then.

The most politically charged discharge process in the history of the EU began in spring 1998. In March, CONT recommended that the EP delay giving the Commission a discharge for the 1996 budget following another critical report from the Court of Auditors. The issue then became entangled with additional allegations of mismanagement involving Commissioner Cresson and, later, the European Community Humanitarian Office (ECHO). An internal Commission whistle-blower—one of an increasing number to come forward in recent years (see Box 11.3)—added to the politically charged atmosphere (van Buitenen 2000; see also Chapter 5).

The Commission survived a motion of censure, but only because a special committee of independent experts was appointed to investigate the charges of mismanagement. The ultimate result was the resignation of the entire Santer Commission. In an indirect way, the Court of Auditors' highly technical work of auditing therefore contributed to what was a history-making event in the politics of the Union. Most of its activity, however, is directed towards the less dramatic, but still crucial, task of improving the financial management of the EU budget by the institutions and protecting the financial interests of the Union.

Although CONT is the primary interlocutor with the Court of Auditors, the latter has attempted to go beyond this bilateral relationship to work more with the main policy committees of the Parliament, because these are the committees deciding on the

> ### BOX 11.3   EU whistle-blowers
>
> A number of officials working in EU institutions have, over the last decade, made public their concerns about financial management in EU institutions. These whistle-blowers have received considerable exposure in the media, and hence have had high visibility and nuisance value to defenders of the EU's financial controls. The institutions generally responded to the whistle-blowers very defensively, although Vice-President Kinnock felt obliged to establish a whistle-blowers' charter in 1999. Among the whistle-blowers were:
>
> - Paul van Buitenen brought his concerns about financial management to an MEP in 1998. He was suspended from his post, but his revelations led to the downfall of the Santer Commission in 1999. Van Buitenen (2000) first wrote a book on his experiences and later (in 2004) was elected to the EP.
>
> - Marta Andreasen was appointed as chief accountant in the Commission, but was suspended in 2002 when she refused to sign off on the Commission's accounts. She was highly critical of the book-keeping standards in the Commission. The Commission did not accept her intervention as a valid case of whistle-blowing. Commissioner Kinnock considered that the Commission had already been in the process of dealing with the shortcomings in the accounting system that Andreasen had voiced (known as the 'Kinnock reforms') and that she had been suspended following a cumulative breach of staff regulations, including being absent from her post.
>
> - Robert McCoy was a financial controller and internal auditor for the Committee of the Regions (CoR) and, in 2000, reported to his superiors evidence of systematic fraud and embezzlement. Instead of reporting it to OLAF, his superiors removed McCoy from his position. A recent report from the European Ombudsman's office suggested that the CoR and eight other EU institutions have failed to implement internal standards to protect whistle-blowers like McCoy, despite being legally required to since 2014. McCoy received neither formal apology nor compensation from the CoR even though an OLAF interim report found merit in his findings.

annual budget and the big programmes. The 2012 peer review argued strongly in favour of 'good direct communication with the EP's specialised committees' and the need to 'further develop its contact with CONT' beyond the discharge procedure (European Court of Auditors 2014c). This work is being supplemented by direct contacts with other committees, and also joint hearings involving CONT and the relevant EP policy committee. This is one of the main strands of the Court of Auditors' reform process.

OLAF

OLAF exercises the following tasks in the fight against fraud, corruption, or any other activity affecting the financial interests of the EU:

- conducting all of the investigations conferred on the Commission by Community legislation and in third countries through agreements;

- safeguarding the Community against behaviour that might lead to administrative or penal proceedings;
- exercising a coordinating role vis-à-vis the national anti-fraud authorities in the fight against fraud; and
- contributing to the development of methods for combating fraud.

To carry out these tasks, OLAF conducts external investigations in the member states and, where permissible, in third countries. It has the power to conduct internal investigations in the EU institutions when fraud or corruption is suspected.

OLAF's 2004 activity report marked the first five years of this fledgling organization's work. OLAF's case management system listed 3,992 cases during this time, including 1,423 cases that it inherited from UCLAF. The number of cases in any one year rose from 322 in 1999–2000 to 637 in 2003–04 (OLAF 2004: 17). In this period, a very high proportion—73 per cent—related to activities jointly carried out with member state authorities (OLAF 2004: 17). This large share of cases underlines the necessity for EU-level bodies to work with national authorities in the fight against fraud (OLAF 2004: 19). The pattern in more recent years has changed to one whereby three-quarters of all new cases are OLAF's own investigations and a quarter involve assistance to national authorities. Between 2010 and 2014, OLAF opened approximately 240 new cases per year (OLAF 2014). The Eurostat case was one of the most controversial cases involving an investigation by OLAF since its establishment (Savage 2005).

OLAF, like all EU institutions, operates in an institutional environment that is multilevel, cross-national, and very diverse. It has to develop strategies for managing diversity and for dealing with the multiple anti-fraud agencies in Europe. It seeks to work closely with national authorities, not as a substitute for national action, but as a means of more effectively fighting fraud that is transnational in nature. Because much crime and fraud in Europe today has a transnational dimension, OLAF itself is partly a response to transnational pressures. In short, legal Europe is attempting to catch up with criminal Europe.

The institutions in context

Financial control and the larger EU system

The evolution of the Court of Auditors and OLAF in the EU system illustrates how institutions and their external environments interact. These institutions were established at different times, more than twenty years apart, in response to changes in the salience of financial management, control, and accountability in the EU system. The establishment of the Court of Auditors reflected recognition of the supranational nature of the EU budget; that of OLAF, the failure of self-regulation within the

Commission. Both institutions represented a strengthening of the relatively weak organizations that preceded them. The Court of Auditors had to devote considerable organizational energy to becoming a 'living institution'—that is, to becoming embedded in the EU system. The Court of Auditors had to evolve a culture of auditing that was suitable to the extended scale and reach of the Union's financial activities. Like all EU institutions, it had to work with diversity—auditing cultures, attitudes to financial management, differences of professional background, legal arrangements in the member states, and multiple languages.

No less important than internal structures are relationships with other parts of the EU system. The Court is part of the system of financial audit and control that exists in the EU, involving internal financial control, external audit, and measures to combat fraud. It is part of the Union's accountability structures in that CONT relies on reports of the Court of Auditors for its annual discharge process. The Court of Auditors has played its part, albeit a secondary one, in the unfolding drama of EP–Commission relations. The Court of Auditors has gradually established working relationships with all EU institutions and its institutional status gives it the same legal status as the institutions that it audits. Its stronger, formal status in Treaty terms matters in the day-to-day politics of auditing in the Union. That said, the international peer review exercises in 2008 and 2012, and follow-up actions by the Court of Auditors, reflected the Court's ambition to become more visible at EU level, and to establish more systematic engagement with all of the EP's committees and not only CONT. Moreover, as the salience of good financial governance has gained prominence in the Union, and received the backing of the Council and the European Council, the Court of Auditors has turned its attention to enhancing its relationship with national auditing authorities.

OLAF, like the Court of Auditors, is part of the Union's accountability structure with a specific remit to combat fraud and crime. Its remit is based on the clear recognition that there is an important transnational dimension to budgetary fraud in the EU. The establishment of OLAF as an independent unit attached to the Commission, but with a separate chain of command, was a response to the problems the Commission had encountered in conducting internal investigations when there were allegations of fraud by individuals in the Commission's services. Its future is bound up with the creation of a European public prosecutor. The idea, which was floated in 1997 in a Commission-funded study entitled *Corpus Juris* carried out by eight academic lawyers, was later backed by the Commission in a 2001 Green Paper on the protection of the financial interests of the Union.[10] The proposal re-emerged in the Convention on the Future of Europe and formed part of the Constitutional Treaty agreed by the member states in 2004. The Treaty made provision for the creation of the role of European public prosecutor, subject to unanimous agreement in the Council. According to the Constitutional Treaty's provisions, the European public prosecutor would be responsible for 'investigating, prosecuting, and bringing to judgement, where appropriate in liaison with Europol [the European Police Office], the perpetrators of . . . offences against the Union's financial interest'.[11]

The European public prosecutor provisions were controversial and were opposed by a number of countries in the negotiations—notably, the UK and Ireland, which did not want the Union to encroach on their systems of criminal law. Hence there is considerable uncertainty concerning the place of OLAF in the emerging financial architecture of the Union and it remains to be seen whether this will change following Brexit. The creation of the European public prosecutor, if it is established, will alter OLAF's operating environment in a fundamental manner. One could envisage OLAF becoming an investigating arm of the European public prosecutor or being absorbed into a reorganized Europol.

Theory and institutional development

From the outset, scholars of integration paid considerable attention to what they saw as the novel characteristics of the Union's institutional architecture. In fact, institutions were central to neo-functionalist analysis, as well as early studies of the EU's policy process. Not unexpectedly, the growing volume of literature on the factors driving integration—liberal intergovernmentalism, supranational governance/new institutionalism, and social constructivism—all address different dimensions of institutionalization and institutional evolution in the EU. How well do these theories of European integration explain the establishment and evolution of the Court of Auditors and OLAF? Both bodies are non-majoritarian, with a role as guardian of the EU purse, in the case of the Court of Auditors, and of investigating fraud, in the case of OLAF. All political systems have bodies the *raison d'être* of which is supervision and control.

There is very limited theoretical work on the establishment and development of these two institutions. Neither body has loomed large in the evolution of integration theory as such; rather, more general social science theories, especially institutionalist approaches, have been more prominent. Laffan (1999) analysed how the Court of Auditors became a living institution—how it evolved from Treaty provisions to become a fully fledged body. The analysis rested on a historical institutionalist account of the Court of Auditors and its evolution. The significance of path-dependence, a core feature of historical institutionalism, is demonstrated by tracing the manner in which the Court of Auditors developed auditing norms (a logic of appropriateness) and engaged with the other more well-established European institutions (Laffan 1999). The development of the Court of Auditors underlines the unintended consequences of institutional development. The member states may have established the Court of Auditors to oversee their agent, the Commission, in its management of EU monies, but over time the Court of Auditors, because of its audit remit, followed the audit trail into the member states. Kourtikakis (2010: 27–30) also uses historical institutionalism to explain how the EU has copied national institutions in this case the Court of Auditors and the European Ombudsman by focusing on critical junctures and institutional isomorphism.

Pujas (2003) situated his analysis of the development of OLAF within traditional integration theory. He proffered two hypotheses—one derived from neo-functionalism; the other, from liberal intergovernmentalism. According to the first hypothesis, the two supranational institutions, the Commission and the EP, wanted to place fraud on the agenda as a new problem so as to develop a new field of competence for supranational institutions. The alternative hypothesis, based on intergovernmentalism, was that the governments wanted to be in a position to blame the Commission so as to avoid responsibility for the lack of an effective anti-corruption policy (Pujas 2003: 785). Having presented the two hypotheses and the evidence supporting both, Pujas turns to a discussion of inter-institutional and intra-institutional relations that, although not explicit, reads like a historical institutionalist account of the evolution of these relations. Pollack (1997: 116), in his seminal article on delegation and agency within the EU from a principal–agent perspective, includes the Court of Auditors as one 'fire alarm' mechanism of member state oversight of the Commission.

Another important vein of theoretical work that has touched on these institutions is work related to the evolution of the EU as a polity. The growth of EU power has been accompanied by a focus on the impact of the Union on democracy, with a particular emphasis on accountability, as an essential feature of democracy. Laffan (2003) analysed the link between auditing and accountability in the Union. Bovens (2007a) developed a conceptual framework that distinguished among different kinds of accountability, defining auditors as central to administrative accountability. In a related article, he analysed accountability in the EU and suggested that new forms of accountability offered opportunities for learning, but were no substitute for popular control (Bovens 2007b). His conclusion was that although administrative accountability akin to that offered by the Court of Auditors was important, it could not entirely overcome the accountability deficits in the Union.

The impact of the institutions

Given the perennial problems associated with the management of EU finances and highlighted in successive reports by the Court of Auditors and OLAF, it begs the question: just how intractable are the problems associated with financial management in the Union? Establishing effective systems of financial management is a challenge even within states. In the EU, there are additional structural factors—notably, the range of auditing institutions, practices, and cultures in the member states and beyond, the geographical range of EU finances, and the multilingual environment within which the staff of the Court of Auditors and OLAF work.

The reports of the Court from the end of the 1970s did much to highlight management inadequacies in the first place, and the Court of Auditors' constant pressure on the Commission led to an acceptance—albeit tardy—that there were very real problems of financial management in the Union. The Commission responded by strengthening formal systems for overseeing the implementation of the budget. But as

Levy (2000: 187) has concluded, 'moving beyond formal change is a general problem that bedevils most aspects of EU program management'. The Commission continues to enhance its internal management processes and to strengthen its links to the member states. This effort has borne some fruit, as is evident in the annual reports of the Court of Auditors, but continuing evidence of problems—particularly in areas of shared management with the member states—underlines the continuing challenges facing the Commission. Addressing the fragmented accountability structures in the Union is a work in progress. The situation in relation to financial management has improved as a result of the 'critical juncture' of the resignation of the Commission, administrative reform of the Commission, and the enhanced commitment to financial control within the system. The Court of Auditors played a particularly important role in EU institutional politics by altering the balance in relations between the EP and the Commission. Its reports provided CONT with the raw material to exercise the discharge procedure in a manner that strengthened parliamentary control over the Commission. The resignation of the Santer Commission was the most dramatic event to result from the problems of self-regulation in the Commission. Without the slow drip-feed of Court of Auditors reports, it is unlikely that it would have happened. For its part, OLAF has undertaken a large number of investigations in the EU institutions, the member states, and in third countries. These investigations have led to criminal investigations in Romania, the extradition of a Lithuanian national from Lithuania to Belgium, a guilty plea by a multinational company in Lesotho, and an investigation into the use of EU monies by the Palestinian Authority (OLAF 2004: 38–40).

An important trend in the approach of the Court of Auditors is its focus not only on EU budgetary expenditure, but also on areas in which EU expenditure might be limited, but the EU impact high. Audits of organic foods, the EU Emissions Trading System (EU ETS) and the European Banking Authority (EBA), for example, relate to the regulatory, rather than the public finance capacity, of the Union, but are in fields in which the EU exercises considerable public power.

Conclusions

The establishment of the Court of Auditors in 1977 was dependent on the changing nature and funding of the Community budget. In turn, once the Court found an institutional identity and established its approach to auditing, it began to highlight the problems of financial management in the Union. Its effectiveness improved with the internal development of an agreed audit culture and growing human resources. For well over a decade, the Court had to fight to ensure that its findings were taken on board in the Commission, in the Council, and at national level. With the major expansion of the Union's budgetary resources after 1988 and a growing net contributors' club, financial management found its way from the margins of the agenda to centre stage. Gradually, the rules surrounding financial management were strengthened and the member states were forced to accept a tighter regime of financial control. The Court of Auditors, the institutional position of which was strengthened in this period, contributed to, but also benefited from, the growing salience of financial management in the Union. Its reform efforts in recent years suggest that the Court is trying to re-position itself in the institutional landscape by engaging more actively with EU institutions—notably, the EP policy committees—by establishing a stronger communications capacity and by asserting its role in relation to the EU's accountability. The establishment of OLAF in 1999 was a response to the problems of fraud against the financial interests of the Union and, more specifically, to the problems of self-regulation in the Commission. Both the Court of Auditors and OLAF represent institutional innovation in the EU system. Subsequent provisions for a European public prosecutor suggest that the process of institutional innovation continues. Such developments bring the continuing autonomy of national criminal law systems and the need to combat transnational problems sharply into focus.

 ENDNOTES

1. I would like to thank a Member of the Court of Auditors and his staff for valuable feedback on an earlier version of this chapter.

2. See http://ec.europa.eu/budget/annual/index_en.cfm?year=2015

3. Council Regulation (EU, Euratom) No. 883/2013 of 11 September 2013 concerning investigations conducted by the European Anti-Fraud Office (OLAF) and repealing Regulation (EC) No. 1073/1999 of the European Parliament and of the Council and Council Regulation (Euratom) No. 1074/1999, OJ L 248/1/.

4. *Court of Auditors Special Report No. 1/2005 concerning the management of the European Anti-Fraud Office (OLAF), together with the Commission's replies*, OJ C 202/1, 18 August 2005.

5. Art. 286 TFEU.

6. This configuration puts the Court in accordance with Art. 287(4) TFEU.

7. Art. 247 EC.

8. Arts 310–325 TFEU; Council Regulation (EC, Euratom) No. 1605/2002 of 25 June 2002 on the Financial Regulation applicable to the general budget of the European Communities, OJ L 248/1.

9. Art. 287 TFEU.

10. COM(2001) 175 final.

11. Art. III-175 of the Constitutional Treaty.

 FURTHER READING

Levy (2000) is the most in-depth analysis available of financial management in the EU. Laffan (1999, 2003), respectively, analyses the Court of Auditors' relationship with other EU institutions and charts how it became embedded in the Union's institutional system.

Kourtikakis (2010) offers an insightful perspective on the evolution of the Court of Auditors and the European Ombudsman. Pujas (2003) provides insight into EU anti-fraud activities. Recent works on OLAF include Quirke (2010) and White (2010). Castells (2005) analyses the relationship between the Court of Auditors and the member state audit institutions. Ulrich (2016) provides an in-depth historical analysis of the role of MEP Heinrich Aigner in the establishment of the Court.

Castells, A. (2005) 'External audit institutions: The European Court of Auditors and its relationship with national audit institutions of the Member States', in M. Garcia Crespo (ed.) *Public Expenditure Control in Europe: Coordinating Audit Functions in the European Union* (Cheltenham: Edward Elgar), 127-47.

Laffan, B. (1999) 'Becoming a "living institution": The evolution of the European Court of Auditors', *Journal of Common Market Studies*, 37/2: 251–68.

Laffan, B. (2003) 'Auditing and accountability in the European Union', *Journal of European Public Policy*, 10/5: 762–77.

Levy, R. (2000) *Implementing European Union Public Policy* (Cheltenham: Edward Elgar).

Kourtikakis, K. (2010) 'Imitation and supranational politics: Some lessons from the European Ombudsman and the European Court of Auditors', *European Political Science Review*, 2/1: 27–48.

Pujas, V. (2003) 'The European Anti-Fraud Office (OLAF): A European policy to fight against economic and financial fraud?', *Journal of European Public Policy*, 10/5: 778–97.

Quirke, B. (2010) 'Fighting EU fraud: Why do we make life difficult for ourselves?', *Journal of Financial Crime*, 17/1: 61–80.

Ulrich, L.C. (2016) *Roads to Europe: Heinrich Aigner and the Genesis of the European Court of Auditors* (Luxembourg: European Court of Auditors).

White, S. (2010) 'EU anti-fraud enforcement: Overcoming obstacles', *Journal of Financial Crime*, 17/1: 81–99.

 WEB LINKS

http://ec.europa.eu/
The most important web source, which provides access to all of the EU institutions, including the EP, and to the work of the Budgetary Control Committee, which is central to the annual discharge of the budget.

http://eca.europa.eu
The website of the Court of Auditors provides access to the annual reports and special reports of, and a bibliography on, the Court of Auditors. It also offers access to the Budget Directorate and the Financial Control Directorate.

http://ec.europa.eu/anti_fraud
The OLAF website provides an overview of the activities of the organization, including case studies linked to issues such as cigarette smuggling, and also explains how individuals or groups can make informal contact to report fraud.

PART III

Integrating Interests

CHAPTER 12

Police and judicial cooperation: Integrating security interests

Andrew Geddes

▌ Summary

European Union (EU) member states seek to work together on issues such as asylum, refugee protection, migration, border controls, police cooperation, and judicial cooperation. These were once seen as the prerogative of member states; indeed, they are defining features of states' identities as sovereign. This chapter shows how a complex

Cont. ➤

> **Cont.**
>
> process of incremental institutional change established new ways of working on internal security issues and reconfigured the strategic perspective from which these issues are viewed. It shows too how this cooperation has been severely tested by the refugee crisis. In 2015, more than 1 million people crossed the Mediterranean to enter the EU, with 3,700 people reported dead or missing. Of these refugees and migrants, 845,000 moved through Greece. The majority moved because of conflict in the Middle East, particularly in Syria. The refugee crisis was linked to a political crisis for EU institutions and leaders as serious questions were raised about the content and the viability of key components of the EU's approach to security and human rights. From being a policy arena that was not even mentioned in the 1957 Treaty of Rome or 1986 Single European Act (SEA), internal security within an 'area of freedom, security, and justice' (AFSJ) is now a key EU priority. This chapter pinpoints key developments, specifies institutional roles, and explores the relationships over time between changing conceptualizations of security and institutional developments.

Introduction

European cooperation on internal security within the AFSJ is firmly embedded as a key priority of the EU. Significant policy developments in areas such as policing, judicial cooperation, border controls, migration, and asylum have been accompanied in a relatively short period of time by institutional development, transformation, and consolidation. Policy and institutional development signify movement into areas of 'high politics' that impinge directly on state sovereignty. Institutional change has also been informed by reconceptualizations of internal security that have played a powerful role in framing institutional and policy developments. This chapter connects policies, institutions, and ideas over time to analyse the extensive, diverse, and politically contentious range of issues that usually fall within the domain of interior or justice ministries in the member states. They also tend to be seen as closely related to national sovereignty and reside within the domain of the executive branches of national governments, with tendencies towards seclusion and secrecy in decision style. This chapter shows how an institutional style has developed that is 'sectoral', in that it draws from the internal security branches of the member states with some involvement by EU institutions. The result has been the creation of 'transgovernmental' interactions at EU level that have reshaped the settings within which questions of internal security are both conceptualized and acted upon.

There was no mention of internal security in the Paris and Rome Treaties (1951 and 1957, respectively) or in the 1986 Single European Act (SEA). There was, though, 'informal' cooperation between states outside the Treaty framework. It was not until 1993, when the Maastricht Treaty created the justice and home affairs

(JHA) pillar, that there was formal reference to internal security, including immigration, asylum, border controls, and judicial and police cooperation. In 1999, Article 1(5) of the Amsterdam Treaty proclaimed that the EU should be maintained and developed 'as an area of freedom, security and justice . . . within which the free movement of persons is assured' and with 'appropriate measures with respect to external border controls, asylum, immigration and the prevention and combating of crime'.

Key developments post-Lisbon have been the full application of Community decision rules and institutional processes to almost all internal security matters, and the testing of these rules and processes by the refugee crisis. The Lisbon Treaty also makes the Charter of Fundamental Rights binding on member states. The Czech Republic, Poland, and the United Kingdom (UK) (pre-Brexit) secured derogations from the scope of the Charter of Rights. This means that citizens of these countries cannot use the Charter to challenge rights issues in their courts if the basis for their challenge is rights granted to them as EU citizens within the Charter. If they are to issue a challenge, then they must use national laws. Neither can the Charter be used to introduce new rights into the national laws of these countries.

Post-Lisbon institutional changes also sees the JHA portfolio within the Commission separated into 'home affairs' and 'justice' roles. That said, as will be seen, this area of policy does possess a complex and byzantine quality, as evidenced, for example, by Ireland's opt-out from the passport-free travel provisions of the Schengen zone. Box 12.1 provides a timeline of key developments.

BOX 12.1	Timeline of key developments in police and judicial cooperation

1967 **Naples Convention** establishes customs cooperation to tackle fraud

1975 **Trevi** is initially a response to terrorist organizations, but its remit was widened to tackle internal security issues seen as arising from single market integration

1985 **Schengen Agreement**, initially between five member states (Belgium, France, Germany, Luxembourg, and the Netherlands), then becomes the laboratory for 'compensating' internal security measures in the single market

1986 **SEA** proposes a Europe with free movement for people, services, goods, and capital, and provides a further impetus to informal cooperation between member states outside of the formal Treaty framework

1986 **Ad Hoc Group on Immigration** established to explore the migration and asylum implications for non-EU nationals of free movement provisions

1988 **Group of Coordinators** established to coordinate the various informal bodies and groups dealing with internal security issues

Cont. ➤

Cont.	
1993	**Maastricht Treaty** formalizes transgovernmental cooperation by creating the JHA pillar
1999	**Amsterdam Treaty** creates a new Title IV dealing with free movement, migration, asylum, and border controls, while leaving judicial and police cooperation in a recast judicial and police cooperation (JPC) pillar
1999	**Tampere Programme** devised by national interior ministers and sets an ambitious five-year agenda for internal security development
2004	**Hague Programme** provides a further five-year plan for policy development within which increased emphasis is laid on the 'external dimension'—that is, cooperation with non-member states
2009	**Lisbon Treaty** provides for full application of Community decision rules to almost all internal security matters and makes binding the Charter of Fundamental Rights to inform application of the internal security *acquis*
2009	**Stockholm Programme** lays down a further five-year plan (2010–14) that proposes, for example, a common asylum policy and a strong focus on the 'external' dimension of internal security
2014	**Strategic Guidelines for Justice and Home Affairs** cover the period to 2020 and focus mainly on consolidation of existing rules

This chapter addresses two related sets of questions that link institutions, policies, and ideas. First, what impelled the development of EU cooperation on internal security? Why have developments occurred at some points in time and not at others? And what impact have changes in the conceptualization of security and insecurity had on the development of policy? The second set of questions focus on institutional form, and examines the processes that have developed and their response to challenges, such as the refugee crisis.

The meaning of 'security'

Central to the analysis that follows is the relationship between institutions and ideas. To understand EU internal security policy, it is important to probe the meaning of 'security'. Various qualifiers are appended to the term 'security', such as 'internal', 'external', 'state', 'national', 'international', 'human', and 'societal'—but none help us to understand the term itself. Perhaps the EU itself can help in a quest for clarity by providing a definition? There is a strong commitment to develop the EU as an AFSJ. But even in key EU documents such as the 2014 Strategic Guidelines for Justice and Home Affairs (which mapped the EU internal security agenda for the period 2015–20), the meaning of the term can be elusive. The Strategic Guidelines recognize various threats that are seen to confront the member states, such as serious and organized crime, corruption, human trafficking, and people smuggling, and discuss the need to develop 'coherent' policies, while also recognizing the close links between 'internal' and 'external' policies, and thus the importance to EU internal security policy of relations with non-member states. The Guidelines identify internal security as a key EU priority, and as a means to protect citizens and offer effective rights to people inside and outside the EU.

Security is often represented in documents such as the Strategic Guidelines as a key demand made by EU citizens. The development of action on internal security can then be a means for the EU to acquire legitimacy in the eyes of its citizens by taking on this role and responding to the concerns of their citizens. There is a supply side in this particular 'market' too, because institutions, organizations, and processes associated with EU action may themselves have helped to create cultures of insecurity, uncertainty, and risk that then form the basis for arguments for intensified policy action. The refugee crisis provoked an intensification of efforts to work with non-EU members, particularly Turkey, to enhance border controls and to try to stop movement of people from areas affected by conflict in the Middle East, particularly Syria, towards Europe.

These definitional ambiguities could also be seen as creating political opportunities as various actors seek to impose their preferred understandings of security challenges. This way of thinking connects issue 'framing' to mobilizations, and then to the types of policy and institutional response that have developed. Such a constructivist perspective takes ideas seriously in relation to institutional development.

Finally, we need to think about the effects of policy development over time. Decisions about EU internal security cooperation and policy have been made at particular *points in time*. We can also assess the effects of cooperation *over time* and the pace, or *tempo*, of institutional development. By doing so, it is possible to assess the influence of initial decisions about institutional form on later decisions and to assess the ways in which—over time—new EU-level institutional venues have been created, and then have further reshaped ideas about security and insecurity in the EU. A theoretical observation can also be made if we extend this thinking about the effects of cooperation over time. If it is the case that understandings of security and thinking about strategic challenges have been affected by cooperation, then it would also seem to be the case that national preferences can be shaped and reshaped by cooperation at the EU level as a consequence of interactions over time and the emergence of new, shared understandings of European internal security. In such circumstances, preferences are not exogenous to the process, as liberal intergovernmentalists argue; rather, they can be defined and redefined as a result of interaction.

Executive dominance

From its early origins, cooperation on internal security has centred on liaison and interaction between national interior and justice ministries, as well as national security agencies such as police forces. This configuration pinpoints the predominant position of the executive branch of national government and associated agencies. The Commission did seek to play a role in policy development, but found this effort difficult because it was confronted by a weak legal basis for its involvement. Even in the late 1990s, the Commission representatives would leave the room when member states turned their attention to the Schengen area, because it was an issue from which the Commission was excluded. Supranational institutions such as the Commission, Court of Justice, and European Parliament (EP) were effectively excluded from the development of the Schengen system in the 1980s and 1990s. This exclusion is significant because these developments went on crucially to inform the shape and form of cooperation after the Schengen *acquis* was brought into the EU Treaty framework by the Amsterdam Treaty.

We can also specify a little more clearly how cooperation worked and assess its implications. There were actually very specific forms of cooperation that were 'sectoral'—that is, focused on a range of issues linked to internal security, and involving ministers and officials from mainly interior ministries and security agencies. What this specificity means is that distinct patterns of cooperation and working methods have evolved over time. Wallace and Reh (2015) have identified internal security as an example of 'intensive transgovernmentalism', whereby functional interdependence exposes a governance dilemma as member states confront 'transboundary' policy problems with which they would struggle to deal acting alone.[1]

Being 'transboundary' does not determine the shape or form that cooperation on internal security might take. Environmental issues are also transboundary and the EU has made much more significant steps towards common policies in this arena than it has in the area of internal security. By contrast, the EU has preferred to move more tentatively in the arena of internal security because of the political sensitivity of immigration, asylum, policing, and judicial cooperation, which have a strong relation to understandings of national sovereignty and to the legitimate authority of national governments that are concerned to be seen to 'deliver' security to their citizens.

The analytical insight that can be garnered from the preceding discussion is that, instead of being locked into a supranational–intergovernmental dichotomy, the focus on transboundary problems and transgovernmental institutions provides a means of exploring the ways in which functional interdependencies can generate pressures for action. But it also shows that these pressures need not translate into a unique template for cooperation and/or policy development; rather, there are distinct policy styles and ways of working in areas as diverse as the environment and internal security that play a strong role in shaping the scope, form, and content of action.

Informal transgovernmentalism

The Trevi Group

Early traces of internal security cooperation can be found in the Naples Convention of 1967, agreed between the six founding European Economic Community (EEC) member states ('the Six') to deal with customs cooperation. This cooperation was closely linked to the common market because it sought to combat infringements of national customs legislation. Cooperation moved to a different level when member states sought greater coordination in their responses to domestic groups defined as terrorist organizations, such as Basque separatist group ETA (*Euskadi ta Askatasuna*) in Spain, the Red Army Faction in West Germany, the Red Brigades in Italy, and the Irish Republican Army (IRA) in Northern Ireland. National governments sought to cooperate within the Trevi Group, which was set up in 1976 by the then nine member states to promote cooperation between police, security, and intelligence agencies. There are various explanations given for the name 'Trevi': one is that it is an acronym derived from its focus on *Terrorisme, radicalisme, extrémisme et violence internationale*; another is that it is named after the Trevi Fountain in Rome, near which the group first met. Whichever is the case, the key point is that Trevi created patterns and habits of cooperation on internal security to highlight the importance of regular interactions that link internal security officials in member states.

The political leadership and direction for Trevi was set by meetings every six months of interior ministers from the nine member states. This kind of political steering by national ministers is a key feature of EU decision-making, but cannot provide policy and operational details. Consequently, to prepare for these ministerial meetings, senior officials from each member state would meet in May and November—that is, one month before the meeting of ministers. There was also another layer beneath this senior official level, because the detailed groundwork for these higher-level meetings was actually done in working groups. Three such groups were created in 1976. So-called Trevi I focused on anti-terrorism; Trevi II, on police training, including measures to combat football-related violence. A third group dealing with civilian air travel, Trevi III, was largely inert and was redefined in 1985 to focus on serious organized crime, after which it became more active. Two other groups (nuclear safety and civil emergencies) were created, but never actually met. Associated with the work of Trevi in the sense of being kept informed about developments were the 'friends of Trevi': Austria, Canada, Finland, Morocco, Norway, Sweden, Switzerland, and the United States (US).

Early cooperation centred on anti-terrorism, police training, and serious organized crime. Methods of cooperation emerged outside of the formal Treaty framework and were 'transgovernmental', with actors defined by their operation in the field of internal security policy meeting frequently and developing patterns of working. These interactions qualify the idea of a supranational versus intergovernmental dichotomy positing either supranational institutions or the member states, respectively, as being in the driving seat. Transgovernmental interactions are 'sectoral' in that they focus on the specialized function of internal security questions and involve groups of people—officials from national and EU institutions plus people from security agencies—who meet regularly to exchange information and ideas, and may not be directly under the control of cabinets and prime ministers. This distinction does not mean that officials act contrary to the policies or interests of their governments, but can mean that they develop common understandings that shape how problems are understood in the first place, which can then influence how responses develop. Working groups provided a base for interaction and the development of shared understandings between national officials, which, in turn, helped to reshape the context within which planning and decision-making occurred. Member states did not cede responsibility to common institutional processes, but made evident their willingness to work together.

The impact of single market integration

Did the SEA plan to create a European single market—defined as an area without internal frontiers within which people, services, goods, and capital could move freely—also have the effect of impelling cooperation on internal security? There are important linkages between economic integration and internal security cooperation, but there was also a determination that internal security cooperation would occur outside of the Treaty framework, in transgovernmental forums with limited involvement by supranational institutions.

The key development during the 1980s occurred outside of the Treaty framework and prior to the SEA. In June 1985, the Schengen Agreement was signed by Belgium, France, (West) Germany, Luxembourg, and the Netherlands in a riverboat on the River Mosel near to the town of Schengen in Luxembourg. The location was symbolic, because it is where the borders of Luxembourg, Germany, and France meet. The Schengen Agreement marked an ambitious move by five EC member states with a long-standing commitment to deeper political integration. The Schengen Agreement provided for the abolition of border controls between participating states, common rules on migration, asylum, and visas, and the creation of a database—the Schengen Information System (SIS)—to bring together information held in national databases on individuals and property. In 1990, the Schengen Implementing Convention, agreed by the same five states, sought to effect these agreed measures. Monar (2001) has argued that Schengen provided a 'laboratory' for the member states, demonstrating to them the internal security implications of free movement. In May 2005, Austria, Belgium, France, Germany, Luxembourg, the Netherlands, and Spain reached agreement in the Prüm Treaty to step up cooperation in tackling cross-border crime, illegal immigration, and terrorism, by providing reciprocal access to the DNA profiles, fingerprints, and vehicle registration data of participating states (Grabbe 2000; Pastore *et al.* 2006). The Prüm Treaty was signed before the Lisbon Treaty's provisions for 'enhanced cooperation' came into effect. But Prüm (as Schengen did before it) foreshadowed the enhanced cooperation under which a third or more of EU member states can pursue cooperation as long as it does not discriminate against other member states, furthers Treaty objectives, and is not an area that falls within the EU's exclusive competence.

The Amsterdam Treaty imported the Schengen *acquis* directly into the EU. This move points towards the importance of secluded and secretive venues outside of the Treaty framework for the development of measures that are then 'imported' to form part of the EU *acquis*. By 1997, when the Amsterdam Treaty was agreed, all member states except Ireland and the UK had signed the Schengen Agreement.

Informal transgovernmental cooperation in the 1980s

Single market integration also affected the Trevi Group, which initially focused on terrorism and police training. Over time, its role was developed in light of the creation of the single market and the security issues that were seen to be arising as a result of this deeper level of economic integration, which would require the dismantling of internal frontiers. The 'Trevi 92' group worked with an ad hoc group on immigration (created in 1986) to consider the security implications of single market integration. A group of coordinators was established in 1988, consisting of senior officials from each member state, which produced the Palma document that detailed the internal security measures that were seen as necessary to 'compensate' for single-market liberalization.

The ad hoc group on immigration drafted the Dublin Convention (1990), which is the framing document of the European asylum system, and which created key ideas and approaches that have informed policy development since. The right to asylum is protected by the Geneva Convention of 1951, Article 1 of which seeks to protect anyone who:

. . . owing to a well-founded fear of being persecuted for reasons of race, religion, nationality, membership of a particular social group or political opinion, is outside the country of his nationality and is unable or, owing to such fear, is unwilling to avail himself of the protection of that country; or who, not having a nationality and being outside the country of his former habitual residence as a result of such events, is unable or, owing to such fear, is unwilling to return to it.

At the core of the Dublin system is the idea that an asylum application be made in the first country that is entered by the applicant. Any decision made in this first country of entry is final and binding for other member states. This rule means that the European asylum system is supposed to be a 'one-stop' system designed to prevent 'asylum shopping', with applicants moving from one member state to another (Kaunert and Léonard 2012). In the face of large-scale flows from Syria, the German government stated that it would consider asylum applications from Syrians irrespective of where they entered the EU. This decision led hundreds of thousands of people to embark on journeys across south-east Europe in an attempt to reach Germany. The decision also undermined the Dublin asylum system because Germany was prepared to consider the claims of applicants that had arrived in other EU member states in which their claims technically should have been made. The Eurodac system—that is, the European fingerprint database—supports implementation of the Dublin Convention (and its successor, the Dublin II Regulation of 2003). These formed part of the Common European Asylum System developed by 2003 and then further revised through common EU measures by 2013 (Monar 2014).

The context for the development of the Dublin system was the increase in asylum that occurred in the aftermath of the end of the Cold War, particularly to Germany. As with the Syrian refugee crisis, we see concerns about the sharing of responsibility, but also a lack of solidarity between member states. In both the early 1990s and in 2014–15, Germany was concerned that other member states were not ready to embrace the sharing of responsibility or of solidarity through, for example, the distribution of asylum seekers and refugees in a more proportional way across the EU.

Formalized transgovernmentalism

The Maastricht Treaty and the challenges of a wider Europe

The end of the Cold War provided further impetus to the development of EU internal security cooperation. We also begin to see, in the late 1980s and early 1990s, how security issues were redefined, with a move from the state security framework that had prevailed during the Cold War towards a new focus on societal security and associated 'threats', such as immigration, asylum, and transnational organized crime, which also cut across the traditional distinction between 'internal' and 'external' security. Institutional form and decision-making processes were heavily influenced by the patterns of interaction and cooperation created in the 1970s, and by the key role played in these by interior ministries and internal security agencies.

The 1990s saw some fairly apocalyptic predictions of large-scale migration or rampant organized crime from Eastern Europe. Some argued that as many as 25 million people might move from East to West, although the actual number was about 10 per cent of that figure (Codagnone 1999). The key point is that these forecasts of the potential scale of the threat or challenge had important effects on perceptions of internal security and were used as a rationale for strengthened EU-level action to deal with these perceived threats.

The institutional response was the JHA pillar of the Maastricht Treaty. This step was a compromise measure that sought to reconcile states that were firmly opposed to supranational action on issues such as migration and asylum, such as the UK, with those member states, such as Belgium, France, Germany, and the Netherlands, which were more open to the idea of common policy-making on such issues at EU level. The intergovernmental JHA pillar allowed member states to cooperate in nine areas of 'common interest' (see Box 12.2)—that is, areas in which common policies were to be developed. There would also be limited involvement by supranational institutions, with the Commission only loosely associated with policy development, and the EP and Court of Justice largely excluded.

The Maastricht Treaty brought together within the JHA pillar a variety of issues, some of which were issues on which member states had been working together since the late 1960s. It formalized this cooperation, but did so in a way that severely

---

BOX 12.2	Areas of 'common interest' in Maastricht's JHA pillar

- Asylum policy
- Border controls
- Immigration policy, including rules on entry, residence, and movement, as well as family reunion and access to employment by nationals of non-EU member states, or third-country nationals (TCNs) (It also covered unauthorized immigration, residence, and work by TCNs.)
- Combating drug addiction
- Combating fraud
- Judicial cooperation in civil matters
- Judicial cooperation in criminal matters
- Customs cooperation
- Police cooperation for preventing and combating terrorism, unlawful drug trafficking, and other serious forms of international crime

(This also included customs cooperation, in connection with the organization of a Union-wide system for exchanging information within a European police office—that is, Europol.)

---

limited involvement by supranational institutions, and also placed constraints on legal and political accountability at either national or EU levels (Geddes 2008).

Authority was delegated to a complex five-tier structure comprising the JHA Council, the Committee of Permanent Representatives (Coreper), the K4 Committee of senior officials (named after the relevant Treaty Article), steering groups, and working groups. This set-up was later amended to a four-tier structure during the UK presidency in 1998, when steering groups were abolished. Even so, the structures were complex and opaque.

Decisions were to be made by unanimity in the JHA Council, which would be supported by Coreper and the K4 Committee. The K4 Committee and the working groups brought working methods established in the Trevi Group into the EU. Under the JHA pillar, the Commission shared the right of initiative with the member states. A JHA portfolio was created within the then Directorate-General (DG) for Social Affairs. The EP had the right only to be 'regularly informed' of developments and 'consulted' about decisions, while the Court of Justice of the EU had no mandatory jurisdiction over the JHA pillar.

The legal outputs that were possible from the JHA pillar were also very limited in their scope. There was no provision for issuing regulations or directives under the JHA pillar; instead, member states had to rely on other types of instrument. Joint positions and joint actions could define the EU's approach to a particular issue, while conventions in international law could be agreed, which would then need to be

> **BOX 12.3   Europol**
>
> Europol is based in The Hague and has more than 600 staff. Its origins lie in nascent forms of police cooperation established within the Trevi Group, whose remit was subsequently expanded as a result of the perceived security challenges that became associated with single market integration. The Europol Convention agreed in Rome in July 1995 provided a base for cooperation. Europol does not have powers of arrest. Its role is to facilitate information exchange and coordinate investigations. Around 130 liaison officers from national police forces work with Europol. Europol has complex institutional structures. It has a management board that is composed of one high-ranking representative of each member state and the European Commission. Each member has one vote. The management board meets twice-yearly to discuss a wide range of Europol issues and to adopt a general report on Europol activities. These reports are then submitted to the JHA Council for its approval. A director appointed for a four-year term supervises the work of three departments (focusing on operations, governance, and capabilities).

ratified in accordance with constitutional procedures in each member state. Three such conventions were agreed: Schengen; Dublin (dealing with asylum); and Rome (creating Europol—see Box 12.3). All took a long time to move from agreement to ratification. The process of ratification of the Schengen Agreement was delayed by the implications of German reunification, while Dublin took seven years to move from signature to ratification.

Partial communitarization

The Amsterdam Treaty

The Amsterdam Treaty was designed to tackle some of the inadequacies of the Maastricht 'pillar' framework. The Maastricht Treaty was an uneasy compromise born more of the need to strike a deal than of considered reflection on the best way in which to tackle perceived new security challenges. At the most basic level, it seemed that the Maastricht framework did not provide the member states with the tools needed to do the job. For example, the inability to use the Community decision-making method inhibited the effectiveness of cooperation, as demonstrated by the difficulty securing ratification of conventions agreed in international law. Opaqueness and difficulties in holding decision-makers to account were seen as exacerbating the democratic deficit.

During the Amsterdam negotiations, a core group of member states were prepared to see fuller incorporation of internal security issues within the Community, but others, such as the UK and Denmark, were not prepared to take such a step. The solution, as will be seen, was the use of 'flexibility' in the Treaty framework, which allowed the UK, Ireland, and Denmark to opt out of measures on free movement, immigration, and asylum. The UK and Ireland were not Schengen members, while Denmark was. This move can be understood as partial communitarization that extended further powers to the Commission and the Court, but with constraints on decision-making, such as continued use of majority voting in the Council until at least five years after the Treaty came into force.

A key feature of the Amsterdam Treaty was the new Title IV added to the Treaty framework. It brought free movement, migration, asylum, checks at external borders, protection of the rights of nationals of non-member countries (known as third-country nationals, or TCNs), and judicial cooperation in civil matters into the scope of the Community method of decision-making. The Council remained the key decision-maker for five years following ratification of the Treaty (until 2004). This meant that:

- the power to make proposals was shared by the Commission and the member states;
- all decisions required unanimity in the Council; and
- the EP would be consulted before decisions were taken.

The Court of Justice also saw its competences extended to cover Title IV matters, but only following a reference from the highest court of appeal in a member state. This provision constrained the Court of Justice's role in making rulings based on preliminary references from tribunals in member states seeking to apply Community law.

The European Commission did not exercise jurisdiction over the JHA pillar. After 2004, the Commission had sole right of initiative in Title IV (just as in other Community areas of competence) and, following unanimous agreement by the Council, the codecision and qualified majority voting (QMV) procedures could be applied. The 'Return' Directive of 2008,[2] covering expulsion of irregular migrants, was the first measure to be adopted using codecision (renamed under the Lisbon Treaty as the 'ordinary legislative procedure', or OLP).

Objections from the UK and Ireland were accommodated within a protocol added to the Treaty, which made it clear that the two countries were not covered by measures under Title IV and could not be bound by decisions made by other member states. Both countries could, however, opt in to proposals. The protocol was added because the UK and Ireland reserved the right to impose controls on those entering their territory, while other member states within 'Schengenland' were removing such controls. Ireland was keen to participate so far as possible with Title IV measures, while maintaining its common travel area with the UK. The UK government, too, opted into a range of Title IV measures, including all key asylum measures (Papagianni 2001; Geddes 2005; Adler-Nissen 2009a) pre-Brexit. The UK has actually seen the benefits of EU-level action on those forms of migration that its policies have defined as unwanted (asylum seekers and irregular migrants), while not participating in those measures that are were potentially rights-extending (such as the 2003 directive that extended rights equivalent to EU citizens for TCNs legally resident in the Union for a period of five years or more[3]) or measures that impinged on the ability to exercise border controls at the UK's frontier. The government of Denmark also chose not to be covered by Title IV measures. Its position was different because it is a Schengen member state. But governments of a more Eurosceptic and anti-immigration hue were keen to be able to decide whether or not to implement decisions agreed under Title IV in national law that built on the Schengen framework.

The JHA pillar dealt with provisions on JPC in criminal matters, which included racism and xenophobia, terrorism, trafficking in persons and offences against children, drug trafficking, arms trafficking, and corruption and fraud. The aim here was to promote closer cooperation, although the institutional mechanisms for doing so were weak. The instruments for policy action remained joint positions, decisions, framework decisions, and conventions.

In 1999, a DG JHA was established within the Commission that, by 2010, employed more than 600 staff. In 2010, the remit of the DG was split into two, with one new DG dealing with home affairs and another with justice. Viviane Reding, the first Justice Commissioner, made a big impact in her new role in 2010 when she labelled plans to round up and deport Roma from France to Romania 'a disgrace', and issued a letter of formal notice to the French government requesting full information on the transposition of the 2004 Free Movement Directive[4] into French law. Her intervention was grounded in a suspicion that the French were employing ethnic criteria to discriminate against Roma, which would be against EU law (Boswell and Geddes 2011: 195).

The five-year plans

On the basis of the agreement reached at Amsterdam, the interior ministers of the member states met in Tampere, Finland, to draft a five-year policy plan specifying their objectives in the area of internal security policy and cooperation. (See Box 12.1 for a timeline of key developments.)

Tampere

The Tampere Programme specified a number of objectives.[5] First, a 'common migration and asylum policy' was taken to mean efforts to promote partnership with countries of origin, to promote 'fair treatment' of non-EU nationals (TCNs), and to seek better management of migration flows with action to tackle illegal immigration. The second area identified by Tampere was creating 'a genuine European area of justice', including mutual recognition of judicial decisions. The third area was the 'Union-wide fight against crime', which sought to step up cooperation against crime. Finally, Tampere sought stronger external action, with closer integration of the external and internal dimensions of policy. This effort has become evident in what the EU calls its 'global approach to migration'. Lavenex (2006) has noted that migration—typically the domain of interior ministries—has now acquired a significant foreign policy dimension.

Tampere was a powerful agenda-setting document. Political leaders tend not to have the time, ability, or inclination to flesh out the broad policy directions that they provide; they rely on officials to perform this function for them. On the basis of the Tampere conclusions, the Commission and the member states set to work. The Commission, in particular, was keen to stake out a role for itself, to develop credible policy ideas, and to set ambitious targets for realization of the various components of the AFSJ, identified by the Tampere document.

Particular progress was made in the development of common migration and asylum policies, but here, too, we see some distinct features of EU policy development: the dominance of the executive branch of national governments, and the existence of opt-out provisions for the UK, Ireland, and Denmark, but combined with a growing role for supranational institutions. There is an important distinction between free movement for EU citizens, which is covered by EU law, and the regulation of migration by TCNs, which is largely a matter for the member states. In 2013, a total of 3.4 million people immigrated to one of the EU's twenty-eight member states (to become twenty-seven post-Brexit), while at least 2.8 million people emigrated from an EU member state.[6] Of these 3.4 million immigrants, 1.4 million were from non-EU member states (TCNs), 1.2 million were citizens of another member state exercising their right to free movement, and a further 800,000 were returning to the country of which they held citizenship. In the 2000s, Italy, Spain, and the UK were key destination countries both for TCNs and EU free movers.

Between 2000 and 2006, Spain's TCN migrant population rose by 194 per cent to 3.1 million. In 2006 alone, 840,000 people moved to Spain, of whom 500,000 were TCNs. A key issue for these countries has been border controls and efforts to tackle 'irregular' forms of migration—more precisely, those not authorized by migration policies.

After 2012, there were increases in migration by asylum seekers, with Germany and Sweden the key destinations. In 2015, there were more than 1.2 million asylum applications in the EU, with more than half of these in Germany and Sweden.[7]

The Hague

The Hague Programme covered the period 2004–09.[8] It sought to move the EU from standards-setting measures, such as those on asylum, towards a more common approach to key internal security issues, including a common asylum policy. It also sought to deal with admissions policy, which had been an area in which member states had resisted the extension of EU competencies. There was further reinforcement of measures to tackle irregular migration, and to step up cooperation with non-EU member states on migration and asylum as part of the external dimension. This effort included measures to expel and return irregular migrants to their countries of origin. In December 2008, the 'Return' Directive, laying down rules on expulsion, was agreed. It was the first directive in the area of internal security to use the codecision procedure.

In the area of JPC, the Hague Programme sought greater exchange of information, which was indicative of the emphasis laid in EU internal security on the gathering of data through systems such as the SIS and Eurodac. The programme also called for greater use of Europol and the EU's Judicial Cooperation Unit (Eurojust). Greater stress was laid in the Hague Programme on measures to tackle terrorism in terms of prevention, preparedness, and response.

Stockholm

The Stockholm Programme[9] and subsequent action plan prepared by the Commission (European Commission 2010) marked a further development of the plans for the AFSJ in light of earlier developments, and also the revised structure for internal security policy developed in the Constitutional Treaty (which was dropped following 'no' votes in referenda held in France and the Netherlands in 2005). The key internal security elements of the Constitutional Treaty were included within the provisions of the Lisbon Treaty, the main headings being: citizenship and fundamental rights, including strengthening cooperation in law enforcement; border management; civil protection; disaster management; and judicial cooperation. The importance of the 'external dimension' of internal security is a prominent feature of the Stockholm Programme. Its inclusion blurs the distinction between the responsibilities of interior and foreign ministries, and raises questions about how the EU can achieve objectives in non-member states. In the 1990s and 2000s, it was able to transpose fairly effectively its objectives into the national legal frameworks of accession states, because it was able to dangle the carrot of membership in front of them. It cannot offer a membership prospect to countries such as Morocco and Libya, but has been very keen to work with them to help to achieve objectives such as curbs on the flows of irregular migrants. Here, we see that the external dimension of internal security requires issue linkage if agreements are to be reached and if connections are to be made between issues such as migration control and border security, with issues of importance to sending and transit states, such as aid, trade, and development. As Paoletti (2011) shows, this stance gave repressive regimes, such as that in Libya, leverage and the ability to extract concession from the EU, such as funding for major infrastructural projects. These connections with the Gaddafi regime caused embarrassment for EU leaders in the aftermath of the popular uprising that began in 2011 and subsequent military action led by the North Atlantic Treaty Organization (NATO). Border control was a key motive for cooperation and became a concern because of people smuggling operations from Libya following the effective breakdown of governance after 2011.

The Strategic Guidelines

The Strategic Guidelines[10] were an attempt to step back from numerous targets and objectives contained within the Stockholm Programme; instead, the focus was on consolidation of existing measures—although the attempt to be strategic was seriously challenged by the refugee crisis and the difficulties that it provoked in terms of securing cooperation between member states, as well as developing the commitment within the Guidelines to working with non-member states. This external dimension proved very difficult because of the massive displacement caused by the conflict in Syria, estimated at more than 4 million people by summer 2015, with the majority moving to the neighbouring states of Jordan, Lebanon, and Turkey.

Policy development in the AFSJ

We can now examine three areas in which there has been policy development, but distinct ways of working. This distinctiveness illustrates the institutional complexities of internal security cooperation and policy-making at EU level.

Anti-terrorism

Anti-terrorism policy developed in the context of the revised JPC pillar, with a focus on cooperation outside of the Community decision-making processes and a limited role for supranational institutions. Initially, the September 2001 ('9/11') attacks on Washington DC and New York played a powerful role in impelling cooperation, but the institutional base for such cooperation was already established, and the 'meaning' of security had been powerfully defined by interior ministries and security agencies beginning in the 1970s, meaning that there was a powerful institutional repertoire that provided the basis for responses to 9/11 and subsequent terror attacks, such as those in Madrid in 2004 and in London in 2005. Two common positions were agreed in 2001 on the funding of terrorist organizations and the freezing of terrorist assets. A Framework Decision on Combating Terrorism was adopted in mid-2002 that sought to create a common EU-wide definition of 'terrorist organization'. This definition was broad, going beyond that included in United Nations (UN) conventions, and thus was seen by some as having the potential to lead to the application of anti-terrorist laws to public protest more generally, with the risk of trampling on civil liberties. The Madrid attack led to the appointment of an EU anti-terrorism coordinator, an anti-terrorism action plan, and a 'scoreboard' to monitor implementation of measures in the action plan. Following the London attacks, an extraordinary meeting of EU interior ministers was held, at which it was agreed that all measures that had already been agreed should be implemented as a matter of urgency. This list included the European evidence warrant (EEW), the strengthening of the SIS and visa information system, biometric details on passports, stronger efforts to combat terrorist financing, efforts to prevent recruitment and radicalization, and stronger controls on the trade, storage, and transport of explosives. After 2012, concern grew about Muslim citizens of EU member states moving to Iraq and Syria to join with the so-called Islamic State (IS) terrorist organization. The murderous attacks in Paris and Brussels in 2015 and 2016 were carried out by terrorists linked to IS (see Box 12.4). In June 2014, the Council adopted an EU Strategy for Combating Radicalization and Recruitment to Terrorism, with the aim of tackling the causes of radicalization. There have also been efforts to promote EU–US cooperation, which have proven controversial, as Box 12.5 illustrates.

BOX 12.4   The 2015 and 2016 terror attacks on Paris and Brussels

Paris was the scene of two terrorist attacks in 2015 that left more than 140 people dead. On 7 January 2015, two brothers claiming allegiance to the Al Qaeda terrorist group in Yemen murdered eleven people at the offices of the satirical magazine *Charlie Hebdo*. On 11 January, world leaders from forty countries joined nearly 4 million other people to march in solidarity and against the attacks. The tragic events of January were compounded by the devastating attacks on 13 November 2015 on a number of targets across Paris by terrorists linked to IS that saw 130 people murdered. Of these, eighty-nine were killed while attending a rock concert at the Bataclan theatre. Even worse carnage was avoided when a suicide bomber was denied entry to the French national stadium where a France versus Germany football match was being played. He detonated his vest outside the stadium, killing three bystanders. In response to the attacks, President Hollande declared a three-month state of emergency and announced intensified attacks on IS targets in the Middle East. On 22 March 2016, thirty-two people were murdered in Brussels when a series of bombs exploded at Brussels airport and Maalbeek metro station, the latter in the heart of the EU quarter of the city. The perpetrators of this attack—three of whom died in the bombings—had been involved in the November 2015 Paris bombings. Together, the Paris and Brussels attacks drew further attention to weaknesses within the EU Schengen system. They also led to calls for much greater efforts to identify suspects and share information within the Schengen system. This move would include a European passenger name record, with airlines obliged to hand over passenger data to national authorities including for 'internal' Schengen flights.

BOX 12.5	EU–US cooperation post–9/11

Cooperation on anti-terror measures has also involved working closely with the US authorities. This area of cooperation has provided further examples of cooperation in the reserved domain of executive power, with limited legislative or judicial involvement or scope for oversight. Concerns have also been expressed about the abuse of personal data in breach of EU data protection laws. In the post-Lisbon EU, however, we see the EP flexing its muscles in this area, because it has the power to block international agreements.

Bilateral EU–US agreements on extraditions and mutual legal assistance were agreed in 2003, and implemented in the bilateral relations of the member states with the US to take effect in 2010. The extradition agreement specifies extraditable offences, the exchange of information, transmission of documents, and transit rules. It also provides protection against use of the death penalty, because extradition to the US is possible only if the death penalty will not be imposed. The mutual legal assistance agreement provides for exchange of financial information.

Cooperation was further extended when a controversial EU–US agreement, the Passenger Name Record (PNR) Directive, gave American authorities access to passenger data from European airlines. The EP obtained an annulment of the PNR Directive by the Court of Justice on the grounds that greater data protection measures were needed to conform to EU data protection laws. The EP also questioned the Commission's legal jurisdiction to conclude the PNR agreement. The Court of Justice ruled that the Commission did not have the legal authority to do so. The Court of Justice judgment did not deal with privacy and data protection issues, which left scope for bilateral agreements to take the place of the PNR Directive between the US and each EU member state. As part of its 'global approach' on internal security issues, the Commission announced plans in 2010 to revisit the PNR issue both within the EU and with key partners such as the US, Canada, and Australia. The terrorist attacks of 2015–16 led to intensified action to agree sharing of PNR data, including for Schengen 'internal' flights (see Box 12.4).

Using powers granted to it by the Lisbon Treaty in 2010, the EP also acted to block an interim SWIFT data-sharing agreement between the EU and the US. The Society for Worldwide Interbank Financial Telecommunication (SWIFT) is a private company, based in Belgium, which handles international bank transfers. The EP's rejection would affect the ability of the US authorities to access 'bulk' data, but it would still be able to access individual data using the provisions of the agreement on mutual legal assistance. The EP's civil liberties committee indicated that it was unlikely to look favourably on revised Commission proposals if they were not to address fundamental issues of data protection and respect for the rights of EU citizens. Later in 2010, a new version of the agreement was approved by the EP. How far these fundamental issues were resolved remains a matter of argument, but it was an example of the ability of the EP to change the content of a Treaty signed by the Commission and the member states.

Migration, asylum, and border controls

Migration, asylum, and border controls were located within the new Title IV, and subject to application of Community decision rules, with a transitional period until

2004. There were two key policy drives in the aftermath of Amsterdam and Tampere that reflected consolidation of EU efforts to 'securitize' migration: the development of a common asylum policy, and efforts to tackle irregular migration. The Common European Asylum System (CEAS) was put in place in 2003, containing a 'Dublin II' regulation, which brought the one-stop asylum procedure into the framework of EU law plus directives on temporary protection, reception conditions, qualifications to enter the asylum process, and asylum procedures. A revised framework—so-called CEAS II—was in place by 2013. These were criticized for focusing on minimum standards and gave a lot of wiggle room to member states. The refugee crisis provoked a crisis in the Dublin system because, in response to the humanitarian crisis, German Chancellor Angela Merkel announced on 4 September 2015 that all asylum applications by Syrians would be considered, irrespective of the point at which they entered the EU. In September 2015 alone, around 200,000 asylum seekers arrived. In the summer and autumn of 2015, hundreds of thousands of people were moving across Europe to Germany, with tensions at the borders of Greece, Hungary, Austria, Slovenia, Croatia, and Macedonia. The Commission's European Agenda for Migration of May 2015 proposed relocation for asylum seekers (European Commission 2015a). Agreement was reached in 2015, for relocation of up to 160,000 asylum seekers from Greece, Italy, and Hungary to other EU member states. By March 2016, fewer than 700 people had actually been relocated. The UK refused to participate in this mandatory EU scheme, and announced separate plans to take in 20,000 people from Syria between 2015 and 2020. The EU also sought agreement with Turkey to reinforce border controls and to stop movement towards Europe, although Turkey insisted on further assistance with refugees amounting to €3 billion and raised the issue of visa liberalization for Turkish nationals moving to the EU.

The European arrest warrant

The European arrest warrant (EAW) shows how single-market principles in the form of mutual recognition have been applied to internal security. The EAW is a warrant for arrest that is valid throughout the EU. Building on the objectives specified in the Tampere document to step up the fight against crime and to extend the principle of mutual recognition, a framework decision of 2002 was made that entered into force on 1 January 2004. The EAW is designed to speed up the process of extradition and is based on the principle that warrants issued for arrest by national judicial authorities are recognized by other member states. The EAW was used to return Osman Hussain, suspected of involvement in the failed bombings in London in July 2004, to the UK from Italy. More controversially, Andrew Symeou, a British national, was sent to Greece on a manslaughter charge for alleged involvement in a death at a nightclub in 2007. Symeou denied the charge and questions were raised about the evidence, as well as allegations of mistreatment of witnesses by the Greek authorities. Symeou spent eleven months in prison before being released on bail. He was cleared of the charges in June 2011.

The Lisbon Treaty

The implications of the Lisbon Treaty for internal security were profound. The creation of an AFSJ is defined as a competence that is shared with the member states. Almost all internal security matters are made subject to the Community method of decision-making, with use of QMV, codecision (under the OLP) for the EP, and competence for the Court of Justice extended to cover the issuance of preliminary rulings in the areas of judicial cooperation in civil matters, migration, and asylum. And, following a five-year post-ratification break (until 2014), the procedure was extended to all areas previously covered by the JPC pillar, including judicial cooperation in criminal matters, the Eurojust and Europol (see Box 12.3) agencies, and non-operational police cooperation and civil protection. Eurojust was established following a 2002 Council decision to pursue cooperation on serious crime between member states, and to allow for investigations and prosecutions covering the territory of more than one member state. Plans to augment the role of Eurojust by creating the office of a European public prosecutor charged to act against crimes against the EU budget encountered opposition from member states because of questions such as the role of such an office against value-added tax (VAT) fraud, which is a national prerogative (see Chapter 11). A European Asylum Support Office was established by a 2010 regulation to provide operational support to member states when dealing with refugee flows.

Lisbon also introduced an 'emergency brake' mechanism for individual member states with the power to veto measures that are seen to jeopardize its criminal justice system. A system of 'yellow' and 'orange' cards was also introduced, which gave national parliaments the right to return legislative proposals to the European Commission. This system could serve as a check on EU action, but seems more likely to be a way in which legislatures can seek to influence the negotiating positions of national governments. Lisbon also made important organizational and institutional changes, summarized in Box 12.6.

BOX 12.6   Post-Lisbon organizational changes

A Standing Committee on Internal Security (COSI) was created to develop the EU's internal security strategy. COSI is composed of high-level officials from interior ministries. The respective roles of the Standing Committee on Immigration, Frontiers and Asylum (SCIFA) and the Article 36 Committee (CATS) were to be reviewed by January 2012. Reporting to SCIFA and CATS are working groups on: visas; asylum; external frontiers; civil law matters; terrorism; customs cooperation; cooperation in criminal matters; cooperation in substantive criminal law; civil protection; fundamental rights; citizens' rights and free movement of persons; information exchange and data protection; external relations; law enforcement; Schengen; and, finally, general matters, including evaluation.

Conclusions

The introduction to this chapter posed two sets of linked questions that explored the relationship between institutions, policies, and ideas. First, we asked what impelled these developments. We saw a range of factors linked both to the logics of European integration, such as the effects of single market integration, as well as to the resonance of transboundary issues, such as terrorism, in the domestic politics of member states and the perceived need to seek new venues in which to develop responses to these challenges. We then asked why developments occurred at some points in time and not at others. We saw the importance of certain critical junctures in policy development linked to the drive for economic integration that informed Schengen and the SEA, as well as the broader implications of the end of the Cold War and the refugee crisis. But we saw, too, the need to account for the impact of systematic patterns of working together on internal security that developed from the 1970s onwards. These arrangements have changed the setting within which occur both thinking and decision-making about internal security. Thus we need to focus both on the timing of events and on the underlying tempo of institutional development linked to the institutionalization of organizational action at the EU level in the area of internal security.

We can now seek to factor in the role that ideas play in shaping institutional change and policy development. The chapter emphasized how changed conceptualizations of security have played a key role in shaping the EU internal security agenda. But it is also ideas about security advanced by certain actors largely concentrated within the executive branches of member state governments that have played a particularly key role in shaping the policy agenda.

This focus on the important underlying role of ideas about security leads to the second set of questions that have been addressed by this chapter. We saw that the executive branch of member state governments have been key players in policy development. We saw, too, that their role is challenged by the developing responsibilities of the Commission, EP, and Court of Justice in these areas. We have seen how all three have been able to flex their muscles and challenge aspects of policy. This tension became acutely apparent during the refugee crisis, and the attendant debate about borders, security, human rights, and the protection of refugees that illustrated the difficulty formulating a common EU response and the absence of EU-wide solidarity demonstrated by the large flows of refugees to a relatively small number of member states. There has been some rebalance in power relations between the executive, legislative, and judicial branches of government, but the executive branches of national governments still hold the upper hand, while the EP and Court of Justice have more scope to advocate and delineate the parameters of an AFSJ that realigns the relationship between freedom, security, and justice.

ENDNOTES

1. See also Menon and Weatherill (2008).

2. Directive 2008/115/EC of the European Parliament and of the Council of 16 December 2008 on common standards and procedures in Member States for returning illegally staying third-country nationals, OJ L 348/98.

3. Council Directive 2003/109/EC of 25 November 2003 concerning the status of third-country nationals who are long-term residents, OJ L 16/44.

4. Directive 2004/38/EC of the European Parliament and of the Council of 29 April 2004 on the right of citizens of the Union and their family members to move and reside freely within the territory of the Member States, OJ L 158/77.

5. Tampere European Council, 15–16 October 1999, Presidency Conclusions.

6. Eurostat, Migration and Migrant Population Statistics, available online at http://ec.europa.eu/eurostat/statistics-explained/index.php/Migration_and_migrant_population_statistics

7. Eurostat, Asylum Quarterly Report, September 2015, available online at http://ec.europa.eu/eurostat/statistics-explained/index.php/Asylum_quarterly_report

8. The Hague European Council, 4–5 November 2004, Presidency Conclusions.

9. *The Stockholm Programme: An Open and Secure Europe Serving and Protecting Citizens*, OJ C 115/01, 4 May 2010.

10. Council of the EU, Strategic Guidelines on Justice and Home Affairs, available online at http://www.consilium.europa.eu/en/policies/strategic-guidelines-jha/

 FURTHER READING

The most comprehensive guide to the legal framework governing the AFSJ is provided by Peers (2011). Mitsilegas *et al.* (2003) provide a thorough account of the development of the AFSJ. Boswell and Geddes (2011) explore the implications for migration and mobility of emerging EU internal security competencies. Huysmans (2000) provides a sophisticated conceptual account of the securitization of migration, while Lavenex (2006) explores the implications for the governance of migration and asylum of 'external governance'.

Boswell, C., and Geddes, A. (2011) *Migration and Mobility in the European Union* (Basingstoke and New York: Palgrave).

Huysmans, J. (2000) 'The European Union and the securitization of migration', *Journal of Common Market Studies*, 38/5: 751–77.

Lavenex, S. (2006) 'Shifting up and out: The foreign policy of European immigration control', *West European Politics*, 29/2: 329–50.

Mitsilegas, V., Monar, J., and Rees, W. (2003) *The European Union and Internal Security: Guardian of the People?* (New York: Palgrave Macmillan).

Peers, S. (2011) *EU Justice and Home Affairs Law* (3rd edn, Oxford: Oxford University Press).

 WEB LINKS

http://ec.europa.eu/dgs/home-affairs/index_en.htm
http://ec.europa.eu/justice/index_en.htm

In 2010, the Commission divided JHA between two Directorates-General: DG Home Affairs and DG Justice.

http://www.europol.europa.eu/

The Europol website.

http://www.ceps.eu

The Centre for European Policy Studies (CEPS), a Brussels-based think tank, has a section dedicated to JHA on its website.

http://www.statewatch.org

Civil liberties organization Statewatch monitors the growth of the European state.

CHAPTER 13

Common foreign and security policy: Institutionalizing Europe's global role

John Peterson and Niklas Helwig

■ Summary

Amongst all that sets the European Union (EU) apart, its aspirations in foreign policy rank high. No other international organization claims to have a 'common' foreign policy. Leaving aside the (arguable) exception of the North Atlantic Treaty Organization (NATO), none claim an emerging defence policy. The common foreign and security policy (CFSP) seeks to combine the political weight of twenty-eight (twenty-seven, post-Brexit) EU member states in the pursuit of common goals. But European foreign

Cont. ➤

Cont. ➤

policy must integrate a wide range of other policies to be effective. Likewise, any assessment of the EU's role in global affairs must consider CFSP as one policy within a broader external relations toolkit (see Box 13.1). This chapter highlights the CFSP's relative youth (compared to other EU policies), mixed record, and uncertain future. Compared with the rest of what the EU does, foreign policy has resisted pressures for integration. Nonetheless, it has witnessed a significant degree of institutionalization and is an area in which the EU's ambitions remain high.

Introduction

The creation and development of what is now the EU has not only promoted cooperative relations between its member states, but also has given them an opportunity to speak with a common, sometimes single, voice in world politics. Potentially, the Union has the power to influence global events in pursuit of European values and interests. By the early twenty-first century, no other international actor had such a diverse foreign policy 'toolkit' (Everts and Keohane 2003: 177). It could even be argued that the EU's power matched or exceeded that of the United States (US) in every area besides the deployment of military force (Moravcsik 2005: 349).[1] The

Possessing such power is not the same as being able to deploy it effectively. The EU's capacity for external action developed first in trade policy. From the origins of the European Economic Community (EEC), there was a clear connection between the creation of a customs union and a common commercial policy (CCP) towards the rest of the non-EU world (the former was impossible without the latter). Purely functional necessity resulted in the effective delegation by member states of trade policy authority to the EU's institutions, with the European Commission in the lead. Today, the EU acts for the member states in international trade negotiations, including within the World Trade Organization (WTO), usually managing to negotiate as a single bloc (Young and Peterson 2014).

However, there is no obvious connection between (what has become) a single market and a common foreign policy. The EU has its own seat alongside larger member states in key forums such as the Groups of Seven and Twenty (G7 and G20, respectively), and it has 'super-observer' status at the United Nations (UN) General Assembly. But it is absent from others, such as the International Monetary Fund (IMF), where it is represented by its member states (which do seek to coordinate their positions). EU member states have vastly different foreign policy capabilities, and vary in their willingness to employ the EU's complex and often time-consuming procedures. One consequence is stubbornly divided views about the EU's ultimate aim in foreign policy: the *intergovernmental coordination* of pre-existing national foreign policies (at a minimum), or the *supranational governance* of a single European foreign policy (at a maximum).

| BOX 13.1 | Defining 'foreign policy' and 'external relations' |

In ordinary English, 'foreign policy' and 'external relations' mean much the same thing. However, they have quite different meanings in Euro-speak. *External relations* is the term used in Brussels to refer to the foreign affairs responsibilities of the Commission: trade and aid, but also external aspects of other EU policies, such as agriculture, and judicial and police cooperation. Most decisions are taken by the Council on the basis of a Commission proposal, by QMV and with a strong role for the European Parliament (EP).

In contrast, *foreign policy* refers to actions in areas that are normally the remit of national foreign ministries and on which nearly all decisions are taken unanimously. The Commission is fully associated, not least through the High Representative, who now chairs most meetings of EU foreign ministers and is Vice-President of the Commission (see Box 13.4). But the Commission has always occupied a position of weakness compared with those of member states in foreign policy. The EP still has no power—besides budgetary influence and a right to invite heads of EU delegations for exchanges of views—over the CFSP.

CFSP proposals can be made by any member state or the High Representative (with or without the support of the Commission). Traditionally, the Council presidency took the lead, but it lost its role in the CFSP after the adoption of the 2007 Lisbon Treaty. The first two post-Lisbon High Representatives, Catherine Ashton (a British Labour politician) and Federica Mogherini (former Italian foreign minister), tried to steer the EU foreign policy agenda, but were often outflanked or held back by member states.

Since the 1992 Maastricht Treaty, the CFSP, along with the rest of what the EU does, has been the responsibility of a 'single institutional framework'. Thus decisions on the CFSP and external relations are taken by the same people—mainly foreign ministers and heads of state or government, with Commission support—but according to different decision rules. The Lisbon Treaty eliminated the pillar system that made CFSP decision-making distinct from other policies. But, in substance, little has changed: CFSP decisions still require unanimous approval by the European Council or the Foreign Affairs Council (FAC), with limited possibilities for QMV and the option for member states to 'constructively abstain'. Moreover, the Court of Justice of the EU has no jurisdiction on CFSP matters. One of the EU's legal gurus argues that Lisbon 'confirms that CFSP remains clearly subject to different rules and procedures from the other activities of the EU. It therefore remains a second pillar as it was before' (Piris 2010: 260).

When decisions on foreign policy action are taken, EU member states (particularly larger ones) often act like 'normal' nation-states; thus they reject the delegation of foreign and security policy to international bodies except on the basis of unanimity. This intergovernmental approach dominates most other international organizations, such as NATO. At the same time, it has become increasingly recognized within European political classes, and even more so amongst diplomats, that even the largest EU states have limited influence unless they act together with European partners. All EU member states have accepted this reality for decades, but they have drawn different conclusions from it. Most smaller EU states, but also Germany, have argued consistently for a more supranational CFSP—with decisions by qualified majority voting (QMV). Others—France, Spain, Sweden, and the United Kingdom (UK), prior to Brexit—have insisted that EU foreign policy must be made by consensus.

Even as it aspires to a common foreign policy, the EU is unlikely ever to have a *single* foreign policy, in the sense of one that replaces national policies. The CFSP remains only one element in what is often referred to as 'European foreign policy', or the sum total of all external action by EU member states (Keukeleire and Delreux 2014; Hill and Smith 2016). And when the perceived national interests of member states clash, such as over the 2003 Iraq War, there simply is no EU foreign policy, common or otherwise (Hill 2004).

What the CFSP offers is a mechanism for seizing on the 'politics of scale' (Ginsberg 1989, 2001), or the notion that the EU is far more powerful when it speaks with one voice, as opposed to twenty-eight (or twenty-seven, post-Brexit). The EU has even developed something approaching a doctrine for its foreign policy, in the shape of the European Security Strategy (ESS) adopted in 2003 and renewed in 2016 (see Box 13.2). The Union has gone much further in institutionalizing foreign policy cooperation than any other regional organization and even features common diplomatic structures of a kind we usually associate with nation-states only, in the form of the European External Action Service (EEAS) and the High Representative of the Union (see Box 13.4).

BOX 13.2   **The European Security Strategy**

Agreed in the aftermath of painful divisions over the US-led invasion of Iraq, the European Security Strategy (ESS)[2] identifies the key challenges and threats facing the EU. It also highlights the Union's strategic objectives, throwing the EU's weight behind effective multilateralism (especially via the UN), democracy promotion, and respect for human rights and the rule of law. The ESS espouses the need for more active policies across the whole range of 'political, diplomatic, military and civilian, trade and development activities', and an EU strategic culture fostering 'early, rapid, and when necessary, robust intervention' (Council of the European Union 2003: 11).

In 2015, the EU launched a review aimed at writing a new EU global strategy under the leadership of High Representative Mogherini. The initiative reflected consensus that the ESS had not been flattered by the reality check of the following years, as the EU's global environment had become 'more connected, contested and complex' (EEAS 2015: 8). The EU's incoherence in response to the Libyan crisis suggested that EU foreign policy remained prone to divisions of the kind it had suffered over Iraq (Koenig 2011). Similar divisions were exposed in the aftermath of the 2011 Arab Spring, when the instability of the Middle East and North Africa (MENA) region caused a massive influx of refugees onto European soil. The more demanding relationship with Russia, after its aggression in Ukraine from 2014 onwards, was another stress test: divisions between individual member states, with varying relationships with the eastern neighbour, made it difficult for the EU to maintain a common front on Russia. In the circumstances, debates about whether European and US security cultures remained in alignment or in a state of divergence are still live ones (Dannreuther and Peterson 2006).

The origins of CFSP institutions

One of the first laws of politics is that nearly all institutions have unintended effects that their creators neither foresee nor intend. The founding fathers of what is now the EU had little or no ambition to create a new foreign policy power. Foreign policy was thus a bit player in the European project of the early 1950s, which began as an economic enterprise, albeit with a strong political purpose: to make war impossible between Germany and France via the integration of their coal and steel industries. The next major step, the creation of a European Defence Community (EDC) in 1952, sought to harness a still-occupied and distrusted (West) Germany into a European army to bolster Western Europe's defence against the Soviet threat (see Table 13.1). But plans for the EDC collapsed in 1954, following its rejection by the French National Assembly, leading the founding fathers once again to turn to economic integration to fulfil political objectives.

The supranational governance endemic to the European Coal and Steel Community (ECSC) and, later, the EEC, was always unimaginable in the security realm. Defence was left mostly to the NATO and its strictly intergovernmental institutions. However, the coming to power of Charles de Gaulle as French president led to a serious effort to 'intergovernmentalize' the EEC by grafting onto it the so-called Fouchet Plan in 1961–62. De Gaulle's clear intent was to turn the EEC into a voluntary union of member states with extensive national veto powers, action only by unanimity, and no role for supranational institutions in foreign and defence affairs. The Fouchet Plan was rejected by the other EEC five, because some (such as the Netherlands) were unhappy that it excluded the UK and others saw it as a French move against NATO. In any event, the debate on the Fouchet Plan—with intergovernmental co-operation competing for support with the Community method—set a pattern for future debates about European foreign policy.

TABLE 13.1 The expansion of EU foreign policy: A chronology	
Year	**Policy event**
1952	EDC Treaty signed by six founding states of the EEC
1954	EDC Treaty rejected by French National Assembly Brussels Treaty for the Western European Union (WEU) signed by six EEC states plus the UK
1958	Treaty of Rome founding the European Economic Community (EEC) enters into force
1970	EPC mechanism created

Cont. ➤

Cont. ➤	
1971	EPC used to present (for the first time) collective EC positions at the UN
1973	EPC used to develop collective positions toward key allies (such as the US)
1974	First institutionalized regional political dialogues (Euro–Arab)
1975	Helsinki Final Act of the CSCE, in which EPC played a key role
1981	EPC/EC coordinated economic embargo against Argentina during Falklands War
1986	Single European Act agreed, bringing EPC into the EC treaty framework
1989–91	Communist governments fall in Central and Eastern Europe, culminating in German unification (1990) and the collapse of the Soviet Union (1991)
1992	Maastricht Treaty on European Union agreed, with provisions for a CFSP and links to the WEU
1993	Maastricht Treaty (and the CFSP) enters into effect
1997	Amsterdam Treaty agreed, creating High Representative for the CFSP
1998	UK and France agree the St Malo Declaration on European Defence
1999	Cologne and Helsinki summits (respectively) create European Security and Defence Policy (ESDP) and agree to create Rapid Reaction Force
2003–04	Convention on the Future of Europe agrees Constitutional Treaty. First ESDP police mission in Bosnia, followed by ESDP military missions (Macedonia, Democratic Republic of Congo, Bosnia)
2003	US invades Iraq in coalition with some European Union member states; EU is painfully divided
2005	Constitutional Treaty rejected by French and Dutch voters
2006	Lisbon Treaty negotiated by European leaders, retaining much of the Constitutional Treaty's content on external relations
2008	Russian troops move into South Ossetia and Abkhazia, sparking a conflict with Georgia; EU negotiates a ceasefire
2009	Lisbon Treaty ratified by all member states, creating the 'multi-hatted' High Representative of the Union/Vice-President of the Commission, the European External Action Service, and the permanent President of the European Council
2011	A wave of democratic protests and reforms spreads across North Africa, heralding an 'Arab Spring'; the instability of the region, especially in Libya and Syria, triggers an inflow of refugees to Europe via the Mediterranean Sea and the Balkans in subsequent years
2014	Russia annexes Crimea and supports pro-Russian unrest in Eastern Ukraine, causing the EU to rethink its policies in the Eastern Neighbourhood and adopt comprehensive sanctions against Russia

European political cooperation

Interest in foreign policy coordination did not disappear with the Fouchet Plan. Buoyed by the resignation of de Gaulle and the prospect of the Community's first enlargement, EC foreign ministers agreed the 1970 Luxembourg report that established the European political cooperation (EPC) mechanism. The EPC had no basis other than a political declaration (legally non-binding) of the Council. Member states agreed to consult and cooperate on issues of foreign policy, but not on defence and only outside the EEC Treaty framework. For several years, France prevented any discussion of foreign policy within an EEC framework. Foreign ministers were even forced on one occasion in 1975 to hold an EPC meeting in the morning in Copenhagen and then fly to Brussels to reconvene in the afternoon for 'separate' EEC discussions.

Still, the EPC slowly became more institutionalized, with informal rules and substantive policies gradually emerging during the 1970s. There was no shortage of opportunities to put the EPC to the test: common European positions were sought on the Yom Kippur War in the Middle East, relations with the US, crises in Cyprus and Portugal, the Soviet invasion of Afghanistan, and the Iranian revolution. But actual policy output remained modest for two reasons: first, all decisions were made by consensus and just one member state could block or water down any proposal; and second, the EPC had no resources, policy tools, or staff of its own.[3] Some of its early participants therefore viewed it as little more than a diplomats' dining club.

Over time, however, the EPC began to produce substantive policies. The 1980 Venice Declaration on the Middle East affirmed the right of Palestinians to self-determination (in defiance of the US) for the first time. Member states, using both the EPC and EC frameworks, played a leading role in the Conference on Security and Cooperation in Europe (CSCE).[4] Despite US scepticism of what was originally a Soviet initiative, the CSCE produced the Helsinki Final Act in 1975, a political declaration that reaffirmed fundamental rights and freedoms, made border changes permissible only by peaceful means, and opened discussions on ways in which countries treated their citizens and cooperated with their neighbours. Later, the CSCE was regarded as an important factor leading to the end of the Cold War.

Yet the 1970s and 1980s were mostly a time of missed opportunities for European foreign policy. Member states, including France, gradually accepted that a large part of the problem was the separation of the EPC from the EC itself. The EPC had begun to develop its own brand of 'soft law', which allowed its participants to refer to and (with the cooperation of the Commission) draw upon Community instruments such as economic aid and sanctions. These arrangements still remained mostly ad hoc and unsatisfactory.

From the EPC to the CFSP

Over time, an increasing number of member states became less hesitant to use Community instruments and institutions to support EPC objectives. Many also became frustrated by problems rooted in the compartmentalization of economic and political

> **BOX 13.3** **CFSP policy instruments**
>
> In contrast with purely political decisions taken under the EPC, the CFSP provides for legally binding decisions. Prior to the Lisbon Treaty, there were three types of decision: *common positions* (requiring coordinated national actions); *joint actions* (using EC instruments, such as aid and trade); and *common strategies* (providing a longer-term view). Yet the lack of any clear distinction between, say, common positions and joint actions, and the tendency of common strategies to lack substance, led to their reformulation. The Lisbon Treaty specified one legally binding act for all CFSP action: *decisions*, which could define policy Union guidelines, actions, positions, and implementation arrangements. However, there remained no provisions for giving the Commission the right to monitor implementation of the CFSP, besides entrusting the High Representative with ensuring 'implementation of the decisions adopted by the European Council and the Council'; how he or she would do so, besides naming and shaming in cases of blatant non-implementation, remained unclear and proper implementation of the CFSP thus appeared to be 'largely left to the goodwill of Member States' (Piris 2010: 264).

affairs. The Commission became gradually more accepted as a necessary partner in the EPC in order to align Community policies with European foreign policy objectives. Eventually, member states decided that the EPC should be given formal status within the Treaties in the form of the Single European Act (SEA) in 1986.

Yet even the new-model EPC was exposed as inadequate in the face of major challenges such as the fall of the Berlin Wall, war in Yugoslavia, and the Gulf War. The opportunity was taken in the 1992 Maastricht Treaty to strengthen it, by bringing it into the new EU's institutional structure and giving it, for the first time, defence aspirations, all with an ambitious-sounding new name: the 'common foreign and security policy' (see Box 13.3). Maastricht integrated the previously autonomous EPC secretariat (working under the Council presidency) into the General Secretariat of the Council. What it did *not* do, however, was modify the strictly intergovernmental decision-making processes of the EPC. Despite the strong political signal that the EU was getting its act together in foreign policy, little changed in practice.

The evolution of the CFSP structures

The Maastricht Treaty gave birth to the EU, putting into a single Treaty framework the European Community, CFSP, and the newly emerging area of justice and home affairs (JHA) (see Chapter 12). But it kept these policy areas separate by giving the CFSP and JHA their own distinct decision-making procedures and 'pillars' (Pillar II for the CFSP). Maastricht also provided for a common defence policy and gave the Union the right to call on the Western European Union (WEU) (see Table 13.1)—a

European-only alternative to NATO that had been kept alive for various purposes—to undertake military missions on the EU's behalf.

The new Treaty also ensured continuity between the old EPC and new CFSP. Responsibility for managing the CFSP remained with the rotating (between member states) Council presidency, which also remained responsible for its implementation. Decisions could be taken on the proposal of any member state, as well as the Commission, but the Commission's inferior status was formalized by making it only 'fully associated' with the CFSP. While the EU appeared to embrace higher foreign-policy ambitions, it dedicated few new resources to this purpose. The CFSP remained intergovernmental and a matter of (almost exclusively) unanimous agreement. As under the EPC, the Union looked extensively to the policies and instruments of the EC to realize its foreign policy ambitions.

The European Council formally gave the CFSP strategic direction and took the highest profile political decisions (see Chapter 3). Foreign ministers meeting monthly in the General Affairs Council (GAC) took most policy decisions. On CFSP matters, foreign ministers' agendas were prepared as under the EPC by a committee of senior officials, the Political Committee (PoCo), which did the preparatory work that the Committee of Permanent Representatives (Coreper) performed for Pillar I questions. Composed of political directors—very senior diplomats—from national foreign ministries, PoCo normally met once a month, usually in the capital of the presidency, as well as in the margins of foreign ministers' and European Council meetings. PoCo was serviced by a diverse array of working groups of national EU officials covering geographical regions (such as the Middle East) and functional issues (such as non-proliferation).

The CFSP also inherited the Coreu system from the EPC.[5] This encrypted communications network allows for direct communications between national foreign ministries, the Commission, and the Council Secretariat. It became a critical real-time means of exchanging information and views. The longer it operated, the more it became accepted that major foreign policy problems should be discussed at the EU level before national positions were formed. Thus a 'coordination reflex' emerged: consultation before action became the norm and unilateral action was shunned.

The common security and defence policy

The 1997 Treaty of Amsterdam was an opportunity to address some of the defects in the CFSP (Peterson and Sjursen 1998). The Treaty created the High Representative for the CFSP, who would retain the existing post of Secretary-General of the Council, to 'assist' the presidency in managing the CFSP. A new policy planning and early warning unit also was established within the Council Secretariat, bringing together staff from the Council, Commission, WEU, and member states. Some spoke of a nascent EU foreign ministry; more sober analysts noted that the new unit expanded the EU's Brussels-based foreign policy machinery, but kept it under the firm grip of the Council (Allen 1998: 54–5).[6]

In themselves, these changes were not far-reaching. To illustrate, the new policy unit did not supplant or even contribute much to the EU's network of national foreign ministries. What made Amsterdam important and changed the CFSP was less the new provisions than the way in which they were implemented. Amsterdam came into force (in 1999) when the EU was under pressure after its humiliating performance in the Balkans, where it appeared powerless without US political, as well as military, leadership to prevent extensive bloodshed, first in Bosnia and then in Kosovo (Bildt 1998; Holbrooke 2011; Clark 2002). In particular, the exposure of Europe's institutional and military ineffectiveness in Kosovo focused minds on the Union's inability to manage a security crisis without extensive US participation.

The Cologne European Council in 1999 created a new European security and defence policy (ESDP), building on the bilateral UK–French St Malo initiative of the previous year.[7] It also appointed Javier Solana as the CFSP High Representative, thus opting for a heavyweight former Spanish foreign minister and NATO Secretary-General instead of a low-profile official. Six months later, the Helsinki European Council agreed the main features of the EU's defence policy, with substantial knock-on effects for the CFSP (of which ESDP, now called the 'common security and defence policy', or CSDP, forms a part). The so-called headline goal was agreed, specifying the military capabilities that member states would aim to put at the EU's disposal, along with parallel 'civilian and conflict prevention dimensions'.[8]

New politico-military structures had to be grafted onto what was previously a purely civilian organization so as to manage the EU's new military capability. Thus a military committee consisting of senior military officers representing their national chiefs of staff (similar to NATO's arrangements) was set up. It would be serviced by a new military staff made up of military personnel seconded from member states and located in the Council Secretariat. On the political (CFSP) side, PoCo was superseded by a new Political and Security Committee (PSC), consisting of national ambassador-level officials, stationed (significantly) in Brussels and not in their capitals. The PSC would meet regularly (typically twice a week) and take responsibility for the day-to-day management of the CFSP. Uniquely in the EU's institutional set-up, it was given scope to make actual decisions (as opposed to recommendations) on the political control of military operations if the Council so mandated. In its earliest versions, member states frequently appointed relatively junior diplomats to the PSC; 'Progressively, however, the PSC [became] a key posting for career diplomats' (Howorth 2010: 457).

The Lisbon Treaty

These institutional changes, along with the appointment of Solana as High Representative for the CFSP, produced a distinct European foreign policy system. Over time, it became increasingly robust, action-oriented, and Brussels-centred. Still, foreign policy remained an area in which the EU clearly failed to punch at its weight. Perhaps the CFSP's main weakness was the leadership conflicts inherent in a system in which the presidency changed every six months, the High Representative was increasingly seen as the external face of EU foreign policy, but lacked real power, and the Commission remained responsible for many of the instruments needed to make CFSP effective. Thus CFSP reform emerged as a prominent theme of the 2002–03 Convention on the Future of Europe and the Constitutional Treaty that emerged in 2004.

Following its rejection in the 2005 French and Dutch referenda, the Constitutional Treaty looked doomed. Few were more disappointed than those for whom strengthening the EU's foreign policy was a priority. The Constitutional Treaty had proposed to abolish the rotating presidency and transform the High Representative into an EU Minister for Foreign Affairs (MFA), who would also serve as a Vice-President of the Commission in charge of external relations. It also created a new European External Action Service (EEAS) to assist the MFA.

In the end, most of the Constitutional Treaty's foreign policy provisions survived the transition to the Lisbon Treaty that came into force in December 2009. The term 'Minister of Foreign Affairs' was ditched for the less provocative (and more familiar) title High Representative, but the post retained nearly all of the same powers and authority specified in the Constitutional Treaty (see Box 13.4). The EEAS was

---

BOX 13.4   The High Representative

The Lisbon Treaty's High Representative of the Union is meant to enhance the 'continuity', 'coherence', and 'visibility' of the EU's action in the world. The High Representative is triple-hatted (that is, given more than one formal affiliation) as High Representative for CFSP in the Council (as before Lisbon), the Vice-President of the Commission responsible for external relations, and chair of the FAC. The EEAS and the chair of the PSC—the crucial preparatory body on CFSP matters—as well as EU special representatives to specific states or regions work under her or his authority.

The European Council appoints the High Representative by qualified majority, with the agreement of the Commission President. The High Representative serves for a five-year term. As one of the Vice-Presidents of the Commission, he or she needs EP approval, as do other members of the Commission.

The many responsibilities of the office include proposing CFSP decisions and monitoring their implementation, diplomatic missions to crisis regions and strategic partners, countless speeches at international gatherings, and the conduct of international negotiations (such as chairing the Iran nuclear talks). In addition, the office holder tries to steer EU decision-making, for example through regular meetings with Commissioners and in national capitals. The High Representative is also an interlocutor to the EP and reports to its plenary on the CFSP.

Fulfilling such a wide range of tasks posed daunting challenges for the first occupant of the post, Catherine Ashton. Delivering one message was especially demanding, given

Cont. ➤

Cont. ➤

the abundance of actors involved in EU foreign policy. Alongside the High Representative, the Presidents of the European Council and Commission retained their own external representative roles, such as representing the EU in the G7 and G20. Many of the EU's external relations portfolios, such as trade, development cooperation, humanitarian aid, enlargement, and neighbourhood policy, remained in the hands of other Commissioners.

Upon taking office in 2014, Federica Mogherini announced her intention to seek stronger coordination between EU institutions, as well as with member states. The first signs of this new approach were the launch of monthly meetings of Commissioners with external relations portfolios, as well as her tour of EU capitals. Yet Mogherini's first months also revealed the difficulties of providing 'co-leadership' (Helwig and Rüger 2014: 4). Policy initiatives such as an ill-prepared and leaked strategy paper on Russia in early 2015 exposed how difficult it was for EU administrations to think of themselves as unified, strategic foreign policy actors and to coax member states towards a joint approach.

launched in 2010 as a 6,000-strong diplomatic service for the Union, working alongside national embassies (see Box 13.5). Lisbon also contained 'mutual assistance and solidarity clauses', albeit with qualifications to reassure non-NATO members (such as Sweden and Ireland) and a clear statement that, for the twenty-one EU members of the Atlantic Alliance, NATO 'remains the foundation of their collective defence and the forum for its implementation'.[9] Piris (2010: 275) is clear that while the solidarity clause is 'of utmost symbolic and political importance . . . it does not amount to a mutual defence clause and does not change anything in the respective position of each member state vis-à-vis NATO'.

What also did not change were the basic ground rules of the CFSP—notably, that nearly all important decisions would be taken by unanimity. Nor did the new-model High Representative reduce the importance of national foreign ministers or the Council presidency, whose agreement continued to be needed for every common policy. However, the High Representative now assumed a far stronger position than any previous European official to broker agreements and to implement them, once agreed.

BOX 13.5   The EEAS

The EEAS supports the High Representative in the conduct of the CFSP, but also assists the Commission, President of the European Council, and EP in their external activities. The EEAS was launched as an 'autonomous body', bringing together staff from the Commission, Council, and national diplomatic services. The latter provided at least a third of the officials of the EEAS, yet national diplomats—owing to member states' eagerness to control the service—very quickly filled the majority of the leadership positions.

The service is led by an executive secretary-general and three deputies, and comprises several geographical and thematic Directorate-Generals (DGs). The political affairs department, headed by the deputy secretary-general for political affairs, plans and coordinates substantive work. Crisis management structures for the planning and implementation of civilian and military missions were moved from the Council Secretariat to the EEAS, although they were kept separate from the rest of the organizational structure of the service because of the uneasiness among member states regarding integration of this policy area. About 140 delegations worldwide represent the EU politically, coordinating the activities of local member states' delegations, providing political reporting, and implementing EU external financial instruments, for which they also employ about 3,500 Commission officials.

A *de novo* body operating at one remove from the community institutions, the EEAS initially struggled to work efficiently and deliver on its main task: to increase coherence between the CFSP and the external relations of the Commission. Since then, streamlining of the hierarchy and closer cooperation with the Commission Secretariat-General have improved its capabilities. Whether the EEAS is really a European foreign ministry in the making or just an institutional fudge that preserves divisions between the Commission's external relations, the intergovernmental CFSP, and member states' foreign policies remains an open question.

The CFSP in action

One of the abiding features of the EU foreign policy system is its emphasis on consensus: no single official or body enjoys a monopoly over policy initiation. The post-Lisbon High Representative was meant to provide leadership of a kind that the CFSP traditionally had lacked. The basic problems of multiple EU foreign policy representatives, plus inconsistent and often weak leadership and implementation, were prime motivators of the decision to create the new post. Giving the High Representative a foot in both the Commission and Council had in-built institutional contradictions. But it created the potential at least for greater coherence between political ends and economic means.

A more fundamental problem with the CFSP system is that member states are bound by agreed common approaches and have an obligation to consult each other, but retain freedom of action where there is no agreed common policy. Even where EU agreement exists, member states may still act themselves, so long as they do so in accordance with the agreed position. This practice can be seen in the succession of EU foreign ministers who follow each other making the rounds in the Middle East, sometimes to the despair of the High Representative. Put simply, there is no obligation on a member state to conduct its foreign policy 'exclusively', or even primarily, through the CFSP, or even to leave CFSP action exclusively to the High Representative (unless it has been agreed otherwise).

The difficulty of reaching common policies and/or the conviction that (especially) larger member states can achieve better results by other means sometimes leads to the creation of small groups outside the EU. One prominent and traumatic (for the young and fragile CFSP[10]) example was the so-called Contact Group, in which France, Germany, the UK, and (eventually) Italy engaged in multilateral diplomacy after 1994 with the US and Russia on the conflicts in the former Yugoslavia, with other EU member states effectively excluded. Another occurred when France, Germany, and the UK (the 'EU3') gave themselves the task in 2004 of trying to convince Iran to agree to international controls on its nuclear development programme. The inclusion of the UK in both configurations points to an important consequence of Brexit: an EU that no longer includes one of its major diplomatic and military heavyweights will inevitably count for less in global politics.

The Lisbon Treaty did not change the dynamic towards diplomacy led by large European states with the EU marginalized or even excluded altogether. The main diplomatic format for negotiating a ceasefire agreement in Eastern Ukraine after 2014 was the so-called Normandy format, which comprised Germany, France, Russia, and Ukraine, without any EU involvement. Sensitivities between large and small EU member states remain tender. But with enlargement to twenty-eight (twenty-seven, post-Brexit), there is an increasing—if still reluctant—recognition that some member states are more equal than others and similar groups are necessary if the CFSP is to function. In any event, foreign policy for all EU member states has over time become more Europeanized (Wong 2011)—that is, more Brussels-based, frequently linked to EC external economic policies, and increasingly part of the EU's personality.

Instruments and powers

As the rules governing EU foreign policy have expanded over the years, so too have its policy instruments and capabilities. As we have seen, the EPC often involved little more than issuing declarations and coordinating member states' diplomatic activity. Nonetheless, the Euro–Arab Dialogue and CSCE in the mid-1970s were early examples of institutionalized political dialogues. Such dialogues became ways in which to coordinate all EPC (and, later, EC) activities towards an important region or country, such as the Mediterranean or the Central and Eastern Europe countries (CEECs). In particular, trade and cooperation agreements have been linked to broad political goals, particularly democracy, respect for the rule of law, and human rights (Szymanski and Smith 2005; Young and Peterson 2014). These arrangements also enabled the EU to promote regional integration, including in the Middle East, Latin America, and Asia (Smith 2014: 67–94). Each of the EU's 'positive' economic measures (financial aid or trade agreements) involves a negative component as well: the Union's ability to stop aid or to suspend trade negotiations (at a minimum), or to impose diplomatic or economic sanctions (at a maximum—see Box 13.6.).

By the late 2000s, the EU moved to create *strategic partnerships* with major or emerging powers, not least as a way to give itself incentives to agree common

---

BOX 13.6   EU sanctions

Restrictive measures (EU-speak for sanctions) are one of Europe's main coercive foreign policy instruments. The EU is especially drawn to the use of economic sanctions because they make use of the strength of the regional trading bloc as a lever. That the CCP is an exclusive competence of the EU makes sanctions and the compliance of EU member states to the restrictive measures, at least in theory, quicker and easier to handle. Restrictive measures also match the EU's alleged post-modern approach to power in international relations, whereby military strength has lost its primacy, and has been replaced by economic incentives and diplomatic initiatives.

Yet Europe's love affair with sanctions got off to a slow start. During the first twenty years of the EEC's existence, economic sanctions were imposed in only two cases: against Rhodesia in 1965; and against Greece in 1967. Following the creation of the EPC in 1970, the EU imposed sanctions against a growing list of countries: Iran; the Soviet Union; Argentina; Poland; Libya; South Africa; Yugoslavia; and Iraq.

Restrictive measures imposed by the EU have become more sophisticated over time (Portela 2010). *Targeted sanctions* block bank accounts and passports of high-ranking individuals, and were used intensively against the authoritarian regimes of Libya, Egypt, Tunisia, and Syria during the 2011 Arab Spring. *Comprehensive sanctions*, as in the case of the Iran nuclear negotiations, are much more crippling for the targeted economy and often comprise trade embargoes for specific industries.

The EU's sanctions policy received heightened attention during the Ukraine crisis in 2014, when member states agreed for the first time on comprehensive sanctions against one of its major trading partners (Russia). The move was made as a reaction to Russia's disregard of Ukraine's territorial integrity and after the shooting down of a Malaysian Airlines flight by a Russian-made missile over eastern Ukraine. Intense lobbying by the US administration and decisive German leadership (traditionally a country with close economic ties with Russia) were essential. While the EU was praised for its ability to send a strong signal, its unity was still fragile and its long-term strategy of how to engage with Russia remained vague.

---

positions and combine policy instruments in bilateral diplomacy (see Box 13.7). Otherwise, the objectives of these privileged dialogues were left unclear. As Herman Van Rompuy, post-Lisbon President of the European Council, bluntly put it: 'We have strategic partners, now we need a strategy.'[11]

The Maastricht Treaty was important in giving the EU, for the first time, the capacity for military action via recourse to the WEU. Elaborate arrangements were established between the Union and WEU, as well as between the latter and NATO (so that the WEU could call on NATO assets). The only case in which the Union drew upon the WEU's resources in the 1990s was in assisting in the EU's administration of the Bosnian town of Mostar. On the one occasion on which the Union might have asked the WEU to undertake a military operation on its behalf, to defuse a crisis in Albania in 1997, EU foreign ministers were unable to agree and Italy ended up leading a coalition of the willing.

BOX 13.7	Strategic partnerships

The EU has created a dense network of agreements and partnerships that seek not only to advance specific policy matters, but also to create a multilateral, rules-based global order. This wider objective mirrors its own internal nature and habits, and desire to 'export' them to other parts of the world. Partnership and cooperation agreements (PCAs) with third countries provide for cooperation on trade and economic matters, but also on issues such as climate change, poverty reduction, and political reform. The Cotonou Agreement (2000) with seventy-nine African, Caribbean, and Pacific (ACP) countries is one example.

PCAs with countries such as China (1985) and Russia (1994) eventually morphed into strategic partnerships. The EU has upgraded several relationships with ten countries to this status, which might be considered the holy grail of its institutionalized relations. By 2016, the Union had strategic partnerships with (in addition to Russia and China) Brazil, Canada, India, Japan, Mexico, South Africa, South Korea, and the US.

A lack of practical outcomes from these partnerships has been a point of criticism. Climate change (or, in EU-speak, 'climate action') illustrates the point. After more than a decade of strategic partnerships with Brazil, Russia, India, and China (the so-called BRIC countries), all of which focused on environmental policy, the EU found itself shut out of the room by its strategic partners during the most important negotiations at the Copenhagen climate talks in December 2009.

The very meaning of strategic partnerships remained uncertain. Some argued that the EU's designation of this status to Canada, Japan, Mexico, and South Africa risked undermining its relationships with truly global players such as the US and China, and suggested a lack of differentiation. Strategic partnerships had no Treaty basis and thus were left ill-defined, meaning little more than additional summits and meetings.

Strategic partnerships exemplify EU's fixation with 'structural diplomacy' (Smith *et al.* 2015: 5), which is focused on lengthy processes of engaging third countries in dialogues and negotiations. Yet partnerships often fall to pieces when strategic interests collide. In 2015, Russia was erased from the list of strategic partners following its aggression in Ukraine. Instead of treating Russia as a strategic partner, Federica Mogherini suggested Russia should be seen as a 'strategic player' given its indisputable relevance in regional and global politics. Still, the Russia case was yet another blow to the idea of strategic partnerships, which demonstrated that the EU is increasingly active in foreign policy, but that the quality of its diplomacy remains suspect.

Over time, cumbersome procedures for EU–WEU joint action became a source of frustration. Influenced by events in Kosovo, the European Council decided in 1999 that the EU should have its own military capability, after which the WEU's military capability simply fell away. The core tasks of the new ESDP, like those of the WEU before it, were the so-called Petersberg tasks[12]—that is, humanitarian and rescue missions, peacekeeping, and crisis management, including (ambiguously) 'peacemaking'. The ESDP's military cornerstone was the headline goal agreed by the subsequent Helsinki European Council. The EU decided to equip itself with a rapid reaction force (RRF) of 60,000 troops by 2003, which could be deployed with two months' notice and sustained for a year. As was the case for a similar NATO reaction force, the RRF would not be a standing force; rather, EU member states would earmark national troops and capabilities for the force during specific operations, thus 'double' or even 'triple-hatting' them.

After the launch of the RRF, member governments worked to identify shortfalls in European military capabilities and took steps to remedy them, even though the target date of 2003 slipped to 2010. Meanwhile, experience showed that smaller forces—even more rapidly deployable, but for a shorter time—could be useful, as was demonstrated by Operation Artemis in the Democratic Republic of the Congo (Mace 2003). Paralleling steps in NATO towards smaller and more deployable formations, the EU decided in 2004 to create 'battle groups' of up to 1,500 troops. Most combined European resources at the hard end of their military capabilities in specialized areas such as desert or jungle fighting, or dealing with a chemical weapons attack. The aim was to have the battle groups available at near-immediate notice for short-term deployments. However, none had been deployed at the time of writing. Even a plan to deploy a battle group to the Central African Republic to assist a French force in 2013 was abandoned because it would have been led by the UK, which by then was committed to a referendum on its continued EU membership. Spurious stories in the British press about proposals to create a 'European army' were deemed to give UK Eurosceptics too much leverage to make the deployment politically viable (Dempsey 2013). Some argue that specific crises requiring the deployment of a battle group have not yet arisen. But questions inevitably arise as to the relevance or need to create such forces in the first place.

On the civilian side, considerable effort was put into developing the capability to prevent conflicts before they occur and to help failing or post-conflict states with their civilian infrastructures—particularly law and order. A headline goal for rapid-response police—as well as other law enforcement professionals—was established in parallel to the military headline goal. The very first ESDP operation was, in fact, a civilian police mission that the EU took over from the UN in Bosnia in 2003. It was followed by small military operations in Macedonia and Congo later that year, but also a more substantial military commitment in Bosnia (taking over from NATO) in 2004.

Often, efforts to give substance to dramatic 1999 foreign and security policy decisions taken by the European Council in Cologne and Helsinki have lacked conviction. Member states have failed to live up to their ambitious goals (such as the RRF's headline goal). Defence budgets generally have fallen, rather than increased. One rough estimate is that about 70 per cent of the EU's men and women in military uniform are able to be deployed *only* within their national territory (Patten 2010: 11). When Europe chooses to act militarily, as in the case of Libya in 2011, it has continued to rely on NATO, and has been exposed as chronically short of military assets and dependent on US support. Arguably, the gap between capabilities and expectations that has troubled the EU since the creation of the CFSP has widened (Hill 1993, 1998), although probably as a result of increased expectations of the Union as much as, or more than, the slow growth of EU capabilities.[13]

Still, there is no denying progress towards more coherent EU foreign and security policies. The Union's military options, while small-scale, are gradually widening (see Figure 13.1); CSDP (the new term for ESDP since the Lisbon Treaty) can now be deployed 'where NATO as a whole is not engaged'. Obviously, any EU-led military operation will depend on a handful of countries—in the first place, France and possibly Germany (post-Brexit)—with expeditionary military capabilities to mount them. For anything beyond small-scale operations, the EU has to call on NATO assets, but that arguably is a sign of good sense (avoiding duplication) and not

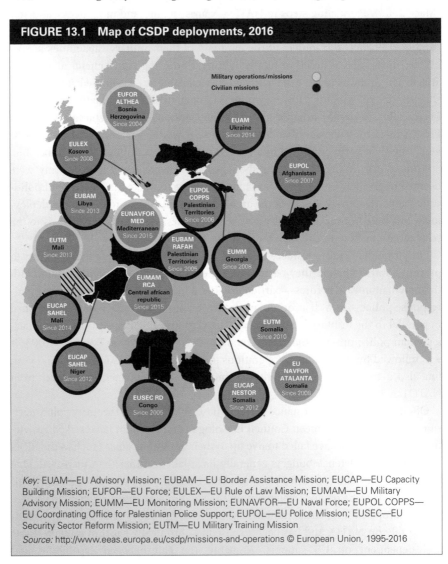

FIGURE 13.1   Map of CSDP deployments, 2016

Key: EUAM—EU Advisory Mission; EUBAM—EU Border Assistance Mission; EUCAP—EU Capacity Building Mission; EUFOR—EU Force; EULEX—EU Rule of Law Mission; EUMAM—EU Military Advisory Mission; EUMM—EU Monitoring Mission; EUNAVFOR—EU Naval Force; EUPOL COPPS—EU Coordinating Office for Palestinian Police Support; EUPOL—EU Police Mission; EUSEC—EU Security Sector Reform Mission; EUTM—EU Military Training Mission

Source: http://www.eeas.europa.eu/csdp/missions-and-operations © European Union, 1995-2016

weakness. The so-called Berlin Plus[14] arrangements between the EU and NATO are far less cumbersome than the old EU–WEU procedures.

To the ambitious, the EU's effort remains disappointingly slow and militarily weak. But the EU's ability to contribute to international security by combining military and civilian dimensions of the CSDP is unique, and certainly beyond what NATO can offer. The advantage of the EU compared to NATO is the availability of a range of instruments including preventive diplomatic actions, as well as the cooperation instruments of the Commission. In 2014, the EU adopted a blueprint on how to deal more effectively with the surge of crises in its periphery dubbed the *Comprehensive Approach to External Conflicts and Crises* (EEAS 2013). The document mapped out how to deploy EU's instruments over the lifetime of a crisis, based on the EU's experience in the fight against piracy off the Horn of Africa (Operation Atalanta). While the logic behind the comprehensive approach is appealing, it has been accused of devaluing military instruments and being a 'smokescreen behind which the EU's CSDP has virtually collapsed' (Witney *et al.* 2014: 6). Presented in a more positive light, the EU is slowly buttressing its 'soft power', or ability to attract or persuade in international affairs (Nye 2004, 2011), with hard power to coerce or deter.[15]

The EU's foreign policy record

The sum total of the EU's foreign policy activity—diplomatic, economic, and military—goes far beyond that of any other regional organization; yet hard, even brutal, questions about whether it results in demonstrable EU influence in world politics cannot be avoided. The EU's record as a foreign policy actor is decidedly mixed.

After early failures, the EU's chief success—in a still-continuing story—has been the Balkans. A large part of Europe's achievement has come from lessons learnt from using enlargement as, in a sense, a tool of foreign policy. Specifically, the Commission used the promise of EU membership to promote reform in the CEECs, and had the 'demonstration effect' of establishing and consolidating democracy, liberalization, and the rule of law. Deliberately transposing this success to the Balkans, the EU has offered the prospect of accession as a way of changing behaviour. The attraction of enlargement has induced Balkan political leaders to pay heed (sometimes intermittently) to political pressure from the EU. To illustrate, progress on curbing corruption and handing over suspected war criminals from the Bosnian War put Croatia in a position in which it became the EU's twenty-eighth (pre-Brexit) member state in 2013. Even Bosnia-Herzegovina itself was preparing an application for EU membership by early 2016. Thus the Union has shown itself to be more powerful because of what it *is*—a geopolitical magnet—than for anything that it actually *does*.

After the 2004–07 enlargements, the Union hoped that it could achieve similar results in other neighbouring countries to the EU's east and south, even though many were not prospective candidates for accession. The EU offered to form special relationships with such states via a new European Neighbourhood Policy (ENP), which combined political, economic, trade, and other policy instruments. At the tenth anniversary of the ENP in 2014, the EU had little reason to celebrate. What was once meant to become a 'ring of friends'—a neighbourhood of prosperous countries with close relations—had become a 'ring of fire'.

Towards the East, the EU's attempt to forge closer ties with six post-Soviet countries of the Eastern Partnership (EaP) initiative—Armenia, Azerbaijan, Belarus, Georgia, Moldova, and Ukraine—led to geopolitical rivalry with Russia. These tensions surfaced at an EaP summit meeting in late 2013, which was meant to seal an association agreement with Ukraine, but instead kicked off a series of events culminating in a war in eastern Ukraine. Under pressure from Moscow, Ukraine's President Yanukovych shelved the association agreement in the last minute, sparking anti-regime (and pro-EU) riots in Kiev that were violently suppressed, leading eventually to the ousting of Yanukovych. Moscow did not stand idle and used the opportunity to annex the Ukrainian peninsula of Crimea, which had a high ethnic-Russian population, was the only warm water Russian naval base, and was seen by Moscow as a part of its motherland. Pro-Russian unrest in the eastern Ukraine Donbass region in 2014 was orchestrated by Moscow and a new Ukrainian government was forced into a military confrontation with armed separatists. The EU finally had to act decisively when a Russian missile hit a Malaysian Airlines flight in Ukrainian airspace, killing 210 EU citizens in July 2014. At the time of writing, the EU had managed a comprehensive sanctions regime against Moscow (see Box 13.6), while Germany and France were in the driver's seat of negotiations on a lasting ceasefire agreement with Ukraine and Russia.

At the same time, the EU had to rethink its strategy in the East. Whether it could maintain its aim of closely associating post-Soviet countries without sparking tensions with Russian President Vladimir Putin remained doubtful. Ultimately, Putin appeared concerned mostly about his power base and ensuring that Western norms of liberalism and democracy did not take hold in the region.

The situation south of Europe did not look much better. The Arab Spring of 2011 exposed how the EU had propped up dictators in Egypt, Libya, Syria, and Tunisia by channelling aid with strings attached, but never 'pulled' on matters of human rights and good governance. Hopes of finding ways in which to assist these countries in transitioning to democratic societies had mostly to be abandoned and replaced by a more interest-driven approach. The war in Syria propelled the rise of the so-called Islamic State of Iraq and Syria (ISIS) terrorist group. By 2016, it controlled huge parts of the north of the country, as well as areas of Iraq, despite an extensive Western bombing campaign that included EU states—especially France after the Paris massacre by ISIS-affiliated operatives in November 2015.

Earlier, the democratization process in Egypt had broken down when a military coup ousted President Mohamed Morsi in 2013. Post-Gaddafi Libya turned into an ungoverned and effectively failed state where ISIS also gained ground, provoking flows of refugees to Europe among which Libya was a major transit point. Europe's refugee crisis led the EU to offer large amounts of aid to Turkey to try to stem the human flow to Europe's shores, despite the erosion of democracy under Turkish President Recep Tayyip Erdoğan. More generally, the EU increasingly turned a blind eye to values such as minority rights and democracy, and returned to supporting autocratic regimes as the lesser evil in the MENA region.

While the loss of EU credibility was considerable, member states' handling of the resulting refugee crisis was even shoddier. Confronted with hundreds of thousands of refugees arriving via boats on the Mediterranean Sea or by foot through the Western Balkans, member states fell into national egoisms instead of agreeing European solutions. Hungary started to build fences on its EU borders, while other member states reinstated temporary intra-European border checks, putting a core achievement of the EU—the passport-free Schengen zone—into jeopardy. The EU's immediate reaction was the creation of a Mediterranean CSDP mission to disrupt and intercept people smugglers operating from the Libyan coast. However, it was clear that more comprehensive solutions were needed in the longer run.

These challenges point towards the strong capacity of the European Council to gather and decide quickly on issues with considerable ramifications, but also highlight how the long-term strategy of the EU's crisis diplomacy often remains unclear. Meanwhile, the EEAS began slowly to play the intended role of a hub that kept the various string of EU's external relations together through its supporting work. It contributed to the technical negotiations of the Iran nuclear deal in 2015 and helped to set up the sanctions regime against Russia. However, without the competences of the Commission or resources of larger national EU foreign ministries, it failed to fuse the national and European dimensions of foreign policy-making consistently.

In general, the CSDP's record has been patchy. Operation Artemis in the Congo (2002) showed that the EU could respond quickly to a UN appeal in a humanitarian crisis and save lives in the process. Operation Atalanta—the first CSDP naval mission—countered piracy and delivered humanitarian aid to the Horn of Africa, bringing a (fragile) stability to Somalia (Peterson and Geddes 2015: 196–7). But the EU police mission to oversee reform of the police in Bosnia was ridiculed as an expensive 'laughing stock' (Lyon 2005). Beyond the EU's neighbourhood, on the wider international stage, the Union's ability to influence events remains very dependent on (if not subordinate to) the US—that is, its success is largely determined by the extent to which, and if so, how, the US is engaged in areas in which they share a foreign policy interest, notably in the Middle East, or on counterterrorism and non-proliferation. An open question following the 2016 UK referendum vote to leave the EU is how the exit of Washington's closest European ally would affect US engagement and foreign policy coordination with Europe.

The institutions in context

One of the CFSP's major problems is that it does not represent or dominate any specific policy problem. Unlike (say) agricultural or competition policy, in which the EU has exclusive competence, the CFSP must often compete with other actors and forums, such as related EU policy domains, other international organizations, and even the independent activities of EU member states. In this sense, the CFSP must often struggle simply to make itself relevant.

The CFSP in the EU system

Foreign policy is effective to the extent that its 'targets' are open to persuasion, influence, or coercion. The EU is no different: its success depends on its ability to supply or withhold resources in exchange for compliant behaviour. However, the CFSP by itself has only limited resources and few instruments of its own. It is therefore most effective when it harnesses resources available as EU instruments. In these cases, Commission involvement is essential, if only because it has the sole right of initiative. Sensitive to its prerogatives, the Commission often bridles at any suggestion that decisions might be taken in CFSP that tell it what to do in other EU policy areas.

Under the Lisbon Treaty, the right of initiative in CFSP is exclusively a matter for the High Representative and the member states, although the High Representative is, after all, a Vice-President of the Commission. EU member states have gone to considerable lengths to maintain their control over CSDP, and to isolate it and their national defence industries from integrative pressures that might push it in the direction of the Community method. However, military and civilian crisis management structures—such as the military committee and the Crises Management and Planning Directorate (CMPD)—now fall under the remit of the High Representative. Furthermore, a European Defence Agency (EDA) was launched in 2004, with the High Representative chairing its board of directors (which consists of European defence ministers), to work on upgrading and integrating the EU's military capabilities.

In foreign policy, what is most interesting is not where the EU is, but where it is in relation to where it started. Not long ago, the mere mention of an EU military capability was unthinkable; today, the CSDP is an accepted growth area for common European action. No other regional international organization possesses its own military component, although some (such as the African Union) have embryonic military capabilities or have made feeble pledges to cooperate on foreign policy issues. Despite all of its problems, the EU has gone further in security and defence policy than any other international organization.

The CFSP and national policies/ministries

Foreign, security, and defence policies are core prerogatives of nation-states. All EU member states have their own foreign and defence ministries and policies (Hocking and Spence 2002). There is little sign that they intend to abandon them. Yet the EU has become a central reference point for national foreign policies, especially for smaller EU states. Since the early 1970s, we have witnessed a gradual contraction of *domaines réservés*, in which former colonial powers regard their own interest and influence as paramount, and a simultaneous expansion of the topics considered appropriate for the CFSP. Virtually no foreign policy topic is considered off limits for EU action. The exception is issues before the UN Security Council, of which Iraq was a prime example: the two European permanent members of the Security Council—the UK and France—often insisted that their UN obligations precluded any coordination of their positions with the EU, let alone accountability to the Union for them (even pre-Brexit).

Otherwise, communication between national capitals—which is crucial to consensus-building—is now highly institutionalized. Since the Lisbon Treaty, national diplomacies have further adapted to the new institutional structures that the EEAS and the High Representative brought to the CFSP, and use the new actors in Brussels as 'power multipliers' (Balfour *et al.* 2015). The growth of the CFSP as a policy domain and the intense networking that takes place within it often make it difficult for outsiders to determine where national foreign policies end and the CFSP begins. Some would even argue that purely national foreign policy preferences—entirely unaffected by EU deliberations—no longer exist (Glarbo 2001).

Theorizing the CFSP

Applying theory to the practice of European foreign policy is daunting. Most theories of European integration or EU policy-making provide partial explanations at best, since the CFSP contains elements of intergovernmentalism, supranationalism, and transgovernmentalism. Equally, for theorists of international relations (IR) more generally, 'the issue of the meaning of European foreign policy cooperation for the international system, and conversely the impact of international relations on the EU, has been of marginal concern' (Hill and Smith 2016: 477).

Realists have struggled to explain the emergence of the CFSP since it challenges the assumption that nation-states remain narrowly concerned with sovereignty concerns: chiefly, their own relative power and security. Still, Rosato (2011) has argued that the emergence of the EPC, and then the CFSP, represented attempts to reign in a resurgent and then reunited Germany, and that integration more generally was an attempt to balance against an external threat: the Soviet Union. More generally, most realists argue that CFSP remains little more than a rhetorical veil for the persistence of national foreign policies.

One of the most compelling theoretical accounts of the CFSP is institutionalism (Smith 2004, 2011). Institutional theory helps to explain not only what is expected, but also what appropriate behaviour is by actors in any social setting. Historical institutionalism offers a kind of moving picture rather than a snapshot (Pierson 1996). This variant of institutionalism stresses the importance of (mostly) incremental changes in terms of their accumulation. Consider the High

Representative's transformation into something akin to an EU minister for foreign affairs, or how the EU started with the EPC and eventually equipped itself with a defence capability. Rational choice institutionalism suggests that member states have few incentives to delegate foreign policy powers to supranational EU institutions, because such steps would do little to reduce their transaction costs (Wagner 2003). When member states delegated elements of policy planning and implementation to actors in Brussels, principal–agent analyses concluded that EU level agency was mostly kept under close control (Dijkstra 2013; Helwig 2015). Sociological institutionalists argue that networks of experts, diplomats, and officials (or *epistemic communities*) reach compromises based on their shared norms, and can significantly influence policy outcomes (Juncos and Pomorska 2011; Cross 2013).

Even constructivist theorists, who reject the causal world view of institutionalism, point out the significance of the formal and informal rules of CFSP in shaping the identity of the European foreign policy community and the norms they promote (Manners 2002; Tonra 2003). However, proponents of this identity-based account of CFSP have to concede that Europe's normative power 'is in for some rough weather' (Gerrits 2009: 77) as the EU's liberal model increasingly comes under stress in a more contested world and differences inside the Union are amplified.

Perhaps more than any other single perspective, institutionalism helps to explain why EU foreign policy institutions have developed to the point at which member states are not only unable, but also unwilling to interrupt a process of further institutionalizing foreign, security, and (now) defence policy cooperation (Hill 2004), even if clear policy successes remain elusive (Howorth 2010, 2014). Among students of IR, consensus is beginning to emerge (slowly) that 'the EU can no longer be treated as a peculiar side-issue in international relations' (Hill and Smith 2016: 458–9). The question remains, however, to what extent the institutionalization of foreign policy inputs (decision-making processes, structures) will truly allow the EU to shape foreign policy outcomes in the conduct of IR.

Conclusions

The history of EU foreign policy is punctuated by critical junctures at which the Union encountered crises and tried to come up with institutional responses to address them. The pattern of crisis-and-response is evident in the chronology of its Treaties since the early 1990s. The collapse of the Berlin Wall, tensions in Yugoslavia, and the first Gulf War led European leaders to try to develop greater foreign policy and military capacities in the Maastricht Treaty. After Bosnia and Kosovo exposed a lack of European crisis management tools, European leaders responded by creating the ESDP via the Amsterdam Treaty in 1999. The persistent inadequacies of the CFSP system—exposed by disunity on Iraq, combined with the 'Big Bang' 2004–07 enlargements and global terrorist threats after the September 2001 ('9/11') terrorist attacks—brought another such response in the Constitutional Treaty in 2004 and its descendant, the Lisbon Treaty. Afterwards, it was still impossible to imagine an effective CFSP without more coalitions of the willing or leadership by larger EU member states, perhaps increasingly in tandem with the High Representative. Stronger leadership was seen as necessary in achieving more coherence in the EU's external policies.

There was no shortage of opportunities, and indeed demands, for the EU to speak with a single voice in the 2010s. Continued tension in the Middle East, the unfinished peace in the Balkans, problems in the Caucasus and other countries close to the EU's borders (Belarus, Moldova, North Africa, Ukraine), the rise of China as a global actor, ongoing disputes with North Korea and (especially) Russia, and the erosion of democracy in the former Soviet Union all put pressure on the EU, even before Brexit meant the departure of one of the EU's previously most powerful member states (especially in foreign and security policy). Yet long before the UK's decision to leave the EU, there was a widespread feeling that things could not go on in foreign policy as before. The first major test of the post-Lisbon CFSP architecture was the 2011 Arab Spring. Europe's response to the crisis and its fallout was disappointing, as the MENA region destabilized, becoming a stronghold for terrorist organizations and autocratic regimes, and source of a massive inflow of migrants. While the responsibility for Europe's failure lies mainly with the member states and their inability to agree on a common approach, EU institutions have had to rethink their strategic approach in the world. The ability of the EU to be unified in the response to the Ukraine crisis is a positive sign of EU actorness. Yet it remains to be seen whether the EU manages its demanding relationship with Russia and the countries in the post-Soviet space in the long term.

As always, institutional reform was a necessary, but far from sufficient, condition for an effective CFSP. Member states, especially large ones, will always weigh the virtues of 'multiplying' their power via common EU action against the difficulties of getting others to agree. Recent enlargements have made consensus-building even more time-consuming than before. The external relations provisions of Lisbon have the potential, at least, to give the CFSP consistent leadership, with international name recognition and authority to pull together the strengths of its member states and the Commission. The EEAS gives the EU, for the first time, 'real' embassies in important national capitals such as Washington DC, Beijing, and Delhi, backed up by real resources. To some extent, the emerging EU diplomatic system even challenges the established standards of state-centric diplomacy (Spence and Bátora 2015). The EU will no doubt have fresh chances to realize its potential in foreign policy—but, on balance, it will likely fall short more often than it will meet expectations.

ENDNOTES

1. See also McCormick (2007).

2. See Council of the EU (2003).

3. In its first years, the EPC was staffed by the foreign ministry of the holder of the Council presidency, reflecting its informal and non-institutionalized status.

4. The CSCE was renamed the Organization for Security and Cooperation in Europe (OSCE) when it was made a standing organization in 1995.

5. Coreu refers both to *correspondant Européen*—that is, a mid-level official in each foreign ministry, responsible for coordination with the Council presidency—and the system used for communication on CFSP matters.

6. See also Spence (2002).

7. This bilateral summit held at a French coastal resort produced a joint declaration by Europe's two major military powers endorsing the creation of an ESDP with the means to allow the EU to act autonomously should NATO decide not to be involved in a military action (see Sloan 2005: 190–3).

8. This phrase refers to 'civilian' (i.e. non-military) policy tools, such as diplomacy or economic sanctions, and command structures, such as EU defence ministers meeting in the Council of Ministers, as well as instruments for preventing conflicts, including the addition of policing or judicial expertise to EU military missions, as was done in the Balkans.

9. Art. 42(7) TEU.

10. Nuttall (1992: 269) notes that the Contact Group 'did after all preserve a facade of EU organizational coherence' through a variety of procedural fixes that linked the participation of EU states to the CFSP as a whole. However, the Contact Group came at a time—during the first year of the CFSP's existence—during which the EU's new mechanisms for foreign policy seemed to be failing more generally.

11. Quoted in *European Voice*, 16 September 2010, p. 11.

12. This designation arose from the Petersberg hotel outside Bonn at which WEU ministers adopted the tasks in 1992.

13. The EU has proved capable of settling, or at least managing, open disputes that have flared with the US (about the relationship with NATO) and Turkey (primarily about Cyprus) externally.

14. 'Berlin Plus' refers to the set of rules and procedures finalized in 2002 to govern EU access to NATO planning and military assets (see Cornish 2004; Sloan 2005).

15. One of the EU's top former foreign policy officials has argued that soft power is wielded only by those who also possess hard power (see Cooper 2004).

FURTHER READING

The most comprehensive of recent works on the EU's international role is Hill and Smith (2016), as well as Keukeleire and Delreux (2014). K. E. Smith (2014) is a useful examination of how the EU pursues its foreign-policy objectives and McCormick (2007) argues that the Union has already achieved 'superpower' status. M. E. Smith (2003) offers an institutionalist treatment of the CFSP, Bretherton and Vogler (2005) survey the EU as a global actor using a constructivist lens, and Rosato (2011) offers a provocative treatment of European integration from a realist perspective. Laïdi (2008) and Howorth (2014) are both useful overviews. For a detailed discussion of EU's emerging diplomatic system, see Balfour *et al.* (2015), as well as Spence and Bátora (2015).

Balfour, R., Carta, C., and Kristi, R. (eds) (2015) *The European External Action Service and National Foreign Ministries: Covergence or Divergence?* (Aldershot: Ashgate).

Bretherton, C., and Vogler, J. (2005) *The European Union as a Global Actor* (2nd edn, London and New York: Routledge).

Hill, C., and Smith, M. (eds) (2016) *International Relations and the European Union* (3rd edn, Oxford and New York: Oxford University Press).

Howorth, J. (2014) *Security and Defence Policy in the European Union* (2nd edn, Basingstoke: Palgrave Macmillan).

Laïdi, Z. (ed) (2008) *EU Foreign Policy in a Globalized World: Normative Power and Social Preferences* (London and New York: Routledge).

McCormick, J. (2007) *The European Superpower* (Basingstoke and New York: Palgrave Macmillan).

Rosato, S. (2011) *Europe United: Power Politics and the Making of the European Community* (Ithaca, NY: Cornell University Press).

Smith, K.E. (2014) *European Union Foreign Policy in a Changing World* (3rd edn, Oxford and Malden, MA: Polity).

Smith, M.E. (2003) *Europe's Foreign and Security Policy: The Institutionalization of Cooperation* (Cambridge: Cambridge University Press).

Spence, S., and Bátora, J. (eds) (2015) *The European External Action Service: European Diplomacy Post-Westphalia* (Houndsmills and New York: Palgrave Macmillan).

 WEB LINKS

http://www.eeas.europa.eu
The website of the EEAS is the best place to get an overview and current updates of EU's activities in the world.

http://www.eeas.europa.eu/security-defence/index_en.htm
The CSDP site of the EEAS has a number of resources, including details on operations, structures, and other documents.

http://www.iss.europa.eu
The Institute for Security Studies (ISS)—the EU's own, internal, Paris-based think tank—produces high-quality analyses of foreign and security policy issues that are all available online.

http://ecfr.eu/
The European Council on Foreign Relations publishes topical analysis of current issues in European foreign policy.

http://carnegieeurope.eu/
The Brussels branch of the Carnegie Endowment for International Peace provides insightful analyses and also runs a daily blog on Europe and its global activities.

CHAPTER 14

Coreper: National interests and the logic of appropriateness

Jeffrey Lewis

▌ Summary

The Committee of Permanent Representatives (Coreper) originated as a diplomatic forum to meet regularly and prepare meetings of the Council of Ministers. It quickly and quietly evolved into a locus of continuous negotiation and *de facto* decision-making, gaining a reputation as 'the place to do the deal'. This reputation is based on insulation from domestic audiences and an unrivalled ability to make deals stick across a range of issue areas and policy subjects. Most importantly, Coreper spotlights the process of integrating interests in a collective decision-making system with its own organizational culture, norms, and style of discourse. Coreper is an institutional environment in which group-community standards create what neo-institutionalists call a 'logic of appropriateness', which informs bargaining behaviour and influences everyday decision-making outcomes.

Introduction

This chapter addresses the role of Coreper in the European Union (EU). According to one analyst, 'the caliber and effectiveness of permanent representation officials determine to a great extent how countries fare in the EU' (Dinan 2010: 216); another claims that the members of Coreper are 'among the great unsung heroes' of European integration (Westlake 1999: xxiv). Both observations offer a useful entry point to understanding Coreper and how it functions. First, it is a pivotal actor in everyday EU decision-making. For this reason, member states consider Coreper one of the most important postings in Brussels. Second, in what may seem counter-intuitive in light of the first point, Coreper is less visible than most other institutions in the EU. As this chapter will clarify, Coreper's importance as an institutional actor is related to its ability to avoid the spotlight over the years, and to work behind the scenes at finding agreements and forging compromise.

Coreper is the site in EU decision-making where national interests and European solutions interact more frequently, more intensively, and across more issue areas than any other. To work effectively, the Committee relies on a culture of consensus-based decision-making: an informal, intangible quality of the institutional environment and a critical component in the permanent representatives' ability to 'find solutions'. Coreper is also something of a chimera. To some, it resembles a bastion of intergovernmentalism; to others, it appears less like inter-state bargaining than a haven for Eurocrats to 'go native'. Neither view, in such stark terms, is accurate nor is either view entirely wrong. In an authoritative study of the Council system, Hayes-Renshaw and Wallace (2006: 332) note 'a continuous tension between the home affiliation and the pull of the collective forum'. From a theoretical perspective, negotiation in Coreper is often a subtle blend of both the 'logic of consequences' and the 'logic of appropriateness'.[1] Viewed through a neo-institutionalist lens, it is precisely this tension that makes Coreper so interesting to study.

According to the EU's Treaties, Coreper is 'responsible for preparing the work of the Council and for carrying out the tasks assigned to it'.[2] From this austere mandate, Coreper has acquired a significant role in EU decision-making. Among its assigned tasks is the remit to 'endeavour to reach agreement at its level to be submitted to the Council for adoption'.[3] In institutionalist language, there is an obligation of result that the permanent representatives find is an unwritten part of the job description. As one ambassador explained, 'there is a high collective interest in getting results and reaching solutions. This is in addition to representing the national interest'.[4] Another said: 'If we have to take it to the Council, there is a sense that we have failed'.[5]

In many ways, Coreper is the ideal institutional site to examine national interests in the context of everyday EU decision-making. With few exceptions (see 'Contestation'), Coreper is the needle's eye through which the legislative output of the Council flows. Because a defining trait of the Council is its sectoral differentiation, pursuing the 'national interest' across its operating formations requires complex national systems of interest intermediation and inter-ministerial coordination. The permanent representatives have a cross-Council negotiating mandate that functions as an essential aggregation mechanism in everyday EU decision-making. The EU ambassadors and deputies are thus critical interlocutors in the ability of a member state to pursue what Anderson (1999: 6) calls a 'milieu goal' in Brussels, or the ability to 'ensure that government policy objectives are consistent, both within Europe and across the national and supranational levels'.

The chapter proceeds as follows. In the next section, we examine how the permanent representatives acquired such a central position in the EU system. We then sketch out the structure of Coreper, including how it works and has changed over time. Next, the Committee's main powers—namely, *de facto* decision-making and an institutional capacity for integrating interests—are examined. We move on to consider how different theories account for Coreper's development as a collective decision-making environment, and whether consensus practices are based on active, calculative choice or have become more durably internalized and taken for granted. A brief concluding section looks at the wider implications for theory of an institutional body that so explicitly straddles and blurs the boundary between the national and European levels.

Coreper's origins

Although no mention was made in the Treaty of Paris about the creation of a preparatory body, the need for such a body became apparent less than six months after the Treaty entered into force in July 1952. At the first meeting of the Special Council of Ministers (September 1952), the ad hoc group on the organization of the Council's work was instructed to come up with a proposal for a preparatory committee. The Coordinating Commission, or Cocor (from the French *Commission de coordination du conseil des ministres*), was the result. The formal decision to create Cocor was taken by the Special Council of Ministers in February 1953. But it was only with the 1957 Treaty of Rome that the legal basis for a preparatory committee was established (under Article 151).

The first Cocor meeting was held in March 1953. Cocor began to meet monthly in Luxembourg, with representatives travelling back and forth from their national capitals. Cocor diplomacy was premised on mutual trust, a spirit of accommodation, and an equality of voice between big and small states. Ernst Haas (1958: 491)[6] drew a sharp distinction between Cocor and the brand of diplomacy found at, for example, the Council of Europe, equating the former with the 'principle of a novel community-type organ'.

From the earliest proposals to set up a permanent preparatory body, the issue of delegating formal decision-making authority was allowed to remain ambiguous. This non-debate was evident at the 1956 intergovernmental conference (IGC),

---

BOX 14.1   **Constitutive politics and the Spaak Committee**

The creation of a permanent Brussels-based body composed of high-ranking civil servants was based on a proposal from the Committee of the Heads of Delegations, popularly
known as the 'Spaak Committee' after its chair, industrious Belgian Foreign Minister Paul-
Henri Spaak. The Spaak Committee, set up by the foreign ministers at Messina (June
1955) to discuss future steps in European integration, began meeting intensively at the
Château de Val Duchesse outside Brussels in July 1955. Eight months of talks produced
the Spaak Report (April 1956). The recommendations of the Spaak Report were approved
by the foreign ministers' meeting in Venice (May 1956) and, after further IGC negotiations
(again led by the Spaak Committee), culminated in the Treaty of Rome (March 1957). In
one of the lesser-known political coups in the history of the EU, it was the Spaak Committee that strongly endorsed a permanent negotiating body. For the most part, the Committee's members were the same individuals who would become the first permanent
representatives. Noël (1966: 88) hints at the novelty of this move, whereby the Spaak
Committee morphed into what would become Coreper, since the interim committee
contained many of the same personnel and 'preserved the same atmosphere and spirit'.
In short, the Spaak Committee and the creation of Coreper are a remarkable example of
'constitutive politics' in the institutional history of European integration.[7]

---

where the design of a new, permanent, Brussels-based committee was negotiated
(see Box 14.1). Over the course of discussions, it became clear that there was agreement among the foreign ministers *not* to create a Brussels-body composed of deputy
ministers; instead, they agreed that the permanent delegations should be headed by
high-ranking diplomats. But there was little discussion of what substantive form the
permanent representatives' role should take and the issue was left open. Articles 151
and 121 of the Treaty of Rome reflect this ambiguity, allowing simply that the Council's rules of procedure shall 'provide for the establishment of a committee composed
of representatives of member states. The Council shall determine the task and competence of that committee'.

Early on, the open-ended nature of Coreper's authority set off alarm bells at the
Commission. Following the January 1958 decision to begin the work of the Committee without precisely defining its tasks and powers, the Commission asked for clarification of Coreper's role (de Zwaan 1995: 75). In March 1958, Belgian Foreign Minister
Larock, acting as Council President, defended the Council's provisional rules of procedure and assured Commission President Hallstein that they ruled out the possibility of delegating decisional authority to Coreper (Noël 1967: 228–9). There were
similar questions raised in the European Parliament (EP), with some members concerned that the Committee could usurp the Commission's right of initiative (de
Zwaan 1995: 75). Since these early years, the Commission—in particular, the Secretary-General's office, with Emile Noël at the helm from 1958 to 1987—would come to
view the permanent representatives as potential allies in a common cause. One Commission official stated: 'We consider Coreper more as an ally than something we have

to fight with'.[8] Coreper is often the strategic point of inroad to the Council, since the Commission prefers to have detailed substantive discussions with the permanent representatives, who (unlike many ministers) are also well versed in the legal intricacies of the Treaty. Jacques Delors, while Commission President, often personally appeared in Coreper to explain and 'sell' key single-market proposals to the permanent representatives before they were presented at the ministerial level.[9]

After the late 1950s, Coreper, quietly and often unnoticed, acquired a reputation for forging compromise and finding solutions across an ever-growing range of issues. This standing was contrary to its reputation in academic circles: integration researchers typically characterized Coreper as an embodiment of intergovernmentalism and hardball bargaining (Webb 1977: 18–19; Weiler 1981: 285). As the European Community deepened, Coreper acquired new responsibilities and general policy competences (Noël and Étienne 1971). Agricultural policy was an exception because of the highly technical nature of administering the common agricultural policy (CAP) and, in 1960, the Special Committee on Agriculture (SCA) was established to take over this specialized policy field.[10] The deepening process created exponential pressures for Coreper to develop *de facto* legislative competences to minimize policy-making bottlenecks and impart coherence to the segmentation of the Council's work. The bifurcation of Coreper in 1962 into Coreper I and II (see 'Structure of the institution') was a realization of this burgeoning workload. But, contrary to conventional intergovernmentalist accounts, the Committee institutionalized a deliberative, consensual style of decision-making based on 'thick' bonds of trust, understanding, responsiveness, and a willingness to compromise. Serving as a gatekeeper for the Council's work was not simply about paving the way for ministers to find agreements; increasingly, it also meant the ability to dispose of large quantities of business by forging consensus out of seemingly irreconcilable national positions (see Box 14.2).

Structure of the institution

In structural location, Coreper occupies a unique institutional vantage point in the EU system. Vertically placed between the experts and the ministers, and horizontally situated with cross-Council policy responsibilities, the permanent representatives obtain a broad overview of the Council's work. Compared with the experts meeting in the working groups, they are political heavyweights; unlike ministers, however, they are policy generalists *and* experts in the substantive questions of a file. In his classic study of Coreper, Joseph Salmon (1971: 642) referred to this unique perspective as the *vue d'ensemble* ('aggregate view'). The institutional perspective of the *vue d'ensemble* is a qualitative feature of Coreper, part of its organizational culture, and a kind of cognitive map that newcomers must learn to read and navigate to be successful.

BOX 14.2	The paradox of 'crisis': The 1965–66 empty chair and consensus-seeking habits

The 'empty chair' crisis occurred when French President de Gaulle recalled his EU negotiators to Paris over a disagreement regarding CAP funding and the anticipated use of majority voting in the Council. The episode has long held mythical status as an intergovernmental control mechanism at the heart of protecting 'very important' national interests. The resulting Luxembourg compromise (never part of the *acquis*, but rather a press release published in the *Bulletin of the EEC*[11]) is seen as instilling a kind of conservatism in making EU decisions, since any member could invoke veto rights where important interests were at stake. Aside from the fact that scholars (and practitioners) continue to disagree on the lessons to be drawn from what amounted to more of a 'cryptic plan' (Golub 2006: 280), or an agreement to disagree, new archival research portrays the crisis as more of a historical turning point that cemented a social order premised on mutual trust and expectations for consensus-seeking. Further, the evidence shows that Coreper was central in the habituation of these practices.

First, the July 1965–January 1966 'empty chair' was not literal, because French Deputy Permanent Representative Maurice Ulrich remained in Brussels (Palayret *et al.* 2006: 35). Procedurally, the use of the written procedure helped to keep decisions flowing— and the Five (remaining of the Six) agreed to brief the French (via Ulrich) on all negotiations during their absence (Ludlow 2006: 99).

Second, the crisis had the curious effect of testing *and* tempering the spirit of trust and accommodation. Retrospective accounts are consistent in stressing the self-restraint practised in finding a resolution without engaging in brinkmanship (Hayes-Renshaw and Wallace 2006: 318–19). Especially fascinating is evidence that French negotiators deliberately restrained initial positions advanced by de Gaulle to avoid 'permanent harm' to French interests (Ludlow 2006: 202).

Third, by the early 1960s, Coreper's role was already very central to the Council's work (Ludlow 1997). But the crisis had the effect of enhancing the institution's 'clubbiness'. As one insider recounts, 'the months of the crisis were to lead to a curious reinforcement of the trust between the various players involved in finding the solution' (Davignon 2006: 18). The unwritten mandate granted by member states to their EU permanent representatives to 'find solutions' was constituted by the psychological discomfort of confrontation found in this case.

Thus the Council's most existential decision-making crisis had the paradoxical effect of reinforcing consensus-seeking. According to Ludlow (2006: 106), 'the rebuilding of trust observable at the level of Coreper soon began to feed through both to the Council of Ministers, and, still more gradually, to those parts of the national administrations entrusted with the making of European policy'. Echoing this transition, Council scholars conclude that 'the adroitness of the Compromise marks the introduction of sophisticated procedural politics' (Hayes-Renshaw and Wallace 2006: 319), which are practised by the weekly deliberations of the permanent representatives. The habits of consensus-seeking and the social environment whereby Coreper diplomacy reproduces it was ironically confirmed by the *Sturm und Drang* of the empty chair crisis.

Defined narrowly, Coreper consists of fifty-six members, who are jointly referred to as the 'permanent representatives'. This cohort includes twenty-eight EU permanent representatives (also known as the 'EU ambassadors') and twenty-eight deputy permanent representatives (both to become twenty-seven post-Brexit). The Committee meets in two formats, confusingly named Coreper I (deputies) and Coreper II (ambassadors). The Commission is always represented in both Committee formats. But such a narrow definition would miss how Coreper is embedded in a much more extensive network of national delegations in Brussels, known as the 'EU permanent representations' (Permreps). At a glance, the Permreps look like embassies, but as integration has deepened, they have grown in size and coverage to become microcosms of the national governments, and 'veritable administrative melting-pots' (Hayes-Renshaw *et al.* 1989: 128). For example, the Permreps also staff an ambassador-level official for the Political and Security Committee (PSC—see Chapter 13), and several high-ranking military officers for the work covered by the EU Military Committee. Permreps has also become the nerve centre to manage the duties of the rotating EU presidency and delegations often swell by 25 per cent or more to handle the workload.

Since 1975, a group of assistants to the ambassadors, known as the 'Antici counsellors' (Anticis), have finalized and prepared the agendas for weekly Coreper II meetings. The Anticis also act as advisers to their ambassadors, minimizing the element of surprise by floating ideas and testing arguments before or at the margins of meetings, and drafting reports to send back home. In 1993, the deputies formalized a similar group of assistants, known as the 'Mertens counsellors' (Mertens). The Antici and Mertens counsellors are emblematic of a wider array of transgovernmental networking that takes place among national administrations through the Permreps. This networking extends to common foreign and security policy (CFSP) and justice and home affairs (JHA) counsellors, and, now, military attachés who work on European security and defence policy (ESDP) matters. In general, the permanent representations are a mechanism for socialization to the EU, training new generations of diplomats and policy specialists, orchestrating presidencies, and educating national administrations to open their minds to the reality of EU decision-making (Lewis 2005; Heisenberg 2007).

Coreper I and II

Coreper is split into two formations based on a functional division of labour (see Table 14.1). Both meet weekly and each have their own councils to prepare. Coreper II is composed of the ambassadors and is responsible for the monthly General Affairs Council (GAC), as well as issues with horizontal, institutional, and financial implications. What is more, discussions range widely, shifting from (say) canned tuna to relations with Russia. Coreper II is also closely implicated in multiannual budget negotiations and, historically, with IGCs (often serving as a delegation's personal representative).

TABLE 14.1 Responsibilities of Coreper I and II

Coreper II—Ambassadors

General affairs and external relations
Justice and home affairs
Multi-annual budget negotiations
Structural and cohesion funds
Institutional and horizontal questions
Association agreements and development
Accession
Trilogues and conciliation in relevant areas of OLP
IGC personal representatives*

Coreper I—Deputies

Internal market
Environment
Employment, social policy, health, and consumer affairs
Competitiveness
Transport, telecommunications, and energy
Industry and research
Education, youth, culture, and sport
Fisheries
Agriculture (veterinary and plant-health questions)
Trilogues and conciliation in relevant areas of OLP

*Varies by member state and IGC

Coreper I is made up of the deputies and is responsible for the misleadingly la-belled 'technical' councils, such as those for competitiveness, environment, and em-ployment, social policy, health, and consumer affairs. While decisions are quite 'technical', such as setting sustainable catch limits every December for the common fisheries policy (CFP), this work is often intensely political. Coreper is also respon-sible for representing the Council during ordinary legislative procedure (OLP) nego-tiations (formerly known as 'codecision'—see Chapter 6). This duty includes 'early reading' negotiations, known as 'trilogues', as well as the formal conciliation process when EP–Council disagreements prevail. As representatives of the presidency, the chairs of Coreper I and II hold particularly active roles in managing trilogue negotia-tions with the EP and Commission (European Parliament 2014a: 19). Pre-Lisbon, the Coreper I deputies were more engaged than the ambassadors given the policy areas to which codecision applied. As much as 50 per cent of the deputies' time be-came devoted to codecision matters (Bostock 2002: 223). Post-Lisbon, and the ex-tension of codecision to dozens of new legal bases in the form of the OLP, ambassadors in Coreper II are now similarly involved in policy matters that cover, for example, the multiannual financial framework and aspects of JHA, such as immigration, asylum, and visas. A tipping point seems to have been reached during the 2013 Irish presidency when the Coreper II ambassador was engaged in as many, or more, OLP files than his Coreper I colleague (Jacobs 2015: 5).

So who *are* the EU permanent representatives? Ambassadors are almost invariably senior-ranking diplomats from the ministries of foreign affairs. For most member states, the deputy is also recruited from foreign affairs; exceptions include Germany, for which the deputy always comes from economic affairs, and the United Kingdom (UK), for which the deputy frequently came (pre-Brexit) from the Department for Business, Innovation and Skills (BIS). The EU permanent representatives are selected from the highest tier of career diplomats and senior civil servants, usually with a considerable background in European affairs. The member states control appointments and there is no approval process in Brussels. Appointments are typically made after a recommendation, or at least tacit approval, from the head of state or government. Such high-level political selection contributes enormously to the credibility (and confidence) of the permanent representatives to negotiate in Brussels. In European diplomatic circles, Coreper is considered a top posting. EU permanent representatives rank the position on par or slightly above postings to Washington DC, New York, and Paris.

Coreper appointments are also noteworthy for their length of tenure and the absence of partisan politics. The average tenure is five years—slightly longer than the typical three- or four-year diplomatic rotation. But some permanent representatives remain in Brussels for much longer, upwards of a decade or beyond. For example, since 1958, Belgium has had eight ambassadors; Germany, seven deputies. Permanent representatives, unlike their masters, the ministers, are typically insulated from electoral politics and shifts in government (with some exceptions, such as Portugal and Greece—see Perez and Scherpereel 2015). Longer non-partisan appointments provide 'continuity in the representation of interests' (de Zwaan 1995: 17).

Contestation

Since 1958, Coreper has been the senior preparatory forum of the Council. The vertical channels of coordination have placed the permanent representatives in clear command of how files are routed to the ministers. They are gatekeepers with 'cast-iron Treaty authority' (Nicoll 1994: 195). While, on paper, all Treaty reforms have reconfirmed Coreper's senior preparatory status, two developments are contesting this position in practice.

Since the early 1990s, everyday EU decision-making has seen the intensification of rivalries between preparatory bodies (Lewis 2000). Scholars observe that the proliferation of decision-making bodies results in the Council losing its 'old focality' (Genschel and Jachtenfuchs 2016: 47; Bickerton *et al.* 2015b). There are, for example, occasional turf battles over foreign policy competences between Coreper II and the PSC. In other policy areas, Coreper II has permanently conceded responsibility of the Economics and Financial Affairs Council (Ecofin) and the Eurogroup of euro area finance ministers to the Economic and Finance Committee (EFC) and its

Eurogroup working group (EGWG). EFC reports are not, as a rule, even copied to the permanent representatives; they are sent directly to finance ministers. Hastened by the crisis management needed in recent years, the bureaucratic network embedding finance ministries in the surveillance of national economic policies and the policy coordination agenda has elevated the EFC and EGWG to effectively bypass the input of the Coreper II ambassadors (Puetter 2014: 118, 192–5). Other, less serious, boundary disputes involve the Coordinating Committee in judicial and police cooperation in criminal matters (formerly known as the 'Article 36 Committee', or CATS) and JHA matters, and the Trade Policy Committee (formerly the 'Article 133 Committee') over administration of the common commercial policy (CCP). Coreper has become more proactive (perhaps even defensive) in establishing policy boundaries and clarifying its senior preparatory status. The Council's rules of procedure are now more detailed in laying out Coreper's right to 'ensure consistency of the European Union's policies and actions'.[12]

A second source of contestation is the relative decline of the foreign ministers and GAC. For the first several decades of European integration, general affairs was *primus inter pares* ('first among equals'). But the process of deepening had the effect of raising the stature and importance of other sectoral councils. By the 1990s, the GAC had lost its claim to be providing leadership or acting as an overall coordinator of EU affairs (Gomez and Peterson 2001). Some hold that Ecofin has supplanted the GAC as the senior formation of the Council. For most member states, this shift reflects the domestic inter-ministerial balance of power that has seen an eclipse of foreign affairs relative to the growing ascent of the finance, economics, justice, and interior ministries in EU affairs (Hocking 1999; Hocking and Spence 2002). The weakening of the GAC affects Coreper as well, since, in past decades, the foreign ministries had primacy in staffing and instructing the Brussels' Permreps. The impact today is evident, for example, in the Ecofin/Eurogroup linkages with the EFC/EGWG that bypass Coreper and can be interpreted as a new infrastructure for a finance-dominated network directly connected to European Council summitry. Some Permrep officials perceive this general pattern of contestation as weakening Coreper's institutional role and, perhaps more intangibly, the *vue d'ensemble* mentioned earlier. Others recognize a certain amount of 'turf fighting' among preparatory groups, but still see a more complementary relationship and division of labour slowly normalizing.

Powers of the institution

The formal rules delineating Coreper's functions are as understated as the original Treaty basis to 'prepare' the Council's work. In rational choice imagery, Coreper's power is shrouded intentionally by 'incomplete contracting' and an unwritten delegated authority to find workable solutions. From a sociological institutionalist perspective, this delegated authority gives the permanent representatives network-like power in two areas in particular: *de facto* decision-making, and the institutional capacities to integrate interests.

De facto decision-makers

As the Council's senior preparatory forum, Coreper is a place where many EU decisions are effectively made. But the permanent representatives have no *formal* decision-making authority: juridical decision-making authority is a power exclusively reserved for the ministers and formal voting is expressly prohibited at any other level of the Council. In practice, or *de facto*, however, Coreper has evolved into a veritable decision-making factory. There are ways around the formality of *de jure* voting, such as the 'indicative vote' of how a delegation would vote if the matter were put before the ministers. More common is the tactful packaging of a discussion by the presidency, in which the chair will ask 'I assume no one else requests the floor?' or state 'A sufficient majority exists'. No vote is taken. There is no raising of hands. But many agreements are reached in this manner and decisions thus are made.

Participants claim that the overwhelming bulk of decisions are made by consensus (see Chapter 4). Even under conditions of qualified majority voting (QMV), permanent representatives regularly spend extra time to 'bring everyone on board'. Pushing for a vote is considered inappropriate in most cases and the 'consensus assumption' is a reflexive habit. A clear example of this consensus reflex can be seen in the legislative record of the 1992 project. Of the 260 single market measures subject to QMV, approximately 220 were adopted without a vote at all (de Schoutheete 2000: 9–10). Spending extra time and not pushing for a vote are considered 'the right things to do', offering a clear illustration of the logic of appropriateness in Coreper's institutional setting.

The most surprising finding here is not that civil servants have been delegated *de facto* decisional authority, but that the density of this mechanism in maintaining the output and performance across so many policy fields of the Council's work. The intangible power to make *de facto* decisions derives from the role perception to 'find solutions' and a sense of responsibility to deliver results. Signs of this responsibility and the mandate on which it rests can be traced back to the dog days of Eurosclerosis and the heads of state or government who innovated European Council summitry. In particular, the communiqué of the 1974 Paris Summit holds: 'Greater latitude will be given to the Permanent Representatives so that only the most important political problems need be discussed in the Council'.[13] It was during this same period that integration researchers began to observe that Coreper resembled 'a Council of Ministers in permanent session' (Busch and Puchala 1976: 240).

We turn now to *how* Coreper is able to reach so many decisions and what is potentially the group's most valuable contribution to EU decision-making: its capacity for integrating interests.

Integrating interests

Continuous negotiation

Coreper's structural position imparts continuity in the representation of interests that would otherwise be difficult to match. Not only is Coreper distinguishable by the issue intensity of negotiations, but also the permanent representatives' involvement across different domains of EU decision-making is pervasive. In addition to weekly meetings, the permanent representatives sit beside their ministers during Council sessions, briefing them beforehand and offering tactical suggestions. They attend European Council summits as behind-the-scenes consultants.[14] They monitor the proceedings of the working groups and offer specific points of strategy or emphasis. The ambassadors are also closely involved in monitoring cooperation and association agreements, cooperation councils (including Euro–Med conferences and Euro–Asian summits), and accession negotiations. And the evolution of the OLP negotiation network has intensified contacts between members of the European Parliament (MEPs) and Coreper. This trend is reflected in the 1,557 trilogues held between 2009 and 2014 that clearly influenced the high rate of early first reading agreements (85 per cent) and dramatically lowered the rate of conciliation cases to 2 per cent of the total (compared to 22 per cent of the total between 1999–2004; Jacobs 2015: 5).

All of this creates a dynamic of continuity in Coreper's work, reinforced through weekly meetings. Added into the mix is the regular cycle of Coreper I and II luncheons, held by Coreper II before the monthly GAC and also on a topical or ad hoc basis, usually two or so per six-month presidency. Lunches can function as long-term strategic planning sessions, often with a European Commissioner invited as a guest. More frequently, and because attendance is so tightly restricted, lunches are used to tackle the thorniest of problems (Butler 1986: 30). Last, but not least, are the informal Coreper trips hosted by the presidency, which precede European Council summits. Trips are long weekends of socializing, 'rich in food and culture', used to reinforce interpersonal relations and the bonds of trust—a kind of 'oiling of the mechanism'. Taken together, the continuity of negotiation and recurring face-to-face contact builds an institutional memory in Coreper from which permanent representatives learn to draw.

Instruction, voice, and insulation

Permanent representatives are under 'instruction' from their national capitals. In principle, for every agenda item, there is an instruction setting, at a minimum, what is and is not acceptable as an outcome. Again in principle, this instruction is arrived at after domestic coordination through the relevant line ministries and often through an inter-ministerial coordination mechanism.[15] In practice, the instruction process is more complex, especially in temporal sequence. For starters, most instructions have in-built flexibility. Of course, there are certain taboo areas (institutional reform, fiscal policy) and national sensitivities. But, here, permanent representatives claim not even to need instructions, because they already know what positions to take.

More fundamental to this story is the degree to which permanent representatives acquire an institutionalized voice in the instruction process itself (Lewis 2014). Some generic patterns include, first, departing from instructions and making recommendations back to the capital for changes. The power of recommendations obviously varies by issue area and the personal authority of a permanent representative. But they are most effective in areas in which there is a risk of becoming isolated or, under the shadow of the vote, disregarded in a possible compromise. Second, the capitals often signal that a margin of manoeuvre exists. Sometimes, permanent representatives are told not to take an instruction seriously or that the position in the printed instruction can be disregarded. Third, when there is a political need to avoid confrontation or politicization at the level of the ministers, permanent representatives (sometimes even told 'avoid Council') will have a freer hand in making deals and selling success at home (Lewis 1998). Fourth, there are times when the capital does not know or cannot decide. In these instances, the permanent representatives are causally contributing to the definition of what national interests in the EU context are. One Antici counsellor stated: 'Instructions already contain a big Brussels element in them, and sometimes they are Brussels instructions, because the first ten lines of our report imply an instruction . . . sometimes they just copy our reports into instructions'.[16]

It can even happen that permanent representatives disregard their instructions. According to one ambassador:

It happens . . . [S]ometimes the capital gets nervous, they have various lobbies behind it usually. We also have to keep in mind that what has been built up over the last forty years is important. That a file should go. That we should proceed forward. This is constantly a factor in what we do. Often we have much more at stake than the dossier.[17]

While it is important to avoid an overly socialized view of the permanent representatives, one should not underestimate the relative autonomy that Coreper, as a collective forum, can obtain in selling results back home to their authorities. Some permanent representatives are known to joke about being regarded back home as the 'permanent traitor'. This somewhat cheeky image in fact highlights one of the truly distinctive features of Coreper: the degree of insulation from the normal currents of domestic constituent pressures. As one ambassador put it, 'Coreper is the only forum in the EU where representatives don't have a domestic turf to defend'. 'Because of this,' he went on to add:

It is often politically necessary to present a position knowing it is unrealistic. My minister of finance needs certain arguments to be presented. He has certain pressures from his constituencies. We have to make it look like we fought for this even though we both know it will lead nowhere. I will present it, and if it receives no support, I will drop it.[18]

Meetings are treated with an air of confidentiality, and many sensitive national positions are ironed out in restricted sessions in which the permanent representatives can speak frankly and in confidence that what is said will not be reported to the capitals or the media. Insulation is a structural feature of Coreper that affords the group collective capacities to reshape domestic constraints. It can include group discussion on how an agreement will be packaged and sold to the authorities back home. As a group, the Committee can engage in transgovernmental bargaining tactics, such as the 'plotting' of a compromise in the collective interest of finding solutions. 'To get new instructions we have to show [the capital] we have a black eye', an ambassador explained. 'We can ask Coreper for help with this; it is one of our standard practices'.[19] According to another: 'Sometimes I will deal with impossible instructions, by saying, "Mr Chairman, can I report back the fierce opposition to this?" And sometimes fierceness is exaggerated for effect'.[20] Plotting is a negotiation practice found in Coreper that demonstrates how a collective rationality can reformulate individual, instrumental rationality. In general, underlining opposition (even 'faked outrage') is a tool for the group to deal with recalcitrant bargaining positions. Exaggerating the fierceness of opposition is also a group resource collectively to legitimate or reject arguments, which in turn reflects a dense normative institutional environment.

A dense normative environment

Coreper's institutional capacity to aggregate interests under such a steady workload is facilitated by a dense normative environment. While these norms are almost purely informal in character—meaning that they are unwritten, not linked directly to any clauses in the Treaties, and largely self-enforcing—the group-community standards in Coreper are highly ingrained into the basic ethos of the Committee's work. For example, there is a norm of diffuse reciprocity, or the balancing of concessions over an extended shadow of the future. Diffuse reciprocity can take many forms, including concessions and derogations, or 'going out on a limb' to persuade the capital for changes or a compromise. Dropping reserves or abstaining (rather than submitting a 'no' vote) are also political gestures that can be filed away and later returned in kind.

An even more basic norm is 'thick trust' and the expectation to speak frankly. Trustworthiness through honest dealings is reconfirmed weekly through the normal cycle of meetings, trips, and lunches.[21] Thick trust is especially important during end-game negotiations and restricted sessions when the group collectively legitimates or rejects arguments based on deliberative processes, such as principled reasoning, standards of fairness, or justifications for special consideration.

There is also a norm of mutual responsiveness that is best described as a shared purpose to understand each other's problems. Mutual responsiveness is another form of collective legitimation, whereby arguments are accepted or rejected by the group. Mutual responsiveness works within broad normative parameters, on the one hand, recognizing that everyone has certain problems that require special consideration, but on the other, that no one can be a *demandeur* too often and expect anyone to listen. This rule is such a basic one that Coreper newcomers report learning the practice after attending only a few meetings.

Norm socialization and the style of discourse

EU norms are internalized through a multilevel process of socialization. At the micro level, new participants in Coreper go through a process of adaptation and learning what one scholar calls the 'family rules' (Pouliot 2011: 549). Coreper has a shared discourse with its own key phrases, such as when a delegation is signalling a willingness to compromise or requesting special consideration. Learning the discourse is an important socialization mechanism for newcomers who join the club (Peterson and Jones 1999: 34; Novak 2013: 1100–1). As one ambassador explained:

There is a Coreper language with its own code words and code phrases. When used, this language is clearly understood by everyone. For example, if I have bad instructions that I'm against, I can say, 'But of course the presidency has to take its responsibilities', which means put it to a vote and I'll lose, I accept this.[22]

There are, however, complex social psychological factors at work, as well as background ('scope') conditions for norm socialization. They include a shared identification with the legitimacy of the institution and the rules in question. If a forum such as Coreper did not also have a well-endowed tradition to practise mutual responsiveness and deal with sensitive domestic concerns by spending extra time and collectively legitimating individual arguments, then we would not expect to see the levels of trust required for such consensus-based decision-making hold up for long.

Norm socialization is especially relevant for the cohort of new Coreper members from (mostly) Central and Eastern Europe countries (CEECs) who arrived after 2004. Despite early estimations that increased heterogeneity and unwieldy size would pose problems for the Council's club-like settings, evidence to date underscores a conscious effort by newcomers to acclimatize to EU decision-making norms. The best overall indicator is the stability of consensus-based outcomes, with historical averages for contested votes less than 15 per cent of all legislative acts (Mattila 2009; Hertz 2010). While adding more members does tend to increase transaction costs for negotiation and may decrease the speed of reaching decisions, it has not altered long-standing traditions of consensus-seeking behaviour nor has it thus far led to more reliance on formal voting (Hertz and Leuffen 2011).

Socialization dynamics in Coreper track with recent international relations research that finds institutional environments can instil 'mimicking' and 'social influence' behaviours: novices seek, first, to get by in an uncertain environment (that is, to copy what others are doing); second, over time, behaviours become more durably internalized as practising the accepted norms leads to influence and social capital (Johnston 2008). Indeed, the Council even has built-in mechanisms to promote norm socialization, such as the 'active observer' period, which begins one year prior to formal accession to allow delegations to attend meetings, including Coreper, to allow them to learn the ropes (Juncos and Pomorska 2007; Lempp 2007).

The rotating presidency is another mechanism for norm socialization. For new-comers, their inaugural presidency is judged a veritable 'entrance exam' (Elgström and Tallberg 2003: 194), which involves exposing hundreds of national civil serv-ants to EU realities, often spearheaded through the permanent representation and usually several years in advance. Running an effective presidency is a way of proving one's European credentials. The pattern of earnest effort by novice members tells us that this achievement is considered a clear route to building a good reputation and social capital in Brussels.

There is also evidence that Coreper makes new use of existing procedures to build mutual confidence and avert contested outcomes. One example is the upsurge in reading formal statements into the minutes of legislative acts since 2005. Some argue that the use of 'formal statements' serves as a viable outlet for expressing political dissatisfaction without the need for contesting a vote (Hagemann and de Clerck-Sachsse 2007). In other words, an informal norm to voice dissent through formal statements helps to sustain the consensus culture, as well as to send positive signals from newcomers that they are willing to uphold existing norms. Another adaptation is intensified informal contacts and the coordination of positions outside of the weekly meetings themselves. A seasoned deputy noted: 'Much has shifted to an in-formal circuit. I spend much more time on the telephone: "I have a point, can you support me?"'[23] An ambassador reached a similar conclusion: 'It is inevitable that more will be done outside the meetings rather than in the room'.[24] There are also more procedural rules on working methods—'who does not speak agrees' carries new normative weight in an EU of twenty-eight (twenty-seven post-Brexit)—and a higher usage of the formal written procedure to handle routine administrative busi-ness. But, overall, the evidence to date points to the durability of consensus prac-tices. The incentives to build a good reputation are still strong, and compel newcomers to acclimatize and internalize collective norms.

Accountability

There is a common perception that decision-making in Brussels is remote, opaque, and even undemocratic. Given Coreper's role in everyday decision-making, it is somewhat surprising that, in all of the discussions to address the EU's democratic deficit since the early 1990s, Coreper has remained largely unmentioned. But given Coreper's workload and the need for insulation from the politicization effects dis-cussed, it is clear why member states are reluctant to tinker with such fine-tuned mechanisms. There are occasional suggestions that emanate from a capital that per-haps a new Coreper III of ministers or deputy prime ministers might work to democ-ratize the system. But support for this idea has never gained much momentum.

It is also easy to push the image of an all-powerful, unaccountable group of back-room decision-makers too far. Committee members are accountable to their minis-ters for the positions taken in negotiations and there is always a possibility (although specific examples are extremely hard to come by) that a minister can undo a deal done at Coreper level. If permanent representatives were to stray too far or be overruled by their ministers, they would quickly lose credibility in Coreper and in their home capitals. There are also signs of more direct institutional links to domestic politics, seen in the number of Permreps who now have a formal liaison for communication with their national parliament (including Greece, Hungary, Ireland, and Latvia).

Whether such an indirect system of accountability is a sustainable form of governance can be debated. Following the post-2004 enlargements, many believe the EU will need to rely even more on the few, but vitally important, negotiation forums that are based on a club-like and insulated atmosphere. Collective norms guide appropriate behaviour and rule out a range of instrumental tactics (such as pushing for a vote, making veto threats, and so on). Coreper is the exemplar of this, but it is not alone. An intriguing analogue in macroeconomic and euro area policy-making is the EFC, which brings national central bank and finance officials together—*in camera*, with no note-takers, and under the long tradition of doing everything by consensus. Another example that covers foreign policy is the professional ethos of the PSC ambassadors, described as a veritable 'consensus-generating machine' (Bickerton 2012: 31; Howorth 2011). Even with the revolutionary change that the OLP has on the EU's legislative process, we still see a heavy reliance on informal and closed-door settings, such as the trilogue methodology, to work out areas of compromise between the Council and EP versions of a proposal. In an EU of twenty-eight (twenty-seven post-Brexit), the need for a mechanism like Coreper is greater than ever.

Theorizing Coreper

Although, in Chapter 1, the editors of this volume describe Coreper as an 'awkward case' for scholars, the institution's hybridity offers a rich laboratory for testing theories of the new institutionalism and, arguably, finding considerable nuance in a range of complementary explanations. Rational choice theories offer compelling explanations for patterns of principal–agent delegation and the strategic rationale for creating *de facto* decision-makers. The insulated, club-like setting of Coreper offers strong empirical confirmation for the argument of David Stasavage (2004: 670) that states will often 'shun transparency' in international negotiations, since openness can act as 'an incentive for representatives to "posture" by adopting uncompromising bargaining positions'. Finding collective solutions and 'getting on with it' is an unspoken mandate that gives Coreper its reputation for being results-oriented. There is also convincing evidence that patterns of consensus do not simply fit a 'do the right thing' logic to make everyone content or even mutually accommodative to each other's domestic policy needs. There is also a strategic pattern of 'blame avoidance' when member states are isolated or unconvincing, and a deliberate promotion of insulated decision-making without recourse to formal voting in order to publicly conceal who the winners and losers are (Novak 2013; Smeets 2015).

Historical institutionalism offers insight into the long-term evolution of preparatory authority, especially the emergence of consensus-seeking practices, and the 'lock-in' effects of path-dependent behaviour geared towards compromise and mutual responsiveness (see Box 14.2). The historiography of a dense normative environment for preparatory committees tends to have self-reinforcing effects as a superior method to deliver collective results and prevent bargaining breakdowns (Heisenberg 2007). On this reading, neo-functionalists such as Haas (1958: 490–2) and Lindberg (1963: 77–86, 280) were early pioneers of historical institutionalist thinking, for example in their identification of the Council's distinctive 'procedural code'. The process-tracing methodology of this variant of institutionalist theory is particularly useful in explaining the increased sophistication of the normative environment for voting and consensus practices over time (Novak 2011: 15). At the same time, *how* these norms and rules are learned is a topic in relation to which more sociological theories of institutions have certain home court advantages.

In a sociological institutionalist or constructivist framing, the normative structures of EU preparatory bodies provide a culture of decision-making that is learned and internalized through a process of socialization. Checkel (2005: 804) defines socialization as 'a process of inducting actors into the norms and rules of a given community'. As Johnston (2008) shows, socialization patterns can be disaggregated into a 'range of microprocesses', from 'mimicking' (where newcomers copy group norms to get along in an uncertain environment) to 'social influence' (where newcomers follow group norms for social rewards such as status) and 'persuasion' (where pro-norm behaviour is tied to shared cognitive understandings of the right thing to do—a thicker form of internalization). But as Novak (2013: 1093) points out, 'socialization does not always entail empathy and the willingness to help others'; socialization also acts to delimit inappropriate behaviour in a society, such as making demands without justification, invoking 'very important interests' opportunistically, or pushing for a public vote. Using Goffman's concept of stigmatization, Adler-Nissen (2014: 149) makes a convincing case that 'most societies rely not only on socialization (in the form of emulation, learning, or persuasion)—they also use public sanctioning to construct and display normality'. The professional expertise of EU preparatory groups also serves as a cognitive filter for acceptable ideas and behaviour, a process-level dynamic that Heipertz and Verdun (2010) study using what they call an 'expertocratic approach' that resonates with the international relations (IR) literature on epistemic communities and the newer 'practice turn' (Adler and Pouliot 2011).

Going a bit further, treating committees as social environments that follow 'club rules' invites a more anthropological and ethnographic understanding of institutions (Neumann 2012; Adler-Nissen 2016). In this view, the permanent representatives have evolved consensus practices to the point at which they acquire a 'taken for granted' quality that is a hallmark of Bourdieu's (1977) sociological notion of '*habitus*' (Adler-Nissen 2009b; Pouliot 2011). Pouliot (2008: 257) shows the concept of '*habitus*' fits a distinctive 'logic of practicality', or the 'inarticulate know-how that makes what is to be done self-evident or commonsensical'. Thus *habitus* is different from the more active reflection of what 'ought to be done' inherent to the role-playing logic of appropriateness or the instrumental calculations that make up strategic norm conformity, since it is unconsciously taken-for-granted. Instead, norms are 'performed', rather than 'internalized' as a *sens practique* within a diplomatic field of shared meanings that 'define agency and make action intelligible' (Adler-Nissen 2008: 668; Adler-Nissen 2016). The concept of a *habitus* offers intriguing support for the durability of what Hayes-Renshaw and Wallace (1995: 465) observe as 'the instinctive recourse to behave consensually'. Taken together, these alternative institutionalisms cast a wide net in capturing the complex mixed motives and strategic construction of group-community standards in Coreper.

The 'Janus face' of Coreper

Coreper challenges the conventional dichotomy that sharply demarcates the national and European levels. As state agents, the EU permanent representatives nicely illustrate how national and supranational roles and identifications can become nested and coexist. Interviews with participants consistently confirm that permanent representatives obtain a distinct secondary allegiance to collective, EU decision-making. However, the 'nested' identity concept does not fully capture the quality of the identity configuration found here, because permanent representatives do not self-reflectively see their secondary allegiance as competitive or contradictory to national allegiance. They are not different hats worn at different times or held in juxtaposition to each other, but rather a broadening of the cognitive boundaries of what counts as the 'self' and the 'national interest' (Adler-Nissen 2009b). One deputy stated: 'There is a confidence that I will deliver the goods at home and a confidence to deliver the goods collectively. I must find ways to synthesize the two'.[25] The EU permanent representatives are examples of state agents who have found a way to operationalize what Laffan (2004: 90–4) describes as 'double-hatting'.

Instead of limited conceptualizations of shifts and transfers in identity, what we see in Coreper is a blurring of the boundaries between the national and the European. Describing his own unwritten job description, one deputy claimed, 'I wear a Janus face'.[26] The metaphor of the Janus face nicely captures how permanent representatives perceive their institutional roles and multiple allegiances, to represent national interests *and* participate in making collective decisions according to a deliberative process of negotiation. None of this implies that national identities and interests become marginalized or disappear; rather, what stands out is the infusion of the national with the European and vice versa. To be successful, EU permanent representatives develop a more complex identity configuration informing definitions of self and interest. From a Janus-faced perspective, they act as both state agents and supranational entrepreneurs simultaneously. From an institutional design standpoint, this finding is highly significant as to how the overall system of decision-making functions. As Weiler (1994: 31) so aptly summarized, the system:

... replaces a kind of 'liberal' premise of international society with a communitarian one: the Community as a transnational regime will not simply be a neutral area in which states seek to maximize their benefits but will create a tension between the national self and the collective self.

The implications of this tension for how we think of sovereignty in Europe are also significant. Waever (1995: 412, emphasis original) argues that the EU reconfigures conventional conceptions of national sovereignty because of the 'importance of Europe *in* national identities', in which 'the European dimension is included in national self-conceptions'. The cognitive blurring of boundaries between the national and European layers also fits suggestively with what Risse (2010: 45) describes as a 'marble cake' concept of multiple identities, in which 'identity components blend into each other and are intertwined'. As high-ranking national officials, the permanent representatives offer a striking empirical example of this blurring at the everyday level of EU decision-making.

Conclusions

This chapter has focused on integrating interests in the EU and, in particular, the systemic, policy-setting level at which Coreper operates. Understanding Coreper negotiations requires being alert to the often-subtle interplay of national and community perspectives. The EU permanent representatives are nation-state agents who represent national interests, but who have also internalized collective decision-making rules and norms that inform bargaining behaviour and shape legislative outcomes. The logic of action found in Coreper goes beyond cost–benefit, instrumental interest calculation, and includes a distinctive 'appropriateness' logic based on group-community standards. Given the range of early predictions about enlargement leading to gridlock or worse, it is impressive how this collective decision-making logic persists over time, which in turn supports an argument that norm socialization in forums such as Coreper is an important process-level dimension of European integration. As a key decision-making bottleneck in the Council system, Coreper embodies a culture of consensus-seeking and mutual accommodation of national preferences using group-legitimation standards. The durability of consensus practices ('part of our DNA', as one insider described it[27]) also supports a reading closer to the sociological meaning of *habitus* that is largely taken for granted as practical knowledge of 'how we do things'.

At the same time, while the Committee's normative environment is highly institutionalized, it is also based almost exclusively on informal rules and norms. As such, it is subject to a very different process of change from, say, that of revising the Treaties or changing the formal voting rules. If members were to alter the calculus of whom they appoint to Coreper (and the Permreps) and/or to begin to challenge established decision-making norms (by, say, pushing for a vote under QMV, or refusing to explain and justify positions), the Council *could* develop a more rigid 'veto culture' or divide into different voting blocks along geographic or gross domestic product (GDP) lines. In such scenarios, the organizational culture and normative environment would change. The 'double-hatting' identity configuration of the EU permanent representatives could be altered as well. If Coreper were to develop into a body in which voting weights and instrumental cost–benefit calculations ruled the day, rather than consensus-driven deliberation and debate, we could see system-wide effects (and unintended consequences) on how effectively the Union can operate.

ENDNOTES

1. March and Olsen (1989) offer the classic distinction between logics of consequences and appropriateness. In the former, 'the only obligations recognized by individuals are those created through consent and contracts grounded in calculated consequential advantage'; in the latter, individuals are 'acting in accordance with rules and practices that are socially constructed, publicly known, anticipated, and accepted' (March and Olsen 1989: 951–2).

2. Art. 240 TFEU.

3. Art. 19(2) of the Rules of Procedure of the Council, Council Decision 2009/937/EU, OJ L 325/35, 11 December 2009.

4. Interview, Brussels, 12 July 1996.

5. Interview, Brussels, 26 May 2000.

6. See also Haas (1960).

7. Anderson (1997: 81) defines 'constitutive politics' as the 'processes and outcomes that establish or amend EU rules of the game', as distinct from 'regulative politics', which are the 'processes and outcomes that take place within established, routinized areas of EU activity'.

8. Interview, Brussels, 21 April 1997.

9. Interview, Brussels, 15 May 2000. This practice sharply contrasts with Commission President Hallstein 'who was known to snub the Permanent Representatives . . . by sending them his assistants' (Palayret *et al.* 2006: 27).

10. Other partial exemptions from Coreper's remit involve macroeconomic policy coordination (the specialty of the EFC, Eurogroup Working Group, and Economic Policy Committee), military planning (managed by the Military Committee), and certain aspects of foreign policy, especially crisis management (the focus of the Political and Security Committee). See the section on 'Contestation' for more.

11. Bulletin EEC 3/66.

12. Art. 19(1) of the Rules of Procedure, with a footnote that adds 'in particular for matters where substantive preparation is undertaken in other fora'.

13. Bulletin of the EC, 12–1974, point 1104.7.

14. By current convention, only the Coreper II ambassador representing the rotating presidency is invited to the European Council meeting itself.

15. Such as the *Secrétariat Général du Comité Inter-ministériel pour les Questions de Coopération Economique Européenne* (SGCI) in France/French.

16. Interview, Brussels, 22 May 1996.

17. Interview, Brussels, 18 May 2000.

18. Interview, Brussels, 15 May 2000.

19. Interview, Brussels, 15 May 2000.

20. Interview, Brussels, 26 May 2000.

21. As Putnam (1993: 171) explains, thick trust is a key interpersonal ingredient of 'social capital', which tends to develop in 'small, close-knit communities' based on 'a belief that rests on intimate familiarity with this individual'.

22. Interview, Brussels, 15 May 2000.

23. Interview, Brussels, 27 May 2003.

24. Interview, Brussels, 27 May 2003.

25. Interview, Brussels, 7 July 1996.

26. Interview, Brussels, 20 February 1996.

27. Telephone interview, 22 September 2015.

FURTHER READING

For an excellent treatment of Coreper's role in EU decision-making, see Hayes-Renshaw and Wallace (2006). De Zwaan (1995) offers the most comprehensive study available in English, although it tends toward the descriptive and legalistic. Hayes-Renshaw *et al.* (1989) is a classic. See also Bostock (2002) and Mentler (1996, in German). Menon's (2004) edited volume, with short reflections by all eight UK ambassadors, offers an insider perspective on what many used to say was (pre-Brexit) the smoothest-run Permrep in Brussels. New accounts of the empty chair crisis include Ludlow (2006) and Palayret *et al.* (2006). A range of sophisticated interpretations that help to explain the role of EU committees in producing a consensus culture can be found in Smeets (2015), Kleine (2013), Häge (2013), Novak (2013), Bickerton (2012), and Heisenberg (2007). On the historical evolution of EU committee structures, see Knudsen and Rasmussen (2008). For more on multiple identities and how to conceptualize different configurations of identity in the context of the EU, see Risse (2010).

Bickerton, C. (2012) *European Integration: From Nation-States to Member States* (Oxford and New York: Oxford University Press).

Bostock, D. (2002) 'Coreper revisited', *Journal of Common Market Studies*, 40/2: 215–34.

De Zwaan, J. (1995) *The Permanent Representatives Committee: Its Role in European Union Decision-Making* (Amsterdam: Elsevier).

Häge, F. (2013) *Bureaucrats as Law-Makers: Committee Decision-Making in the EU Council of Ministers* (London and New York: Routledge).

Hayes-Renshaw, F., and Wallace, H. (2006) *The Council of Ministers* (2nd edn, Basingstoke and New York: Palgrave).

Hayes-Renshaw, F., Lequesne, C., and Mayor Lopez, P. (1989) 'The permanent representations of the member states to the European Communities', *Journal of Common Market Studies*, 28/2: 119–37.

Heisenberg, D. (2007) 'Informal decision-making in the Council: The secret of the EU's success?', in S. Meunier and K. McNamara (eds) *The State of the European Union 8: Making History* (Oxford and New York: Oxford University Press), 67–87.

Kleine, M. (2013) *Informal Governance in the European Union: How Governments Make International Organizations Work* (Ithaca, NY: Cornell University Press).

Knudsen, A.-C., and Rasmussen, M. (2008) 'A European political system in the making 1958-1970: The relevance of emerging committee structures', *Journal of European Integration History*, 14/1: 51–67.

Ludlow, N.P. (2006) *The European Community and the Crises of the 1960s: Negotiating the Gaullist Challenge* (London and New York: Routledge).

Menon, A. (2004) *Britain and European Integration: Views from within* (Oxford: Blackwell).

Mentler, M. (1996) *Der Auschuss der Sta'ndigen Vertreter bei den Europäischen Gemein-schaften* (Baden-Baden: Nomos).

Novak, S. (2013) 'The silence of ministers: Consensus and blame avoidance in the Council of the European Union', *Journal of Common Market Studies*, 51/6: 1091–1107.

Palayret, J.-M., Wallace, H., and Winand, P. (2006) *Visions, Votes, and Vetoes: The Empty Chair Crisis and the Luxembourg Compromise Forty Years on* (Brussels: Peter Lang).

Risse, T. (2010) *A Community of Europeans? Transnational Identities and Public Spheres* (Ithaca, NY: Cornell University Press).

Smeets, S. (2015) *Negotiations in the EU Council of Ministers: 'And All Must Have Prizes'* (Colchester: ECPR Press).

 WEB LINKS

http://www.consilium.europa.eu

The best online resource for monitoring Coreper's work is the Council's website, which has a 'full meeting calendar' that can be sorted by configuration, including Coreper I and II. In addition, the 'documents' link includes the agendas for each meeting. For an online directory of Coreper personnel (including valuable contact information for arranging interviews at the permanent representations), select 'Contact: Who Is Who', then choose the link for Coreper.

http://www.europarl.europa.eu/code/default_en.htm

For more on OLP activity that involves Coreper, consult the EP's website on 'Conciliations and Codecision'.

CHAPTER 15

European parties: A powerful caucus in the European Parliament and beyond

Tapio Raunio

▍ Summary

The party system of the European Parliament (EP) is dominated by the two main European party families: centre-Right conservatives and Christian democrats, on the one hand, and centre-Left social democrats on the other. In the early 1950s, members of the European Parliament (MEPs) decided to form party-political groups instead of national blocs to counterbalance the dominance of national interests in the Council. Since then, the party groups have gradually, but consistently, consolidated their positions in the Parliament, primarily by introducing procedural reforms that enable them to make effective use of the EP's legislative and appointment powers. At the same time, the shape of the party system has become more stable—at least as far as the main groups are concerned. Nevertheless, national parties remain influential within party groups, not least through their control of candidate selection.

Introduction

Compared with parties in EU member state legislatures, the party groups of the EP operate in a very different institutional environment. While the Parliament is involved in the appointment of the Commission and can force it to resign, there is nonetheless no real EU government accountable to the Parliament. There are no coherent and hierarchically organized European-level parties; instead, MEPs are elected from lists drawn up by national parties and on the basis of largely national electoral campaigns. The social and cultural heterogeneity of the EU is reflected in the internal diversity of the groups, with around 200 national parties from twenty-eight member states winning seats in the Parliament in the 2014 elections. The party groups are thus firmly embedded in the political systems of the EU member states. However, despite the existence of such factors, EP party groups have gradually, over the decades, consolidated their position in the Parliament, primarily through introducing procedural reforms that enable them to make effective use of the EP's legislative powers. At the same time, the shape of the party system has become more stable, at least as far as the main groups are concerned. One can thus talk of the 'institutionalization' of the EP party system.

A word on nomenclature is warranted here. EP 'party groups' and 'Europarties' are terms that sound synonymous, but are not. *Party groups*, as the name suggests, exist only within the EP; their purpose is to bring together groups of MEPs to pursue, among other things, a common position on EU legislation. *Europarties* are extra-parliamentary—that is, they exist beyond the EP. They bring together politicians from the EP and beyond to pursue shared political objectives and, in the 2014 EP election, to field candidates for the post of Commission President. There is considerable scope for confusion here, because EP party groups and Europarties sometimes have similar sounding names. The European People's Party is a Europarty, which brings together centre-Right politicians from across the EU, including German Chancellor Angela Merkel, Commission President Jean-Claude Juncker, and European Council President Donald Tusk. The European People's Party Group, in contrast, describes only those MEPs who work together in the EP. It comprises MEPs from national political parties affiliated with the Europarty, the European People's Party, but also some MEPs from national political parties that are not aligned with any Europarty.

The chapter begins by examining the shape of the EP party system, the structure of the party groups, and the role of national parties within them. It shows that while the Left–Right dimension constitutes the main cleavage in the chamber, the dominant coalition is formed between the two large groups—the centre-Right European People's Party (EPP) and the centre-Left Social Democrats (S&D). Next, we examine parties at the European level and argue that, without any real executive office at stake in European elections, the vertical linkage function of the party groups—that of connecting voters to the EU policy process—remains poorly developed. However, the *Spitzenkandidaten* ('lead candidates') initiative, whereby the Europarties put forward their own candidates for the Commission President in the 2014 elections, represents an interesting step in the direction of European-level parliamentary democracy. Also, in horizontal terms, the EP party groups and the Europarties perform an important function by integrating political interests across the Union. The chapter also looks at the state of research on the EP party system, highlighting the need to understand how coalitions are formed in the committees and the plenary.

The shape of the EP party system

The Common Assembly of the European Coal and Steel Community (ECSC), the predecessor of the Parliament, held its inaugural session in September 1952. In the first important vote held in the Assembly, to elect its President, the members had already split along group lines instead of voting as national blocs. This decision to form party groups crossing national lines needs to be understood in light of developments in the early 1950s. First, the creation of the High Authority (the predecessor of the Commission) and the Assembly marked the emergence of more supranational institutions, in contrast to those of the intergovernmental Council of Europe (particularly its Consultative Assembly). Second, national interests in the ECSC were already represented in the Council of Ministers and the Assembly sought to counterbalance this through its party-political structure.

Throughout its history up to the present day (Box 15.1 summarizes EP groups after the 2014 elections), the EP party system has been based on the Left–Right dimension, the main cleavage in almost all European countries. The seating order in the chamber reflects this divide, with the social democrats and former communists on the left side of the hemicycle, the greens and liberals in the middle, and Christian democrats and conservatives on the right. Table 15.1 shows the distribution of seats between party families in the Parliament between 1979 (the date of the first direct EP elections) and 2014. Initially, the party system consisted of only three groups: socialists/social democrats (the Party of European Socialists, or PES); Christian democrats/conservatives (the EPP); and liberals (the European Liberal, Democrat and Reform Party, or ELDR)—the three main party families in EU member states. The Christian democrat group was the largest group until 1975, when the British Labour Party joined the socialist group; after the 1999 EP elections, the former overtook the latter once again.[1]

BOX 15.1	Party groups in the 2014–19 European Parliament

European People's Party (EPP, 217 seats)

The EPP is a mix of Christian democrats and conservatives, joining together parties from all EU member states. The largest national party is the German Christian Democratic Union/Christian Social Union (CDU/CSU). The conservative wing of the group has strengthened over the years, with the entry of parties such as the Italian Forza Italia, the French (Gaullist)

Cont. ➤

Cont.

The Republicans, the British Conservatives (which left the group in 2009 to form the ECR group—as we shall see), and particularly the controversial Hungarian party Fidesz (the Hungarian Civic Alliance). Despite the numerical growth of conservative forces in the group, the EPP has traditionally and consistently been in favour of closer European integration.

Progressive Alliance of Socialists and Democrats (S&D, 190 seats)

This group of the Party of European Socialists (PES) brings together social democratic and socialist parties from all EU countries. The largest party delegations are the Italian Democratic Party, the German Social Democrats, and—until the United Kingdom (UK) implements the outcome of its 2016 referendum vote on EU membership—the British Labour Party. The group supports further integration, primarily because, with monetary union and deeper economic integration, the defence of traditional goals of the Left—such as social and environmental legislation, and employment policies—require European-level action to complement national measures.

European Conservatives and Reformists (ECR, 74 seats)

This conservative group was formed after the 2009 elections when the British Conservatives broke away from the EPP group. It is affiliated with the European-level Alliance of European Conservatives and Reformists (AECR). The ECR has members from sixteen countries and it benefited from the wave of Eurosceptic votes in the 2014 election. The two largest national parties following this election were the British Conservatives and the Polish Law and Justice Party, although the former will exit this group once the UK formally leaves the EU. The group can be categorized as Eurosceptic, but it does not share the hard-line anti-integrationist views of the EFDD.

Alliance of Liberals and Democrats for Europe (ALDE, 70 seats)

The liberal group consists of various liberal and centrist parties, and has come to occupy a pivotal role between the two largest groups. After the 2004 elections, the group changed its name from European Liberal, Democrat, and Reform Party (ELDR) to the Alliance of Liberals and Democrats for Europe (ALDE), which is also the official name of the liberals' Europarty. The group brings together MEPs from twenty-one member states and it has traditionally been a firm advocate of deeper integration.

Confederal Group of the European United Left/Nordic Green Left (EUL–NGL, 52 seats)

The EUL–NGL brings together a variety of Left-socialist and former communist parties, around half of which belong to the Party of the European Left (EL), from fourteen member states. The euro crisis and austerity measures contributed to the success of EUL–NGL in the 2014 elections, and the main parties in the group are the Left Party from Germany, the Greek Coalition of the Radical Left (Syriza), and the Spanish Podemos. The EUL–NGL is divided over the desirability of further integration.

Greens/European Free Alliance (G/EFA, 50 seats)

This group is an alliance between the European Green Party (EGP) and the various regionalist parties of the European Free Alliance (EFA). The regionalist parties—such as the Scottish National Party (pre-Brexit) and the Catalan parties—do not have enough seats to form a group of their own and thus sit with the greens. The greens have, in recent years, become strongly pro-EU, for similar reasons to the social democrats. The group unites MEPs from seventeen countries and the largest party is the German Alliance '90/The Greens.

Europe of Freedom and Direct Democracy (EFDD, 45 seats)

The EFDD is the parliamentary group of the Alliance for Direct Democracy in Europe (ADDE). The group is the larger of the predominantly Eurosceptic groups in the Parliament, bringing together anti-EU lists and parties from seven countries, including the Italian Five Star Movement.

Europe of Nations and Freedom (ENF, 39 seats)

Established in the summer of 2015, ENF joins together various nationalistic far-Right anti-immigration parties from eight countries. Over half of the MEPs come from the French Front National, with other parties including the Dutch Party for Freedom, the Austrian Freedom Party, and the Italian Northern League.

Note: The seat shares are correct as at September 2015. Fourteen MEPs did not belong to any of the groups, sitting instead as 'independent' or 'non-attached' MEPs.

TABLE 15.1   Party groups in the European Parliament, 1979–2014

Party family	Seat distribution after each round of elections							
	1979	1984	1989	1994	1999	2004	2009	2014
Social democrats/ Socialists	113	130	180	198	180	200	184	191
Christian democrats/ Conservatives	107	110	121	157	233	268	265	221
Liberals	40	31	49	43	50	88	84	67
Conservatives	86	79	54	53	21	27	54	70
Communists/ Radical left	44	41	42	28	42	41	35	52
Greens/ Regionalists		20	43	23	48	42	55	50

Cont. ➤

Cont.								
Eurosceptics				19	16	37	32	48
Extreme right		16	17					
Others	11			19	20			
Non-attached	9	7	12	27	16	29	27	52
Total	410	434	518	567	626	732	736	751

For the first time since the introduction of direct elections, the EPP became, after the 1999 elections, the largest group in the chamber. The EPP has continued to be the largest group since then—a development explained partly by the difficulties that centre-Left parties have faced throughout Europe in recent years. The conservative wing of the group has been strengthened since the 1990s, but the party that had most difficulties in fitting into the group was undoubtedly the British Conservatives, the views of which, particularly on European integration, were quite different from those of the group majority (Maurer *et al.* 2008).[2] The centre-Left social democratic group was the biggest in the Parliament from 1975 to the 1999 elections. The formation of the centre-Left group (S&D after the 2009 elections) presented far fewer problems, because almost each member state has an electorally significant centre-Left social democratic party.

Moving to the medium-sized groups, the liberal group (ALDE) has a strongly pro-European philosophy, and this stance has occasionally created problems between the group majority and the centre parties from the Nordic countries that are more Euro-sceptic than the group majority. The greens achieved an electoral breakthrough in 1989 and have since then formed a group of their own in the Parliament. The region-alist parties of the European Free Alliance (EFA) have never mustered enough seats to form their own group; hence their MEPs have mainly joined forces with the greens. Communists, or the radical Left, have formed a group under various labels since 1973. The title 'Nordic Green Left' was added to the group name Confederal Group of the European United Left after the 1995 enlargement, because the Finnish and Swedish Left parties wanted to emphasize their separate identity within the then otherwise largely Mediterranean group. The group has traditionally been a quite loose alliance, and the group stated in its constituent declaration that EUL–NGL 'is a forum for cooperation between its different political components, each of which retains its own independent identity and commitment to its own positions' (quoted in Hudson 2012: 37).

Eurosceptic parties have formed groups since the 1994 elections, but such strongly anti-EU political forces have remained very much in the minority in the Parliament. However, in the 2014 elections, Eurosceptic parties performed notably well in a large number of member states, with the Eurosceptics on the Right mainly against loss of national sovereignty and multiculturalism, while the vote for the Left-leaning

Eurosceptics was primarily explained by the euro crisis and austerity measures in the Mediterranean countries (Treib 2014; Hobolt 2015). The conservatives, however, are a party family that displays a milder version of opposition to further integration, have formed a group under various names ever since the UK joined the then European Community, and following the 2014 EP elections, the ECR was the third largest group in the chamber. Finally, the non-attached MEPs have normally represented various extreme Right or nationalist parties, which had a group of their own between 1984 and 1994 (and for a short period in 2007), and again from summer 2015 onwards in the form of the Europe of Nations and Freedom group.

The EP party system has, throughout the history of the directly elected Parliament, been effectively dominated by the centre-Right EPP and the social democratic PES. After the 2014 election, however, their combined seat share fell to 55 per cent of MEPs. This duopoly is nicely illustrated by the system of electing the President of the Parliament. With the exception of the 1999–2004 Parliament, the PES and EPP have shared the presidency since 1989. For example, in the 2009–14 electoral term, the first President was Jerzy Buzek from the EPP, with Martin Schultz from the S&D group replacing him at mid-term in January 2012.[3] The party system has also become more stable and predictable. In addition to the three groups that have been present in the chamber from the 1950s, the groups of the greens (including the regionalists), the conservatives, the radical Left, and the Eurosceptics have also become 'institutionalized' in the chamber since the first direct elections.

Internal organization

The EP's rules of procedure, the standing orders of the Parliament, set numerical criteria for group formation. Following the 2014 elections, a political group must comprise at least twenty-five MEPs from at least a quarter of the member states.[4] Apart from ideological ties (McElroy and Benoit 2010, 2012), the availability of considerable financial, material, and procedural benefits has provided further incentives for group formation. While the money from the Parliament may appear inconsequential in absolute terms, it has nevertheless been crucial for certain smaller parties—such as regionalist and green parties—which often do not have access to comparable resources at the national level. Material benefits include, for example, office space and staff.

Group staff perform a variety of duties, ranging from routine administration to drafting background memos, following developments in committees, and drawing up whips in plenaries. In addition, each MEP has several assistants (normally at least three, financed from the EP budget), and both the committee and the EP staff assist groups and MEPs. Turning to procedural rights, appointments to committees and intra-parliamentary leadership positions, and the allocation of reports and plenary speaking time, are based on the rule of proportionality between the groups. Certain plenary actions, such as tabling amendments or oral questions, require the backing of a committee, a party group, or at least forty MEPs. The larger party groups have thus, over time, introduced changes to the EP rules of procedure that have further marginalized the smaller party groups and individual MEPs (Kreppel 2002), while party groups have in a similar fashion reformed their own rules through adopting more centralized procedures (Bressanelli 2014: 57–76). Non-attached representatives in particular are procedurally marginalized in the chamber.

Group cohesion

Three factors tend to work against cohesion within party groups in the Parliament: the balance of power between the EU institutions; the rules for candidate selection; and the internal heterogeneity of the groups. A key element in producing unitary group action in national legislatures is the fact that governments depend on the support of the parliamentary majority. The EP party groups lack this motive. While the Commission has to be approved by the Parliament and can be brought down by it (as happened indirectly in 1999), the composition of the Commission is only partly based on the outcome of the European elections.

Second, 'centralized nomination procedures should lead to greater party cohesion' (Bowler *et al.* 1999: 8). National parties, and not EP groups or Europarties, control candidate selection. Therefore national parties possess the ultimate sanction against MEPs. This applies particularly to countries using closed lists or mixed systems, in which electors choose between pre-ordered party lists. Interestingly, while links between national parties and their MEPs have traditionally been rather loose (Raunio 2000), there is nowadays greater policy coordination between MEPs and their parties, with case studies on British and German parties in particular confirming this trend, but national parties nonetheless largely refrain from 'mandating' their MEPs (Blomgren 2003; Bailer 2009). Voting behaviour in the Parliament provides further evidence of the influence of national parties. Research indicates that when MEPs receive conflicting voting instructions from national parties and their EP groups, they are more likely to side with their national party, particularly in parties in which the leadership has more or better opportunities to punish and reward its MEPs (such as through more centralized candidate selection or closed lists):

Despite the fact that the parliamentary principals in the EP control important benefits—such as committee assignments and speaking time—it is the principals that control candidate selection (the national parties) who ultimately determine how MEPs behave. When the national parties in the same parliamentary group decide to vote together, the EP parties look highly cohesive. But when these parties take opposing policy positions, the cohesion of the EP parties break down.

(Hix 2002: 696)

Hence we can expect that MEPs who are seeking re-election will be particularly re-luctant to ignore national party guidelines and that this attentiveness to national party positions will be more evident in the run-up to European elections (Lindstädt *et al.* 2011). Likewise, we expect MEPs seeking to return to domestic politics to de-fect from group positions more often (Meserve *et al.* 2009).

Finally, of all legislatures, the heterogeneity of the Parliament is probably matched only by that of the Indian Congress. Around 200 national parties from twenty-eight member states won seats in the 2014 elections. Such a high level of geographical and ideological diversity, not to mention the problems involved in communicating in more than twenty official languages, presents a formidable challenge for the groups.

However, roll-call analyses show that the groups do achieve high levels of cohe-sion, with average cohesion levels of around 85–90 per cent and some groups even above 90 per cent (Hix *et al.* 2007). In comparative terms, the EP groups are on aver-age less cohesive than party groups in the EU member state legislatures, but have tended to be more cohesive than parties in the United States' (US) Congress. What accounts for this relatively unitary behaviour? Until the 1990s, one could argue that because most votes in the Parliament had little, if any, impact, it did not really matter how MEPs voted. According to this line of reasoning, the fragile foundations of group cohesion would be put to the test once the Parliament acquired real legislative powers. However, in reality, group cohesion has remained stable while the EP has gained new powers.

The explanation that follows for high cohesion levels focuses on policy influence, and on how group organization is tailored to face the twin challenge of internal het-erogeneity and the strong position of national parties. Decision-making within groups can be described as rather consensual, with groups putting much effort into building positions that are acceptable to all, or nearly all, parties in the group. Unlike national party leaders, EP group chairs do not control or even influence candidate selection nor can they promise lucrative ministerial portfolios or well-paid civil ser-vice jobs. Groups have whips, but their main job is reminding MEPs of group posi-tions and indicating which votes are important. While the groups have fairly similar organizational structures to their counterparts in national parliaments, with leaders, executive committees, and working parties, the groups can nevertheless be charac-terized as non-hierarchical and non-centralized.

Balancing national and group interests

At the start of the five-year legislative term, the groups elect their leaders (chairs or presidents), who usually occupy the post until the next elections, or even longer. The chairs represent their group in the Conference of Presidents, the body responsible for setting the Parliament's agenda and for organizational decisions. In the 2014–19 Parliament, the G/EFA, EFDD, and EFN groups have two co-chairs. The number of vice-chairs varies between the groups. The executive committee of the group is the Bureau, which normally includes the group chair and vice-chairs, heads, and possible additional members of national party delegations; other potential members include the treasurer or committee coordinators. The Bureau is responsible for organizational and administrative issues, and prepares policy decisions for group meetings. It plays a key role in facilitating group consensus. In their discussion on factionalism within national parties, Bowler *et al.* (1999: 15) argue that:

[T]here are reasons for thinking that factions can help rank-and-file members discipline their leadership, either by providing faction leaders to take part in policy discussions (reporting back to their members) or by making it clear to party leaders that a block of votes will desert if some policy line is crossed. In this sense, factions help party leaders understand where their support or opposition lies within the party and the levels of this support or opposition.

The same dynamic is at work in the EP groups. When one replaces factions with national party delegations, we see that, by guaranteeing most national delegations representation in the executive committee, the group leadership learns about the positions of national parties and the intensity of their preferences. The groups convene regularly in Brussels prior to the plenary week, as well as during plenaries. The meetings in Brussels constitute a 'group week', usually lasting two or three days. When individual MEPs or national parties feel that they cannot follow the group position, they are expected to make this clear in the group meetings. MEPs also use plenary speeches for explaining why they dissented from the group line, defending their behaviour that is often motivated by national party-political considerations (Proksch and Slapin 2015: 148–62). Party groups have also established working groups for examining specific policy areas and for coordinating group policy on those issues.

National party delegations are the cornerstones upon which the groups are based. Some smaller groups are indeed no more than loose coalitions of national parties, while one can occasionally see divisions along national lines even in the older and more organized groups. Most national delegations have their own staff, elect their chairs, and convene prior to group meetings. However, the impact of national parties is mitigated by two factors. First, national parties are seldom unitary actors themselves. National parties throughout the EU are, to a varying extent, internally divided over integration and these divisions are reproduced in the Parliament. Good examples are the British Conservative and Labour delegations. Second, the majority of bills and resolutions do not produce divisions along national lines. Much of the Parliament's agenda is taken up by traditional socio-economic matters, such as internal market legislation, not by constitutional matters or redistributive decisions, such as the allocation of structural funds.

But the most important reason why MEPs and national party delegations vote with their group most of the time is policy influence. After all, the main rationale for group formation in any parliament is that it helps like-minded legislators to achieve their policy goals. Cohesive group action is essential for achieving the group's objectives, while cooperative behaviour within groups helps MEPs to pursue their own policy goals. Moreover, given the huge number of amendments and final resolutions voted upon in plenaries, the voting cues provided by groups and their whips, and particularly group members in the responsible EP committee, are an essential source of guidance for MEPs (Ringe 2010).

To summarize, the desire to influence EU policy and the relatively non-hierarchical group structure, based on institutionalized interaction between the leadership, the committees (see below), and the national party delegations, facilitates group cohesion. It is occasionally claimed that the accommodation of national viewpoints leads to lowest-common-denominator decisions. However, these policy compromises are a prerequisite for the Parliament to influence EU legislation.

Coalition politics and parliamentary committees

Committees are established to make parliaments more efficient. They facilitate specialization, and thereby enhance a parliament's ability to influence legislation and hold the government accountable. While there is much variation among European legislatures, most parliaments have strengthened the role of committees in order to reduce the informational advantage of the executive (Mattson and Strøm 1995; Martin 2014).

The same applies to the EP (Mamadouh and Raunio 2003; Whitaker 2011; Yordanova 2013). Unlike many national constitutions, the EU Treaties leave it up to the Parliament to design its internal rules. The EP has structured and reformed its internal organization so as to make the most of its hard-won powers in the EU political system (Kreppel 2002). As the EP has gained new powers, the full chamber has delegated more authority to committees. The thrust of legislative work is done in committees that are also key forums for holding institutions such as the Commission and the European Central Bank (ECB) to account, and in shaping the EU's budget and monitoring its implementation. Committees are well resourced in terms of staff and, when we include also party group staff, MEPs' personal assistants, and a research service that provides assistance to MEPs, it is clear that the Parliament has prioritized policy expertise when deciding its internal organization and rules. Importantly, committees and obviously the plenary meet in public, and hence inject much-needed transparency to EU decision-making. The 2014–19 Parliament has twenty committees.

Parliament's positions are, in most cases in practice, decided in the committees before the plenary stage. Because committees enjoy extensive procedural power inside the Parliament, both party groups and national parties have stronger incentives for influencing committee proceedings. Representation on committees is roughly proportional to group size, with committee memberships and chairs reallocated at mid-term (after two-and-a-half years). Research on committee appointments by Bowler and Farrell (1995: 227) shows that:

[T]he share of committee places is proportional by both nationality and ideological bloc. Within these limits, set by allocations along ideological or national lines, there is scope for the kinds of specialized membership and recruitment made in the US Congress.[5]

Within committees are four positions of authority: chair; vice-chairs; party group coordinators; and *rapporteurs*. Committees elect their own chairs, but in practice party groups decide the allocation of chairs and vice-chairs, with the d'Hondt method[6] used for distributing the chairs. Chair allocation is thus broadly proportional, again reflecting procedures used in most national parliaments (Mattson and Strøm 1995). Party group coordinators are responsible for coordinating the work of their groups in the committees. Together with the committee chair, the coordinators negotiate the distribution of rapporteurships between the groups.

Turning to the passage of legislation, when the draft act arrives in the Parliament from the Commission, a committee is designated as responsible for producing a report on the issue, with one or more committees assigned as opinion-giving committees. Committees use an auction-like points system for distributing reports to the groups, with group coordinators making bids on behalf of their groups. The allocation of reports is also roughly proportional to group strength in the Parliament. However, because the total points of each group is proportional to its seat share in the chamber, the most expensive reports (those that 'cost' the most points), such as those on the EU budget or on important pieces of codecision legislation, often are drafted by MEPs from the two largest groups, EPP and S&D. While both EP party groups and national parties are using rapporteurships for achieving their policy objectives, the policy expertise of MEPs is also taken into account when allocating reports to MEPs (Bowler and Farrell 1995; Mamadouh and Raunio 2003; Yoshinaka *et al.* 2010; Whitaker 2011; Daniel 2013; Yordanova 2013).

The *rapporteur* must be prepared to make compromises. Majority-building as early as the stage at which reports are drafted helps to facilitate the smooth passage of the report in the committee and in the plenary. The draft report, together with amendments (tabled by any member), is voted upon in the committee. Committee decision-making has been characterized as consensual (Settembri and Neuhold 2009). Pragmatic scrutiny and cooperation between EPP and S&D means that most issues are essentially pre-cooked at the committee stage—thus paving the way for plenary votes adopted by 'supermajorities' (Bressanelli 2014: 148–62; Bowler and McElroy 2015). Before the plenary, the groups decide their positions: what amendments to propose, and whether or not to support the report. National party delegations often hold their own meetings prior to the group meetings. Finally, the report and amendments (by the responsible committee, a party group, or at least forty members) are voted upon in the plenary.

Party groups monitor committee proceedings, with group coordinators and perhaps working parties playing key roles. The procedures for allocating committee chairs, seats, and reports, all roughly based on proportionality, can also be seen as mechanisms for the party groups to control committees. Importantly, national parties are key players in allocating committee seats and reports, and there are signs that they are, to an increasing extent, using committee assignments to achieve their policy goals. Nonetheless, party group influence within committees is ultimately based on coordination mechanisms instead of hierarchical structures for controlling MEP behaviour in the committees. Delegating authority to backbenchers through committee work and reports can also be understood as a key way of rewarding group members and tying them into the formation of group positions (Mamadouh and Raunio 2003; Settembri and Neuhold 2009; Ringe 2010; Whitaker 2011; Yordanova 2013; Roger and Winzen 2015).

Coalition-building at the plenary stage is more clearly driven by partisan concerns. Roll-call analyses show that the main cleavage structuring competition in the Parliament is the familiar Left–Right dimension, with the anti/pro-integration dimension constituting the second main structure of competition in the Parliament (Hix *et al.* 2007).[7] While the primary decision rule in the Parliament is simple majority, for certain issues (mainly budget amendments and second-reading legislative amendments adopted under the codecision procedure), the EP needs to have absolute majorities (50 per cent plus one additional MEP). This absolute majority requirement facilitates cooperation between the two main groups, EPP and S&D, which, between them, controlled around two-thirds of the seats until the 2014 elections. Cooperation between EPP and S&D is also influenced by inter-institutional considerations, because the Parliament has needed to moderate its resolutions in order to get its amendments accepted by the Council and the Commission (Kreppel 2002). Competition on the Left–Right continuum has benefited the smaller groups. This advantage has applied particularly to the liberals: situated ideologically between the EPP and S&D, the liberals have often been in a pivotal position in forming winning coalitions. Recent enlargements have not really changed either group cohesion levels or coalition patterns in the chamber. Party cohesion has remained stable, as the two main groups continue to vote together around two-thirds or 70 per cent of the time, and representatives from new member states do not defect any more from their group than do average MEPs (Hix and Noury 2009; Lindstädt *et al.* 2011; Bressanelli 2014; Bowler and McElroy 2015). But how MEPs vote hardly matters from the point of view of EP elections, as is argued in the next section.

Electoral accountability

Voting decisions in EP elections are heavily influenced by the domestic party-political environment. The primacy of domestic factors results in part from the strategies of national parties, which control candidate selection and carry out the electoral campaigns. Most national parties have so far fought EP elections on domestic issues, although the euro crisis introduced a stronger 'European element' to the 2014 elections. National parties are mainly based on the traditional social cleavages recognized in political science literature and, because the anti/pro-integration dimension tends to cut across these cleavages, parties often experience internal fragmentation on EU questions.[8] Moreover, survey data shows that parties are, on average, more representative of their voters on traditional Left–Right matters than on issues related to European integration, with the parties more supportive of integration than the electorate (Mattila and Raunio 2012). Hence established parties have an incentive to contest the elections along the familiar Left–Right dimension and to downplay contestation over integration. Indeed, in most member states, parties have preferred not to engage in debates over the EU—and where such debates have taken place, this contestation has often benefited smaller parties at the expense of mainstream governing parties (Szczerbiak and Taggart 2008).

Elections to the Parliament are therefore scarcely 'European': they are held during the same week, and the candidates compete for seats in an EU institution, but there is no common electoral system[9] or EU-wide candidate lists, constituency boundaries do not cross national borders, and campaigning is conducted by national parties on the basis of largely national agendas.[10] So national politics is reproduced in EP elections, with the same set of actors and largely also the same set of issues. But, interestingly, recent evidence points in the direction of the EU, as an issue, becoming increasingly politicized and salient. This trend has also become apparent in European elections, as demonstrated by the increasing importance of the EU as an issue in explaining citizens' voting behaviour. Analysing the 2004 and 2009 EP elections, Hobolt *et al.* (2009: 111) showed how preference congruence between parties and their supporters over EU impacted on the vote shares of national parties:

[G]overning parties may lose votes because of the disconnect between major governing parties and their voters on the issue of EU integration, and the fact that EP elections make this issue, and therefore this disconnect, more prominent. On both the contextual and individual levels, it appears that Europe can matter when voters go to the polls. Governing-party voters who are more sceptical about further integration are more likely to defect or abstain in EP elections.[11]

However, while parties thus have a good reason to take the EU seriously, these developments need to be understood in the context of the second-order logic of EP elections, with smaller and opposition parties gaining votes at the expense of mainstream and government parties (Reif and Schmitt 1980; van der Eijk *et al.* 1996; Manow and Döring 2007; Schmitt 2009; Hix and Marsh 2011; Hong 2015).

Europarties and their *Spitzenkandidaten*

The main party groups in the Parliament are either officially, or in practice, the parliamentary wings of their Europarties (see Box 15.1). Article 138a of the 1992 Maastricht Treaty assigned political parties a specific role to play in the political system of the European Union: 'Political parties at the European level are important as a factor for integration within the Union. They contribute to forming a European awareness and to expressing the political will of the citizens of the Union'. This 'Party Article' was subsequently included as Article 10(4) of the 2007 Lisbon Treaty: 'Political parties at European level contribute to forming European political awareness and to expressing the will of citizens of the Union.'

The constitutional recognition in the form of the Party Article in the Maastricht Treaty contributed to the consolidation of Europarties. With the exception of the EPP, which had already been founded back in 1976, the other federations of national parties were quickly turned into Europarties. The Confederation of Socialist Parties of the European Community (CSP), founded in 1974, was transformed into the PES in November 1992. The Federation of European Liberal, Democrat and Reform Parties, founded in 1976, became the ELDR in December 1993, changing its name to ALDE in 2012. The European Federation of Green Parties (EFGP) was established in June 1993, changing its name to the EGP in 2004. In addition, a number of other Europarties, such as ADDE, AECR, EFA, and EL, have been established since the introduction in 2004 of public funding of Europarties from the EU's budget (Johansson and Raunio 2005).

It is still more realistic to describe Europarties as federations of national parties or as party networks, at least when comparing them with the often centralized and hierarchical parties found at the national level. At the same time, there can be no doubt that the Europarties are a force to be reckoned with in European politics and their influence extends beyond the Parliament. Internally, Europarties have introduced organizational changes that reduce their dependence on individual member parties. In particular, (qualified) majority voting is now the standard decision rule in the main organs of the Europarties. The policy influence of Europarties is difficult to measure, and depends on their internal cohesion and the willingness of national member parties to pursue and implement the agreed policy objectives. The empowerment of the Parliament, in terms both of legislative powers and of holding the Commission accountable, means that the Europarties' EP groups are in a key position to influence the EU policy process. More broadly, the Europarties serve as important arenas for the diffusion of ideas and policy coordination. Particularly the meetings of party leaders, held usually at the same venue as the summits of the European Council, enable national parties to coordinate their actions prior to the summits.[12] Hence Europarties have influenced Treaty reforms and other major European-level policy decisions, as well as appointments to top jobs in EU institutions. This point applies especially to the EPP, which has been the largest Europarty since the turn of the millennium, as we shall discuss. Moreover, Europarties prepare the ground for future enlargements by integrating interests from the prospective member states. Through their membership in the Europarties, parties from the applicant countries engage in partisan cooperation that is important in nurturing wider, pan-European political allegiances (Hix and Lord 1997; Ladrech 2000; Johansson and Zervakis 2002; Lightfoot 2005; Hanley 2008; Bressanelli 2014; Timus and Lightfoot 2014; Johansson 2016).

Advocates of EU level democracy have argued that Europarties should be elevated to a decisive role in European governance. Indeed, there has emerged quite a lively debate about whether the EP should become a fully fledged 'federal' parliament that elects and controls a genuine EU government. The defenders of such a parliamentary model argue that, because the EU already possesses significant authority over a broad range of policy areas, the choice of who exercises such authority should be based on competition between political forces—in this scenario, essentially Europarties contesting the EP elections (Follesdal and Hix 2006; Hix 2008). In this parliamentary model, the government (the Commission) would be accountable to the EP and could be voted out of office by the latter—as already happens. Europarties would put forward their candidates for the Commission President (the EU's 'prime minister'). These candidates would campaign on the basis of their Europarties' manifestos. After receiving the support of the Parliament, the winning candidate would form his or her government, with the other party groups forming the parliamentary opposition.[13] More cautious voices argue that this is not the right way in which to address the democratic deficit, partly on account of the lack of common European identity and because issues that are most salient to voters are still decided nationally (Moravcsik 2002). Others have pointed out that installing party government at the EU level may not be a good solution in an era during which political parties are facing serious difficulties in the context of national democracies (Mair and Thomassen 2010).

In the 2014 elections, the Europarties and their EP groups took a bold and controversial step in this direction by putting forward *Spitzenkandidaten*, or 'lead candidates', for the Commission President (see also Chapter 6). Jean-Claude Juncker, the lead candidate of the largest party group, EPP, was eventually appointed as the new head of the Commission.[14] This initiative was criticized heavily by Eurosceptics, with the EP (again) accused of overstepping its formal competences. For example, then British Prime Minister David Cameron talked of 'a power grab through the back door' that was never agreed upon by member states, and which would both shift power from the European Council to the Parliament and politicize the Commission (Cameron 2014). Cameron was certainly right in claiming that the *Spitzenkandidaten* process will strengthen the role of party politics in the Commission, but again the change should not be exaggerated, because party politics already strongly influences the composition of the Commission. Because both the Commission and its president must be approved by the Parliament before they can take office, the EP has explicitly demanded that the voice of the voters not be ignored in the make-up of the Commission. Hence the wording of Article 17(7) of the Lisbon Treaty, according to which the European Council, acting by a qualified majority, shall propose to the Parliament a candidate for Commission president after 'taking into account' the election results, merely gave Treaty status to a practice dating back to mid-1990s. Because the EPP is the largest group and centre-Right groups control the majority of the seats (and centre-Right cabinets dominate the Council), the partisan composition of the Commissions appointed since 2004 has leaned toward the centre-Right, with a clear majority of the Commissioners and the President representing either EPP or ALDE member parties. Not surprisingly, there has consequently been a firm centre-Right grip on EU politics that has unquestionably left its mark on legislation. Whether this undermines the role of the Commission as a neutral upholder of EU law and common interest is open to debate, but at least the *Spitzenkandidaten* procedure—and, more broadly, the politicization of the Commission—has the potential to strengthen the 'electoral connection' between voters and Brussels, thus making it easier to assign credit and blame in EU decision-making (Hobolt 2014; Schmitt *et al.* 2015). Europarties may thus not be familiar to European voters, but party politics clearly matters in EU politics.

Theorizing the EP party groups

The EP has become one of the most researched parliaments in the world; it is certainly the EU institution about which we know the most. This result is largely explained by the openness of the Parliament, which enables scholars to gather data on various aspects of the Parliament's work. However, while scholars have developed sophisticated theoretical models for understanding voting behaviour and party performance in European elections, the empowerment of the EP, the distribution of committee positions and rapporteurships, and roll-call voting in the plenary (Yordanova 2011; Hix and Høyland 2013), party groups remain something of a black box, both theoretically and empirically. This applies to both their internal decision-making and their coalition formation.

Longitudinal analyses of both cohesion and coalition formation indicate stability: groups have maintained their rather high levels of unity (as measured by voting in the plenary), and most resolutions in the chamber are passed by comfortable 'super-majorities' or 'grand coalitions' between EPP and S&D, and possibly other groups (Bowler and McElroy 2015). The grand coalition is numerically the safest way in which to build winning coalitions in the chamber (especially when the decision rule is absolute majority), but the dominance of the grand coalition suggests that the two large groups work routinely together beyond cooperating in individual issues, probably mainly at the committee stage. Uncovering the mechanisms of such regular cooperation, and its linkages to decision-making inside EPP and S&D groups, would result in much better understanding of how the Parliament forms its positions.

The 'grand coalition' indicates, in turn, substantial differences between party groups. Considering the strong influence of EPP and S&D, the smaller groups may either choose to cooperate with them or to offer a parliamentary 'opposition' by voting against them. The former option is mainly exercised by more centrist groups such as ALDE, G/EFA or ECR, whereas the Eurosceptic groups (especially EFDD and ENF) and the radical Left (EUL–NGL) more often favour the latter alternative, voicing their opposition to the adopted measures or using the Parliament and the job of an MEP primarily as a platform for providing information about the EU (and its failures) to their electorates (Jensen and Spoon 2010; Whitaker and Lynch 2014; Brack 2015). Future research should thus delve deeper into such variation between groups, both in terms of their coalition strategies and internal dynamics.

Conclusions

The party groups in the EP are often underestimated, or even ridiculed, by national media. Certainly, from the outside, these groups may appear to be somewhat strange creatures. After all, they bring together representatives from as many as twenty-eight countries (pre-Brexit), with a plethora of languages spoken in the Parliament's meeting rooms and corridors.

However, such characterizations are quite simply not accurate. The Parliament as an institution has structured its internal organization so as to maximize its influence in the EU. The thrust of legislative work is done in the committees, in which individual *rapporteurs* draft reports that form the basis for parliamentary resolutions. In a similar fashion, the party groups have designed their internal organization and divided labour within them so as to balance the interests of the whole group, the national parties, and the individual MEPs. And research clearly shows that the EP groups have indeed mastered the art both of bargaining with other EU institutions and of achieving unitary group behaviour.

Another often-aired claim is that MEPs and their national parties live in different worlds, with lack of will and conflicting preferences over integration preventing meaningful cooperation. While there is some truth to such arguments, these divisions do not mean that MEPs are divorced from their national parties or constituencies. On the contrary, MEPs remain firmly connected to national politics through a variety of channels, with most of them holding simultaneously various offices in their parties (either at the local, district, or national level), and maintaining active links with their party organizations and voters. Moreover, it is interesting to note that, overall, the preferences of national MPs and MEPs over integration are quite similar, and that, contrary to much accepted wisdom, MEPs do not 'go native' in Brussels—that is, become considerably more pro-European than their party comrades back home (Scully 2005). At the same time, we see more European politicians building their careers at the EU level. No doubt linked to the empowerment of the Parliament (see Chapter 6), turnover of MEPs has decreased, with a higher share of politicians building careers in the EP—and with these individuals also more likely to wield influence in the Parliament through holding leadership positions or acting as *rapporteurs* (Whitaker 2014; Daniel 2015). This development should contribute both to the policy expertise of the party groups and to the influence of the EP vis-à-vis the other EU institutions.

The biggest, and most demanding, challenge for the party groups is to connect with EU citizens. This point applies both to connecting vertically with the citizens in individual EU countries and to forging horizontal cross-national linkages. First, considering the lack of a common EU-wide identity and the absence of any real European government, EP elections are bound to remain 'second-order' contests in comparison with elections to national parliaments. This status means also that the party groups in the Parliament will remain unknown to most Europeans. Second, while the Europarties and their EP groups undoubtedly perform an important role by integrating political interests across the Union, this integrative function takes place almost exclusively among national political elites, thus leaving the electorate to focus mainly on national or local politics. The need to establish a stronger connection between citizens and the EU was a key argument behind the *Spitzenkandidaten* initiative, but for now Europeans do not know how and to what extent the Europarties and their EP party groups influence EU policies.

ENDNOTES

1. For analyses of party groups in the pre-1979 Parliament, see van Oudenhove (1965), Fitzmaurice (1975), and Pridham and Pridham (1981).

2. In fact, the title 'European Democrats' was added to the EPP's group name after the 1999 elections so that the Tories could maintain their separate identity in the otherwise strongly pro-integrationist EPP group. Before the 2004 elections, the group struck a deal with the Conservatives, who had threatened to leave the group and ally with other conservative parties that are critical of further integration. This deal caused a lot of controversy in the group—and resulted in a section of MEPs defecting to the ELDR after the 2004 elections. According to that deal, the Conservatives had a right to voice their own views on European constitutional and institutional matters, and had more favourable financing and staffing terms within the group, including the right to one of the group's vice-presidencies.

3. Schultz continued as the President after the 2014 elections. This cosy pact was temporarily suspended after the 1999 elections, when a centre-right coalition elected Nicole Fontaine (EPP) as the new President in July 1999. Imitating the deals between EPP and PES, the EPP and ELDR struck an agreement according to which the Liberals would support Fontaine and the EPP would, in turn, back the candidacy of ELDR group leader Pat Cox at mid-term in January 2002.

4. Groups comprising MEPs from only one country (such as Forza Europa in 1994–95) have not been permitted since the 1999 elections.

5. See also McElroy (2006); Yordanova (2013).

6. Named after its inventor, the Belgian mathematician Victor d'Hondt, the method is used for allocating seats in electoral systems based on proportional representation. The party group winning most seats in the Parliament gets the first committee chair, and the number of seats held by that group is then divided by two and compared with the seat shares of the other groups. The group with most seats at this point receives the second committee chair. The process continues until all committee chairs have been allocated.

7. See also McElroy and Benoit (2012). There is also a debate concerning the validity of the roll-call data. Because recorded votes represent only a sample of the totality of votes in the Parliament, the representativeness of that sample is a crucial matter (Carrubba *et al.* 2006; Finke 2015; Yordanova and Mühlböck 2015).

8. See, for example, Hix and Lord (1997); Hix (1999); Marks and Wilson (2000); Marks and Steenbergen (2004).

9. The design of the electoral system impacts on MEPs' contacts with their electorates, with MEPs from more 'open' systems paying more attention to individual voters and constituency interests (Farrell and Scully 2007, 2010).

10. Europarties already have now election manifestos, but these can be counterproductive for national parties. In their discussion of parties in the US House of Representatives, Cox and McCubbins (1993) argue that members of Congress have an incentive to be loyal to their party groups, because the reputation of their groups is important in terms of re-election. Distancing oneself, or the national party, from the Europarty can hence be a wise electoral strategy for national parties, especially in those member states in which the public is less supportive of European integration.

11. See also De Vries *et al.* (2011); Hobolt and Spoon (2012); Hong (2015).

12. While scholars have paid more attention to the role of parties and party preferences in EU decision-making since the late 1990s, this strand of research is still quite undeveloped, particularly in terms of measuring and explaining party links between the EP, Council, the Commission, and even the European Council (see Lindberg *et al.* 2011).

13. For a more detailed illustration of how such a parliamentary model would work, see Hix (2008: 166–78). An alternative approach would be that of having a direct election of the Commission President. In such a 'presidential' model, the candidates would also be put forward by Europarties (Decker and Sonnicksen 2011).

14. The other lead candidates were Ska Keller (EGP), Martin Schulz (PES), Alexis Tsipras (EL), and Guy Verhofstadt (ALDE).

 FURTHER READING

The first book to focus on the role of political parties in the EU, Hix and Lord (1997) remains relevant today, with chapters on national parties, EP party groups, and Europarties, while Bressanelli (2014) offers a more recent analysis of Europarties and EP party groups. Kreppel (2002) provides a data-rich account of the development of the EP's party system. Comparing the electoral systems used in EP elections, Farrell and Scully (2007) analyse how the design of the electoral systems impacts on the composition of the Parliament, and the attitudes and behaviour of the MEPs. Based on a large data-set of roll-call votes since the 1979 elections, Hix *et al.* (2007) explain party group voting in the chamber, with particular focus on voting cohesion and coalition formation. Ringe (2010) examines how MEPs make decisions in the Parliament, with particular focus on the interaction between committees and party groups. Whitaker (2011) and Yordanova (2013) offer systematic treatments of the EP's committees, analysing how EP party groups and national parties use the committees to further their policy objectives.

Bressanelli, E. (2014) *Europarties after Enlargement: Organization, Ideology and Competition* (Basingstoke: Palgrave Macmillan).

Farrell, D.M., and Scully, R. (2007) *Representing Europe's Citizens? Electoral Institutions and the Failure of Parliamentary Representation* (Oxford: Oxford University Press).

Hix, S., and Lord, C. (1997) *Political Parties in the European Union* (Basingstoke: Macmillan).

Hix, S., Noury, A.G., and Roland, G. (2007) *Democratic Politics in the European Parliament* (Cambridge: Cambridge University Press).

Kreppel, A. (2002) *The European Parliament and the Supranational Party System: A Study of Institutional Development* (Cambridge: Cambridge University Press).

Ringe, N. (2010) *Who Decides, and How? Preferences, Uncertainty, and Policy Choice in the European Parliament* (Oxford: Oxford University Press).

Whitaker, R. (2011) *The European Parliament's Committees: National Party Control and Legislative Empowerment* (Abingdon: Routledge).

Yordanova, N. (2013) *Organising the European Parliament: The Role and Legislative Influence of Committees* (Colchester: ECPR Press).

 WEB LINKS

http://www.aldeparty.eu

http://www.epp.eu

http://europeangreens.eu

http://www.socialistsanddemocrats.eu/

The homepages of the four main Europarties—Alliance of Liberals and Democrats for Europe; European People's Party; European Green Party; Party of European Socialists—provide a brief history of the parties, their election and policy programmes, and links to national member parties, the EP party group, and affiliated organizations.

http://www.votewatch.eu

Votewatch is a constantly updated website using statistics from the EP's homepage to provide comprehensive data on the attendance, voting, and other activities of MEPs, party groups, and national parties. It also includes data on behaviour in the Council of member state governments.

CHAPTER 16

Social and regional interests: The Economic and Social Committee and the Committee of the Regions

Carolyn Rowe and Charlie Jeffery

■ Summary

Since its founding, the European integration project has provided for the formal inclusion of social and regional interests through, first, the European Economic and Social Committee (EESC), created in 1957, and more recently, a Committee of the Regions (CoR), established in 1994. While neither has full institutional status nor codecision rights, they provide a focal point for organized social and regional interests. Their impact, however, remains debatable. Minor 'successes' in shaping policy outcomes by no means suggest a role and function on a par with the Commission, European Parliament (EP), or European Council. The validity of the EESC and CoR has been questioned, because interest groups have shown themselves able to engage in the policy process without a formalized representative structure. Nonetheless, such is their symbolic force that they have weathered the recent crises that have tested the European Union (EU). Despite calls for reform of the EU's system of governance, the EESC and CoR remain seemingly insulated from such debates and their future seems secure.

Introduction

The EESC and the CoR are two formal bodies that were established to represent two specific sets of interests within the EU's inter-institutional nexus: the interests of employers and employees, and regional interests, respectively. Neither enjoys full institutional status, and each instead relies largely on goodwill and informal contacts to gain access to the heart of the decision-making process. As the number of competing interests in Brussels grows, both bodies are faced with the need to maintain their relevance. Squeezed to the margins of the policy process, existential questions now cast a very large shadow over their roles, functions, and operations. What is their relevance in the contemporary European political system? What value do they add to EU decision-making?

This chapter considers the role and purpose of these two bodies. It begins with a historical consideration of their establishment, and examines the extent to which the context in which they were founded continues to provide a rationale and legitimacy for their operation. The chapter then looks at the manner in which the operations of both bodies have had to develop over time in response to shifting institutional circumstances. The development of both bodies tells the story of how interest mediation in the EU has expanded, pushing these formal vehicles of social and regional interest representations to the fringes of policy networks. The chapter then moves on to an analysis of the contemporary operation of both bodies, assessing how they contribute to European politics and analysing their real added value.

Although launched in very different eras, the EESC and CoR have a remarkable amount in common. Much of this commonality was deliberate: the EESC served as the institutional template for the establishment of the CoR. The internal structures of the two bodies are similar, as is their advisory status. They share a newly renovated headquarters at the heart of the EU district in Brussels and sizeable permanent secretariats of more than 500 officials to support the work of their members. More fundamentally, they have had similar founding rationales: securing this degree of transnational input was felt, at the time of their creation, to be valuable for the European decision-making process. In neither case, though, have many observers been convinced that this rationale of added value has been delivered.

The origins and history of the EESC and CoR

The EESC and CoR were each fashioned in Treaty negotiations held at critical stages in the European integration process. The 1957 Treaty of Rome, which established the EESC, built out radically in 1958 from the narrow foundations of the European Coal and Steel Community (ECSC) to inaugurate a much wider project of economic integration. The Maastricht Treaty of 1992, which provided for the creation of a committee of regional interests in the EU, was an ambitious response to market deepening, new global economic pressures, and, above all, the collapse of the Iron Curtain. At such critical moments as these, negotiating agendas are fluid and windows of opportunity for new, and often unanticipated, initiatives can emerge. The EESC and CoR both fall into this category.

The idea of establishing an economic and social committee as part of the new European Economic Community (EEC) emerged only in 1956 and was finally agreed just two months before the Treaty of Rome was concluded in March 1957 (Smismans 2000: 4). It was introduced to the agenda by two of the smaller players in the negotiations, Belgium and the Netherlands. Their aim was to reproduce the corporatist models provided by their domestic social and economic councils—forums for consulting business and trade unions in economic policy-making—in the new EEC framework. The proposals fell on fertile ground: five of the founding six member states (except West Germany) had similar domestic institutions (Lodge and Herman 1980: 267).[1] Germany originally opposed the proposal because of its negative experience of a similar economic and social body, the *Reichswirtschaftsrat*, during the Weimar Republic (Hrbek 1993: 127).

Two other factors argued for an EESC and led to its adoption against West German opposition. First, the idea of bringing in the expertise of the 'social partners' of business and labour to economic decision-making was consistent with both the predominantly economic logic of the early stages of the integration process and the prevailing climate of corporatist interest representation. 'Europe' could even lend its own example in the form of the Consultative Committee, comprising representatives of employers and workers (and also of traders and consumers), which had been established to support the work of the ECSC.

Second, the proposed ECSC Assembly, the forerunner to the EP, was to be indirectly elected, at least initially, and limited to a consultative role. As such, it did not provide 'normal' parliamentary channels for bringing interest-group influence to bear on European decision-making, in that there was no clear parliamentary focal point for lobbying activity. In this sense, some felt that the EESC was needed as a

supplementary *representative* body for the new Community, perhaps even 'as an in-
cipient parliamentary-legislative assembly—the third organ in a tri-cameral legislature alongside the Council of Ministers and a European Parliament linked to the
Commission' (Lodge and Herman 1980: 267).

The idea of establishing a committee of European regional interests developed
traction throughout the 1980s. The Single European Act (SEA) of 1986 had ushered
in a new suite of policy responsibilities for the European level of governance, sustained by the activist Commission presidency of Jacques Delors. This expanded
agenda saw European competence creep into the spheres of authority of many of
Europe's local and regional governments. Furthermore, local and regional governments found themselves responsible for on-the-ground implementation of many
new European policies, decisions over which they had little input, amidst heighten-
ing tensions over the legitimate sphere of European competence. 'Strong' regions—
that is, territorial entities with their own autonomous governing capacities—were
disproportionately affected by the shifts of policy responsibility upwards to the European level following the implementation of the SEA. These regions were, understandably, in the vanguard of pressuring the European institutions for change,
through some kind of formal compensation for their lost responsibilities. Those
member states of the regions that had been most affected as a result—Germany, Belgium, and Spain in particular—came under domestic pressure to push for some form
of regional institution in Brussels.

Whatever the tensions over legitimacy, the SEA had created a new framework of
political cooperation amongst levels of authority across the member states of the
European Community. As the scope of these policies grew, regional and local governments were inevitably drawn in as desirable partners in policy-making. In certain
fields—in particular, structural policy after the reforms of 1988—this role became
increasingly formalized, leading to the coining of the term 'multilevel governance'
(Marks 1993).

At the same time, governance within EU member states came under pressure, increasing the salience of local and regional actors within new policy paradigms. Patterns of governance within the member states were being recalibrated in ways that
upgraded the significance of sub-state governments. Globalization was felt, in some
circles, to make redundant traditional forms of economic policy intervention by central governments, and to require more differentiated economic strategies tailored to
local and regional strengths. In some member states, movements for regional autonomy (re-)emerged to prominence. In each case, the result was a growing capacity
among regional and local governments to engage in policy-making processes, at
both the domestic and the European levels. In other words, the new multilevel governance emerged from the convergence of new trends of sub-state political mobilization launched from both above and below. From the 'bottom up', strong regions were
putting pressure on their national governments to secure a stronger and more direct
foothold in the policy process of the EU; from the top down, the functional rationale
supporting a regional committee—'to improve the poor implementation of regional

policy by member states by involving other stakeholders in its design and execution'
(Warleigh 1999: 10)—was essentially the same technocratic impulse that had earlier
argued for the inclusion of the economic expertise of interest groups, via the EESC,
into economic policy.

Many of the reasons given for the CoR's lacklustre performance on the EU institutional scene following the hype that surrounded its creation were attributed by commentators to the original institutional design and its flaws. In the eventual
compromise that secured its creation by the Maastricht Treaty, those championing a
third level of European decision-making had had to give way to a watered-down
format that saw local mayors and councillors sit alongside the presidents of powerful
and economically important regions and historic nations. But this compromise also
reflected a strategic political decision: that powerful sets of interests in Europe did
not wish to see the CoR, or the sub-state level more broadly, develop into genuinely
influential policy actors.

In the initial days of its operation, the CoR, with only a consultative role to play,
depended for a large extent on its relations with the Commission, the Council, and
the EP for its formal relevance (Domorenok 2009: 146). The instability of this institutional position was aggravated further by the decision to make the Committee a
representative vehicle for *all* subnational territorial interests from the member states,
seating presidents of the German *Länder* or Spanish *Communidades Autonomas*
alongside town councillors from municipalities with around 250 residents. Common positions on policy issues were difficult to establish given the diverse sets of
interests represented in the CoR.

These internal divisions threatened to tear apart the newly created consultative
body. Instead, they served merely to weaken the body's potential as a significant
actor in EU affairs. Its most powerful actors, and the collective power that they
could wield in cooperation with a coalition of regional interests from other member
states, chose rather to pursue their interests in alternative venues. The most powerful sub-state actors simply bypassed the CoR as a force for interest representation
and instead acted through more direct channels in Brussels, such as their own permanent representations in the city (Rowe 2011), or through coalitions of similar,
powerful regional actors, such as the Conference of Presidents of Regions with Legislative Power (RegLeg), the political network of EU regions with legislative
competences.

The overall effect was to marginalize the CoR, pushing it to the fringes of EU
policy debates. Clearly, the EESC and the CoR are not the only routes available
through which social and regional interests can bring their concerns to bear in Europe, and the range of alternative vehicles for interest representation has expanded
greatly since the two advisory bodies were established. Both interest groups and regional and local authorities routinely use alternative routes to access EU decision-
making. These alternative routes offer, for some at least, greater returns than working
through the EESC or CoR alone and are logically given preference, impacting on
both the credibility and the function and operation of both organizations.

The function and operation of the EESC and CoR

Both the CoR and EESC have formal roles as 'consultative committees'. The CoR was established in the model of the EESC, which pre-dated it by almost forty years. Yet both the EESC and the CoR have developed an operational remit today that takes them slightly beyond the scope of their original purpose. Because their Treaty positions were circumscribed in vague terms, both the EESC and the CoR have made use of their limited degree of institutional leeway to carve out a position of some authority within shifting patterns of EU governance.

Formal powers

The EESC was not generously endowed at the outset. The 1957 Rome Treaty provided for mandatory consultation of the Committee by both the Council and the Commission, in certain specified fields, and optional consultation in other areas in which the institutions considered such consultation appropriate (see Box 16.1). The Amsterdam Treaty also opened up the possibility for the EESC to be consulted by the EP, although this happens only rarely. The list of areas in which consultation is mandatory has expanded over time, in particular since the SEA. It includes agriculture, the free movement of labour, internal market issues, economic and social cohesion, social policy, regional policy, the environment, research and technological development, employment policy, equal opportunities, and public health. The 2007 Lisbon Treaty expanded the policy areas in which the EESC must be consulted to cover sports policy, European space policy, and energy. Optional consultation allows the EESC to be consulted where the Council, Commission, or EP 'consider it appropriate', and can thus cover any other aspect of the Treaties.[2] Crucially, the right to give opinions does not extend to a right to have those opinions heard: neither the Commission nor the Council, nor indeed the EP, is obliged to give any feedback on EESC opinions, let alone to take them into account.

BOX 16.1	EU policy fields in which EESC consultation is mandatory

- Agricultural policy
- Free movement of persons and services
- Transport policy
- Harmonization of indirect taxation
- Approximation of laws on the internal market
- Employment policy
- Social policy, education, vocational training and youth
- Public health

- Consumer protection
- Trans-European networks
- Industrial policy
- Economic, social and territorial cohesion
- Research and technological development and space
- The environment

Source: http://www.europarl.europa.eu/atyourservice/en/displayFtu.html?ftuId=
FTU_1.3.13.html

The 2001 Nice Treaty established a new category of members to the EESC—namely, consumers. Thus the EESC's representative focus was considerably broadened. Consumers legitimately could be considered to constitute the most significant organized civil society representatives across the EU.

The CoR was initially given more or less the same set of powers as the EESC, although the range of policy areas on which the EU institutions were obliged to consult the CoR was smaller than that of the EESC (see Box 16.2). Mandatory referrals naturally covered a rather different group of policy fields, reflecting the CoR's local and regional remit. The initial fields for mandatory consultation related to education, training, and youth, economic and social cohesion, the structural funds, trans-European networks, public health, and culture. These have been extended incrementally through Treaty revision, and now cover aspects of employment policy, social policy, and the environment, with the Lisbon Treaty also allowing for mandatory consultation on energy and climate change policy.

BOX 16.2   EU policy fields in which CoR consultation is mandatory

- Transport
- Employment
- Social policy
- Education, vocational training, youth, and sport
- Culture
- Public health
- Trans-European networks
- Economic, social, and territorial cohesion
- Environment and climate change
- Energy

Source: https://portal.cor.europa.eu/subsidiarity/whatis/Pages/defaultPolicy.aspx

The CoR is informed when the EESC is being consulted on legislative proposals. In cases in which it considers that specific regional interests are involved, it may also issue an opinion on the matter. This provision essentially extends the fields of mandatory consultation of the CoR to match those of the EESC, particularly in issues concerning agriculture.

The CoR also has the possibility to draft 'own initiative' opinions in areas of concern that are not covered by the list of policy fields for mandatory consultation. This right was granted to the CoR on its inception. In contrast, the EESC had to wait thirty-five years, until the signing of the Maastricht Treaty, to be afforded such an opportunity (Warleigh 1999: 20).

Composition of the EESC

The memberships of the EESC and the CoR have always mirrored each other, and continue to do so. Following the accession of Croatia in 2013, both had 350 members, with membership distributed according to the size of the member state. Thus France, Germany, Italy, and the United Kingdom (UK)—pre-Brexit—each have the largest national delegations to each body, with twenty-four members each, whilst Cyprus, Luxembourg, and Malta have the smallest delegations, made up of only five members each (see Box 16.3).[3]

The EESC was established to provide for a permanent dialogue between the principal social and economic actors in Europe, and those groupings have not changed dramatically since the body's inception in 1957. The original EESC brought together members from national socio-economic organizations, divided into three groups: Group I, employers' organizations (the 'employers' group'); Group II, trade unions

BOX 16.3	National memberships of the EESC and CoR
Country	**Number of seats**
France, Germany, Italy, UK*	24
Poland, Spain	21
Romania	15
Austria, Belgium, Bulgaria, Czech Republic, Greece, Hungary, Netherlands, Portugal, Sweden	12
Croatia, Denmark, Finland, Ireland, Lithuania, Slovakia	9
Latvia, Slovenia	7
Estonia	6
Cyprus, Luxembourg, Malta	5

*Prior to the UK's withdrawal from the EU

(the 'workers' group'); and Group III, 'various interests' (that is, actors who did not fall naturally into either of the other group categories and who were drawn from a broad range of civil society groupings). This last section tends to cover fields such as the social economy, consumer and environmental organizations, agricultural organizations, groups representing small business, and so on. The groups (I, II, III) function largely along the lines of the political groups found in the EP or the CoR. Their role is principally to discuss the work programme of the EESC and to develop outline positions on proposals ahead of full consideration in plenary sessions. Since 2010, members have been appointed for a five-year term, aligning the EESC with the norm in the EU institutions.

The sections of the EESC are where the bread-and-butter work is carried out. In this way, they are similar to the thematic commissions of the CoR or the committees of the EP: they undertake full analysis of policy proposals from the EU institutions, and draft opinions and recommendations. Within the EESC, the sections (rather than political groups, as elsewhere) appoint an individual as *rapporteur* on a proposal, whose job it is to guide the process of drafting the opinion on that issue.

Each section is made up of a membership that cross-cuts group membership. At present, there are six thematic sections, each responsible for a set of policy areas. Because the sections draw in members from all three of the groups within the EESC, it is here that the 'social dialogue' between workers and employers, which is at the core of the EESC's remit, is technically facilitated.

Beyond these formal subject committees, the EESC also sets up ad hoc groups to consider broader issues of thematic concern. For example, it has launched a Consultative Commission on Industrial Change (CCMI), three 'observatories' that monitor the single market, the labour market, and sustainable development in the EU, and a steering committee on the Europe 2020 strategy for sustainable growth. All act as advisory committees, and produce reports for wider consideration within the EU institutions and the decision-making process at large. Plenary meetings are held over a two-day period, around ten times per year, and take place in the EP's Brussels building. The agendas of plenary sessions tend to focus on the consideration of reports and the adoption of opinions.

Composition of the CoR

Members of the CoR are appointed by national governments, who propose lists of members to the Council for adoption (see Box 16.4). At the point of its creation, there was no obligation for members appointed to the CoR to be elected representatives in their home regional or local authority. However, most member states developed an informal system for delegation that demanded some position of elected authority, and in those countries with clearly defined political regions, at least half of the CoR seats were allocated to regional politicians (Nugent 2010: 231).

BOX 16.4 **French members of the EESC**

The twenty-four French members of the EESC at the time of writing are drawn from organized groups in France that represent the three pillars of the EESC's representation: employers, workers, and 'various interests' (this last loosely covering other types of socio-economic interest group). At the time of writing, these include those listed in Table 16.1.

TABLE 16.1 French members of the EESC

Name	Professional affiliation	EESC group membership
Emmanuelle Butaud-Stubbs	Delegate-General, Union of Textile Industries	Group I (Employers)
Laure Batut	Member of the International and European Affairs Department, General Confederation of Labour—Workers' Power	Group II (Workers)
Christiane Basset	Vice-President of the National Union of Family Associations (UNAF)	Group III (Various Interests)

As in the EP, policy proposals are considered in detail in subject committees, known within the CoR as 'commissions'. Membership of each commission cross-cuts national and party affiliations. The CoR currently operates on the basis of six thematic subject committees, each of which considers policy proposals in a certain sphere of activity (see Box 16.5). Again, they are referred to internally by an acronym.

BOX 16.5 **Commissions of the CoR**

- Commission for Citizenship, Governance, Institutional and External Affairs (CIVEX)
- Commission for Territorial Cohesion Policy and EU Budget (COTER)
- Commission for Economic Policy (ECON)
- Commission for Environment, Climate Change and Energy (ENVE)
- Commission for Natural Resources (NAT)
- Commission for Social Policy, Education, Employment, Research and Culture (SEDEC)

Internally, at an organizational level, successive restructuring procedures have seen the CoR be reshaped to take on a more politicized role than that originally envisaged for it. Since 2006, the CoR has begun to approximate the political procedures of the EP, being organized internally on the basis of political groups. Between them, these political groups share out the lead roles on opinion drafting and appointing the *rapporteurs* for each issue on the basis of a size-related points system, as is done in the EP. The establishment of strong political groups as the basis of administration within the CoR has largely superseded the position of national delegations to the CoR. It has also facilitated stronger ties between the CoR and EP, particularly on the drafting of opinions. Overall, then, the internal organization of the CoR has become increasingly sophisticated to reflect the growing scope of its work (Schönlau 2008: 20).

Members of the CoR (see Box 16.6) are organized into five political groups at the time of writing, mirroring the largest groups in the EP, alongside a small subset of non-aligned members. Four of these political groups are familiar from the EP: liberals (Alliance of Liberals and Democrats for Europe, or ALDE); socialists (Party of European Socialists, or PES); centre-Right (European People's Party, or EPP); and the more right of centre European Conservatives and Reformists Group (ECR). The CoR also has a fifth group, known as the European Alliance (EA), which comprises an ad hoc mixture of independents, greens, and minority nationalists. There are significantly fewer political groups in the CoR than in the EP because the national systems of delegating members to the CoR introduces something of an automatic filtering process. As of 2016, the EPP was the largest political grouping within the CoR, with 129 members; the PES, 120; the ALDE group, 39; the ECR, 16; and the European Alliance, 21 (see Chapter 15).

BOX 16.6   **French members of the CoR**

The French delegation to the CoR consists of twenty-four members and an equal number of alternates. The current distribution of seats, both for members and alternates, is listed in Table 16.2.

TABLE 16.2 French members of the CoR

French delegation	Members	Alternates
Regions	12	12
Departments	6	6
Municipalities	6	6

Members of this delegation are proposed by the Association of French Regions (Association des Régions de France), the Assembly of French Departments (Assemblée des Départements de France) and the Association of French Mayors (Association des Maires de France), and appointed by the French prime minister.

Leadership of the EESC

At a planning and operational level, the EESC is guided by a managerial bureau. The bureau is made up of thirty-six members, along with the President and two Vice-Presidents. The President has oversight for the political work of the EESC and is largely responsible for providing the guidelines for that work. The President is also the figure responsible for the external representation of the Committee, interacting with the other institutions on the Committee's behalf, as well as member states and other bodies.

The Vice-Presidents support and assist the President in their roles. Vice-presidential positions are held by members of the two groups that do not hold the presidency. The distribution of functions within the bureau, sections, and any study groups that are established always strives to strike a balance between the three groups (Smismans 2000). The President, two Vice-Presidents, and the members of the bureau itself are elected on a two-yearly basis, and take-up of the position rotates between the three groups. The other members include the president of each of the functional sections and each of the representative groups.

Leadership of the CoR

The organizational structure of the CoR is very similar to that of the EESC. At a political level, the CoR is managed by a bureau, constituted, as of 2016, by sixty members of the Assembly. The President, elected for a two-and-a-half-year term of office since Lisbon, is supported by a First Vice-President and one Vice-President from each of the member states. Alongside these members, there are then four chairs of the political groups represented within the CoR. Finally, the bureau is supported by twenty-seven further ordinary members of the CoR. Overall, the composition of the bureau reflects the national and political balances within the CoR.

The bureau then meets around seven times per year to manage planning functions, such as the agendas for plenary sessions, to draw up the CoR's policy programme, to allocate opinions to the various subject commissions, and to decide when to draft own-initiative opinions. The CoR holds fewer plenary sessions than the EESC: around five per year. Like EESC plenaries, however, full sessions of the CoR are also held in the EP premises in Brussels.

The EESC in practice

Despite the limited power that it had been given, there were confident expectations in the EESC that its 'accumulated expertise would be valued and exploited by the EC's institutions' and that it would be able to develop a representative role as a 'mediator on behalf of national economic and social interests vis-à-vis the Commission and the Council of Ministers' (Lodge and Herman 1980: 269). Neither expectation was fulfilled. For the Council of Ministers, the EESC was a body to be regarded with scepticism and disdain. Its output was regarded, for the most part, as simply reinforcing the supranational agenda of the European Commission and thus was prone to run up against the buffers of intergovernmentalism. As such, the EESC remains on the fringes of the European policy debate, with a limited impact on decisions. It has effectively been relegated to the status of yet another EU lobby group, struggling to compete with other consultative bodies and organized interests in Brussels.

Nonetheless, it has had its successes and these have been widely championed. For example, an EESC report on a Community charter of basic social rights formed the basis of the Commission's proposals on the Social Charter that were accepted at the Strasbourg summit in 1989. This episode marked the first time in its history that the EESC had been able to set the agenda decisively and before the usual decision-making process had begun. Building on this achievement, the EESC was an early proponent on the issue of fundamental rights in the EU. It continues to hold this example up as its key area of influence in the European sphere across all of its marketing literature; the EU Charter of Fundamental Rights, the EESC claims, was largely the outcome of its own internal debates and subsequent opinion on the issue of fundamental rights.

Largely in recognition of its increasing marginalization and in view also of the source of its one true success, the EESC leadership in the 1990s began to shift towards presenting itself and its own role in the EU slightly differently, as a leading representative of European civil society. Throughout the 1990s, the European Commission began to engage more systematically with civil society organizations (CSOs) in policy fields such as environmental and development policy. This mode of interaction was perceived as a legitimizing force for the Commission. It subsequently developed a new normative discourse on the role of these organizations, coining the concept of 'civil dialogue' in 1996 to plead for increased interaction with CSOs (Smismans 2003: 484).

It was at this point that the EESC began to stress the value that it could add to this concept of a European civil dialogue, based on the strength of its own cross-national, multi-sectoral composition. Subsequent presidencies of the EESC began to give priority to the so-called Citizen's Europe initiative, organizing hearings that, it was claimed, gave voice to the real aspirations of the European citizens. This approach faltered, however, given the badly focused and top-down character of the hearings (Smismans 1999: 557). Nonetheless, the EESC's new focus on civil society persevered. By the late 1990s, the EESC began to tagline itself as the 'forum of organized civil society'. Since 2003, the former Economic and Social Committee (ESC), referred to informally as 'Ecosoc', has called itself the European Economic and Social Committee (EESC), largely to help to differentiate it from the numerous economic and social committees that operate in the member states.

The EESC's current leadership regards the role of the Committee as threefold, with its status as a civil society representative body at the heart of its mission. First, the

EESC aims to ensure that European policies and legislation better reflect economic, social, and civic concerns, by drawing on the knowledge and expertise of its members. Second, its leaders argue that its existence and operation helps to promote a 'more participatory EU', given that it acts as 'organized civil society's institutional forum'. Finally, the EESC presents itself as advancing the role of CSOs and participatory democracy in Europe.[4] National economic and social councils exist in twenty-two of the EU's member states, and these bodies are core partners for the EESC, providing a network for their activities and a range of contacts with whom the EESC's own committees and consultative bodies interact.

Despite its composition, the EESC does not operate as an expert body within the institutional configuration of the EU, undertaking rather a more representative role. The opinions that the EESC prepares are by no means merely technical; rather, they reflect compromises between the EU's principal socio-economic actors. These compromises are not political ones, such as those found elsewhere in the formal decision-making process and even internally within the CoR, the EESC's 'sister' institution. Their real added value comes from the fact that they are instead driven by a consensus-finding process amongst the leading socio-economic actors in an EU policy area, which can itself be useful (Hönnige and Panke 2013). But it is from its status as the formal locus of organized interests in the single market that the Committee continues to derive its own self-image, even if stakeholders within other institutions might prefer greater technical expertise to be reflected in their opinions.

The CoR in practice

The initial output of the CoR was deemed to be of little added value for the general policy-making process of the Community, underpinning further a sense of marginalization. Its opinions were widely regarded as bland, of low quality, and 'invariably call[ing] for an increased sub-national participation in the EU policy-making process, but little else' (Farrows and McCarthy 1997: 26). Some major improvements have been noted over time, however. The majority of opinions produced are delivered today on the basis of either mandatory or optional inter-institutional consultations, rather than as a result of own-initiative proposals from the CoR itself (Domorenok 2009: 152). This practice has helped to achieve a degree of focus in the output of the CoR, with an increased emphasis on delivering advice where its expertise would be welcomed.

The CoR's confused birth gave rise to a situation of ambiguity in which it was not exactly clear what it was really for. However, successive Treaty revisions and a process of internal reordering have subtly altered the role and status of the CoR, allowing the body to define its objectives more clearly. The 1997 Amsterdam Treaty extended its remit to cover legislation in around two-thirds of the EU's policy fields. But it was the 2001 Treaty of Nice that really marked a qualitative step forward in the status of the CoR, with the inclusion of a new provision that CoR members should hold some form of electoral accountability in their home localities. The Committee was thus to consist of 'representatives of regional and local bodies who either hold a regional or local authority electoral mandate or are politically accountable to an elected assembly'.[5]

The ratification and entry into force of the Lisbon Treaty in 2009 finally delivered one of the CoR's core objectives: securing its right to defend its own prerogatives before the Court of Justice of the EU. Of equal note is the right, also enshrined in the Lisbon Treaty, for the CoR to bring actions before the Court in cases in which it views legislation as having breached the principle of subsidiarity, effectively turning the CoR into the EU's subsidiarity 'watchdog'. This move, on its own, was viewed as a hugely significant advance by the CoR's supporters. Not only did it fulfil, fifteen years after its inception, one of the CoR's longest-standing aims, but it also finally elevated the CoR above the status of the EESC. Further, the EU definition of the subsidiarity principle has, since Lisbon, explicitly contained a reference to the local and regional dimensions of EU politics and policies. This emphasis has further strengthened the CoR leadership's approach to subsidiarity and increased the institution's political action in the realm of subsidiarity. For instance, the subsidiarity monitoring network allows for an enhanced and early focus on political dossiers that are considered relevant in terms of subsidiarity.

In line with this more powerful role as the subsidiarity watchdog for the EU, the CoR has, since 2009, participated in the assessment of the territorial impact made by certain legislative proposals put forward by the European Commission. The effect has been to give the CoR enhanced capacity to shape and influence EU decision-making during the pre-legislative phase.

The Lisbon Treaty also provided for further changes that were perceived as having strengthened the CoR and its role in the European legislative process. First, the Treaty increased its members' term of office from four to five years, bringing the CoR in line with other EU institutions—notably, the EP and the Commission. In addition, the Lisbon Treaty saw a widening of the CoR's area of consultation to include new policy areas: energy and climate change. Consultation rights were also strengthened, so that the CoR can now be consulted by the EP, as well as by the Commission and Council of Ministers, in the areas of common concern set out by the EU Treaties.

At a more abstract level, the Lisbon Treaty wrote into law the fundamental objective of 'territorial cohesion' in the EU. This shift marked a further step change for the CoR's inter-institutional relations, as it continues to promote territorial cohesion through its own work and operation. In a separate move that articulates this objective more precisely, the Treaty on European Union (TEU) was revised to enshrine the right to local and regional self-government in EU law.[6]

However, it is at the level of internal organization that the primary change has taken place over the course of the CoR's existence. Observers feared at the outset that internal divisions within the CoR—northern versus southern European regions; strong versus weak; rich versus poor; and so on—would prevent the new body from developing a clear sense of purpose. Yet while these internal disparities have encouraged the stronger, constitutionally empowered regions at the very least to prioritize alternative channels of interest mediation in the EU, dividing lines have not proven as destructive as was first feared. Indeed, despite all of these obvious lines of conflict that the CoR's original template design established, they have today been replaced by real lines of conflict between the sets of actors who strive to achieve influence within the body: the political groups and the national delegations (Hönnige and Kaiser 2003).

The CoR's original institutional composition did not include political groups. As an advisory body, it established *national* delegations to represent territorial interests on a member state by member state basis. On that model, the two most important organizational structures were the national delegations and thematic commissions. However, over the years, the operation of the CoR and its leaderships have seen the body evolve in a more 'politicized' direction, with lines of conflict opening up between the interests of party groups, along much the same lines as party groups within the EP. Today, the party groups are the most significant structures within the CoR, a development that few expected (Christiansen 1996). This development has had a substantial impact on inter-institutional relations: the operation of the main party groupings within both the CoR and the EP has inevitably led to closer links between these two bodies than with either the Commission or the Council of Ministers. Through contacts at the level of secretariats and individual *rapporteurs*, the political groups try to bring the positions of the institutions closer together and thereby to increase the chance that the consultative output of the CoR is taken into account in the wider EU decision-making process.

In terms of impact, it is difficult for the CoR to improve on its engagement with the principal decision-making institutions of the EU (Commission, Council, EP), given that its opinions are generally sent only by internal post. There is no formal mechanism in place for follow-up discussions nor for feedback from the decision-making institutions themselves. In recognition of this shortcoming, targeted steps have been taken to secure greater impact in the policy process. For example, on any opinion produced, a core set of the recommendations that it entails are now also printed on the outside, so that even if the opinion itself is not widely read, its overall message can have some potential impact on the desk of whichever official to whom it is sent. This change may seem minor, but it is a significant one.

Of even more significance is the degree to which links with the European Commission, the most important champion and partner of the CoR since its inception, have incrementally been strengthened. There is an upward exchange of staff between the two, with many Commission officials having spent several years in the CoR, giving them a sensitivity to the CoR's outputs that is missing from interaction with the EP, for instance. The incumbent secretary-general, the highest-ranking position in the secretariat of the CoR, for instance, is a former Commission official. Further, on average, two Commissioners now attend each of the CoR's plenary sessions and the Commission President takes part in at least one each year. In addition, the use of non-mandatory referrals by the European Commission to the CoR has also risen sharply (Schönlau 2008: 23).

The EESC and the CoR in context

Evidently, both the EESC and the CoR have developed their roles within the institutional architecture of the EU in ways that go beyond the initial activity foreseen for them at the moment of their founding. Their operation and functions today show that these bodies have adapted to the changing nature of European governance, and demonstrate how they have sought to carve out roles for themselves, whilst continuing to face calls for their closure. Dissenting views on the value added of both organizations, the CoR and EESC alike, are not uncommon and periodically make headline news. For example, in 2011, in its position paper on the new EU budget post-2013, the (liberal) ALDE group of the EP called for both a radical shake-up of the CoR and possible abolition of the EESC (ALDE 2011).

Against this background of constant debate about their legitimacy, both the CoR and the EESC have increasingly bought into the narrative of 'participatory democracy' and 'input legitimacy' within the EU (Schmidt 2013). Both have sought to maximize their civil society and grass-roots connections as an entry ticket to wider policy negotiations. Their representative structures, both bodies claim, facilitate better connections between Europe's decision-makers and citizens; this claim underpins their argument for greater status as policy actors in the institutional framework of the EU. Some commentators continue to argue that the EESC and the CoR are important only at a symbolic level, in that it is useful for the EU to recognize the territorial disparity of its member states through a formal committee that discusses regional and local perspectives on policy. Others suggest that both bodies do have a legitimate role to play in European decision-making, largely on account of their representative characters (Smismans 2000). These views stress that it does add something to the legitimacy of the European policy process if the decision-making system incorporates a formalized, permanent committee of economic and social interests (Schönlau 2008).

Since the early 1990s, the concept of a European civil society, broadly defined, has become common currency within the EU's discourse, yet (unsurprisingly perhaps) some institutions and bodies have held on more firmly to these notions than others. For the Commission, the normative dialogue on stronger engagement with civil society actors in social policy decisions has gradually spread to all of its Directorates-General (DGs), and forms the basis of its policy on interaction with external representatives (Smismans 2003). For the EESC and, to a lesser degree, the CoR, the growing notion of a civil dialogue allowed them to reinforce their strategies to gain a stronger voice in European affairs, by emphasizing their connection to grass-roots concerns in the member states, both with regard to social and economic partners, and to local and regional authorities. In light of this new approach, the EESC began to present itself more forcefully as an institutional expression of the organizations making up civil society. In fact, the EESC currently markets itself with the strapline 'a bridge between Europe and organized civil society'.[7] It emphasizes that its operation helps to strengthen the EU's democratic legitimacy and effectiveness by enabling CSOs from the member states to express their views at the European level. But the Committee's focus is not restricted to the EU member states: like the CoR, the EESC has an active external relations agenda. It engages in civil society dialogue such as round tables with Brazil, China, and India, and connects regularly with civil society groups in the European neighbourhood, all carried out under an annual operational budget of around €120 million per year.

In more general terms, both organizations emphasize the validity of their engagement with the community outside the Brussels 'loop'. That community extends to European civil society, and local and regional authorities.

Again, beyond its original remit as an advisory body, the CoR has developed a profile as a facilitator of regional engagement, leading on particular issues of note and championing certain objectives that it selects, in cooperation with various other regional stakeholders. Chief amongst the new activities that embrace wider regional support in Brussels are regular forums on thematic issues such as communications, transport policy, and social innovation, the Europe 2020 monitoring platform, and a subsidiarity monitoring network. It also extends to the annual open days hosted in Brussels, and a series of workshops and seminars under a general theme with a regional and local angle organized by both the Commission and the CoR in Brussels. These interactions with the large community of so-called local and regional stakeholders in Brussels—regional representations, non-governmental organizations (NGOs), city government officials, associations of regions with shared sectoral concerns, and so on—comes in addition to the regularized interactions between the CoR and its stakeholder community in Brussels, through the more formalized system of 'structured dialogue'—that is, regularized interaction on thematic points of mutual concern.

A final issue to note is the CoR's increasing engagement not only in the sectoral policy issues and not only with a clear territorial cohesion dimension, but also in the external affairs of the Union. CIVEX in particular has a remit to consider engagement in the EU's international affairs, for example promoting the development of decentralized cooperation globally. A clear marker of the growing international ambitions of the CoR is its role in establishing the Euro–Mediterranean Assembly of Local and Regional Authorities (known more commonly by its French acronym ARLEM), providing a local and regional dimension to the EU's ongoing integration efforts in the Euro–Med area. It exists alongside a similar assembly for the European Neighbourhood Policy (ENP) countries, known as the Conference of Regional and Local Authorities for the Eastern Partnership (CORLEAP). The ongoing political crises in both these regions have sustained the CoR's remit to extend further its activities in the EU's external relations—a role not foreseen by the architects of the CoR's original institutional position.

All of this activity blurs somewhat the distinction between the CoR's formally prescribed role, as set out in the EU Treaties, and its ambitions—or, more precisely, the ambitions of recent CoR leaderships that have steered the body in this direction. With an increased emphasis on the CoR's ability to connect disparate groups and promote shared policy agendas through dialogue and discussion, the CoR begins to take on a role as something of a platform rather than an actor in EU affairs. Whilst the networking and collaborative activities do, at times, feed into the more formal work of the CoR—namely, the drafting of opinions—this is not always the case. As such, the CoR's position in the institutional configuration of the EU remains unclear, whatever the added value of these 'softer' activities in the policy sphere may be. All of this ambiguity provides further grist to the mill of those who seek to disband the organization, and fuels the drive within the CoR to outline its own impact through measurable successes and targets delivered. For the member states, the EESC and CoR present no demonstrable cause for concern, other than perhaps the financial implications of their operation, although the EESC and CoR together represent just 2.56 per cent of the EU's overall administration budget. For this reason, debates surrounding their future have limited salience in national politics—and even less so since the rise in value of 'civil society' arguments, or indeed the mood music of delivering 'real' subsidiarity, as outlined by Commission President Jean-Claude Juncker during his 2014 inaugural address to the EP.[8] The 'hands-off' approach to management of the EESC and CoR has provided both organizations with the scope to develop their roles in new directions since their establishment.

Ultimately, however, each of these organization is only one of a number of channels that social or regional interests can exploit to engage with the European decision-making process. Both share an uncomfortable position on the margins of EU legislative circles. Despite ambitions to shape policy outcomes, both remain restricted and challenged in that aim, largely superseded today by the vast number of 'civil society' actors that operate as independent lobbyists in the Brussels arena.

Despite all of this extensive undertaking and the notional high-level nods in support of the CoR's activities—such as Commission President Barroso being one of the first signatories to the CoR's European Charter for Multilevel Governance in 2014—there is little evidence to suggest that the CoR is succeeding in its aim to have a fuller impact in the EU policy process. A recent study found only limited evidence of 'impact' in any real sense and that impact only if a number of conditions were met: that the CoR produce its own policy recommendations quickly, that the recommendations are of a sufficient quality to be taken seriously, and that the CoR's recommendations resonate with the addressees' own prior positions on the issue (Hönnige and Panke 2013: 452). In particular circumstances, principally when policies with a clearly identifiable local and regional impact are being developed, there is evidence to show that the EU's main decision-making bodies, especially the Commission, do give the CoR's opinions serious consideration (Carroll 2011). Under other conditions, such as when the Commission already has a clearly focused line on policy proposals or when the dossier has already garnered an EP response before the CoR has delivered its opinion, the influence of the CoR is likely to be both 'diffuse and weak' (Tatham 2008).

Theorizing the EESC and the CoR

Whilst these two consultative committees in the EU policy process remain just that—partners for consultation—rather than centres of any real political authority, it is not unsurprising that academic interest in the work of both the EESC and the CoR does not feature heavily in the scholarly literature on the EU. Neither are 'institutions' in the classic sense of empowered decision-making actors. The history of both institutions' creation has also determined the extent to which theorizing on the EESC and the CoR has remained limited; neither was created on the basis of any real institutional vacuum, but rather to satisfy the demands of various organized actors within the EU—that is, employers, workers and sub-state entities. These actors have endowed, and continue to endow, the EESC and the CoR with a powerful symbolic presence. In a political process that sets out to be consensus-oriented, all EU leaders want to be seen to be taking seriously the interests of producers, employers, workers, and, of course, local and regional authorities. Their symbolic status has also largely insulated the EESC and CoR from the effects of the financial and euro crises that have upset the EU's own power balance in recent years.

Theorizing on the EU's consultative committees has therefore been preoccupied with two important questions: why do they exist, and do they really make any difference? Theoretical models have been deployed only on occasion, to explore their coming into being (Warleigh 1999; Carroll 2011) or the development of their role (Domorenok 2009). Most recently, for example, Panke *et al.* (2015) developed a model constructed from insights drawn from new institutionalist literature. Yet none of these explorations have yielded noteworthy insights or driven forward these models. Hooghe and Marks (2001) and Bache (2008) use the CoR as an element in the construction of theoretical models of 'multilevel governance' (MLG), a form of network governance that encompasses multiple interactions between empowered actors (Piatonni 2009; Stephenson 2013). These insights relate to the full range of channels through which sub-state actors across the EU were able to exert influence and engage in the policy-making process.

Notably, early academic excitement about MLG and the construction of a 'Europe of the Regions' has waned in scholarly work on the EU (Elias 2008). In fact, the usage of the term has become so commonplace and so widely applied that it is at risk of becoming a useful descriptor that is applicable across all manner of governance contexts, ultimately referring to different things in different arenas (Stephenson 2013). Within the EU, the CoR has become an initiator and driver itself of reflection on MLG in its original conceptualization, although it is a poorly disguised shorthand for an argument in favour of greater powers for itself. With a sizeable research budget at its disposal, in recent years the CoR has financed scholarly research on both MLG as a governing concept and its applicability in the context of the CoR's own role, using this terminology to design a hypothetical framework for fuller political engagement in the EU's policy process (CoR 2012). As such, the CoR has cultivated a role for itself as something of a 'champion of the cause' for scholarship on MLG, latching onto this as a route by which the body itself might potentially gain greater political impact. Whilst the CoR still promotes its ability to legitimize EU decision-making through its role as the collective voice of those governments 'closest to the people', there is an ongoing parallel agenda for legitimacy-building through the development of the theoretical dimension of a system of governance whereby the CoR could envisage a much greater role than is currently the case in practice.

This agenda has informed much of the policy output of the CoR on MLG and shaped a number of practical initiatives. Building further on a 2009 White Paper on Multilevel Governance, in 2011 the CoR presented an Opinion Paper on Building a European Culture of Multilevel Governance, which outlined concrete steps for achieving rather ambitious aims such as a renewal of the Community method, based on 'a more inclusive process and the establishment of multilevel governance'.[9] This paper set out plans for a 'scoreboard' on MLG, aimed at measuring the extent to which its main principles have been taken into account. The initiative was launched with enthusiasm in 2011, although its outputs waned subsequently. The scoreboard was then followed by an EU Charter for Multilevel Governance in Europe, published in 2014, which aims to garner support through a drive to secure signatories who demonstrate their political commitment to MLG by signing. Most recently, the CoR has produced grand publications on identifying 'best practice' in the implementation of MLG across the EU's suite of policy fields.[10]

The CoR has therefore worked to instrumentalize the concept of MLG as a very politicized objective of securing greater influence both for itself, and for local and regional actors in the EU within the EU's policy process.[11] Its agenda does not extend to achieving further influence for its sister institution, the EESC. But whilst MLG was first conceptualized simply as an academic frame for capturing the reality of complex governing interactions across multiple arenas and, as such, retains the character of a theoretical perspective rather than a fully fledged theory, the CoR is promoting the notion of MLG as a political objective and a marker of 'good governance'.

Conclusion

The EESC and the CoR have developed roles in practice that deviate somewhat from the visions held by the initial supporters and champions of their creation. Neither has moved to take on a stronger formal position as a codecision-maker in the European legislative process. But both have cultivated niche roles that anchor them firmly in the policy circles that feed into the wider processes of thinking on European issues and which ultimately launch new policy agendas. Both retain important symbolic functions at the EU level, and have sought to maximize the opportunities afforded to them through debates on European governance, civil-society dialogue, and MLG.

Neither organization has stood still since its creation; rather, each has sought actively to secure some form of engagement in the European policy process that is appropriate to its membership and representative focus. The question remains, however: what is their added value in an open policy process with a burgeoning private lobbying sector and new groups of collective interests emerging all of the time? This question continues to raise the notion of 'impact' as a driver of the activities of both the EESC and CoR, even if that impact is difficult to categorize and even more slippery to pin down.

Nonetheless, both the EESC and CoR have managed to cultivate an approach to engagement in European policy issues that has some wider resonance in the stakeholder community. Both organizations have scope to develop new activities and even roles, thanks largely to the 'hands-off' approach to their management taken by national governments. Both have, on occasion, managed to shape policy outcomes in their favour. This influence does suggest some degree of dynamism inherent to both organizations that should secure their future in an increasingly complex system of EU governance.

ENDNOTES

1. See also Schmitter and Lehmbruch (1979); Lehmbruch and Schmitter (1982).
2. Art. 304 TFEU.
3. The numbers per country are detailed in Protocol 36 TFEU.
4. EESC mission statement, available online at http://www.eesc.europa.eu/resources/docs/mission-statement.pdf
5. Art. 300 TFEU.
6. Art. 4(2) TEU.
7. See, respectively, http://www.eesc.europa.eu and https://portal.cor.europa.eu/mlgcharter/Pages/MLG-charter.aspx
8. Opening statement by Jean-Claude Juncker at the European Parliament Plenary Session, 15 July 2014.
9. CoR Opinion, *Building a European Culture of Multilevel Governance: Follow-up to the Committee of the Regions'* White Paper, CdR 273/2011 fin.
10. See, e.g., Committee of the Regions (2013).
11. See, e.g., the CoR Mission Statement, available online at http://cor.europa.eu/en/about/Documents/Mission%20statement/EN.pdf, which states that one of its principal aims is to 'promote multi-level governance'.

FURTHER READING

There are few systematic investigations of either the EESC or CoR on their own; most studies put these bodies into comparative perspective or address them within the context of investigations into the nature of European governance. The analysis presented by Warleigh

(1999) of the CoR is a useful starting point for understanding the body itself. Smismans (2000) provides an equally insightful starting point for analysis of the EESC. Hooghe and Marks (2001) locate the emergence of the CoR within a broader, comparative investigation of emergent patterns of multilevel governance in the EU, and Stephenson (2013) offers a comprehensive overview of how that concept has been taken forward in a number of different analytical directions. Jeffery (2000) offers some insights into the impact of increased regional representation on European governance. Rowe (2011) considers the tensions that promote regional engagement in Brussels, both through the CoR and through alternative channels of representation. Greenwood's (2011) study of more contemporary lobbying in the EU helps to clarify the nature of the interest mediation carried out by both the EESC and the CoR. A most helpful analysis of the contemporary role played by both the EESC and the CoR is found in a recent study by Panke *et al.* (2015).

Greenwood, J. (2011) *Interest Representation in the European Union* (3rd edn, Basingstoke and New York: Palgrave Macmillan).

Hooghe, L., and Marks, G. (2001) *Multi-Level Governance and European Integration* (Oxford and Boulder, CO: Rowman & Littlefield).

Jeffery, C. (2000) 'Sub-national mobilization and European integration: Does it make any difference?', *Journal of Common Market Studies*, 38/1: 1–23.

Panke, D., Hönnig, C., and Gollub, J. (2015) *Consultative Committees in the European Union: No Vote—No Influence?* (Colchester: ECPR Press).

Rowe, C. (2011) *Regional Representations in the EU: Between Diplomacy and Interest Representation* (Basingstoke and New York: Palgrave Macmillan).

Smismans, S. (2000) 'The European Economic and Social Committee: Towards deliberative democracy via a functional assembly', *European Integration Online Papers (EIoP)*, 4/12.

Stephenson, P. (2013) 'Twenty years of multi-level governance: Where does it come from? What is it? Where is it going?', *Journal of European Public Policy*, 20/6: 817–37.

Warleigh, A. (1999) *The Committee of the Regions: Institutionalising Multi-Level Governance?* (London: Kogan Page).

 WEB LINKS

http://www.cor.europa.eu/

http://www.eesc.europa.eu/

Full information on the activities of the EESC and the CoR can be obtained from their respective websites.

CHAPTER 17

Conclusion: EU institutions in theory and practice

John Peterson and Dermot Hodson

▌ Summary

Amidst so much uncertainty about the future of the European Union (EU), it is easy to forget that—institutionally, if not politically, speaking—it has endured over six decades and has adapted to changing circumstances. Equally, we should not underestimate the severity of the difficulties it presently faces, including the euro and migration crises, conflict in Syria and Ukraine, and the outcome of the 2016 referendum in the United Kingdom (UK), the implementation of which is being termed 'Brexit'. EU institutions remain irrevocably interdependent and obliged to work together to deliver collective governance even as they and European governments try to solve multiple crises that sap political time and attention. The capacity of the Union's institutions to govern collectively is increasingly called into question. One upshot is frequent creation of *de novo* institutions as EU governments seek new ways of solving policy problems without turning to the traditional Community method. But it is no panacea. Multiple variants of institutional theory shed light on EU institutions, as our authors show, but it is wise to reflect on whether 'we are all institutionalists now'—and if so, whether that is desirable.

Introduction

In late 2015, George Soros—business magnate, philanthropist, and commentator—argued that the EU faced no fewer than five crises at once: the threat of the UK's exit (subsequently realized), the euro, Greece, migration, and Ukraine. The UK's vote in June 2016 to leave the EU was, according to French Prime Minister Manuel Valls, 'an explosive shock. At stake is the break-up, pure and simple, of the union'.[1] No system of governance is very good at solving crises, let alone so many at once: crises tend to reinforce one another, and political time and attention are limited. 'What can be done', Soros (2015: 2) asked, 'to arrest and reverse the process of disintegration?'

In truth, the EU rarely has been free of crises of one kind or another. To illustrate, ten years before Soros' clarion call, the failure of the EU's Constitutional Treaty following referenda held in two founding member states cast a pallor of gloom over the Union. Institutional reforms such as creating a permanent President of the European Council, a High Representative commanding real resources in foreign policy, and an empowered European Parliament (EP) were all blocked. Yet all of these innovations eventually took effect when the Lisbon Treaty entered into force in late 2009.

Of course, Lisbon's transformation of the institutional environment hardly means that European integration is irreversible or that predictions about its future are safe. Indicative was that the agenda of a pivotal EU summit in February 2016 contained only two issues: the refugee crisis and a deal on the UK's renegotiation over its terms of membership. Meanwhile, negotiations on a political settlement in Ukraine with Russia were on a knife edge, while those on halting the bloodbath in Syria were at an impasse. The eurozone economy was slowly recovering from its second recession since the global financial crisis, but Greece's sovereign debt crisis was in no sense resolved. In 2011, Sir Stephen Wall, a former UK permanent representative pronounced: 'We have seen the high point of the European Union. With a bit of luck it will last our lifetime. But it's on the way out. After all, very few institutions last forever.'[2] Sound familiar?

In this chapter, we lift our gaze and reflect on where the EU as an institutional system has been and where it is going. We do no gazing into crystal balls; instead, we identify what is enduring about the character of the EU's institutions, however fragile the wider political process of European integration now seems. Chapter 1 began by stressing how extraordinary the Union's institutions are—but it also argued that the EU's formal and informal bodies are not as complex as is often claimed. EU institutions can, and should, be understood using the traditional theories and concepts of international relations (IR) and politics, because they offer competing insights and perspectives on why EU institutions were created and what they do.

General theories of politics and IR also help us to grapple with one of the great puzzles of modern politics: why has Europe (uniquely) chosen such an ambitious, elaborate, and contested system of collective governance? These approaches (as opposed to those focused exclusively on European integration) remind us that Europe is a comparatively crowded and resource-poor part of the world, populated by a rich variety of densely populated states, most of them small, whose histories are closely intertwined, but marked above all by conflict (much of it bloody). It would be difficult to argue that states in Europe were ever more interdependent than they are today. More than most regions in the world, Europe must cooperate to prosper, or even to survive (Dogan 1994). Collectively governing Europe is never easy. But nor is it optional.

The historical focus of this volume's contributions reminds us that European integration began with strikingly narrow economic objectives: first, to manage joint production of coal and steel; and then, to develop a common market. Yet the institutions designed to deliver on these goals were innovative and ambitious. Earlier instances of European cooperation, such as the Council of Europe, were built on intergovernmental institutions (see Chapter 1). In contrast, the European Coal and Steel Community (ECSC) included powerful supranational institutions operating at arm's length from national governments, while also envisaging a role for transnational institutions accountable to voters and pressure groups. Now, as then, this design generates tensions between those who wish to reinforce institutions in competing intergovernmental, supranational, and transnational directions (see Chapter 1). As Dehousse and Magnette argue in Chapter 2, conflict over the design of institutions—reminiscent of eighteenth-century debates in the United States (US) between federalists and anti-federalists—has defined European integration and shaped its near-constant process of institutional change over the past thirty years.

Since the 1950s, the EU has taken on an enormous number of new tasks. As it has done so, it has expanded its membership to include a far larger and more diverse collection of states than anyone could have imagined at the beginning, or that its institutional system was ever intended to accommodate. Yet an official who worked for the ECSC in the 1950s would see much that is institutionally familiar in today's EU. He or she would instantly recognize the Council of Ministers and the Court of Justice, and see a strong family resemblance between the High Authority and the Commission, on the one hand, and the Common Assembly and EP, on the other. Perhaps precisely for this reason, institutionalizing collective governance in the EU has become a steadily more difficult—and thus politicized—process that has produced many more and more diverse institutions. Moves to extend the EU's remit to matters of monetary, foreign, defence, and internal security policies (amongst others) have led to more diverse institutional choices. Rather than framing the question as a black-or-white one—'do we want to cede more power to the traditional Community institutions?'—national governments have increasingly turned to *de novo* institutions to carry out specific policy tasks at one remove from other EU institutions. As we noted in Chapter 1, one consequence is that the number of EU institutions has increased from four in 1951 to around sixty in 2016.

This volume has tried to cut through the complexity by approaching each institution in a roughly similar way. Four basic themes have emerged. First, the EU's institutions are irrevocably interdependent. Regardless of how much they compete for power and influence, they are doomed to succeed or fail together. Second, the capacity of EU institutions to govern Europe collectively is increasingly being called into question. The difficulties of managing the euro, as well as an unprecedented influx of migrants, have cast doubt on the ability of the system to generate policies that both work and are seen to work. Third, the process of embedding what is national into what is European has become a far more complicated process than it was when, say, the decision was taken in the 1960s to create a common agricultural policy (CAP) to replace national policies. One result is that (again) member governments have experimented with new forms of *de novo* institutions to achieve collective governance— but, in doing so, they have added to the EU's complexity. Fourth, this volume has shown that the EU institutional system has served as a catalyst for theory-building and testing. Our understanding of how the Union works and (crucially) *why* it works as it does has been greatly enriched as a result. However, the dominance of institutional approaches warrants reflection as to whether other theoretical perspectives are being overlooked.

We develop each of these themes in this final chapter and conclude by grappling with perhaps the most urgent question facing students of the EU's institutional system: can it be made more accountable and more legitimate in the eyes of European citizens? Put another way, can it become a more accepted, respected pivot of political life in Europe, or must it remain a target of the same populist protests that fed the UK's referendum vote to leave the EU and have affected other international organizations, such as the World Trade Organization (WTO) or International Monetary Fund (IMF), as well as national systems of government in Europe and beyond? Our essential argument is that the EU's institutions are arguably the most innovative attempt to secure legitimacy for international cooperation. Nonetheless, further innovation is likely to be required if the EU system is to succeed—or even, perhaps, to survive.

Institutional interdependence

A central theme of this book has been that none of the institutions of the EU is independent and free to act autonomously. The idea of intergovernmental institutions 'bad', supranational institutions 'good', and—increasingly—transnational institutions 'better' seems to be an article of faith for some EU scholars (Mattli and Stone Sweet 2012: 14). The chapters in this volume caution against such rigidity. The EU has always depended on the interaction between different types of institution. It is simplistic to suggest that the EU would function better simply if it were to cede more power to bodies such as the Commission or EP. Moreover, it has become increasingly difficult to identify EU institutions according to one of these three ideal types (intergovernmental, supranational, transnational). To illustrate, the Commission is no longer the archetypal supranational institution it once was: for instance, consider the High Representative's divided loyalty to the College and Council of Ministers and the EP's role in nominating the Commission President. Likewise, quintessentially intergovernmental bodies such as the Committee of Permanent Representatives (Coreper), the Council of Ministers, and the European Council have fine-tuned working methods that seem to some to be more supranational than inter-governmental in character (see Chapters 3, 4, and 14).

We can (usefully) classify EU institutions as executive, legislative, or judicial bod-ies. There is, however, no clear Montesquiean separation of powers in the EU system (see Chapter 1). Instead, EU institutions are interlinked and interdependent. Argu-ably, their powers are *combined* more than they are separated. Every contribution to this volume acknowledges the relationship between the institution(s) in question and other elements in the EU's institutional system. The effect has been to highlight the collective responsibility that the Union's institutions assume for EU policies. It is not only the members of the college of Commissioners who must formally and pub-licly support all decisions of the Commission. More generally, if often informally, all components in the EU's institutional system are cogs in a network of mutually reliant actors who determine how the EU decides policy (Keohane and Hoffmann 1991: 13–15). Even bodies with a high degree of statutory independence, such as the Eu-ropean Central Bank (ECB), are inextricably linked to the EU institutional system. Consider how, as the euro crisis intensified, the ECB was drawn deeper and deeper into EU policy-making (see Chapter 9). ECB President Mario Draghi was left in no doubt of this dynamic in 2015 when a protestor leapt onto the table at one of his typi-cally professorial press conferences and cried, 'End the ECB dictatorship!'

Although it protects some bodies from political interference, the design of the EU's system demands that actors within each of its institutions heed and respond to actors in the other institutions. The Lisbon Treaty explicitly states that the 'institutions shall practice mutual sincere cooperation'.[3] Even the Court of Justice, which fosters an image of distant independence, ultimately depends on the goodwill of the mem-ber states and their courts to implement its judgments (see Chapter 7). Whatever talk there may be of the decline of the Commission, it is hard to see how the Council could prosper without a Commission strong enough to make proposals, broker deals, and sometimes accept criticism for the results. In particular, the need for col-lective governance to maintain the Union's economic clout internationally is some-times so clear that EU member governments are obliged to stand by the institutional system they have created even when its basic authority is questioned and they them-selves appear to attack it.

A good example was the quotas agreed on imports of Chinese textiles after the decades-old international Multi-Fibre Agreement was discontinued in 2004. All EU member governments publicly supported the Commission's attempt to protect against a flood of Chinese imports (or at least did not condemn it) when new quotas were agreed, despite the preference of several member states for a more liberal ap-proach (that is, increases in Chinese imports to satisfy EU consumers). Later, the Commission, and especially Trade Commissioner Peter Mandelson, were blamed by EU governments when the quotas were filled far faster than projected by mid-2005, leaving many European retailers howling. Yet EU governments had mandated the

Commission to negotiate the quotas and were themselves integral parts of the Brussels system that was attacked by much of the European press for the chaos of the 'bra wars' (Heron 2007).

Turf battles go hand in hand with the EU's system of collective governance. In fact, they are one of its most harmful pathologies. At times, the EU's institutions can seem more concerned with expanding their own remits than with ensuring that the EU turns out effective policies. Yet, as Hooghe and Rauh show in Chapter 8, compelling evidence suggests that even the Commission—often seen as the most fervent turf-battler and remit expander—is populated by officials who mostly want the EU to work better.

In any case, the EU's institutions have become increasingly collectively accountable for the work of the Union. Within Council working groups (see Chapter 4), as well as in Coreper (see Chapter 14), national views are merged into agreed positions. Afterwards, national actors are reluctant to reveal the range of views that preceded a decision. The Council often stubbornly defends its common position in codecision with the EP even when it has been accepted with difficulty by some member states. After conciliation produces agreement, it often becomes hard to separate out who was responsible for what. Codecision has not only become (literally) the EU's 'ordinary' decision procedure (see Chapter 6), but also firmly established that most major legislative decisions are made collectively by the Commission, Council, and Parliament. While much is made of the political differences between the EU's main institutions, none can do its job without the others and there is little prospect for a well-functioning Union unless they find ways to work together.

Capacity: Decline or renewal?

A second underlying theme of this book has been the emergence of new questions about whether the EU's institutions are up to the job(s) that they have been given. Even before the Union's membership expanded to twenty-eight (after Brexit, twenty-seven) member states, it was tempting to ask whether European integration had peaked—that is, even if the EU had fostered international cooperation of a kind unprecedented in modern history, was it time to accept that it could never work as well again? It is worth reviewing the arguments presented in this volume that give rise to such stark and disturbing questions.

The leadership problem

This book has highlighted the non-hierarchical character of the EU, and its lack of both government and opposition. European political parties have become increasingly powerful over the last decade (see Chapter 15). But no single grouping can claim to govern the Union nor does any institution enjoy a monopoly over the EU's executive powers (see Chapter 1). There is no cabinet, no single executive. The European Council is the most important locus of executive power in the EU and its powerful influence on the direction of EU policy-making has been plain to see in recent years (see Chapter 3). Here, the 2007 Lisbon Treaty has had a major impact. The 2009 appointment of Herman Van Rompuy as the first full-time President of the European Council was belittled by some; it is now widely agreed that Van Rompuy 'provided continuity and gave the work of the European Council the appearance of seamlessness and flow at an unexpectedly challenging time' (Dinan 2011: 110). His successor, Donald Tusk, played a key role in the 2015 settlement when Greece threatened to crash out of the eurozone and again in negotiating a text to try to mollify UK concerns (unsuccessfully) ahead of its 2016 referendum on continued EU membership.

Still, the EU will probably always fall short of strong or clear political leadership (Hayward 2008; McNamara 2015). Leadership remains a highly contested commodity, as we can see if we consider the various candidates to provide it: the Commission, the Council presidency, or the European Council, and the multiple individuals representing each of them. In the 2010s, the Commission became less like a proto-government and more like any other international bureaucracy, although Jean-Claude Juncker—with his vision of a new-model 'political' Commission—had ambitions to lead where he could (see Chapter 5). The Council presidency's position was conspicuously weakened post-Lisbon in that it was no longer responsible for organizing or chairing European Councils and lost 'ownership' of the common foreign and security policy (CFSP) to the High Representative. Again, the most likely candidate to supply leadership remains the European Council. But it is able to achieve only what member states want it to achieve, with agreements often hammered out bilaterally beyond its walls. While Tusk certainly concentrated the minds of the EU heads of state or governments to keep Greece in the euro in 2015, it is doubtful that he changed any. Where national differences are deeply rooted, even the most skilled broker often cannot forge consensus, as illustrated by Tusk's candid admission in September 2015 that Europe had lost control of its borders amidst a flood of migrants.

It might be argued that institutions do not lead, leaders must lead. It is up to the EU's member governments, individually or in alliances, to provide political direction. If we take this view, we inevitably end up asking whether past sources of leadership—such as the Franco–German alliance—can persist. Two of the fundamental lessons of this volume help us to frame, if not answer, this question. First, we have seen that powers are now more widely shared amongst the EU's institutions than ever before, making it more difficult for one member state or any group of them to give political impulses that resonate across the Union's institutional system. Second, while crises may still give scope for Franco–German leadership, strong, decisive action at the EU level often requires political agency from multiple sources. This dynamic can be seen in the multitude of voices that speak for the EU on the international stage, ranging from the presidents of the European Council, the Commission, the Council of Ministers, the Eurogroup, and the ECB to individual Commissioners or member state ministers acting alone or in concert. Confusion about who really speaks for Europe shapes the calculations of non-Europeans about how important the Union really is. The point was exemplified by how the EU's High Representative and the foreign ministers of France, Germany, and the UK all participated in the so-called P5 + 1 negotiations with Iran on its nuclear programme. Insiders reported that Iranian participants were baffled by the formula of having the EU's High Representative chair negotiations. Yet Catherine Ashton and her successor, Federica Mogherini, played an integral part in one in the most important diplomatic deals of the twenty-first century thus far—something that would have been unthinkable to EU watchers twenty years ago. Nevertheless, the evolution of the EU towards a more diverse political and institutional system raises profound doubts about whether the Union of the future can rely on past sources of political leadership.

The management problem

The EU's lack of hierarchy has benefits. It sustains participation by many parties because the policy agenda seems (in appearance, at least) remarkably open. No one wins all the time and even losers in policy debates can become winners by shifting the agenda towards new policies that mitigate or cancel out past ones. Ultimately, collective governance is unsustainable in the absence of compromise: we can expect those who lose policy arguments to compromise today only if they can hope to be winners in tomorrow's policy debates.

Yet the EU's lack of hierarchy creates problems of management, as well as political drift. At earlier stages in its evolution, member states might have looked to the Commission or the Council to manage most EU policy-making. But the reality is different now: no genuine hierarchy of policy goals exists and there is no body or institution able to impose one. The problem is exacerbated when, as at the time of writing, the EU was confronting multiple crises at the same time.

Especially in an enlarged Union, the lack of hierarchy often means that the EU goes to almost absurd lengths to accommodate every voice. The American delegation headed by George W. Bush that visited Brussels in 2005 was bemused by the approximately seventy different speeches to which they were subjected by EU representatives in the course of a few days of meetings. The severity of the management costs of the EU's hyper-pluralism has been highlighted perceptively by Metcalfe (2000). Put simply, the EU's institutional system—whatever its virtues—is a recipe for undermanagement. Regardless of how high and mighty the European Council looks, much EU governance occurs within horizontally structured and often highly autonomous policy networks that preside over individual policy sectors (Peterson and Bomberg 2001; Jordan and Schout 2006). The EU's main institutions are well represented in most of them (especially since codecision marked a substantial upgrade in the EP's powers) and inter-institutional politics occur within them: agents of the

Commission, EP, and Council can be relied upon to defend their institutions' prerogatives and priorities staunchly. Nevertheless, responsibility is still shared for *outcomes*. As such, none of the EU's individual institutions have strong incentives to invest in the capacity of networks to manage the policy agenda: to set priorities, to follow up past initiatives, and to ensure effective implementation.

Moreover, the Union's management problem almost naturally gets worse over time. There is little to suggest that Metcalfe's (2000: 824) summary of the reasons why is any less valid now than it was when he offered it at the turn of the millennium:

[A] combination of factors operating within the EU's institutional framework creates political incentives to take on more tasks while imposing constraints on the acquisition and development of capacities for managing them effectively. In the Council, political decision-makers too readily assume the existence of management capacities and governance structures to implement policies or dodge the difficult issues about who should provide them. The Commission has been more interested in staking out new territorial claims than insisting on the resources for discharging responsibilities effectively.

Weak management usually means poor coordination and a lack of priorities. Witness the increasing inability of the General Affairs Council (GAC) to impose direction on or set priorities for EU policy-making (see Chapter 4). One possibility is that EU member states eventually will choose arrangements that mirror those in the European Council and Foreign Affairs Council (FAC) by appointing full-time chairs. The Eurogroup, which brings together national finance ministers of euro members, took a step in this direction when they appointed one of their members in 2005 to a fixed term of office as chair rather than rotating the presidency between member states every six months. The chair chosen in 2013, Jeroen Dijsselbloem, simultaneously served as Dutch finance minister, and it can have been little short of impossible to manage both a national and European portfolio at the height of the euro crisis. For this reason, the so-called Five Presidents' Report on completing monetary union called for the creation of a permanent Eurogroup President in 2015 (Juncker *et al.* 2015). It remained to be seen whether the idea would be taken up, but it hinted at the possibility of a future system of cabinet governance in which all versions of the Council had their own 'permanent' chairs to take charge of the day-to-day management of business.

One way in which to deal with this management problem has been to increase political and financial scrutiny by agents looking right across the EU's system of collective governance. A good example is the European Ombudsman, who has become an important figure in forcing EU institutions to march to the sound of a single drum on a range of issues of (mal)administration.[4] Another is the empowerment of the Court of Auditors and the creation of the European Anti-Fraud Office (OLAF), which both could be taken as evidence that, from a rather modest beginning, the EU has adopted a much tighter and uniform regime of financial control in recent years (see Chapter 11).

The problem of integrating interests

Until the 1980s, the task of integrating interests was a relatively simple one of integrating the national interests of its member states. The then European Community primarily dealt with narrowly circumscribed areas of policy marked out for collective governance, such as the CAP and external trade. Policy-making was an elite-driven exercise, more or less monopolized by national executives working with the Commission. The EP was an assembly of seconded national parliamentarians. The Economic and Social Committee was a pseudo-corporatist talking shop. Both were easily ignorable by the Council. The Commission was always less ignorable, and took pains to ingratiate itself with broad social and political interests, while trying to integrate them into Europe-wide associations. But not until the Delors era did the Commission make common cause with pan-European interests, such as the European Round Table of Industrialists (ERT) as part of efforts to complete the single market.

Now, the problem of integrating interests is far more acute. The EU's policy agenda has expanded enormously. More societal interests have a stake in EU policy-making and demand a voice in the process. The direct election of members of the European Parliament (MEPs) since 1979 and the emergence of the EP as co-legislator with the Council has reinforced this trend by establishing a powerful transnational institution at the heart of the Union. In the 1990s, Shackleton (1997: 70, emphasis original) noted that the EU had (at the time) only recently been transformed from 'a system concerned with the *administration of things* to one concerned with the *governance of people*'. The speed of developments since makes this moment now seem a long time ago. The EU has since become a far more important purveyor of public goods. Yet the Union has made fewer, shorter strides towards integrating societal interests compared to the steps it has taken to subject new policies to collective governance.

Two caveats must be offered here. One is that the EU system does a remarkably proficient job of integrating the *institutional* interests of its main players. No important EU policy can be agreed—outside of a few sectors such as competition—without a large measure of consensus spanning the Council, the Commission, and the EP. Even the EU's more recent institutions, which tend to privilege national interests and are overwhelmingly staffed by national officials, provide the Commission and the EP with channels for input. A good example is the Stockholm Programme on justice and home affairs (JHA), which brought together both national foreign affairs and JHA officials to assess terrorist threats from particular countries, but with annual assessments of whether liaison on counter-terrorism with foreign governments is effectively carried out by the Commission.[5] Collective institutional responsibility for EU policy, which must be a central goal of any effective system of collective governance, is something the EU does rather well.

Second, the EU's institutional system has, over time, become better at integrating sectoral interests. A key feature of modern international cooperation is the emergence of various kinds of policy-specialized transgovernmental networks, populated by actors who have more in common with each other than with officials who specialize in other policy areas, even those who share their nationality (Ruggie 2002; Slaughter 2009). The implication is that the EU must integrate a far wider diversity of more differentially concerned 'national interests' than was the case for most of its history. On the basis of this test, Coreper has become an effective integrator of the interests of increasingly more divided and less single-minded national civil services. Meanwhile, the growing popularity of strong, independent EU agencies offers a mechanism for the integration of functional interests in an era of 'sectoral unbundling'.

At the same time, Part III of this volume contains plenty of proof of the EU's failure to integrate wider societal interests effectively. Pan-European party groups in the EP remain very far from commanding the loyalty and support of European citizens (see Chapter 15). It is a strain to conclude that the European Economic and Social Committee (EESC) is even worth having, and the Committee of the Regions (CoR) is at best but one of a number of channels for regional interests to make their mark and by no means the most important one (see Chapter 16).

From the Community to the Union method?

Despite all of the Union's problems, there are reasons to be optimistic about the future of the EU's institutions. One is the EU's proven capacity for improvization (Peterson and Bomberg 2001: 58–9). Traditionally, only when faced with a crisis has the Union been able to innovate. Although it has been much-repeated since the post-2008 financial crisis, Stanford economist Paul Romer seems to have coined the phrase 'a crisis is a terrible thing to waste'.[6] The EU bears living testimony to this injunction, from the Treaty of Rome's attempt to revive the idea of European integration after the failure of the European Defence Community (EDC) to the numerous reforms enacted in light of the euro crisis.

As problems facing the EU have intensified, so has its capacity for institutional experimentation. Debate raged across Europe about whether measures taken to contain the eurozone crisis—such as creating (what became) the European Stability Mechanism (ESM) to support eurozone countries that experienced financial difficulties—were in the best tradition of EU improvisation or revealed the failure of European leaders to get 'out ahead' of powerful market forces. But the debate also placed on the EU's agenda previously unimaginable proposals to move towards a banking union, Commission scrutiny of draft national budgets, and even a common eurozone treasury. This spoke to what UK Chancellor George Osborne (hardly a staunch Euro-enthusiast) referred to as the 'remorseless logic' of European integration (Osborne 2014).

Another reason to think that European integration is more than an historical artefact is the variety of new methods that have become alternatives to the standard

Community method of delegating to the EU's legislative institutions. Admirers of the Community method often pour scorn on such alternatives. But they at least signal that EU member governments remain willing to extend collective governance to the point of institutionalizing new policy cooperation, even if it results in strange and awkward new institutions.

As such, one of the central themes of this book has been how much more varied and complex the institutionalization of collective European governance has become. Take, as examples, the ESM, European border agency Frontex, and the European External Action Service (EEAS). Despite their obvious differences, all three eschew the delegation of powers to traditional Community institutions along classic lines. All preserve a role for individual member states that is stronger and less challengeable by other EU's institutions than is the case under the Community method (Wallace and Reh 2015).

The origins of the Community method can be traced back to Lindberg (1965: 62), who coined the term to describe the 'hard bargaining and horse trading, tenacious defence of national interests, and persistent reluctance by the governments to grant any more authority to the central institutions than was unavoidable'. This approach contrasted with what Lindberg (1965: 62) referred to as 'Community romanticism', by which he meant the view 'that governments made real sacrifices of national interest with a view to achieving Community consensus'. Thus the term 'Community method' was intended to inject a sense of realism into views about what the institutions of the fledgling European Community did.

There is no commonly agreed definition of the Community method today, but the best known is found in the Commission's White Paper on European Governance (European Commission 2001b). According to this definition, the Commission's primary role is to propose policy and legislation, and to represent the EU in international negotiations. The Council and the EP, meanwhile, adopt legislative and budgetary acts, with decisions by the former typically based on qualified majority voting (QMV). Responsibility for policy execution falls either to the Commission or national authorities, with the Court of Justice tasked with upholding the rule of EU law throughout.

In retrospect, we can see that the Community method has been under threat since the early 1990s (Devuyst 2005). Moreover, there is nothing new about the EU being used for narrow and ostensibly 'national' purposes 'to extend the policy resources available to the member states' (Wallace 2010: 89). A key question for students of EU institutions is thus how the Union's system of collective governance should work if not according to the Community method. Some scholars look to the literature on Europeanization to understand the changing organizational logic of the EU (Graziano and Vink 2007; Sedelmeier 2011; Börzel and Risse 2012; Bulmer and Lequesne 2016). Others point towards the emergence of a new 'Union method' (Chang 2013), which combines the Community method with what German Chancellor Angela Merkel has called 'coordinated action in a spirit of solidarity' (Merkel 2010: 7).

Perhaps the prime illustration in this volume of the Union method in action is the increasingly ubiquitous role of the European Council (see Chapter 3), even if we might doubt how much it really controls or even monitors. Another is the enhanced role of national parliaments in EU decision-making, manifest in the 'yellow card' system created by the Lisbon Treaty, which allows national legislators to band together to challenge unwanted EU proposals. To these examples could be added how Coreper has assumed an essential role at the interface between the EU and its member states, and incidentally has gone from being a collection of 'bad guys' to one of 'good guys' in the eyes of those who are most enthusiastic about European integration.

More challenging for the idea of the Union method is the rise of *de novo* bodies in recent decades (see Chapter 1). One view of these new institutions, many with distinctive remits or compositions, is that they are actually a new form of supranational institution and, by implication, a means to revive the Community method (Schimmelfennig 2015b). But this view rests uneasily with the embedding of national authorities in the decision-making structures of such bodies. For example, the board of governors of the ESM consists of finance ministers of participating members, with representatives from the Commission and ECB invited to attend its meetings only as observers.

An alternative take on *de novo* bodies is that they are a response to the EU's legitimacy problems (Bickerton *et al.* 2015a). From this perspective, EU member states' recourse to institutional experimentation marks an attempt to extend collective governance without being seen to transfer powers in a straight and linear way to traditional Community institutions. A key question for the future is whether this trend will continue or whether, alternatively, we might see a reconsolidation of policy-making via the Community method. Wolfgang Schäuble—German finance minister and an ardent supporter of deeper integration—was among those to push for Treaty change to bring the various ad hoc intergovernmental institutions created in response to the euro crisis under the Treaties and thus under the control of supranational institutions. However, at the time of writing, there was little appetite among the heads of state or government for a large-scale change given the very real prospect that one or more member state would reject any Treaty change. We thus must ask whether the EU's collective system of governance can survive if member states continue to be more intent on working around, rather than resolving, its persistent problems of legitimacy.

Where the Community method survives or has been extended, levers for national influence have been retained and guarded jealously. A critical case here is JHA, one of the few areas of policy-making that has seen the powers of the Commission and Court of Justice extended in recent decades. In reality, JHA has never been a straightforward case of communitarization, because member states have retained a large measure of control over the most sensitive internal security questions (Wolff 2015). The persistence of national controls can be seen in relation to the EU's common approach to asylum, which worked reasonably well until the European migration crisis of 2015, but then buckled. The Commission's initial attempts to relocate migrants across EU member states fell short, putting severe strain on the Schengen system and leaving both the Community and Union methods in a perilous state.

In the final analysis, we cannot predict where the EU is headed in institutional terms. But it is clear that the Union and its member states will face more hard choices about whether and how cooperation is institutionalized in the years ahead. The choices made could have profound consequences in determining the durability of the EU.

Theorizing EU institutions: Are we all institutionalists now?

If this book has grappled with one theoretical question above all others, it is this: in what ways do institutions matter? Nearly all contributors to this volume have drawn on the insights of institutional theory in at least one of the variants described in Chapter 1. This outcome should come as no surprise—this book, after all, is an in-depth study of EU institutions—but the range of the theoretical approaches surveyed is still striking.

In line with institutional theory, we have seen that institutions—how they are constructed, how they work, and how they interact—are a powerful determinant of EU politics. A close reading of this volume yields one heuristic point above all others: the process of collective governance in Europe cannot be understood without intimate knowledge of the EU's institutions and policies. Moreover, themes that emerge from a scan across the full landscape of the EU's institutions are, we would submit, central to the study of European integration more generally and include the following:

- There is considerable scope for institutional *agency* in EU politics, which inevitably makes inter-institutional competition a primary feature of EU policy-making. The ill-tempered dispute between the European Council and EP over the *Spitzenkandidaten* ('lead candidate') method of nominating Juncker points, above all, to the considerable political weight that Commission presidents wield (see Chapters 5 and 6), as well as how the EP often manages to 'squeeze out' power in areas in which it previously lacked it (Corbett *et al.* 2015: 61). The conflict could easily rear its head again when it comes time to appoint Juncker's successor.

- The EU's institutional system generates *multiple identities*, the importance of which cannot be discounted in policy debates. To take a prominent example, Angela Merkel showed genuine leadership in extolling the virtues of a *Willkommenskultur* in the teeth of Europe's migrant crisis and earned—in the judgement of *The Economist*—the mantle of 'the indispensable European', while being chosen as *Time* magazine's 2015 Person of the Year.[7] Yet she was forced to accept multiple German domestic policy measures to limit asylum seekers from achieving refugee status or bringing their close relatives to Germany in early 2016, when polls suggested that more than 80 per cent of Germans thought her government had mishandled the refugee crisis.[8]

- *Path-dependence* can be powerful in the EU's institutional system to the extent that it becomes hard not to be pessimistic about the system's ability to cope with the Union's need for localized solutions to dissimilar policy problems.

- Austerity was imposed on multiple EU states during the eurozone crisis in exchange for EU–IMF bailouts—including on Greece, a comparatively closed economy that has long lacked competitiveness in international markets, as well as Ireland, one of the world's most open economies that traded more with non-eurozone countries than with those who shared the currency. Ireland's rapid recovery from its fiscal crisis compared to that of Greece had less to do with the former's greater acceptance of austerity than the underlying strength of its economy.

- One implication of the strength of path-dependence in the EU is that *principal–agent relationships* are often troubled and contested, with inevitable policy costs. In accepting that the Commission would scrutinize national draft fiscal budgets, member states had to accept that, inevitably, there would be conflict in agreeing changes to proposed national budgets as the new agent (the Commission) responsible for oversight on the part of principals (member states) took different views about what was or was not fiscally responsible. In 2016, in the case of Portugal—which had required EU assistance during the eurozone crisis—the Commission narrowly avoided outright conflict with a new anti-austerity Portuguese government. In a typical euro compromise, the Commission approved Portugal's draft budget (which was initially deemed overly profligate) in exchange for an agreement that it would continue to monitor Portuguese public spending.

This survey of the EU's institutions, like institutional theory itself, might seem to paint a sombre, downbeat, pessimistic picture of modern politics. Prominent themes include inertia, pathology, turf battles, and so on. Yet, as suggested by work that applies institutionalist theory to international organizations (Keohane 1998; Ikenberry 2009; Peters 2011), it is possible to view international institutions—including those of the EU—as purveyors of innovative solutions to the problems of modern governance. While they often seem trapped by path-dependency, the EU's institutions are usually better able than European governments to embrace long-term solutions to problems such as global warming, the aging of the European workforce, or fostering civil society in Europe's neighbourhood. To illustrate, it is difficult to imagine that any EU government could have, on its own, developed the ten-year Europe 2020 strategy with its headline goal of 'smart, sustainable, inclusive growth', and detailed commitments to better coordination of national and EU policies.[9]

EU institutions almost always outperform their international counterparts in terms of efficiency and effectiveness. Consider, for example, the rapidity with which the Council and EP agreed on legally binding commitments to reduce greenhouse gas emissions compared to the long years of negotiation within the United Nations (UN) before agreement on the much-less-binding Paris Agreement was reached in 2015. For these reasons, students of politics and IR—however much their eyes may glaze over at the mention of terms such as 'codecision'—have much to learn from the study of EU institutions. Indeed, seminal scholars such as March and Olsen (1989) and Pierson (1996) have cut their theoretical teeth on case studies of EU institutions that had general applicability in wider studies of politics and IR. In this sense, students of EU institutions have become theory-makers, as well as theory-takers, in ways to which they aspired in the heyday of integration theory, but never quite achieved.

Yet amidst these three cheers for institutionalism, we caution our readers to consider what happened after Richard Nixon's infamous claim in 1971, 'We're all Keynesians now.'[10] What ensued was the long era of Reagan, Thatcher, and monetarist economics—the latter almost a mirror image of Keynesianism—in the 1980s. If we are 'all institutionalists now', might not this be the harbinger of some 'post-institutionalist' turn in the study of the EU? Theoretical paradigms come and go in social science, and the dominance of institutionalism should not be taken for granted. One warning sign is that the new institutionalism has increasingly become a battle between ever-increasing numbers of institutionalisms that are distinguished by ever decreasing differences.

Consider, for example, an (early) critique by Blyth (1997) of how different variants of the (then) new institutionalism considered the impact of ideas on political outcomes.[11] By this account, multiple institutionalists were guilty of reducing ideas to ' "filler" to shore up . . . already existing research programs rather than treat[ing] them as objects of investigation in their own right' (Blyth 1997: 229). As the shift from Keynesianism to monetarism demonstrated, ideas can be powerful determinants of political outcomes that can overwhelm institutions, and the path-dependency, inertia, and turf battles to which they give rise.

We do not discount the possibility of an eventual shift away from institutionalist studies of the EU. To illustrate, one contender to mainstream institutionalist analysis of the EU is the 'varieties of capitalism', an influential school of comparative political economy that sees institutions as emerging in a bottom-up manner in accordance with the underlying model of capitalism rather than as something imposed from the top down by policy-makers (Hall and Soskice 2001). Applied to EU institutions, the varieties of capitalism school generates important insights into why particular member states favour different institutional arrangements, as in Fioretos's (2001) link between German firms' reliance on financing through banks and Germany's reticence about extending the single market to financial services. A strength of this approach is that it shows just how difficult it is for EU institutions to govern collectively, when such governing imposes one-size-fits-all policies on diverse models of capitalism (Bickerton et al. 2015a). A limitation of the varieties of capitalism school is that it tends to emphasize the incompatibility of EU institutions with national models of capitalism (Johnston and Regan 2016) and so struggles to explain why member states would choose to create such institutions in the first place. Too often, this puzzle is accounted for by overblown claims about the power of neoliberal ideas to override national interests (Hall 2008).

Still, the UK's referendum vote in 2016 to leave the EU serves as a powerful reminder that we can take neither EU institutions nor the claims of institutional theories for granted. For all of the power vested in bodies such as the Commission, Court of Justice, and EP over the last sixty years, these institutions were essentially powerless as British politicians fought for and against the UK's continued membership of the Union. If EU institutions featured at all in the referendum debate, it was as cartoon caricatures of unelected bureaucrats in Brussels—a depiction that did no justice to the combination of intergovernmental, supranational, and transnational bodies that govern the EU. Institutional theory struggles to explain why the UK prime minister even called the referendum, other than perhaps as a rare and misplaced attempt by a head of state or government to tie his hands in a two-level game (Hodson and Maher 2014). Theorists have their work cut out to understand exactly how the UK will extricate itself from more than four decades of dense institutional cooperation with EU partners. Andrew Moravscsik (2016), arguably the leading theorist of European integration, has suggested that the UK's relationship with European countries could be much the same before and after Brexit, while Daniel Drezner, a leading light in the study of international political economy, suggests that Brexit has turned our understanding of international relations on its head (Beauchamp 2016). Both scholars cannot be right.

Conclusion: The accountability conundrum

If there is a single burning question that arises from studying the EU's institutions, it might be the accountability question: how can the Union's institutions, in the absence of a truly European polity, become more accountable to citizens and thus a more legitimate level of governance? One view advocates direct, transnational democracy, such as by instituting the direct election of the President of the Commission (Hix 2008), empowering national parliaments in EU decision-making, or by fostering truly pan-European political parties (see Chapter 15). The *Spitzenkandidaten* method of nominating the Commission President (see Chapters 5 and 6) represents an important step in this direction. Yet, at the time of writing, it had done more to embolden the Commission and EP as political actors than to connect Europe to its citizens. Turnout at the 2014 EP elections was around 43 per cent (compared to 62 per cent in 1979) and just 13 per cent in one of the EU's newest member states, Slovakia. All eyes are now on the 2019 EP elections to see if the contest for the Commission presidency, and an EP majority, can capture the public imagination.

It might be easier to envisage European political leaders better able to sell the EU's institutions to its citizens. It is commonplace to criticize the current generation of EU leaders for their lack of commitment to the European project. Yet twenty-first-century Europe's political class has been populated by articulate and committed pro-Europeans who have faced crises of which their predecessors could not have dreamt in their worst nightmares. A prime example is Angela Merkel, who was crucial to political agreement on the Lisbon Treaty, was staunch in insisting that defence of the euro was in the German interest, and showed political courage during the refugee crisis. Moreover, some amongst the EU's recently most fluent political communicators—Barroso, Van Rompuy, Draghi, Juncker, Mogherini—have made effective mouthpieces of posts that either did not exist or had been transformed since the heroic epoch of European integration in the 1980s.

Yet the EU's accountability problem persists and, as the UK's vote to leave the EU suggests, it might prove fatal to the Union. Member governments accept the need to pool sovereignty at the EU level to achieve collective governance. But they refuse to create clear, straight, simple lines of accountability of the sort that allow citizens to throw out a government they previously have elected and substitute an opposition (Peterson 1997). It is a challenge that could lead us to conclude that the EU's institutional system is on the verge of breakdown, especially given recent enlargements to include poorer states whose citizens have little-to-no experience of multiculturalism, or the integration of migrants, combined with declining enthusiasm for the EU in Europe's more mature democracies. Add to the equation unrest over the consequences of the decisions taken to defend the Schengen system or the euro and the result is a classic collective action problem, in which 'free-riders'—consider the cases of Hungary or Greece—fail to act in the interests of the collective (Olson 2009).

Of course, the collective action problems of all international organizations grow as their membership increases. But no international organization is as powerful as the EU and thus none faces such demands for accountability according to democratic standards. To its credit, the EU has gone further than any other international body in its attempt to secure legitimacy. No other international body boasts such intensive involvement from national governments in its intergovernmental institutions. None have such powerful supranational institutions capable of locking in the benefits of cooperation between sovereign states. Only the EU boasts such a powerful transnational institution as the EP, the world's only directly elected multinational parliament. And yet none of this has been sufficient to legitimate the EU's extraordinary experiment in governance beyond the nation-state.

Taking the analogy further, the EU's institutions could be viewed as prototypes for global institutions that might one day govern something like a 'single', global market. It is easy to stretch this analogy too far and to be seduced by the naive, Wilsonian vision of world government that was widely embraced in the interwar period, only to be challenged by realist IR theorists in the 1950s as intellectually bankrupt. Yet it was precisely then that the EU embarked on its extraordinary mission of institution-building in the pursuit of collective governance. One long-term effect has been to mark out the EU's institutions as models for other international organizations that need to be made more accountable and subject to democratic controls. The view of Keohane (1998), perhaps the most influential of all IR scholars, is that the task of democratizing international organizations is not that much more challenging than was the task of creating and institutionalizing democracy at the domestic level during the passing of the era of the 'divine right of kings' in the seventeenth and eighteenth centuries. This view might be dismissed as naive (or peculiarly American), but its existence shows us both that there is much about the EU's institutional system that is admired (as well as much that is heartily disliked) *and* that the Union's democratic conundrum reflects wider problems of democratizing global governance.

As we have seen, the EU's institutions sometimes—perhaps even often—facilitate collective governance on divisive issues such as market liberalization, climate change, and the EU's relations with the world in ways that are politically ingenious. When the EU's institutions work well together, the Union's policy process takes on a sort of epileptic charm, much like good jazz music, blending European traditions, languages, and experiences. When EU institutions work badly, the experience is closer to free jazz, a cacophonous and atonal mix of music that causes all but aficionados to switch off their radios. Historically, its institutions have worked well enough to ensure that the EU—however uncertain its future may appear—remains the champion of those who wish and hope for more and more effective collective governance internationally.

ENDNOTES

1. Quoted in *Financial Times*, 25 June 2016.
2. Quoted in Kettle (2011).
3. Art. 13 TEU.
4. The Ombudsman has assumed extensive powers under Art. 228 TFEU to examine cases of maladministration and, more generally, has felt free to criticize the way in which the institutions operate. Most have in turn felt obliged to respond and to improve their working methods, such as recruitment procedures or responses to public requests for information.
5. See *The Stockholm Programme: An Open and Secure Europe Serving and Protecting Citizens*, available online at https://ec.europa.eu/anti-trafficking/eu-policy/stockholm-programme-open-and-secure-europe-serving-and-protecting-citizens-0_en. The Stockholm Programme was succeeded by Strategic Guidelines for JHA in 2014 (see Chapter 12).
6. Quoted in Rosenthal (2009).
7. See *The Economist* (2015) and Gibbs (2015).
8. See Faiola (2016).
9. For more information, see http://ec.europa.eu/europe2020/europe-2020-in-a-nutshell/index_en.htm
10. It turns out that Nixon actually said 'I am now a Keynesian' and that the 'we're all Keynesians now' quip came from a 1965 cover story in *Time* that attributed it to the economist Milton Friedman (Bartlett 2013).
11. Interestingly, the author was later one of the most trenchant critics of the austerity programmes that took force in Europe after 2008.

❚ REFERENCES

Adams, M., de Waele, H., Meeusen, J., and Straetmans, G. (2013) *Judging Europe's Judges: The Legitimacy of the Case Law of the European Court of Justice* (London: Bloomsbury).

Adler, E., and Pouliot, V. (2011) 'International practices', *International Theory*, 3/1: 1–36.

Adler-Nissen, R. (2008) 'The diplomacy of opting out: A Bourdieudian approach to national integration strategies', *Journal of Common Market Studies*, 46/3, 663–84.

Adler-Nissen, R. (2009a) 'Behind the scenes of differentiated integration: Circumventing national opt-outs in Justice and Home Affairs', *Journal of European Public Policy*, 16/1: 62–80.

Adler-Nissen, R. (2009b) 'Late sovereign diplomacy', *The Hague Journal of Diplomacy*, 4/2: 121–41.

Adler-Nissen, R. (2014) 'Stigma management in international relations: Transgressive identities, norms, and order in international society', *International Organization*, 68/1: 143–76.

Adler-Nissen, R. (2016) 'Towards a practice turn in EU studies: The everyday of European integration', *Journal of Common Market Studies*, 54/1: 87–103.

Allen, D. (1998) 'Who speaks for Europe? The search for an effective and coherent external policy', in J. Peterson and H. Sjursen (eds) *A Common Foreign Policy for Europe* (London: Routledge): 41–58.

Alliance of Liberals and Democrats for Europe (ALDE) (2011) *Position Paper on Budget Post 2013* (Brussels: Alliance of Liberals and Democrats for Europe).

Alter, K.J. (1998) 'Who are the "masters of the treaty"? European governments and the European Court of Justice', *International Organization*, 52/1: 121–47.

Alter, K.J. (2001) *Establishing the Supremacy of European Law: The Making of an International Rule of Law in Europe* (Oxford: Oxford University Press).

Amtenbrink, F., and Van Duin, K.P. (2009) 'The European Central Bank before the European Parliament: Theory and practice after ten years of monetary dialogue', *European Law Review*, 34/4: 561–83.

Anderson, J.J. (1997) 'Hard interests, soft power, and Germany's changing role in Europe', in P. Katzenstein (ed.) *Tamed Power: Germany in Europe* (Ithaca, NY: Cornell University Press): 80–107.

Anderson, J. (1999) *German Unification and the Union of Europe: The Domestic Politics of Integration Policy* (Cambridge: Cambridge University Press).

Andrews, D. (2003) 'The Committee of Central Bank Governors as a source of rules', *Journal of European Public Policy*, 10/6: 956–73.

Arestis, P., and Sawyer, M. (2001) 'Will the euro bring economic crisis to Europe?', Levy Economics Institute of Bard College Working Paper No. 322.

Armstrong, K.A., and Bulmer, S. (1998) *The Governance of the Single European Market* (Manchester: Manchester University Press).

Atkins, R., Daneshkhu, S., and Parker, S. (2005) 'Eurozone ministers say rates must stay on hold', *Financial Times*, 30 November.

Auel, K. (2007) 'Democratic accountability and national parliaments: Redefining the impact of parliamentary scrutiny in EU affairs', *European Law Journal*, 13/4: 487–504.

Avant, D.D., Finnemore, M., and Sell, S.K. (2010) *Who Governs the Globe?* (Cambridge: Cambridge University Press).

Bache, I. (2008) 'Europeanization and multi-level governance: Empirical findings and conceptual challenges', ARENA Working Papers No 16.

Bailer, S. (2009) 'The puzzle of continuing party group cohesion in the European Parliament after Eastern enlargement', in K. Benoit and D. Giannetti (eds) *Intra-Party Politics and Coalition Governments* (London: Routledge): 192–204.

Balfour, R., Carta, C., and Raik, K. (2015) *The European External Action Service and National Foreign Ministries: Convergence or Divergence?* (Aldershot: Ashgate).

Balint, T., Bauer, M.W., and Knill, C. (2008) 'Bureaucratic change in the European administrative space: The case of the European Commission', *West European Politics*, 31/4: 677–700.

Ban, C. (2013) *Management and Culture in an Enlarged European Commission: From Diversity to Unity?* (Basingstoke: Palgrave Macmillan).

Barroso, J.M. (2007) 'Better institutions for better results', Speech 07/203 (Brussels: European Commission).

Bartlett, B. (2013) 'Keynes and Keynesianism', *Economix: Explaining the Science of Everyday Life, The New York Times,* 14 May, available online at http://economix.blogs.nytimes.com/2013/05/14/keynes-and-keynesianism/

Bauer, M.W. (2002) 'Reforming the European Commission: A (missed?) academic opportunity', *European Integration Online Papers (EIoP)*, 6(8).

BBC News (2004) 'MEPs approve revamped Commission', 18 November, available online at http://news.bbc.co.uk/1/hi/world/europe/4021499.stm

Beach, D. (2008) 'The facilitator of efficient negotiations in the Council: The impact of the Council Secretariat', in D. Naurin and H. Wallace (eds) *Unveiling the Council of the European Union* (Basingstoke: Palgrave Macmillan): 219–37.

Beauchamp, Z. (2016) 'Brexit is terrifying—and no, not because of the economics', *Vox World*, 24 June.

Benedetto, G. (2013) 'The EU budget after Lisbon: Rigidity and reduced spending?', *Journal of Public Policy*, 33/3: 345–69.

Best, E., Christiansen, T., and Settembrini, P. (eds) (2008) *The Institutions of the Enlarged European Union: Continuity and Change* (Cheltenham: Edward Elgar).

Beyers, J. (2005) 'Multiple embeddedness and socialization in Europe: The case of Council officials', *International Organization*, 59/4: 899–936.

Beyers, J., and Kerremans, B. (2004) 'Bureaucrats, politicians, and societal interests: How is European policy making politicized?', *Comparative Political Studies*, 37/10: 1119–50.

Bickerton, C.J. (2012) *European Integration: From Nation-States to Member States* (Oxford: Oxford University Press).

Bickerton, C.J., Hodson, D., and Puetter, U. (eds) (2015a) *The New Intergovernmentalism: States and Supranational Actors in the Post Maastricht Era* (Oxford: Oxford University Press).

Bickerton, C.J., Hodson, D., and Puetter, U. (2015b) 'The new intergovernmentalism: European integration in the post-Maastricht era', *Journal of Common Market Studies*, 53/4: 703–22.

Biesenbender, J. (2011) 'The dynamics of treaty change: Measuring the distribution of power in the European Union?', *European Integration online Papers (EIoP)*, 15/1.

Bildt, C. (1998) *Peace Journey: The Struggle for Peace in Bosnia* (London: Weidenfeld & Nicolson).

Billiet, S., Hodson, D., and Maher, I. (2009) 'The principal-agent approach to EU studies: Apply liberally but handle with care', *Comparative European Politics*, 7/4: 409–13.

Blomgren, M. (2003) *Cross-Pressure and Political Representation in Europe: A Comparative Study of MEPs and the Intra-Party Arena* (Umeå: Department of Political Science).

Blom-Hansen, J., and Brandsma, G.J. (2009) 'The EU comitology system: Intergovernmental bargaining and deliberative supranationalism?', *Journal of Common Market Studies*, 47/4: 719–40.

Blondel, J. (1970) 'Legislative behaviour: Some steps towards a cross-national measurement', *Government and Opposition*, 5/01: 67–85.

Blyth, M. (1997) ' "Any more bright ideas?" The ideational turn of comparative political economy', *Comparative Politics*, 29/1: 229–50.

Borrás, S., and Jacobsson, K. (2004) 'The open method of co-ordination and new governance patterns in the EU', *Journal of European Public Policy*, 11/2: 185–208.

Börzel, T.A., and Risse, T. (2012) 'From Europeanisation to diffusion: Introduction', *West European Politics*, 35/1: 1–19.

Bostock, D. (2002) 'Coreper revisited', *Journal of Common Market Studies*, 40/2: 215–34.

Boswell, C., and Geddes, A. (2011) *Migration and Mobility in the European Union* (Basingstoke: Palgrave Macmillan).

Bourdieu, P. (1977) *Outline of a Theory of Practice* (Cambridge: Cambridge University Press).

Bovens, M. (2007a) 'Analysing and assessing accountability: A conceptual framework', *European Law Journal*, 13/4: 447–68.

Bovens, M. (2007b) 'New forms of accountability and EU-governance', *Comparative European Politics*, 5/1: 104–20.

Bowler, S., and Farrell, D.M. (1995) 'The organizing of the European Parliament: Committees, specialization and co-ordination', *British Journal of Political Science*, 25/2: 219–43.

Bowler, S., and McElroy, G. (2015) 'Political group cohesion and "hurrah" voting in the European Parliament', *Journal of European Public Policy*, 22/9: 1355–65.

Bowler, S., Farrell, D. M., and Katz, R. S. (1999) 'Party cohesion, party discipline, and parliaments' in S. Bowler, D. Farrell and R.S. Katz (eds) *Party Discipline and Parliamentary Government* (Columbus, OH: Ohio State University Press): 3–22.

Brack, N. (2015) 'The roles of Eurosceptic members of the European Parliament and their implications for the EU', *International Political Science Review*, 36/3: 337–50.

Braun, B. (2015) 'Preparedness, crisis management and policy change: The euro area at the critical juncture of 2008-2013', *British Journal of Politics and International Relations*, 17/3: 419–41.

Bressanelli, E. (2014) *Europarties after Enlargement: Organization, Ideology and Competition* (Basingstoke: Palgrave Macmillan).

Bretherton, C., and Vogler, J. (2005) *The European Union as a Global Actor* (2nd edn, London: Routledge).

Brittan, L. (2000) *A Diet of Brussels: The Changing Face of Europe* (London: Little, Brown).

Buiter, W.H. (1999) 'Alice in Euroland', *Journal of Common Market Studies*, 37/2: 181–209.

Buiter, W., and Rahbari, E. (2011) 'Global growth generators: Moving beyond "emerging markets" and "BRIC" ', Centre for Economic Policy Research Policy Insight No. 55.

Bulmer, S., and Lequesne, C. (eds) (2016) *The Member States of the European Union* (Oxford: Oxford University Press).

Bulmer, S., and Wessels, W. (1987) *The European Council: Decision Making in European Politics* (Basingstoke: Palgrave Macmillan).

Burley, A.M., and Mattli, W. (1993) 'Europe before the Court: A political theory of legal integration', *International Organization*, 47/1: 41–76.

Burrows, N., and Greaves, R. (2007) *The Advocate General and EC Law* (Oxford: Oxford University Press).

Busch, P., and Puchala, D. (1976) 'Interests, influence, and integration political structure in the European Communities', *Comparative Political Studies*, 9/3: 235–54.

Butler, M. (1986) *Europe: More than a Continent* (London: William Heinemann).

Cameron, D. (2013) *EU Speech at Bloomberg* (London: Office of the Prime Minister).

Cameron, D. (2014) 'No one voted for Mr Juncker', *European Voice*, 13 June, available online at http://www.politico.eu/article/no-one-voted-for-mr-juncker/

Campbell, J. (1983) *Roy Jenkins: A Biography* (London: Weidenfeld & Nicolson).

Carroll, W.E. (2011) 'The Committee of the Regions: A functional analysis of the CoR's institutional capacity', *Regional & Federal Studies*, 21/3: 341–54.

Carrubba, C.J., Gabel, M., Murrah, L., Clough, R., Montgomery, E., and Schambach, R. (2006) 'Off the record: Unrecorded legislative votes, selection bias and roll-call vote analysis', *British Journal of Political Science*, 36/4: 691–704.

Castells, A. (2005) 'External audit institutions: The European Court of Auditors and its relationship with national audit institutions of the member states', in M. Garcia Crespo (ed.) *Public Expenditure Control in Europe* (Cheltenham: Edward Elgar): 127–47.

Cederman, L.-E. (2001) 'Nationalism and bounded integration: What it would take to construct a European demos', *European Journal of International Relations*, 7/2: 139–74.

Chamon, M. (2011) 'EU agencies between Meroni and Romano or the devil and the deep blue sea', *Common Market Law Review*, 48/4: 1055–75.

Chang, M. (2013) 'Fiscal policy coordination and the future of the Community Method', *Journal of European Integration*, 35/3: 255–69.

Chappell, L. (2006) 'Comparing political institutions: Revealing the gendered "logic of appropriateness"', *Politics & Gender*, 2/2: 223–35.

Checkel, J.T. (2005) 'International institutions and socialization in Europe: Introduction and framework', *International Organization*, 59/4: 801–26.

Chorley, M. (2012) 'European Union STILL wasting billions every year as auditors refuse to sign off accounts for 18th year in a row', *Daily Mail*, 6 November.

Christiansen, T. (1996) 'Second thoughts on Europe's "third level": The European Union's Committee of the Regions', *Publius: The Journal of Federalism*, 26/1: 93–116.

Claeys, G. (2015) ' "Juncker Plan": The EIB in the driver's seat', *Bruegel Blog*, 30 June, available online at http://bruegel.org/2015/06/juncker-plan-the-eib-in-the-drivers-seat/

Clark, W.K. (2002) *Waging Modern War: Bosnia, Kosovo, and the Future of Combat* (New York: Public Affairs).

Cockfield, A. (1994) *The European Union: creating the single market* (London: John Wiley & Son Ltd.)

Codagnone, C. (1999) 'The new migration in Russia in the 1990s', in K. Koser and H. Lutz (eds) *The New Migration in Europe: Social Constructions and Social Realities* (Basingstoke: Palgrave Macmillan): 39–59.

Coen, D., and Thatcher, M. (2008) 'Network governance and multi-level delegation: European networks of regulatory agencies', *Journal of Public Policy*, 28/1: 49–71.

Committee for the Study of Economic and Monetary Union (1989) *Report on Economic and Monetary Union in the European Community*, available online at http://ec.europa.eu/economy_finance/publications/publication6161_en.pdf

Committee of Independent Experts (1999a) *First Report on Allegations Regarding Fraud, Mismanagement and Nepotism in the European Commission*, 15 March, available online at http://www.europarl.europa.eu/experts/pdf/reporten.pdf

Committee of Independent Experts (1999b) *Second Report on Reform of the Commission: Analysis of Current Practice and Proposals for Tackling Mismanagement, Irregularities and Fraud*, 10 September (2 vols), available online at http://www.europarl.europa.eu/experts/pdf/rep2-2en.pdf

Committee of the Regions (2012) *Scoreboard for Monitoring Multilevel Governance (MLG) at the European Union Level*, 2nd edn, available online at http://cor.europa.eu/en/activities/governance/Documents/scoreboard-2012-executive-summary.pdf

Committee of the Regions (2013) *Multilevel Governance (MLG) in EU Policies: Best Practices at the European Level*, available online at http://cor.europa.eu/en/activities/governance/Documents/mlg-brochure-best-practices-2013.pdf

Conway, G. (2011) 'Recovering a separation of powers in the European Union', *European Law Journal*, 17/3: 304–22.

Coombes, D.L. (1970) *Politics and Bureaucracy in the European Community* (London: George Allen & Unwin).

Cooper, I. (2013) 'Bicameral or tricameral? National parliaments and representative democracy in the European Union', *Journal of European Integration*, 35/5: 531–46.

Cooper, R. (2004) 'Hard power, soft power and the goals of diplomacy', in D. Held and M. Koenig-Archibug (eds) *American Power in the 21st Century* (Oxford: Polity): 167–80.

Corbett, R. (1993) *The Treaty of Maastricht: From Conception to Ratification—A Comprehensive Reference Guide* (London: Longman).

Corbett, R. (1998) *The European Parliament's Role in Closer Integration* (Basingstoke: Palgrave).

Corbett, R. (2012) 'Democracy in the European Union', in E. Bomberg, J. Peterson and R. Corbett (eds) *The European Union: How Does it Work?* (3rd edn, Oxford: Oxford University Press): 141–60.

Corbett, R. (2015) 'Democracy in the European Union', in D. Kenealy, J. Peterson, and R. Corbett (eds) *The European Union: How Does It Work?* (4th edn, Oxford: Oxford University Press): 141–62.

Corbett, R., Jacobs, F., Neville, D., and Shackleton, M. (eds) (2016) *The European Parliament* (9th edn, London: John Harper).

Corbett, R., Peterson, J., and Kenealy, D. (2015) 'The EU's institutions', in D. Kenealy, J. Peterson, and R. Corbert (eds) *The European Union: How Does It Work?* (Oxford: Oxford University Press): 47–71.

Cornish, P. (2004) 'NATO: The practice and politics of transformation', *International Affairs*, 80/1: 53–74.

Costa, O. (2001) *Le parlement européen, assemblée délibérante* (Brussels: Editions de l'Université de Bruxelles).

Council of Ministers (1966) 'Final Communiqué of the extraordinary session of the Council', *Bulletin of the European Communities*, 3: 5–11.

Council of the European Union (2003) *A Secure Europe in a Better World: European Security Strategy*, available online at https://www.consilium.europa.eu/uedocs/cmsUpload/78367.pdf

Council of the European Union (2015) *Annual Report on Access to Documents, 2014*, available online at http://www.consilium.europa.eu/en/documents-publications/publications/2015/council-annual-report-access-documents-2014/

Court of Justice of the European Union (2015) *Court of Justice of the European Union Annual Report 2014*, available online at http://curia.europa.eu/jcms/upload/docs/application/pdf/2015-03/en_ra14.pdf

Cour-Thimann, P., and Winkler, B. (2012) 'The ECB's non-standard monetary policy measures: The role of institutional factors and financial structure', *Oxford Review of Economic Policy*, 28/4: 765–803.

Cowles, M.G. (2003) 'Non-state actors and false dichotomies: Reviewing IR/IPE Approaches to European Integration', *Journal of European Public Policy*, 10/1: 102–20.

Cowles, M.G., and Curtis, S. (2004) 'Developments in European integration theory: The EU as "other"', in M.G. Cowles and D. Dinan (eds) *Developments in the European Union* (Basingstoke: Palgrave Macmillan): 296–305.

Cox, G.W., and McCubbins, M.D. (1993) *Legislative Leviathan: Party Government in the House* (Berkeley, CA: University of California Press).

Craig, P., and de Búrca, G. (2015) *EU Law: Text, Cases, And Materials* (6th edn, Oxford: Oxford University Press).

Crespy, A., and Schmidt, V. (2014) 'The clash of titans: France, Germany and the discursive double game of EMU reform', *Journal of European Public Policy*, 21/8: 1085–101.

Crombez, C., Steunenberg, B., and Corbett, R. (2000) 'Understanding the EU legislative process: Political scientists' and practitioners' perspectives', *European Union Politics*, 1/3: 363–81.

Cross, J.P. (2013) 'Striking a pose: Transparency and position taking in the Council of the European Union', *European Journal of Political Research*, 52/3: 291–315.

Cross, M. (2013) 'The military dimension of European security: An epistemic Community approach', *Millennium: Journal of International Studies*, 42/1: 35–64.

Curtin, D. (2014) 'Challenging executive dominance in European democracy', *The Modern Law Review*, 77/1: 1–32.

Dahl, R.A. (1999) 'Can international organizations be democratic? A skeptic's view', in I. Shapiro and C. Hacker-Cordon (eds) *Democracy's Edges* (Cambridge: Cambridge University Press): 19–36.

Daniel, W.T. (2013) 'When the agent knows better than the principal: The effect of education and seniority on European Parliament *Rapporteur* Assignment', *Journal of Common Market Studies*, 51/5: 832–48.

Daniel, W.T. (2015) *Career Behaviour and the European Parliament: All Roads Lead through Brussels?* (Oxford: Oxford University Press).

Dannreuther, R., and Peterson, J. (eds) (2006) *Security Strategy and Transatlantic Relations* (London: Routledge).

Davey, M., and Walsh, M.W. (2013) 'Billions in debt, Detroit tumbles into insolvency', *The New York Times*, 18 July.

Davignon, E. (2006) 'Foreword', in J.M. Palayret, H.S. Wallace and P. Winand (eds) *Visions, Votes, and Vetoes: The Empty Chair Crisis and the Luxembourg Compromise Forty Years on* (Brussels: Peter Lang): 15–19.

De Boissieu, P., Cloos, J., Christoffersen, P.S., van Middelaar, L., Keller-Noëllet, J., Milton, G., Roger, C., Blanchet, T., David G., and Gillissen, A. (2015) *National Leaders and the Making of Europe: Key Episodes in the Life of the European Council* (London: John Harper).

De Gaulle, C. (1970) *Discours et messages, tome IV: Pour l'effort* (Paris: Plon).

De Grauwe, P. (2016) *Economics of Monetary Union* (11th edn, Oxford: Oxford University Press).

De Montesquieu, C.B. (2011) *The Spirit of Laws* (New York: Cosimo).

De Ruyt, J. (1987) *L'acte unique européen* (Brussels: Editions de l'Université Libre de Bruxelles).

De Schoutheete, P. (2000) *The Case for Europe: Unity, Diversity, and Democracy in the European Union* (Boulder, CO: Lynne Rienner).

De Schoutheete, P., and Wallace, H.S. (2002) *The European Council* (Paris: Notre Europe).

De Vries, C.E., Van der Brug, W., Van Egmond, M.H., and Van der Eijk, C. (2011) 'Individual and contextual variation in EU issue voting: The role of political information', *Electoral Studies*, 30/1: 16–28.

De Wilde, P., and Zürn, M. (2012) 'Can the politicization of European integration be reversed?', *Journal of Common Market Studies*, 50/1: 137–53.

De Zwaan, J.W. (1995) *The Permanent Representatives Committee: Its Role in European Union Decision-Making* (Amsterdam: Elsevier).

Decker, F. and Sonnicksen, J. (2011) 'An alternative approach to European Union democratization: Re-examining the direct election of the Commission President', *Government and Opposition*, 46/2: 168–91.

Dehaene, J.-L., von Weizsäcker, R., and Simon, D. (1999) *The Institutional Implications of Enlargement: Report to the European Commission*, available online at http://www.esi2.us. es/~mbilbao/pdffiles/repigc99.pdf

Dehousse, R. (1988) 'Completing the Single Market: Institutional constraints and challenges', in R. Bieber, R. Dehousse, J. Pinder, and J.H.H. Weiler (eds) *1992:One European Market? A Critical Analysis of the Commission's Internal Market Strategy* (Baden-Baden: Nomos): 336–45.

Dehousse, R. (1995) 'Constitutional reform in the European Community: Are there alternatives to the majoritarian avenue?', *West European Politics*, 18/3: 118–36.

Dehousse, R. (1998) *The European Court of Justice: The Politics of Judicial Integration*, (Basingstoke: Palgrave Macmillan).

Dehousse, R. (2004) *L'Europe sans Bruxelles? Une analyse de la méthode ouverte de coordination* (Paris: Notre Europe).

Dehousse, R. (2005) *La fin de l'Europe* (Paris: Flammarion).

Dehousse, R. (ed.) (2011) *The 'Community Method': Obstinate or Obsolete?* (Basingstoke: Palgrave Macmillan).

Dehousse, R. (2016) 'Why has EU macroeconomic governance become more supranational?', *Journal of European Integration*, 38/5: 617–31.

Dehousse, R., and Majone, G. (1994) 'The institutional dynamics of European integration: From the Single Act to the Maastricht Treaty', in S. Martin (ed.) *The Construction of Europe: Essays in Honour of Emile Noël* (Dordrecht: Springer): 91–112.

Delors, J. (2004) *Mémoires* (Paris: Plon).

Dempsey, J. (2013) 'The depressing saga of Europe's battle groups', *Carnegie Europe*, 19 December.

Deroose, S., Hodson, D., and Kuhlmann, J. (2007) 'The legitimation of EMU: Lessons from the early years of the euro', *Review of International Political Economy*, 14/5: 800–19.

Devuyst, Y. (1999) 'The Community Method after Amsterdam', *Journal of Common Market Studies*, 37/1: 109–20.

Devuyst, Y. (2005) *The European Union Transformed: Community Method and Institutional Evolution from the Schuman Plan to the Constitution for Europe* (Brussels: Peter Lang).

Dijkstra, H. (2010) 'Explaining variation in the role of the EU Council Secretariat in first and second pillar policy-making', *Journal of European Public Policy*, 17/4: 527–44.

Dijkstra, H. (2013) *Policy-Making in EU Security and Defense: An Institutional Perspective* (Basingstoke: Palgrave Macmillan).

Dinan, D. (ed.) (2000) *Encyclopedia of the European Union* (London: Macmillan).

Dinan, D. (2010) *Ever Closer Union* (4th edn, Basingstoke: Palgrave Macmillan).

Dinan, D. (2011) 'Governance and institutions: Implementing the Lisbon Treaty in the shadow of the euro crisis', *Journal of Common Market Studies*, 49/1: 103–21.

Dogan, M. (1994) 'The decline of nationalisms within western Europe', *Comparative Politics*, 26/3: 281–305.

Domorenok, E. (2009) 'The Committee of the Regions: In search of identity', *Regional and Federal Studies*, 19/1: 143–63.

Donovan, D., and Murphy, A.E. (2013) *The Fall of the Celtic Tiger: Ireland and the Euro Debt Crisis* (Oxford: Oxford University Press).

Dooge, J. (1985) *Interim Report by Ad Hoc Committee on Institutional Affairs to the European Council, Dublin, 3–4 December* (Brussels: European Council).

Doutriaux, Y. and Lequesne, C. (2013) *Les institutions de l'Union européenne après la crise de l'euro* (Paris: La Documentation Française).

Duchêne, F. (1994) *Jean Monnet: The First Statesman of Interdependence* (New York: Norton).

Dumoulin, M. (2007) *The European Commission, 1958–72: History and Memories* (Luxembourg: Office for Official Publications of the European Communities Luxembourg).

Dunne, P., Everett, M., and Stuart, R. (2015) 'The Expanded Asset Purchase Programme: What, why and how of Euro Area QE', *Central Bank of Ireland Quarterly Bulletin*, 3: 51–71.

Duthel, H. (2010) *European Debt Crisis 2011: Portugal, Ireland, Italy, Greece, Spain and Belgium* (Berlin: epubli).

Dyson, K., and Featherstone, K. (1999) *The Road to Maastricht* (Oxford: Oxford University Press).

Eberlein, B., and Grande, E. (2005) 'Beyond delegation: Transnational regulatory regimes and the EU regulatory state', *Journal of European Public Policy*, 12/1: 89–112.

Economist, The (2015) 'The indispensable European', 7 November.

Egeberg, M. (2003) *Organising Institutional Autonomy in a Political Context: Enduring Tensions in the European Commission's Development* (Oslo: ARENA).

Eichengreen, B. (2010) 'The breakup of the euro area', in A. Alesina and F. Giavazzi (eds) *Europe and the Euro* (Chicago, IL: University of Chicago Press): 11–51.

Elias, A. (2008) 'Introduction: Whatever happened to the Europe of the Regions? Revisiting the regional dimension of European politics', *Regional & Federal Studies*, 18/5: 483–92.

Elgström, O., and Tallberg, J. (2003) 'Conclusion: Rationalist and sociological perspectives on the Council Presidency', in O. Elgström (ed.) *European Union Council Presidencies: A Comparative Approach* (London and New York: Routledge): 191–205.

Elster, J. (1998) *Deliberative Democracy* (Cambridge: Cambridge University Press).

Epstein, R.A., and Rhodes, M. (2014) 'International in life, national in death? Banking nationalism on the road to banking union', Kolleg-Forschergruppe Working Paper No. 61.

EU Heads of State or Government (2010) 'Statement by EU Heads of State or Government', Brussels, 11 February.

European Bank for Reconstruction and Development (2012) *Annual Report 2011* (London: European Bank for Reconstruction and Development).

European Central Bank (2003) 'The ECB's monetary policy strategy', Press release, 8 May.

European Central Bank (2015) *Annual Report for 2015* (Frankfurt am Main: ECB).

European Commission (2000) *Reforming the European Commission: A White Paper*, COM (2000) 200 final.

European Commission (2001a) *Report from the Commission on the Working of the Committees during 2000* COM (2001) 783 final.

European Commission (2001b) *European Governance: A White Paper*, COM (2001) 428 final.

European Commission (2009) *Evaluation of the EU Decentralised Agencies in 2009: Vol. III—Individual Agencies*, available online at http://europa.eu/agencies/documents/agency_level_findings_en.pdf

European Commission (2010) *Delivering an Area of Freedom, Security and Justice for Europe's Citizens Action Plan Implementing the Stockholm Programme*, COM (2010) 171 final.

European Commission (2015a) *A European Agenda for Migration*, COM (2015) 240 final.

European Commission (2015b) *Report from the Commission on the Working of Committees during 2014*, COM(2015) 418 final.

European Commission (2016) 'The European Citizens' Initiative: Official register', available online at http://ec.europa.eu/citizens-initiative/public/welcome

European Court of Auditors (1981) *Study of the Financial System of the European Communities*, 15 December, OJ C 342/24.

European Court of Auditors (2010) *Annual Activity Report 2009* (Luxembourg: European Court of Auditors).

European Court of Auditors (2014a) *Gaps, Overlaps and Challenges: A Landscape Review of EU Accountability and Public Audit Arrangements 2014* (Luxembourg: European Court of Auditors).

European Court of Auditors (2014b) *Making the Best Use of EU Money: A Landscape Review of the Risks to the Financial Management of the EU Budget* (Luxembourg: European Court of Auditors).

European Court of Auditors (2014c) *International Peer Review of the European Court of Auditors* (Luxembourg: European Court of Auditors).

European Court of Auditors (2015) *2015 Work Programme* (Luxembourg: European Court of Auditors).

European External Action Service (2013) *The EU's Comprehensive Approach to External Conflicts and Crises*, 11 December, available online at http://www.eeas.europa.eu/statements/docs/2013/131211_03_en.pdf

European External Action Service (2015) *The European Union in a Changing Global Environment* (Brussels: EEAS).

European Ombudsman (2015) 'Ombudsman opens investigation to promote transparency of "trilogies"', Press release no. 9/2015, 28 May.

European Parliament (2014a) *EU, Euratom: Definitive Adoption of the European Union's General Budget for the Financial Year 2014*, 20 February, OJ L 51/1.

European Parliament (2014b) *Activity Report on Codecision and Conciliation, 14 July 2009–30 June 2014 (7th Parliamentary Term)*, available online at http://www.europarl.europa.eu/code/information/activity_reports/activity_report_2009_2014_en.pdf

Everts, S., and Keohane, D. (2003) 'The European Convention and EU foreign policy: Learning from failure', *Survival*, 45/3: 167–86.

Fabbrini, S. (2013) 'Intergovernmentalism and its limits: Assessing the European Union's answer to the euro crisis', *Comparative Political Studies*, 46/9: 1003–29.

Fabbrini, S. (2015) *Which European Union? Europe after the Euro Crisis* (Cambridge: Cambridge University Press).

Faiola, A. (2016) 'Could Europe's refugee crisis be the undoing of Angela Merkel?', *Washington Post*, 4 February.

Falkner, G. (2016) 'Fines against member states: An effective new tool in EU infringement proceedings?', *Comparative European Politics*, 14/1: 36–52.

Farrell, D.M., and Scully, R. (2007) *Representing Europe's Citizens? Electoral Institutions and the Failure of Parliamentary Representation* (Oxford: Oxford University Press).

Farrell, D.M., and Scully, R. (2010) 'The European Parliament: One parliament, several modes of political representation on the ground?', *Journal of European Public Policy*, 17/1: 36–54.

Farrell, H., and Héritier, A. (2007) 'Codecision and institutional change', *West European Politics*, 30/2: 285–300.

Farrows, M., and McCarthy, R. (1997) 'Opinion formulation and impact in the Committee of the Regions', *Regional and Federal Studies*, 7/1: 23–49.

Fasone, C. (2012) 'The struggle of the European Parliament to participate in the new economic governance', EUI Working Papers RSCAS 2012/45.

Finke, D. (2015) 'Why do European political groups call the roll?', *Party Politics*, 21/5: 750–62.

Fioretos, O. (2001) 'The domestic sources of multilateral preferences: Varieties of capitalism in the European Community', in P.A. Hall and D. Soskice (eds) *Varieties of Capitalism: The Institutional Foundations of Comparative Advantage* (Oxford: Oxford University Press): 213–44.

Fitzmaurice, J. (1975) *The Party Groups in the European Parliament* (Farnham: Ashgate).

Fligstein, N., and Mara-Drita, I. (1996) 'How to make a market: Reflections on the attempt to create a Single Market in the European Union', *American Journal of Sociology*, 102/1: 1–33.

Follesdal, A., and Hix, S. (2006) 'Why there is a democratic deficit in the EU: A response to Majone and Moravcsik', *Journal of Common Market Studies*, 44/3: 533–62.

Freedman, J.O. (1978) *Crisis and Legitimacy: The Administrative Process and American Government* (Cambridge: Cambridge University Press).

Galloway, D. (2014) 'Classifying secrets in the EU', *Journal of Common Market Studies*, 52/3: 568–83.

García, N.P., and Priestley, J. (2015) *The Making of a European President* (Basingstoke: Palgrave Macmillan).

Garrett, G. (1995) 'The politics of legal integration in the European Union', *International Organization*, 49/1: 171–81.

Garrett, G., Kelemen, R.D., and Schulz, H. (1998) 'The European Court of Justice, national governments, and legal integration in the European Union', *International Organization*, 52/01: 149–76.

Gatsios, K., and Seabright, P. (1989) 'Regulation in the European Community', *Oxford Review of Economic Policy*, 5/2: 37–60.

Geddes, A. (2005) 'Getting the best of both worlds? Britain, the EU and migration policy', *International Affairs*, 81/4: 723–40.

Geddes, A. (2008) *Immigration and European Integration: Beyond Fortress Europe?* (Manchester: Manchester University Press).

Genschel, P., and Jachtenfuchs, M. (2016) 'More integration, less federation: The European integration of core state powers', *Journal of European Public Policy*, 23/1: 32–59.

Geradin, D., Munoz, R., and Petit, N. (2005) *Regulation through Agencies in the EU: A New Paradigm of European Governance* (Cheltenham: Edward Elgar).

Gerrats, P.M.E. (2008) 'Credibility and transparency', *ECB Economic Papers 330* (Frankfurt AM: ECB).

Gerrits, A. (2009) *Normative Power Europe in a Changing World: A Discussion* (The Hague: Netherlands Institute of International Relations, Clingendael).

Gibbs, N. (2015) 'Person of the Year: Angela Merkel', *Time*, 21 December.

Ginsberg, R.H. (1989) *Foreign Policy Actions of the European Community: The Politics of Scale* (Lanham, MD: Rowman & Littlefield).

Ginsberg, R.H. (2001) *The European Union in International Politics: Baptism by Fire* (Lanham, MD: Rowman & Littlefield).

Giscard d'Estaing, V. (1988) *Le pouvoir et la vie* (Paris: Compagnie).

Giscard d'Estaing, V. (2002) 'Introductory speech by President V. Giscard d'Estaing to the Convention on the Future of Europe', 26 February.

Glarbo, K. (2001) 'Reconstructing a common European foreign policy', in T. Christiansen, K.E. Jørgensen, and A. Wiener (eds) *The Social Construction of Europe* (London: Sage): 140–57.

Goebel, R.J. (2005) 'Court of Justice oversight over the European Central Bank: Delimiting the ECB's constitutional autonomy and independence in the *OLAF* judgment', *Fordham International Law*, 29: 600–54.

Goetze, S., and Rittberger, B. (2010) 'A matter of habit and quest: The sociological foundations of empowering the European Parliament', *Comparative European Politics*, 8/1: 37–54.

Golub, J. (1999) 'In the shadow of the vote? Decision making in the European Community', *International Organization*, 53/4: 733–64.

Golub, J. (2006) 'Did the Luxembourg Compromise Have Any Consequences?' In Palayret, J-M. Wallace, H. and Winand, P. (eds) *Visions, Votes and Vetoes: The Empty Chair Crisis and the Luxembourg Compromise Forty Years On* (Brussels: P.I.E. Peter Lang), pp. 279–99.

Gomez, R., and Peterson, J. (2001) 'The EU's impossibly busy foreign ministers: "No one is in control"', *European Foreign Affairs Review*, 6/1: 53–74.

Gouldner, A.W. (1957) 'Cosmopolitans and locals: Toward an analysis of latent social roles', *Administrative Science Quarterly*, 2/3: 281–306.

Grabbe, H. (2000) 'The sharp edges of Europe: Extending Schengen eastwards', *International Affairs*, 76/3: 519–36.

Graziano, P., and Vink, M. (2007) *Europeanization: New Research Agendas* (Basingstoke: Palgrave).

Greenwood, J. (2011) *Interest Representation in the European Union* (3rd edn, Basingstoke and New York: Palgrave Macmillan).

Griffiths, R.T. (2000) *Europe's First Constitution: The European Political Community, 1952–1954* (London: Federal Trust).

Groenleer, M. (2009) *The Autonomy of European Union Agencies: A Comparative Study of Institutional Development* (Delft: Eburon Uitgeverij BV).

Grønbech-Jensen, C. (1998) 'The Scandinavian tradition of open government and the European Union: Problems of compatibility?', *Journal of European Public Policy*, 5/1: 185–99.

Haas, E.B. (1958) *The Uniting of Europe: Political, Economic and Social Forces, 1950–1957* (London: Stevens & Sons).

Haas, E.B. (1960) *Consensus Formation in the Council of Europe* (Berkeley, CA: University of California).

Häge, F.M. (2007) 'Committee decision-making in the Council of the European Union', *European Union Politics*, 8/3: 299–328.

Häge, F.M. (2008) 'Who decides in the Council of the European Union?', *Journal of Common Market Studies*, 46/3: 533–58.

Häge, F.M. (2011) 'The European Union policy-making dataset', *European Union Politics*, 12/3: 455–77.

Häge, F.M. (2013) 'Coalition building and consensus in the Council of the European Union', *British Journal of Political Science*, 43/3: 481–504.

Hagemann, S. (2008) 'Voting, statements and coalition-building in the Council from 1999 to 2006', in D. Naurin and H. Wallace (eds) *Unveiling the Council of the European Union* (Basingstoke: Palgrave Macmillan): 36–63.

Hagemann, S., and de Clerck-Sachsse, C. (2007) *Old Rules, New Game: Decision-Making in the Council of Ministers after the 2004 Enlargement* (Brussels: Centre for European Policy Studies).

Hagemann, S., and Høyland, B. (2010) 'Bicameral politics in the European Union', *Journal of Common Market Studies*, 48/4: 811–33.

Hall, P.A. (1997) 'The role of interests, institutions, and ideas in the comparative political economy of the industrialized nations', in M.I. Lichbach and A.S. Zuckerman (eds) *Comparative Politics: Rationality, Culture, and Structure* (Cambridge: Cambridge University Press): 174–207.

Hall, P.A. (2008) 'The evolution of varieties of capitalism in Europe', in B. Hancké, M. Rhodes, and M. Thatcher (eds) *Beyond Varieties of Capitalism: Conflict, Contradictions, and Complementarities in the European Economy* (Oxford: Oxford University Press): 89–121.

Hall, P.A. (2012) 'The economics and politics of the euro crisis', *German Politics*, 21/4: 355–71.

Hall, P.A., and Soskice, D. (2001) 'An introduction to varieties of capitalism', in P.A. Hall and D. Soskice (eds) *Varieties of Capitalism. The Institutional Foundations of Comparative Advantage* (Oxford: Oxford University Press): 1–70.

Hall, P.A., and Taylor, R.C. (1996) 'Political science and the three new institutionalisms', *Political Studies*, 44/5: 936–57.

Hancisse, L., McMenamin, A., Perera, M., and Patz, R. (2014) *The European Union's Integrity System* (Brussels: Transparency International EU Office).

Hanley, D. (2008) *Beyond the Nation State* (Basingstoke: Palgrave Macmillan).

Hartlapp, M., Metz, J., and Rauh, C. (2013) 'Linking agenda setting to coordination structures: Bureaucratic politics inside the European Commission', *Journal of European Integration*, 35/4: 325–41.

Hartlapp, M., Metz, J., and Rauh, C. (2014) *Which Policy for Europe? Power and Conflict inside the European Commission* (Oxford: Oxford University Press).

Hawk, B.E., and Laudati, L.L. (1996) 'Antitrust federalism in the United States and decentralization of competition law enforcement in the European Union: A comparison', *Fordham International Law Journal*, 20/1: 18–49

Hayes-Renshaw, F. (1999) 'The European Council and the Council of Ministers', in L. Cram, D. Dinan, and N. Nugent (eds) *Developments in the European Union* (Basingstoke: Palgrave): 23–43.

Hayes-Renshaw, F. (2015) 'How policies are made', in D. Kenealy, J. Peterson, and R. Corbett (eds) *The European Union: How Does It Work?* (Oxford: Oxford University Press): 118–40.

Hayes-Renshaw, F., and Wallace, H. (1995) 'Executive power in the European Union: The functions and limits of the Council of Ministers', *Journal of European Public Policy*, 2/4: 559–82.

Hayes-Renshaw, F., and Wallace, H. (1997) *The Council of Ministers* (Basingstoke: Palgrave Macmillan).

Hayes-Renshaw, F., and Wallace, H. (2006) *The Council of Ministers* (2nd edn, Basingstoke: Palgrave Macmillan).

Hayes-Renshaw, F., Lequesne, C., and Mayor Lopez, P. (1989) 'The permanent representations of the member states to the European Communities', *Journal of Common Market Studies*, 28/2: 119–37.

Hayward, J. (ed.) (2008) *Leaderless Europe* (Oxford: Oxford University Press).

Heipertz, M., and Verdun, A. (2010) *Ruling Europe: The Politics of the Stability and Growth Pact* (Cambridge: Cambridge University Press).

Heisenberg, D. (2007) 'Informal decision-making in the Council: The secret of the EUs success', in S. Meunier and K. McNamara (eds) *Making History. European Integration and Institutional Change at Fifty* (Oxford: Oxford University Press): 67–89.

Helwig, N. (2015) *The High Representative of the Union: The Constrained Agent of Europe's Foreign Policy* (Berlin: epubli GmbH).

Helwig, N., and Rüger, C. (2014) 'In search of a role for the High Representative: The legacy of Catherine Ashton', *The International Spectator*, 49/4: 1–17.

Henning, C.R. (2015) 'The ECB as a strategic actor: Central banking in a politically fragmented monetary union', in J.A. Caporaso and M. Rhodes (eds) *Europe's Crises: Economic and Political Challenges of the Monetary Union* (Oxford: Oxford University Press): 167–99.

Héritier, A. (2007) *Explaining Institutional Change in Europe* (Oxford: Oxford University Press).

Héritier, A. (2015) 'Covert integration in the European Union', in J. Richardson and S. Mazey (eds) *European Union: Power and Policy-Making* (London: Routledge): 351–70.

Herman, V., and Lodge, J. (1978) 'Democratic legitimacy and direct elections to the European Parliament', *West European Politics*, 1/2: 226–51.

Heron, T. (2007) 'European trade diplomacy and the politics of global development: Reflections on the EU-China "bra wars" dispute', *Government and Opposition*, 42/2: 190–214.

Hertz, R.F. (2010) 'Still pedaling? The impact of Eastern enlargement on European Union decision-making', Dissertation, Eidgenössische Technische Hochschule ETH Zürich, Nr. 19253.

Hertz, R.F., and Leuffen, D. (2011) 'Too big to run? Analysing the impact of enlargement on the speed of EU decision-making', *European Union Politics*, 12/2: 193–215.

Hill, C. (1993) 'The capability-expectations gap, or conceptualizing Europe's international role', *Journal of Common Market Studies*, 31/3: 305–28.

Hill, C. (1998) 'Closing the capabilities-expectations gap?', in J. Peterson and H. Sjursen (eds) *A Common Foreign Policy for Europe?* (London: Routledge): 18–38.

Hill, C. (2004) 'Renationalizing or regrouping? EU foreign policy since 11 September 2001', *Journal of Common Market Studies*, 42/1: 143–63.

Hill, C., and Smith, M. (eds) (2011) *International Relations and the European Union* (2nd edn, Oxford: Oxford University Press).

Hill, C., and Smith, M. (eds) (2016) *International Relations and the European Union* (3rd edn, Oxford and New York: Oxford University Press).

Hill & Knowlton (2000) *The European Commission 2000–2005: One Year On* (Brussels: Hill & Knowlton).

Hix, S. (1999) 'Dimensions and alignments in European Union politics: Cognitive constraints and partisan responses', *European Journal of Political Research*, 35/1: 59–106.

Hix, S. (2002) 'Parliamentary behavior with two principals: Preferences, parties, and voting in the European Parliament', *American Journal of Political Science*, 46/3: 588–98.

Hix, S. (2008) *What's Wrong with the EU and How to Fix It* (Cambridge: Polity).

Hix, S., and Bartolini, S. (2006) *Politics: The Right or the Wrong Sort of Medicine for the EU?* (Paris: Notre Europe).

Hix, S., and Høyland, B. (2011) *The Political System of the European Union* (3rd edn, Basingstoke: Palgrave Macmillan).

Hix, S., and Høyland, B. (2013) 'Empowerment of the European Parliament' *Annual Review of Political Science*, 16: 171–89.

Hix, S., and Lord, C. (1997) *Political Parties in the European Union* (Basingstoke: Palgrave Macmillan).

Hix, S., and Marsh, M. (2011) 'Second-order effects plus pan-European political swings: An analysis of European Parliament elections across time', *Electoral Studies*, 30/1: 3–15.

Hix, S., and Noury, A. (2009) 'After enlargement: Voting patterns in the sixth European Parliament', *Legislative Studies Quarterly*, 34/2: 159–74.

Hix, S., Noury, A.G., and Roland, G. (2007) *Democratic Politics in the European Parliament* (Cambridge: Cambridge University Press).

Hobolt, S.B. (2014) 'A vote for the President? The role of *Spitzenkandidaten* in the 2014 European Parliament elections', *Journal of European Public Policy*, 21/10: 1528–40.

Hobolt, S.B. (2015) 'The 2014 European Parliament elections: Divided in unity?', *Journal of Common Market Studies*, 53/S1: 6–21.

Hobolt, S.B., and Spoon, J.J. (2012) 'Motivating the European voter: Parties, issues and campaigns in European Parliament elections', *European Journal of Political Research*, 51/6: 701–27.

Hobolt, S.B., Spoon, J.-J., and Tilley, J. (2009) 'A vote against Europe? Explaining defection at the 1999 and 2004 European Parliament elections', *British Journal of Political Science*, 39/1: 93–115.

Hocking, B. (1999) *Foreign Ministries: Change and Adaptation* (Basingstoke: Palgrave Macmillan).

Hocking, B., and Spence, D. (eds) (2002) *Foreign Ministries in the European Union: Integrating Diplomats* (Basingstoke: Palgrave Macmillan).

Hodson, D. (2011) *Governing the Euro Area in Good Times and Bad* (Oxford: Oxford University Press).

Hodson, D. (2013a) 'The little engine that wouldn't: Supranational entrepreneurship and the Barroso Commission', *Journal of European Integration*, 35/3: 301–14.

Hodson, D. (2013b) 'The eurozone in 2012: "Whatever it takes to preserve the euro"?', *Journal of Common Market Studies*, 51/1: 183–200.

Hodson, D. (2015a) 'The IMF as a *de facto* institution of the EU: A multiple supervisor approach', *Review of International Political Economy*, 22/3: 570–98.

Hodson, D. (2015b) 'Policy-making under economic and monetary union: Crisis, change and continuity', in H. Wallace, M. A. Pollack, and A. R. Young (eds) *Policy Making in the European Union* (Oxford: Oxford University Press): 166–95.

Hodson, D. (2016) 'Eurozone governance: From the Greek drama of 2015 to the Five Presidents' Report', *Journal of Common Market Studies*, 54/1: 150–66.

Hodson, D., and Maher, I. (2014) 'British brinkmanship and Gaelic games: EU treaty ratification in the UK and Ireland from a two-level game perspective', *British Journal of Politics & International Relations*, 16/4: 645–61.

Hodson, D., and Puetter, U. (2016) 'The euro crisis and European integration', in M. Cini and N. Pérez-Solórzano Borragán (eds) *European Union Politics* (Oxford: Oxford University): 365–79.

Hoffmann, S. (1966) 'Obstinate or obsolete? The fate of the nation-state and the case of Western Europe', *Daedalus*, 95/3: 862–915.

Hoffmann, S. (1995) *The European Sisyphus: Essays on Europe, 1964–1994* (Boulder, CO: Westview).

Hoffmann, S., Keohane, R.O., and Mearsheimer, J.J. (1990) 'Back to the future, part II: International relations theory and post-Cold War Europe', *International Security*, 15/2: 191–9.

Holbrooke, R. (2011) *To End a War* (New York: The Modern Library).

Hong, G. (2015) 'Explaining vote switching to niche parties in the 2009 European Parliament elections', *European Union Politics*, 16/4: 514–35.

Hönnige, C., and Kaiser, A. (2003) 'Opening the black box: Decision-making in the Committee of the Regions', *Regional and Federal Studies*, 13/2: 1–29.

Hönnige, C., and Panke, D. (2013) 'The Committee of the Regions and the European Economic and Social Committee: How influential are consultative committees in the European Union?', *Journal of Common Market Studies*, 51/3: 352–71.

Hood, C. (1991) 'A public management for all seasons?', *Public Administration*, 69/1: 3–19.

Hooghe, L. (2002) *The European Commission and the Integration of Europe: Images of Governance* (Cambridge: Cambridge University Press).

Hooghe, L. (2005) 'Many roads lead to international norms, but few via international socialization: A case study of the European Commission', *International Organization*, 59/4: 861–98.

Hooghe, L. (2012) 'Images of Europe: How Commission officials conceive their institution's role', *Journal of Common Market Studies*, 50/1: 87–111.

Hooghe, L., and Marks, G. (2001) *Multi-Level Governance and European Integration* (Lanham, MD: Rowman & Littlefield).

Hooghe, L., and Marks, G. (2009) 'A postfunctionalist theory of European integration: From permissive consensus to constraining dissensus', *British Journal of Political Science*, 39/1: 1–23.

Hooghe, L., and Marks, G. (2012) 'Politicization', in E. Jones, S. Weatherill, and A. Menon (eds) *Handbook on the European Union* (Oxford: Oxford University Press): 840–53.

Hooghe, L., Marks, G., Lenz, T., Bezuijen, J., Ceka, B., and Derderyan, S. (forthcoming) *A Postfunctionalist Theory of Governance: Measuring International Authority, Vol. III* (Oxford: Oxford University Press).

Hosli, M.O. (1995) 'The balance between small and large: Effects of a double-majority system on voting power in the European Union', *International Studies Quarterly*, 39/3: 351–70.

House of Lords (2001) *The European Court of Auditors: The Case for Reform*, 12th Report, 3 April (London: HMSO).

House of Lords (2004) *Strengthening OLAF, the European Anti-Fraud Office*, 24th Report, 13 July (London: HMSO).

Howarth, D., and Quaglia, L. (2016) *The Political Economy of European Banking Union* (Oxford: Oxford University Press).

Howorth, J. (2010) 'The EU as a global actor: Grand strategy for a global grand bargain?', *Journal of Common Market Studies*, 48/3: 355–74.

Howorth, J. (2011) 'The Political and Security Committee: A case study in "supranational Intergovernmentalism"', in R. Dehousse (ed.) *The 'Community Method', Obstinate or Obsolete?* (Basingstoke: Palgrave Macmillan): 91–117.

Howorth, J. (2014) *Security and Defence Policy in the European Union* (2nd edn, Basingstoke: Palgrave Macmillan).

Høyland, B., and Hansen, V.W. (2014) 'Issue-specific policy-positions and voting in the Council', *European Union Politics*, 15/1: 59–81.

Hrbek, R. (1993) 'La function consultative dans la République Fédérale d'Allemagne', in J. Vandamme (ed.) *Fonction consultative professionnelle et dialogue social dans la communauté européenne* (Brussels: Presses Universitaires Européennes): 121–36.

Hudson, K. (2012) *The New European Left: A Socialism for the Twenty-first Century?* (Basingstoke: Palgrave Macmillan).

Huysmans, J. (2000) 'The European Union and the securitization of migration', *Journal of Common Market Studies*, 38/5: 751–77.

Ikenberry, G.J. (2009) *After Victory: Institutions, Strategic Restraint, and the Rebuilding of Order after Major Wars* (Princeton, NJ: Princeton University Press).

Ioannou, D., Leblond, P., and Niemann, A. (2015) 'Introduction: European integration and the crisis—Practice and theory', *Journal of European Public Policy*, 22/2: 155–76.

Issing, O. (2008) *The Birth of the Euro* (Cambridge: Cambridge University Press).

Jacobs, F. (2015) 'Developments in European Parliament handling of European Union legislation since the Treaty of Lisbon', Paper presented at the European Union Studies Association Fourteenth Biennial Conference, 5–7 March, Boston, MA.

Jacqué, J.P. (2004) 'Les principes constitutionnels fondamentaux dans le projet de traité établissant la constitution européenne', in L.S. Rossi (ed.) *Vers une nouvelle architecture de l'union européenne* (Brussels: Bruylant): 157–67.

Jeffery, C. (2000) 'Sub-national mobilization and European integration: Does it make any difference?', *Journal of Common Market Studies*, 38/1: 1–23.

Jenkins, R. (1989) *European Diary* (London: Collins).

Jensen, C.B., andSpoon, J.J. (2010) 'Thinking locally, acting supranationally: Niche party behaviour in the European Parliament', *European Journal of Political Research*, 49/2: 174–201.

Joana, J., and Smith, A. (2002) *Les commissaires européens: Technocrates, diplomates ou politiques?* (Paris: Presses de sciences PO).

Joerges, C., and Vos, E. (1998) *EU Committees: Social Regulation, Law and Politics* (Oxford: Hart).

Johansson, K.M. (2016) 'Europarty influence and its limits: The case of the European People's Party and the Amsterdam Treaty', *Journal of European Integration*, 38/1: 79–94.

Johansson, K.M., and Raunio, T. (2005) 'Regulating Europarties cross-party coalitions capitalizing on incomplete contracts', *Party Politics*, 11/5: 515–34.

Johansson, K.M., and Zervakis, P.A. (2002) *European Political Parties between Cooperation and Integration* (Baden-Baden: Nomos).

Johnson, B. (2016) 'I cannot stress too much that Britain is part of Europe—and always will be', *The Telegraph*, 26 June.

Johnston, A., and Regan, A. (2016) 'European monetary integration and the incompatibility of national varieties of capitalism', *Journal of Common Market Studies*, 54/2: 318–36.

Johnston, A.I. (2008) *Social States: China in International Institutions, 1980–2000* (Princeton, NJ: Princeton University Press).

Jones, E. (2014) *The Year the European Crisis Ended* (Basingstoke: Palgrave Macmillan).

Jordan, A., and Schout, A. (2006) *The Coordination of the European Union: Exploring the Capacities of Networked Governance* (Oxford: Oxford University Press).

Jørgensen, K.E., and Laatikainen, K.V. (eds) (2013) *Routledge Handbook on the European Union and International Institutions* (London: Routledge).

Josselin, D., and Wallace, W. (2001) 'Non-state actors in world politics: A framework', in D. Josselin and W. Wallace (eds) *Non-State Actors in World Politics* (Basingstoke: Palgrave): 1–20.

Judge, D., and Earnshaw, D. (2008) *The European Parliament* (Basingstoke: Palgrave Macmillan).

Juncker, J.-C. (2014) *A New Start for Europe: My Agenda for Jobs, Growth, Fairness and Democratic Change* (Brussels: European Commission).

Juncker, J.-C., Tusk, D., Dijsselbloem, J., Draghi, M., and Schulz, M. (2015) *Completing Europe's Economic and Monetary Union* (Brussels: European Commission).

Juncos, A.E., and Pomorska, K. (2007) 'The deadlock that never happened: The impact of enlargement on the Common Foreign and Security Policy Council working groups', *European Political Economy Review*, 6(Mar): 3–30.

Juncos, A.E., and Pomorska, K. (2011) 'Invisible and unaccountable? National representatives and Council officials in EU foreign policy', *Journal of European Public Policy*, 18/8: 1096–114.

Juncos, A.E., and Pomorska, K. (2013) '"In the face of adversity": Explaining the attitudes of EEAS officials vis-à-vis the new service', *Journal of European Public Policy*, 20/9: 1332–49.

Karyotis, G., and Gerodimos, R. (2015) *The Politics of Extreme Austerity: Greece in the Eurozone Crisis* (Basingstoke: Palgrave Macmillan).

Kassim, H. (2004) 'The Kinnock reforms in perspective: Why reforming the Commission is an heroic, but thankless, task', *Public Policy and Administration*, 19/3: 25–41.

Kassim, H., and Menon, A. (2004) 'EU member states and the Prodi Commission', in D.G. Dimitrakopoulos (ed.) *The Changing European Commission* (Manchester: Manchester University Press): 15–32.

Kassim, H., Peterson, J., Bauer, M.W., Connolly, S., Dehousse, R., Hooghe, L., and Thompson, A. (2013) *The European Commission of the Twenty-First Century* (Oxford: Oxford University Press).

Kaunert, C., and Léonard, S. (2012) 'The development of the EU asylum policy: Venue-shopping in perspective', *Journal of European Public Policy*, 19/9: 1396–413.

Kelemen, D.R. (2002) 'The politics of "Eurocratic" structure and the new European agencies', *West European Politics*, 25/4: 93–118.

Kelemen, R.D. (2005) 'The politics of Eurocracy: Building a new European state?', in N. Jabko and C. Parsons (eds) *The State of the European Union, Vol. 7: With US or against US? European Trends in American Perspective* (Oxford: Oxford University Press): 173–89.

Kelemen, R.D., and Tarrant, A.D. (2011) 'The political foundations of the Eurocracy', *West European Politics*, 34/5: 922–47.

Keohane, R.O. (1998) 'International institutions: Can interdependence work?', *Foreign Policy*, Spring: 82–94.

Keohane, R.O., and Hoffmann, S. (1991) *The New European Community: Decision Making and Institutional Change* (Boulder, CO: Westview Press).

Kerremans, B. (1996) 'Do institutions make a difference? Non-institutionalism, neo-institutionalism, and the logic of common decision-making in the European Union', *Governance*, 9/2: 217–40.

Kettle, M. (2011) 'Greece, Schengen, Nato: It's time to admit the European dream is over', *The Guardian*, 23 June.

Keukeleire, S., and Delreux, T. (2014) *The Foreign Policy of the European Union* (Basingstoke: Palgrave Macmillan).

Kingdon, J.W., and Thurber, J.A. (1984) *Agendas, Alternatives, and Public Policies* (Boston, MA: Little, Brown).

Kleine, M. (2013) *Informal Governance in the European Union: How Governments Make International Organizations Work* (Ithaca, NY: Cornell University Press).

Knudsen, A., and Rasmussen, M. (2008) 'A European political system in the making 1958–1970: The relevance of emerging committee structures', *Journal of European Integration History*, 14/1: 51–68.

Koenig, N. (2011) 'The EU and the Libyan crisis: In quest of coherence?', *The International Spectator*, 46/4: 11–30.

Koenig-Archibugi, M. (2002) 'Mapping global governance', in D. Held and A. McGrew (eds) *Governing Globalization: Power, Authority and Global Governance* (Cambridge: Polity Press): 46–69.

Kohler-Koch, B. (2000) 'Framing: The bottleneck of constructing legitimate institutions', *Journal of European Public Policy*, 7/4: 513–31.

Kohler-Koch, B., and Eising, R. (1999) *The Transformation of Governance in the European Union* (London: Routledge)

Kourtikakis, K. (2010) 'Imitation and supranational politics: Some lessons from the European Ombudsman and the European Court of Auditors', *European Political Science Review*, 2/1: 27–48.

Kousis, M. (2014) 'The transnational dimension of the Greek protest campaign against Troika memoranda and austerity policies, 2010-2012', in D. della Porta and A. Mattoni (eds) *Spreading Protests: Social Movements in Times of Crisis* (Colchester: ECPR Press): 139–70.

Kreppel, A. (2002) *The European Parliament and Supranational Party System: A Study in Institutional Development* (Cambridge: Cambridge University Press).

Ladrech, R. (2000) *Social Democracy and the Challenge of European Union* (Boulder, CO: Lynne Rienner).

Laffan, B. (1997) *The Finances of the Union* (London: Macmillan).

Laffan, B. (1999) 'Becoming a "living institution": The evolution of the European Court of Auditors', *Journal of Common Market Studies*, 37/2: 251–68.

Laffan, B. (2003) 'Auditing and accountability in the European Union', *Journal of European Public Policy*, 10/5: 762–77.

Laffan, B. (2004) 'The European Union and its institutions as "identity builders"', in R.K. Herrmann, T. Risse, and M.B. Brewe (eds) *Transnational Identities: Becoming European in the EU* (Oxford: Rowan & Littlefield): 75–96.

Laïdi, Z. (2008) *EU Foreign Policy in a Globalized World: Normative Power and Social Preferences* (London: Routledge).

Lavenex, S. (2006) 'Shifting up and out: The foreign policy of European immigration control', *West European Politics*, 29/2: 329–50.

Lehmbruch, G., and Schmitter, P. (1982) *Patterns of Corporatist Policy-making* (Beverly Hills, CA: Sage).

Lempp, J. (2007) '"Coreper enlarged": How enlargement affected the functioning of the Committee of Permanent Representatives', *European Political Economy Review*, 6/Mar: 31–52.

Lenaerts, K. (1991) 'Some reflections on the separation of powers in the European Community', *Common Market Law Review*, 28/1: 11–35.

Levy, R. (2000) *Implementing European Union Public Policy* (Cheltenham: Edward Elgar).

Lewis, J. (1998) 'Is the "hard bargaining" image of the Council misleading? The Committee of Permanent Representatives and the Local Elections Directive', *Journal of Common Market Studies*, 36/4: 379–504.

Lewis, J. (2000) 'The methods of Community in EU decision-making and administrative rivalry in the Council's infrastructure', *Journal of European Public Policy*, 7/2: 261–89.

Lewis, J. (2005) 'The Janus face of Brussels: Socialization and everyday decision making in the European Union', *International Organization*, 59/4: 937–71.

Lewis, J. (2014) 'COREPER: Linking capitals and Brussels', in T. Blom and S. Vanhoonacker (eds) *The Politics of Information: The Case of the European Union* (Basingstoke: Palgrave Macmillan): 65–77.

Lightfoot, S. (2005) *Europeanizing Social Democracy? The Rise of the Party of European Socialists* (London: Routledge).

Lijphart, A. (2012) *Patterns of Democracy: Government Forms and Performance in Thirty-Six Countries* (New Haven, CT: Yale University Press).

Lindberg, B., Rasmussen, A., and Warntjen, A. (2013) *The Role of Political Parties in the European Union* (London: Routledge).

Lindberg, L.N. (1963) *The Political Dynamics of European Economic Integration* (Stanford, CA: Stanford University Press).

Lindberg, L.N. (1965) 'Decision making and integration in the European Community', *International Organization*, 19/1: 56–80.

Lindstädt, R., Slapin, J.B., and Vander Wielen, R.J. (2011) 'Balancing competing demands: Position taking and election proximity in the European Parliament', *Legislative Studies Quarterly*, 36/1: 37–70.

Linz, J.J. (1998) 'Democracy's time constraints', *International Political Science Review*, 19/1: 19–37.

Livingstone, E. (2015) 'Jean-Claude Juncker urges stronger Commission role on euro', *Politico*, 15 December, available online at http://www.politico.eu/article/juncker-stronger-commission-role-euro-crisis-banking-parliament-speech/

Lock, T. (2015) *The European Court of Justice and International Courts* (Oxford: Oxford University Press).

Lodge, J., and Herman, V. (1980) 'The Economic and Social Committee in EEC decision making', *International Organization*, 34/2: 265–84.

Ludlow, N.P. (1997) *Dealing with Britain: The Six and the First UK Application to the EEC* (Cambridge: Cambridge University Press).

Ludlow, N.P. (2006) *The European Community and the Crises of the 1960s: Negotiating the Gaullist Challenge* (London: Routledge).

Ludlow, N.P. (2016) *Roy Jenkins and the European Commission Presidency, 1976–1980: At the Heart of Europe* (Basingstoke: Palgrave Macmillan).

Ludlow, P. (1991) 'The European Commission', in R.O. Keohane and S. Hoffmann (eds) *The New European Community: Decision-Making and Institutional Change* (Boulder, CO: Westview): 85–132.

Ludlow, P. (1992) 'Europe's Institutions: Europe's Politics', in G.F. Treverton (ed.) *The Shape of the New Europe* (New York: Council on Foreign Relations): 59–91.

Ludlow, P. (2000) *A View from Brussels: Briefing Notes on the European Councils* (Brussels: EuroComment).

Lyon, J. (2005) 'EU's Bosnia police mission is "laughing stock"', *European Voice*, 15 September.

Mace, C. (2003) 'Operation Artemis: Mission improbable?', *European Security Review*, 18 July.

MacMullen, A. (1999) 'Fraud, mismanagement and nepotism: The Committee of Independent Experts and the fall of the European Commission 1999', *Crime, Law and Social Change*, 31/3: 193–208.

MacMullen, A. (2000) 'European Commissioners: National routes to a European elite', in N. Nugent (ed.) *At the Heart of the Union: Studies of the European Commission* (Basingstoke: Palgrave Macmillan): 28–50.

Maduro, M., and Azoulai, L. (2010) *The Past and Future of EU Law: The Classics of EU Law Revisited on the 50th Anniversary of the Rome Treaty* (London: Bloomsbury).

Maes, I. (2006) 'The ascent of the European Commission as an actor in the monetary integration process in the 1960s', *Scottish Journal of Political Economy*, 53/2: 222–41.

Magnette, P. (2001) 'Appointing and censuring the European Commission: The adaptation of parliamentary institutions to the community context', *European Law Journal*, 7/3: 292–310.

Magnette, P. (2005a) *What Is the European Union?* (Basingstoke: Palgrave Macmillan).

Magnette, P. (2005b) 'In the name of simplification: Coping with constitutional conflicts in the Convention on the Future of Europe', *European Law Journal*, 11/4: 332–51.

Magnette, P., and Nicolaïdis, K. (2004) 'The European Convention: Bargaining in the shadow of rhetoric', *West European Politics*, 27/3: 381–404.

Maher, I. (2007) 'Regulation and modes of governance in EC competition law: What's new in enforcement', *Fordham International Law Journal*, 31/6: 1713.

Mair, P., and Thomassen, J. (2010) 'Political representation and government in the European Union', *Journal of European Public Policy*, 17/1: 20–35.

Majone, G. (1998) 'Europe's "democratic deficit": The question of standards', *European Law Journal*, 4/1: 5–28.

Majone, G. (ed) (2003) *Risk Regulation in the European Union: Between Enlargement and the Internationalization* (Florence: EUI).

Majone, G. (2005) *Dilemmas of European Integration: The Ambiguities and Pitfalls of Integration by Stealth* (Oxford: Oxford University Press).

Mamadouh, V., and Raunio, T. (2003) 'The committee system: Powers, appointments and report allocation', *Journal of Common Market Studies*, 41/2: 333–51.

Mandelson, P. (2005) 'The idea of Europe: Can we make it live again?', UACES-EPC Future of Europe Lecture, Brussels, 20 July.

Manners, I. (2002) 'Normative power Europe: A contradiction in terms?', *Journal of Common Market Studies*, 40/2: 235–58.

Manow, P., and Döring, H. (2007) 'Electoral and mechanical causes of divided government in the European Union', *Comparative Political Studies*, 41/10: 1349–70.

March, J.G., and Olsen, J.P. (1989) *Discovering Institutions: The Organizational Basis of Politics* (New York: Free Press).

March, J.G., and Olsen, J.P. (2004) 'The logic of appropriateness', ARENA Working Papers No. 04/09.

Marks, G. (1993) 'Structural policy and multilevel governance in the EC', in A.W. Cafruny and G.G. Rosenthal (eds) *The State of the European Community*, Vol. 2 (Boulder, CO: Lynne Rienner): 391–410.

Marks, G., and Steenbergen, M.R. (2004) *European Integration and Political Conflict* (Cambridge: Cambridge University Press).

Marks, G., and Wilson, C.J. (2000) 'The past in the present: A cleavage theory of party response to European integration', *British Journal of Political Science*, 30/3: 333–59.

Marks, G., Hooghe, L., and Blank, K. (1996) 'European integration from the 1980s: State-centric v. multi-level governance', *Journal of Common Market Studies*, 34/3: 341–78.

Martin, S. (2014) 'Committees', in S. Martin, T. Saalfeld, and K. Strøm (eds) *The Oxford Handbook of Legislative Studies* (Oxford: Oxford University Press): 352–68.

Matthijs, M. (2014) 'Mediterranean blues: The crisis in southern Europe', *Journal of Democracy*, 25/1: 101–15.

Mattila, M. (2009) 'Roll call analysis of voting in the European Union Council of Ministers after the 2004 Enlargement', *European Journal of Political Research*, 48/6: 840–57.

Mattila, M., and Raunio, T. (2012) 'Drifting further apart: National parties and their electorates on the EU dimension', *West European Politics*, 35/3: 589–606.

Mattli, W. (1999) *The Logic of Regional Integration: Europe and beyond* (Cambridge: Cambridge University Press).

Mattli, W., and Stone Sweet, A. (2012) 'Regional integration and the evolution of the European polity: On the fiftieth anniversary of the *Journal of Common Market Studies*', *Journal of Common Market Studies*, 50/1: 1–17.

Mattson, I., and Strøm, K. (1995) 'Parliamentary committees', in H. Döring (ed.) *Parliaments and Majority Rule in Western Europe* (Frankfurt: Campus): 249–307.

Maurer, A. (2003) 'The legislative powers and impact of the European Parliament', *Journal of Common Market Studies*, 41/2: 227–47.

Maurer, A., Parkes, R., and Wagner, M. (2008) 'Explaining group membership in the European Parliament: The British Conservatives and the Movement for European Reform', *Journal of European Public Policy*, 15/2: 246–62.

McCormick, J. (2007) *The European Superpower* (Basingstoke: Palgrave Macmillan).

McCubbins, M.D., Noll, R.G., and Weingast, B.R. (1987) 'Administrative procedures as instruments of political control', *Journal of Law, Economics, & Organization*, 3/2: 243–77.

McElroy, G. (2006) 'Committee representation in the European Parliament', *European Union Politics*, 7/1: 5–29.

McElroy, G., and Benoit, K. (2010) 'Party policy and group affiliation in the European Parliament', *British Journal of Political Science*, 40/2: 377–98.

McElroy, G., and Benoit, K. (2012) 'Policy positioning in the European Parliament', *European Union Politics*, 13/1: 150–67.

McNamara, K.R. (1998) *The Currency of Ideas: Monetary Politics in the European Union* (Cambridge: Cambridge University Press).

McNamara, K.R. (2002) 'Rational fictions: Central bank independence and the social logic of delegation', *West European Politics*, 25/1: 37–76.

McNamara, K.R. (2015) *The Politics of Everyday Europe: Constructing Authority in the European Union* (Oxford: Oxford University Press).

Meade, E.E. (2003) 'A (critical) appraisal of the ECB's voting reform', *Intereconomics*, 38/3: 129–31.

Menon, A. (ed.) (2004) *Britain and European Integration: Views from within* (Hoboken, NJ: Blackwell).

Menon, A., and Weatherill, S. (2008) 'Transnational legitimacy in a globalising world: How the European Union rescues its states', *Western European Politics*, 31/3: 397–416.

Mentler, M. (1996) *Der Ausschuss der ständigen Vertreter bei den europäischen Gemeinschaften* (Baden-Baden: Nomos).

Merkel, A. (2010) *Speech by Federal Chancellor Angela Merkel at the Opening Ceremony of the 61st Academic Year of the College of Europe, Bruges 2 November* (Bruges: College of Europe).

Meserve, S.A., Pemstein, D., and Bernhard, W.T. (2009) 'Political ambition and legislative behavior in the European Parliament', *The Journal of Politics*, 71/3: 1015–32.

Metcalfe, L. (2000) 'Reforming the Commission: Will organizational efficiency produce effective governance?' *Journal of Common Market Studies*, 38/5: 817–41.

Metz, J. (2015) *The European Commission, Expert Groups, and the Policy Process: Demystifying Technocratic Governance* (Basingstoke: Palgrave Macmillan).

Milward, A.S. (1992) *The European Rescue of the Nation-State* (London: Routledge).

Ministry of the President (2010) *Public Employment in European Union Member States* (Madrid: Ministry of the President).

Mitsilegas, V., Monar, J., and Rees, W. (2003) *The European Union and Internal Security: Guardian of the People?* (Basingstoke: Palgrave Macmillan).

Monar, J. (2001) 'The dynamics of justice and home affairs: Laboratories, driving factors and costs', *Journal of Common Market Studies*, 39/4: 747–64.

Monar, J. (2014) 'The EU's growing external role in the AFSJ domain: Factors, framework and forms of action', *Cambridge Review of International Affairs*, 27/1: 147–66.

Monnet, J. (1978) *Memoirs* (London: Collins).

Moravcsik, A. (1991) 'Negotiating the Single European Act: National interests and conventional statecraft in the European Community', *International Organization*, 45/1: 19–56.

Moravcsik, A. (1993) 'Preferences and power in the European Community: A liberal intergovernmentalist approach', *Journal of Common Market Studies*, 31/4: 373–524.

Moravcsik, A. (1998) *The Choice for Europe: Social Purpose and State Power from Messina to Maastricht* (Ithaca, NY: Cornell University Press).

Moravcsik, A. (1999) '"Is something rotten in the state of Denmark?" Constructivism and European integration', *Journal of European Public Policy*, 6/4: 569–81.

Moravcsik, A. (2002) 'Reassessing Legitimacy in the European Union', *Journal of Common Market Studies*, 40/4: 503–24.

Moravcsik, A. (2005) 'The European constitutional compromise and the neofunctionalist legacy', *Journal of European Public Policy*, 12/2: 349–86.

Moravcsik, A. (2012) 'Europe after the crisis', *Foreign Affairs*, 91/3: 54–68.

Moravcsik, A. (2016) 'The great Brexit kabuki: A masterclass in political theatre', *Financial Times*, 8 April.

Moravcsik, A., and Nicolaïdis, K. (1999) 'Explaining the Treaty of Amsterdam: Interests, influence, institutions', *Journal of Common Market Studies*, 37/1: 59–85.

Moschella, M., and Lombardi, D. (2015) 'The government bond buying programmes of the European Central Bank: An analysis of their policy settings', *Journal of European Public Policy*, 23/6: 1–20.

Narjes, K.-H. (1998) 'Walter Hallstein and the early phase of the EEC', in W. Loth, W. Wallace, and W. Wessels (eds) *Walter Hallstein: The Forgotten European?* (Basingstoke: Palgrave): 109–30.

Naurin, D., and Lindahl, R. (2008) 'East-North-South: Coalition-building in the Council before and after enlargement', in D. Naurin and H. Wallace (eds) *Unveiling the Council of the European Union* (Basingstoke: Palgrave Macmillan): 64–78.

Naurin, D., and Wallace, H. (2008) *Unveiling the Council of the European Union: Games Governments Play in Brussels* (Basingstoke: Palgrave Macmillan).

Nelsen, B.F., and Stubb, A. (eds) (1994) *The European Union: Readings on the Theory and Practice of European Integration* (Boulder, CO: Lynne Rienner).

Neumann, I.B. (2012) *At Home with the Diplomats: Inside a European Foreign Ministry* (Ithaca, NY: Cornell University Press).

Nicolaïdis, K. (2013) 'European democracy and its crisis', *Journal of Common Market Studies*, 51/2: 351–69.

Nicoll, W. (1994) 'Representing the states', in A. Duff, J. Pinder, and R. Pryce (eds) *Maastricht and Beyond: Building the European Union* (London: Routledge): 190–206.

Niemann, A. (2006) *Explaining Decisions in the European Union* (Cambridge: Cambridge University Press).

Niemann, A., and Ioannou, D. (2015) 'European economic integration in times of crisis: A case of neofunctionalism?', *Journal of European Public Policy*, 22/2: 196–218.

Noël, E. (1966) 'The Permanent Representatives Committee', Lecture delivered to the Institute of European Studies, Université Libre de Bruxelles, 19 and 21 April. Reprinted in European Commission (ed.) *A Tribute to Emile Noël: Secretary-General of the European Commission from 1958 to 1987* (Luxembourg: Office for Official Publications of the European Communities): 87–124.

Noël, E. (1967) 'The Committee of Permanent Representatives', *Journal of Common Market Studies*, 5/3: 219–51.

Noël, E., and Étienne, H. (1971) 'The Permanent Representatives Committee and the "deepening" of the Communities', *Government and Opposition*, 6/4: 322–47.

Norman, P. (2003) *The Accidental Constitution: The Story of the European Convention* (Brussels: Eurocomment).

North, D. (1991) 'Institutions', *Journal of Economic Perspectives*, 5/1: 540–55.

Norton, P. (1990) 'Parliaments: A framework for analysis', *West European Politics*, 13/3: 1–9.

Norton, P. (2013) *Parliament in British Politics* (Basingstoke: Palgrave Macmillan).

Novak, S. (2011) *Qualified Majority Voting from the Single European Act to the Present Day: An Unexpected Permanence* (Paris: Notre Europe).

Novak, S. (2013) 'The silence of ministers: Consensus and blame avoidance in the Council of the European Union', *Journal of Common Market Studies*, 51/6: 1091–107.

Nugent, N. (1999) *The Politics and Government of the European Union* (4th edn, Basingstoke: Palgrave Macmillan).

Nugent, N. (2010) *The Government and Politics of the European Union* (7th edn, Basingstoke: Palgrave Macmillan).

Nugent, N., and Rhinard, M. (2015) *The European Commission* (Basingstoke: Palgrave Macmillan).

Nuttall, S.J. (1992) *European Political Co-operation* (Oxford: Oxford University Press).

Nye, J.S. (2004) *Soft Power: The Means to Success in World Politics* (New York: Public Affairs).

Nye, J.S. (2011) *The Future of Power* (New York: Public Affairs).

Nye, J.S., and Keohane, R.O. (1971) 'Transnational relations and world politics: An introduction', *International Organization*, 25/3: 329–49.

OLAF (2004) *Report by the European Anti-Fraud Office (OLAF), Fifth Activity Report for the Year Ending June 2004* (Brussels: OLAF).

OLAF (2014) *The OLAF Annual Report: Fourteenth Report of the European Anti-Fraud Office, 1 January to 31 December 2013* (Brussels: OLAF).

Olsen, J.P. (2002) 'Reforming European institutions of governance', *Journal of Common Market Studies*, 40/4: 581–602.

Olson, M. (2009) *The Logic of Collective Action* (Cambridge, MA: Harvard University Press).

Ortega, E., and Peñalosa, J. (2012) 'The Spanish economic crisis: Key factors and growth challenges in the euro area', *Banco de Espana Occasional Papers*, 12/1.

Osborne, G. (2014) 'Extracts from the Chancellor's Speech on Europe', Open Europe Conference, London, 15 January, available online at https://www.gov.uk/government/speeches/extracts-from-the-chancellors-speech-on-europe

Padoa-Schioppa, T., Emerson, M., King, M., Milleron, J.C., Paelinck, J.H.P., Papademos, L.D., Pastor, A., and Scharpf, F.W. (1987) *Efficiency, Stability, and Equity: A Strategy for the Evolution of the Economic System of the European Community* (Oxford: Oxford University Press).

Page, E.C. (1997) *People Who Run Europe* (Oxford: Clarendon Press).

Pagoulatos, G., and Quaglia, L. (2013) 'Turning the crisis on its head: Sovereign debt crisis as banking crisis in Italy and Greece', in I. Hardie and D. Howarth (eds) *Market-Based Banking and the International Financial Crisis* (Oxford: Oxford University Press): 179–200.

Palayret, J.M., Wallace, H.S., and Winand, P. (2006) *Visions, Votes, and Vetoes: The Empty Chair Crisis and the Luxembourg Compromise Forty Years on* (Brussels: Peter Lang).

Palmer, M. (1977) 'The role of a directly elected European Parliament', *The World Today*, 33/4: 122–30.

Panagiotarea, E. (2013) *Greece in the Euro: Economic Delinquency or System Failure?* (Colchester: ECPR Press).

Panke, D., Hönnig, C., and Gollub, J. (2015) *Consultative Committees in the European Union: No Vote—No Influence?* (Colchester: ECPR Press).

Paoletti, E. (2011) *The Migration of Power and North—South Inequalities: The Case of Italy and Libya* (Basingstoke: Palgrave Macmillan).

Papagianni, G. (2001) 'Flexibility in justice and home affairs: An old phenomenon taking new forms', in B. De Witte, D. Hanf, and V. Ellen (eds) *The Many Faces of Differentiation in EU Law* (New York: Intersentia): 101–28.

Parsons, C. (2003) *A Certain Idea of Europe* (Ithaca, NY: Cornell University Press).

Pastore, F., Monzini, P., and Sciortino, G. (2006) 'Schengen's soft underbelly? Irregular migration and human smuggling across land and sea borders to Italy', *International Migration*, 44/4: 95–119.

Patten, C. (2010) 'What is Europe to do?', *New York Review of Books*, 57/4: 11–12.

Pedler, R.H., and Schaefer, G.F. (eds) (1996) *Shaping European Law and Policy: The Role of Committees and Comitology in the Political Process* (Maastricht: European Institute of Public Administration).

Peers, S. (2011) *EU Justice and Home Affairs Law* (Oxford: Oxford University Press).

Pereira, P.T., and Wemans, L. (2012) 'Portugal and the global financial crisis: Short-sighted politics, deteriorating public finances and the bailout imperative', School of Economics and Management Technical University of Lisbon Working Paper No. 26/2012/DE/UECE.

Perez, L.K., and Scherpereel, J.A. (2015) 'The effects of ministerial turnover on the vertical articulation of power in the Council of the EU', Paper presented at the European Union Studies Association Fourteenth Biennial Conference, 5–7 March, Boston, MA.

Pescatore, P. (1987) 'Some critical remarks on the "Single European Act"', *Common Market Law Review*, 24/1: 9–18.

Peters, B.G. (2011) *Institutional Theory in Political Science: The New Institutionalism* (London: Bloomsbury).

Peterson, J. (1997) 'The European Union: Pooled sovereignty, divided accountability', *Political Studies*, 45/3: 559–78.

Peterson, J. (1999) 'The Santer era: The European Commission in normative, historical and theoretical perspective', *Journal of European Public Policy*, 6/1: 36–65.

Peterson, J. (2004) 'The Prodi Commission: Fresh start or free fall?', in D.G. Dimitrako-poulos (ed.) *The Changing European Commission* (Manchester: Manchester University Press): 15–32.

Peterson, J. (2006) 'Conclusion: Where does the Commission stand today?', in D. Spence and G. Edwards (eds) *The European Commission* (London: John Harper): 502–19.

Peterson, J. (2008) 'José Manuel Barroso: Political scientist, ECPR member', *European Political Science*, 7/1: 54–77.

Peterson, J. (2009) 'Policy networks', in A. Wiener and T. Diez (eds) *European Integration Theory* (2nd edn, Oxford: Oxford University Press): 105–24.

Peterson, J. (2015) 'The Commission and the new intergovernmentalism: Calm within the storm?', in C.J. Bickerton, D. Hodson, and U. Puetter (eds) *The New Intergovernmentalism: States and Supranational Actors in the Post-Maastricht Era* (Oxford: Oxford University Press): 185–207.

Peterson, J. (2016) 'Juncker's political European Commission and an EU in crisis' *Journal of Common Market Studies*, early view.

Peterson, J. (2017) 'Juncker's political commission and an EU in crisis', *Journal of Common Market Studies* at http://onlinelibrary.wiley.com.ezproxy.is.ed.ac.uk/doi/10.1111/jcms.12435/full

Peterson, J., and Bomberg, E. (1999) *Decision-Making in the European Union* (Basingstoke: Palgrave Macmillan).

Peterson, J., and Bomberg, E. (2001) 'The EU after the 1990s: Explaining continuity and change', in M. Green Cowles and M. Smith (eds) *The State of the European Union, Vol. V: Risks, Reform, Resistance or Revival?* (Oxford: Oxford University Press): 19–41.

Peterson, J., and Geddes, A. (2015) 'The EU as a security actor', in D. Kenealy, J. Peterson, and R. Corbett (eds) *The European Union: How Does It Work?* (4th edn, Oxford: Oxford University Press): 187–207.

Peterson, J., and Jones, E. (1999) 'Decision making in an enlarging European Union', in J. Sperling (ed.) *Two Tiers or Two Speeds? The European Security Order and the Enlargement of the European Union and NATO* (Manchester: Manchester University Press): 25–45.

Peterson, J., and Sjursen, H. (1998) *A Common Foreign Policy for Europe: Competing Visions of the CFSP* (London: Routledge).

Pianta, M., and Gerbaudo, P. (2015) 'In search of European alternatives: Anti-austerity protests in Europe', in M. Kaldor, S. Selchow, and T. Murray-Leach (eds) *Subterranean Politics in Europe* (Basingstoke: Palgrave MacMillan): 31–59.

Piatonni, S. (2009) *The Committee of the Regions White Paper on Multilevel Governance: Some Reflections* (Brussels: Committee of the Regions).

Pierson, P. (1996) 'The path to European integration: A historical institutionalist analysis', *Comparative Political Studies*, 29/2: 123–63.

Pinder, J. (1992) 'Federalism versus nationalism: The European Community and the new Europe', *New European Law Review*, 1: 239–55.

Piris, J.-C. (2010) *The Lisbon Treaty: A Legal and Political Analysis* (Cambridge: Cambridge University Press).

Pollack, M.A. (1997) 'Delegation, agency, and agenda setting in the European Community', *International Organization*, 51/1: 99–134.

Pollack, M.A. (2001) 'International relations theory and European integration', *Journal of Common Market Studies*, 39/2: 221–44.

Pollack, M.A. (2003) *The Engines of European Integration: Delegation, Agency, and Agenda Setting in the EU* (Oxford: Oxford University Press).

Pollack, M.A. (2008) 'The new institutionalisms and European integration', *ConWEB: Webpapers on Constitutionalism and Governance Beyond the State*, 1.

Pollak, J., and Slominski, P. (2015) 'The European Parliament: Adversary or accomplice of the new intergovernmentalism?', in C.J. Bickerton, D. Hodson, and U. Puetter (eds) *The New Intergovernmentalism: States and Supranational Actors in the Post-Maastricht Era* (Oxford: Oxford University Press): 245–62.

Ponzano, P., Hermanin, C., Corona, D., and Europe, N. (2012) *The Power of Initiative of the European Commission: A Progressive Erosion?* (Paris: Notre Europe).

Portela, C. (2010) *European Union Sanctions and Foreign Policy: When and Why Do They Work?* (London: Routledge).

Pouliot, V. (2008) 'The logic of practicality: A theory of practice of security communities', *International Organization*, 62/2: 257.

Pouliot, V. (2011) 'Diplomats as permanent representatives: The practical logics of the multilateral pecking order', *International Journal*, 66/3: 543–61.

Pridham, G., and Pridham, P. (1981) *Transnational Party Co-operation and European Integration: The Process towards Direct Elections* (London: HarperCollins).

Proksch, S.-O., and Slapin, J.B. (2015) *The Politics of Parliamentary Debate* (Cambridge: Cambridge University Press).

Puetter, U. (2006) *The Eurogroup: How a Secretive Circle of Finance Ministers Shape European Economic Governance* (Manchester: Manchester University Press).

Puetter, U. (2014) *The European Council and the Council: New Intergovernmentalism and Institutional Change* (Oxford: Oxford University Press).

Puetter, U. (2015) 'The European Council: The centre of new intergovernmentalism', in C.J. Bickerton, D. Hodson, and U. Puetter (eds) *The New Intergovernmentalism: States and Supranational Actors in the Post Maastricht Era* (Oxford: Oxford University Press): 165–84.

Pujas, V. (2003) 'The European Anti-Fraud Office (OLAF): A European policy to fight against economic and financial fraud?', *Journal of European Public Policy*, 10/5: 778–97.

Putnam, R. (1993) *Making Democracy Work: Civic Traditions in Modern Italy* (Princeton, NJ: Princeton University Press).

Quaglia, L. (2009) 'Political science and the "Cinderellas" of economic and monetary union: Payment services and clearing and settlement', *Journal of European Public Policy*, 16/4: 523–39.

Quintyn, M., Ramirez, S.L., and Taylor, M. (2007) 'The fear of freedom: Politicians and the independence and accountability of financial sector supervisors', *IMF Working Papers*, 7/25: 1–50.

Quirke, B. (2010) 'OLAF's role in the fight against fraud in the European Union: Do too many cooks spoil the broth?', *Crime, Law and Social Change*, 53/1: 97–108.

Randzio-Plath, C. (2000) *A New Political Culture in the EU: Democratic Accountability of the ECB* (Bonn: ZEI—Center for European Integration Studies, University of Bonn).

Rasmussen, A. (2007) 'Early conclusion in the co-decision legislative procedure', EUI Max Weber Programme Working Paper No. 2007/31.

Rasmussen, A., Burns, C., and Reh, C. (2013) 'Twenty years of legislative codecision in the European Union', *Journal of European Public Policy*, 20/7, Special Issue.

Rauh, C. (2016) *A Responsive Technocracy? EU Politicisation and the Consumer Policies of the European Commission* (Colchester: ECPR).

Rauh, C., and Zürn, M. (2014) 'Zur Politisierung der EU in der Krise', in M. Heidenreich (ed.) *Krise der europäischen Vergesellschaftung?* (Berlin: Springer): 121–45.

Raunio, T. (2000) 'Losing independence or finally gaining recognition? Contacts between MEPs and national parties', *Party Politics*, 6/2: 211–23.

Reh, C., Héritier, A., Bressanelli, E., and Koop, C. (2013) 'The informal politics of legislation: Explaining secluded decision making in the European Union', *Comparative Political Studies*, 46/9: 1112–42.

Reif, K., and Schmitt, H. (1980) 'Nine second-order national elections: A conceptual framework for the analysis of European election results', *European Journal of Political Research*, 8/1: 3–44.

Reinhart, C., and Rogoff, K. (2013) 'Financial and sovereign debt crises: Some lessons learned and those forgotten', IMF Working Paper No. WP/13/266.

Ringe, N. (2010) *Who Decides, and How? Preferences, Uncertainty, and Policy Choice in the European Parliament* (Oxford: Oxford University Press).

Risse, T. (2009) 'Social constructivism and European integration', in A. Wiener and T. Risse (eds) *European Integration Theory* (Oxford: Oxford University Press): 159–76.

Risse, T. (2010) *A Community of Europeans: Transnational Identities and Public Spheres* (Ithaca, NY: Cornell University Press).

Rittberger, B. (2001) 'Which institutions for post-war Europe? Explaining the institutional design of Europe's first community', *Journal of European Public Policy*, 8/5: 573–708.

Rittberger, B. (2003) 'The creation and empowerment of the European Parliament', *Journal of Common Market Studies*, 41/2: 203–25.

Rittberger, B. (2005) *Building Europe's Parliament: Democratic Representation beyond the Nation State* (Oxford: Oxford University Press).

Rittberger, B., and Schimmelfennig, F. (2006) 'Explaining the constitutionalization of the European Union', *Journal of European Public Policy*, 13/8: 1148–67.

Rittberger, B., and Wonka, A. (2010) 'Credibility, complexity and uncertainty: Explaining the institutional independence of 29 EU agencies', *West European Politics*, 33/3: 730–52.

Roederer-Rynning, C., and Greenwood, J. (2015) 'The culture of trilogues', *Journal of European Public Policy*, 22/8: 1148–65.

Roger, L., and Winzen, T. (2015) 'Party groups and committee negotiations in the European Parliament: Outside attention and the anticipation of plenary conflict', *Journal of European Public Policy*, 22/3: 391–408.

Rosamond, B. (2000) *Theories of European Integration* (Basingstoke: Palgrave Macmillan).

Rosato, S. (2011) *Europe United: Power Politics and the Making of the European Community* (Ithaca, NY: Cornell University Press).

Rosenthal, J. (2009) 'A terrible thing to waste', *New York Times Magazine*, 31 July.

Ross, G. (1995) *Jacques Delors and European Integration* (Cambridge: Cambridge University Press).

Rowe, C. (2011) *Regional Representations in the EU: Between Diplomacy and Interest Mediation* (Basingstoke: Palgrave Macmillan).

Ruggie, J.G. (1982) 'International regimes, transactions, and change: Embedded liberalism in the postwar economic order', *International Organization*, 36/2: 379–415.

Ruggie, J.G. (2002) *Constructing the World Polity: Essays on International Institutionalisation* (London: Routledge).

Salmon, J. (1971) 'Les représentations et missions permanents auprès de la CEE et de l'EURATOM', in M. Virally, P. Gerbet, and J. Salmon (eds) *Les missions permanentes auprès des organisations internationales* (Brussels: Dotation Carnegie pour la paix internationale): 684–7.

Sandalow, T., and Stein, E. (1982) *Courts and Free Markets: Perspectives from the United States and Europe* (Oxford: Oxford University Press).

Sandholtz, W., and Sweet Stone, A. (2012) 'Neo-functionalism and supranational governance', in E. Jones, A. Menon, and S. Weatherill (eds) *The Oxford Handbook of the European Union* (Oxford: Oxford University Press): 18–34.

Sauger, N., Brouard, S., and Grossman, E. (2007) *Les Français contre l'Europe? Les sens du référendum du 29 mai 2005* (Paris: Presses de Sciences Po).

Savage, J.D. (2005) *Making the EMU: The Politics of Budgetary Surveillance and the Enforcement of Maastricht* (Oxford University Press Oxford).

Savage, J.D., and Verdun, A. (2016) 'Strengthening the European Commission's budgetary and economic surveillance capacity since Greece and the euro area crisis: A study of five Directorates-General', *Journal of European Public Policy*, 23/1: 101–18.

Scharpf, F.W. (1999) *Governing in Europe: Effective and Democratic?* (Oxford: Oxford University Press).

Scharpf, F.W. (2011) 'Monetary union, fiscal crisis and the pre-emption of democracy', *Journal for Comparative Government and European Policy*, 9/2: 163–98.

Schimmelfennig, F. (2015a) 'Liberal intergovernmentalism and the euro area crisis', *Journal of European Public Policy*, 22/2: 177–95.

Schimmelfennig, F. (2015b) 'What's the news in "new Intergovernmentalism"? A critique of Bickerton, Hodson and Puetter', *Journal of Common Market Studies*, 53/4: 723–30.

Schmidt, V.A. (2008) 'Discursive institutionalism: The explanatory power of ideas and discourse', *Annual Review of Political Science*, 11/1: 303–26.

Schmidt, V.A. (2013) 'Democracy and legitimacy in the European Union revisited: Input, output and "throughput"', *Political Studies*, 61/1: 2–22.

Schmidt, V.A. (2014) 'Speaking to the markets or to the people? A discursive institutionalist analysis of the EU's sovereign debt crisis', *British Journal of Politics and International Relations*, 16/1: 188–209.

Schmitt, H. (2009) 'European Parliament elections after eastern enlargement: Introduction', *Journal of European Integration*, 31/5: 525–35.

Schmitt, H., Hobolt, S.B., and Popa, S.A. (2015) 'Does personalization increase turnout? *Spitzenkandidaten* in the 2014 European Parliament elections', *European Union Politics*, 16/3: 347–68.

Schmitter, P., and Lehmbruch, G. (1979) *Trends towards Corporatist Intermediation* (Beverly Hills, CA: Sage).

Schönlau, J. (2008) 'The CoR at 15: What role in a multi-level democracy?' Unpublished paper, RECON.

Schön-Quinvalin, E. (2011) *Reforming the European Commission* (Basingstoke: Palgrave Macmillan).

Scully, R. (2005) *Becoming Europeans? Attitudes, Behaviour, and Socialization in the European Parliament* (Oxford: Oxford University Press).

Sedelmeier, U. (2011) 'The differential impact of the European Union on European politics', in E. Jones, P.M. Heywood, M. Rhodes, and U. Sedelmeier (eds) *Developments in European Politics* (2nd edn, Basingstoke: Palgrave): 28–44.

Settembri, P., and Neuhold, C. (2009) 'Achieving consensus through committees: Does the European Parliament manage?', *Journal of Common Market Studies*, 47/1: 127–51.

Shackleton, M. (1997) 'The internal legitimacy crisis of the European Union', in A.W. Cafruny and C. Lankowski (eds) *Europe's Ambiguous Unity: Conflict and Consensus in the Post-Maastricht Era* (Boulder, CO, and London: Lynne Rienner): 69–84.

Shapiro, M. (1997) 'The problems of independent agencies in the United States and the European Union', *Journal of European Public Policy*, 4/2: 276–7.

Siedentop, L. (2001) *Democracy in Europe* (New York: Columbia University Press).

Slaughter, A.-M. (2009) *A New World Order* (Princeton, NJ: Princeton University Press).

Sloan, S.R. (2005) *NATO, the European Union, and the Atlantic Community: The Transatlantic Bargain Challenged* (Lanham, MD: Rowman & Littlefield).

Smeets, S. (2015) *Negotiations in the EU Council of Ministers: And All Must Have Prizes* (Colchester: ECPR Press).

Smismans, S. (1999) 'An Economic and Social Committee for the citizen, or a citizen for the Economic and Social Committee?', *European Public Law*, 5/4: 557–82.

Smismans, S. (2000) 'The European Economic and Social Committee: Towards deliberative democracy via a functional assembly', *European Integration online Papers (EIoP)*, 4/12.

Smismans, S. (2003) 'European civil society: Shaped by discourses and institutional interests', *European Law Journal*, 9/4: 373–95.

Smith, J. (1999) *Europe's Elected Parliament* (Sheffield: Sheffield Academic Press).

Smith, K.E. (2014) *European Union Foreign Policy in a Changing World* (3rd edn, Oxford and Malden, MA: Polity).

Smith, M.E. (2003) *Europe's Foreign and Security Policy: The Institutionalization of Cooperation* (Cambridge: Cambridge University Press).

Smith, M.E. (2004) *Europe's Foreign and Security Policy: The Institutionalization of Cooperation* (Cambridge: Cambridge University Press).

Smith, M.E. (2011) 'A liberal grand strategy in a realist world? Power, purpose and the EU's changing global role', *Journal of European Public Policy*, 18/2: 144–63.

Smith, M.E. (2013) 'The European External Action Service and the security-development nexus: Organizing for effectiveness or incoherence?', *Journal of European Public Policy*, 20/9: 1299–315.

Smith, M.E, Keukeleire, S., and Vanhoonacker, S. (2015) *The Diplomatic System of the European Union: Evolution, Change and Challenges* (London: Routledge).

Solana, J. (2002) *Preparing the Council for Enlargement*, S0044/02, Brussels: Council of the European Union, General Secretariat.

Soros, G. (2015) 'Ukraine and Europe: What should be done?', *New York Review of Books*, 8 October.

Spaak, P.H. (1969) *Combats Inachéves* (two vols, Paris: Fayard).

Spence, D. (1991) 'Enlargement without accession: The EC's response to German unification', Royal Institute of International Affairs London Discussion Paper No. 36.

Spence, D. (2002) 'The evolving role of foreign ministries in the conduct of European Union affairs', in B. Hocking and D. Spence (eds) *Foreign Ministries in the European Union* (Basingstoke: Palgrave Macmillan): 18–36.

Spence, D., and Bátora, J. (2015) *The European External Action Service: European Diplomacy Post-Westphalia* (Basingstoke: Palgrave Macmillan).

Spence, D., and Edwards, G. (eds) (2006) *The European Commission* (London: John Harper).

Stacey, J. (2003) 'Displacement of the Council via informal dynamics? Comparing the Commission and Parliament', *Journal of European Public Policy*, 10/6: 936–55.

Stasavage, D. (2004) 'Open-door or closed-door? Transparency in domestic and international bargaining', *International Organization*, 58/4: 567–704.

Stein, E. (1981) 'Lawyers, judges, and the making of a transnational constitution', *American Journal of International Law*, 75/1: 1–27.

Steinbach, A. (2010) 'The Lisbon judgment of the German Federal Constitutional Court: New guidance on the limits of European integration?', *German Law Journal*, 11/4: 367–90.

Steinmo, S. (2004) 'Néo-institutionnalismes', in L. Boussaguet, S. Jacquot, and P. Ravinet (eds) *Dictionnaire des politiques publiques* (Paris: Presses de Sciences Po): 290–8.

Stephenson, P. (2013) 'Twenty years of multi-level governance: Where does it come from? What is it? Where is it going?', *Journal of European Public Policy*, 20/6: 817–37.

Stewart, R.B. (1975) 'The reformation of American administrative law', *Harvard Law Review*, 88: 1667–813.

Stone Sweet, A., and Sandholtz, W. (1998) *European Integration and Supranational Governance* (Oxford: Oxford University Press).

Stone Sweet, A., Sandholtz, W., and Fligstein, N. (2001)*The Institutionalization of Europe* (Oxford: Oxford University Press).

Strasser, D. (1992) *The Finances of Europe* (Luxembourg: Office for Official Publications of the European Communities).

Suvarierol, S. (2009) 'Networking in Brussels: Nationality over a glass of wine', *Journal of Common Market Studies*, 47/2: 311–35.

Szczerbiak, A., and Taggart, P. (2008) *Opposing Europe? The Comparative Party Politics of Euroscepticism, Vol. 2: Comparative and Theoretical Perspectives* (Oxford: Oxford University Press).

Szymanski, M., and Smith, M.E. (2005) 'Coherence and conditionality in European foreign policy: Negotiating the EU-Mexico Global Agreement', *Journal of Common Market Studies*, 43/1: 171–92.

Tallberg, J. (2003) *European Governance and Supranational Institutions: Making States Comply* (London: Routledge).

Tallberg, J. (2010) 'The power of the chair: Formal leadership in international cooperation', *International Studies Quarterly*, 54/1: 241–65.

Tatham, M. (2008) 'Going solo: Direct regional representation in the European Union', *Regional and Federal Studies*, 18/5: 393–515.

Taulègne, B. (1993) *Le Conseil Européen* (Paris: P.U.F.).

Taylor, J.B. (1995) 'The monetary transmission mechanism: An empirical framework', *The Journal of Economic Perspectives*, 9/4: 11–26.

Timuş, N., and Lightfoot, D. (2014) 'Europarties: Between the processes of "deepening"and 'widening"', *Acta Politica*, 49/1: 1–4.

Tonra, B. (2003) 'Constructing the CFSP: The utility of a cognitive approach', *Journal of Common Market Studies*, 41/4: 731–56.

Torrent, R. (1999) 'Whom is the European Central Bank the central bank of? Reaction to Zilioli and Selmayr', *Common Market Law Review*, 36/6: 1229–41.

Trieb, O. (2014) 'The voter says no, but nobody listens: Causes and consequences of the Eurosceptic vote in the 2014 European elections', *Journal of European Public Policy*, 21/10: 1541–54.

Tsakatika, M. (2005) 'Claims to legitimacy: The European Commission between continuity and change', *Journal of Common Market Studies*, 43/1: 193–220.

Tsebelis, G., and Garrett, G. (2001) 'The institutional foundations of intergovernmentalism and supranationalism in the European Union', *International Organization*, 55/2: 357–90.

Ulrich, L. (2016) *Roads to Europe: Heinrich Aigner and the Genesis of the European Court of Auditors* (Luxembourg: European Court of Auditors).

Union of International Organizations (2015) *Yearbook of International Organizations, 2014/2015* (41st edn, Leiden: Brill).

Urwin, D. (1994) *The Community of Europe: A History of European Integration* (London: Routledge).

Van Buitenen, P. (2000) *Blowing the Whistle: One Man's Fight against Fraud in the European Commission* (London: Politico's).

Van der Eijk, C., Franklin, M.N., and Ackaert, J. (1996) *Choosing Europe? The European Electorate and National Politics in the Face of Union* (Ann Arbor, MI: University of Michigan Press).

Van Middelaar, L. (2013) *The Passage to Europe: How a Continent Became a Union* (New Haven, CT: Yale University Press).

Van Oudenhove, G. (1965) *The Political Parties in the European Parliament: The First Ten Years, September 1952–September 1962* (Leyden: Sijthoff).

Van Rompuy, H. (2010) 'Speech by the President of the European Council, Mr Herman Van Rompuy pronounced today at the "Klausurtagung" of the CSU-Landesgruppe Wildbad Kreuth, Germany', Wilbad Kreuth, 7 January.

Van Rompuy, H. (2014) *Europe in the Storm: Promise and Prejudice* (Leuven: Davidsfonds).

Vanhoonacker, S., and Pomorska, K. (2013) 'The European External Action Service and agenda-setting in European foreign policy', *Journal of European Public Policy*, 20/9: 1316–31.

Vedel, G. (1972) *Report of the Working Party Examining the Problem of the Enlargement of the Powers of the European Parliament* (Brussels: Commission of the European Communities).

Verdun, A. (1999) 'The role of the Delors Committee in the creation of EMU: An epistemic community?' *Journal of European Public Policy*, 6/2: 308–28.

Verdun, A. (2015) 'A historical institutionalist explanation of the EU's responses to the euro area financial crisis', *Journal of European Public Policy*, 22/2: 219–37.

Verdun, A., and Christiansen, T. (2000) 'Policies, institutions and the euro: Dilemmas of legitimacy', in C. Crouch (ed.) *After the Euro: Shaping Institutions for Governance in the Wake of European Monetary Union* (Oxford: Oxford University Press): 162–78.

Voermans, W. (2010) 'Birth of a legislature: The EU Parliament after the Lisbon Treaty', *The Brown Journal of World Affairs*, 17/2: 163–80.

Vollaard, H. (2014) 'Explaining European disintegration', *Journal of Common Market Studies*, 52/5: 1142–59.

Votewatch Europe (2012) *Agreeing to Disagree: The Voting Records of EU Member States in the Council since 2009* (Brussels: VoteWatch Europe).

Waever, O. (1995) 'Identity, integration and security: Solving the sovereignty puzzle in EU studies', *Journal of International Affairs*, 48/2: 389–431.

Wagner, W. (2003) 'Why the EU's common foreign and security policy will remain intergovernmental: A rationalist institutional choice analysis of European crisis management policy', *Journal of European Public Policy*, 10/4: 576–95.

Wallace, H. (2010) 'An institutional anatomy and five policy modes', in M.A. Pollack, H. Wallace, and A.R. Young (eds) *Policy-Making in the European Union* (6th edn, Oxford: Oxford University Press): 69–104.

Wallace, H., and Reh, C. (2015) 'An institutional anatomy and five policy modes', in M.A. Pollack, H. Wallace, and A.R. Young (eds) *Policy-Making in the European Union* (7th edn, Oxford: Oxford University Press): 72–112.

Wallace, H., and Wallace, W. (eds) (2000) *Policy-Making in the European Union* (5th edn, Oxford: Oxford University Press).

Wallace, H.S. (1980) *Budgetary Politics: The Finances of the European Communities* (London: George Allen & Unwin).

Warleigh, A. (1999) *The Committee of the Regions: Institutionalising Multi-Level Governance?* (London: Kogan Page).

Warntjen, A. (2008) 'Steering, but not dominating: The impact of the Council presidency on EU legislation', in D. Naurin and H. Wallace (eds) *Unveiling the Council of the European Union* (Basingstoke: Palgrave Macmillan): 203–18.

Warntjen, A. (2010) 'Between bargaining and deliberation: Decision-making in the Council of the European Union', *Journal of European Public Policy*, 17/5: 565–79.

Webb, C. (1977) 'Introduction: Variations on a theoretical theme', in H. Wallace, W. Wallace, and C. Webb (eds) *Policy-Making in the European Communities* (London: John Wiley & Sons): 1–32.

Webber, D. (2014) 'How likely is it that the European Union will disintegrate? A critical analysis of competing theoretical perspectives', *European Journal of International Relations*, 20/2: 341–65.

Weiler, J.H. (1981) 'The Community system: The dual character of supranationalism', *Yearbook of European Law*, 1/1: 267–306.

Weiler, J.H. (1986) 'Eurocracy and distrust: Some questions concerning the role of the European Court of Justice in the protection of fundamental human rights within the legal order of the European Communities', *Washington Law Review*, 61: 1103.

Weiler, J.H. (1994) 'Fin-de-siècle Europe', in D.M. Curtin, T. Heukels, and H.G. Schermers (eds) *Institutional Dynamics of European Integration: Essays in Honour of Henry G. Schermers* (Dordrecht: Martinus Nijhoff): 203–16.

Weiler, J.H. (1999) *The Constitution of Europe: "Do the New Clothes Have an Emperor?" and Other Essays on European Integration* (Cambridge: Cambridge University Press).

Weiss, T.G. (2007) *The Oxford Handbook on the United Nations* (Oxford: Oxford University Press).

Wendt, A. (1992) 'Anarchy is what states make of it: The social construction of power politics', *International Organization*, 46/2: 391–425.

Werts, J. (1992) *The European Council* (The Hague: TMC Asser Instituut).

Wessels, W. (2016) *The European Council* (Basingstoke: Palgrave Macmillan).

Westlake, M. (1999) *The Council of the European Union* (London: Catermill).

Westlake, M., and Galloway, D. (2005) *The Council of the European Union* (3rd edn, London: John Harper).

Whitaker, R. (2011) *The European Parliament's Committees: National Party Influence and Legislative Empowerment* (Abingdon: Taylor & Francis).

Whitaker, R. (2014) 'Tenure, turnover and careers in the European Parliament: MEPs as policy-seekers', *Journal of European Public Policy*, 21/10: 1509–27.

Whitaker, R., and Lynch, P. (2014) 'Understanding the formation and actions of Eurosceptic groups in the European Parliament: Pragmatism, principles and publicity', *Government and Opposition*, 49/2: 232–63.

White, S. (2010) 'EU anti-fraud enforcement: Overcoming obstacles', *Journal of Financial Crime*, 17/1: 81–99.

Wiener, A., and Diez, T. (eds) (2009) *European Integration Theory* (2nd edn, Oxford and New York: Oxford University Press).

Williams, A. (2015) 'EBRD to invest in Greece', *European Bank for Reconstruction and Development News*, 3 March.

Winnett, R. (2009) 'William Hague interview: Gordon Brown could be forced into European referendum', *The Telegraph*, 10 April.

Witney, N., Leonard, M., Godement, F., Levy, D., Liik, K., and Tcherneva, V. (2014) 'Rebooting EU foreign policy', *European Centre for Foreign Relations Policy Brief*, 3 October.

Wolff, S. (2015) 'Integrating in justice and home affairs', in C.J. Bickerton, D. Hodson, and U. Puetter (eds) *The New Intergovernmentalism: States and Supranational Actors in the Post-Maastricht Era* (Oxford: Oxford University Press): 129–45.

Wong, R. (2011) 'The Europeanization of foreign policy', in C. Hill and M. Smith (eds) *International Relations and the European Union* (2nd edn, Oxford and New York: Oxford University Press): 134–53.

Yiangou, J., O'Keeffe, M., and Glöckler, G. (2013) '"Tough love": How the ECB's monetary financing prohibition pushes deeper euro area integration', *Journal of European Integration*, 35/3: 223–37.

Yordanova, N. (2011) 'The European Parliament: In need of a theory', *European Union Politics*, 1/4: 597–617.

Yordanova, N. (2013) *Organising the European Parliament: The Role of the Committees and their Legislative Influence* (Colchester: ECPR Press).

Yordanova, N., and Mühlböck, M. (2015) 'Tracing the selection bias in roll call votes: party group cohesion in the European Parliament', *European Political Science Review*, 7/3: 373–99.

Yoshinaka, A., McElroy, G., and Bowler, S. (2010) 'The appointment of *rapporteurs* in the European Parliament', *Legislative Studies Quarterly*, 35/4: 357–86.

Young, A.R., and Peterson, J. (2014) *Parochial Global Europe: 21st Century Trade Politics* (Oxford: Oxford University Press).

Zenios, S.A. (2013) 'The Cyprus Debt: Perfect crisis and a way forward', *Cyprus Economic Policy Review*, 7/1: 3–45.

Zilioli, C., and Selmayr, M. (2000) 'The European Central Bank: An independent specialized organization of Community Law', *Common Market Law Review*, 37/3: 591–643.

Zwart, T., and Verhey, L. (eds) (2003) *Agencies in European and Comparative Law* (Antwerp: Intersentia).

▌ INDEX